PLAYGROUNDS TO THE PROS

PLAYGROUNDS
TO THE
PROS

An Illustrated History of
Sports in Tacoma–Pierce County

Caroline Gallacci ‡ Marc H. Blau ‡ Doug McArthur

THE TACOMA ATHLETIC COMMISSION
TACOMA, WASHINGTON

FOR THE FANS

Published by
Tacoma Athletic Commission
P.O. Box 11304
Tacoma, Washington 98411
www.tacomaathletic.com

Distributed by
University of Washington Press
P.O. Box 50096
Seattle, Washington 98145-5096
www.washington.edu/uwpress

ISBN 0-295-98477-5
Library of Congress Control Number: 2004113036

Book design: Karen Schober
Copy editor: Kris Fulsaas
Indexer: Carolyn Acheson
Produced by Unleashed Book Development
www.unleashedbooks.com

Cover photograph: *L. to R., unknown, Marv Rickert, Del Holmes, and Milt Cadinha, members of the 1941 Tacoma Tigers baseball team (courtesy Byron Rickert).*
Back cover photographs: *clockwise, from top, Stadium Bowl action (SSM), Pat Galbraith (SSM), Tacoma Stars' forward Preki (courtesy Tacoma News Tribune), the 1948 Tacoma Fuelerettes (courtesy Pat Strachan Stavig), and Pat Lesser Harbottle (courtesy John and Pat Harbottle).*

Photography sources appear in captions, all of which constitute a continuation of this copyright page information. The following collections graciously contributed most of the photographs for this history: Marc Blau (MB); Shanaman Sports Museum (SSM); Pacific Lutheran University Athletic Department (PLU); University of Puget Sound Athletic Department (UPS); and the Tacoma Public Library (TPL).

A Word from the Authors

One thing that I discovered while writing this sports history is how research of the past sparks memory, especially mine of my own family. Although I knew that one of my aunts had tried archery early in life, it was not until recently that I learned my great-grandfather played semi-pro baseball in Cleveland, Ohio. I had forgotten, too, that my father started out as a physical education major at Willamette University in Salem, Oregon, and my mother dreamt in the 1930s of playing professional basketball. Until my older sister showed me a photograph of proof, I did not know that she won a bowling trophy while in high school. As the history of my family shows, sports play an important role in all of our lives. And I hope this book will help readers remember.

—Caroline Denyer Gallacci

One can never really understand the magnitude of a project such as this until it is actually undertaken. I had absolutely no idea of what I was getting into when I suggested the Tacoma Athletic Commission create a history of sports in the county. And while I pride myself on being a local sports junkie and historian, I hadn't realized how much, in fact, I did *not* know.

There are many people who opened up their homes and hearts over the years and allowed their memories to be mined. Without their willingness to share, this book would lack the stories and personalities that make up its essence. Indeed, some very dear friends passed away before the stories they shared with me could be published for you: baseball players Al Pentecost, Sonny Bailey, Floyd "Lefty" Isekite, Earl Kuper, Marion Oppelt, and Joey Johns. I also want to single out both Jim Price and David Eskenazi whose shared devotion to baseball, as well as their knowledge and photos, enhance the chapters on baseball significantly.

Others who were gracious with their time include Dick Greco, Cy Greenlaw, Lornie Merkle, Ruth Canale Ward, Lowell Butson, Joan Mahon Allard, Jeanne Walters, Vince Hanson, Ruggles Larson, and Pat McMurtry who was a wealth of boxing knowledge.

My mother Maybelle, whose love of family history and writing skills I apparently inherited, served me well on this project. And I have to thank my father Kurt, who introduced me to a multitude of sports as a youngster and never hesitated to encourage my involvement, despite his unfamiliarity with many activities due to his European upbringing. My daughter C.J. and son Chad have listened to more stories and seen enough sports memorabilia to last them a lifetime; I appreciate their patience. And I cannot thank my wife Cheryl enough, for encouraging and allowing me to immerse myself in this project for the better part of three years. Without her support and understanding of my passion for our sports heritage—and without the countless athletes and coaches who made our history what it is, as well as the commitment of TAC—this book would not have become a reality.

—Marc H. Blau

For almost 65 years I have been deeply involved with sports in Tacoma and Pierce County, but it has taken my writing assignments for this book to see and truly appreciate the impact that the thousands of athletes, coaches, and fans have had on the lives of so many others in our community. My research here uncovered dozens of stories about people whose history either had been forgotten or never officially recorded, except by newspaper accounts of games and tournaments at the time. In interviews with the family members of deceased athletes, I learned how much their honors and achievements in sport had meant to their loved ones. I soon realized that some of this history we are sharing today should have been written years ago, when many more of our sports heroes could have enjoyed it, too. Of course, though they may be gone, they are not forgotten. Hopefully, this book will enable them to live on in the collective memories of our community.

—Doug McArthur

CONTENTS

The contributions of five key individuals have shaped our community's sports heritage more significantly than any other participants. Their collective passion for sports, desire to provide opportunities for both recreational and competitive participation, and dedication to improve the quality of life in Tacoma–Pierce County are unparalleled.

This is not to downplay, by any means, the great individual and team achievements of all our area's athletes, coaches, and other participants. But while conducting research for this book, the names of these five sportsmen continued to emerge with great regularity. All members at one time of the Tacoma Athletic Commission (TAC), each of these "Fabulous Five" deserve a salute and our thanks for embodying the TAC's motto to be "dedicated to sports and civic betterment."

Ben Cheney (1905–1971)

Benjamin Bradbury Cheney was a man for all sports seasons. He was an innovative businessman and a philanthropist who never forgot his humble beginnings. He also loved sports and at every opportunity sponsored local athletes and teams, especially those in baseball. "In Tacoma it is difficult to imagine the state of baseball and its history," notes one website, "had Ben Cheney not been one of us, one of baseball's best fans ever."

He was born in 1905 in Lima, Montana, a small town near the Montana–Idaho border. Family tragedies left him in the care of his paternal grandparents, Benjamin F. and Rebecca Cheney, who in 1911 moved to South Bend, Washington, to open a photography studio. While growing up on Willapa Bay, Ben dreamed of playing professional sports. Because his local high school did not offer baseball, he was drawn to Father Victor Couverette, a Roman Catholic priest whose organized recreational baseball teams provided an outlet for the teenager. Ben defined himself later as a "good field, no hit" shortstop and had recognized eventually that he would never play professional baseball.

Just about every Willapa Bay youngster was introduced to work in the timber industry, and Ben Cheney was no exception. He left high school before graduating with his class of 1924 to work as a choke setter for the Columbia Box and Lumber Company. Then at the age of 19, he left South Bend and headed to Tacoma to attend the Knapp Business School. He returned to the lumber business after leaving Knapp, when he began his professional career as a stenographer for the Dempsey Lumber Company.

Frugality was what made Cheney wealthy. He saved enough of his salary during the course of 12 years to form his own business, Cheney Lumber Company, in 1936. His specialty was milled railroad ties. Bothered by the timber waste that accrued in the milling process, however, he aimed to do something about it.

Cheney's solution came by observing the changing domestic architectural styles of the 1920s and 1930s, such as the popular "bungalow." New housing needed eight-foot framing so using the extra timber, he created Cheney "Studs." Mills soon blossomed in National (near Eatonville in Pierce County), Tacoma, Willapa Harbor, Vancouver, and Chehalis. Then he moved south to Myrtle Point and Central Point in Oregon and to Aracata, Pondosa, and Greenville in California.

His economic success lead to Cheney's philanthropy which encompassed his love of baseball. The sport was never far from his mind, even while developing his lumber empire, when he could often be found playing on local amateur teams. Cheney soon funded youth sports programs wherever there was a Cheney Stud Mill. Thousands of youngsters living in the Pacific Coast states were able to play sports thanks to his economic support. "Ben was the greatest friend of youth that Tacoma ever had," sports historian Doug McArthur told Cheney's biographer Med Nicholson. By the time Cheney died in 1971, "it was conservatively estimated that 5,000 young persons of both sexes had participated in baseball, football, basketball, soccer, bowling, and hockey programs sponsored by the Cheney Lumber Company." There is also longevity to his sponsorships: The Seattle Studs team, now playing in baseball's Pacific International League, was founded in 1954 by Cheney.

In fact, the Cheney Studs name was everywhere in Tacoma amateur sports in the 1950s. The Tacoma Cheney Studs baseball and basketball teams competed for champi-

Tom Cross (L.) and Clay Huntington (R.) look over as Ben Cheney (sitting R.) completes the purchase of Cheney Field (formerly Tiger Park) with Omar Bratrud of the Metropolitan Park District (SSM, 1063).

Tom Cross (L.) and Lornie Merkle were top basketball officials in the community and instrumental in the recruiting, training, and development of officials for all sports in the area (SSM, 1198).

onship honors during this time. There was also a Washington Cheney Studs team made up of the most talented baseball players in the Puget Sound region. Lincoln High School graduate Luther Carr was a member of the team in 1955 and one of the first African-Americans to play in the region, pointing to Ben Cheney's commitment to integration.

In 1959, after both the New York Giants and the Brooklyn Dodgers moved to California, Cheney headed to the big leagues. There was a small interest available for sale in the new San Francisco Giants and Cheney bought it, and then bought additional shares to become the teams' second largest stockholder. He was like a kid in a candy store, playing with the Giants during spring training and serving as first-base coach during an exhibition game in Tacoma. His team stock purchases were an example of his knack for good timing: In 1962, the year he became a major owner and board member of the franchise, "his" Giants won the National League pennant.

All the while Cheney never forgot his adopted hometown. His family home remained on Browns Point and he contributed to the construction of the neighborhood's Methodist church. He also developed a camp for the Tacoma Boys Club. His commitment to bringing professional baseball to Tacoma, however, was his greatest sports contribution to the city.

While the full story is told elsewhere in this history, it's important to note that were it not for Ben Cheney, Tacoma would not be home today to a AAA professional baseball franchise playing in the Pacific Coast League. He made it happen in 1960 by financially guaranteeing the construction of a stadium on time and with a budget of $870,000, paltry by today's standards. Cheney acted as the general contractor for the endeavor, and photographs taken at the time portray a man with a mission. He constructed the facility in only three months, and because he did, Tacoma honored him by naming the new baseball park Cheney Stadium.

"He was well liked, but shy and quiet," a former classmate told Med Nicholson. Cheney also modestly believed that his wealth and talents were there to give to others and he gave generously throughout his lifetime. In 1955, he established the Ben B. Cheney Foundation "to carry on his hopes and dreams for the people and communities that he knew and loved." Ben Cheney died in 1971, but the foundation lives on and will continue giving on behalf of this quiet kid from South Bend.

Tom Cross (1920–2003)

When it came to sports, Tacoma native Tom Cross reached beyond playing, coaching, and refereeing. He was one of the most influential sports program directors for parks and recreation departments in both Tacoma and Pierce County, largely responsible for making them the successful and essential programs they are today, and retired after 34 years of service to local residents. He also taught a course in leisure studies at the University of Puget Sound that imparted his belief that sports are as important in American society as cultural arts, good literature, or a degree in business administration. "I enjoyed my work," he said shortly before he died in December of 2003. "I could hardly wait to get up in the morning."

In these various roles, Cross was an inspiration to others, urging them to pursue sports careers of their own. Jan Wolcott, current director of Pierce County Parks and Recreation, and Marc Blau, former manager of community centers for the same agency, were two of his protégés. "Those of us who worked for him," Blau explains, "found a way to stay involved in sports and recreation for years. There is no doubt of the overall influence he had on the lives of people involved in sports and recreation. His contribution may have been more profound and comprehensive than any other person in the history of Tacoma."

Tom Cross was born on September 16, 1920. By the time he graduated from Stadium High School in 1938, he was an accomplished basketball player and a second-team All-State performer his senior year. At the College of Puget Sound, he was the spark on a team that won the Northwest Conference Championship in 1939–1940 and he was named to the All-Northwest Conference 2nd team while being the second leading scorer in the conference.

In 1942 the CPS phys-ed department received a phone call from Rainier High School. The conversation that followed clearly had an impact on the remainder of Cross's life and career. The high school wanted two officials for one of their games and for which they were offering three bucks each! Cross was one of the students who took the offer and 60 years later, he was still officiating and was considered by many to be the "Father of Officiating" in the state. He helped create officials's organizations to serve high school sports throughout Washington. Cross also refereed PAC-10 basketball (1948–64) and football (1948–73), worked Rose Bowl games in 1963 and 1973, continued as a PAC-10 observer, and served as the first official timer for Seattle Seahawks football games.

Cross was introduced to the wonders of sports administration during World War II. "He thought he would be driving a truck," his obituary explained. But instead the army "assigned him to supervise a recreation center on post." After the war, and before he was able to apply what he had learned during his military service, he had to complete his college degree at Puget Sound. He combined his studies with coaching the Logger basketball team and playing on the professional Tacoma Mountaineers of the Pacific Coast Basketball Conference. While this particular team barely survived a season, as the years went by Cross never missed an opportunity to play. When former players of the Cheney Studs formed the Stud Old Timers in the early sixties, Cross continued playing with them until he was 55, still dazzling the crowd with a majestic high-arching two-handed set shot which he appropriately named the "heel-clicker." The game for these players at this age, Cross once recalled, was "trot down and walk back."

Cross felt, however, that his most important contribution to sports in Pierce County was his creation and development of the programs that still exist today: He started out in 1947

as athletic director for the Metropolitan Park District of Tacoma and then moved to the Pierce County Parks and Recreation Department in 1958 until his retirement in 1981. In running both programs—no matter the age, sex, or sport involved—Cross would find a way to maximize the number of sports offered for the greatest number of people, at the least cost. His true sports love was in these recreation ranks. He loved playing and organizing games and leagues for those who simply played for fun, no matter what the level of competition or the sport. In and out of his roles as athletic director, he helped provide facilities when there were none. He found sponsors. He encouraged local businessmen to donate funds to build or improve facilities and fields. If there weren't enough teams to form a league in a given sport, he would call on old friends and teammates to put one together. Naturally he played, too. He became "Mr. Recreation!"

And, oh, how he lived up to that title. He was instrumental in the development of Peck Field, Tacoma's first multifield softball facility which had lights and a schedule that often included 12 games a night. He was the driving force behind Heidelberg Park, providing a lighted diamond for Tacoma baseball teams. Along with his boss Tom Lantz, then Superintendent of Recreation for Tacoma, Cross opened Titlow and South End Swim Pools. Prior to that he succeeded in lighting Franklin Park for night softball games and preserved Tiger Park for night baseball after Tacoma's pro team departed. (It was often rumored that he and Clay Huntington even mortgaged their homes for Tiger Park, but neither man ever confessed to such a thing—although they later convinced Ben Cheney to bail them out and turn it into the first Cheney Field.) Certainly, the opening of Sprinker Recreation Center's ball field complex in 1969 followed by the ice arena and indoor tennis and racquetball courts in 1976 was another one of his crowning achievements.

It was Cross's drive, willingness to call on old friends, and love of the game that got slowpitch softball its start in Tacoma. His Stud Old Timers joined three other teams to organize the first league in Northwest history. Legendary names like John Heinrick, Marv Harshman, Marv Tommervik, Frank Gillihan, and George Wise all played. The 14-inch ball prevailed for many years after its introduction in the late 40s. Cross played fastpitch, however, when he was younger. He was a slingshot-style pitcher for teams including the Cammaranos, Teamsters, and Stoplight Tavern. He was most effective from that 37-foot mound. He even played touch football, quarterbacking Pat's Place to numerous league titles by looking one way and passing another, an old basketball trick he learned on Tacoma playgrounds.

When he wasn't playing or promoting sports and recreation, Cross was coaching. Among his proudest accomplishments he listed the formation of age-group baseball, starting at age 11. It kept local baseball from succumbing to the pressures which Little League play threatened to bring to Tacoma. Later, when his third-grade daughter Chris asked him "how come you don't have teams for girls?" the Lassie League was born. He also helped form and coach kids in the Junior Olympics Track & Field program on Wednesday evenings at Lincoln Bowl in which hundreds of boys and girls participated. Ditto for the Daffodil Festival activities, ranging

Clay Huntington broadcast Tigers baseball and Rockets hockey games (SSM, 1605).

from marble and horseshoe tournaments to badminton, handball, and table tennis competitions.

"In my lifetime," sports historian Doug McArthur told the *News Tribune* when Cross died, "I can't remember anyone who had more impact on the youth of the community. When there weren't programs in recreation and sports, he created them. He fostered and encouraged us to participate in it, and he made sure there were facilities when there weren't any."

Tom Cross also viewed his own accomplishments within a broader context of national history. He understood, for instance, the important role schools played in the early development of playgrounds and swimming pools. He also saw how the influx of families during and after World War II stretched parks and recreation programs to their limits, leading not just to the creation of the Pierce County Parks and Recreation Department but to additional parks programs within the county's many jurisdictions. He championed the importance of these programs and the ways in which they can anchor a community.

His legacy runs like a thread through this sports history and is honored by numerous Halls of Fame inductions for his various sports' achievements. He is commemorated officially by the Tom Cross Ballfields at Sprinker Recreation Center, an endowment fund in his name established by the Greater Tacoma Community Foundation. "I think he's probably as much of a legend as anybody in the Tacoma area," Marv Harshman told the *News Tribune*. "He gave a lifetime to Tacoma…He was a great official…He was a first-class person." McArthur agrees, "I've never known a man with so many friends. To be around him simply was a joy."

Clay Huntington (1922)

The media has been a crucial partner in the development, promotion, and even the invention of sports. Through newspapers first, then radio and television, fans are now linked to their favorite sport and athletes in ways inconceivable one hundred years ago. As a sports journalist and broadcaster, Tacoma's Clay Huntington was just such a link for local fans, as well as an important voice in leading various efforts to make sure the county had the sports facilities it needed.

Clay Huntington's model was undoubtedly his grandfather Samuel Adams Huntington, who was both a journalist and a promoter of sports facilities during the early years of the 20th century. Samuel brought his family from British Columbia to the City of Destiny, published a promotional weekly called *The Sound*, and in 1910 helped lead the Tacoma Chamber of Commerce's effort to fund the construction of Stadium Bowl, the city's first sports arena.

The family went back to Canada at the beginning of World War I, but Clay's father later returned to Tacoma. "I got my start in broadcasting at the age of 10 or 11," explains Clay. "The neighborhood gang would play games in a vacant lot that we converted into a football and baseball field, and we attached a hoop to an old barn at the end of the lot for basketball. When I wasn't playing, I'd climb up into a tree and sit on the branches overlooking the field and practice my play-by-play of the games. Jerry Geehan, Tacoma's first sports broadcaster, was an idol of mine and so I followed his broadcasting of events throughout the 30s. The first sportscast that I ever did was in the fall of 1941 on KTBI. It was a 15-minute show sponsored by Kreme Krust Bread and Bert's Men's Wear and my two guests were Vic and LaVerne Martineau. I've been involved in the business ever since."

While attending high school, Huntington launched his reporting career by writing and editing the Lincoln High School newspaper. By 1942 he was a journalism student at the University of Washington while also reporting the results of local high school games. He must have made an impression on sports enthusiasts because, just before his war service in the Navy began, this teenager found himself in Mayor Harry P. Cain's office helping to form the Tacoma Athletic Commission.

By war's end, Huntington was certain that a combination of sports writing and radio announcing was his calling. He became the Saturday sports editor for the *Tacoma Times* while also taking journalism courses from Murray Morgan at the College of Puget Sound. He remained at the *Times* while attending CPS until the *News Tribune* purchased the newspaper in 1949. Gradually he shifted from the printed sports page to radio and television announcing, a career that lasted into the 1990s.

Throughout the years his radio voice could be heard reporting local football, basketball, and baseball games for KMO, KTBI, and KTNT. In the 1950s, before the time of on-site play-by-play broadcasting, he re-created major league baseball games with Rod Belcher over a 14-station network that covered Washington, Oregon, and Alaska. In 1953, he entered the realm of television announcing for both channels 11 and 13. Along the way, he also encouraged other sports broadcasters, including Bob Blackburn, who was the voice of the Oregon State Beavers and the Pacific Coast League Portland Beavers before moving to Seattle.

Sports broadcasting has not been, however, the end-all of Clay Huntington's career. Like his grandfather before him, he had a sense of community that took him from behind the mic to a more public stage. Indeed, when asked what his proudest sports moment was, he pointed to his grandfather's efforts to fund the Stadium Bowl and compared his own role 50 years later to help fund the construction of Cheney Stadium and bring AAA baseball back to Tacoma. His effort has led to over 40 years of Pacific Coast League baseball in Tacoma.

Huntington also helped fund other sports facilities, including Heidelberg Park with Tom Cross. While Cross created the sports programs, he rousted local donors into providing the money needed to build the facilities.

His contributions to the community also include the promotion of sports history: He initiated the Tacoma–Pierce County Sports Hall of Fame in 1957 and in 1960 with the support of then-Governor Albert Rosellini, expanded this honor roll with the creation of the State of Washington Sports Hall of Fame. Huntington was also instrumental in the creation of the Shanaman Sports Museum of Tacoma–Pierce County.

Today Clay Huntington continues his broadcasting career through his own radio station, one that continues to provide coverage of all local sports, whether high school, college, or professional. Because he started sports writing and sportscasting as a youth, he is very attuned to the future generations of sports talent. To make sure that today's youngsters can succeed, in 2000 the Tacoma Athletic Commission established the Clay Huntington Scholarship Award to help high school graduates in their pursuit of sports broadcasting and journalism. As of this writing boys and girls from Peninsula, Gig Harbor, and Spanaway Lake High Schools are well on their way toward continuing the traditions begun by Huntington more than 60 years ago.

Doug McArthur (1929)

Doug McArthur was three years old when he got hooked on sports. His father, who worked for the St. Paul and Tacoma Lumber Company, had been sent to Deming, Washington, to manage one of the company's mills. The Depression, however, forced the closure of the mill and the abandonment of the company town. The McArthur family found themselves practically alone in the wilderness of eastern Whatcom County. Their only link to the outside world was a radio.

Seattle Rainiers baseball games were a part of their listening repertoire. "I grew up on [sportscaster] Leo Lassen," McArthur says. "Boys are interested in sports whether they play or not. That is how I became interested in sports—totally detached from any opportunity to play." He also became interested in sports statistics at an early age, something that proved valuable when he first turned to broadcasting as a career and then later became a sports historian.

"For a lot of us in that era it was a childhood fantasy to be a sports broadcaster," McArthur explains, "unless you had great athletic ability." His family returned to Tacoma in time for McArthur to attend Stewart Junior High and become a 1946 graduate of Lincoln. He loved to play baseball but questioned his own athletic prowess. He considered himself an "over-achiever, but not a great player," decided on a career as a pharmacist, and enrolled at Washington State University. After only one week, however, he decided to change to communications—which led to his long career in sportscasting and sports administration and promotion.

Like Clay Huntington before him, McArthur went to the College of Puget Sound and became another one of Murray Morgan's students. He actually had the benefit of both Murray and his wife Rosa's instructions. McArthur would tape his attempts at sportscasting, and Murray would have Rosa listen to it and provide a critique from the perspective of a novice sports fan. From these exercises, McArthur learned the importance of clarity on the air. "If you get too close to a sport," he says, "you forget what people may or may not know." You must be able to "paint the word picture."

McArthur served in the Korean War, graduated from the Armed Forces Information School in New York in 1954, returned to Tacoma and, in 1956, became sports director at KTAC radio. That's when sportscasting, public relations,

administration, and promotion became the combined essence of his career. He was Superintendent of Public Recreation and Supervisor of Athletics for the Tacoma Public Schools and the Metropolitan Park District in the early 1960s. Between 1966 and 1978 he was Director of Athletics at the University of Puget Sound, a position that later led to his induction into the Logger Athletic Hall of Fame.

McArthur is quick to pick his two most memorable sports moments. As coach of the 1956 Stanley's Shoemen, he was blessed with a team that successively won their last 13 games to claim the state, regional, and national amateur baseball championships. "It was the first time a West Coast team had ever won at that level," he says, "and I was so proud Tacoma could be represented that way. The headlines in Battle Creek, Michigan, said 'Tacoma is King!'"

He also fondly remembers the national basketball championship won by the UPS Loggers while he was Director of Athletics there. "We won the Division II NCAA title in Evansville, Indiana, and no other Northwest team had ever done that. We also beat five Division I teams along the way. I was so proud of that program."

Doug McArthur managed the Cheney Studs in 1957 (courtesy Doug McArthur).

McArthur eventually formed his own company, one that combined his love of sports with broadcasting, public relations, and promotion. He began by purchasing the broadcasting rights for Tacoma's professional, college, and high school sports, along with those for the Portland Timbers soccer games. Among the recruited announcers used in these broadcasts were Art Popham and Bob Robertson. But there was more to his company's portfolio. McArthur was one of the founders and the 13-year tournament director of the LPGA Safeco Golf Classic, and he was also a force behind the development of the Tacoma Dome.

Proponents of the Dome project approached him following the past failures of voters to fund the facility. There was need for a full-time promoter, especially since the community was divided over its location. McArthur simply removed this issue from the discussion by focusing on the need for a multipurpose facility, period. "We told the voters that we'd put wheels on it and move it around the city if necessary," he says. Viewing the proposal within this context proved to be a way to unite the community resulting in a 70% affirmative vote after years of rejection. "I firmly believe that if you tell the whole story and tell it truthfully," he says, "that we have a supportive community. I found that clearly with the Dome campaign."

"I have never been a star in any sport," Doug McArthur says, "but I have played a lot of sports and I think it is the feeling of achieving things together [that is so important]. There is a magic to sports. Sports bring out the little kid in us. I've had an opportunity to do everything in my life that has been enjoyable for me."

Stan Naccarato (1928)

Stan Naccarato may have asked more Tacomans for more sponsorship dollars than anyone else in our history, and rarely did he experience rejection. When Doug McArthur asked Naccarato to sponsor his amateur baseball team in 1956, Naccarato couldn't say no. When the resulting Stanley's Shoemen won the national amateur championship in Battle Creek, Michigan, it was "one of the highlights of my career" he has said. "Being a part of that was a great experience in the world of sports." And it proved to be only one among many.

Naccarato was born in Tacoma in 1928 and grew up in Spanaway. His interest in sports began classically by playing catch in the yard with his father. By the time he graduated from Clover Park High School in 1946, he had already spent four years playing on a semi-pro baseball team sponsored by Western State Hospital. He showed great promise when, in 1946, the Cincinnati Reds signed him on as a pitcher for the Ogden Reds of the Pioneer League. During three years of play he notched a 33–10 record, but his career came to a quick end due to an injury in his right shoulder. He returned to Tacoma and joined Morley Brotman in selling shoes.

"I am a people person," he explains, and this underscores everything he accomplished following his departure from the Red's franchise. "From boxing to anything I've done from the outside looking in, or the inside looking out, there has always been a fascination" with sports as a very human endeavor. Naccarato acknowledges that the competitiveness of games can certainly get the adrenaline flowing, but more important, he feels, is the experience a family can have together watching a baseball game in Cheney Stadium.

It would be impossible to list everything that Naccarato has done on behalf of Tacoma sports. He has chaired the Tacoma Athletic Commission twice. For more than 40 years he has been Master of Ceremonies and chairman of boxing's Golden Gloves tournaments. Over a 25-year period he served five governors as a Washington State Athletic Commissioner and chairman governing Professional Boxing and Wrestling. He has helped raise money for countless organizations and causes, ranging from new turf on Stadium Bowl's field to Mary Bridge Children's Hospital to treatment and prevention of leukemia, diabetes, and heart disease. At present he is the liaison between the Puyallup Tribe and the City of Tacoma.

What Naccarato considers his most important contribution to local sports begins with the Chicago Cubs and its 1971 decision "in the dead of night" to move its Tacoma franchise to Wichita, Kansas. Naccarato led the effort to save baseball for the city. In 16 hours, he and 19 other investors raised the $100,000 needed to keep the Cubs team here. Then for 20 years Naccarato was president and general manager of the various Tacoma teams—the Twins, Yankees, Tugs, and Tigers—and in the process won "every award there was to win in the national association." In 1975, for example, he was

General Manager of the Year and was awarded the Charley McPhail Promotional Trophy and The Sporting News General Manager of the Year award. At that time, no one in the 77-year history of the national association had won all three major awards in one year.

Another memorable moment began when Naccarato saw his first medium-sized multi-purpose "dome" in California. He decided to start selling the idea to Tacomans and helped raised the first round of campaign funds to build a "dome of our own." He then again teamed with McArthur to campaign for it. The result was a 70% "yes" vote, the biggest approval margin in the city's history. As it was for Tom Cross, the reward for him was "seeing things in Tacoma that wouldn't have been there otherwise, of being a part of it."

"I wouldn't be here today if it were not for sports," Naccarato believes. He is a wealth of knowledge, especially when talking about how economics and the increasing role played by national sports and media organizations have changed the playing field. There is a danger, in his view, that the concern for the bottom line might destroy the best things about sports, especially in Tacoma.

He worries, because of his love for the City of Destiny. "You can see my love for my town," Naccarato says. "I think it is as beautiful here as San Francisco. I will sell it to everybody. I always will. I've had a love affair with this town for my whole life. I was offered a job by George Steinbrenner with the New York Yankees, and I stayed in Tacoma because you couldn't pay me enough money to go to New York. This is my town!"

Stan Naccarato has been a major force in the promotion and philanthropic support of sports in the community (SSM).

INTRODUCTION

The concept for this book, *Playgrounds to the Pros,* evolved over time just like the individual sports histories that it describes. Its impetus, however, can be attributed specifically to the idea for a sports museum in Tacoma which had existed since the early 1980s. It was no surprise when the Tacoma Athletic Commission, an ardent promoter of sports endeavors in Tacoma since 1943, committed to ensuring that the museum become a reality. The TAC was compelled to recreate the history of sports so that its rich heritage could be passed on, allowing current and future generations to understand the evolution of Tacoma's sports traditions.

As artifacts were accumulated for display purposes, it became a priority to learn the stories behind the objects and record the information for posterity. It wasn't enough to acquire an old baseball glove—we wanted to know who it belonged to, what kind of a player he was, when he played in the area, who his teammates were, and much more. Occasionally someone would give us vintage 16-mm film footage of a football game played in Stadium Bowl, a downhill run by Gretchen Kunigk-Fraser, or a Freddie Steele or Pat McMurtry fight.

Now celebrating ten years of existence, the Shanaman Sports Museum allows visitors to enjoy viewing uniforms, game equipment, championship rings, trophies, vintage photos, and much, much more. A book, however, allows us to recognize and explore with more depth the accomplishments of athletes, coaches, officials, and other individuals who have made significant contributions to our sports history.

This book is also about sharing the successes and the failures of athletic competition. It is about thanking coaches who dedicate their lives to teaching boys, girls, men, and women how to become the very best they can be—both on and off the field of play. It is about recognizing the athletes who perform and accomplish feats that perhaps they never thought were achievable. It is about the people in leadership positions who organize and create programs to encourage participation and who work diligently to make sure there are places to play, such as ballfields, gymnasiums, tennis courts, ice arenas, golf courses, and swimming pools. It is about the officials who provide a fair playing environment, and it is about the fans—parents, grandparents, aunts, uncles, siblings, and friends who support the participants.

Flashing across the pages of Tacoma's colorful sports history is a razzle-dazzle procession of athletes, coaches, officials, and administrators—professional and amateur—who have molded our sports heritage. The late Dan Walton, who chronicled the local sports scene for decades as sports editor of *The Tacoma News Tribune*, once wrote, "Name your sport, and Tacoma has it!" Without a doubt, the athletes of Tacoma–Pierce County have forged a tradition of excellence of which we can all be proud.

On behalf of the Tacoma Athletic Commission, we are pleased to present this gift of *Playgrounds to the Pros: An Illustrated History of Sports in Tacoma–Pierce County* to the community. Read on and enjoy!

Steve Brightman was a longtime member of the Lakewood Curling Club (courtesy Arline Brightman).

RIGHT: Midget auto racing at Athletic Park in the mid-1940s (courtesy Nick Nickolas).

Dick Kunkle, a longtime sportswriter for the Tacoma News Tribune, *is credited with the concept for the Sound-to-Narrows race and the Star Track state high school championships (PLU).*

RIGHT: Boys' basketball game with official Jack Johnson, ca. 1955 (photo by Clarence Seman, courtesy the Cheney Family).

THE PLAYING FIELD
PART I

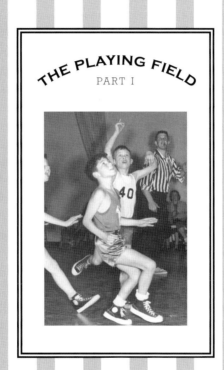

CHAPTER 1

THE TACOMA ATHLETIC COMMISSION:
DEDICATED TO SPORTS AND CIVIC BETTERMENT

Cheney Studs catcher Bob Maguinez listens closely to the ground rules from umpires Stan Naccarato (L.) and Lornie Merkle (R.), while an opposing coach looks on (SSM, 2000.8.3).

When Junior Archery Champion Sonny Johns needed $250 to travel to the 1939 national tournament in St. Paul, Minnesota, he turned to the Tacoma Optimist Club for help. To get a successful fund-raising campaign underway, the Tacoma Chamber of Commerce (TCC) donated $50. Such was the role that many local service clubs and commercial organizations played in helping athletes in the years prior to World War II.

Besides groups such as the Optimists, Pierce County communities and Tacoma neighborhood organizations raised money to fund sports and recreational facilities and to sponsor teams. In 1915, for example, the Lincoln Athletic Club was formed for football players living in the neighborhood south of Tacoma's downtown. A year later the South Tacoma Athletic and Commercial Club formed, providing gridiron competition against the Tahoma Athletic Club. Rollin Dennis, a local attorney and star player at Whitworth College (then located in the city's north end), coached the South Tacoma team.

By the 1930s, sports and recreation enthusiasts were taking advantage of federal New Deal programs to fund the construction of facilities. From the Longbranch Peninsula to Eatonville and Buckley, local communities turned to the Works Projects Administration (WPA) for help. Because this was a time when educators viewed sports as a way to instill cooperation and teamwork in the young, many of these facilities were constructed as part of new schools.

The War Years

The focus of local sports changed, however, with the United States' entry into World War II on December 7, 1941. Even before the onset of hostilities, explained urban historian Philip Funigiello, federal officials "anticipated that industrial expansion, the movement of populations to centers of defense activity, and the general dislocation attending the growth of boom-towns would create new social problems and intensify old ones." For this reason, Mark A. McClosky, head of the federal Division of Recreation, encouraged local community recreation programs so as to "maintain full worker productivity and to combat the disruptive effects of transient populations upon cities and towns." This was polite rhetoric. The "disruptive effects of transient populations" really meant prostitution that could result in diseases, which would make employees unable to work and enlisted personnel unable to perform their military duties.

One of the tools the American armed forces used to mitigate any potential disruptive effects was to declare cities off-limits to military personnel if the high command thought that liberty in a particular city would prove detrimental to the fighting forces. Cities, of course, wanted to avoid the declaration and worked with federal officials in what was called a policy of suppression. Within this context, sports were an alternative to the red-light districts found in any city in the country.

Tacoma Mayor Harry P. Cain was well aware of this federal program. The formation of the Tacoma Athletic War Commission (TAWC) was a result of his wish not to see the city declared off-limits, by providing recreational alternatives to those entertainments available on the streets. Cain also saw the organization as a tool to promote sports locally while funding athletic equipment for military personnel stationed at nearby Fort Lewis and McChord Air Force Base (AFB).

TAWC was officially formed on December 30, 1942, with former Gonzaga football player Doug Dyckman as its first chairperson. Representatives of Tacoma businesspeople, coaches, and the sports media joined him on the board: Irving Thomas, Will Maylon, Elbert Forbes, and Everett Jensen were among the business representatives. John Wycoff ran existing sports programs in Tacoma's shipyards; Harry Satterlee was secretary of the International Brotherhood of Teamsters Local 313.

Bob Abel, then president of baseball's Western International League (WIL), and Bill Herdman, bowler and

The Tacoma Athletic Commission sponsored the annual Fourth of July Fireworks; L. to R., George Sheridan, unknown, unknown, Stadium High athletic director Murray Healy, Bob Danhauser (SSM, 2002.17.32).

groundskeeper at Stadium High School, were also members of the commission, along with coaches Baron Barofsky and John Heinrick. Representing the media were Jerry Geehan, who had begun his radio broadcasting career in 1932; Larry Huseby, another pioneer sportscaster; and Elliott Metcalf and Dan Walton, sports reporters for the *Tacoma Times* and the *Tacoma Ledger,* respectively. And, finally, there was 17-year-old Clay Huntington, a cub reporter who became one of the most influential members of the local sports scene.

The commission's first responsibility was to foster sports partnerships with Fort Lewis and McChord AFB. Thus the first event sponsored by the new organization was an exhibition basketball game between the famed Harlem Globetrotters and the newly formed Fort Lewis Warriors. On January 1, 1943, more than 2,500 people paid 85 cents to attend the game at the Tacoma Armory. Fort Lewis won by a score of 36–28, and the military base received from the commission $850 for recreational equipment.

Additional sports events during the war years funded many military units overseas. One such recipient was a construction battalion stationed in the South Pacific and com-

manded by Tacoma native Richard C. Holbrook. Thanks for the supply of boxing, baseball, and basketball equipment came from the chaplain, N. P. Jacobson: "Athletics play a most important role in the off duty hours of our men and officers alike and such gear will find constant use." To show their appreciation, the Seabees called their sports teams the Loggers because Tacoma was considered the lumber capital of the world at that time.

Local funding also allowed local wounded GIs the opportunity to attend sporting events or just to go fishing on Puget Sound. "Many of them never have been on salt water," sportswriter Dan Walton noted at the time. "Some of them never went fishing before. It makes you feel good inside to have so many of them come up and tell you how much they enjoyed the trips. Some say it's the most fun they've had since joining the army."

Many sports events were inaugurated or sponsored by TAWC during the war years. Some were designed to fund athletic equipment for the military; others were geared

Headquarters for the Tacoma Athletic Commission was once the Top of the Ocean Restaurant (SSM, 1850).

The Tacoma Athletic Commission sponsored an annual Oyster Drive (SSM, 1538).

toward efforts to assist local schools. The Grid-Go-Round and the Hoop-Go-Round were two projects introduced by TAWC in 1943. These interscholastic games brought together high school football and basketball teams from all over the county in a quick competition to determine which team was the best. Those paying to attend were assured that half of the gate receipts funded athletic programs in the participating schools.

TAWC also sponsored sports events as a part of local war bond campaigns. In 1945, during the Mighty Seventh war loan drive, the organization—in conjunction with the Pierce County War Finance Committee—provided an evening of boxing. Featured in the ring was Jack Dempsey, then a Coast Guard commander, who both fought and refereed. The price to see the show was the purchase of a war bond.

By the early months of 1945, it was clear that the efforts of TAWC had fulfilled the commission's original charge. In that year, Tacoma City League basketball teams, along with the Shelton Naval Air Station, battled the Harlem Globetrotters during the latter team's second visit to the city. Other sports organizations also quickly became local partners. Among those credited in newspaper reports of the time were the Tacoma Sportsmen Club, the Tacoma Golf Association, the Tacoma Lawn Tennis Club, and the Tacoma Employers Baseball League. In addition, in 1944 the combined park and school boards created the Tacoma Recreation Commission, with Tom Lantz as director, who served as the first president of the Washington Recreation and Parks Society.

From TAWC to TAC

With the end of the war, TAWC decided to continue its efforts under a new name that continues to be used today: the Tacoma Athletic Commission (TAC). Mayor Cain endorsed the move: "The Tacoma War Athletic Commission was created to bring athletic treats to servicemen stationed at home and to use its profits for the benefit of servicemen serving abroad. The commission has accomplished completely what it set out to do. … Now that the shooting war is over, the commission will emphasize the importance of presenting to Tacoma the best athletic contests obtainable."

Jerry Geehan, sports broadcaster and then chairperson of TAC, elaborated on the future goals of the organization. The first order of business, he explained, was to "build or buy a suitable building for a club, then convert part of it into a gaming room, part into a bar, and part into a club room, and perhaps part of it for lodging of its bachelor members." While looking for a new meeting place, TAC planned to continue with the sporting events that the organization had sponsored in the past, including the Grid- and Hoop-Go-Rounds, boxing matches, the Harlem Globetrotters basketball exhibition game, and Sound Off, the first staged army show in Tacoma.

In 1948, TAC president Howard Smith proudly announced "the three rather choice bits of sports entertainment in which the organization is participating." The activities were the Tacoma Open Golf tournament at Fircrest, the 1948 Grid-Go-Round in Lincoln Bowl, and the Penn State–Washington State football game held in Stadium Bowl.

Jack Shapiro was chair of the September golfing event, with a purse of $12,000. Explained Smith, "There'll be warmer competition by more 'big name' golfers for more cash than has ever been laid on the line in the entire Puget Sound area." During the Grid-Go-Round, also held in September, the reconstructed Lincoln Bowl was dedicated, a ceremony that included the inauguration of a new electronically operated scoreboard donated by TAC. Although

TAC didn't sponsor the November Penn State–Washington State game (Penn State won, 7–0), the organization took credit for having the game transferred from Pullman to Tacoma. "In that connection," Smith boasted, "Spokane made a strong bid for the game but TAC's superior persuasion prevailed."

In 1948 the work of TAC went beyond these sports events. The organization provided athletic equipment for the Washington State Training School in Chehalis and hosted the International Powerboat Race from Tacoma to Vancouver, British Columbia. It cosponsored the 1948 Washington State Badminton Tournament and sponsored the opening ceremonies for both the WIL and Pacific Coast Hockey League (PCHL). TAC was fast becoming one of the "finest athletic promoters in the United States," as the organization claimed on its podium banner.

The year 1948 was a busy one for TAC. In addition to sponsoring a multitude of sports activities, the organization purchased the Top of the Ocean building for its headquarters. Located northwest of the Old Tacoma Dock on Ruston Way, it was built in 1946 with a design unique to the city. C. A. Kenworthy was its architect and Tacoma Boat Mart was the general contractor for the structure designed to resemble an ocean liner. The first-floor restaurant had a capacity of 700 people and a floating dock that could accommodate up to 20 yachts and where seaplanes could find moorage. TAC purchased the building and six adjacent lots for $156,000, with plans to keep the restaurant and dance floor open to the general public. The commission's headquarters were on the second floor.

By this time, TAC had developed a pattern of sports and entertainment events designed to help fund local athletic programs and individuals. For example, the organization began to sponsor the Golden Gloves boxing tournaments in 1949 (under the guidance of Ray Kelly and Scotty Weinstone), earning credit for sponsoring the second-oldest such program in the country. That same year, in Lincoln Bowl, it offered the citizens of Tacoma a Fourth of July spectacle, including vaudeville acts and pyrotechnics. TAC also held a water carnival in 1949 off its Top of the Ocean headquarters featuring, among other events, an outboard motor race from Point Defiance across Commencement Bay to Browns Point and a 15-

mile race between Tacoma- and Seattle-based water-skiers.

In 1953 the commission sponsored a women's handicap bowling tournament, in addition to college and high school track and field meets at Fort Lewis. TAC also sponsored the men's Northwest softball tournament held in September that year. TAC continued to import sports celebrities as a part of fund-raising events, but by the 1960s entertainment personalities also became part of the package. Willie Mays, Sandy Koufax, Arnold Palmer, and Joe Namath were a few of the athletes featured during these years, alongside celebrities such as Roy Rogers, Gene Autry, Bob Hope, and Bing Crosby, who, born in Tacoma, was considered one of the city's favorite sons.

In January 1950, however, TAC suffered from the havoc that winter storms can play on the south shore of Commencement Bay: a blizzard caused extensive property damage to the Top of the Ocean building. At first the commission considered a massive building campaign, one that would shelter the structure from damaging north winds. The plan, designed by the architectural firm of Lance, McGuire, and Muri, consisted of a 150-foot by 170-foot retaining wall that would surround the Top of the Ocean building and contain a swimming pool flanked by landscaping and boat moorage.

The plan never materialized. Instead, TAC moved its headquarters downtown. "TAC Opening New Quarters," headlined the *Tacoma News Tribune* in 1956. More than 400 members were expected to attend an evening of festivities, ceremonies, and dancing in the new building at 735 Commerce Street.

Before this move, in 1951 TAC issued its first report to the citizens of Tacoma. "The report tells a clear and emphatic story of an extensive program of civic activity," explained the *Tacoma News Tribune* in May that year. "The booklet … not only reports on the activity as a whole but also concentrates on the 1950 accomplishments and stresses its hopes and aims for the future." The report listed close to 1,800 individuals whose yearly membership fees also contributed to TAC's goals.

"Here's to the Future—Let's Spend It Together," began the report. "Perhaps never since the day of its founding has the Tacoma Athletic Commission had as great an opportu-

JANUARY 27, 1947: NEWS RELEASE

There are those nonresidents who would have people believe Tacoma is a one-horse town and that citizens are home in bed when streets are rolled up at curfew time, but the recently organized Tacoma Athletic Commission is out to prove that a fallacy.

TAC, a nonprofit group, is an outgrowth of the old Tacoma Athletic War Commission organized in December 1942 for the purpose of raising funds through various sports contests and other enterprises to furnish athletic and other recreational equipment for troops overseas and at home.

TAWC put on shows and conducted other events in the city, and money derived went into the purchase of equipment for the soldiers.

A public address system was purchased and donated to Madigan Hospital, and a piano was given to the USS aircraft carrier *Vella Gulf* for no reason other than the craft had been built in Tacoma shipyards.

In three years TAWC spent more than $40,000 on athletic equipment for the armed forces and has received numerous letters of appreciation from American troops all over the world.

The Tacoma Athletic Commission came into existence shortly after the war ended and is now set to take up in peacetime where TAWC left off at the cessation of hostilities.

Plans have been made and a lease already signed for new clubrooms in a downtown Tacoma building from where the organization will direct its enterprise.

Officials said TAC will promote athletic contests and engage in other civic affairs to raise funds for charity and other worthwhile causes. Money derived from these events will be equally divided between charitable organizations. and the remainder will go to TAC to stage additional events.

The organization, composed of men from all walks of life, is presently negotiating for a major football game to be played between two prominent collegiate teams at the Tacoma stadium this season and has numerous sports events scheduled for the coming year. Already it has sponsored basketball games between the Harlem Globetrotters and the Kansas City All-Stars pitted against local teams.

On the humorous side of the books, TAC recently sent a toilet seat for the governor's mansion at New York's capital after Governor Dewey said the state was unable to provide one. The action was publicized all over the country, and an army paper at Saipan even devoted its entire four pages to the story.

One of the organizations receiving donations from TAC is the Sister Kenny Foundation for the fight against infantile paralysis.

Membership now numbers approximately 500 persons, and officials are soon to start a drive to get the first 1,000 in the fold.

"Tacoma is an up-and-coming, live-wire town," officials said. "And we aim to put it in its proper place among other cities of the nation."

—Jack B. Evans,
United Press Staff Correspondent, January 27, 1947

nity to be of service to its community and its nation as it has today." Then followed a list of its goals, still in effect today:

We propose to create and attract for Tacoma more major sports events of national caliber and to work unceasingly for the development of the proper facilities and stadiums in which to stage them.

We propose to work even more closely with the public schools, the Department of Recreation and all youth organizations to provide our youth with more places to play and a comprehensive program of guided sports activity.

We propose to develop a close association with the armed forces of the area to create an effective sports program for the men and women stationed here and to bring all those in uniform into an active and friendly contact with our own civilian sports.

Tacoma–Pierce County Sports Hall of Fame

In 1957 Clay Huntington, the youngest voice on the Tacoma Athletic War Commission from 1942, conceived the idea of honoring local athletes through a Tacoma–Pierce County Sports Hall of Fame. Baseball's Bob Johnson, championship boxer Freddie Steele, and Olympic gold medal skier Gretchen Kunigk-Fraser were the first inductees on an honor roll that now includes nearly 100 athletes.

Huntington was also the mind behind the formation of the State of Washington Sports Hall of Fame in 1960. Then-Governor Albert Rossellini commissioned an honor roll of those athletes who, through their outstanding sports achievements, have brought national acclaim both to themselves and to the state of Washington. The list is long, with more than 135 athletes inducted.

The Tacoma Dome

From the earliest days of Tacoma's history, its citizens longed for an indoor multipurpose facility that could accommodate a wide array of activities from sports to entertainment, trade exhibitions, and conventions. Over time, and until the completion of the Tacoma Dome in 1983, various places were used for such public gatherings. In the 1890s, Tacoma businesspeople constructed an exhibition hall for trade shows near present-day Tacoma Avenue and

North Seventh Street, but a fire soon destroyed it. Throughout the 20th century, both high school bowls and their gymnasiums, the Tacoma Armory at South 11th and Yakima, the University of Puget Sound (UPS) Fieldhouse, and the Exposition Hall still located on Portland Avenue provided places where spectator sports reigned supreme. With increasing numbers of sports participants and enthusiasts amid a growing Tacoma–Pierce County population, however, less land was available for this traditional piecemeal development of major sports and entertainment venues.

Tacoma's desire for a facility was first expressed in a 1940s report entitled "Tacoma the City We Build." In canvassing local neighborhood and business organizations at the time, city planners discovered that of all the possible public works needed locally, a "civic auditorium" was highest on the list. From then on, until the completion of the Tacoma Dome, the questions always were: where would the facility be located, and how much would it would cost? There were many false starts along the way, beginning in 1967.

Former Tacoma Athletic Commission directors Stan Naccarato (foreground) and, L. to R., Ben Cheney, Pete Stojack, and Howard Pratt promote the annual Grid-Go-Round event (SSM, 2002.17.5).

"It all started casually enough," *Tacoma New Tribune*'s Jim Metcalf reported that year, "with some thinking-out-loud type remarks by County Commissioner Pat Gallagher at a Civic Arts Commission meeting about the possibilities of an all-sports stadium in Pierce County." To get things moving, the commissioners appointed a committee "to deal with a firm which wants to build a stadium with a retractable glass roof." The plan was abandoned, due in part to the realization that those initiating the effort wanted to introduce dog racing to Washingtonians as a gambling sport. There was also some uncertainty about attracting a major-league football or baseball team to the new facility. The citizens' committee, composed primarily of bankers, concluded that without the backing of major-league sports, the endeavor was doomed.

The second attempt to get the ball rolling was in 1976, when the county and city governments appointed another committee to spark the project. The group, headed by Booth

Tacoma Athletic Commission presented the annual State of Washington Sports Hall of Fame banquet at the Temple Theatre, ca. 1960s (SSM, Loc.1143).

Gardner, assumed that the new facility would be constructed near Cheney Stadium on land formerly used for local soapbox derby racing and owned by the Metropolitan Park District. What was needed, therefore, was citizen approval of a $14 million bond issue. In November 1976, voters rejected the proposal.

By 1980 voters had changed their minds and approved a $27.95 million proposal to construct what became the Tacoma Dome. By this time, Tacomans were convinced that a multipurpose facility could serve as a catalyst for economic revitalization downtown. A group known as the Tacoma Minidome Committee headed the election campaign. But unlike in the past, the Tacoma Athletic Commission got involved and played a significant role in assuring the successful outcome. Stan Naccarato, chairman of this committee, specifically "laid the bond issue's success at the feet of … Doug McArthur, who coordinated all bond issue promotions through his advertising agency, MAC-Northwest." When interviewed, McArthur admitted that one of the high points of his career was his role in the construction of the dome. Tacoma businessman Morley Brotman and sports writer Stan Farber were two others who helped see that the bond issue passed.

Before the measure was put to the voters, however, two concerns had to be resolved. One was the location of the facility. Between 1976 and 1979, proponents of seven different sites campaigned for the honor. Besides the Metropolitan Park District land near Cheney Stadium, other possibilities were in the Hawthorne area, Lincoln Heights, Tacoma Community College, Wapato Hills, the Thea Foss Waterway, and downtown Tacoma. Debating these options divided the various community and business organizations whose support was needed for a successful bond drive.

In September 1979, a consensus finally was reached. *Tacoma News Tribune* publisher Elbert Baker II is credited with bringing all sides together: he established a group composed of representatives from the Chamber of Commerce, the Downtown Tacoma Association, TAC, and the city council and advised them to reach a decision. "Civic leaders endorse Hawthorne minidome" headlined the newspaper on September 14, 1979, following the meeting. "Putting aside past differences, an ad hoc committee of

Tacoma community leaders today unanimously endorsed a triangular site in the Hawthorne neighborhood abutting Interstate 5 as the site for a proposed minidome sports and convention center."

The second concern was the dome's construction material. On the lighter side of the debate, one local pundit suggested that the architects make "the dome in the shape of Mt. Rainier, so Tacoma could name it Mount Tacoma and right the old wrong that labeled 'their mountain' Mount Rainier." Concrete, fabric, or wood, however, were the real contenders for the dome's roof material. Wood—inspired by

the Northern Arizona University Ensphere—was the winner of the competition. A year following the approval of the bond issue, the city selected Tacoma Dome Associates (TDA) as the successful bidder for the project. Dr. Wendell Rossman, architect-designer of the Arizona facility, joined Tacoma architect James McGranahan to form TDA. Merit Construction Company, headed by Jimmy Zarelli, built the structure. Zarelli's passion for sports was obvious: he was one of the Tacomans who invested in the Tacoma baseball team in 1971 to keep them from moving. He served as president of Baseball Tacoma from its inception until his death

Jerry Geehan interviews Sonja Heinie and Tyrone Power in 1937 during the filming of "Thin Ice" at Paradise on Mount Rainier (SSM, 302).

in August 1985. As a cheerleader for the concept of the Dome, Zarelli led the construction team to make it become a reality—within budget and on schedule. Someone wrote at the time that "if the Dome had a father, it would be Mr. Zarelli," and that moniker fit him well.

When the bond issue campaign was underway in 1980, Doug McArthur, speaking on behalf of TAC, said that if the voters said yes "and if the environmental-impact statements clear all hurdles in record time—and if no court tests surface—and if contractors stay on schedule—the minidome could be ready for business in 1983." He was right. In 1983 the Tacoma Dome opened for business, and since that time it has hosted thousands of sports events ranging from Seattle Sonics basketball to professional soccer and hockey games, Golden Glove boxing competitions, wrestling, and high school basketball and football championships.

Shanaman Sports Museum

The fund-raising campaign for the Tacoma Dome left a surplus in TAC's coffers. The funds were put in a trust for a much longed-for sports museum. Through the combined efforts of Clay Huntington, Marc Blau, and the City of Tacoma, along with grants from the Elbert Baker and Ben B. Cheney Foundations and several generous contributions from local businesses and individuals, the museum fund expanded and then was topped off by local businessman Fred Shanaman Jr. The Shanaman Sports Museum, one of TAC's most recent projects, opened its doors to the public in 1994 in the Tacoma Dome. This visual history of sports is yet another gift to the community from TAC.

Members of the 1956 Cheney Studs football team try to find themselves in a photo following their annual end-of-the-season banquet (SSM, 2002.17.30).

Athletic Awards and Other Contributions

As the 20th century neared its end, the commission began to sponsor awards for young athletes who have made significant contributions to their sport. TAC honors Pierce County High School Athletes of the Year, choosing from the many talented students initially selected as Athletes of the Month. The Hannula Award, so named for champion swimming coach Dick Hannula, is presented annually to the Pierce County amateur adult athlete of the year. Future sportscasters and journalists also are honored by means of the TAC-sponsored Clay Huntington Scholarship Award.

For 60 years, TAC—first as the Tacoma Athletic War Commission—has been promoting sports. The wartime needs of civilians and soldiers provided the impetus behind the organization's creation. By viewing sports as both entertainment and competition, by providing sports equipment and facilities, and by sponsoring attractive local events, the commission has been able to economically assist sports teams and individual athletes with its contributions, now totaling millions of dollars. And the giving continues, with its most recent contributions going to the Tom Cross Ballfields at Sprinker Recreation Center and the Bob Maguinez Ballfield at Heidelberg Park. TAC is "dedicated to sports and civic betterment." This is what it has done in the past, and this is what it will continue to do in the future.

TACOMA ATHLETIC COMMISSION, PAST PRESIDENTS
FOR MORE INFORMATION ON THE TAC, VISIT WWW.TACOMAATHLETIC.COM.

1944: Doug Dyckman Sr.	1965: Roger McDonald	1986: Dan Inveen
1945: John P. Heinrick	1966: Tom Cross	1987: Ed Fallon
1946: Jerry Waechter	1967: Stan Naccarato	1988: Nick Weinstein
1947: Jerry Geehan	1968: Stan Naccarato	1989: Jerry Plancich
1948: Howard Smith	1969: Hal Brotman	1990: Jack Johnson
1949: Frank Gillihan	1970: Hal Brotman	1991: Dennis Faker
1950: Frank Walters	1971: Frank Ruffo	1992: Rich Berndt
1951: Dave Tuell Sr.	1972: Dick Greco	1993: George Nordi
1952: Jim Peterson	1973: Hank Semmern	1994: George Nordi
1953: Dillard Howell	1974: Hank Semmern	1995: Dr. Greg Plancich
1954: Ples Irwin	1975: Tom Paine	1996: Dr. Greg Plancich
1955: Dr. Charles Larson	1976: Tom Paine	1997: Herb Brown
1956: Dick Beckman	1977: Del Smith	1998: Joe Macaluso
1957: Clay Huntington	1978: Morris McCollum	1999: Scott Nordi
1958: Clay Huntington	1979: Wayne Thronson	2000: Scott Nordi
1959: Morley Brotman	1980: Greg Pratt	2001: Mike Medrzycki
1960: Jim Rondeau	1981: Jim Maniatis	2002: Kevin Kalal
1961: Neil Hoff	1982: Doug McArthur	2003: Tony Anderson
1962: Heil Hoff	1983: Don Smith	2004: Tony Anderson
1963: Bill Gazecki	1984: Bud Barnes	2005: Tony Anderson
1964: Marv Tommervik	1985: Jerry Beitz	

CHAPTER 2

PUBLIC PARKS, PLAYGROUNDS, AND ORGANIZED SPORTS

Golden Gloves 1957 champions pose with the embossed briefcases they received as awards (SSM, 2002.17.13).

When Pierce County was first being settled, sports were pretty much a private affair, and organized sports, when they came into being, were the domain of the well-to-do. Over time, numerous organizations emerged, many developing their own facilities. Those who could afford it participated in a wide array of sports, from archery and riflery to golf, foxhunting, and baseball. In the 19th century, the only genuinely public sport was horse racing. The track was located west of Tacoma's downtown on land just north of present-day University of Puget Sound (UPS).

For years the notion that local governments should assume any responsibility for sports programs was a novel idea, and it was not until the turn of the 20th century that municipalities began to change their thinking. By this time, cities realized that they must play a role in the socialization of the so-called masses. By creating playgrounds and sports programs to channel the energies of young people into worthwhile endeavors, the Metropolitan Park District of Tacoma established the first public sports program in the city, but it took years of citizen nudging before the district developed the facilities and created the programs needed so that young people had a place to play.

The creation of public parks in Tacoma began through private developers donating land for this purpose. Clinton P. Ferry was the first when, in 1883, he provided for a neighborhood park within his new subdivision. Other property owners followed suit. When the Northern Pacific Railroad selected the emerging city as the site for its terminus in 1873, it formed the Tacoma Land Company (TLC) to determine both how the railroad's land was to be developed and how the new city was to be governed. Parks were part of TLC's concept of a well-planned city, and Wright, Garfield, Lincoln, and McKinley Parks are its most well-known results.

In 1888 TLC lent its political clout to convince Congress to donate Point Defiance to the city for a park. President Ulysses S. Grant had originally set aside the land for a military reservation. When it became clear that the army had no plans for the site, local citizens petitioned Congress to use the land for a park. The wish was granted, with the understanding that should the military ever need the site, the federal government could reclaim the land.

Whenever TLC designated property to the city parks, the deeds always included a proviso that defined how the land was to be used. If TLC's instructions were not followed, ownership of the property reverted back to it. With the 1886 grant for Wright Park, for instance, the proviso mandated municipal participation in park development and maintenance and the creation of an agency to oversee the development of parks in the city. By 1890 Tacoma owned more than 700 acres of parkland but had yet to establish an overseer. Therefore, in 1890, the Tacoma City Council created a Board of Park Commissioners to "take charge and exercise control over all parks belonging to the city."

Funding Parks

It took money to develop and maintain Tacoma's growing system of parks. Funding for the endeavor came from the city's budget, but by the turn of the 20th century it became clear that there would never be enough money to cover the costs of creating the parks originally envisioned by Tacoma's commissioners. Stuart Rice, chair of the Board of Park Commissioners in 1907, proposed creating a separate taxing district as a solution to the problem. His model was the local school district, which had its own taxing authority and operated independently of city government.

The Washington State Legislature, however, had to

Ben Cheney lends a helping hand to two boys hustling to get to football practice (courtesy the Cheney Family).

authorize the use of taxing powers for this purpose. Rice wrote the needed legislation and lobbied for its passage. In March 1907, his statute became law. Within a month, local voters approved the creation of the Metropolitan Park District of Tacoma and Pierce County and elected its first board, mandated to oversee its operations.

When the park board began its work, sports were not part of its plan. Public parks were to be quiet places of nature, not an environment wherein children could play. Indeed, in 1909, the board asked "the Superintendent of Public Schools to have the teachers take up the matter of children running over the grass in the parks." The idea of providing baseball fields in the neighborhoods was vetoed as well because local residents thought that children playing baseball would lower their property values. Instead, children used the streets and landscaped parking strips in front of people's homes for their games. Neighbors, in response, tried to get the city council to pass an ordinance prohibiting boys from playing in the streets.

Playgrounds Needed

The need for a public sports facility and playgrounds arose at the time voters created the new park district, when a baseball park was proposed. "Public outcry had been aroused over the temporary occupation by the baseball management of a strip of Lincoln Park," editorialized the *Tacoma Daily News* in March 1907. "Baseball is essentially a public enterprise when properly managed, and the News believes the Tacoma team is going to be properly managed." When kicked out of Lincoln Park, the Tacoma team tried McKinley Park, only to face a city council order of trespass. "Tacoma is without a park of any description in which high school and other amateur athletic organizations may hold their meets," the *News* reported later in the month. "Instead of having league baseball in common with all other cities of the country, the city is apparently endeavoring to keep from having it forced upon it."

Another issue was vandalism. In Tacoma, complaints had been made of "shooting, damaging the statuary … in the parks. The large lions at the entrance of Wright Park have been used as targets. … In Ferry Park a gang of mischievous boys amuse themselves by throwing stones at the ornaments." Children clearly needed alternative ways to expend their energy. "There was little for the children to do in the cities," explained one proponent of playgrounds. "In this time of idleness the devil has found much for idle hands to do." Tacoma was, in other words, beginning to see the need for playgrounds.

What energized the discussion in 1907 was W. W. Seymour's $10,000 grant to the city, a donation that was to be used for some park purpose. Seymour's investments in a wide array of economic ventures had made him a wealthy man, and his temperament made him a local philanthropist. When he made his contribution to the Metropolitan Park District's board, he left it up to a committee to determine how the money should be spent. His only requirement was that it should go to something to benefit the young people of Tacoma.

Tacoma High School students petitioned for a new athletic field. One teacher from the school proposed the construction of a boy's gymnasium to keep troublemakers off the street. Competing with the student's petition, the

Tacoma Boosters urged the creation of playgrounds, especially after the organization was approached by those wanting to outlaw playing in the streets. "We want to go slow before we do anything that will keep the boys from playing ball," said Booster Tom J. Fleetwood. "They've got to have a place to play, and some of the little chaps have no other place but the street. I am not going to stand for anything that will shut them out of a playground. The boys have got to have a place to play."

The winner of the funds was a conservatory in Wright Park. But the idea that public playgrounds and supervised play were significant responsibilities of the Metropolitan Park District survived the debate over how to use Seymour's donation. Indeed, Tacoma's mayor at the time, George P. Wright, claimed that playgrounds were really where Seymour wanted his money to go. "What I wish we could do," Wright said, "is to follow out what I know was Mr. Seymour's wishes. His gift was the result of an inspiration received while he was in Chicago: the public playgrounds for children, where they can find a place to play without going in the street. The trouble is that the money given out is not sufficient to purchase the grounds and maintain them in the central part of the city."

Stadium Bowl, Lincoln Bowl, and Sparks Field

Both playgrounds and sports programs for children ultimately came into being through the combined efforts of the Tacoma park and school district boards. From the early years of Tacoma's history, the question of where young people could play group sports was a nagging concern. This was even more important when sports became an extracurricular activity for high school students. But playing fields for the young was not the only reason that Tacomans eventually clamored for an outdoor arena. Local teams needed a venue. In addition, Tacoma needed a place where people could gather en masse for special events and entertainment.

The story of how the Stadium Bowl came to be begins with school architect Frederick Heath, who submitted his plans for a high school athletic field to the Tacoma School Board in 1907. Adjacent to the new Tacoma High School site was a rugged gulch that Heath considered ideal for the development, one modeled in part on the Roman Coliseum.

Local citizens had raised $50,000 by the end of 1908 for the construction of the facility.

A two-day festival held on June 10 and 11, 1910, celebrated the completion of the stadium. "Four thousand children formed a living American flag and 7,000 executed carefully rehearsed dances, exercises and drills before 25,000 cheering fans," reported the *Tacoma Daily Ledger*. The next day, a track meet between Tacoma High School students and competitors from Seattle entertained the crowd. The two events signaled the future uses of the arena. Since then, the bowl has seen military exhibitions, carnivals, performances by John Philip Sousa's band, and the speeches of presidents. Reportedly, Babe Ruth hit a baseball from the bowl into Commencement Bay. College and high school football players have graced its field, as have professional baseball teams.

One high school stadium and one athletic field were not enough for Tacoma, however. At the same time that Tacoma High School's new arena was completed, parents in the south end were petitioning the school board for a new high school. In September 1911, the board agreed to a site located near Lincoln Park and named the new school Lincoln Park High School. The building, another one of Frederick Heath's masterpieces, opened in 1913.

It took seven years to build an athletic field, the first Lincoln "bowl," north of the high school. Compared to Stadium Bowl, this facility was quite primitive, but it served a useful purpose at a crucial time. School board minutes for December 1917 report "another slide of earth at the Stadium [Bowl] from Cliff Avenue … covering a portion of the railway tracks and damaging the railroad coal bunkers." Tacomans were faced with having no sports venue for a period, and the creation of a new athletic field at Lincoln filled this void.

By the 1930s, events held in the Lincoln athletic field were just as attractive to Tacomans as those held in the restored Stadium Bowl. In 1936 the City Baseball League offered to install floodlights in return for a five-year lease of Lincoln's field. The school board accepted the offer. The baseball league's lease, however, was agreed to with some hesitation, for at the same time the board was planning the construction of a new Lincoln Bowl.

The endeavor had begun in 1933, when the Tacoma School District sought federal New Deal funding for the city's second major athletic field. The Works Projects Administration (WPA), however, would not approve a grant covering the anticipated $235,000 cost for the structure without local financial support. Voters approved the needed increase in property taxes in March 1940, making the Lincoln Bowl a reality. George Leif was the architect, with J. Arnston the project engineer.

Construction began a year later. "Athletic Bowl at Lincoln High School Taking Shape," a *Tacoma News Tribune* headline reported in May 1941. By October the same year, the *Tacoma Times* told readers that "It Won't Be Long Now, Men … When completed which will not be long, it will present another asset to the city. The South End, home of athletic patronage here, has long needed such a field." And

Brian Sternberg was the 1963 TAC's Athlete of the Year; looking on are Clay Huntington, George Prescott, Marv Tommervik, Jack Sonntag, Sternberg, Howard Pratt, and AP Sports Editor Jack Hewins (SSM, 1526).

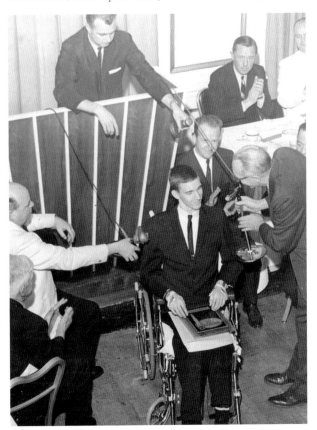

though the newspaper reporters anticipated football games in the Lincoln Bowl by the end of the year, it was not to be, because the United States entered World War II instead. By this time, the excavation for the facility was completed but not much else.

It took another 20 years to complete Lincoln Bowl. By 1947, work had begun again, but it was not until the early 1960s that the excavated Lincoln Gulch was filled to form the arena visible today. The project was aided by the construction of the I-5 freeway. "Lincoln Gulch is no more," reported the *Tacoma News Tribune*'s Dick Stansfield in 1960. "And Lincoln Bowl is now really a bowl. … All this is courtesy of the Tacoma Freeway. … Contractors … needed a place to dump earth. Lincoln gulch was available. … The visual change is staggering, possibilities for the area enormous."

Tacoma was not, however, the only Pierce County community to build a good outdoor athletic field devoted to school sports. In 1923, close to the time that plans were underway at Lincoln, the Puyallup school board purchased land near Meeker Elementary School for both a playground and an athletic field for high school students. At first, students named the facility Viking Field, to match the mascot adopted by the high school for all of its extracurricular activities. In 1970, however, the school board "decided to rename a number of schools and other facilities in the district to honor persons who had given outstanding service to the students of Puyallup." In the process, it changed the name of Viking Field to memorialize Carl Sparks because the former coach and athletic director had played a major role in shaping the lives of high school athletes.

Intercity School Sports

The Tacoma School District board was also the first to introduce physical education programs to the city, especially for high school students. "Physical culture" was added to the high school curriculum in 1897, with the construction of tennis courts the first item on the board's agenda. Prior to the 1920s, competitions crossed jurisdictional lines for intercity events.

Intercity sports were banned, however, after a 1913 episode entailing, according to a Tacoma newspaper writer, "disgraceful scenes in which drunken students" wreaked havoc in the Carlton Hotel. "There should be no inter-city sports," the news editor continued in his 1927 article. "A high school contest at a considerable distance from Tacoma would be something which no parent would regard with particular favor in this day of automobiles and pocket flasks." Whether local high school students should compete in intercity events was a rather hot issue at the turn of the 20th century. The Tacoma School Board decided to put the matter before the voters in 1927, with an election result firmly in favor of intercity sports.

The public also pushed for playgrounds. Beginning in 1911, ad hoc committees, members of Parent Teacher Associations, and local neighborhood organizations all went before the school board at one time or another asking for land for public playgrounds. As a result, by the 1930s the Tacoma School District had established a pattern of playgrounds located adjacent to or near most elementary schools in the city. The Metropolitan Park District continued to amass land for playgrounds during this same period.

The park and school districts assumed an informal part-

"CHILDREN MUST HAVE PLAYGROUNDS"

W. W. Seymour Says Need Is Imperative: He Tells of Similar Undertakings in Other Cities and of the Good that Will Be Accomplished.

"Whether public playgrounds should be provided for the children of Tacoma," said W. W. Seymour to the News today, "is not a question about which there can be any argument. That concerning the subject which cannot be too strongly emphasized is the educational value of play properly directed.

"It is conceded that all children must play, and if boys cannot find any other place in which to indulge in their sports, they necessarily have to take to the streets. The largest cities of the country, notably New York and Chicago, have only recently and at great cost, in condemning properties for the purpose, established playgrounds for children. I visited some of those in Chicago. They have nine of them. They are called squares and are from two to three acres in area. They are under the supervision of a board of commissioners appointed by the judges of the courts. These playgrounds are equipped with buildings used as gymnasiums, swimming pools, reading and rest rooms. In one I visited there is a restaurant operated by the commissioners where lunches were

sold at cost. It has also a wading pond for little girls and sand heaps for them to play in. The older boys are provided with places for ball playing, running, and other athletic sports, which they can enjoy under the direction of those whose duties are to see that the games are carried on in a fair and manly manner.

"It is not so much that the boys are kept off the streets by having a playground as that they are afforded the means of playing under conditions which, while giving them all the benefits, eliminate the temptations. There is no cheating, fighting, or rough talk allowed. There is nothing that is more calculated to make boys strong and manly as a good square game of baseball.

"I am heartily in favor of having playgrounds for the children in Tacoma. The city is growing so rapidly that no time should be lost in securing such advantages for boys and girls. As time goes on, the difficulty and cost of solving the problem, which must of necessity confront this city as it has other large centers of population, will be increased."

—*Tacoma Daily News*, April 15, 1907

Young boys bat the ball around at a local baseball camp in 1965 (SSM, 2001.26.15).

nership that led to organized and supervised recreation throughout the city. Ferry Park became "the first junior sponsored playground in Tacoma under the impetus of the great playground movement." This endeavor went beyond the development and use of playground facilities. In 1934, for example, the Metropolitan Park District agreed to sponsor boys' clubs for a two-month trial period, using school gymnasiums for the program. To formalize the relationship, in 1944 the combined park and school district boards created the Tacoma Recreation Commission, with Tom Lantz as its director.

Sprinker Recreation Center

By the end of World War II, Tacomans had established the framework for the sports programs that would follow. But demographics were pointing to a new need outside the city's boundaries. Throughout the 20th century, the population of Pierce County had been growing faster than that of the City of Tacoma. The war accelerated this trend. And sports were an important part of these outlying communities from the begin-

ning, which can be seen in old photographs of local baseball teams. By the 1940s, the Tacoma Athletic War Commission included teams from Pierce County towns in its Hoop-Go-Round. Indeed, the December 1943 event was held in Clover Park High School's new gymnasium in Lakewood.

In 1958 Pierce County Commissioners created the Pierce County Parks and Recreation Department, with Tom Cross as its first director. The department's purpose was to meet the recreational needs of people living within the unincorporated areas of Pierce County, using an inherited system of parks created in the past. Spanaway Park is probably the most significant of these bequests. Another was located on the north shore of American Lake, where over the years crew enthusiasts have found a home.

Pierce County Parks continued Tacoma's program of supervised play for children, such as swimming classes at county beaches and tennis on area courts. A strong emphasis also was placed on the cooperation and teamwork so necessary to sports. As in Tacoma, a partnership arose between the park department and the various county school districts with active sports leagues in basketball, wrestling, softball, and football.

With time, Pierce County expanded its sports and recreation programs and created new golf courses, community centers, and recreational facilities, including Sprinker Recreation Center, completed in 1976. Tom Cross is credited with creating this significant multipurpose facility. In the early 1960s, he envisioned undeveloped land across from Spanaway Park at Military Road as something that could be a haven for sports enthusiasts. Softball, baseball, ice skating, tennis, archery, football, and horseshoes were just some of the activities he felt would make it a place where families could enjoy recreational activities all in one location. The outdoor portion opened in 1969 and was named to honor Harry Sprinker, an avid sports enthusiast and Pierce County commissioner at the time the complex was under construction. The indoor center opened in 1976, and the ice arena hosted the compulsory figures competition for the U.S. Figure Skating Association's national championships in 1987. It was also the practice rink for the Tacoma Rockets of the Western Hockey League and the Tacoma Sabercats of the West Coast Hockey League.

Other Sports Facilities

Tacoma and Pierce County residents have been instrumental in the development of sports and recreational facilities. Many individuals who pioneered local endeavors came from places where parks and play fields were hard to come by because the land was already consumed by houses, business blocks, and industrial complexes. Given this awareness, their cry for more sports and recreational facilities began early and has never stopped.

Heidelberg Park, Peck Athletic Field, and Cheney Field are all part of the outcome of this local effort. So, too, are the Harry Lang Stadium in Lakewood, the South End Recreation Area softball complex near Mount Tahoma High School, and countless school sports facilities extend-

Ref Chuck Gilmur (L.) follows the action at a UPS Logger football game (UPS).

ing from Buckley to the Gig Harbor peninsula. Pierce County's history is also commemorated at Fort Steilacoom Park, where soccer players now compete on land once a part of America's first military base in the Pacific Northwest.

By the end of the 20th century, the notion that municipal and county governments should play a role in sports was firmly established. Without countywide school district support, young men and women would not have the opportunity to test their mettle in their sport of choice. By the end of the 20th century, just about every city and town in the county had created parks and playgrounds for the enjoyment of everyone, from toddler-age T-ball enthusiasts to seniors running marathons. Through the collective and persistent efforts of many local citizens, the city and county now have many places to play.

CHAPTER 3

UMPIRES AND REFEREES:
THE SILENT SERVICE

Umpire Clarence Stave was known for his jester-like performance whenever he was behind the plate at semipro baseball games (MB).

Every sport has rules and ways to interpret them when infractions occur. This simple fact underlines the essential premise of sportsmanship: it matters not whether you win a game but how you play. Honesty and decency are a part of the equation too, and it is the umpires' and referees' responsibility to make sure that in the enthusiasm of the moment, players remember the rules and behave.

Wayne Gardner, who refereed volleyball for more than 70 years, discovered early in life that playing the sport also meant being an arbiter from time to time. To referee, he once told a reporter, was a good way to learn the game. Jimmy Rondeau, one of the top referees for Tacoma's Golden Gloves and who refereed George Foreman's fight against Ken Norton in Caracas, Venezuela, put another spin on the profession. While he oversaw matches at the federal penitentiary on McNeil Island, wardens ask him to be liberal in interpreting the rules when cellblock rowdies were in the ring, so that inmates would wear out their anger in the ring against each other rather than the wardens.

The referee's task is not an easy one, however, because unlike other kinds of arbitrators, the sports official's goal is to be unnoticed in the contest. Obviously this is not possible all the time, especially when fans, players, or the media differ with a call. In 1913, for example, one newspaper reporter questioned the impartiality of an official during a Tacoma-Seattle soccer game. He accused the official of making his decisions to benefit Seattle because a relative of his was on the team. The reporter's point was that there was a need for impartial officials, and with time his wish materialized.

Tom Cross

In Tacoma and Pierce County there have been more than 2000 officials, considered some of the best guardians of the rules of sports and sportsmanship. Among so many, it is a challenge to single out any one of them for historical accolades, but Tom Cross is often cited as model and mentor. "He was an icon," said Jan Wolcott, current director of Pierce County Parks and one of the many officials influenced by Cross. "It was a learning experience to work with him."

Cross sat on both sides of the sports fence. He played several sports for fun and wanted to make sure that everyone around him enjoyed sports as much as he did. From 1947, when he took his first job as athletic supervisor of Tacoma's Metropolitan Park District, until 1981, when he retired as Pierce County's first Parks and Recreation director, his mantra was sports.

Cross's work led him to referee. In that role he achieved a regional reputation by officiating at Pacific-8 Conference basketball (1948–1964) and football (1948–1976) games. He was also the organizational force behind the creation of the Washington Officials Association (WOA) in 1946 to cover football and basketball and is considered the first assigning secretary of the Western Washington Officials Association serving the greater Tacoma–Pierce County area.

Ken Jones, longtime president of WOA, explained why Cross considered the organization crucial to officiating: prior to this time, each school decided on its referees or umpires for a game, a process subject to criticism. A local officials governing body, however, could prepare a pool of officials to meet the individual needs of those playing sports. With this in mind, Cross proposed an organization that could recruit, train, and then assign officials based on their ability to impartially arbitrate the rules of various games.

Cross was an inductee into the WOA Hall of Fame in 2003, as well as the first official inducted into the Washington Interscholastic Activities Association (WIAA) Hall of Fame in 2004, because of his commitment to interscholastic and intercollegiate sports. Along the way, he periodically shared with reporters his most memorable moments. For example, when asked by *Tacoma News Tribune* sports editor Earl Luebker in 1975, Cross defined his most exciting time as a referee: the 1963 Southern California–Wisconsin Rose Bowl game when Cal won 42–37. "We ran out of footballs," Cross remembered; "we used 24, and the game must have lasted 400 hours." Before it was over, the lights had to be turned on in the stadium.

Other Notables

Sometimes Cross shared the field with Marv Tommervik, one of Pacific Lutheran University (PLU)'s greatest players and coaches. Together, they considered a 1969 Southern California–Stanford game as the most memorable. "Southern Cal won it 26–24 on Ray Ayala's 34-yard field goal with no time left," Luebker reported. "That was one of the most thrilling, stunning games I've ever seen," Tommervik remembered. "Stanford had scored, to go ahead 24–23, with just a little more than a minute to go."

Cross and Tommervik also share honors as recipients of the WOA award for meritorious service. Established in 1966, the award is given to those whom their peers consider the best in the business. Cross received his in 1976, Tommervik in 1978.

Ken Jones singled out some of the most memorable officials: Joe Salatino, Lornie Merkle, Dale Bloom, Jerry Snarski, Dean Haner, and Jack Johnson, along with Tom Cross. Jack Johnson was the first National Football League (NFL) official from Tacoma. After 10 years as a Pac-10 football official, Aaron Pointer enjoyed a 17-year career in the NFL as a head linesman, retiring in 2003. This was Pointer's second successful venture in athletics; he played professional baseball for 10 seasons including time with the Houston Astros and Chicago Cubs. After winning a Pacific Coast League championship with the Tacoma Cubs in 1969, the rangy centerfielder finished his playing career in

CHAPTER SPONSORED BY TOM TOMMERVIK:

Making sure athletes played by the rules was just one part of Marv Tommervik's career as a football official, says his son Tom, who dedicates the history of Tacoma-area officials to him. A past president of the Washington Officials Association, Marv also traveled around the state helping interpret new rules. He officiated at the high school and small college level and traveled from coast to coast for 25 years as a Pac-10 Division I football official, which included officiating at two Rose Bowls.

Japan before returning to Tacoma, where he worked for 25 years with the Pierce County Parks & Recreation Department. And, if the name Pointer rings a bell, it's because his sisters are the Pointer Sisters of pop music fame. But there are others, too. Buddy Horton, for example, has refereed Pacific-10 Conference women's basketball and then switched sports to become a part of the NFL officials' roster. Kirk Dornan enjoyed a successful Pac-10 football career before joining the ranks of the NFL. Jay Stricherz has officiated football for 26 years and was the referee of the first BCS championship game, matching Tennessee and Florida State. He also has a Cotton bowl game to his credit. Tom Cross considered Ron Storaasli, a basketball referee, the best he had ever seen. Bruce Alexander is the only National Basketball Association (NBA) referee from Tacoma. Walt Gogan was the first nationally rated volleyball official from the city; Teri Wood was the second.

Women Officials

Cross also actively recruited women officials. Suzanne Koenig answered the call in the early 1960s and officiated women's basketball for 24 years. When she began, the women's game was played outside the realm of local inter-scholastic sports, through park department and church leagues. However, following Title IX of the Education Amendments of 1972, which prohibits discrimination on the basis of sex, and the aggressive introduction of women's sports into the realm of scholastic and collegiate competition, Koenig was able to watch female athletics grow with the times. When interviewed in 2004, she said her greatest joy as an official was watching women's basketball improve both in terms of coaching and playing ability.

Koenig also provided a reason why maintaining a corps of women officials remains a challenge. "Men view officiating as recreation," she explained. For them, "it is a way to keep their hand in a sport; women, on the other hand, have to balance the rearing of children with their time on the court or field." Whereas the local male officials during Koenig's time congregated at the Cloverleaf Tavern with coaches from both sides of the game "to hash through the plays" over beer and pizza, women went home to "pay the babysitter and resume their domestic responsibilities."

Women referees were also unlikely candidates for a sportswriter's interview. Men, on the other hand, had an open forum, and every official had stories to tell as a keeper of the rules of sports.

Lornie Merkle points out the ground rules to manager Doug McArthur of the Cheney Studs while partner Frank Morrone looks on (SSM, 1199).

Lornie Merkle

Lornie Merkle graduated from Bellarmine High School in 1934 with hopes of a sports career. However, when his brother could not referee a football game and asked him to take his place, he became an official overnight. He earned $1 his first time out. Merkle remembered how he became an official during the early years of the 20th century and the challenges he faced when he stopped playing the game and started interpreting its rules. "I made money and I enjoyed it," Merkle said in 2002. By the time he retired in 1976, he had officiated in some 4,500 football and basketball games over the course of almost 40 years. He could be found at local high school games and also as a referee for Pac-8 games.

"Coaches determined who they wanted to referee their contests," Merkle noted when explaining how he was able to officiate for so long. "You had to be on their list to work." Coaches selected those whom they respected as impartial, guys who knew the rules even when those changed.

Respect didn't mean that coaches and Merkle always agreed once the game began. One of his favorite photographs shows a local coach arguing in his face over Merkle's knowledge of the rules. "In the old days," he told *News Tribune* reporter John Lawrence, "sometimes you had to run for the exit after the game or lock yourself in the nearest room."

Merkle's retirement surprised many coaches, but he departed the scene without any regrets. "I know it sounds corny, but I owe them [the coaches] a debt of gratitude for putting up with me for all those years. My calls were bad, but they suited my personality," Merkle noted. "He has umpired forever," said the program when Merkle received his Meritorious Service Award in 1977. "Those of us who played when he did [officiated] will never forget him."

The Officiating System

By the time Merkle retired, the question of who could officiate was evolving into the system used today, one emphasizing WOA's goals when it first organized in 1946. Local coaches are no longer allowed to determine the officials' roster. Instead, potential referees and umpires have to undergo a training regime that ranges from rules clinics to on-field— or on-court—experience. "This program specifically pertains to high-profile sports such as basketball and football," noted Pierce County Parks Director Wolcott when explaining the new system.

Beyond training, officials are judged by their peers under a rating system. Wolcott considers this endeavor the most important part of the process, one that maintains the integrity of the profession. An umpire or referee must know the rules and be aware of where he or she is on the playing field or court. An umpire or referee must also maintain a professional stance that communicates impartiality to the most argumentative coach or irate fan.

Worst Call?

Reporters are always tempted to ask umpires or referees if they rememeber their worst call. For Lornie Merkle, it happened during a UPS-PLU football game when he got so confused about a play after he tossed his flag on the ground that he did not make any call at all. "The writers about jumped out of the press box," Merkle remembered. "Then I

went home, and there they were running the game on TV, and there I was, blowing the call. When I woke up the next day, there's a two-column box in the *TNT* about how I blew the call. … And you ask me if I remember my worst call?"

For Tom Cross, it was a regionally televised game between the University of California and the University of Southern California. "It involved a situation where the ball had been kicked around in the end zone. I called it a safety. The cannon had gone off and the score was posted on the board, but the other officials jarred my memory on the rules." The error was quickly corrected by the other officials "and things worked out all right."

Motivation

Why be a referee or an umpire? For Ken Jones, who has been a referee for 35 years, the activity is a tremendous release. As a land use planning consultant, most of what he does in the workaday world is mental and officebound. As an official, he gets exercise and satisfaction from giving something back to the athletic community. Marc Blau, a 1997 recipient of the National Federation Distinguished Volleyball Official Award, concurs: "Officiating is a perfect opportunity to give back to a sport that one personally enjoys."

"It certainly isn't for the money," said Jan Wolcott. "I love to be involved in football and basketball." As a result, he has spent 26 years assigning officials for the two sports, as well as officiating himself. Blau agreed that "the vast majority of people choose to referee because it is fun and they love being around sports and young people."

Blau also reflected on what it personally means to be a sports official. "After 30 years of officiating, I am still waiting to call the perfect game. To be a good official, you have to respect what coaches go through to prepare for a game. You have to understand that it is not easy managing so many different personalities, dealing with parents, and putting together a good game plan. At the same time, I hope that through my interaction and approach with the coaches, they will recognize that I take my job seriously."

CHAPTER 4

SPORTSWRITERS AND BROADCASTERS

Jerry Geehan began his broadcasting career at KVI radio in 1932 (MB).

On a cold autumn day in 1887, a newspaper reporter watched Harvard and Yale alumni batting an old boxing glove around with a stick. The reporter, George Hancock, tied the laces of the boxing glove together to form a ball, marked off bases and a pitcher's box inside the gymnasium of Chicago's Farragut Boat Club, and in the process invented the game of softball.

In 1933 a *Dayton Daily News* photographer, Myron E. Scott, watched three boys racing their homemade engine-less cars down one of the hills of that Ohio city. He saw a contest in the making and introduced Americans to the soapbox derby.

The association between sports and the media has always been a tigh tone, but how the connection became such an integral partnership relates less to playing games and more to economics and technology. As the American economy grew following the Civil War, so too did a worker's income. This enabled families to make purchases once considered unattainable. They could now afford to attend or participate in sports events. Improved literacy meant that families could read about sports in their local newspapers.

Newspaper Sports Sections Emerge

By the turn of the 20th century, improved technologies governing the production of newspapers and the creation of the "penny press" revolutionized the relationship between sports and the media. What had begun as small items scattered within the hodgepodge of a newspaper's reporting became a separate sports section, with some written by reporters whose reputations equaled the best novelists of the day.

Tacoma's Marshall Hunt, son of Tacoma newspaperman Herbert Hunt, was one such writer. As sports editor for the *New York Daily News*, his assignment was covering Babe Ruth. "Not the Yankees," *News Tribune* reporter John Bailey explained at the time of Hunt's death, "but Babe Ruth himself. He became the Babe's companion and confidant."

Those were the days "of the swashbuckling press corps," local sports columnist Dan Walton remembered. "They wrote of people and characters and not of dry statistics. Often they wrote in purple phrases. They didn't spare the adjectives. And the fans ate it up." Walton knew, for he too was a product of the same golden age of sports writers after he became sports editor for the *Tacoma Ledger* in 1921. By

Elliott Metcalf, the Tacoma Times Sports Editor (SSM, 2000.2.6).

the time of his death in 1976, Walton had spent decades writing for both the *Ledger* and then the *News Tribune*. His "Sports Log" column (including sections titled Chips, Splinters, and Driftwood) remains a rich source on the events and personalities of the era.

Contemporaries of Walton included sports columnists Elliot Metcalf and Nelson R. Hong. Hong preceded Metcalf as sports editor at the *Tacoma News Tribune* in 1930. Until 1937, when the *Tribune* purchased the *Ledger,* Hong's "Between You and Me" column entertained readers as much as did Walton's in the competing newspaper. When Walton retired in the early 1970s, Earl Luebker took his place. Like the sports writers before him, he had a lot more interest in the people who played the sports than the outcome of the game. His sports awards were numerous, including Washington State Sports Writer of the Year in 1974 and the Jim Murray Sports Writer Award. In 1996 he was inducted into the PLU Sports Hall of Fame.

Countless other sports writers have informed and entertained local readers over the years. George Washington "Biddy" Bishop and J. Ernest Knight were two of the earliest. Dave James, Howard Clifford, Jack Sareault, Mike Ingraham, Don Davison, John Lawrence, Dick Kunkle, Stan Farber, Ed Honeywell, Art Thiel, and John McGrath are only a few of the others, some of whom are still writing today.

Radio Broadcasts

Until the 1920s, only the written word informed the public about its favorite sports. The introduction of radio (and, later, television) added a new dimension to reporting by giving the listener (or viewer) the opportunity to experience a sports event firsthand. Early sports commentators had voices of velvet and nerves of steel. Their words built memorable images that captured imaginations. Armed with statistical cards, a wealth of knowledge, a microphone, and an abiding love of the game, sportscasters made listening to (or watching) a sporting event in the living room almost as exciting as being there in person.

One of the earliest sports broadcasts in Tacoma did not actually come over the radio. In the early 1920s, before

World Series games were locally aired, fans gathered outside the *Tacoma Ledger* building on St. Helens Street to watch the progress of the game. According to Sonny Bailey, a former Tacoma baseball player, "They erected a big baseball diamond billboard and use a moving ping-pong ball to represent a baseball. The *Ledger* received the teletype update on the game action and it was re-created with the ping-pong ball on that billboard." Another baseball player, Verne Champagne, remembered, "A thousand people filled the street, even in the rain. Babe Ruth was playing in those days, and when he hit a home run the ball would go over the billboard fence."

Ping-pong balls and billboards were replaced by radio broadcasts after the medium came to Tacoma in 1922. One of the first local stations was 7XV, which operated out of the home of Howard Reichert on North Ninth and L Streets. However, reporting of sports events was not on its early schedule, which included news reports and musical programs. As the 1920s came to a close, two stations gave radio its first commercial broadcasts in Tacoma. KGB, owned by the *Tacoma Ledger* and Mullins Electric, and KDZE, with its equipment on the roof of the Winthrop Hotel, both brought the world to Tacoma via the airwaves.

Commercial radio introduced Tacoma not only to a new form of entertainment, but to the personalities behind the microphone as well. One of the most popular voices belonged to Jerry Geehan, the founding father of West Coast sports broadcasting and the first baseball announcer in Tacoma. Geehan recalled that "my career actually began at Lincoln High School as master of ceremonies of a weekly junior broadcast."

Two major radio stations developed during this time: KMO and KVI. Geehan was hired by KVI in 1932, shortly after he graduated from high school. He was responsible for broadcasting City League baseball games from Lincoln Bowl, as well as all high school sporting events. He became sports director at KVI, later moving to KMO in 1938 to broadcast Western International League (WIL) baseball, sponsored by the cereal Wheaties. Along with a daily radio sportscast, he announced College of Puget Sound (now UPS) and Pacific Lutheran College (now PLU) football and basketball games.

When Geehan moved to KMO, he essentially switched jobs with a fellow Lincoln High School graduate, Larry Huseby. Huseby combined news and sportscasting first at KMO and then at KVI.

In 1936, while Geehan was announcing ski races at Mount Rainier, he interviewed Sonja Heinie and Tyrone Power, who were then filming the movie *Thin Ice*. "They were both very easy to get along with," recalled Geehan. "I spent much time with them playing bridge." He also interviewed Al Ulbrickson that year. The longtime University of Washington (UW) crew coach had just returned from the Berlin Olympics, where his rowers had won a gold medal.

One of Geehan's most memorable moments in broadcasting was the PLU-Gonzaga football game in 1940. Geehan remembered that "PLU was a huge underdog, but they won with a last-minute field goal by Marv Harshman." Geehan also recalled being refused permission to broadcast a Freddie Steele fight. "We did the fight anyway—live from the top of a motor home outside the stadium."

Geehan became the KMO sales manager in 1943 and later was general manager for both KMO radio and Channel 13 television. In the late 1950s, a group headed by Geehan purchased KTAC. He spent 37 years in Tacoma radio and television but also remained active in community and professional affairs, including serving as president of the board of the Washington State Broadcasters. The media personalities who succeeded him, however, were Geehan's greatest source of pride. "We hired Don Hill, Clay Huntington, Doug McArthur, Rod Belcher, Bob Robertson, and Bill O'Mara. Hiring these men was the highlight of my career."

Sports Announcers

While Jerry Geehan was busy broadcasting WIL baseball games in the 1930s, Phil Goldwater was making a name for himself in the press box at Lincoln Bowl. He was both the official scorekeeper and the public address announcer for all Timber and City League baseball games. Harry Jordan was also a well-known sportscaster and KMO sports announcer during what has been called the Geehan Era. At the same time, Ed Meager was the Athletic Park announcer for the WIL games. His keen sense of observation and acrid wit made him a popular announcer and later contributed to his success as a political news writer for the Tacoma Times newspaper between 1937 and 1941.

Other noteworthy writer-broadcasters of this era included Elliot Metcalf, who broadcast local boxing matches and was also a highly respected sports writer for both the *Tacoma News Tribune* and the *Tacoma Times*. John McCallum, another local favorite, attended Lincoln High School and Washington State University (WSU) before

Jerry Geehan joined KMO Radio in 1938, broadcasting Western International League and local college baseball games (MB).

adding his colorful commentary to local sports broadcasts. His collection of facts and anecdotes served him well as the sports host on KIRO radio. He spent 50 years as a sportswriter and historian, writing a multitude of books on sports history. Charlie Bryant was also a well-known Tacoma Tigers broadcaster on KVI during the early 1940s.

Tacoma radio was in its prime in the 1940s and 1950s. Mason Halligan began his career in 1942 as a sports writer for the weekly *Spotlight Review*. As a broadcaster he worked for KTBI and KTAC, with wrestling and auto racing his

specialties. In 1946 Bob Field reported hockey from the Tacoma Ice Palace; his popular play-by-play broadcasts often rang with enthusiasm as he shouted "He scores!"

Clay Huntington provided color commentary for Rockets hockey and Tigers baseball broadcasts. He completed his military service and then began a broadcasting career that included high school sports, as well as PLU and UPS games, many while still a UPS student himself. Huntington recalled some creative experiences from those early days. "We broadcast a Clover Park–Kirkland game out of the front seat of a car in the rain, and during the Peninsula High School field dedication ceremony, we broadcast from a fir tree."

There was also the memorable Whitworth-PLU game in the early 1950s. "The fog enveloped the field, but Marv Harshman continued the game," Huntington remembered, "and the announcer couldn't see. Toward the end of the game, Ron Billings [PLU All-American and later coach at Lincoln High School] scored a touchdown, but it wasn't announced for another 10 minutes. Even Tom Cross, the referee, wasn't sure they had scored!"

Later Huntington added Seattle Rainiers baseball telecasts, the Seattle Americans televised hockey games, and Tacoma Giants baseball to his broadcasting repertoire. He also wrote for the *Tacoma Times* in the late 1950s. According to Doug McArthur, one of Huntington's favorite baseball expressions was "the deuces prevail!" McArthur explained, "That meant it was two and two on the batter with two outs."

Huntington started his radio broadcasting career at KTBI. Sponsored by a bakery, he was the "Jordan's Breadcaster" for the Tacoma Tigers Baseball Club from 1946 to 1951 and provided the color commentary for the Tacoma Rockets Hockey Club from 1946 to 1953. Huntington was also one of the key figures in bringing Pacific Coast League (PCL) baseball back to Tacoma in 1960. The next year he started KLAY FM radio station with Stan Naccarato, one he still owns.

Rod Belcher also got his start as a broadcaster during the late 1940s. In 1946 he was hired as KMO's sports announcer. Geehan, station manager at the time, allowed Belcher to make his broadcasting debut during a UPS–University of Pacific game in Stadium Bowl. Both teams

From L. to R., Elliott Metcalf, Tacoma Times Sports Editor; Jack Kearns, famed fight manager; Dan Walton, Tacoma News Tribune Sports Editor (SSM, 1974).

appeared on the field in red jerseys. It was decided that Pacific would wear their gray warm-up sweats, on which numbers were stenciled only 3 inches high, making it nearly impossible to identify the players. Belcher survived the initiation and went on to broadcast two or three football games a week. During basketball season, the number of games doubled. He later became the voice of the '49ers, but not before changing his name to Rod Hughes. His real last name was considered inappropriate because the football team's sponsor was a beer company.

Belcher and Huntington were joined by John Jarstad for broadcasts of the UW and Seattle University games during the 1950s. Jarstad was also the KTVW TV announcer for the Seattle Rainiers baseball team between 1955 and 1958. His first year with the team was a historic season that resulted in a PCL title that was not determined until the dramatic next-to-last game. Jarstad was the first sports director for KOMO TV and did many fishing and skiing broadcasts, oftentimes with his own photography.

Pat O'Day, another Tacoman who graduated from Lincoln High School, credits both Huntington and Belcher for his own broadcasting career. As a youngster in the mid-1940s, he hung around the two at the KMO studio while his father, a minister, broadcast a weekly religious program.

Bob Robertson enjoyed a successful career on both television and radio, providing coverage for the Tacoma Tigers as well as Washington State University football and basketball (SSM, 1475).

"I stood behind Huntington in the press box of high school games," O'Day remembered, "and hung on his every word." O'Day is most recognized locally as the voice of hydroplane racing.

Bob Robertson also has his roots in Tacoma as a pioneer broadcaster, beginning at KMO in the early 1950s. He covered high school games and was the KSTW Channel 11 sports anchor. Robertson was WSU's voice of the Cougars from 1964 to 1968 and from 1972 to the present; from 1969 to 1971, ignoring cross-state rivalries, he was the voice of the Huskies. The list of his broadcasting exploits covers many major sports in the region: PCL baseball on television in Seattle and Tacoma (1958–1968); Seattle Totems (1958–59), Seattle Sounders (1972–74), and Tacoma Stars (1989–92) soccer and hockey games; and Tacoma Tigers and Seattle Rainiers baseball games (1984–1997). Robertson, acknowledged as one of the top play-by-play announcers in the Northwest, has been named Washington

Sportscaster of the Year 12 times. In 2004 Robertson received the Chris Schenkel Award from the National Football Foundation and the College Football Hall of Fame, the first announcer west of Kansas to be so honored. "Always be a good sport, be a good sport *all ways,*" Robertson reminded his listeners at the end of every broadcast.

Travails of Teletype

During the 1960s, re-creating game play by means of the telephone, especially when teams were on the road, was still a part of broadcasting. This provided unique drama when reporting Tacoma Giants games. At the time, Don Hill did the play-by-play announcing, and Doug McArthur provided the color commentary. McArthur recalled that "Don took the Booster Club to Hawaii to watch the series. The second game was in Maui, where there was no teletype, so Don called at the end of each inning and I then re-created it. The game was tied and went into extra innings. Because of the time difference, it was about 2:30 a.m. I got the report that Milt Smith of Hawaii was up to bat, the count was 3–2. Smith proceeded to foul 15 pitches, then hit a grand slam home run to win the game."

McArthur remembered thinking, "Everyone is tired; I'll just report the grand slam and skip the 15 fouls. But I remembered that Ed Honeywell, the *News Tribune* sports columnist, was a stickler for details and would report everything, so I came up with a re-creation of every conceivable type of foul—all 15 of them." The following morning, McArthur raced to get the paper and see whether Ed Honeywell had reported all the fouls. When McArthur opened the paper to the sports page, it said, "Because of the late hour of the game, Ed Honeywell's report did not make the paper today."

McArthur began as a statistician for Clay Huntington in the early 1950s but moved to full-time announcing when Huntington's schedule became too much for one person. In 1956, after graduating from UPS, McArthur was hired by Jerry Geehan as KTAC sports director. In that capacity, he broadcast local high school and college football and basketball games. He also reported the 1956 National Association of Intercollegiate Athletics (NAIA) championship PLU basketball game, when the university placed second in the nation, in addition to the National Collegiate Athletic Association

(NCAA) finals when UPS won the national championship.

Don Hill's voice and cheery "How about that, Giants fans?" was long familiar to baseball followers in Tacoma. He covered the Tacoma Giants, Cubs, and Twins games on KTAC and KTNT. His first game in Tacoma was also the first game for the Tacoma Giants in the PCL in 1960. Between 1960 and 1984, he logged 3,572 games or re-creations of Tacoma baseball events. His wife, Connie, was instrumental in the success of his re-creations of road games. With the help of a correspondent at the ballpark who called in a play-by-play account of each inning, Connie taped the conversation and took shorthand notes. She then quickly transcribed the action and delivered it to her husband at the microphone. Hill then reported the information with the added drama, sizzle, and sparkle that gave radio broadcasting its appeal.

Bill Doane and Jerry Howarth, the only announcer to make it to professional sports, as the voice of the Toronto Blue Jays, were local broadcasters in the 1970s. So too were Ed Bowman, Art Popham, Bud Blair, and Tom Beuning. Popham was a popular Tacoma baseball play-by-play broadcaster from 1976 to 1984. During that time, he broadcast games for the Twins, Yankees, Tugs, and Tigers. He began his career as a bat boy for the Kansas City Athletics. At the age of 20, he was the public relations director for the team. He followed the As to Oakland in 1970 but by 1976 was in our City of Destiny broadcasting over KMO radio, where he covered PCL games, UPS sports, and high school games. Popham and McArthur also created the "Live from the Leaf" sports program, which aired from the Cloverleaf Tavern every Friday night from 1977 until 1981. Fans were updated on late-breaking scores; local high school, college, and professional sports action was reviewed; and local sports figures were interviewed. The pattern of this early sports program is now a given for both radio and television sports reporting.

Television and Beyond

Changing priorities in radio programming, the rising popularity of television, and the emergence of cable networks have decreased the role that radio now plays in sports broadcasting. But Tacoma was still producing its fair share of broadcasters as the 20th century ended. Tom Glasgow, a for-mer Mount Tahoma High and PLU graduate, began his career while still in college, as a broadcaster for PLU basketball. He later produced the Wayne Cody program for KIRO TV and became a sports anchor. Steve Thomas, before moving on to reporting Seahawks games, attended Franklin Pierce High School and was a broadcaster for KTNT. By the 1990s Adam Gordon, Scott Ellingson, Dick Calvert, and John Lynch were additional reminders that sports needs broadcasters and that Tacoma and Pierce County can produce its fair share.

Various forms of mass media—newspapers, radio, television, and now the Internet—have informed, educated, and entertained sports enthusiasts and competitors. Were it not for the hundreds of local sports writers, publicists, broadcasters, and photographers, the history of sports could not be written.

Sports photographer Morley Brotman, longtime owner of Morley Studios (SSM, 1050).

Joe Hemel played first base at WSU, 1947–48 (SSM, 1997.17.2).

RIGHT: Sonny Johns takes a practice shot in preparation for an upcoming competition (SSM, 2003.7.5).

THE SPORTS
PART II

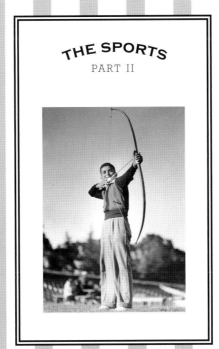

Little Sonny Johns stands tall with some of his tournament awards (SSM, 2003.7.7).

CHAPTER 6

ARCHERY

In 1942 Dorothy Axtelle of Tacoma was the state women's archery champion; she held the national women's title in her junior year (Richards Studio Collection, TPL, Image D12971-6).

The modern age of archery began in 1828 with the formation of the United Bowmen Club in Philadelphia. Then, in 1879, the American National Archery Association was formed. Initially the sport was reserved for the elite, who gathered in local parks to shoot arrows at targets. Dressed in their Sunday best, these archers viewed the activity as part of their social status. Modern American bow hunting, on the other hand, grew out of economic necessity after the Civil War, when disarmed former soldiers in the South used the bow and arrow to obtain meat for the family table.

One of the founders of Washington state archery was Glenn St. Charles, who with his family owned Northwest Archery in Des Moines, Washington. In 1957 St. Charles became one of the founding members of the Pope and Young Club, which to this day is the official repository of records for bow hunting.

Present-day archers are divided into bow hunters, field target shooters, and 3-D target competitors. Today there are some 2,000 members, representing 37 clubs, in the Washington State Archery Association. Two of these clubs, the Puyallup Skookum Archers and the Tacoma Archery Club, are located in Pierce County. The Tacoma Archery Club developed as one component of the Tacoma Sportsmen Club. Competitions were held at a range constructed at the sportsmen's facility at 903 Commerce and at Jefferson Park.

The most famous archer of this era was young Sonny Johns, one of two sons born to Aniella and Harry C. Johns, who owned the Archery Manufacturing and Sales Company in Tacoma. Harry and his sons built the Monte Vista archery range located at the intersection of Union Avenue and Steilacoom Boulevard, where the Tacoma Advertising Club took motion pictures of the facility as part of a *Life* Magazine project. It was no accident, therefore, that Sonny took to the sport at an early age and became a national champion in 1938 when he was only 13 years old. That year he also won the Pacific Northwest junior crown, in the process shooting two perfect scores, the first time the feat had been achieved by a youngster. By the end of the year, he became the National Archery Association's junior champion, winning just about every competition possible for a boy his age.

Johns became a national celebrity. "He is a member of the Six Point Gold Club," reported the *Tacoma Ledger-News Tribune* in 1939, "the most exclusive archery organization in the United States." He "has received hundreds of requests for pictures and information on himself from archery fans all over the world," the newspaper continued, and "his picture has appeared in practically every American pictorial magazine and newspaper and brings this city worlds of publicity." Johns's parents were asked to have him endorse food products, a request denied because "much of the fun for the youngster would be taken out of the sport if he were to commercialize on his abilities while still in school."

World War II cut Sonny Johns' archery competition short, as it did for many young athletes of the era. In October 1942, at the age of 18, Johns joined the Navy and remained there for the duration, leaving his archery exploits behind.

As Sonny Johns' career wound down, Henry Lange began to interest Puyallup Valley residents in the sport. Lange, who worked for the Bureau of Indian Affairs, constructed a small target range in the Edgewood area of eastern Pierce County. In 1951 he was able to encourage a number of Puyallup-area sportsmen to establish the Skookum Archers Club (SAC), an organization that formally incorporated in 1959. Charter members included Ed Arnold, Frank Marcoe, and Bill Stoner, a local sporting-goods store owner as well as a future mayor of Puyallup and member of the Pierce County Council.

National Championships in August of 1938 in San Francisco (SSM, 2003.7.3).

By the 1960s, SAC had its own range, located on Shaw Road near Puyallup, a facility that has been in operation for more than 50 years. It became a gathering place for what the club called "one of Puyallup's newest recreation facilities." That year the Skookums held an open house featuring archery demonstrations and tours of the new range. For several years, it also hosted a target tournament at Fife High School in conjunction with the annual Daffodil Festival.

Over the years, SAC sponsored many men's and women's championship competitors. Diane Brereton and Carolyn Elder are two of the top female pros in the state. Brereton, a four-time North American champion in field archery, was ranked among the top 10 in the country. She was also a former state director of the National Field Archery Association (NFAA). Elder won numerous indoor and outdoor state, regional, and national titles. In 1996 she won the Indoor Nationals at Tulsa, Oklahoma, and was ranked the top finger shooter in the country.

Dan Croft, a member of the Tacoma Sportsmen Club, achieved several national and state records. In 1996 at Watkins Glen, New York, he broke the existing NFAA record, and Puyallup's Bob Davis finished 12th. In the 1990s, Croft also held the record for the Washington State Field Archery tournament and shared with Castle Rock's Jerry Adams the state record of 285 points for the Indoor Blue Face competition. Croft scored 728 points out of a total of 900 to also become the record holder for the Washington State Target competition.

At the time of his death in 1992, Bill Brereton, Diane's husband, was credited with bringing the North American Field Archery Championships to Washington. The list of his involvement in archery organizations is lengthy: SAC, Washington State Archery Association (WSAA), NFAA, and the Professional Archers Association—in which he was a charter member—are only a few. Because of his contribution to the sport, Brereton was awarded the highest honor that WSAA offers for tournament play. He was also awarded the NFAA Medal of Merit, the second highest national award granted by this organization. Clearly, over the years Pierce County archers have made their mark as local, regional, and national competitors.

CHAPTER 6

AUTOMOBILE RACING

This 1913 Montamara Festo Road Race trophy was presented to winner Jimmy Parsons (courtesy Dr. Wayne D. Herstad).

Organized automobile racing began in the United States on Thanksgiving Day, 1895. Sponsored by newspapers for promotional purposes, drivers raced from Chicago to Evanston, Illinois, and back at a speed of approximately 10 miles per hour. By the turn of the 19th century, both automobile road racing and track racing were established sports in the United States, with the Indianapolis 500—first run in 1911—the cornerstone of the competition. From the end of World War I onward, various forms of racing evolved.

In the spring of 1912, the Tacoma Carnival Association (TCA) was looking for something to invigorate its newly created Montamara Festo, a mountain-sea festival. The association, formed in 1907, was responsible for the July Fourth Independence Day festivities and other events. Its president, A. B. Howe, was approached by Arthur Pritchard, head of the Tacoma Automobile Club, who proposed that an automobile race culminate the Montamara Festo the next year. Indianapolis had had great success with its 500-mile auto race in 1911, so local businesspeople were all in favor of the idea. However, they did not want just local auto races, they wanted a major national auto-racing event.

Because most auto races were held in the Midwest, on the East Coast, or in Southern California, Tacoma offered a total purse of $25,000—at the time, one of the largest—to draw the biggest names in auto racing to the Northwest. The scheme worked; in 1912 famed race-car drivers such as Earl Cooper, "Terrible" Teddy Tetzlaff, Ralph Mulford, Eddie Pullen, and Hughie Hughes competed, driving cars from Fiat, Benz, Stutz, Mercer, Ford, Maxwell, and more. In those days, most cars carried both a driver and a mechanic.

TCA used the prairie of Lakeview for the location of the track, which is now the site of Clover Park Technical College. At the end of the Montamara Festo's parades and fireworks, the automobile races began under the control of famed starter Fred J. Wagner. There were four races along a 5-mile course: Lakeview Avenue to Steilacoom Boulevard to Gravelly Lake Drive to 111th and back to Lakeview Avenue. The 100- and 150-mile races were run concurrently, with the driver ahead at the 100-mile mark considered the winner of the 100-mile race. The 200- and 250-mile races were also run concurrently. The winners of the first four races were Bob Evans in a Flanders, Eddie Pullen in a Mercer, Earl Cooper in a Stutz, and Teddy Tetzlaff in a Fiat.

The fifth race, the 250-mile Montamarathon Free-for-All, was held the next day and won by Teddy Tetzlaff in his giant red Fiat, with an average speed of 66.08 miles per hour. One of the other race-car drivers stated, "You never raced against Tetzlaff, you chased him." Tetzlaff's philosophy was, "Put the gas pedal to the metal and don't let it up until the race is over or the car blows up."

TCA was pleased with the large crowds and overall response to the 1912 auto races. The organization had even made a profit, and it began planning the 1913 race. For the next 11 years, the most prominent competitors and the best race cars in the nation came to the new Tacoma Motor Speedway for competitions sanctioned by the American Automobile Association (AAA). The City of Destiny became one of only two class-A tracks in the nation—the other was in Indianapolis.

In 1913 the course was reduced in size from 5 miles to 3.5 miles, turning at 100th Street instead of 111th and then returning to Lakeview Avenue, so people in the grandstand could see more of the race. The number of races was reduced from five to three. The first race was a 100-mile race sponsored by the Tacoma Automobile Club, called the Intercity Trophy Race. Open to drivers from Washington, Oregon, Idaho, and British Columbia, it was won by Seattle driver

Earl DeVore drove this National in the first-ever race at the Tacoma Speedway in 1912 (courtesy Dr. Wayne D. Herstad).

Jim Parsons in a Stutz, averaging 65.28 mph. The second, open to all drivers, was the 200-mile Potlatch Trophy Race, sponsored by the Seattle Potlatch Association; it was won by Earl Cooper, also in a Stutz, at an average speed of 71.03 mph. The third race was the 250-mile Montamarathon Trophy Race, sponsored by TCA. It was again won by Earl Cooper in his Stutz No. 8, at an average speed of 70.75 mph. An estimated 40,000 spectators came to see the races in 1913.

The world record for a mile on a dirt track was broken at Tacoma Motor speedway that same year by famed race-car driver "Wild" Bob Berman, racing against the clock in a 200-horsepower Benz called the Blitzen Benz. He covered the mile distance in 35.2 seconds, crossing the finish line at 140 mph.

It was also the year for the first serious Tacoma Motor Speedway accident, on the 123rd lap of the Montamarathon. Bert Dingley bought the Fiat that Teddy Tetzlaff had driven to victory in 1912 when he won the Montamarathon. Dingley took out the engine and replaced it with a Pope-Hartford engine and radiator. People approaching his car from the rear always thought it was the Fiat. On realizing that it was not a Fiat anymore, most people would say, "Oh, no." After hearing this many times, Dingley decided to name his car the Ono. In the 1913 race, Dingley blew a tire and flipped the Ono. He was severely injured and spent the next six months in a Tacoma hospital; his mechanic escaped serious injury. During Dingley's recuperation, he became a celebrity and wrote many articles for the local newspapers.

In 1914 the recently formed Tacoma Speedway Association (TSA) created a new 2-mile track, along with a new grandstand, at Lakeview Avenue and Steilacoom Boulevard. However, the track remained a dirt one, shaped much like a capital D. But soon racetracks around the country started building board tracks, because smoother board tracks enabled cars to achieve higher speeds. So in 1915 the Tacoma Motor Speedway surface was covered with two million board feet of 2x4s placed end to end with a 5/8-inch gap between them.

Perhaps as a result of the new speeds, the Montamarathon that year was marked by tragedy. Billy "Coal Oil"

Carlson and his mechanic, Paul Franzer, were killed when the right front tire blew on Carlson's Maxwell race car at the 116th-mile mark. The car went flying and the driver and mechanic were thrown 30 feet in the air. Maxwell automobile race-car manager Ray Harroun, the 1911 Indianapolis winner, immediately pulled all Maxwell cars from any future races throughout the country.

Famed race-car driver Barney Oldfield came to Tacoma for the first time in 1915. He brought three cars with him: a Fiat Cyclone, which he raced against an airplane flown by DeLloyd Thompson; a front-drive Christie, which he raced against the clock; and a Peugeot, which placed third in the Potlatch Trophy Race.

The race format changed in 1916, when the recently formed TSA decided to have three races on different days of the year: Memorial Day, Fourth of July, and August 5. The Memorial, or Decoration, Day race of May 30 was postponed to June 4 because of rain. The events of that day consisted of a grand outdoor automobile show and parade, a women's contest, and 20- and 30-mile grudge races.

Grudge races, very in vogue, were intense rivalries between cities. Ulysses Aubrey of Tacoma was pitted against Jim Parsons of Seattle, the favorite because he had just purchased the Earl Cooper Stutz No. 8 race car that had previously won the 1913 and 1914 Montamarathons. However, Aubrey had hidden under the hood of his smaller Mercer chassis a specially built 450-cubic-inch Stutz Wisconsin racing engine. Aubrey easily won both races, to the thrill of the Tacoma fans.

A grudge rematch between Aubrey and Parsons was scheduled for the 1916 July Fourth race. It was to be run in three heats, two of 35 miles each and one of 30 miles. The grandstand was filled with anticipation, but the races did not take place: Parsons' race car cracked a piston pin and could not run. A "Fat Man" race took place, however. Men weighing more than 200 pounds had to run 100 yards, start their cars, and race around the track once. Another headliner of July Fourth was a head-on collision of two powerful railroad locomotives. A milelong track was placed in front of the grandstand and, because the main grudge auto races weren't run, the officials put the name of Tacoma on one train and Seattle on the other. As the collision dust cleared, the Tacoma train had one wheel off the track, so the Seattle train was declared the winner of the grudge race.

On August 5, the third and final Tacoma Motor Speedway event featured a 300-mile $10,000-purse Montamarathon, and once again the biggest names in racing came: Tommy Milton, Ralph DePalma, Barney Oldfield, Dave Lewis—and a young man just making a name for himself in auto racing, Eddie Rickenbacker. Rickenbacker won the 300-mile Montamarathon with an average speed of 86.56 mph in a Maxwell race car. (Rickenbacker had purchased the fleet of Maxwells after the company had officially stopped racing them in 1915.) He gave up racing in 1917 with the outbreak of World War I, became a fighter ace by shooting down 26 enemy planes, and later won the Congressional Medal of Honor.

By 1916 racecars were getting more sophisticated. Stripped-down production automobiles with two-wheeled mechanical brakes gave way to eight-cylinder cars with four-wheel hydraulic brakes. Driver safety was not a factor for many years to come. Cloth coveralls, leather helmets, and glass goggles were all the protection they had. Only a few cars had a wire-mesh windscreen. Barney Oldfield stated that the reason he always had a cigar between his teeth when he raced was that the cigar acted as a shock absorber and kept his teeth from rattling together and chipping.

During World War I, some tracks, including Indianapolis, closed down for the duration. In 1918, however, Tacomans organized a Fourth of July racing program to honor America's allies in the war. Each car displayed a flag representing the various countries. Cliff Durant in his Chevrolet represented Belgium; Eddie Pullen in his Mercer, France; Dave Lewis in his Duesenberg, Great Britain; Eddie Hearne, also in a Duesenberg, Italy; and Earl Cooper in his Stutz represented America. The three races—25-, 50-, and 75-mile events—were called the Liberty Sweepstakes. Durant won the first two; Hearne won the third. Durant's car advertised "Chevrolet" on its side, but there was nothing Chevy about the car. Durant had purchased two Stutz cars from Earl Cooper, but since his father was president of General Motors, he couldn't go around winning races in a Stutz thus the disguise.

In 1920 another tragedy hit the Tacoma Motor Speed-

way when fire destroyed the grandstand. Firefighters considered it arson but, unfortunately, the facility was not insured. Tacoma businesspeople, not wanting to lose the track, pooled their resources and provided the money to build a new grandstand for the start of the races on July 5 that year. The new stands were much larger, with one portion covered. A tunnel was also built from the grandstand under the track to the infield. A large water tower with an official scoreboard was also erected.

The total purse for the 1920 race was $22,500, with a first prize of $10,000. The format was returned to one major race of 115 laps, or 223 miles. It included the top race-car drivers in the nation: Ralph DePalma, Roscoe Sarles, Jimmy Murphy, Joe Boyer, and Tommy Milton. Milton won the race in a Duesenberg, with an average speed of 93.294 mph. Milton, who had only one eye, always memorized the eye charts so he could pass the vision tests. However, his vision disability never stopped him from winning Tacoma and Indianapolis races and becoming the national champion; in fact, he won again in 1921.

By the next year, however, the wooden board track was starting to show its age, not only from the pounding of the race cars, but also from the damp Northwest weather. Sometimes the gapped 2x4s broke under the pressure of a race car and were thrown crosswise into the path of oncoming cars. Track carpenters made constant repairs.

One of the most exciting races at the Tacoma Motor Speedway was held on the worn track in 1922. It consisted of 125 laps, or 242.5 miles. Tommy Milton, who had won in 1920 and 1921, was the favorite to repeat his win for the third consecutive time. Roscoe Sarles, who had taken second in 1921, was eager to beat Milton, and Jimmy Murphy, who had won the French Grand Prix in 1921, was also there. But when the dust cleared, it was Murphy who squeaked out one of the closest victories in Tacoma Motor Speedway history, winning with an average speed of 94.51 mph, over Milton's 94.45 mph.

Given the excitement of the 1922 race, fans eagerly awaited the next year. TSA, however, was out of money. The fire of 1920, the many needed track repairs, and the cost of providing the winner's purse all played a role in the organization's decision to suspend racing at the track.

(There was also a rumor that someone had absconded with some of the gate receipts.)

In the 11 seasons of racing at the Tacoma Motor Speedway, the city had hosted 28 races with more than 80 different drivers and entertained crowds approaching a half million. The total distance of all events was more than 4,000 miles, and more than $275,000 was awarded in prizes. The national prominence of the speedway helped to put Tacoma on the map.

After the speedway closed in 1922, auto racing continued in Pierce County on new tracks encompassing even newer events. Throughout the decades of the 20th century, drivers raced on fixed tracks and established roads, competing in a wide array of events. Speed was the goal when it came to automobile racing, and as early as the 1920s, cars were designed to capture the land-speed record beyond what might be achieved on a competitive track.

In most places, stock-car racing refers to somewhat stock-appearing cars (usually with fenders and full bodies) racing on oval tracks, either dirt or paved. The races are

A view of the old tower at Tacoma Speedway with the Stutz Pace Car driven by Barney Oldfield leading the pack in 1922, which included Jimmy Murphy in car 35 (courtesy Dr. Wayne D. Herstad).

CHAPTER SPONSORED BY
BILL CAMMARANO:

The history of automobile racing is sponsored by Bill Cammarano, "honoring those who gave me great memories," including: Jim Crews, Butch Dennison, Dave Fogg, Jerry Grant, Dennis Kitts, Pete Lovely, Mel McGouy, John McIntire, Bill Seidleman, Ed Shefchik, Louie Shefchik, Cliff Spaulding, Dave Tatom, the late Wade Althuser, Syd Carr, Tom Carstens, Russ Congdon, Dave Dipolito, Leo Dobry, Joe Henderson, Burleigh Hillman, Dennis Long, and Col. Tex Roberts. Of the following memorable tracks, only Pacific Raceways is still open for racing today: Athletic Park, Bremerton Airport, Gray Field, Pacific Raceways, Payne Field, SeaTac Speedway, Shelton Airport, Spanaway Speedway, and Thun Field.

booked and measured in laps—one trip around the track is a lap. In some cases, the races are held on road courses.

Drag racing consists of two cars racing head to head down a straight, normally quarter-mile track. A drag race entails a series of qualification runs and then eliminations, with the top 16 cars running a series of single elimination events; the winner is the final undefeated car. There's considerable variety in drag racing, with several classes of cars, including Midget, Sprint Car, Championship ("Champ") Car, and Late Model Sportsman.

Hot rodding isn't really a kind of racing. People, usually kids, modified their cars in both appearance and speed for the road. Eventually they moved to the racetracks, where the cars were sometimes booked as hot rods or, more commonly, roadsters because on the track, most of the cars were based on roadster body styles. Hot rodding is still around and never really died, but that type of racing lasted only a couple of years after WWII.

In open-wheel racing, cars do not have fenders or full bodies. In short-track racing, open-wheel racing is done with midgets, sprint cars, and championship (Indy 500) cars, along with some classes in road racing (see later in this chapter).

Midget Racing

In the 1930s a new form of racing took the country by storm. The cars were called Midgets, miniature versions of the Indianapolis 500 cars of the time. A group of California Midget racers staged an exhibition at the 1935 Puyallup Fair, and within a year local enthusiasts were determined to bring Midget racing to the Pacific Northwest. With the clo-

sure of the Tacoma Motor Speedway in 1922, the major challenge was to create a track.

Bobby Rowe, a former major-league hockey star and former owner of the Tacoma Tigers Baseball Club, provided the leadership. Through his efforts, the baseball park located at 14th and Sprague, then used for motorcycle racing, became the venue for the Midget races. The first race at the

Bob McLees was a member of the Seidelman Racing Enterprises team who here drove for the longtime midget sponsor and owner Jim Crews of Crews Auto Parts (courtesy Bill Seidelman).

renamed Speedway Royale was held on May 12, 1936. Most of the drivers were veterans of the traveling Northwest Big Car (now called Sprint Car) circuit, but many were on the track for the first time. Spectators cheered as Tacoma's Dave Dippolito recorded the fastest qualifying time and followed with a victory in the B main event, while crowd favorite "Swede" Lindskog won the Helmet Dash. Heat race winners that day were Bill Spaulding, Bert Blomgren, and Ralph Thompson. Northwest veteran Tony West capped the evening with his win in the 25-lap feature event.

Nine days later, Portland held its first Midget race, and Seattle joined the circuit in June. Northwest Midget racing was underway. The season continued successfully throughout the summer, but Speedway Royale was not included in the following year's schedule. The Midgets did not return to Tacoma until just prior to World War II.

In 1942 Midget racers returned to Pierce County on a one-fifth-mile oval on a former rodeo grounds near 99th Street and South Tacoma Way. Then the realities of World War II stopped competition. At the end of the war, races were held again at the Speedway Royale site, though by then it was called Athletic Park. Chick Barbo won the first postwar championship, in 1946. The Washington Midget Racing Association (WMRA), formed in those early postwar years, is still the sanctioning body for Midget racing in Washington and one of the oldest racing associations in the nation.

Local drivers made the Washington circuit as tough as any in the nation. Shorty Templeton, Jack Turner, and Bob Gregg were inducted into the National Midget Racing Hall of Fame; Allan Heath became a legend in West Coast open-wheel racing. Tom Carstens also made his debut in the postwar years as an owner and sponsor of Midget car racing. He later became the first executive of the Northwest Region of the Sports Car Club of America (SCCA).

The first WMRA Midget event at Spanaway Speedway was held in 1960, two years after Jim Crews began sponsoring Midget racers through his Crews Auto Parts business. In 1968 Crews acquired an Offenhauser-powered Midget driven by Kenny Petersen, one of the finest drivers in the area, and in 1969 he won the WMRA championship. After that, Crews sponsored a champ dirt car driven by Indy 500 driver Sam Sessions in Springfield, Illinois. Crews contin-

ued as a car owner in WMRA until 2001; he employed virtually every top Northwest Midget driver. Crews, who also served as a club official, is considered one of the most knowledgeable people in Northwest auto racing.

Brothers Arnie Starks and Mike Starks both raced with WMRA in the '70s. Arnie's son John later became a four-time WMRA champion, turning in consistent drives in the U. S. Auto Club's (USAC) Silver Crown Division. John's brother, Dean, is one of the top car builders and mechanics in the Northwest. Ed Shefchik won a WMRA championship driving for Jim Crews and is one of the primary Midget owners on the West Coast. Shefchik gave Kasey Kahne his first Midget ride. Ed's son Louie was also a top WMRA driver before becoming one of the most respected vehicle fabricators in the nation.

Jalopies and Roadsters

While the Midget races continued in Seattle, Portland, and Yakima in the late 1930s, Pierce County racing primarily featured cut-down street cars called jalopies. This type of racing was governed by the Northwest Jalopy Racing Association. The cars ran tracks such as Mile B Speedway, a half-mile dirt track in Spanaway that was later developed as Spanaway Speedway. With the drivers building more powerful motors and better suspension systems, the jalopies evolved into roadsters governed by the Tacoma Roadster Racing Association. Roadster drivers were popularly called Dopesters, and their automobiles were, according to one 1941 newspaper account, "specially built and 'pepped up' by gears, gadgets, high compression heads, etc." Leading Dopester racers in 1941 were Seattle's Lloyd Blair and 'Crash' McCrackers. Competitions were held at the Steilacoom Track located near the former Tacoma Motor Speedway.

Pete Lovely began driving roadsters in both Washington and Oregon during the late 1940s. He moved on to sports cars, becoming a force in national and regional events. By 1969 he acquired a Lotus and moved into the exotic world of Formula One racing. Lovely's first efforts gave him a seventh-place finish in Canada and a ninth in Mexico. In 1970 he placed 10th in England. These results were amazing for an independent racer, and his effort remains the only link between Tacoma and the lofty sport of Formula One racing.

The Indianapolis 500

For several years during the 1930s, Indy cars required a riding mechanic. The two-man Champ Cars of that era were kind of a throwback to the teens, when most cars carried a mechanic and driver. But Tacoma's major tie to the Indianapolis 500 was rooted in the postwar racing boom. In 1948 sprint-car owner Leo Dobry fulfilled his dream of owning and sponsoring a car to compete in the Indy. Dobry ordered a new Kurtis Kraft Champ Car to be delivered to the California shop of Hal Cole, who would build the car and drive it in the 500. Other than Cole, the effort was all local. Ralph Taylor, another sprint car veteran, was enlisted as crew chief and immediately left for California to assist in construction.

In late April, the car arrived at Dobry's Standard Auto Parts, and after a week of public appearances, the "City of Tacoma Special" headed for Indianapolis in its custom see-through trailer. Taylor, Tom Carstens, and Joe Henderson formed the enthusiastic crew. On race day, Cole turned in the best drive of his Indy career as the "City of Tacoma" moved into the top 10 at the 350-mile mark. Cole finished sixth, surprising all the "experts" and generating a great deal of Northwest interest in the car. After two unsuccessful appearances on the Championship Trail, the car returned to Tacoma.

The following year, Spokane's Athletic Roundtable offered Dobry a $5,000 sponsorship to run the car in the 1949 Indy as "Esmeralda" in honor of their mascot, a donkey. Dave Fogg, a Midget racer and hot-rod racer and at the

Eddie Rickenbacker in his Maxwell (#1) won the 300-mile 1916 Montamarathon race with an average speed of 86.56 miles per hour; Tom Milton finished second in his Duesenberg (#12, far L.), with Omar Toft in his Omar-Duesenberg (#5) and Barney Oldfield in his Delage (#3) on the line (courtesy Dr. Wayne D. Herstad).

time a member of the Tacoma Young Men's Business Club (YMBC), was enraged that a Tacoma-based race car would be running at the Indianapolis 500 for Spokane. He persuaded the YMBC board to sponsor the car instead, and he formed a committee to raise the necessary funds.

"The *Tacoma Times* [Fogg remembered that in those days, Tacoma was home to two newspapers] gave us lots of publicity. We ran raffles and put on a big parade through downtown Tacoma. The parade included more motorcycles seen in downtown Tacoma before or since. The final event was a big dance at the Tacoma Armory that also featured many money-raising concessions. I don't recall how much was raised, but it was enough that Leo turned down the Spokane offer and the race car was emblazoned with the name 'City of Tacoma.'"

Dobry made several changes to his team for the 1949 race. Jack Beckley replaced Ralph Taylor as crew chief; California roadster driver Jack McGrath replaced Cole. Fogg joined Carstens, Henderson, and "Tex" Roberts, an Air Corps officer and Midget-racing veteran, as crew. The team was ready on opening day, and newcomer McGrath gave the car the ride of its life. When the Pole Day qualifications ended, only the NOVIs were faster. The NOVI was a supercharged V-8 racing engine named for the Michigan town the engine builder lived in (the story was that the name came from an old railroad marker sign: No. VI). NOVIs came on the racing scene right after WWII. There were about only four of the engines, installed in a lot of different chassis. At the time Dobry's car was at Indy, the NOVIs, which were pretty new, were installed in very sleek front-wheel-drive chassis. They were incredibly powerful and the fastest cars around, but they usually either crashed or broke. The NOVI engines were around until the '60s.

For the 1949 race, in Tex Roberts's words, "a bunch of hillbillies from the Northwest" were on the front row of the most important racing event in the world. Mechanical troubles eliminated the "City of Tacoma" early in the 500, and after a few unsuccessful showings at other Championship Trail events, the car again returned to Tacoma.

Dobry continued to campaign the car regionally, and in 1952 George Hammond, a part-time racer whose real job was driving a tour bus at Pikes Peak, Colorado, gave Dobry his only national championship win, in the Pikes Peak Hillclimb.

Bill Seidelman Jr., then a student at Lincoln High School, got his first taste of racing while serving as Dobry's gofer. Seidelman was a second-generation racer; his father, Bill Sr., was a riding mechanic in the 1930s era of two-man Champ Cars who raced motorcycles before giving it up when he married. He continued as a builder and mechanic, starting with the Midget boom of the '30s. Bill Jr. confined his activities to building and wrenching in Midgets, Sprint Cars such as Dobry's, and Champ Cars when USAC was the major open-wheel sanctioning body in the country—it is now the most diversified auto-racing sanctioning body in the world. Both of Bill Jr.'s sons, Mark and Glen, actually raced, with Mark winning the first USAC-Washington supermodified event at Spanaway Speedway in 1985. Both Mark and Glen have since retired from the cockpit, but Glen's sons, Nick and Tony, are keeping the four-generation open-wheel racing tradition alive as drivers in WMRA.

Spanaway Speedway

Racing in Spanaway began in the 1930s at the old Mile B Speedway, and in 1940 the newspaper announced a new course for a June "Jalopy Circus." The track was located south of Military Road seven blocks east of Spanaway Park. Some of the drivers for the 1940 event were Guy Perry, Jerry Stillman, Gene Carden, Brady Rice, and "Snooks" Dayton.

Then in 1956, Dick Boness convinced his dad and brother to construct a racetrack on their family dairy farm, which included the site of the long-forgotten Mile B Speedway. After Mile B Speedway had closed, it had become overgrown. There hadn't been much there—no grandstands, concessions, or restrooms—but at one time you could still see the outline of the track in the ground. The Bonesses called their new track Spanaway Speedway. Despite the land's racing history, the neighbors wanted the new racetrack declared a nuisance, a 7-foot fence removed, and the court to declare that "no auto races or any other business be conducted there." But their attempt to ban automobile racing failed, and Spanaway Speedway survived into the 21st century.

The Bonesses's track, initially an unlit half-mile dirt oval, was first used by racing members of the Valley Stock

Car Association. The original members of this group were listed on a plaque displayed at the speedway until the track closed in 2003, but the real honor for them and the Boness family was in creating the longest-operating racing facility in Tacoma and Pierce County. After two years, the track became a paved ¼-mile oval, and lights were added shortly thereafter. Spanaway Speedway, which retained this configuration for the balance of its existence, was home to a wide array of racing events.

In 1977, for example, the Jackie Marcoe Memorial Mid-Season Championship Stock Car race was held at Spanaway. Local racers included Bill Sauls and Butch Mentry of Puyallup, Tacoma's Gordy Ferguson and Steve Detweiller, and Sumner's Pat Maschek. The winners' names were engraved on a trophy donated by the Marcoe family to honor 14-year-old Jackie, who was killed in an automobile accident on his way to the track in 1975.

Women also graced the Spanaway Speedway, and in the 1990s the woman to beat was "Demolition Ma'am" Joann Keefe. "She's a 47-year-old grandmother of four," the *News Tribune* reported. "A part-time waitress who once ran her own flower shop. A nice lady with a kind smile and a warm heart." She was also a devil on wheels when she competed in the Powder Puff class of demolition derby drivers. Grandma Joann was Rookie Driver of the Year in 1987 and, in 1991, the first woman to race Thunder Cars (a "bump to pass" class) at the Spanaway Speedway. The next year she won the season championship and in 1993 finished the season in a three-way tie for first. "She's fast," Thunder Car driver Randy Keller told the *News Tribune*. "You've got to be careful because she's sneaky. … She's plowed me a few times," pointing to the fact that Joann Keefe raced against both men and women.

Spanaway native Derrike Cope, the 1990 winner of the Daytona 500, raced Stock Cars at the speedway; Tom Sneva and his family raced Supermodifieds there. Winston Cup driver Chad Little raced Super Stock Cars at Spanaway; Mike Bliss raced both Midgets and Supermodifieds before he moved east and won the USAC Silver Crown and National Association for Stock Car Auto Racing (NASCAR) Craftsman Truck series titles. Seven-time Indy 500 participant and many-time Supermodified titlist Davey Hamilton also raced Midgets at Spanaway.

Tacoma's Ron Eaton started his illustrious career at the track and moved on to become one of the top drivers in NASCAR's Winston West Division and a three-time champion in the NASCAR Northwest Tour. At one point, he raced in both the V-eight and six-cylinder classes, winning the season championship in both. Eaton's first race was at the local speedway in 1965, and he credits Spanaway with being the place where he learned to race.

While the so-called major events came and went, Spanaway Speedway provided weekly racing action for area fans. The track ran upward of four nights per week by the early and mid-1980s, and the pits were often jammed with more than 100 cars. A new generation of Northwest drivers made their mark in the racing world. Future Winston West champion Dirk Stevens from Olympia and Bremerton's Bob Fox, a West Coast champion in the NASCAR Super Stock Cars, appeared at the speedway, joining Eaton and Hershel McGriff as future NASCAR champions. Rebel Jackson Jr., whose father, Rebel Sr., was one of the initial competitors at the Spanaway facility, won his first main event at Spanaway before becoming one of the top Supermodified drivers in the country. Seattle's Rick Moss, currently a seven-time WMRA champion and winningest driver in the club's history, battled Puyallup's Dennis Kitts, a four-time WMRA titlist, over the years in Spanaway Midget competition. Kitts, a former go-kart racer at Elk Plain, won at Spanaway in everything from Midgets to Supermodifieds to Street Stock Cars to figure-8 machines. (Figure-8 cars are stock cars with heavy "armor" on their sides that race on a track with a figure-8 configuration. The center intersection provides excitement as the cars try to avoid each other on the track!)

The Spanaway facility also featured many drivers who limited their racing activities to local and regional competition. Tacoma native Don McLeod, a national roller-skating champion as a kid and a baseball prospect in high school, started racing on motorcycles. He moved to Modified Stock Cars before posting five Washington Racing Association (WRA) Sprint Car championships. An industrial accident sidelined McLeod in 1984, but he returned in 1990 to capture the Western States Supermodified Tour title. Dick Boness described McLeod as "a very competitive driver, hard on tires, but he was a great showman. He was great with the kids and popular with the public."

Ken Longley drove Stock Cars for four decades to become the winningest driver in the track's history. Starting at Spanaway in 1962, he won nine championships in a variety of Stock-Car classes and racing associations. "Longley was the master with the six-cylinder," Boness said in 1999. "One year he even drove a six-cylinder car in an eight-cylinder class but said he knew Spanaway Speedway so well, that would even the playing field." Longley also raced in the NASCAR Northwest Tour for several years but will forever be associated with Spanaway.

Jackie Kuper, who won four Stock-Car titles at the track, is considered one of the true gentlemen of the sport and one of the top five competitors in Spanaway Speedway history. Tacoma's Mac McTaggert, a racer since the late '40s, was one of the major stars of the early days at Spanaway but

continued his career in the Supermodifieds until the '90s.

The speedway has also featured some prominent Pierce County racing families. Bill Sauls started as a top competitor before becoming track manager and an official for several racing associations. His son, Mike, has long been one of the top Late-Model Sportsman and Superstock drivers in the area, while Mike's son, Jay, is just starting his career behind the wheel.

Racing continued to evolve at Spanaway Speedway throughout the '80s and '90s. Truck racing become a popular attraction, along with several other new forms of the auto sport. In the Vintage Modified Racing Association competitions, all of the entries had to have an American-made body dating from 1948 or earlier. Drivers sometimes were recruited from unexpected places: Bill Bruton, who drove a 1921 Model A Ford, was a chiropractor who was introduced

Billy "Coal Oil" Maxwell and his mechanic Paul Franzer tragically were killed in this 1915 Montamarathon race at the Tacoma Speedway (courtesy Dr. Wayne D. Herstad).

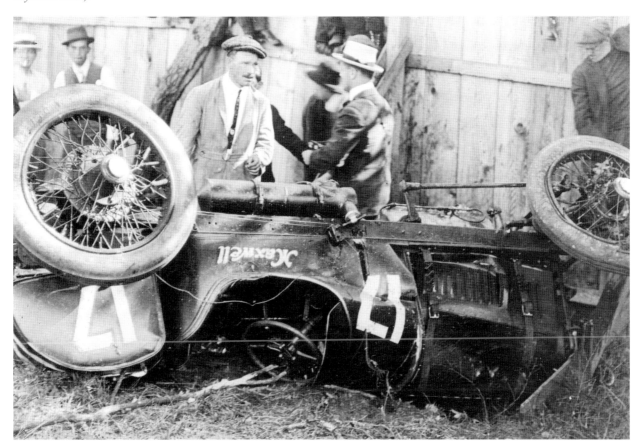

to the sport by one of his patients. A customer at John Volk's valve-grinding business led him to vintage racing and the restoration of a 1937 Chevrolet. The customer, Eric McClain, became his driver. For these guys, racing was a hobby meant to be fun.

Throughout most of its history, the Spanaway Speedway's ownership remained in the hands of the Boness family. Dick Boness eventually wanted to sell the facility to Pierce County Parks and retire. Instead, the land was sold to a developer who planned to construct some 200 houses on the site. After a few years of racing under lease arrangements with the new property owner, promoter Dan Pikron was forced to close the track forever in 2003—after it had provided racing thrills to Pierce County for almost 50 years.

Daytona 500

When brothers Don Cope and Jerry Cope moved from San Diego to Spanaway in 1964, they were already seasoned racers, having been involved, along with brother Guy, in drag racing since the mid-1950s. The family, including Don's son Darren, continued to drag race until 1979 when Don bought a Late-Model Sportsman. Darren drove and his brother Derrike, recuperating from a baseball knee injury, got involved helping on the car. When Derrike decided to start driving, no one could have guessed that it would lead to the biggest single win for a Northwest driver.

After racing with NASCAR in the Northwest, Derrike moved to the southeastern heart of NASCAR in the mid-1980s. The Winston Cup series starts each season with its biggest event in February, the Daytona 500, probably the most competitive single event in all of motor sports. In 1990, on the last of the 200 laps, Cope ran a solid second behind Dale Earnhart Sr. Then another racer blew his transmission, scattering debris across the track. Both Earnhart and Cope drove through it, with Earnhart suffering a flat tire entering the third turn. When Earnhart pulled up to get out of the way, Cope passed him and maintained the lead for the final quarter lap, despite his own flat tire, scoring the biggest prize in Stock-Car racing. Later that year, Cope also won in Dover, Delaware.

Cope continues to race the premier division of NASCAR, and in 2004 he had full season sponsorship for the first time in several years. Although he hasn't yet

regained the winning magic of the 1990 season, his Daytona victory remains the biggest auto-racing win any Pierce County driver has posted so far. But his two nieces, Angela and Amber, have kept the family name active in Northwest racing circles. Both have competed successfully in go-karts and are now moving into Late-Model Stock Cars, with their eye on NASCAR in the near future.

Drag Racing

Fans of the movie American Graffiti remember the closing scene: two hot rods drag racing along a rural road while the sun rises over Modesto, California. Young people growing up in Pierce County in the 1950s could easily relate, for the earliest drag racing in the area paralleled what was shown on the screen. The Goose, an area near the State Game Farm north of Steilacoom Lake, was the place. Here in February 1955, some 150 teenage boys gathered to watch a boy from Lincoln High School and one from Clover Park High School race to see who could go faster. Onlookers brought weapons ranging from 10-inch bolts to can openers, but Pierce County sheriff officers stopped the potential melee. "If these hotrods were under supervision on a regular drag strip," Sargeant Earl Olson told a reporter at the time, "things like this couldn't happen."

Hot rodders had only the runways on Gray Field at Fort Lewis to legally race. The alternative at the time was the streets and roads of Tacoma and Pierce County. Six hot-rod clubs soon combined to become the Tacoma Timers, with the goal of establishing a drag-racing course. Operating under supervision of the Tacoma Police Department, the Timers sponsored fund-raising events and explored possible locations for a racing strip.

Drag racing found its home when the Puyallup Raceway finally opened in 1960, but the venture barely lasted a decade as racers traveled elsewhere to compete. Most went to the Seattle International Raceway (SIR), located near Kent in King County. Al Swindahl's Chassis Components Corporation, located in South Tacoma, remained the prime builder of chassis for the nation's top drag racers since 1965. His clients included some of the top drivers of the National Hot Rod Association (NHRA), including Gary Ormsby, Joe Amato, Don Prudhomme, and Shirley Muldowney.

If the Seidelmans are the first family of Pierce County oval-track open-wheel racing, the Austins hold drag-racing honors. Of drag racers, Pat Austin's career is the most impressive. His father, Walt, raced hot rods in the '50s and

BUILT FOR SPEED

Not all Pierce County racing enthusiasts were satisfied with the status quo of Vintage cars, Midgets, dragsters, Formula Cars, or demolition derbies. Some were obsessed with land-speed records, creating cars that would eventually transcend the sound barrier. Tacoma's first entrant appeared in 1954: the Thomas brothers—Jim, John, and Richard—designed a speed demon for drag racing. They were members of the Century Toppers, a group of drivers able to hold a car at 100 miles per hour over a quarter mile from a standing start. The year before, the brothers had taken their car to the Bonneville Salt Flats in Utah, where it reached the speed of 142 mph. When asked how it felt to drive at such speeds, brother John Thomas, a Boeing employee, told the *News Tribune* that "it doesn't scare me half as much as driving to work through that traffic every day."

Almost a half century later, Spanaway's Ed Shadle is geared to challenge the world land-speed record for automobiles. Bates Technical College students who are helping to prepare the car claim that Shadle "will have to maneuver his jet-powered turbo car, the North American Eagle, at approximately 800 miles per hour through a measured mile twice [to break the record]. ... It also means he will break the sound barrier—quite a challenge compared to his first soapbox derby competition in 1954." As of this writing, work continues on the car, with speed trials planned for 2005.

gained regional and national prominence as an owner, builder, and crew chief on a Top Fuel Dragster in the '60s, so Pat grew up surrounded by the drag-racing community. He started his career in Alcohol Funny Cars (which burn alcohol instead of gas), and after a short time competing regionally, he picked up his first national win in 1986. His first national championship followed in 1987. With his reputation in the Alcohol Funny Cars firmly established, Austin moved into the Top Fuel Dragsters.

In 1991 he purchased Gary Ormsby's equipment and began racing in both classes. Austin enjoyed unprecedented success, and in 1991 in Topeka, Kansas, he became the only NHRA driver to win two eliminator titles at a single event. He duplicated the feat the following year in Phoenix, Arizona. Austin ranks fourth on the all-time NHRA winners list and was named 13th of the Top 50 Drivers in the first 50 years of NHRA competition. In the words of Bob Frey, one of the selection panel members, "He's young enough that he could overtake [John] Force's records, if he decides to race some more. For years, when Pat showed up, everyone else was running for second place."

Austin's racing team, based at the Pro Max Performance Center in South Tacoma, is a family affair. In addition to father Walt, Pat is quick to credit brother Mike for much of his success. Mike had a brief career in dragsters in the mid-1990s and scored a win in each of his two years, but his technical and diagnostic skills are more critical to the success of the Austin family team. Every family member shares the success of this top-flight racing operation.

Bucky Austin, Pat's uncle, also carved out a great career in NHRA competition, winning 15 national events in addition to many divisional events.

Road Racing

By the mid-1980s, auto racing was becoming increasingly popular across the nation. The Sports Car Club of America (SCCA) sanctioned a wide variety of racing events, both amateur and professional. Formula Cars are usually open-wheel cars (no fenders or full bodies, open cockpit) with engine and other limitations specified by rule. "Formula" refers to the rules package; it's based on the European system—what we call usually Grand Prix racing is Formula

One. Sports Cars are usually racing classes based somewhat on production cars with fenders and sometimes closed bodies (think Porsche). In general, Formula Cars are open wheel, Sports Cars have fenders.

In the '80s various cities, including Tacoma, began to explore the economic benefits of conducting racing events on city streets. In Tacoma, the attempt resulted in both the Tacoma Grand Prix and the Toyota Olympus Rally. Both events had short lifespans (two years apiece), but each has a special place in Pierce County auto racing.

The Tacoma Grand Prix featured Stock Cars and open-wheeled Formula Cars on a street course around the perimeter of the Tacoma Dome. Gig Harbor's Riley Hopkins, with Tacoma City Council support, formed a nonprofit organiza-

tion and signed Schuck's Auto Supply as the primary sponsor, then designed a 1.5-mile course. The Dome was the garage for the racers, and in the days leading up to the event, all car classes filled the building with a wide variety of exotic racing machinery. KOMO (Seattle) and KATU (Portland) formed a two-station network for live television coverage, and Bobby Unser signed on as grand marshall and TV color commentator. When the track opened on August 1986, Hopkins and his dedicated associates had accomplished the unthinkable: the race was a reality.

The event featured NASCAR's Winston West cars along with a full supporting card of SCCA Formula and Sports Cars. The field contained a good representation of Northwest drivers. The Winston West field included

The Austin & Rogers AA/GD burns it up at Arlington Dragstrip in the mid-60s (courtesy Walt Austin Racing).

Tacoma's Ron Rainwater and Ron Eaton and Spanaway's Derrike Cope, back after his initial foray into the NASCAR Winston Cup circuit. Gary Gove joined Hopkins in the Formula Atlantic field; Mel Kemper in the Russell Formula Mazdas and Gerald Parker in the Pro Sport 2000 class also represented the host city.

On race day the cool, cloudy weather was blamed for the disappointingly small crowd, but it no doubt improved the reliability of the racing machinery. Cope was the pole sitter—the driver in the number-one position, inside the front row; in most major series, the driver with the fastest qualifying time is the pole sitter. Cope and Northwest legend Herschel McGriff staged a long battle for the lead, but when Cope was forced to pit-stop for gas with 14 laps remaining, McGriff, in his 40th year of racing, took over and held on, besting Cope by six seconds. The first Tacoma Grand Prix was history, and despite some operational problems and a substantial financial deficit, it was considered an artistic success. A return engagement was booked—same time, next year.

If the Tacoma Grand Prix was Riley Hopkins' dream, the Olympus Rally was John Nagle's obsession. Without noticeable support from anyone but participating racers, racing enthusiast Nagle planned for 20 years the now little-known event. By 1986 the Olympus Rally was the oldest continuously contested rally in the country, and the international sanctioning body included the race on its schedule as the final event. The SCCA series, which features exotic locales such as Monte Carlo, Greece, and Kenya, decided the Drivers Championship here in the Northwest. Although it attracts little attention in the United States, international rallying draws huge crowds worldwide, and the racing press from all over the world, including all the major wire services, converged on race headquarters at the Sheraton Tacoma. The four-day, 39-stage event covered 850 miles overall, with 343 miles at high speed. The drivers raced primarily on logging or secondary roads from Tacoma through Olympia, Raymond, and Westport before the finish in Olympia.

Fifty-one driver-and-navigator teams left the Tacoma Dome on Thursday night and completed five stages before spending the night in Olympia. Day two consisted of 11 stages over 180 miles of back roads through the Black Hills,

with another night spent in Olympia. Saturday's run consisted of 14 stages going west, with the overnight stop in Westport. The event concluded with a ceremonial finish at the state capital after a 12-stage run eastward on Sunday. Finland's Makku Alen in a Lancia had edged Juha Kankkunen of Finland in his Peugeot by less than 1 minute, 30 seconds. The event was another "artistic success," but it didn't create much of a stir on the local scene. Despite these mixed results, a similar event was scheduled for the following June.

The 1987 edition of the Toyota Olympus Rally again awarded points toward the world championship. The course, which was changed in an attempt to draw more spectators, included 44 stages with an overall length of 1,087.34 miles. The event started in Seattle, moved to Tacoma, then to Westport and back to Tacoma. When the four-day program ended, Kankkunen took the win by 12 seconds over Italy's Massimo Biasion, with Alen another 30 seconds back. The event again generated little local interest, so the rally returned to its regional status. Yet it marked the only time Pierce County auto racing had a part in a major international series since the glory days of the Tacoma Motor Speedway.

About six weeks after the second international rally, the Schuck's Tacoma Grand Prix returned for its second appearance. Spectator facilities had been improved, as had the course, to provide better passing opportunities. With Cope in New York for a Winston Cup event, Tacoma's Eaton and Rainwater represented the local hopes for the event.

Race day was hot, with temperatures in the 80s. Tacoma businessman and racing enthusiast Bill Cammarano brought out his restored 1915 Ralph DePalma Stutz for a two-lap tour of the course, and racing was underway. When the vintage Formula One machines took the course, fans had a chance to see three-time world champion Sir Jack Brabham lead early in the event. Tacoma's Pete Lovely drove his Lotus 48 to a solid third-place finish in the Vintage event. In the featured NASCAR race, McGriff led early, but Spokane's Chad Little, on his way to a successful career with NASCAR in the Southeast, prevailed, taking the checker for his first street-course win.

Again, the event was judged a technical success, but organizational and promotional problems persisted. Despite a cut in admission prices, attendance was very disappointing. There was also a certain amount of friction between NASCAR, which provided the most popular attraction, and SCCA, which provided most of the volunteer help and the support classes. An overriding concern was the large deficit, reported at more than $900,000, remaining from the first event. After two years, the Tacoma Grand Prix was also history.

With the demise of Spanaway Speedway and Pierce County's increasing population density, area auto racing is changing dramatically. Although its future is uncertain, auto racing has survived for more than 90 years in the area, and though it may take on a new face, it will certainly continue to be a major presence on the local sports scene for the next 90 years.

George Hammond drives Leo Dobry's champ car to win the 1950 Pike's Peak Hill Climb (courtesy Dave Fogg).

CHAPTER 7

BADMINTON

Peter Collins, U.S. Junior National Champion in the singles 16-and-under division (courtesy Liz Collins).

Badminton is a spin-off of a sport called battledore, which was played in China, ancient Greece, and India about 2,000 years ago. The present version of the game, developed in India, was originally called poona. This game was brought back to England in 1873 by British colonial officials who saw the game being played, were delighted at how easy it was to play, and enjoyed the free-spirited atmosphere that it induced.

Once the game was in England, the Duke of Beaufort took such a liking to it that he arranged to have it played regularly at his Gloucestershire country estate, which was known as Badminton. Ever since, badminton has lived on as a sport, synonymous with the name of this beautiful English country home.

Badminton was introduced to Canada and the United States in 1890, but it wasn't until 1931 that the Canadian Badminton Association was formed, followed in 1936 by the U.S. Badminton Association. Highlighting the expansion of the sport was the International Badminton Challenge Cup for men in 1939, more popularly known as the Thomas Cup. In 1956 its counterpart for women was introduced as the Uber Cup. Both cups were named after the founders and presidents of the International Badminton Federation, Sir

George Thomas and Mrs. H. S. Uber.

Although badminton was initially thought of as an outdoor game, weather conditions such as wind and sun, along with the unevenness of grass and dirt surfaces, forced the game indoors. Badminton requires individual strength, endurance, accuracy, and player finesse—attributes more apparent in a controlled indoor environment.

Local badminton enthusiasts with instructor Lyle Morton (back row, center) (courtesy Pam Morton Iseri).

In 1972 badminton found favor with the Olympic Committee and appeared as a demonstration sport at the Olympic Games in Munich, Germany. At the 1988 Olympic Games in Seoul, Korea, it was an exhibition sport and in 1992 in Barcelona, Spain, badminton became a full-fledged medal sport and has remained so ever since.

One of the first venues in Tacoma to host badminton games was the Point Defiance Pavilion, which had only a concrete floor to play on. Games were later moved to Lincoln and Wilson High Schools. Some of the stalwart players of the '30s included Al Beeler, Lyle Morton, Jack DuPriest, and Francis Chapman, one of the top lefthanders around.

A headline in the *Tacoma Ledger* newspaper on October 4, 1931, reads, "Tacoma Girls Take up Badminton, New

Lyle Morton hustles during a rally while onlookers from the military enjoy the action (courtesy Pam Morton Iseri).

Sport." The article goes on to say, "Badminton, an English game, is being introduced at the YWCA this fall. It is played similar to tennis, but the equipment differs in that one uses a small racket, similar to a squash racket, and a shuttle, which is made up of 14 to 16 feathers fixed in a cork one inch in diameter. What a trick it is to keep this little shuttle flying over the net! It is lots of fun and is fascinating to play."

On April 2, 1933, the first annual badminton tournament was held at the pavilion, with Lyle Morton and Carolyn Fringess winning singles titles and Morton and Francis Chapman teaming up for the men's doubles title. Three years later, Morton defeated Jack DuPriest, 15–2, 15–6, at the Mason Methodist Church gymnasium to capture the men's singles City Badminton Championship. He then teamed up with Chapman to win another doubles crown, downing DuPriest and Lawrence McCamant, 15–11 and 17–15. Frances Walton successfully defended her women's single title by besting Margaret Jackson, 11–2, 9–11, and 11–4, in the final. Jackson and Betty Culbert won the women's doubles title, defeating a Mrs. Richardson and Alice Grimes, 11–3, 11–5.

The first Daffodil Festival Badminton Tournament was held in 1948 to encourage students, who were playing badminton in intramural school programs, to participate in tournament competition. The Daffodil event replaced the city tournament as the premier badminton competition in the area. Decades later, Chapman was still at it, capturing the men's singles title in the annual 1956 Daffodil tournament by scoring a 15–6, 15–2 victory over Verne Swanson at Lincoln High School. Lyle Morton's influence in the game continued, although his son Bill lost 15–7, 15–13 to Jerry Dorman in the boys' singles event and daughter Pam was downed by Judy Diseth, 11–4, 7–11, 11–5, for the girls' singles title. Pam came back, however, to win the girls' doubles final with partner Joan Wallis, and then the 14-year-old teamed up with Chapman to win the unique mixed handicap doubles over Paul Larsen and Pat Mercereau.

Since the 1960s, Stan Olsen, Bill Udall, Doug Bassett, John and Jackie Wohn, and Joe and Renate Moelders have developed this traditional event into one of the most highly competitive tournaments in the state.

Badminton in Tacoma–Pierce County has endured many venue changes over the years but has managed to survive, thanks to a long list of enthusiastic supporters. Players found space for weekly practices at Fife, Lincoln, Wilson, and Curtis High Schools; the University of Puget Sound; Tacoma Community College; and McCarver Junior High before finding a home at the Lakewood Community Center in 1980. With encouragement from the Pierce County Parks and Recreation Department, and to help make the center its permanent home, Joe Moelders founded the Tacoma Badminton Club in 1984.

Probably the most successful badminton player ever to come out of Tacoma was Ken Nelson, a 1968 graduate of Wilson High School. Formerly from Port Angeles, a noted hotbed for producing badminton players, Ken participated in national competition for 13- to 16-year olds in singles, doubles, and mixed doubles events. He won nine consecutive junior U.S. national titles.

Peter Collins was only six when his mother, Liz, first took him to Badminton Club night at the Lakewood Community Center. Nine years later, Collins became the U.S. Junior National Champion in the singles 16-and-under division. He also won the mixed doubles title in 1996.

Senior club members also enjoyed success at the national level. In 1999 Lynn Larson and Gary Stensland teamed up to win the U.S. National Grandmaster Doubles. Larson also placed second in the Grandmaster Singles and third in both the Grandmaster Mixed Doubles and in the Masters Mixed Doubles national championships.

Today the Tacoma Badminton Club meets regularly Monday evenings at the Lakewood Community Center, with a core group of 40 members responsible for maintaining the organization. The Daffodil Classic enjoys a well-deserved reputation as a prestigious regional tournament, drawing competition from throughout Washington, Oregon, and British Columbia. Despite its nomadic existence for many years, the Tacoma Badminton Club has endured the challenge of being a well-kept secret.

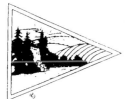

CHAPTER 8

BASEBALL:
THE EARLY YEARS AND AMATEURS

Monte Geiger was one of the mainstays of the Cheney Studs pitching corps over the years (SSM, 1080).

Before million-dollar contracts, commercial endorsements, and Cheney Stadium "Tiger dogs," people in Tacoma just played pure baseball.

The city was only a mixture of tree stumps and makeshift buildings when the Tacoma Invincibles were formed on August 8, 1874. Their reign was short lived—they played their last game 12 days later—but by this time other communities had formed their own teams, and Pierce County baseball was on its way. Orting teams started playing as early as 1876 and had their own ballpark; the Fats and the Leans team of 1891 was even competing against other ball clubs from Wilkeson, Carbonado, Buckley, and Puyallup.

In the summer of 1885, a baseball field was developed at 11th and L Streets, sponsored by Tacoma baseball enthusiast John S. Baker. The field was for the benefit of the Tacoma Athletic Club (TAC), a private organization for the city's business elite. Some citizens, however, frowned upon playing baseball on Sundays. Nevertheless, both children and adults were creating baseball fields in city streets as well as any available vacant lot. Residents sought to ban the game, however, at least in their own neighborhoods, and especially when played by those not eligible for membership in TAC.

By the start of the 20th century, both the City of Tacoma and the Metropolitan Park District had acquired land for recreational purposes. The construction of Stadium and Lincoln Bowls also added to the possible places where young and old alike could play the nation's number-one sport.

Teams sprang up all over the city. One of the most memorable was the Amocats (Tacoma spelled backward). Led by Frank Leslie between 1901 and 1906, they were touted as the greatest amateur team ever to be assembled. In their first 24 games, the Amocats were beaten only three times. Not only were they good, they were cocky. Walter Johnson, who later became a Hall of Fame pitcher for the Washington Senators in the American League, sat on the Amocats bench because Leslie thought he wasn't good enough to play. In one memorable game, batter "Goo" Campbell made history by knocking in two runs on a three-base bunt!

League organization was loose in the early days, but that didn't prevent the 1915 South Tacoma Tigers from representing the West Coast in the Amateur Baseball Championship of the World. Walter Holmberg managed the team that included catcher Lester Patterson, Fuzzy

DeMarais, and Jack Farrell; pitchers Orville Eley, Harry Helmecke, Oscar "Ocky" Haugland (also a leading home-run hitter in the city for years), and Nick Dahl; infielders Eddie McTighe, Allan Browne, Oscar "Ocky" Jensen, Paul Shager, and Roy Wilkowski (later the 1925 City League batting champion, with a .459 average); and outfielders Hank Crowl, Jule Shager, Walter Hagerdorn, and Urban Woods.

The Tigers went by ship to San Francisco to meet the White Autos of Cleveland; 5,000 games had been played in cities across the country to determine these two final contestants. Although Tacoma won the first game, Cleveland ultimately won the series. The loss, however, did not dampen the spirits of baseball fans in Tacoma.

The 1920s: Leagues Form

The first official meeting of the Tacoma City Baseball League was held on April 27, 1921. The league was organized by the Tacoma Commercial Club with Art Graham, Dr. James Egan, and Charles Winegar as its officers. The original teams were sponsored by Standard Oil, Tacoma Grocery, Fairmont, Sound Tire Company, Northern Pacific Railroad, and Wheeler-Osgood Company. The league grew rapidly. Within a year, Teddy's Tigers, Kay Street, Tacoma Avenue, Smelter Athletic Club, Milwaukee RailRoad, LaMunas, and the American Legion teams had been added to the lineup. Games were played in Stadium Bowl before the league moved to Lincoln Bowl in 1926. Athletic Park (now Peck Field) was also the site of many games.

This 1903 championship Tacoma Amateurs baseball team includes: front row, L. to R., Ed Hall, Glen Matthew, Elmer Gibbs; middle row, L. to R., Ralph Votaw, Lind Messinger, Chet Strayer, Mr. Case, Fremont Campbell, Joe Dickson; back row, L. to R., Leo Teats, Frank Hollis, Ed Corey (SSM, 1337).

Memorable ball players on those early league teams included "Ching" Johnson, Al Greco, Herman Tenzler, Al Libke Sr. (known for stealing 14 bases one season), Eddie Carlson (a small but strong catcher—he could throw to all the bases without standing), Stan "Fuzzy" Elliott (who, while still a teenager, pitched against the famed House of David Club), Cliff Marker (who once hit four home runs in one game at Athletic Park), Ocky Jensen, and Heinie Jansen.

Cecil Erb, a Teddy's Tigers pitcher, led the league in 1922 with six perfect games. That season, he won every game he pitched. Louie Balsano was another legend. He earned his reputation as a slugger; in 1925, as a Kay Street first baseman, he was the Tacoma City League batting champion. In 44 games, his 61 hits included three home runs, two triples, and 22 doubles. He also won the batting title in 1923.

Bob Johnson, former major leaguer with the Philadelphia A's, also coached the 1949 Tacoma Tigers (MB).

Former teammates recalled that Balsano loved to sleep. Al Pentecost, who played in the Timber League with Balsano, remembered fondly that "every Sunday we would be waiting for him to go down to Kelso, or Longview, or Centralia. Three or four guys would have to go and roll him out of bed. It was worth it, though. Boy, could he hit!" Old-timers insist that Balsano was perhaps the greatest hitter Tacoma ever developed. Lou's brother Frank was a well-known Kay Street pitcher.

Catcher Sammy Cappa stood only 5 feet 4 inches and weighed less than 135 pounds but was a master behind the plate. In a doubleheader against Grays Harbor in 1925, he threw the same player out six of the seven times he attempted to steal a base. Cappa played for Kay Street as well as other area teams before retiring in 1930 to work in the upholstery business. He once told sportswriter Ed Honeywell that the best pitchers he had played with were "Lefty" Isekite, Stan Hansen ("he had great stuff, great control"), Harley Franklin, "Biscuits" Beesaw, Ocky Haugland ("you could catch his pitches from a rocking chair"), and Vern Votaw.

It wasn't only the players who made names for themselves in the 1920s; Tacoma City League managers were quite a colorful group. Selected by the owner of the firm that sponsored the team, they often were "the guy with the car" who could provide transportation. There were Warnie Brooks of McKinley Hill, Bert Ohiser (the musically talented manager of Sixth Avenue), Fern Hill's baseball enthusiast Dr. J. W. Van Valsah, and "Hong" Armstrong of Tacoma Avenue. Leo Kellogg, Billy Ryan, and Heine Jansen were well-known managers of the Kay Street club, and "Shouting Shorty" Couch was the fiery, plump leader of the 23rd Street Skidoos. Their personalities, fierce competitiveness, and love of the game were critical to the popularity of early-day baseball in Tacoma.

Another colorful baseball personality, umpire Clarence Stave, entered the scene in 1924. Stave, who had a flair for the dramatic, developed into one of the most popular attractions on the Tacoma diamonds for the next 25 years. Left-hander Louie Balsano once hit Stave with a practice swing and knocked him down. When Balsano took the plate after that, it didn't matter where the pitch was thrown; it was "strike one, two, three, you're out!" Balsano was more careful in future games.

Verne Champagne, who played under Stave's watch, recalled Stave "putting on quite a performance at a McNeil Island game. When Frank Ruffo came up to bat, the pitcher threw one over Frank's head and Stave called it a strike. Ruffo would pretend to get into a big argument with Stave. It was all prearranged, of course," explained Champagne. "The bat had been broken earlier and taped together, and during the heat of the argument, Frank would pretend to break the bat over his knee. It always brought down the house."

And the fans loved it when Stave set up mock fights with other players at Lincoln Bowl. Once he pulled a cheap watch out of his pocket and the player grabbed it, threw it down, and stomped on it. According to Al Pentecost, "Anything could happen with Clarence behind the plate!"

As the 1920s came to a close, baseball continued to gain in popularity. The Timber League included small logging towns with lumber mills, such as Chehalis, Shelton, Kelso, Longview, Hoquiam, Aberdeen, Everett, and Tacoma; they played games on Sundays. The Valley League's teams represented small towns located in the valley areas of Pierce County and surrounding communities, such as Carbonado, Puyallup, Sumner, Yelm, Eatonville, Roy, South Prairie, Rocky Ridge, Spanaway, Morton, and Black Diamond; they provided expanded opportunities and more competition for Tacoma teams. The Twilight League included teams such as Superior Dairy, Cammarano Brothers, Publix Garage, Kimball's Sporting Goods, Olympic Ice Cream, Johnson Paint, and Pacific Match. The Industrial League teams' makeup was mostly players who worked together.

Exhibition Games

Barnstorming teams and major-league stars often came to town for exhibition games in this era. For instance, on October 18, 1924, Babe Ruth and Bob Meusel of the New York Yankees were on hand for a game between the triumphant Tacoma City League All-Stars and the Timber League All-Stars. They returned in 1927 with Earle Combs to play the Tacoma Tigers. It was during one of these visits that, according to local folklore, the Babe hit a ball into Commencement Bay from Stadium Bowl.

For years, the House of David, a religious colony

founded in 1903 in Benton Harbor, Michigan, fielded a popular traveling team that toured the United States. With their on-field antics and long hair and beards, which they were forbidden to cut or shave as a code of faith, they were a curiosity everywhere. They always played to capacity crowds. One year, according to Verne Champagne, they brought Olympics track and field star "Babe" Didrickson Zaharias with them as a pitcher. "She started warming up like a girl," Champagne recalled, "and everyone in the stands laughed and booed. Then she rared back and let one go and nearly put the catcher on his rear!"

Champagne also told of the time the Tokyo Giants played before a capacity crowd in the Lincoln Bowl during the mid-'30s. He remembered that game well. "I never saw so much bowing!" he said. "The Giants lined up on the baseline before the game started and bowed to the fans. The base men would bow if you stole a base. They would bow to the umpire on every close call. It used to really embarrass our guys—all that bowing. They were so polite!"

The Kansas City Monarchs had one of the finest traveling teams to visit Tacoma. The Monarchs were a black team assembled long before the integration of the major leagues in 1947, and Satchel Paige gained his greatest fame pitching for them during World War II. Tacoma also had a black Community League team, Monty's Independents, which played in the early '30s; the integrated Longshoremen's team, which played in the City League in 1924, included Jimmie Claxton and Ernie Tanner. Claxton later played professionally. They were followed into the City League by Jess Brooks and Jack Tanner, Ernie Tanner's son.

The 1930s: A Poor Man's Sport

The Depression contributed greatly to the growth and popularity of amateur ball in the '30s. According to Pat Rooney, former player in the City League and with the professional Tacoma Tigers, "Baseball was a poor man's sport. It was inexpensive fun, both for players and spectators. They would pass the hat at games or sometimes charge a dime or quarter. Officials decided on the hat-passing method out of consideration for the unemployed and the realization that sufficient funds could be derived from those able to pay a dime or so when the hat is sent on parade."

People in the neighborhood walked to the stadium to watch their favorite teams. It was not unusual for players to play in several leagues at the same time, especially in the late 1920s and '30s, and some continued playing, coaching, and managing into the '40s.

Sports columnist Elliott Metcalf singled out league hitter Jess Brooks, Larry "Noisy" Arcuri, and George "Gabby" Roket, a 16-year-old first baseman who continued to play into the 1940s, as some of the exciting players to watch. Brooks especially was an exceptional talent. He hit .522 in one championship series and stole six bases. He could pitch as well, hurling a shutout against the University of Washington (UW) while playing at the University of Puget Sound (UPS) in the mid-'30s.

Floyd "Lefty" Isekite was remembered by his teammates and opponents as one of Tacoma's all-time great pitchers. Known as the "strikeout king," Isekite played for Cammarano Brothers, Kimball's, and, in 1934, Pacific Match, for whom he led the Tacoma City League with 85 strikeouts in 105 innings. Isekite went on to have a successful career with the Tacoma Tigers of the Western International League from 1937 to 1940.

Sonny Bailey, who played with Isekite on several teams, remembered that "Lefty was not only a great pitcher, he was a tireless bus driver as well. He would get up early in the morning and drive a rickety old team bus to someplace like Yakima and then pitch an entire game. Every time I caught a good one in the field, Lefty would turn around on the mound and tip his hat to me."

South Tacoma Tigers sightsee in 1915 San Francisco, where they traveled to play in the World Championships (MB).

Sportswriter Dan Walton once referred to Bailey himself as "the gazelle of the gardens." He played in the City League for Cammarano Brothers, Kimball's, Olympic Ice Cream, and Jack 'n' Jill. He also competed in the Northwest League and on Industrial League teams. Bailey recalled that "anytime they needed someone, I was ready. At one point, I was playing in three leagues—one league twice a week, another twice a week, and the Sunday league on the weekend."

Despite Bailey's success, his older brother wouldn't lend him his Bill Doak baseball mitt, named after a former St. Louis Cardinals pitching star. "[Those mitts] were the best," remembered Bailey fondly. "You could pound it and make a nice pocket in the center. It cost $8.50; most of the others cost around $2. That's why Howard wouldn't share."

In the 1930s, Verne Champagne played for both the semipro Tacoma Tigers (Timber League) and Tacoma White Sox (Northwest League), as well as for Kimball's Sporting Goods. He gained his reputation as a center fielder but occasionally played other positions. Champagne remembered a White Sox game in which he was catching for Charlie Wry. Umpire Clarence Stave eloquently announced the battery as "Wry and Champagne." According to Champagne, "The crowd thought we were the bartenders!"

The 1934 season was a big one for Al Pentecost. Playing for Publix Garage, he led the City League pitchers with an earned run average (ERA) of 1.60. There was tough competition in the league that year. Ocky Haugland was pitching for Superior Dairy, Isekite was with Pacific Match, and Vern Votaw also was a contender. Pentecost had played three seasons as a shortstop back in the '20s in the Timber League and City League. In 1927 he played pro ball with the Waterloo team in the Mississippi Valley League, and he also played for Olympic Ice Cream and Kay Street, as well as with Carbonado in the Valley League.

It was with the Carbonado team in 1933, playing Mercer Island in the state tournament, that Pentecost was mistaken for Santa Claus.

"The stands were full of people. Many of them were drinking and partying. They were having a great time, especially the guys sitting in front of my sister and Aunt Bertha," recalled Pentecost. "When the announcer recited my name in the batting order, the guys thought he said 'Santa Claus'

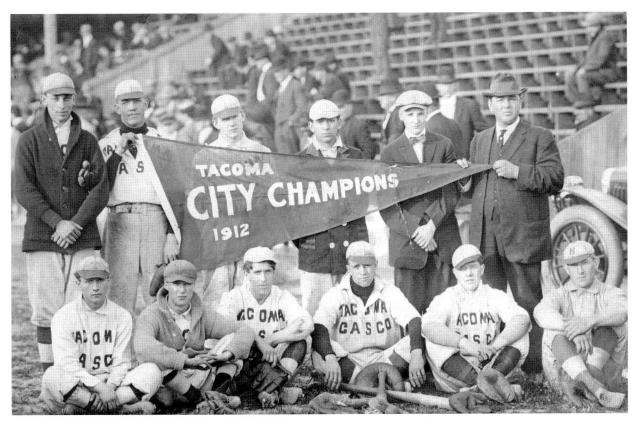

1912 Tacoma Tigers City League championship team (MB).

rather than 'Pentecost.' They had a good time joking and laughing about having Santa Claus in the game, until I came up to bat at the bottom of the first inning with the bases loaded and no outs. We were using those big bottle bats. They were big, long bats, wide and cut down short to the handle. I swung at the pitch and thought it would be a sacrifice fly, but it went over the right-field fence. I didn't even realize it until I heard everyone in the stands yelling."

"I found out later that when I hit the home run, my Aunt Bertha leaned forward and started beating on the shoulders of the guys in front, yelling, 'Now what do think of Santy Claus, huh? Now what do you think of Santy Claus?' I guess they weren't laughing anymore."

Joe Pasquan has been called an early-day Mickey Mantle. Gilly Portmann was a second baseman who was always ready to throw a base runner out. Other standouts included first baseman Joe Spadafore, pitcher Marion Oppelt, and infielder Joe Salatino, considered by many to

be one of the most versatile athletes of his time. Les Bishop in 1935 had 21 consecutive hits at the start of the season. Stan Wallace won the 1935 and 1936 Valley League batting titles with .490 and .591 averages. Hal Lennox, Joe Mlachnik (a highly respected shortstop), Neil Mazza, Rick Lewis, and Jimmy Ennis also made their mark on the diamond, as did pitcher Cy Ball and catcher Frank "Bush" Tobin. When Tobin was catching, it is rumored that his voice carried to Fife!

Lee Keirstead, Paul "Doc" Wotten, Bane Browse, Joey Peterson, Bill Moe, Fred "Buzz" Doane, Primo Artoe, Vic Krause, Frank Brozovich (1934 City League batting champion), and Phil Sarboe were other notable players.

The 1937 Johnson Paint team, managed by the inimitable John Heinrick, was especially memorable. It was the first team from Tacoma to travel beyond the West Coast to participate in the National Baseball Congress tournament in Wichita, Kansas, with a team that included Fred Hutchinson, Earl Johnson, Joe Dailey, Cy Greenlaw, Joe Salatino, Loris Baker, Hal Lee, Rick Lewis, Andy Padovan, Morry Abbott, Erling Tollefson, Frank Ruffo, Jim Ennis, Rudy Tollefson, Doug Hendry, and Joe Mlachnik. Hutchinson and Johnson later pitched several years in the major leagues, while Greenlaw and Abbott became standouts for the professional Tacoma Tigers.

To raise funds for the trip to Kansas, Johnson Paint played an exhibition game against an All-Star League team. A crowd of some 3,500 fans gathered in Lincoln Bowl to watch Freddie Steele, middleweight boxing champion of the world (see chapter 16, Boxing), play three innings as right fielder for the Painters. Once they were in Wichita, the team won their first three games, against Fairfax, Alabama; Waynesboro, Mississippi; and Wichita. The Painters finished fifth after losing to Buford, Georgia, and Dormant, Pennsylvania. This venture into national amateur play, however, would not be the last for a Tacoma team.

The tradition of outstanding managers established by the Tacoma City League in the '20s (see The 1920s: Leagues Form, earlier in this chapter) continued in the '30s. Ocky Haugland managed Superior Dairy and filled in as a player when needed. Al Pentecost still took the mound several times after he became the manager for Publix Garage. Haugland and Pentecost were actually rival managers of a City League All-Star game that was played before 12,000 fans in Stadium Bowl in 1933. Other managers of the decade included longtime pro outfielder Cy Neighbors, Willard Carpy, John Mazzuca, Bert Woodard, and John Heinrick, who is remembered as one of the all-time great coaches in Tacoma history. Heinrick managed the 1934 Pacific Match team and the Johnson Paint team that played in the 1937 National Baseball Congress tournament. His career also included coaching the semipro Tacoma Tigers, serving as president of the City League, a stretch as athletic director at Stadium High School, and coach and athletic director at UPS.

Tacoma's 1956 Stanley's Shoemen was the first West Coast team to win a national amateur baseball championship in 1956: back row, L. to R., Gordy Grubert, Jack Johnson, Dick Schlosstein, Monte Geiger, Dale Bloom, Jim Gallwas, Mike Dillon, Max Braman, Tom Montgomery; front row, L. to R., Ron Storaasli, Pat Dillon, George Grant, Manly Mitchell, coach Doug McArthur, Earl Hyder, Jim Harney, Bob Maguinez, Dick Montgomery (SSM, 2067).

Baseball in the Family

In some cases, amateur baseball was a family affair. Sonny Bailey's brother Howard preceded him on the diamond, as did Dick Greco's uncle Al and Vern Kohout's brother Robert. Brothers Frank Ruffo and Ernie Ruffo were standout ballplayers, as were slugger Frank Burkland and his brother Ray, Frank Balsano and Lou Balsano, Joe Hermsen and Frank Hermsen, Dick Salatino and Joe Salatino, Harold Larson and Kordyll Larson, and Crosetto brothers Walter, Paul, and Julius. Bill Feldman and George Feldman were active as infielder and pitcher, respectively.

The Tollefson brothers had a significant impact in Tacoma: "Hustling Harold," Thor, Rudy (a great shortstop who went on to be an All-Conference player at UW), and Erling (who was as good at the plate as he was at first base). Both Al Libke and Bill Libke were unforgettable ball players: Bill was known for his elusive drop pitch, and Al was a great competitor who excelled as a catcher and in the outfield. The Johnson brothers, Bob and Roy, went on to have noteworthy professional baseball careers, and Bob returned to manage the Tacoma Tigers in 1949. George Mosolf and Jimmy Mosolf were baseball standouts who were followed by their cousins, the Rooney brothers: Tom, George, Jim, and Pat. Other family competitors included Bill Otto and Jack Otto, Ed Chila and John Chila, Joe Thiel and George Thiel, Les Bishop and Lon Bishop, Whit Lees and Wes Lees, Rhine Thaut and Henry "Dutch" Thaut, and the Haugland brothers, Hal, Vic, and Oscar.

Road Trips

One unusual element of playing baseball in the early days was the interesting road trips that were required. Sonny Bailey remembers one particular trip to Carbonado: "The ball field was small and surrounded by trees and high grass. We would hit a nice clean ball way out there, and before we could make it to the base, the ball—a dirty old thing—would already be there. We never could prove it, but we knew they had those balls hidden like Easter eggs. But we didn't say too much, either. After all, they fed us after the game!"

Bailey also recalled going to Cle Elum with his brother Howard, who drove the team in his 1919 Essex. "He had one of the only cars that would make it over the pass," explained Bailey. "The fans sat along the sidelines; a lot of them had been drinking moonshine, and some had guns. When someone got a hit, they whooped and hollered and shot their guns in the air. It looked like the Fourth of July. They were just having fun. A few got drunk and they would just fall asleep in the grass and everybody stepped over them."

A much-anticipated event for Tacoma-area ball players was a trip to McNeil Island to play the prison teams. Verne Champagne recalled, "I was never counted so many times in my life! They would count you when you got on the boat, when you got on the truck to go to the penitentiary, when you got off the truck, [when you went] into the locker room, out of the locker room, onto the field, off the field, into the locker room, out of the shower!" Ernie Ruffo added that "it was all worth it, though; we had great games and the food was wonderful!" McNeil Island games were a tradition that continued for years. Al Pentecost, who played and managed for 26 years, recalled going back with the old-timers' group in the mid-'50s when "most of us were in our 40s and 50s."

A trip to Victoria created a league joke that was hard to live down for Heinie Hademan, a Timber League reserve catcher. In the early '30s, teams were occasionally invited up to Victoria, British Columbia, to play a doubleheader. Victoria paid them $150, so teams would take as few players as possible, which allowed more money for each player. When the Tacoma players were ready to leave Vancouver Island, they could not find Harold Lennox, their catcher. Because they had to go directly to a game in Olympia, they had no choice but to leave him behind and instead use Hademan at the next game. Hademan had such short, stubby fingers that the pitcher couldn't see him flashing signals. So they wrapped white tape on his fingertips to make them more noticeable. After that, infielders around the league, when they turned around to show their teammates the count, would frequently show just the stubs of their fingers.

The 1940s: Decline in the War Years

Just as the political climate of the '30s promoted the popularity of baseball, the events of the '40s contributed to its temporary decline. The 1940s began with high hopes, enthusiasm, and many of the same players and managers who had been involved in City League ball for two decades. Art Berg,

CHAPTER SPONSORED BY

THE BEN B. CHENEY FOUNDATION:

Ben B. Cheney devoted himself to his work, his family, and his community and was a tireless businessman and innovator. As the founder of Cheney Lumber Company, he standardized building stud length at eight feet, reducing discarded and wasted wood at mills around the country. But this lumber innovator's passion was athletics, especially the game of baseball. He helped to bring a Pacific Coast League franchise to Tacoma and played a key role in building Tacoma's ballpark, Cheney Stadium.

Cheney's love of sports was not confined to his own interests. Throughout the small logging communities of Washington, Oregon, and California many young people played on athletic teams sponsored by Cheney Lumber. In fact more than 5,000 youngsters developed their skills while participating in its programs. Today many of these participants still retain the enthusiasm, self-discipline, and team spirit that come from athletic involvement.

A few years after Cheney's death in 1971, the Ben B. Cheney Foundation began active grant making. The Foundation's work supports a wide range of needs in the communities where the Cheney Lumber Company once was active. By the end of 2003 the Foundation had made 3,640 grants to just over 1,100 organizations totaling nearly $54.7 million.

standout first baseman of Superior Dairy, led the 1940 league with a .491 average and also had the most putouts. Dave Minnitti of Cammarano Brothers and Stan Wallace of GMC Trucks weren't far behind in hitting averages. Les Bishop led the way with the most runs batted in. The Smelter Athletic Club, Johnson's Paint, Cammarano Brothers, GMC Trucks, and Turf Smoke Shop were the leading teams of that season.

In July 1941, Tacoma Truckers coach John Heinrick invited the famed Kansas City Monarchs to play an exhibition game against his squad. Heinrick bolstered his chances by also asking Jess Brooks, former Tacoman and UPS star, to temporarily leave his Everett team and join them against the Monarchs, a team he had played for several years earlier. Ray Spurgeon, a young catcher from Lincoln High School, was also invited to participate, taking a break from his Olympia team. The starting lineup included outfielders Brooks, Rick Lewis, and Dave Minnitti and infielders Erling Tollefson at first, John Milroy at second, George Wise at shortstop, and Marv Tommervik at third. Hal Schimling earned the catching duties and Billy Sewell drew mound duty for the Truckers, opposing the great Satchel Paige of the Kansas City team.

Milroy remembered "seeing that team drive up in an old broken-down bus, but right behind them in an expensive car with a good-looking girl sitting next to him came Satchel Paige. I was at bat and Paige threw a couple of questionable pitches that umpire Clarence Stave called balls. Paige called a time-out and wandered in to talk to Stave. I remember Satchel saying, 'You know, I have to pitch every day and so I can't waste pitches. I need you to call these strikes because I can't afford to throw extra pitches. We can have a good time out here or not. I like to let these boys get a hit every now and then, but if you aren't going to help me out there, I will just strike every one of them out!'

"I already had a hit off Paige earlier in the game," said Milroy, "so to hear this was a little deflating. He then proceeded to strike me out, although Billy Sewell pitched a great game and we beat Kansas City, 3–1."

As the '40s progressed, the young men of Tacoma had more serious matters to contemplate. Thoughts of runs batted in (RBIs) and road trips to Shelton were replaced by concerns over the increasing threat of involvement with the war

in Europe. City League teams had a difficult time maintaining a full complement of players, because many men had enlisted or been drafted for military service. The lights went out on the fields and the cheering fans were silent.

There were exceptions, of course. The Shipbuilders Athletic Club (SAC) put together a Tacoma team that had outstanding players from past years as well as some younger men. Their 1944 team included Dave Goodman (1938 Western International League batting chamnpion), Cleve Ramsey, "Lefty" Isekite, Joe Salatino, Bill Turnbull, Pip Koehler, George Wise, Mason Longmire, Earl Porter, Bobby Garretson, Bill Feldman, Jim Martin, Harry Hall, Les Hall, Eddie Carlson, Gene Hansen, and Roy Johnson. Many of them had played professionally, primarily in the Western International League (WIL).

The professional Tacoma Tigers and some WIL teams continued to play until the league disbanded during the war. The Tigers provided an outlet for several homegrown ballplayers. Morry Abbott, who played for them from 1939 to 1942, is remembered as one of the greatest sluggers in Tacoma history. "Lefty" Isekite, a Stadium High graduate and a Tiger from 1937 to 1940, was named to the All-Star team three times. Dick Greco, a longtime City Leaguer, joined the Tigers in 1946 immediately after the war. Greco became a superstar in the lower minor leagues and is remembered as an inspiration to many young ballplayers.

1937 Tigers' player-manager Eddie Taylor hits against Vancouver's Maple Leafs at Athletic Park (Richards Studio Collection, TPL, Image D102-6).

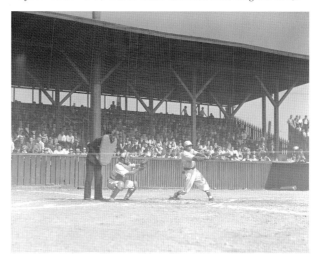

Dave Molitor, who played for both Olympic Ice Cream and the Turf Smoke Shop in 1940, played with the Tigers in 1942 and '46 and was with the Cubs organization and Los Angeles in the late '40s.

Earl Kuper, a Tigers catcher from 1946 to 1948, led the WIL in hitting in 1947, with a .389 average. Dave Minnitti spent a season with the Tigers before returning to Cammarano Brothers in 1949. Popular Cy Greenlaw, formerly with Johnson Paint of the Tacoma City League, starred with the Tigers after the war.

The 1950s: The Postwar Years

After an absence of several years, the City League made its much-anticipated return in 1949. There were a few changes. Primarily, the newly organized teams were sponsored by communities or neighborhoods, as they had been decades earlier, rather than by individual business firms. Kay Street, 26th and Proctor, Sixth Avenue, 38th Street, McKinley Hill, and South Tacoma were all represented. Many of the managers' names also conjured up memories of prewar games: George Wise, Earl Kuper, Frank "Bush" Tobin, Art Berg, Ray Spurgeon, and Gus Paine took control of the teams, while John Heinrick assumed the presidency of the league.

These experienced managers also recruited many seasoned ballplayers, in addition to younger men. Kay Street had the Salatino brothers, Art Viafore, Dave Minnitti, and Al Otto. Sixth Avenue's roster included Berg at first base, while 38th Street claimed Marv Scott and Marion Oppelt. The McKinley Hill team included Gilly Portmann, as well as Tobin, the catcher, and Bob Kohout, a former Dodgers farmhand. Pat Rooney played first base for South Tacoma, and E. M. Torrance joined them as a pitcher. Rooney, on high school graduation, played the 1942 season for the Tigers at first base before returning home to play in the City League in 1949. Rooney remembered the kindness of other team members, namely his hero, Jess Brooks, and Gilly Portmann, who "was really helpful to me as a new young player. He even lent me his bat one time; I never have forgotten that."

Fierce competition defined City League baseball during the early 1950s. Veteran pitcher Marion Oppelt of the 38th Street team and South Tacoma pitcher Dale Bloom, fresh out of high school, led the race for City League leadership in 1950. Of the six league teams, four were still tied for first place after the first 10 games. Extra innings often were needed to decide games.

Behind the scenes, Tom Cross, Clay Huntington, Willard Carpy, and Roland Tollefson helped rejuvenate baseball in the area. Carpy and Tollefson reorganized the Valley League. Their enthusiasm spread, encouraging as many as 30 teams to compete across Pierce County. Cross, responsible for the park district athletic programs, kept the Sunset League going, playing during the week at twilight hours in neighborhood fields. Tacoma's only lighted baseball facility, Tiger Park, was idled by the demise of the Tigers' WIL franchise, and neither Lincoln nor Stadium Bowl could be used for baseball any longer.

This prompted Cross to join forces with Huntington, the former radio voice of the Tigers, to buy the field and eight players still on the Tacoma Tigers roster for just under $40,000. Rumor was that they mortgaged their homes without the knowledge of their wives. Later, they convinced Tacoma lumberman Ben Cheney to purchase the park at South 38th and Lawrence and renamed it Cheney Field.

The Valley and Sunset Leagues gathered momentum. Spanaway had maintained a strong Valley League presence, thanks to a team history dating back to 1919 when Ocky Larsen Sr. played for the Spanaway Merchants. In the 1930s, the Spanaway Athletic Club became the team sponsor and Ray Brammer the team batboy. He went on to play and manage the postwar Spanaway entries. Early games were played at the town's grade school field, but by 1950, the present-day parking lot at Lake Spanaway Golf Course was the venue. The team built the field itself, and the coach used his own car to drag the infield. At games, the fans passed the hat to pay the umpires.

More than 80 players comprise the list of former Spanaway team members. Five of them—Brammer, Jack Bratlie, Howie Davis, Andy Ketter, and Chuck Loete—have been inducted into the Pierce County Baseball Hall of Fame. Brammer and Ketter were originally from Roy; Loete and another star player, Jack Justice, were from Kapowsin. Justice managed the Spanaway nine from 1945 to 1949 and brought his son Gary along to be batboy. Gary Justice became one of the top TV news anchors in the Northwest, for KIRO television.

Baseball fever was at a high pitch in Pierce County in the '50s. Every small town seemed to have a team in the Valley League, and the rivalries were keen. Community pride was at a postwar all-time high, and player camaraderie (among both friend and foe) was strong and lasting. The same could also be said for the City and Sunset Leagues throughout the decade.

Although specific communities sponsored the teams, players moved back and forth from team to team and between leagues. One day you could be rooting for the likes of Frank Bonaro playing championship ball for Edgewood in the Valley League, only to find him later playing on the City League's Kay Street team.

The Tacoma City League was a collection of neighborhood teams defined by commercial areas based on the earlier

expansion of citywide streetcar lines. The teams were a mixture of high school, college, semipro, and former professional players. Kay Street was a sort of king of the hill for players, while Edgewood was the spawning ground, and the Olde Pilsner team was a finale.

The nucleus of the Kay Street team during its dominance was formed by Pete Sabutis, Hal Schimling, Cliff Schiesz, Frank Morrone, Dave Minnitti, Ed Yusko, Gus Paine, Frank Bonaro, Earl Birnel, Dick Browse, Fred Rickert, Larry Rask, Hank Semmern, Dick Salatino, Frank Osborne, Vic Martineau, and Vern Martineau. Rickert came from Vaughn on the Longbranch Peninsula; Bonaro formed a threesome with Minnitti and Morrone, who all later umpired together.

The Edgewood team was initially a product of the local farmers' granges—a collection of teams and players whose history had yet to be written. Phil's Tavern was the first

The Tacoma Tigers played in the 1934 Northwest League: back row, L. to R., Vern Votaw, Frank Ruffo, coach John Heinrick, Forrest Weingard, Joe Spadafore, Vern Champagne; front row, L. to R., Wes Lees, Hal Lennox, Hoefert, Joe Mlachnik, Cecil Erb, Rudy Tollefson (MB).

name for the Edgewood players, of which Phil Lelli, brother-in-law of Kay Street's Hal Schimling, was the sponsor. It was not long before Hal was recruiting Kay Street players for Phil's team.

The Olde Pilsner team grew from former players of both Edgewood and Kay Street. Les Herzog, who later assembled Portland Avenue neighborhood teams, used Schimling, Sabutis, Semmern, and Scheisz as the nucleus of what proved to be a winning team. Dale Bloom, Tom Absher, Ron Billings, Frank Karwoski, and Bob Jamison were other players. So too was Bob Johnson, former Tacoma Tigers manager.

An exception to the constant rotation was the Fort Lewis Employees Association (FLEA) Club. From 1947 to 1952, only 23 different players donned the FLEA uniform. Bill Gibson Sr., at the prodding of his son Bill Jr., was the coach for the duration. Frank McCabe was a favorite pitcher, but it was the Harkness boys who made the FLEA Club a family affair: Dave Sr., Ray, Val, and Gene all played on the 1947 team. By 1956, after the FLEA Club stopped playing, Dave Jr. was added to the roster of the Boilermakers Local 568 team, representing the town of Roy in the Valley League.

Two younger teams then emerged. George Wise picked the cream of the crop from the local high schools under the banner of the Tacoma Sportsmen Club, many of whom were standouts on Stadium's 1946 state championship squad, and they were an immediate success. The veteran "Kay Street–Edgewood" stranglehold on first place in the Sunset and Valley Leagues was challenged by Wise's choices of all-star talent.

Another new contender developed from young talent: Doug McArthur, a local baseball enthusiast and UPS student, organized a team of Lincoln High graduates, and Busch's Drive-In sponsored their entry in the Valley and Sunset Leagues. They didn't win much at first (in fact, they lost their Valley League opener, 18–0), but it didn't take them many years to capture both league championships and represent Tacoma in the state semipro tournament in Bellingham.

A former professional pitcher and fellow Lincoln grad, Vern Kohout, had joined the Drive-Ins as a player-coach and also coached UPS in the Evergreen Conference. Most of the Drive-In players came from UPS and Pacific Lutheran University (PLU); many missed a couple of seasons because of service obligations during the Korean conflict.

In 1955 the majority of that team had come home and were reunited under the sponsorship of Western State Hospital. Mal Stevens, the recreation director at Western State, agreed to sponsor the team to provide Sunday games for the enjoyment of the patients at the institution. A Valley League championship proved most enjoyable for all.

There were other games to be played during the week, however, in the Tacoma City League and the powerful Sea-Tac League, and the team needed sponsorship for that phase of its schedule. Stan Naccarato, whose potential major-league pitching career was cut short by an arm injury, came to the rescue. He convinced his business partner, Morley Brotman, that Stanley's Shoes would benefit from entry in the top two amateur baseball circuits in the state. Thus, the Shoemen were born.

McArthur had convinced many of the best young players in Pierce County to remain together to challenge the established championship-caliber teams assembled by the Seattle Cheney Studs and Tacoma's Woodworth Contractors. A heated three-cornered rivalry that would stretch all the way to Battle Creek, Michigan, and impact several national amateur championships began to unfold at Tacoma's new Cheney Field.

The Shoemen featured a strong pitching staff led by former Lincoln High ace Dale Bloom and Stadium High star Mike Dillon, both with professional experience but reinstated as amateurs. Knuckleball artist Max Braman and lefties Dick Mongomery and Manly Mitchell completed the pitching staff. PLU's Jack Johnson, another former pro prospect, was the catcher. A trio of Stadium High grads, Bob Maguinez, Gordy Hersey, and Dick Schlosstein; Lincoln High grads Earl Hyder, Russ Wilkerson, and Ron Storaasli; and Bellarmine Prep alum Jim Gallwas formed the nucleus of the starting lineup. Wilkerson and Maguinez had starred collegiately at UPS, Storaasli at PLU, Gallwas at Seattle University (SU), Hersey at Washington State University (WSU), and Schlosstein at the University of Oregon.

Former professionals Bill Funk and Marv Scott coached the Woodworth entry. That roster featured ex-WSU pitching star Rod Keough, youthful left-hander Maury Galbraith (a

Bellarmine Prep star), and strong right-hander Harold Larson, a Stadium High grad. Catchers Al Featherstone (Lincoln High) and Arley Kangas (Stadium High and WSU) were behind the plate, and veterans such as Chuck Loete, Jim Rediske (both former PLU stars), and Al Maul (an ex-professional with the Bremerton Bluejackets) supplied the savvy and the power. A young outfielder from Peninsula High, Mel Manley, was a bright addition to the team.

The Studs were a college All-Star team assembled by Joe Budnick of Seattle. Tacomans George Grant and Luther Carr, both UW stars, teamed with the ace pitchers of SU and UW, George Kritsonis and Monte Geiger, to round out this national contender.

In a six-year span, only once, in 1957, did one of the three Tacoma or Seattle powers fail to play for the American Amateur Baseball Congress national championship. The Studs were runner-up in 1955, the Shoemen won it all in '56, Woodworth was runner-up in '58, the Studs were sec-

ond again in '59, and the Studs took the title in 1960. The Shoemen had a 36–8 record in winning City League and Valley League (as Western State) championships in '55 and a 50–11 mark in 1956 while winning state, regional and national tournaments.

The Shoemen survived two big local setbacks before winning their last 13 games to claim those titles. The fun began when they won the first-half City League crown, but Woodworth took the second-half title. A three-game playoff followed, and the archrivals split the opening two games.

With Shoemen hitting star Bob Maguinez at the plate and the tying runs on base, umpire Sandy Moore would not honor a Maguinez request for time-out during the decision. Maguinez stepped out of the batter's box and Moore called a strike. That prompted a visit from McArthur, who was coaching third base.

The home-plate argument that ensued resulted in McArthur and Maguinez both being tossed from the game.

THE LITTLE GIANTS OF THE SOUTH END BOYS CLUB

Shortly after the opening of the South End Boys Club in June 1954, I was contacted by Tom Cross about a program started at McNeil Island regarding the sponsorship of kids' sports. This was coordinated by Cy Rubado. As part of the program, the inmates—with their own resources—purchased uniforms and sports gear for baseball.

The South End Boys Club was selected, and the inmates had a contest to name the team: It was the "Little Giants." We fielded the team, kept the prison population informed about the games, and sent them pictures. The team was invited to the island with another local team, and we played a game before a large [captive] audience. All players were treated to lunch in the prison cafeteria following the game.

The inmates were so taken with the program that the sponsorship was expanded to include basketball and football. The kids visiting the island looked forward to it and were very well greeted by the inmates and the prison staff.

Once a year, the prison population held an open house for many of the Tacoma [sports] leaders and it was always well attended. Mayor John Anderson, called Big John by the inmates, was always the hit of the evening. Several members of the Little Giants program were invited as well.

Some notables from the Little Giants program were Ahmad Rashad and Ron Cey. The Little Giants program was also written up in the Wilson Sporting Goods magazine. The program went on for many years, but finally it was stopped by regulations coming down from higher authority.

—Don Danielson, former director of Boys and
Girls Club of Tacoma–Pierce County

As the disagreement carried on, Moore gave McArthur two minutes to leave the field. "I had to find a pinch hitter, " McArthur remembered. "I turned to Dale Bloom to act as manager and had to get our pinch hitter from the right-field bullpen, where he was warming up a pitcher. Then I couldn't find my street shoes in the dugout. The next thing I knew, the ump had forfeited the game."

Woodworth's disputed championship gave the Contractors a state tournament berth, but Tacoma had two entries coming and the Shoemen also qualified. Initially they said no, but City League Commissioner Tom Cross convinced McArthur and his team to compete.

The Shoemen lost a 3–1 decision to Geiger and the defending state champion Studs in the opener and were faced with a "one loss and you're out" tournament future. With heads high, they congratulated the Cheney team and

started over in the loser's bracket. "An amazing thing then happened," McArthur acknowledged. "We had been so concerned about not losing that failing to win became almost too much for us. After that loss, we were relaxed and quit thinking about losing. We never lost again!"

The 13-game winning streak meant Tacoma had its first-ever national baseball champions.

Bloom pitched the state, regional, and national championship games as the Shoemen two-timed Cheney 9–4 and 17–2 in the final games at state, edged Portland, Oregon, 4–3 in the regional final in South Dakota, and blasted East Chicago, Indiana, 10–0 for the national crown.

Catcher Jack Johnson edged outfield teammate Bob Maguinez for Most Valuable Player at the regionals. Outfielder Ron Storaasli was state MVP. Center fielder Earl Hyder completed the outfield, which McArthur still rates as the best trio of outfielders ever assembled on one Tacoma team. All three sported batting averages near .400 in the 61-game season.

Tacoma's player Bliss races to first but is thrown out as Strieb makes the play, umpire Wright makes the call, and first base coach Stevens looks on (courtesy David Eskenazi).

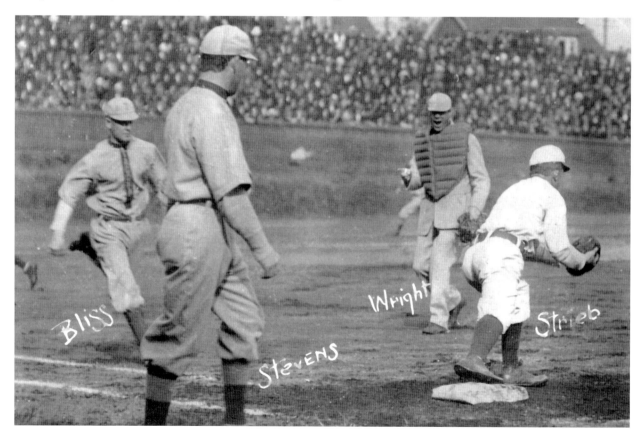

This Valley Forge team played in the Timber League in 1929: back row, L. to R., manager A.CA. "Butch" Sonntag, unknown, Milt Woodard, unknown, unknown, Tony Banaszak Sr.; front row, L. to R., unknown, unknown, unknown, unknown, Whit or Wes Lees; foreground, mascot unknown (SSM, 258.12).

The Shoemen's tournament infield was excellent as well. Jim Gallwas at third base and Dick Schlosstein at first base had been season-long regulars for the Shoemen, but Russ Wilkerson and Gordy Hersey could not get clear from employment obligations to make the regional and national trip. Replacement players were allowed, and the Shoes picked up Cheney Studs stars George Grant and Jim Harney, a double-play combination that sparkled throughout the tournaments. All four had starred at Northwest colleges.

Pitchers Monte Geiger, also added from the Studs, and Mike Dillon both won crucial games along the way. Dillon handcuffed the host Battle Creek, Michigan, team in the national opener, 4–1, yielding just three hits and whiffing 10 without giving up a walk. Geiger outlasted defending national champion Houston, Texas, 7–6 in the semifinals,

despite a freakish ninth inning. The Texans managed three runs on a blooper, which was caught but ruled to be trapped, and a dropped fly ball. Then, with the tying run at second, Geiger coaxed a shallow fly out of the Texas clean-up hitter, and Storaasli raced under it for the final out.

Two years later, the Woodworth Contractors had their chance. Marv Scott, one of the best baseball coaches in Tacoma's history, was serious about winning it all. During regional play, he told a Rapid City, South Dakota, reporter that the Contractors "didn't come to South Dakota just to see Mount Rushmore and we're not going to Battle Creek just to eat corn flakes." Woodworth almost accomplished its mission, finishing second and losing a tough 1–0 decision to Cincinnati in the championship game.

Scott's favorite story from that trip pertains to a game to

be played against Cincinnati. During the bus ride to the park, Scott asked pitcher Don Carlson to "come up in the front seat with me so you can hop off the bus and maybe get a few extra minutes to warm up." "Why coach," Carlson said, "I can warm up in the bus and beat these guys!"

When the Cheney Studs won the American Amateur Baseball Congress (AABC) championship in 1960, two Tacomans played key roles: Bob Maguinez and Earl Hyder. Both had played in that tournament with the Shoemen in '56 and the Contractors in '58.

The 1960s and Beyond

Adult baseball, amateur and semipro, started to lose its allure, however, with the increased popularity of slowpitch softball in the late '50s and the return of the professional Pacific Coast League baseball and the Tacoma Giants in 1960.

But there was one last hurrah, which came in 1996 when the Tacoma Timbers took second place in the National Baseball Congress (semipro) World Series in Wichita, Kansas. The Tacomans went through the winner's bracket undefeated, needing just one win in two games to take home the title, but they dropped both and finished as runners-up.

Appropriately, Brad Cheney was the person responsible for the Timbers' five years of success in the Pacific International League (PIL). Son of legendary baseball enthusiast Ben Cheney, Brad was a batboy for the powerful Cheney Studs teams of the '50s and later coached at Charles Wright Academy and UPS. The Timbers were coached by Barry Aden (180–61 in all five years of their existence), and he described the championship games as "the ugliest seven hours of baseball in my entire life." The opponent was the El Dorado Broncos, who hailed from just 30 miles away, and they had 10,000 fans in the stands. The Timbers had beaten the Broncos, 9–3, early in the tournament but dropped 6–3 and 13–8 decisions in 58-degree weather and rain. It was 100 degrees all week, and the Timbers had won six straight to gain the final round, only to cool off when the temperature dropped.

Several of the Timbers signed professionally and have played in the major leagues. Willie Bloomquist of South Kitsap and the Seattle Mariners is one. So is Justin Leone, the former St. Martin's College star who made his major-league debut with the Seattle Mariners in 2004 via the 3A franchise in Tacoma. Others include Justin Bachman, who played for the Anaheim Angels; Randy Choate with the New York Yankees; David Riske with the Cleveland Indians; and Jeff Zimmerman, who advanced to pitch for the Texas Rangers.

Now a multimillion-dollar industry, baseball has come a long way from local sandlots, but it remains America's favorite sport. Some prefer to remember baseball the way it was, however: a game played by local teams in small towns across the country, a game in which neighbors came to cheer for their favorite team and a hat was passed to pay the umpires. The players were friends, neighbors, and genuine role models for the next generation of young ballplayers. Some prefer to remember a time when competition and camaraderie were more important than compensation. Many feel this was when baseball was at its best, and this was Tacoma–Pierce County baseball from the 1920s to the 1960s.

Oscar Jensen played for the South Tacoma Tigers in 1915 (MB).

CHAPTER 9

BASEBALL:
TACOMA'S PRO TEAMS

Longbranch native Marv Rickert played outfield for the Tacoma Tigers in 1942, enjoyed six years in the major leagues, and played for the Boston Braves in the 1948 World Series (SSM, 2043).

Professional baseball reached the Northwest region of the United States in 1890, when Tacoma joined Seattle, Portland, and Spokane Falls for the inaugural season of the Pacific Northwest League (PNL). Although world wars, financial crises, and periods of poor attendance sometimes interrupted play, Tacoma's baseball history spans more than 110 years. And today the game enjoys its greatest success since the city became a permanent member of the Pacific Coast League (PCL) in 1960.

The original PNL, according to one of its founders, John S. Barnes, was developed as a promotion for the Northern Pacific Railroad. Barnes, 34 at the time, had managed St. Paul's franchise in the original Northwestern League, forerunner of the American Association in the Midwest. Barnes reached Spokane Falls on March 9, 1890, and, after visiting with prospective backers, he and Herbert Moore, whose associates were mostly partners in that city's transit company, left for Tacoma.

There, on March 14, in Captain Dodge's gun store, the league was born under the protection of baseball's ruling National Association. The Tacoma franchise was awarded to W. F. Carson, while Seattle's went to a former semipro

player, W. H. Thornell, and Moore's group took the Spokane Falls club. W. F. "Senator" Morgan, who had made his reputation in bicycle racing, received the Portland franchise.

Barnes took over as the team's business manager at Spokane Falls, which did not officially shorten its name for another year. William H. Lucas, who had founded the Northwestern League's Duluth franchise, followed Barnes to the West and took up the reins at Tacoma.

Tacoma's first home grounds were established on a packed yellow-clay field at 11th & L Streets, formally named Tacoma Baseball Park, in the neighborhood known today as the Hilltop. The opening game, May 3, against Seattle, was preceded by a parade that included a 27-piece band. Admission was 50 cents and a seat in the grandstand was an additional 25 cents.

Under rules of the day, the home team had the choice of batting first or second, and Tacoma captain J. J. McCabe, the second baseman, elected to have his team hit first.

After the Giants, as they were called, went out, Seattle scored four runs. Tacoma answered with two in the second inning and three in the sixth for a 5–4 lead. However, Seattle scored twice in the seventh before McCabe homered with the bases empty to tie the score in the top of the ninth. Then, in the last half of the inning, Gordon Whitely scored on a single to give Seattle a 7–6 victory.

Tacoma rebounded from this initial loss to win its next seven games and take over first place. The streak ended with an 11–9 loss in 10 innings at Spokane Falls. Those two teams dueled through the spring and into summer before Spokane Falls, fortified by stars from the Texas League, which had disbanded, swept a late-July series and pulled away to win the championship. Tacoma's first team, after winning 43 games and losing 41, finished six and a half games behind but comfortably ahead of third-place Seattle.

Former major-league catcher Billy Earle topped Tacoma with a .307 batting average. Teammate Al Manassau, who later umpired in the big leagues, led the league with 57 steals. Frank March was Tacoma's best pitcher, winning 21 games, and he topped the PNL with 197 strikeouts.

Manager Lucas did not fare so well. First, Tacoma's directors declined to renew his contract. Then, at the league's annual meeting, the owners blacklisted him for sowing dissension; then they elected W. B. Bushnell, one of Tacoma's directors, as their new president. Later, in March, Bushnell, whose Union Ice Company also did business in Oregon, bought a majority interest in the Portland franchise.

The *Tacoma Daily Ledger* predicted that the team of 1891, from all indications, would be a daisy. The concept caught on, but the team was a disaster. Only Frank March and Jack Fanning, another good pitcher, returned. When play began, the so-called Daisies settled into last place.

Jack Colbern of the 1938 Tacoma Tigers slides in just ahead of the tag (MB).

On May 16, Tacoma did beat Seattle, 6–5, on the 11th Street grounds in a 22-inning game hailed as the longest in minor-league pro history at that time. But by mid-September, Spokane led the standings by three and a half games, with 10 games to play. The Eastern Washington club lost eight of the 10, however, and Portland came on to win the pennant on the next-to-last day. Tacoma remained in last place and finished with a 38–60 record.

The 1892 team was much better.

Billy (Farmer) Works, a prominent Texas League outfielder, first baseman and manager, was the new man in charge. He imported several fine prospects, including future hall-of-famer Clark Griffith, a handsome, right-handed pitcher who was a veteran of five professional seasons at the age of 22, and outfielder Billy Goodenough, who earned a major-league trial by hitting .374.

The Daisies finished second in both halves of a split season and posted the best overall record. However, hampered by the financial uncertainties that led to the Panic of 1893, the league folded before the schedule was complete.

Tacoma participated in attempts to revive the PNL in 1896 and in 1898. About a week after play began in 1898, Spokane right-hander George Darby pitched a 15–0 perfect game at Tacoma, with the visitors scoring 13 of their 15 runs in the eighth inning. But the league folded again at the end of July, and there was no more professional baseball in Washington or Oregon until Lucas and Texas League founder John McCloskey put together a coalition that survived, with a few setbacks, for more than two decades.

The Dawn of a New Century

On February 22, 1901, the PNL was reborn as a class D affiliate of the National Association, with the original four cities. Lucas returned to the Northwest to serve as president, secretary, and treasurer. McCloskey managed Tacoma, which played on the old grounds at 11th and L Streets. Former major-league catcher Dan Dugdale, who had been involved in the 1898 revival, handled the Seattle franchise.

For the first time, some teams had official names: Tacoma adopted Tigers, and the name stuck for more than half a century.

Portland led the pennant race almost from opening day, led by pitchers George Engel and Bill Salisbury, with 28 wins, each finishing 16 games ahead of Tacoma. Tigers third baseman Charley McIntyre won the batting title with a .341 average. Teammate Jimmy St. Vrain, a left-handed pitcher, won 27 games.

Lucas and McCloskey, both expansion-minded, spent the off-season drumming up additional backers. By the time the 1902 season rolled around, McCloskey was in charge of a new franchise in Butte, the prosperous Montana mining center. Helena, the state capital, also gained admission, increasing league membership to six teams. Infielder Jay Andrews managed Tacoma.

With only one holdover, Tacoma didn't have much of a club. McIntyre had followed McCloskey to Butte, and Andrews, who took his place at third, probably was his own best player. Butte won the championship. The Tigers failed to contend and finished fifth, winning 48 games and losing 72.

Shortly before Christmas, the Portland team's president, Chester A. Whitemore, announced that he was quitting the PNL in favor of the California State League, which had bolted from the National Association, established franchises at Seattle and Portland, and renamed itself the Pacific Coast League (PCL). When the National Association affirmed the PNL's rights to those cities, PNL tried to fight off the invaders. They added competing teams in Los Angeles and San Francisco, awarded a new Portland franchise, and transformed their organization into the Pacific National League.

Additional territory elevated the PNL to class A status, equal to the best minor leagues in the country, but it did not guarantee greater support in the league's smallest markets or adequate interest in its new, more populous ones. PNL acted within its rights, but expansion made no financial sense. Travel included 2,400-mile jaunts between Montana and Los Angeles, and salaries soared, so few observers believed the PNL had much chance against the PCL's interlopers.

Despite attempts to effect a merger, both leagues' owners refused to back down. So the season began, with head-to-head games on adjacent grounds in San Francisco and Los Angeles.

The Montana teams spent the first six weeks on the road, four of them with little or no income in California. By late May, there was talk that the schedule was being manipulated to foster a merger that would exclude Tacoma and Spokane, as well as Butte and Helena. At the end of June, PNL shifted the debt-ridden Portland franchise to Salt Lake City.

In the season's most interesting game, played at Tacoma on July 11, the Tigers and Spokane battled 16 innings to a 3–3 tie, with both pitchers, Tacoma's Sailor Loucks and Bill Dammann of Spokane, going the distance.

Tacoma, in sixth place, and Helena gave up their franchises after the game of Sunday, August 6. Five days later, the California clubs folded, leaving Seattle, Spokane, Salt Lake City, and Butte to play out the schedule.

On February 2, 1904, PCL, having claimed a clear-cut, if unsanctioned, victory, gained admittance to the National Association. In addition to Seattle and Portland, the PCL gained territorial rights to Tacoma and exercised them by sending the second-place Sacramento franchise north.

Tacoma added Jimmy St. Vrain, Spokane first baseman Lou Nordyke, and Mike Lynch, a standout with the local PNL club, to nine holdovers from Sacramento's team. The resulting aggregation brought the city its first pro championship by finishing first in both halves of a 224-game split season. The Tigers posted a 66–46 record for the first half and a 64–48 mark for the second.

Although St. Vrain won 19 games, he couldn't hold a candle to teammates Bobby Keefe and Orvie Overall, who won 34 and 32, respectively. Shortstop Truck Eagan, who became a PCL immortal, led the league with 25 home runs.

However, inadequate financing and poor attendance brought the franchise down. By July 1905, with the Tigers well on the way toward repeating their first-half title, there were reports that they would relocate to Spokane. Not long before the end of another exhausting schedule of more than 220 games, the PCL shifted the franchise back to Sacramento. Then, adding insult to injury, Los Angeles, the second-half champion, won five of six games in the postseason playoff series against the transplanted Tacoma/Sacramento club.

Dapper George Shreeder, proprietor of the Olympic Club, a popular saloon, and the Tacoma team's principal stockholder, realigned himself with Lucas, whose PNL circuit had evolved into the Northwestern League (NL).

Shreeder, after acquiring the Everett franchise, convinced Lynch to stay on as player-manager. A hard-drinking taskmaster, Lynch became the city's first long-term professional baseball figure.

Bringing the Everett team south proved a timely move. Led by Lynch, who took the batting title with a .355 mark, and Ike Butler, whose 20 pitching victories included 12 in a row, Tacoma won the 90-game NL pennant race by eight and a half games.

On April 30, Lynch auditioned an 18-year-old pitcher from Southern California named Walter Johnson. After Grays Harbor beat the young right-hander 4–3, Lynch sent him home. That summer and part of the next, Johnson pitched for a semipro team in Weiser, Idaho, then joined the Washington Senators, won 416 games, and became an original member of the Baseball Hall of Fame—facts Lynch would never live down.

After second-place finishes in 1907, when the NL expanded to six teams, and in 1908, Tacoma's franchise again declined. The Tigers finished last or next to last in each of the next six seasons. Even after the team's fortunes improved, lack of success at the box office led to several changes in ownership.

Shreeder, flush with the success of 1906, equipped his 1907 team with a new ballpark, Athletic Park at 14th Street and Sprague, and new uniforms, which were black with red trim, white hats, and blue and white socks.

The Tigers won 90 games, more than any rival. They played 13 games more than Aberdeen and lost eight of them, however, so the Black Cats claimed the pennant.

Butler still led the league with a whopping 32 wins. Phil Deller finished 27–15 with 11 shutouts. Jack Burnett was hitting .326 at midseason when he was sold to the St. Louis Cardinals. Yakima native Hunky Shaw wound up as the top regular at .278.

Butler won 19 more games in 1908, and Al Carson won 21, but the Tigers had a hard time staying above .500 with a team that batted only .211. Nevertheless, they finished second, seven and a half games behind Vancouver, British Columbia.

After the season, Dan Dugdale lured Lynch to Seattle with an astonishing $3,000 contract, and Russ Hall, who

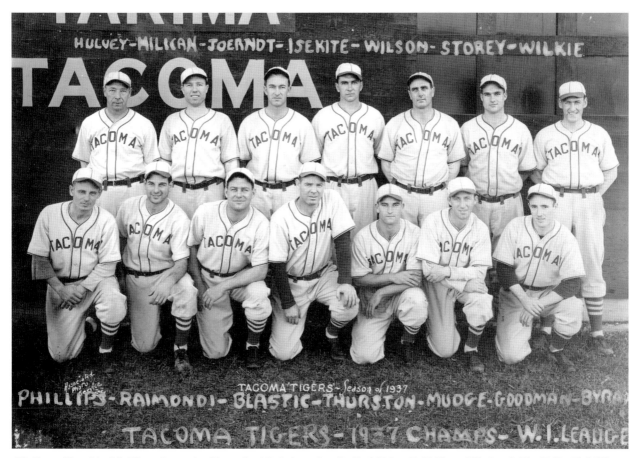

The Tacoma Tigers joined the Western International League in 1937: back row, L. to R., Hank Hulvey, Fred Milican, Ashley Joerndt, Floyd Isekite, Hack Wilson, Harvey Storey, Aldon Wilkie; front row, L. to R., Elmer Phillips, Ernie Raimondi, Hank Blastic, Hollis Thurston, Al Mudge, Dave Goodman, Abe Byram (MB).

had spent two years at Butte after running Seattle's PCL franchise, replaced Lynch at Tacoma. Seattle, last in 1908, finished first in 1909. Tacoma was far last with a 64–111 record, though the team had a bright spot in a young lefty, Jesse Baker. Baker, who had been born in a log cabin on Anderson Island, lost 26 games, 23 of them before he was traded to Spokane. Despite his poor record, he led the league with 249 strikeouts.

1910: Another Decade of Ups and Downs

Tacoma's 1910 and 1911 teams were also inept at the plate but both wound up just below the .500 mark. The Tigers placed a poor third among four teams in 1910. They were fifth of six in 1911.

Portland native Bert Hall and Fred Annis were the top pitchers both years. Hall, an early master of the forkball,

claimed 20 of the team's 73 victories in 1910. Annis, an 18-game winner in 1910, won 15 more in 1911.

In 1910 Baker, now pitching for Spokane, turned in two of the league's greatest pitching feats, both at Tacoma's expense. On June 14, he struck out 15 and drove in the winning run to beat the Tigers, 2–1, in 15 innings. Then, in September, he worked the last 16 1/3 innings of a 4–1, 19-inning Spokane triumph, striking out the side to end the game.

After Seattle skidded back to last place, Dugdale cleaned house, releasing Lynch and engineering the ouster of his old ally, NL president W. H. Lucas, in the hope that less vigilance against rowdy play would stimulate attendance. When George Shreeder, who had faded into the background, regained control of Tacoma's franchise, Lynch returned to manage.

Players from various teams in the City League get ready for pre-game introductions prior to the 1949 opener at Tiger Park (MB).

On opening day of the 1911 NL season, Victoria defeated Tacoma, 3–0, as rookie Tom Lane twirled a no-hitter, beaning Lynch and throwing out his arm. (Lane never recovered.)

Lynch almost didn't make it through the first 10 days. After the rough and ready Irishman assaulted umpire Jack Ward, new league president Bob Lindsay suspended him for the rest of the season. However, when Shreeder argued it had been Ward, not Lynch, who was under the influence, Lindsay fired Ward and reinstated Lynch a couple weeks later.

But a last-place finish in 1912 cost Lynch his job and Shreeder a good deal of money, paving the way for former major-league star Joe McGinnity to become part owner and manager. Still a useful pitcher at the age of 42, McGinnity relied heavily on slow curveballs and made a record 68 appearances, worked 436 innings, and won 22 games, three of them in one week at Spokane. Outfielder Cy Neighbors,

who had hit .308 for the 1912 Tigers, batted .287 and again finished among the league's top 10 as the Tigers improved to 75 victories.

But by 1914, the entire league was losing ground, bogged down by the public's growing interest in automobiles and motion pictures. Portland surrendered its PCL franchise to Ballard, Washington. Then, after war broke out in Europe, attendance in the Canadian cities fell off so dramatically that the season was shortened by two weeks. McGinnity's Tacoma Tigers improved offensively, but they barely won 40 percent of their games.

The season included one memorable game. On May 9, at Tacoma, McGinnity defeated Spokane's future Hall of Fame pitcher, Stan Coveleski, 6–2, with the help of 10 putouts by left fielder Ten Million, the oddly named son of a Seattle judge. During the game, rookie George Kelly, stationed in right field for the visitors, turned a sinking liner off the bat of Neighbors into a triple play. Years later, McGinnity, Coveleski, and Kelly were elected to the Hall of Fame. Million became a noted Seattle-area sports official.

Neighbors finished fourth in batting, with a .315 mark, and third baseman Fred McMullin, in his third season as a regular, hit .293. Six years later, McMullin was one of eight Chicago White Sox banned for life in the aftermath of the 1919 World Series scandal. McGinnity again won 20 games, one more than teammate Izzy Kaufman.

Wartime concerns continued to overshadow baseball in 1915, when Seattle attorney Bob Blewett, who had been a left-handed pitcher for the 1903 Tacoma Tigers, took over as league president. Victoria and Aberdeen, which had since acquired the Portland/Ballard franchise, disbanded, while Vancouver barely survived. Tacoma's players accepted a 10 percent pay cut.

Nonetheless, the Tigers enjoyed their best season in years. They won 85 games and finished second, four games behind Seattle, which came from last place with the help of an 18-game winning streak. Kaufman won 25 games and McGinnity won 21, after blanking Vancouver in both games of a doubleheader on closing day.

The 1916 schedule was reduced by several weeks, and succeeding seasons were even shorter. After the United States entered World War I in 1917, the military draft chipped away at teams already crippled by sagging gate receipts. On the weekend following Independence Day, with leagues expiring across the country, the NL's owners voted to suspend operations after the games of Sunday, July 15. The Tigers wound up third, with a 38–35 record.

Tacoma's Harry Harper, acquired from Spokane after hitting .317 in 1916, won the batting title with a .382 average.

TACOMA PRO BASEBALL: FUN FACTS

- Tacoma's pro teams have an overall record of 3,171–3,187 (.499) from 1960 to 2003.

- On September 1, 2004, Tacoma first baseman A. J. Zapp hit the deepest home run in the 45-year history of Cheney Stadium. His solo run went over the 29-foot-high wall in centerfield, which is 425 feet from home plate, and sailed an estimated 505 feet.

- Dick Phillips is the only Tacoma player to be named the Pacific Coast League MVP. Phillips earned the honor in 1961 when he hit .267 with 16 home runs and 98 RBIs for the Giants franchise.

- Dick Estelle threw two no-hitters for the Tacoma Giants, one each in 1964 and 1965.

- Adrian Garrett belted 43 home runs in 1971 for the Tacoma Cubs, including 19 at Cheney Stadium.

- Burt Hooton of the Tacoma Cubs struck out 19 batters against Eugene, Oregon, on August 17, 1971, at Cheney Stadium.

- The Tacoma Tigers roster featured three consecutive American League Rookies of the Year for the Oakland Athletics: Jose Canseco (1984), Mark McGwire (1985), and Walt Weiss (1986). McGwire played third base for the Tigers before moving to first base with the Oakland A's.

- Troy Neel is the only Tacoma player to ever win the PCL batting title, hitting .351 in 1992 for the Tigers. Brian Raabe broke Neel's franchise record when he batted .352 in 1997 for the Rainiers, and a 19-year-old, Alex Rodriguez, hit .360 with 15 home runs and 45 RBIs in 54 for the Tacoma team in 1995.

- John Halama threw a perfect game for the Rainiers on July 7, 2001, at Cheney Stadium against the Calgary Cannons. It was the first nine-inning, perfect game in the PCL's 99-year history! Three days earlier, Brett Tomko had fired a no-hitter for Tacoma in Oklahoma City.

Rookie right-hander Herman Pillette, who went on to play 23 years in the PCL, won 13 games and shared the league lead.

Only nine minor leagues began the 1918 season, and those had lost many of their best men to military service or the shipyards, which supported excellent amateur teams built around professional players. However, dreary weather and the reduced talent level took their toll. On May 25, Hall announced that Tacoma was quitting the newly reorganized Pacific Coast International League (PCIL). The Tigers were in second place with a 13–9 record. Stevens was first in hitting with a .369 average.

Although the war ended in November, economic problems and staffing shortages left pro baseball looking like a chancy business for 1919. The PCIL, with Victoria joining Seattle, Tacoma, and Vancouver, tried operating weekends only but collapsed after playing fewer than 30 games.

Tacoma was among six cities represented when the PCIL tried for a third time in 1920 and finally completed a season. Tacoma posted a winning 66–53 record, but Athletic Park burned down on Sunday, May 23, and the Tigers, after charging to the front with 10 straight wins in late July, lost 12 of their last 18 starts and finished fourth. Bert Cole was the league's best pitcher, earning a major-league berth with Detroit after posting a 24–7 record and hitting .315.

The 1920s and '30s

Tacoma had another good club in 1921, finishing second to Yakima in both halves of a split season after Seattle and Spokane dropped out and left the PCIL with four teams. Infielder George "Boots" Grantham, on the verge of a substantial big-league career, batted .360 in 40 games. Charlie Mullen, who had played on Seattle's great 1908 Broadway High School team, managed the Tigers, played first base, and finished fourth among PCIL regulars with a .335 mark.

Another reorganization preceded the 1922 season: Tacoma and Vancouver joined two Canadian rivals, Calgary

Superior Dairy played Beacon Oil for the City League championship at Lincoln Bowl in the 1930s (MB).

and Edmonton, in a four-team circuit dubbed the Western International League (WIL). But by mid-June, hobbled by high travel costs, the league was history, and Pierce County fans saw no more pro ball until Tacoma and five other cities formed a new Western International League, affectionately called the Willy League, as the Depression began to wind down in 1937.

The reborn WIL, not unlike the PCIL, placed franchises in Tacoma, Spokane, Yakima, and Vancouver. Lewiston, Idaho, about 90 miles south of Spokane, also agreed to participate, but it wasn't until the last moment that a Wenatchee franchise completed the six-team field.

Roger W. Peck, a Tacoma banker who had coached at UPS, was elected president of the new class B circuit. Yakima's Hunky Shaw, whose lengthy playing career had begun with Tacoma 30 years before, served as vice president. Veteran PCL infielder Eddie Taylor was named as Tacoma's manager. Games were played at Athletic Park, which had a rebuilt grandstand and also had become the home of the semipro Tacoma City League.

The city's baseball fortunes took an immediate upswing. Even though the Tigers never finished first in the regular-season standings, they claimed playoff titles in three of the league's first four years.

WIL play began on April 27, 1937. On May 30, at Tacoma, left-hander Aldon Wilkie of the Tigers pitched a seven-inning no-hitter and completed a doubleheader sweep by defeating Wenatchee, 4–0. Hollis "Sloppy" Thurston, a good-hitting former big-league pitcher and longtime PCL standout, succeeded Taylor at the midpoint and became Tacoma's regular first baseman. After several other personnel changes, the Tigers took the second half by winning 42 games and losing 25. They then whipped Wenatchee four games to one in the playoff.

Harvey Storey, who played both third base and shortstop, was Tacoma's best batter. The 21-year-old Oregonian hit .347 with 51 doubles, 18 homers, 121 runs, 108 RBIs, and 20 stolen bases. Outfielder Dave Goodman, who joined Storey on the all-WIL team, batted .308, while Wilkie also won 15 games, pitched five shutouts, and finished second with 213 strikeouts. He was joined by "Lefty" Isekite, a hard-throwing, 28-year-old Stadium High School graduate who had

been signed out of the Timber League. But it was Hank Hulvey who was top pitcher: the 40-year-old right-hander combined a 15–9 record with a league-leading 2.33 ERA.

Following the season, Peck resigned as league president to take a financial interest in the Tacoma franchise. He retained an active role for several years, and when new grounds were built following World War II, Athletic Park was converted into the softball complex that now bears his name.

Despite fine seasons by Goodman and Isekite, Tacoma wound up last in 1938. Goodman won the batting title with a .337 mark and stole 33 bases. Isekite won 16 games, took the first of his three straight league strikeout titles by fanning 248, and placed second with a 2.01 ERA. The squad included outfielder Marv Rickert, a 17-year-old Long Branch native beginning a pro career that would include six seasons in the major leagues.

In 1939 league home-run production nearly tripled and a rebuilt offense vaulted Tacoma into second place. The Tigers, who had homered only 31 times in 1938, clouted 108—37 of them by Morry Abbott, a newcomer whose total stood as the all-time WIL record. Abbott also drove in 123 runs and scored 116.

Catcher Neil Clifford batted .328, first baseman Bob Garretson hit .315, and rookie Herm Reich, on his way to a long PCL career, contributed 18 home runs and 91 RBIs. "Lefty" Isekite won 18 games to go with a league-leading 3.29 ERA, the strikeout title, and 25 complete games. He even pitched a no-hitter on July 11, when he defeated league-leading Wenatchee, 3–0.

In the Shaughnessy playoffs that had replaced the split-season format, Tacoma rallied to win three of four games from fourth-place Spokane, then tamed Wenatchee with three successive victories in Tacoma. Walt Mattos stole home to decide the opener, 8–7. Ralph Mountain's ninth-inning RBI single ended game two with Tacoma on top, 8–7. Earl Porter, 9–2 during the regular season, won the third game, 3–1. Tacoma wrapped up the title with a 5–3 triumph in 10 innings. Bob Garretson, who had become the player-manager, doubled to start the winning rally. After a pair of walks, two runners crossed the plate following Jack Colbern's squeeze bunt. Floyd Bevens, who had relieved in the ninth, took the loss.

I WAS A TACOMA GIANTS BATBOY

When I was growing up in Tacoma in 1960, the San Francisco Giants moved their 3A Pacific Coast League (PCL) team from Phoenix to Tacoma to play in a brand-new baseball park. They conducted a contest to select the batboys for the team in that first summer. I knew that I had to try to win, so my grandfather helped me write a short essay titled "Why I want to be the Tacoma Giants' batboy." I mailed it to the Giants and waited.

Ten finalists gathered one afternoon at KTAC's offices in downtown Tacoma to visit with representatives of the team and the radio station. Mark Wojahn won the contest to be the first batboy for the Giants, but I finished second, which meant that I would be batboy for the visiting teams when they came to town to play. I was more excited than disappointed that I did not get the home batboy position. After all, I would get to see legendary players such as Dusty Rhodes and newcomers such as Juan Marichal and the Alou brothers [Matty and Jesus], and when the San Francisco Giants played their annual exhibition with Tacoma, I would get to see Willie Mays and be his batboy. Wow! That was some thrill for a 13-year-old who loved baseball.

As the two batboys, Mark and I had a regular routine. We arrived at Cheney Stadium in the late afternoon and dressed in our real Giants flannels—old uniforms from the San Francisco Giants, just like the ones Tacoma players wore. Before batting practice, we carried equipment to the field, including the players' bats and balls for hitting and fielding practice, the catcher's gear, and towels and water for the bench. We always made certain that the dugout looked good. The Tacoma trainer, Leo Hughes, was our boss, and he became a kind of father figure when we were at the stadium. During practice before games, we visited with players, chased down balls in the outfield, and then cleaned things up again around the dugout before the games started. Sometimes Red Davis, the Giants' manager, even invited us to take batting practice with the team.

During the games, we got the bats off the field after a player had been to the plate, returned bats and helmets to their places in the dugout, refilled the water jugs, and shuffled equipment between the clubhouse and dugout. The best part was sitting on the bench between innings and talking with the ballplayers. Mark had the Giants, but I had all the other PCL players who came to town—from Vancouver, British Columbia, in the north to San Diego in the south.

Of course, we both had our favorites. Danny O'Connell, Tacoma's second baseman in 1960, was in the twilight of his career, but he often let me take fielding practice with him, which was a great thrill for a Little League infielder. Being the batboy for visiting teams, I also got to work with two great players from the Spokane Indians: Willie Davis and Frank Howard, a giant of a man physically but always gentle in voice and manner.

Next year, Mark and I were asked to work in the clubhouses, where we had to unpack all of the equipment that came to town with each team. The bus would arrive after the players had been dropped off at the team's hotel, and the trainer, who also doubled as the team's equipment manager, helped me unload the bus. I unpacked uniforms, gloves and bats, and all the other gear the team carried. If they had been on the road rather than at home before visiting, that first day also meant many loads of laundry. We had several washers and dryers under the stands between the clubhouses.

As another service to the visiting teams, I brought in food and drinks for the players. I could not begin to count the number of sandwiches that my mom and I made on Sunday mornings to feed the players between games in the afternoon. I would lay out the meal on long tables late in the first game and then watch the players strip it bare in a matter of minutes; they used to tell me that our egg salad and tuna sandwiches were the best in the PCL.

When the game ended and players left for the hotel, my busiest time started. I had to pick up after 25 players, plus managers and coaches. The uniforms always got washed and the shoes got cleaned and polished. I had to straighten out the locker room, clean the facilities, and sweep and mop the floors so that everything was ready for the next day. My day seldom ended before midnight.

Some bonuses came with my work in the clubhouse. I could watch as many games as I wanted, and I had my own small office where I kept food and supplies for the players. During spring games, it also was a quiet place to study. I got to visit with players, especially the pitchers who got knocked out of games early. The expletives often flew around the clubhouse when they stormed in after getting pulled. They damned the Giants who hit them hard, or the manager who took them out of the game, or anyone else they could blame. Sometimes we talked and occasionally we played board or card games. Usually I just listened and kept the beverages coming.

In 1962 I kept my spot in the visitors' clubhouse while my younger brother Tom took charge of the Giants' clubhouse. We also began to train another brother, Kevin, who started young and helped on both sides, depending on which one of us needed help.

Through the 1960s, Tacoma played at a high level in the PCL, even winning the league crown in 1961. But what was most important to me was that Tacoma had a team and that the visiting players needed my help in the clubhouse. That work paid my way through prep school and college—and, unlike most of my classmates, I never had to look for a summer job. I saw many soon-to-be-famous players pass through the halls of Cheney Stadium.

For example, Lou Piniella came to Tacoma with the visiting Portland Beavers on several occasions in the mid-'60s—he was in the Cleveland farm system. On one memorable night, "Sweet" Lou struck out in the ninth inning. He ran off the field and out of the dugout even before the game ended, still with his bat in hand. When he entered the clubhouse, he took a quick right turn toward the lockers, and on the way he demolished a bat rack, showing better bat speed and power than he had displayed that night in the game. Then he demolished two lockers before he calmed down a bit. I just stood to the side and watched. Years later, when Piniella showed his famous temper as manager of the Seattle Mariners, I thought back to that night in Tacoma. I guess I could say that I saw Lou Piniella in action long before the world got a full look at him. But he played the game with great flair.

The arrival of the Giants in Tacoma in 1960 meant a great deal to many people, including me and my brothers, who carried on the clubhouse tradition into the 1970s.

—Stephen Kneeshaw

Ken Higdon was also a Tacoma batboy, starting in 1978 for the Yankees. He went on to the major leagues as clubhouse manager for the Anaheim Angels who won the 2002 World Series—resulting in a coveted championship ring for Higdon!

The 1940s

The 1940 Tigers, preseason favorites, were hampered by injuries and finished fourth. Isekite finally made the All–Western International League team after posting an 18–9 record to go with another strikeout title, a second-place finish in ERA, and 24 complete games. Rookie outfielder Tony Firpo, who had starred in football and baseball at the University of California, was Tacoma's other All-WIL pick, batting .353 with 87 RBIs in 115 games. In the play-offs, the Tigers, nearly back at full strength, defeated Yakima, two games to one, then turned back Spokane's talented-filled regular-season champions, three games to two.

Isekite, who owned the Indians, gave Tacoma a 7–5 victory before 5,000 fans when the title series opened at Spokane's Ferris Field on Saturday, September 14. After the Indians won the second and third games, play shifted to Tacoma. There, after a rainout, Isekite struck out 11 on the

way to a four-hit, 8–1 triumph. Then the Tigers polished off the Indians, 5–2, for the title. Catcher Bill Brenner was the hero, tripling home two runs in the sixth inning, then scoring on a passed ball.

Almost the entire Tigers roster was overhauled before the 1941 season. The resulting team, managed by career minor-leaguer Horace "Pip" Koehler, lacked a dominating pitcher and adequate offense. The Tigers won only 58 games and finished fifth. The brightest moments came when Del Holmes, Bryant Stephens, and Mel Marlowe set a league record by pitching consecutive shutouts at Wenatchee. But with another world war again casting a shadow over the country, Yakima and Wenatchee dropped out of the league before play began in 1942, leaving only four teams. Tacoma (77–64) led the league in runs but finished second, six and a half games behind Vancouver. Because of staffing shortages, the WIL, along with most

Dick Greco and his wife Evelyn were married at home plate (courtesy Dick Greco).

other clubs, did not operate for the remainder of the war.

When play resumed in 1946, the WIL grew to eight teams for the first time. Tacoma's new club played on new grounds, Tiger Park, built at 38th and Lawrence for an estimated $150,000 by the team's new owner, Enoch Alexson. The Tigers finished fourth. Not surprisingly, after a three-year layoff, there weren't many familiar faces. Nineteen-year-old catcher Dick Kemper was the star, placing second in batting, with a .355 mark and 106 RBIs.

The most intriguing squad member was Bob Hedington, who posted a 6–6 pitching record and, although he didn't qualify for the title, had the league's best ERA at 3.06. Hedington also played 20 games at first base, 20 more at second, 12 at third, and 21 in the outfield. The Seattle native was a defensive liability at almost every one of those positions, and he hit .314.

Cy Greenlaw was the new workhorse pitcher. The left-hander won 18 games, as did major-league castoff Steve Gerkin. Greenlaw's victories included a seven-inning, 3–0 no-hit triumph over Yakima on Memorial Day.

CHAPTER SPONSORED BY
STAN NACCARATO:

Longtime General Manager of the Tacoma Baseball Club, Stan Naccarato briefly played himself in the minors with the Ogden, Utah, Reds of the Pioneer League before an arm injury curtailed a promising career. In 1976 he captured *The Sporting News'* Class AAA Executive of the Year Award, while his team the Tacoma Twins ball club was named the "#1 Franchise in America," surpassing more than 200 minor league teams. That year the team also claimed the Minor Leagues' President's Trophy and the Larry MacPhail Promotional Trophy. An unprecedented achievement, the three awards never before had been won simultaneously by the same organization, under the same GM—a promising career indeed!

In 1947 Earl Kuper, Greenlaw's cousin, became Tacoma's number-one catcher and won the WIL batting crown with a record .389 average. Glenn Stetter, who had taken the title for Wenatchee in 1946, placed sixth at .351. Hedington became the regular third baseman and hit .339 with 115 RBIs. Dick Greco, who replaced Morry Abbott in the previous season, belted 21 home runs and drove in 102 runs.

Despite impressive numbers in what had become a high-octane league, the Tigers wound up no better than sixth, thanks to the WIL's leakiest defense and uncertain pitching. Newcomer Gordon Walden won 19 games and rated 10th in ERA, but Greenlaw was hit hard and won only seven.

Tacoma finished fourth in 1948, 11 games over .500 but 13 ½ games behind Spokane. For the first time, the Tigers led in batting, tying one record with 107 triples and setting another by going 125 games without being shut out. Greco batted .346 and drove in 126 runs, and pitcher George Nicholas went 14–7.

The Tigers skidded downward again in 1949, winding up seventh, 36 ½ games off the pace. Former American League slugger Bob Johnson, who had lived in the area for years, became the player-manager but, at age 42, could play only part-time. Greco led the league with 33 home runs while driving in 118 runs and scoring 123. Catcher Jack Warren, property of Seattle's PCL club, crushed the ball until the Rainiers recalled him; he hit .363 with 86 RBIs in 82 games.

The season included the worst inning in Tacoma's baseball history: On June 15, Spokane assaulted the Tigers with 16 runs as 21 batters produced 12 hits and 16 RBIs during a third-inning barrage. The Indians, who went on to win, 20–14, broke five WIL marks and topped major-league one-inning standards for runs, batters, and RBIs.

The 1950s

In 1950 the San Diego Padres, which had purchased the Tacoma franchise two years earlier, brought back manager Jim Brillheart, a longtime minor-league pitching star who had handled the team for most of the 1948 season. The Tigers improved dramatically, winning 90 games and losing 58 to finish one game behind Yakima's repeat champions.

Greco enjoyed his best year, finishing second in the batting race at .360. He hammered 36 home runs, one short of Morry Abbott's league record. He also drove in an astonishing 154 runs and broke the record for double plays by an outfielder, with 10.

Two newcomers did nearly as well. First baseman Wellington "Wimpy" Quinn, who had starred for Wenatchee before the war, hit .315 and drove in 110 runs. Ron Gifford, the new second baseman, hit .312, walked 129 times, and scored 115 runs.

Holdover lefty Bob Kerrigan was the mainstay of the pitching staff, putting together a brilliant 26–7 season. Kerrigan pitched four shutouts and ranked ninth with a 3.40 ERA. The ERA title went to teammate Tom Kipp, who posted a 2.76 mark.

Although Brillheart remained for 1951, Greco finally moved up the ladder after four and a half seasons, and the Tigers were left with a punchless offense and not much pitching. Aging Vince DiMaggio, the first of three brothers who played standout big-league ball, spent half the season with Tacoma, but he hit only .225 with five homers.

With television sets flooding the country and the other owners planning to upgrade the league to class A status, the Padres sold the debt-ridden franchise to a group of Lewiston, Idaho, businessmen who moved the team to their Idaho city.

The 1960s and Beyond

Professional baseball returned to Tacoma in 1960, when the city accepted the PCL's Phoenix franchise, a farm club of the National League's San Francisco Giants. W. D. "Rosy" Ryan, general manager of the Phoenix Giants, had called Clay Huntington, past president of the Tacoma Athletic Commission (TAC), with a proposal: If the city would build a new stadium in time for the 1960 season, Ryan would move the Phoenix team. The combined efforts of Morley Brotman, TAC president after Huntington, and Ben Cheney—along with a wealth of city and county officials— led to the construction of Tacoma's "100-day Wonder," Cheney Stadium. Brotman put together the financing plan for a ballpark to be built at what was then called the Heidelberg recreational area. Motivated by lumber magnate, philanthropist, and sportsman Cheney, who donated $100,000,

Hal Schimling caught for the Tacoma Tigers as well as several other teams in the City and Valley Leagues (MB).

the city built a modern facility that still serves as the team's home. The new field featured light standards and wooden seats taken from Seals Stadium, which had been the longtime home of San Francisco's PCL team.

Workers took only three months and 14 days to complete construction in time for the April 16, 1960, opening game between the Tacoma Giants and the Portland Beavers. (Fort Lewis soldiers had to dry out the water-soaked field using napalm fire and "Herman Nelson" heaters before the opening pitch.) Two months later, during a Tacoma-Vancouver game, the city officially named the new ballpark after Cheney. A life-size bronze statue of him watching a game was unveiled in the reserved seating section in 1995.

Tacoma holds the longest continual membership in the PCL (1960–2004), and more than 10 million fans have enjoyed watching 3A baseball at Cheney Stadium. The park

BASEBALL FANS

There is no hall of fame for fans, but for Stan Naccarato, Jerry Lilly is a likely candidate. "A piece of baseball's heart is lost" was how *News Tribune* reporter C. R. Roberts defined Lilly's death in 1996. Lilly was an usher at Cheney Stadium, "a character, an institution. He was as much a part of the ballpark as the hot dogs, the peanuts, and second base. His jokes could make an umpire laugh."

Don Sheperdson is another Cheney fixture. He began selling hot dogs when it first opened and was still there in 2004, selling programs to the fans as they entered the park.

And then there is Anne Jacksich. She developed a love for baseball as a child growing up in Kellogg, Idaho, where she remembered the miners emerging from the coal pits, taking a sauna, and then heading to the diamond for a game. This experience as a youngster instilled loyalty for the local team, no matter where she lived later in life. "While others were rooting for the New York Yankees," the 84-year-old explained in 2004, she "cheered for the Spokane Indians" first and then the Tacoma Tigers.

Her record for rarely missing a local baseball game began when she worked in concessions for the Tiger games. When Cheney Stadium opened, she was there. Since that time, she has never missed an opening game or the season finale. Indeed, in 42 years of local baseball, Jacksich has missed only 11 games.

When asked about her love of the sport, Jacksich replied that "baseball must stay in Tacoma." There should be a booster club to welcome minor-league players to the City of Destiny, she said. She proved her point from her front-row, first-base seat near the Tacoma Rainiers dugout. From her well-positioned vantage point, she took on the responsibility of welcoming new players to the city.

has been the home of seven different major-league organizations: Tacoma Giants (San Francisco) 1960–1965, Tacoma Cubs (Chicago, NL) 1966–1971, Tacoma Twins (Minnesota) 1972–1977, Tacoma Yankees (New York, AL) 1978, Tacoma Tugs/Tigers (Cleveland) 1979–1980, Tacoma Tigers (Oakland) 1981–1994, and the current Tacoma Rainiers (Seattle) 1995–present.

Four of Tacoma's modern-era clubs have won the PCL championship. The 1961 Giants were led by legendary minor-league manager John "Red" Davis and had the best record in Tacoma's modern history (97–57). The Tacoma Cubs defeated Eugene, Oregon, to win the PCL title in 1969. The Cubs posted a record of 86–60 and were managed by Whitey Lockman, who tallied 269 career wins as Tacoma's manager. Dave Myers surpassed Lockman by amassing 367 wins in five seasons as the manager of the Rainiers (1996–2000).

The Tacoma Yankees, managed by Mike Ferraro, were 80–57 in 1978 and were declared co-champions with Albuquerque when weather halted the championship series. Dan Rohn was the skipper of the Tacoma Rainiers in 2001, guiding the team to a 85–59 record and a co-championship with New Orleans. (The playoff series was canceled in the aftermath of the terrorist actions on September 11, 2001.) Named PCL Manager of the Year in 2004, his second similar honor in four seasons with the Tacoma Rainiers, Rohn is now number-two in managerial wins during Tacoma's PCL tenure.

The Tacoma Giants alumni include three Baseball Hall of Famers: Gaylord Perry, Juan Marichal, and Willie McCovey, all of whom played for the 1960 team. Perry also pitched for Tacoma in 1961 through 1963.

Other top players to don Tacoma threads include Giants team members Dusty Rhodes, Gil Garrido, Ron Herbel, John Pregenzer, Cap Peterson, brothers Matty and Jesus

Alou, Dick Phillips, and Tom Haller; for the Cubs, Mike White, Aaron Pointer, Clarence Jones, Billy Connors, Larry Gura, Dick LeMay, and Jim Colbern; for the Twins, Tom Kelly, Mark Wiley, Mike Brooks, Jim Nettles, Charlie Manuel, Rick Renick, Jim Van Wyck, Craig Kusick, Lyman Bostock, Bill Ralston, Jack Maloof, and Randy Bass; Yankees members Brian Doyle, Domingo Ramos, and Jim Beattie; Tigers members Tony Phillips, Mike Gallego, Bert Bradley, Bill Krueger, Jose Canseco, Mark McGwire, Walt Weiss, Scott Brosius, Troy Neel, and Felix Jose; and for the Rainiers, Alex Rodriguez, Ron Villone, Gil Meche, Jose Cruz Jr., Raul Ibanez, Jason Varitek, Derek Lowe, and Bucky Jacobson.

Stan Naccarato is credited with saving Tacoma's franchise when he led a group of local investors to purchase the team at the end of the 1971 season. He served as the team's general manager and was named Minor League Executive of the Year in 1975. Tacoma also earned that year's President's Trophy, which honors the country's best minor-league organization. The club was then sold to George and Sue Foster prior to the 1991 season.

Through 2004, Tacoma has fielded pro ballclubs for more than 83 seasons. Seven championships and a pair of playoff titles have made it all worthwhile. And, boosted by being the Triple A affiliate for the Seattle Mariners, the City of Destiny has become the senior active member of the PCL lineup. Here's to 80 seasons more!

A Mt. Tahoma High and WSU grad, Ron Cey was co-MVP in the 1981 World Series while starring at third base for the Los Angeles Dodgers (courtesy Tacoma News Tribune).

CHAPTER 10

BASEBALL:
HIGH SCHOOL AND COLLEGE PLAYERS

Nick Dahl, Stadium High School, 1911 (MB).

While high school and college team championships haven't been numerous in Tacoma–Pierce County baseball annals, top individual performances have been plentiful over the years. From old-timers such as Joe Salatino, Lou Balsano, Jim Mosolf, Stan "Fuzzy" Elliott, Frank Ruffo, Jess Brooks, Sonny Bailey, George Wise, and Floyd "Lefty" Isekite to more recent players such as Ron Cey, Mike Blowers, Doug Sisk, Steve Whitaker, and Rich Hand, Pierce County schools boast a stellar roster of outstanding baseball talent.

Some of the prep stars of the 1920s through 1940s included Frank Morrone, Bryce Lilly, Bob Zurfluh, Billy Sewell, Les Bishop, Neil Mazza, Joe Hemel, and Pete Sabutis of Lincoln High; Barney McFadden of Lincoln and Kapowsin Highs; Chuck Loete and Earl Kuper of Kapowsin; Jim Rediske and Rick Lewis of Roy High; Andy Helling of Sumner High; Cliff Schiesz and Vern Morris of Bellarmine Prep; and Pete Mello of Fife High.

Three of the city's best players were at WSU together in the mid '40s. Fife's Don Paul and Lincoln's Bobby McGuire and Gordy Brunswick were in the starting outfield when the Cougars played Texas for the national championship and the next year challenged USC in a playoff for the Pacific

Coast crown. All three went on to professional careers although Paul chose to pursue football.

As the 1950s unfolded and the opportunities to play locally increased, a slew of Pierce County brother acts emerged: Bellarmine's battery of Vic and Vern Martineau, Stadium pitchers Hank and Don Semmern, Eatonville's Don and Duane Rose, Clover Park's Ron and Don May, Stadium's infield combo Garry and Gordy Hersey, Clover Park's Jim and Jack Pelander, Lincoln's outfield duo Dave and Luther Carr, Wilson's Bill and Terry Parker, Lakes' Bill and Greg Saxton, and Orting's Bill and Dan Hobert. At Roy High School the Ketter brothers and the Harkness brothers dominated the lineups for years. There were even a couple father-son pairings: Catcher Harry Marnsfield starred at Stadium while son Rich caught for Clover Park. Jerry Henderson and his son Colin were Puyallup grads both of whom later starred at WSU.

Then, as now, pitchers were coveted by the pro scouts. Larry Labounty starred at both Lincoln and Stadium Highs (he transferred to the latter). Lincoln had southpaws Ken Schulz, Ron Goerger, and Ken Jones, as well as right-handers Rance Rolfe, Art Viafore, and Dale Bloom. Bellarmine Prep featured two more lefties, Larry Loughlin and Maury

Tiger Park, home of the Western International League's Tacoma Tigers from 1946–1951 (photo by Harry Boersig, MB).

Galbraith, while Stadium relied on Harry Nygard and Harold Larson. Wilson's Mark Crandall and Mt. Tahoma's Ed Shedrock waged many dramatic duels. Keith Predmore was Eatonville's ace and Fife had Dave Hall.

On the receiving end of those pitches were some terrific catchers. Lincoln boasted Ray Spurgeon, Al Featherstone, and Jerry Murphy. Wilson had Butch Dunlap and Stadium had Arley Kangas, considered one of the best ever.

Position players of the 1950s and early '60s were too numerous to name but some young men were unforgettable, such as Stadium infielder Earl Birnel. In fact, he's still playing on national championship over-75 slowpitch teams, after starring at shortstop for Stadium and UPS. Former Lincoln shortstop Joe Stortini also continues to swing a bat. Denny Brand of Wilson and George Grant of Stadium both went on to become infield stars at UW. Lincoln's Dick Lack

and Peninsula's Mel Manley were chosen to all-state teams, while Cap Peterson of Clover Park was signed right out of high school as a San Francisco "bonus baby." And the ultimate position player of the time? Fred Rickert, who played every position on the field for Vaughn High School.

State Championships

Stadium High School's 1936 team, coached by John Heinrick, left no doubt about their state championship claim, though unofficial: the state did not introduce high school tournament play until 1973. The Tigers enjoyed an undefeated season, led by unbeaten pitchers Mel Gillespie and Al Libke Jr., who also played first base. Libke later signed with the Seattle Rainiers of the Pacific Coast League (PCL) and went on to play with the Cincinnati Reds. In his rookie year, he led the Reds in hitting, was second in runs batted in

(RBIs), had a 20-game hitting streak, and led all National League outfielders with six double plays. Marv Scott, who later had a winning coaching career at Wilson and Stadium High Schools, was the shortstop and Jack Tanner, later a Superior Court judge, was in centerfield.

Tanner remembered the unofficial playoffs as a three-game affair hosted by Pomeroy High School, which a week earlier had defeated North Central of Spokane, 7–3, to become the Eastern Washington champion. Stadium had topped Longview, 10–3, for the Western Washington honor.

Gillespie opened on the mound for the Stadium Tigers in the first contest and whiffed nine, allowing just five hits in a 10–1 win. Libke hurled the second game, in which Stadium prevailed in a much tighter contest, 5–3. Libke struck out eight Pomeroy Pirates, and second baseman Paul Barrager hit his second homer of the series, a three-run shot, for the margin of victory. Even though the unofficial state crown now belonged to Stadium, the two teams decided to play a third game because the Tigers had traveled so far for the series. It ended 1–1 and was called after seven innings.

The 1941 Lincoln Abes were described in one account as "the finest Abe nine since the national pastime staged its return to Tacoma prep circles in 1936." They finished their season 28–4 and won the powerful Cross-State League crown and the unofficial state championship in a playoff series with Walla Walla and Bellingham at Athletic Park in Tacoma. Lincoln won 4–0 and 8–2 decisions in those two contests. Steve Grassi and Dick "Swanny" Swanson were standout pitchers for the Abes, whose other stars included Ray Spurgeon behind the plate, Pat Rooney at first base, and sophomores Ed Bemis, Dick Browse, and Tak Ikeda in the outfield.

The 1946 Stadium Tigers trekked to Walla Walla to claim their state championship behind the stellar pitching of Harry Nygard. The ace right-hander was signed by the Tacoma Tigers on graduation in 1947 and played professionally for three seasons before arm problems ended his career. His four-game heroics during Stadium's title march probably didn't help his longevity, but it certainly was impressive at the time. On the Friday before the playoffs, Nygard pitched nine innings to beat Bellarmine, and on Tuesday he hurled 10 innings to trim Renton and earn the

trip east. On Friday he went another nine, whiffing 17 in a 4–0 whitewash of Bellingham. One day later, he blanked John Rogers High of Spokane, 14–0, to complete four games, 37 innings, and four victories in eight days.

Nygard wasn't a one-man team. Stadium had other outstanding players, such as pitcher Don Semmern, shortstop Garry Hersey, second baseman Gordy Bendick, and an outfield that included football stars Walt Espeland and Ray Spalding.

Coach Bob Summers readily acknowledged his limited baseball experience and counted on team captain Hersey to make out the starting lineups. He also asked football coach John Heinrick, the successful coach of the 1936 state champion Stadium baseball squad, to accompany his team to the playoffs.

Lincoln's 1948 and 1949 bids were led by pitchers Art Viafore, Al Otto, Rance Rolfe, and Dale Bloom, in addition to a who's who of future college talent. Rolfe and Bloom both signed pro contracts and Viafore was a college ace at the University of Puget Sound (UPS), where he played with Dick Palamidessi, Russ Wilkerson, and Joe Stortini. Glenn Huffman, Ron Billings, Frank Karwoski, and Dick Larson all played at Pacific Lutheran University (PLU), and Bill Geppert caught at WSU. The Abes won Cross-State League titles both years before bowing to Yakima at state.

But it was almost 30 years before the official Washington Interscholastic Athletics Association (WIAA) state championship game at the 4A level matched Clover Park against Kennedy of Seattle. Merle Hagbo coached the Clover Park Warriors to an unbeaten season, until Kennedy managed a 2–1 victory in the title game. Clover Park finished with a 27–1 record, one of Hagbo's best in 33 years at Clover Park.

Top players on that runner-up team were third baseman Phil Westendorf, who played at WSU and signed with the Kansas City Royals, and Ron Gee, who was an All-Conference player at Clover Park, Green River Community College, and Whitworth College. Pitcher Joe Keller and catcher Randy Peterson also were outstanding.

In 1974 Lakes High School took the 4A title under coach Ed Hardenbrook. The Lancers ended the year with a 23–4 record and defeated Wilson High of Tacoma and

Kelso High in regional play. The championship round was played at Sick's Stadium in Seattle, and Lakes blanked both opponents. Mike Wholey improved his season record to 10–2 with a 0.24 earned run average (ERA) in a 3–0 semifinal decision over Central Valley High of Spokane. Scott Brunick followed that by shutting out Juanita High, 2–0, for the crown. Hardenbrook joined Clover Park's Hagbo in the State Coaches Hall of Fame in 1988.

The 1979 Lancers also advanced to the state title game, but Woodway took a 10–0 verdict to end the Lakes season at 23–10. Catcher Mike Larson and versatile Eric Garrett were the top players on that team. Garrett signed a professional contract with the Oakland Athletics.

Orting had three outstanding seasons from 1976 to 1978, compiling a 77–11 record under head coach Jerry

Rick Austin, a graduate of Lakes High School, pitched at WSU, where he was the 1968 Cougars' top hurler, before going on to pitch in the majors for Cleveland and Milwaukee. (SSM, 2000.4.58).

Thacker, formerly a star shortstop at UPS. The 1976 team, led by shortstop Gary Balmer, beat Ephrata for its first-ever state 1A baseball title, 8–3. Trailing 3–1 in the fifth inning, Orting tied the score on Balmer's RBI and then came up with five runs in the seventh inning. Tim Harpster was the winning pitcher, and Eric Shrum went four for four in the game. Balmer later played at National Association of Interscholastic Athletics (NAIA) powerhouse Lewis-Clark State College, where he became an All-American in 1983. He also had the distinction of playing in two state championship games that year: he was also Orting's quarterback in the football state finals—and Thacker coached both teams.

Thacker's claim to fame in the championship season was twice defeating both Enumclaw and Wilson Highs, two upper-classification schools with solid baseball programs. In 1977 Ephrata turned the tables on Orting with a 9–3 win in the final, and the Cardinals lost the regional final in '78.

Bob Lightfoot started a 21-year coaching career at Wilson High School by winning the 1977 4A state championship in his first year. He finished coaching in 1997 with 327 wins, 147 losses, nine state tournament appearances, five Narrows League titles, and three West Central district crowns. He was selected Coach of the Year six times.

In the 1977 title game, the Wilson Rams trimmed Redmond, 6–5, at Sick's Stadium, the last championship game played in that historic setting. A suicide squeeze play that didn't work as planned produced the winning tally for Wilson. With Ken Lamb running at third and Tab Lively at the plate, Lightfoot called for the squeeze, but the pitch was so high and outside that Lively couldn't get his bat on the ball. The Redmond catcher managed to grab it, but Lamb, with a great jump off third, slid home under the tag.

Catcher Henry Bender, an All-State performer on that team, was the Seattle Mariners' second-draft choice. His 400-foot two-run homer—the winning blast in a 6–4 semifinal victory over Kent-Meridian—carried the fence, plus two rows of cars parked in the street. Wilson's pitching ace was Mike Maxwell, who finished the season unbeaten in 10 games. Centerfielder Brian Sonneman, who played only one year of high school baseball, led the hitters as a senior with a .400 average.

Charles Wright Academy barged into the state baseball spotlight in 1979. The Wright nine took state runner-up honors that year and again in 1981 and 1982. In 1980 they acquired a 1A championship with an unblemished 29–0 record. Coach Larry Marshall, who later coached at Spanaway Lake High School and Pacific Lutheran University (PLU), compiled a 123–33–1 record and won four Nisqually League titles in six years, 1976 to 1982, at Charles Wright.

Russ Schmidtke, a southpaw pitcher, was key to the Charles Wright success. He pitched complete championship games three years in a row in 1979, 1980, and 1981. The 1980 win was precious because the final score was 1–0 and completed an amazing 29–0 season. Charles Wright won its first nine games in 1981 for a 38-game winning streak but lost the championship battle with Ephrata, 3–2, in the Kingdome. Shortstop Tony Haertl was another top player on those teams.

Brad Cheney, son of one of Tacoma's most generous baseball supporters, Ben Cheney, played for Charles Wright in 1976 and 1977. He joined Marshall's coaching staff from 1978 to 1980, the most successful baseball era in Tarriers history.

Gig Harbor High School earned Pierce County a 3A state championship when it scored four runs in the seventh inning to down Capital High of Olympia, 9–8, in 1997. The Tides finished the season with a record of 23–2 under coach Pete Jansen, who remains the coach after 15 seasons. The teams stars were Matt Gardner, a left-handed pitcher and centerfielder, and third-baseman Tim Friedman. Friedman established almost every offensive record in school history, including a .534 batting average and a 20-game hitting streak.

Franklin Pierce High School was runner-up in the 3A event in 1981. The Cardinals lost to Eastmont of Wenatchee, 4–0, on four unearned runs. Franklin Pierce had won the regional title with a 4–0 decision over Hanford behind Dave Reed's 10 strikeouts and a three-run first-inning homer by Arnie Peterson.

Coaches

Pierce County has been blessed with an array of outstanding high school baseball coaches. Among the most respected were Marv Scott at Stadium and Wilson and Bill Mullen at Lincoln.

Scott began his 21-year coaching career at Stadium in 1947 on his retirement from professional baseball with the 1946 Tacoma Tigers. He moved to Wilson in 1959, the first year of its program, before retiring in 1967. At Wilson he won four City League titles, a feat that his successor, Dick Palamidessi, repeated in the next nine years.

Bill Mullen was not only a coaching legend at Lincoln High, he was one of the most beloved coaches in the city. Mullen didn't keep a lot of statistics or records in his 16 years with the Abes, but when Marv Scott's teams didn't win a championship, Mullen's did. His Cross-State League champions of 1948 and '49 included some of the best all-around athletes in Lincoln High history, and many of them starred locally in college at UPS and PLU.

One of Mullen's favorite teams was his so-called Italian Team, whom he talked about for years. Mullen had a strict rule against using profanity, but he long suspected that when certain players began conversing in Italian, they were getting away with something. Even though they didn't all actually play on the same team, he grouped them together in his memory: Giovanni Tomasi, Dick Colombini, Art Viafore, Dick Palamidessi, Jimmy Tallariti, and Joe Stortini.

Carl "Kak" Wasmund was the first baseball coach at Puyallup High, and he served in that capacity for eight years. Andy Helling coached at Puyallup for 18 years and was a three-time choice as South Puget Sound League (SPSL) Coach of the Year while winning three league titles. Four of his players signed pro contracts, and Steve Sand pitched at Southern Cal under Hall of Fame Coach Rod Dedeaux.

Neighboring Rogers High had two coaches who spanned 31 years following Jim Tevis, the first of the Rams' mentors. Bruce Nichols, named SPSL Coach of the Year in 1987, and Dave Tate, who took his teams to four state tournaments and finished as high as fourth in 1993, combined to keep Rogers competitive.

Bill Melton coached at Bethel for eight years when the Braves won two SPSL titles and made two state tournament appearances in the '80s. Mike Blowers, who later enjoyed a long major-league career with the Yankees, Mariners, and Dodgers, was the biggest of the Braves' stars. Other top players Melton coached included Todd Lawber,

JAPANESE BASEBALL

Pierce County's Japanese baseball players and teams were part of a cultural network that encompassed the whole Pacific Northwest. Local teams were initially organized by the Issei, or first generation immigrants, many of whom had learned to play the game in Japan.

Seattle formed the Nippons in 1904. Tacoma's Japanese merchants organized the Mikados two years later. Russ Hall, a former baseball player later to manage the Tacoma Tigers team, coached the Mikados team as it barnstormed throughout California, Oregon, and Alaska when not competing locally. Soon additional teams, the Columbians and the Union Laundry, formed and joined a competitive milieu that included teams from both Oregon and Washington. By the mid-1930s, the Asians had organized the Japanese American Pacific Northwest Baseball Tournament, held in Seattle on the Fourth of July, to conclude the yearly season of play.

The segregated teams formed because the Japanese were excluded from joining the white leagues. Even so, the two leagues played against each other. The best of the Japanese players competed yearly against Tacoma's white semiprofessional champions. In 1905 a team from Waseda University in Japan played Whitworth College—then located in Tacoma—to a 2–0 win.

During the early years of the 20th century, West Coast governments, aided by the courts, were seeking to disenfranchise both the Issei and their American-born children, the Nisei. Attempts were made to ban Japanese immigration, to prevent Japanese children from attending public schools, and to prohibit the Issei from owning land. During these troubled times, baseball, a game that both cultures appreciate and embrace,

acted as a tonic. The ensuing cultural exchange was an international effort. The Waseda University team returned to Tacoma six more times before the outbreak of World War II.

In addition, Americans embarked on what a 1910 *Daily Ledger* report called the "baseball invasion of the orient." That year Joe Dryer, former owner of the Tacoma Cubs in the Washington State League, offered to schedule games between teams in Japan and American players. "Dryer has been corresponding with Mique Fisher, the former Tacoma Tigers manager, who last year took a team to Japan," the *Ledger* continued. Fisher had assured Dryer "that the trip would be practical and might easily be arranged. Japanese leaders in Tacoma have also written letters to influential friends in Japan, endorsing the scheme and asking that it be given support." The team was comprised of white players representing the Northwestern and Pacific Coast Leagues.

By the 1920s, Nisei players began to dominate local Japanese baseball. The reminiscences of Seichi Konzo reflect how the newer generations used baseball as a way to assimilate themselves into American culture. Konzo and his friend Hito Okada were baseball nuts, he said in 1988. "Under the sponsorship of Carl Miyazaki, we formed the Tacoma Taiyo team, and every Sunday we played baseball with teams from Fife, Selleck, and Steilacoom and a host of other teams, including blacks and Indians. We seldom won, but we enjoyed the camaraderie."

Okada and Konzo were the first Nisei on the Stadium High School baseball team in 1922, and Okada won the Good Sportsmanship award his senior year. While in college, John Galbraith of the Eatonville Lumber Company recruited the two to play summer ball for the company team. Joining them were Tetsu Kawazoe and his brother Yae. They, along with the other Japanese players, also worked in the mill or fought forest fires when not playing baseball.

Baseball was more than just an organized sport for many young Japanese. In the 1930s, games were sophisticated social events where players were courted for membership in various social clubs, and they in turn courted the young Japanese women who attended the Sunday games, dances, and picnics. Nisei saw baseball as a way of being American, of being a part of a youth culture that also included such things as dancing to the tunes of Benny Goodman or swooning over Bing Crosby.

For the Japanese, the baseball music temporarily died on December 7, 1941. Within months, both Issei and Nisei were on their way to concentration camps in Idaho and eastern California. Although the military administrators of the camps allowed the internees to play baseball, it was not the same. The internment destroyed the community bonds that had held the teams together.

Japanese baseball was reintroduced in Tacoma following the war. As Japan gradually became a trading partner with the United States, West Coast cities adopted sister cities in the Asian country as a way to enhance international relations. Baseball became a part of the local program in 1988 when Takeshi Ikeda from Tacoma and Hiroshi Yaskawa from Kitakyushu, Japan, created the Sister City Baseball Exchange.

In many ways, today's baseball players are reliving the times before the war when Waseda University played in Tacoma and local teams reciprocated by playing baseball in Japan. Now, however, more young players have an opportunity to participate. By 2003 nearly 700 players from Tacoma and Kitakyushu have played baseball through the exchange. "The games won and lost are probably even, but the final score is not important," said Tony Anderson, chairman of the project. What is important is the interaction between the players and the opportunity to learn more about the cultures of Japan and America.

who played at Portland State University, and pitcher Kelly Slopak, who played at Nevada-Reno.

Dave Hall, a standout pitcher at Fife High School in his playing days, coached the Trojans from 1969 to 1976 and won three league titles. Among his better players were two sets of brothers: Sheldon Ireland and Roland Ireland, both catchers, and Arnie Grab and Randy Grab. Rob Hatley, Dan Luthala, and John Mello also contributed to the Trojans' success, similarly to their fathers Bud Hatley, Fran Luthala, and Pete Mello years before them.

Marco Malich continues to coach at Peninsula High after more than 25 years with the Seahawks. Through 2003, he had a career record of 336 wins and 168 losses. His teams have won 11 league titles and made 10 state tournament

appearances. Among his players were three top catchers. Todd Logan played at Eastern Washington University (EWU) and was drafted by the Minnesota Twins. John Fuller was drafted by Cincinnati. Sean Bagley was selected by the Chicago White Sox. Pitcher Denny Gillich played college baseball at Santa Clara.

Former Tacoma Giant and 1963–64 San Francisco Giants pitcher John Pregenzer returned to Pierce County following his major-league career and coached at Orting, Washington, and Franklin Pierce High Schools. During his brief major-league career, Pregenzer became famous for a popular fan club that originated in San Francisco and drew him national recognition. He was named to Tacoma's all-time All-Star squad as a relief pitcher, along with teammate Eddie Fisher, in 1984.

Holly Gee, who was deeply involved in youth baseball in Lakewood for many years, was the first director of Lakewood Recreation, a 1952 baseball program that gave 1,000 boys a year an opportunity to play the game each summer. He also coached Clover Park High School for six years and American Legion and Connie Mack teams for five more. Gee helped develop several outstanding players while winning three SPSL titles and one PSL championship in 1964. His prize pupils were Cap Peterson, who played for the San Francisco Giants, Washington Senators, and Cleveland Indians, and Bill Murphy, who was a New York Yankee and Met.

One of the most intriguing coaching stories in recent years belongs to Roy Young of Foss High School. He combined his coaching talents with groundskeeping abilities and virtually built a new field at Foss by himself. He not only maintains one of the best-groomed prep fields in the state, he also is welcomed as a part-timer on the grounds crews at both Cheney Stadium in Tacoma and Safeco Field in Seattle.

In 17 years at Foss, Young had his best season in 2004, taking his team to the West Central district playoffs with a 17–5 record. Young named Rhett Parker, who was drafted by the Arizona Diamondbacks but instead chose college baseball at the University of Portland, and Josh Schulz, a pitcher for National Collegiate Athletic Association (NCAA) champion Pepperdine, among his top players.

It is John Patrick Heinrick, however, who is widely regarded as one of Tacoma's greatest all-around coaches ever. Heinrick coached Stadium High baseball teams from 1936 to 1944, doubling as football coach at Stadium and basketball coach at nearby UPS. All of his teams were consistent in their high quality of play. In the summer, he

Stadium High School 1939 City High School League Champions: back row, L. to R., coach John Heinrick, John Horst, Matt Kapovich, Bob Schnecker, unknown, unknown, Ray Hagen, Bob Angeline, Lyman Anderson, unknown; middle row, L. to R., Harold Schweinler, Rod Giskie, Bill Turnbull, Jim Philby, Jay Dahl, Gene Walters, Jim Diederich, Bill Demorest, Kergie Omori, Roy Bronzovich; front row, L. to R., George Gunovich, Al Browne, Vince Genna, Ray Montbroussous, John Batt, Bob Roley, Dave Molitor, Jim Darling, Jim Martin, Floyd Marcusson (courtesy the Dr. Marv Tommervik Jr., Family).

coached semipro baseball, and his Johnson Paint City League team of 1937 finished fifth at the national tournament in Wichita, Kansas. Among his many stars at Stadium were three players who went on to play for the Tacoma Tigers: Gene Clough, Marv Scott, and Dick Greco, who became one of the best sluggers in minor-league history.

College Baseball

College baseball in Tacoma experienced only modest success until the late 1960s, when coach Jack McGee assembled a powerhouse team at UPS. And the Loggers eventually played at a Division I NCAA level in the North–Pacific Conference.

The 1967 season found 11 sophomores and 10 freshmen on the squad, and the Loggers rolled to a 27–4 record as NCAA independents, advancing to the Division II NCAA regionals. Freshman pitching sensation Rich Hand, who earlier in the season had whiffed 15 Washington Huskies in a 5–3 win, earned NCAA Division II All-America honors, while Randy Roberts topped the hitters at .321.

In 1968 the Loggers finished 20–6 and were ranked 16th in the nation in Division II, but they were not invited to the NCAA regionals. However, a two-year record of 47–10 foreshadowed the magic of a national tournament appearance in 1969. Early in the season, Hand tossed a one-hitter in a 1–0 win at WSU. The Loggers also spilled Oregon State University, 4–2, behind Hand's six-hitter and a two-run homer by future major-leaguer Mick Kelleher, who led the team with a .362 average.

After beating Chapman University to win the regional title, UPS was on its way to Missouri and the national finals, where the team finished fourth. The Loggers ended the season 23–9. Hand, an All-American for the second straight year, finished his Loggers career with a 21–6 record and a 1.01 ERA.

The Loggers success story continued under Jack McGee, with a run of five straight regional tournament appearances from 1971 to 1975, but further trips to the nationals didn't happen. The 1971 team won 20 games, led by Craig Caskey's 9–2 pitching record and Greg McCollum's .411 batting average, including six homers. The 1972 Loggers were 24–6 behind Caskey's 10-win season and the

.429 hitting of centerfielder Fred Bullert. The 1973 team finished 25–7 with pitching stars Gregg Bemis, 8–2 for the season, and right-hander Pat Cristelli, 6–2 with a 1.58 ERA and 90 strikeouts in 57 innings. Second baseman Alan Asay hit at a .415 clip.

It was UPS's turn to host the NCAA Division II regionals in 1974. The Nor-Pac Conference also was formed with University of Portland, Portland State University, Seattle University, and UPS aboard. The Loggers were the only Division II entrant but won the title.

The 1975 season proved to be a high point in the history of UPS baseball. The Nor-Pac, which UPS had been most ardent in getting organized, attracted University of Idaho, Boise State University, and Gonzaga University. Every school in the "new" seven-team league played at the NCAA Division I level, and the Loggers became a Division I team as a result.

Unbelievably, UPS won the championship with a 20–4 league record and became one of four teams invited to the NCAA's Rocky Mountain Regional Tournament in Tempe, Arizona, with a 28–11 mark, including 26 wins in their last 31 games. All-American hurler Bemis led the way with a 7–0 league record and a 1.04 ERA, including a no-hitter at Portland State.

The Loggers continued to pile up 20-plus-win seasons, including a solid 22–17–2 record in 1978. Outfielder Grady Fuson, now the general manager of the Houston Astros, led the Loggers that season with a .352 average and later coached the UPS team.

The 1979 season was Jack McGee's final, as UPS announced it was phasing out baseball scholarships. The most successful 14 years in the school's baseball history were over. With more than 300 wins, McGee's record easily topped that of any baseball coach in the school's history.

Research discloses only one other UPS championship. In 1936, coach Jimmy Ennis and his Logger nine won the school's first baseball crown when a trio of late-season wins at Whitman resulted in the Northwest Conference title. Catcher Mel Miller, shortstop Erling Tollefson, and second baseman John Milroy were members of the All-Conference team.

Records show three league championships at PLU. The 1948 Lutes, coached by Marv Tommervik, won the Washington Intercollegiate Conference (WInCo) championship with a 19–2 record. Jim Rediske, Chuck Loete, Jack Bratlie, Wes Saxton, Howie Davis, Bud Hatley, Dwayne Rose, Vern Morris, Lowell Knutson, Wayne Brock, Dave Garner, Marv Allen, and Paul Reiman were members of the winning club.

The 1953 Lutherans won the Evergreen Conference (EvCo) crown. Glenn Huffman, whom coach Marv Harshman called "one of the very best all-around athletes in school history," was the leading hitter at .405, and the pitching staff was led by Vern Hanson and Bud Lester. PLU had a 13–3 season record, including 8–0 in league play. A repeat performance in 1954 gave the Lutes back-to-back EvCo championships, again under Harshman's coaching. The year before, "Harsh" had coached PLU to both football and baseball titles while finishing second in basketball.

The most recent Pierce County product to star at PLU was Jason Andrew, a Franklin Pierce High School graduate, who established PLU career pitching records for innings pitched, wins, and strikeouts. He completed the 2004 season, his third in professional baseball, playing in the Texas Rangers' organization.

From Local Schools to the Pros

Amateur, semipro, and professional teams have flourished over the years as a result of local talent. Early standout players included Jim Neeley and Tony Banaszak of Puyallup High School. Neeley set a single-game strikeout record with 17 as a Viking pitcher in 1946, and he played professionally for the Spokane Indians. Banaszak was All-State and All-League for three years. He batted over .500 and broke Neeley's school strikeout record with 19, while allowing no hits or walks in blanking Sumner 14–0. He signed a pro contract with the Boston Braves right out of high school and played in the California League. At Ventura, he hit a grand-slam homer and pitched seven innings to account for a 13–5 win over Bakersfield and finished with a 4–1 pitching record and a 0.71 ERA during his second year of pro ball.

More recent players include Ron Cey, Mike Blowers, Steve Whitaker, and Rich Hand. Cey, Blowers, and Whitaker are among the top position players to come out of Pierce County and leave their mark on the professional baseball world. Hand, Rick Austin, and Doug Sisk, all of whom also played professionally, are among the top pitchers to play from Pierce County.

Before Ron Cey became a six-time major-league All-Star and a 1981 World Series Co–Most Valuable Player with Los Angeles Dodgers teammates Steve Yeager and Pedro Guerrera, he was a three-sport star at Mount Tahoma High School in Tacoma and a superb baseball player at WSU. Cey ranks among the all-time power-hitting third basemen in major-league history. During a 17-year career, mostly with the Dodgers, he hit 316 home runs, including a 30-homer, 116-RBI season in 1977. He played in four World Series and six All-Star games and finished with 316 home runs and 1,139 RBIs in 2,073 major-league games.

Mike Blowers, one of the heroes of the Seattle Mariners' dramatic drive to win the American League West Division title in 1995, collected 24 doubles, 23 homers, and 96 RBIs that season, with three grand-slam home runs and 33 RBIs in August alone. He was a stellar infielder and top hitter for the Bethel High School Braves and later for Tacoma Community College (TCC) and UW.

Steve Whitaker, a 1962 star at Lincoln High who signed with the New York Yankees organization out of high school, hit seven home runs in his first 16 games with the Bronx Bombers. He led the American League in outfield assists in 1967 and batted in front of Mickey Mantle and Roger Maris. After three seasons with the Yankees, he was drafted by Kansas City in the 1968 expansion draft and was then traded to the Seattle Pilots for Lou Piniella before retiring in 1969.

Rich Hand, who handcuffed every NCAA Division I team in the Northwest on his way to All-America status at UPS, was the first-draft pick of the Cleveland Indians in the 1969 amateur draft. As a Lakes High School senior in 1965, Rick Austin was unbeaten, with an impressive 0.21 ERA, and at WSU he was team MVP while earning All-Pac-10 Northern Division and All-America honors. Like Hand, Austin was drafted by Cleveland in the first round of the 1968 draft. Doug Sisk was a Stadium Tiger standout who signed with the New York Mets in 1980 and won a World Series ring in 1986. In his first three seasons in the majors, he had a 2.12 ERA as a top reliever for the Mets. He did not allow a home run during the entire 1986 season.

A pair of left-handed pitchers, Ron Goerger of Lincoln High and Larry Loughlin of Bellarmine Prep, went on to enjoy solid professional careers. Goerger lost only once in three splendid seasons for Lincoln and once pitched three consecutive no-hitters. He signed with the Chicago Cubs in 1956 and played for 10 years, reaching the PCL where he was an All-Star choice at both Salt Lake and Portland. Loughlin likewise had a terrific high school record and pitched briefly for the Philadelphia Phillies in 1967.

Stadium's Bill Funk, Lincoln's Vern Kohout, Clover Park's Stan Naccarato, and Bellarmine's Vic Martineau were among the most successful high school pitchers in Pierce County during the 1940s. Both Funk and Naccarato saw their promising careers cut short by injuries. Drafted by the St. Louis Browns, Funk began his pro career in the Midwest on a staff that included Ryne Duren, Don Larson (of Yankee perfect-game fame), and Bob Turley. Naccarato was unbeaten at Clover Park late in his senior season, only to lose a 1–0 game on an unearned run to Puyallup, his only loss of the year. He was 33–10 as a professional prospect when an arm injury shortened his promising career. Kohout, a slick left-hander who was Lincoln's pitching ace for three

The pitching staff for the 1937 Tacoma Tigers included: L. to R., Hank Hulvey, Joe Malman, Pinckney Mills, Aldon Wilkie, Jerry Johnson (MB).

When not working for the Tacoma News Tribune, Roy Wilkowski (center), a former South Tacoma Tiger who played in the 1915 World Championships, could be found at the ballpark (courtesy Tom McCormick).

years, was selected to be the starting hurler in the annual city versus state All-Star game at the end of his senior year. Martineau later pitched at UPS and for Kay Street in the Tacoma City League, then with the touring House of David All-Stars.

A few seasons later, pitchers Rance Rolfe, Dale Bloom, and Mike Dillon dominated the high school scene. All three signed professionally, but Rolfe and Dillon suffered career-ending injuries in the minors. Bloom and Dillon returned to lead the Stanley's Shoemen of Tacoma to the National Amateur Baseball Association's championship in 1956. The

Shoemen's outfield that year consisted of Earl Hyder and Ron Storaasli, who played at Lincoln under Bill Mullen, and Bob Maguinez, who prepped at Stadium High. All three hit near .400 in high school as well as in the amateur league. Others on that team who starred at higher levels included Gordy Hersey and Dick Schlosstein from Stadium High, Jim Gallwas from Bellarmine, and Russ Wilkerson from Lincoln.

Catcher Arley Kangas, a Stadium High and WSU star, was a standout for Tacoma's Woodworth Contractors, who finished second in the nation in 1958. He was also selected to represent the United States in the 1959 Pan-Am Games, the only Tacoman ever to be so honored. Stadium High shortstop George Grant was another headliner. He starred as a Cheney Studs and a Stanley's Shoemen amateur, then turned down a pro contract with Philadephia to attend UW, where he was outstanding in both basketball and baseball.

The next wave of outstanding Pierce County baseball products is topped by Jon Lester of Bellarmine Prep, one of the more recent stars to sign a pro contract. Following a stellar prep career, he was a second-round pick in 2002 by the Boston Red Sox. The rangy left-hander is considered one of the brightest pitching prospects in the nation.

Lincoln High School standout, Luther Carr was as graceful on the baseball diamond as he was on the football field (courtesy the Cheney Family).

CHAPTER 11

BASKETBALL:
HIGH SCHOOL PLAYERS

A longtime football and basketball coach at Sumner High School, Ed McCoy attended Lincoln High and College of Puget Sound in 1933 (courtesy Sharon McCoy Lyons).

Basketballs bounced around Pierce County for many years before the establishment of state tournaments, from McKenna High School's recreation hall to the tiny gym at Vaughn High. Players learned to shoot "flat" shots because the gym ceilings were so low.

One of the biggest rivalries during those early days was that of Roy and neighboring Eatonville—a challenge that showed when state competition began as they were often among the top teams. Final scores of 9–6 were common back then, and a player hitting double figures in a single game—even just 10 or 11 points—was considered red-hot!

Boys' Championship Teams

Boys' basketball became an established part of the Washington state high school sports curriculum in 1923. The first state tournament was held that year in Hec Edmundson Pavilion at the University of Washington (UW). All classifications of schools, big and small, were included in the 16-team format. Walla Walla defeated Prosser, 21–16, in the final game but the Blue Devils had their toughest test in semifinal action, edging Eatonville 20–19 after two five-minute overtimes. A free throw after the final gun sounded was the margin of victory.

A Tacoma-area team first won a state championship in 1931. In fact, Tacoma's Stadium High won the first-ever "A" tournament while Eatonville prevailed in the initial "B" gathering. The tournaments were held at the same time, bringing 32 teams to the UW campus for 52 games in one giant event.

Eatonville's Cruisers, sparked by all-state star John Clauson, downed Endicott, 24–12, in the title tussle as more than 3,000 fans attended the first-ever small-school "B" championship. A weird schedule caused by so many entries forced coach Hugh Becket's team to play two games on Friday, the Cruisers beating Steptoe, 30–14, at 8 a.m. and stopping Snoqualmie, 25–20, at 9:30 p.m. It was a geniune family affair for the Pierce County entry, which featured three Fitzers: Kenny, Harold, and Marvin.

Stadium won the big-school "A" finale with a 53–20 thrashing of Raymond. The Stadium Tigers finished 19–1 under coach Dave Morris, with ball-handling wizard Bill "Eagle Eye" Lemmon in the backcourt. Dick Nichols and Orv "Tinnie" Johnson were named to the All-State team for the Tigers, and Johnson was the tournament's second-leading scorer after leading the Southwest League in that area during the regular season.

CHAPTER SPONSORED BY

MEL MICELI:

"We had season tickets to the Sonics games, all the baseball teams, everything," says Mel Miceli, whose husband Tom had a lifelong dedication to promoting sports and was involved with the Tacoma Athletic Commission (TAC). He played basketball growing up in New York and continued in the Navy. When he died in October of 2002, his wish was that people send money to the TAC, instead of sending flowers or other condolences. With the donations TAC will create a sports scholarship in honor of Tom's memory, although his sports enthusiasm lives on his own three children, eight grandchildren, and two great grandchildren—all of whom play or have played in one sport or another, notably baseball and basketball. Mel, her son, and son-in-law continue as active members of TAC.

It was 1944 before another Tacoma team contended. Lincoln, an undersized team not expected to make the state event, became the Cinderella entry of that tournament with three surprising victories before dropping the championship game to Spokane's Lewis and Clark, 41–38. Team captain Ray Johnson, All-State performer Bobby McGuire, and Bob Sater, the tallest of the Lincoln lads at 6 feet 2 inches, spearheaded a speedy and tenacious Lincoln team coached by Eddie Schwarz.

Stadium High School's Tigers, under first-year coach Jack Heinrick, won the 1959 championship with a 70–50 thumping of Burlington. Jim Johnson earned the tournament's Most Valuable Player award and was named, with center Herman Washington, to the All-State team. Washington became an All–Evergreen Conference first-team star at Western Washington University (WWU), where he led the team in both scoring and rebounding as a senior.

The Tigers finished that championship season with a 21–3 record behind the smooth floor play and scoring of sophomore "Sweet" Charlie Williams, who in three seasons became the first Tacoma player to score 1,000 points in his prep career. He went on to star at Seattle University (SU), then a Division I National Collegiate Athletics Association (NCAA) power, and later played professionally with Pittsburgh in the American Basketball Association, where he was an All-ABA selection.

The trophy-winning year was even more amazing considering that Stadium played the entire season without a home gymnasium because of renovation work on the school's facility. Many of the Tigers' practices occurred at the University of Puget Sound (UPS) Fieldhouse following Loggers workouts.

Sumner High School provided a remarkable story in 1960, reaching the state "A" title game despite a losing record. The Spartans dropped a 70–56 decision to Chehalis to finish with a 10–14 mark.

Lincoln's turn to again surprise skeptics came in 1968 when the Abes, just 14–6 in the regular season, won three playoff games to challenge Central Valley of Spokane for the title. Coach Ron Billings's unheralded cagers spilled the state's top-ranked Aberdeen Bobcats, 68–53, in the regional final at the UPS Fieldhouse behind 21 points from Dean

Ecklund and 18 more from Jim Womack. Ecklund had 24 points and was named to the All-State team after the Abes dumped Evergreen, 64–62, in the state semifinal. Womack's two free throws with 48 seconds remaining were the winning points. Central Valley took the state championship game, however, defeating Lincoln by a 62–48 score to complete a 25–2 season.

Also in 1968, Eric Schooler was recognized for his role in getting Sumner to the regional round of the state A playoffs for the first time in eight years. The Spartans took Seamount League honors with a 16–1 regular-season record, the best league mark in the program's 78-year history. Schooler averaged 21.7 points per game and capped his season with a 47-point performance against Port Angeles in the regional final.

Bethel topped Bothell, 53–51, to win the 1970 crown with a 21–1 record behind coach Bobby Fincham. Center Bob Niehl averaged 20 points and 17 rebounds a game and was a second team All-State choice. Niehl went on to coach at UPS. Mark Belvin, who had 36 points in the state semifinal win over Quincy, was the league's third leading scorer. Bethel's only loss was to Sumner, in the final league game of the year.

One year later, it was Puyallup's time to shine. The Vikings, coached by Puyallup High School alum Rich Hammermaster, downed Pasco, 54–41, in the battle of champions. The win gave Puyallup a 23–1 season record, the lone loss coming at the hands of Lincoln by a 65–59 count earlier in the season. Puyallup avenged that defeat with a 66–65 decision over the Abes before 6,000 excited fans in the regional tournament at the UPS Fieldhouse. The Vikings used key contributions from Doug Weese and Rick Gienger to top Auburn, 44–43, the next night to advance to the state final. Curtis High School, coached by Gerald Redburg, won the 3A state championship in 1971, thumping Battleground 64–48 to finish the season with a perfect 24–0 record. The Vikings featured a balanced six-player attack led by Tom Hargadon with a 15.2 scoring average. Brian Roach (13.8), Mike Berger (13.2), Mark Wells (12.8), Jim Ball (12.1), and Tom Shoemaker (9.6) were the other five. The Vikings lost by one point to East Bremerton in the regional finals during a 20–2 season the next year to end a 31-game win streak.

Lincoln finally secured a state 3A title in 1975, beating Everett, 63–58, and giving Coach Billings a 25–2 year. All-State star Steve Matzen and guard Chris Coley sparked the Abes to the championship. Matzen tallied 22 points in the title game, and Coley was credited with an outstanding defensive effort in the semifinal, holding Auburn star Rob Stone to only four points on a 1-for-17 shooting night.

The following season Cleveland High School of Seattle, with 7-footer Jawaan Oldham in the lineup, edged the Abes, 42–41, in the championship affair. It was the only loss of the season for Lincoln, which finished 24–1. Cleveland had a 23–1 record, losing to Lincoln, 76–64, earlier in the year at UW's Hec Edmundson Pavilion. A 38–point outburst by Matzen was the deciding factor in that one, putting an end to a 27-game winning streak by the towering Cleveland team. Lincoln's unbeaten string of 38 games was ended by Cleveland in the 3A title showdown.

Matzen was an All-State first-team selection as both a junior and a senior. He was named the state's outstanding player in his senior year and played in a prep All-Star game in New York. As a senior, he averaged 18.2 points per game and led Lincoln in rebounding and assists. He averaged 17.3 points per game as a junior. At 6 feet 4 inches, he was the top rebounder in the 1976 state tournament with 56 in four games, including 11 in the championship game against a Cleveland duo measuring 7 feet 0 inches and 6 feet 8 inches.

In 1980 Garfield High School of Seattle completed a 25–0 season by edging Tacoma's Bellarmine Prep, 59–53, in the state final. Bellarmine's Lions finished 20–5 behind the one-two scoring punch of Bryce McPhee and Doug Thompson, both of whom averaged more than 20 points per game. The Lions beat Puyallup and Federal Way at the eight-team state tournament after spoiling Fort Vancouver's perfect 22–0 record in the regional finale. McPhee was named the MVP of the state high school All-Star game after his senior year at Bellarmine and went on to excel at Gonzaga University.

Curtis twice came close to state 4A titles, losing 47–28 to Mercer Island in 1985 and 51–41 to Garfield a year later. In 1996 Gig Harbor won a state 3A title, defeating West Valley High of Yakima, 60–45, and capping a 25–2 record under longtime head coach Lyle McIntosh. The Tides were led by forward Bryan Kiehl, 2A Player of the Year in 1996, who averaged 17.5 points and 10.9 rebounds per game, and Sam Scholl, MVP of the state tourney. Tacoma's Wilson High School was 1998 runner-up to Garfield by a 78–65 margin.

Pierce County basketball fortunes reached an all-time high in 2000 when Foss and Bethel High Schools faced off in the state championship game. The Foss Falcons, coached by John Ruby, topped the Bethel Braves, 59–47, to claim Foss's first hoop title. Bethel led 38–37 after the third quarter, but Foss fought back and become the first Tacoma school in 25 years to take the crown. Demetrius Crosby had 18 points for Foss, and Kenan Joyce of the Falcons was the tournament MVP.

Another Foss star was Marc Axton, who made 20 out of 21 free throws during the tournament. He averaged 11.4 points per game his junior season and 21.2 as a senior, when Foss finished fourth at state. His career highlights included a two-year tournament free-throw accuracy mark of 44 for 46, plus a 41-point scoring spree in one game against Garfield. Axton went on to star at Eastern Washington University (EWU), leading that school to its first-ever NCAA tournament appearance in March 2004.

Lincoln, led by coach Tim Kelly, returned to dominance the next two years with consecutive state title wins over Ferris High School of Spokane. The 2001 squad capped a 29–1 season with a 61–54 championship victory. Leonard White was the tournament's Most Valuable Player and had 28 points in the championship game. The 2002 Abes ended up 27–2 after beating Ferris, 50–47, with Robert Crawford scoring 11 of his 18 points in the fourth quarter and Andre Anderson adding 13 points. Lincoln's high-scoring Justin Holt was held to just five points in his final game but was tournament MVP. Holt, a 6-foot 6-inch guard with great leaping ability and a key performer in Lincoln's back-to-back championship march, was recruited to Iowa State but later transferred to Virginia Tech.

Small Schools' Class B Championships

With very few "B" schools in the area, it was many years before a Tacoma quintet won small-school honors. Eatonville was second to Monroe in 1952, the Cruisers falling 51–31 on championship night. Orting also came close in 1966 before losing to unbeaten Reardan, 58–55, in the championship contest. It was Orting's only loss in a 25–game season. Tacoma Baptist had a shot at class B state champion Almira-Coulee-Hartline High School in the 1991 title game but lost a 60–52 verdict. And although Laughbon High of Dupont never won a title, its presence was felt on the court by virtue of Ev Cunningham, a 1972 all-state selection who averaged 23.8 points per game.

But in 1998, under coach Michael Bradley, Chief Leschi High School climaxed a 25–3 season with a 70–51 victory over Valley Christian in Spokane. Sophomore guard Branson Brown scored 18 points and Lamont Trent added 17 in the title tussle. In the semifinals, 6-foot 7-inch center Jonathon Redding had 14 points, 17 rebounds, and 10 blocked shots as Chief Leschi downed St. John's–Endicott, 64–43.

Class A Championships

Classification changes occurred due to ever-fluctuating school enrollments, eventually resulting in five different tournaments. Another 42 years passed until the next class A championship was claimed by a Pierce County team: White River's 1973 victory over Omak. Coach Lloyd Blanusa's team, led by 6-foot 7-inch center Phil Hiam, surprised the state with four straight tourney wins after a mediocre 12–11 regular-season mark. The Hornets played tough opponents from higher classifications during the regular season, however, and that experience helped them win the Seamount League title for a second straight year. Hiam averaged 25 points a game at state, and in his final contest, he scored 31 points and added 18 rebounds and six assists.

Leading the Orting Cardinals to a state tournament appearance in 1971, Reid Brown carried an average of 18.2 points per game. In 1974 and 1975, Rob Scheibner averaged 16.3 as a junior and 17.4 points as a senior; during the latter tournament, he was the second-leading scorer, with 21 points per game. Orting won the class A state tournament in 1983 by a 47–45 count over Lynden. Jerry Clyde coached the Cardinals to a 23–3 record that season, which served as the pinnacle of a string of outstanding Orting teams and players. In 1984 Jay Anderson averaged 23 points and eight rebounds per game in the tournament, and a year later he averaged 20.7 points and 12.7 rebounds

in the tourney after scoring 18.5 points per game during the season.

Steilacoom took back-to-back class A championships in 1984 and 1985 under two different coaches: John Medak and Gary Wusterbarth, respectively. The Sentinels chopped Woodland, 68–39, in the championship game to finish 24–2 under Medak, then routed Highland High of Yakima, 78–55, for the 1985 title to end a 23–2 season under first-year coach Wusterbarth.

Two of Steilacoom High's best-ever players supplied much of the firepower. Two-time MVP Rod Whatley averaged 21.8 points and 10.2 rebounds in the 1984 championship and 18 points and 13.2 rebounds in the 1985 tourney. Guard Jeff Staten averaged 15.8 and 14.8 points in the consecutive tournaments and scored 1,128 points in his four-year Steilacoom career. Steilacoom, still coached by Wusterbarth, made one other championship game appearance, losing 46–45 to Zillah in 1994. But the school's Kendrick Holley was twice MVP in the Nisqually League and twice All-Area while averaging 19.1 points and 12.2 rebounds per game in 2002. He had 41 points in one game versus Port Townsend.

Matt Stepan was an All-State choice at Gig Harbor High School in 1992 with a scoring average of 18.2 and school records in free throws attempted and made. Paul Grobins was All-State in 1993 and holds the Pierce County League career scoring record with 1,339 points and 201 three-pointers. Sam Scholl, who later played at TCC and the University of San Diego, left the Tides with a career assist record of 401, including 17 against Franklin Pierce High in 1994. Matt Enloe, who played in 100 games for the Tides, twice earned All-State and All-State tournament honors in 2000.

Producing College Players

State championships aren't the only measurement of Tacoma–Pierce County basketball success, however: many outstanding college players have been produced locally. Tacoma's first "big man" was 6-foot 8-inch Vince Hanson, who led the Lincoln Abes to a fourth-place finish in the 1941 state tournament. Hanson went on to fame at WSU, where he set an all-time scoring record and was named to

Stadium High and Bellarmine Prep hoopsters at battle (MB).

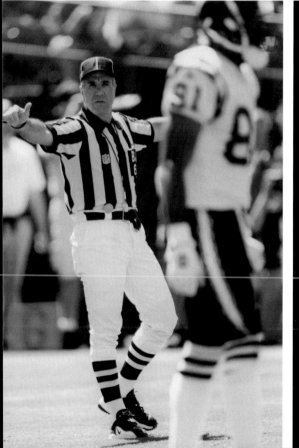

Dan Inveen was a noted Pac-10 football referee when he wasn't serving as athletic director for the Tacoma School District (SSM, 1209).

Kirk Dornan, son of longtime official Duke Dornan, plies his trade as one of Tacoma's NFL officials (SSM, I2003.12.1) .

Pat Austin is crowned the 1995 Top Fuel Champion as part of the National Hot Rod Association Winston Drag Racing U.S. Nationals (SSM, 1986).

The "City of Tacoma" car participated in the famed 1949 Indy 500 race, with crew members, L. to R., Jack Beckley, unknown, Tom Carstens, Dave Fogg, and driver Jack McGrath (courtesy Dave Fogg).

Derrike Cope proudly displays his trophy upon winning the 1990 Daytona 500 (SSM, 2001.17.1).

The start of a 1921 race featured Roscoe Sarles in a Duesenberg, who finished second to winner Tommy Milton in a Durant Special; the pace car (far right) was driven by Ray Harroun, winner of the 1911 Indy 500, and referee Eddie Rickenbacker (courtesy Dr. Wayne D. Herstad).

Pat Austin ranks 4th on the all-time National Hot Rod Association winners list and was named 13th of the Top 50 Drivers in the organization's first 50 years of competition (courtesy Walt Austin Racing).

Leo Dobry on the 1950 Pike's Peak Hill Climb (courtesy Bill Seidelman).

Bert Dingley blows tire and flips his car, the "ONO," on the 123rd lap of the Montamarathon in 1914 (courtesy Dr. Wayne D. Herstad).

The 1937 Johnson Paint team finished 5th at the national championships in Wichita, Kansas: back row, L. to R., Fred Hutchinson, Earl Johnson, Joe Dailey, Cy Greenlaw, Joe Salatino, Loris Baker, Dutch Scheffler; middle row, L. to R., Hal Lee, Rick Lewis, John Heinrick, Andy Padovan, Morry Abbott, Erling Tollefson; front row, L. to R., Frank Ruffo, Jimmy Ennis, batboy Sam Baker, Rudy Tollefson, Doug Hendry, Joe Mlachnik (MB).

The 1969 Tacoma Cubs won the Pacific Coast League championships: front row, L. to R., batboy Charles Spruck, George Sherrod, Al Montreuil, John Lung, Vic LaRose, Mike White, Roger Metzger, batboy Bob Bianchi; middle row, L. to R., Jim Colborn, Jim Dunegan, Ron Piche, Bob Tiefenaur, manager Whitey Lockman, Larry Gura, Rick Bladt, George Pena, Aaron Pointer; back row, L. to R., Chet Trail, Darcy Fast, Archie Reynolds, Roe Skidmore, John Hairston, Dick LeMay, Jim McMath, Randy Bobb, Joe Decker, trainer Gary Nicholson (SSM, 1997.14.9).

A top handball player, Allan Browne also had a lengthy baseball career and played for the South Tacoma Tigers in 1915 (MB).

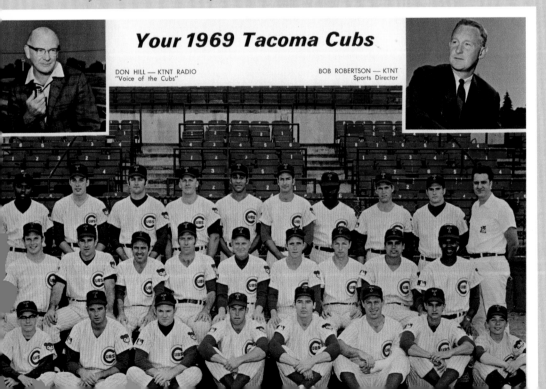

The Violet Oats baseball club, ca. 1908, included brothers Duke and Goo Campbell among its team members (MB).

Casino Ballclub, 1941: back row, L. to R., owner Al Harden, unknown, unknown, Jim Claxton, unknown, Charlie Williams, Lee Stits, Bud Cabell; front row, L. to R., Bob Flowers, Jess Brooks, Jack Tanner, Wardell Canada, Ed Griffin, Jesse Sanders (courtesy Pat Maguinez).

Jon Otness was a Wilson High School and University of Washington standout (photo by Joanie Komura, courtesy University of Washington).

Bob Maguinez, a longtime player, coach, umpire, and scout, played for the 1956 national champion Stanley Shoemen and won another national title in 1960 with the Cheney Studs (SSM, 2000.8.2).

The Pioneer B-and-P Company baseball team, ca. 1905 (SSM).

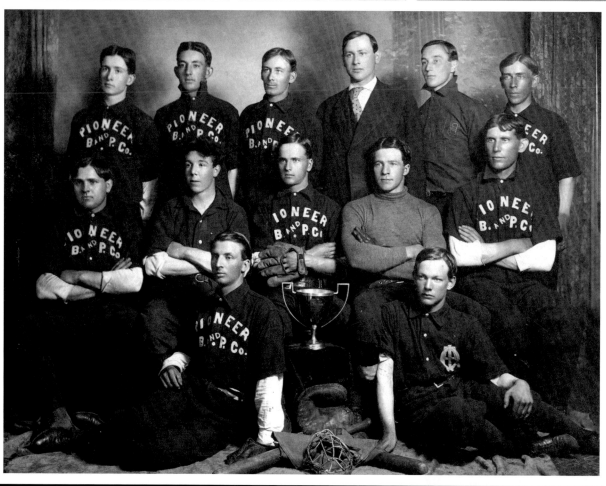

The Orting Cardinals won the 1976 state baseball title with a 25–2 record: back row, L. to R., coach Jerry Thacker, Greg Bickel, unknown, Rob Scheiber, Ron Felker, Dave Hill, Tom Cope, Mike White, manager Lee Seay; front row, L. to R., Jim Rice, Bill Marenco, Bob Hobart, Eric Shrum, Gary Balmer, Tim Harpster, unknown, Chuck White; missing, Jeff Colville and Tom Donahue (courtesy Jerry Thacker).

The Whistle Bottling Company, a forerunner of Cammarano Brothers, played in the Tacoma City League with great success; back row, L. to R., manager Bill Cammarano, Dutch Thaut, unknown, Al Maruca; middle row, L. to R., Howard Bailey, Bill Otto, Jack Zink, Ocky Larson, unknown; front row, L. to R., Rhine Thaut, Ted Lyphardt, Jack Otto, batboy Fred Noble, Fred Wilhelm, Ed Curran, Joe Thiel (SSM, 1350).

The Amocats ("Tacoma" spelled backwards) represented West Coast Grocery and fielded a team from 1903–06 (courtesy F. Lee Campbell).

Perennial All-Star Floyd "Lefty" Isekite is generally considered the greatest strikeout pitcher in our history (MB).

Marion Oppelt (on the mound) in an Oldtimers game at McNeil Prison in the 50s (MB).

Morley Brotman presents the 1957 Washington State Baseball Association's state championship trophy to sponsor Alden Woodworth, as manager Marv Scott looks on; the team finished second in the national championships in 1958 (MB).

The Tacoma Giants won the 1961 Pacific Coast League championship with a 97–57 record (SSM, 1022.00).

Your 1961 Tacoma Giants

DON HILL — KTAC's "Voice of the Giants"

Back Row, left to right—Jim Duffalo, RHP; Bob Perry, OF; John Orsino, C; Bill Hain, IF; Geo. Maranda, RHP; Bud Byerly, Coach-RHP; Rafael Alomar, OF; "Dusty" Rhodes, LF; Leo Hughes, Trainer. **Middle Row**—Gaylord Perry, RHP; Ray Daviault, RHP; Lynn Lovenguth, RHP; Chuck Hiller, IF; John "Red" Davis, Manager; Ron Herbel, RHP; Dom Zanni, RHP; Verle Tiefenthaler, RHP; Eddie Fisher, RHP. **Front Row**—John Goetz, RHP; Gil Garrido, SS; Frank Reveira, Catcher; Richard Keely, Bat boy; Greg

"Indian" Bob Johnson enjoyed a 13-year major league career, 10 years with the American League Philadelphia A's, and a career batting average of .296 with 288 homeruns; he managed the Tacoma Tigers of the Western International League in 1949 (SSM, 1399).

Obak tobacco card of 1910 Tacoma Tiger (SSM).

Catcher Al Ronning puts the tag on a sliding Dick Greco as umpire Clarence Stave readies to make the call (MB).

Roy Wilkowski was the leading hitter in the Tacoma City League in 1915 with a .469 batting average (courtesy Tom McCormick).

The Tacoma Cubs celebrate after winning their 1969 Pacific Coast League title against the Eugene Emeralds; super-fan Ken Still (second from R.) leads the cheers (SSM, 2002.3.1).

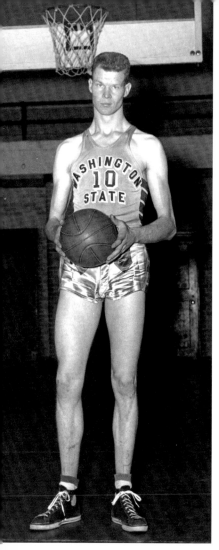

Plywood Tacoma was one of the top amateur basketball teams in the country in the 1970s: L. to R., Gary Wortman, Darron Nelson, LeRoy Sinnes, Steve Anstett, Ted Werner, Jim Van Beek, Mike Dahl, Dave Wortman, Clint Names (SSM, 2001.26.39).

Vince Hanson plied his trade at Lincoln High School before capping his outstanding career at Washington State with selection to the 1945 All–American Collegiate Basketball Team (SSM, 2002.21.1).

The 1945 Stadium High School Tigers were coached by VG Lowman, at top (courtesy David Lowman).

Harry McLaughlin (bottom row, L.) and brother Willie (top row, second from R.) were members of the barnstorming House of David basketball team, which traveled around the country playing in exhibition games. Both played at Clover Park High School and then later for the PLU team coached by Marv Harshman, when Harry was one of the nation's leading scorers in the 1947–48 season (courtesy Leslie McLaughlin Bede).

Members of the 1964 Cheney Studs Courteers: L. to R., George Brown, Jeff Smith, Tom Rogers, Rickey Stewart, John Salatino, Pete Wonders (courtesy the Cheney Family).

Dan Inveen of the Cheney Studs was also basketball coach at Wilson High (SSM, 2000.4.40).

Wing A. C. basketball team, Tacoma City League, 1922 (SSM).

A fine basketball player in his own right, Bruce Alexander was the only individual from Tacoma to ever referee in the NBA, where his flair and style were perfectly suited to the entertainment-conscious league (SSM).

Two familiar foes in the local women's basketball league included the powerful McChord Jets and the Hollywood Boat & Motor team, for whom Delores "Dee" Sagmiller, a Puyallup High grad, gets off a shot (courtesy the Harry Esborg Family).

Curt Peterson played center for the University of Puget Sound's 1976 national basketball championship team (UPS).

John Heinrick (L.), former Stadium High School football and basketball coach, congratulates son Jack on guiding the Tigers to the 1959 state basketball title (SSM, 314).

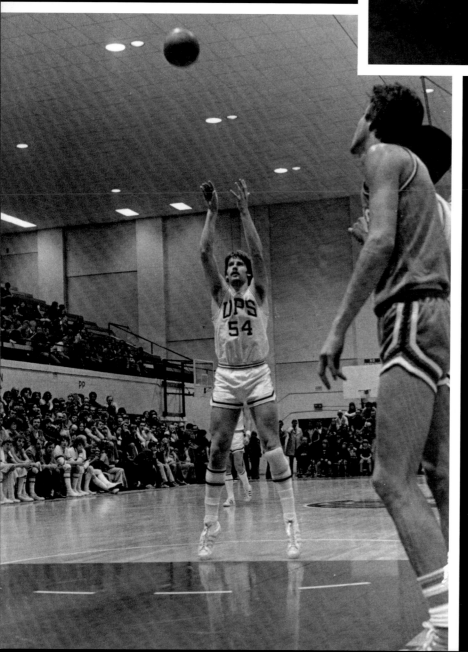

Rick Walker played forward for the University of Puget Sound's 1976 national basketball championship team (UPS).

Matt McCully cuts down the net from the University of Puget Sound's 1976 national basketball championship game; Tim Evans (#34) hoists McCully as Rocky Botts (#20) cheers him on (courtesy Doug McArthur).

Coach Don Moseid was first a standout player for UPS and the Cheney Studs (SSM).

Three key players for the Twang Root Beer team, ca. 1930s, included: Lornie Merkle (#22), Bob Huegel (#24), and Bill Lemmon (#27) (SSM, 2003.6.2).

Clarence Ramsey, a Lincoln High and University of Washington performer (photo by Randy Wingett, courtesy University of Washington).

Sonny Bailey (second from R., with "Fife" on jersey) mixes it up under the hoop in a local 1930s basketball game (courtesy the Bill Bailey Family).

The University of Puget Sound Loggers defeated the University of Tennessee to win the NCAA Division II National Basketball Championships and their season of 27 wins still stands as a school record: back row, L. to R., Phil Hiam, Steve Freimuth, Mike Hanson, Rick Walker, Curt Peterson, Brant Gibler, A.T. Brown; front row, L. to R., Bill Greenheck, Rocky Botts, Mike Kuntz, Mike Strand, Mark Wells, Tim Evans; not pictured, Matt McCully, coach Don Zech, assistant coach Jim Harney (SSM, 1932).

Members of the Little Giants basketball team that played in the Boys Club program: back row, L. to R., Bobby Moore (now Ahmad Rashad), Ron Schmidtke, Jim McAlpine, Jim Berg, coach Jim McCuen; front row, L. to R., Jerry Berg, Steve Sand, unknown, Dick Samlaska (courtesy South End Boys & Girls Club).

Jim and Inigo's 1306 Tavern team won the trophy for "Best Dressed" in 1950: L. to R., Ann Lucchesi, Jo Halko, Evelyn Stein, Dot Pollen, Milly Fleming (SSM).

Tacoma's entry at the 1949 American Bowling Congress national tournament included: L. to R., John Artoe, Earl Johnson, Ted Tadich, Primo Artoe, Urban Schmidt (SSM, 1999.10.2).

Earl Johnson was the first Tacoman to bowl professionally, joining the pro tour in the 1960s, and won five Professional Bowlers Association championships (courtesy American Bowling Congress).

Joe Wilman (courtesy Greater Tacoma Bowling Association).

Universal Cleaners team, ca. 1935 (SSM).

Earl Anthony won 45 Professional Bowling Association titles and was the first bowler in history to reach $1 million in career earnings (courtesy American Bowling Congress).

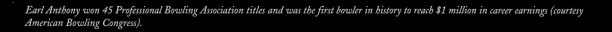

Pat McMurtry (L.) and Willie Pastrano (R.) duke it out in a July 1956 bout in Lincoln Bowl, as referee Davey Ward steps in to separate them (courtesy Pat McMurtry).

Davey Ward (L.) takes instruction from Freddie Steele (MB).

Homer Amundsen gives Pat McMurtry plenty of water before he gets back in the ring (SSM, 1999.14.6).

Leo Randolph, 1976 Olympic Old Medal winner (SSM, 324.05).

George Wright (L.) and Bob McKinney size up each other in a bout at the Tacoma Armory (MB).

Jimmy Rondeau (far R.) was the referee in 1974 when George Foreman (R.) defeated Ken Norton (L.) in Caracas, Venezuela, thus giving Foreman the right to fight Muhammed Ali (courtesy Jim Rondeau).

By 1973, Sugar Ray Seales (L.) was a 1972 Olympic Gold Medalist and an unbeaten pro welterweight vying for the world championship; his half-brother Dale Grant (R.) was named the 1972 U.S. Amateur Boxer of the Year by the Amateur Athletic Union with a record of 290–18 (Richards Studio Collection, TPL, Image D163893–16).

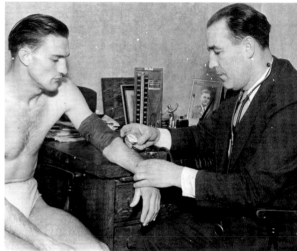

Freddie Steele gets a pre-fight physical (courtesy the Freddie Steele Family).

Ernie Jensen, veteran referee who fought collegiately at the University of Idaho in 1937, monitors the action in this bout between Rudy Garcia (L.) and Joe Lopez (R.) (MB).

The 1954 NCAA boxing champions included Mike McMurtry of Idaho State (far R.) who won the heavyweight division (SSM, 1999.14.5).

Puyallup High grad Brock Huard had an outstanding career for the UW Huskies before entering the NFL with the Seattle Seahawks (photo by Bruce Terami, courtesy University of Washington).

Vince Goldsmith (center), a Mt. Tahoma High grad, was the University of Oregon's MVP in 1979 and 1980 (courtesy Vince Goldsmith).

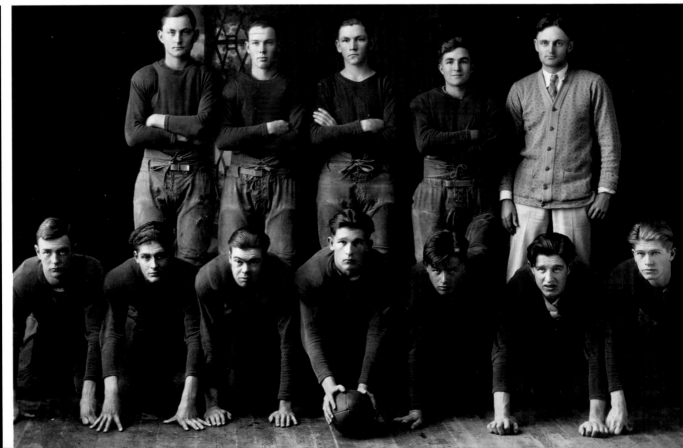

VG Lowman's early coaching career started with football (courtesy David Lowman).

Puyallup High grad Dane Looker is now a wide receiver for the NFL's St. Louis Rams (courtesy Dane Looker).

Jerry Thacker was a top quarterback for the College of Puget Sound Loggers and played with the semipro Tyees before going into coaching (UPS).

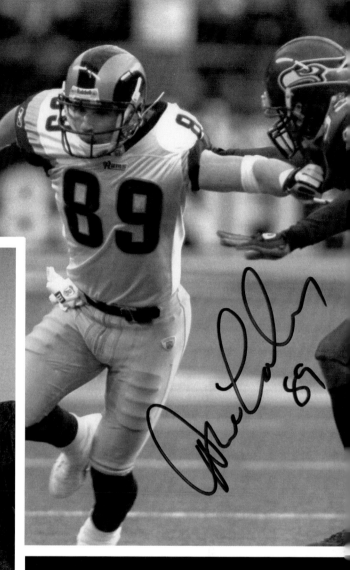

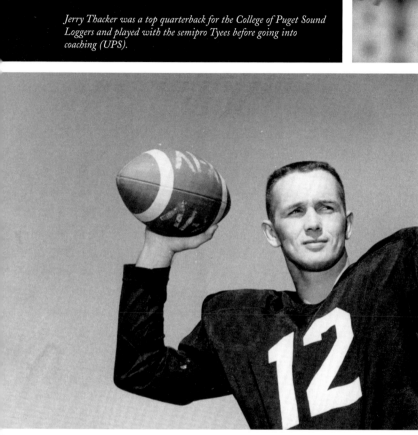

Lute players listen intently to coach Frosty Westering (PLU).

Dan Thurston (#80) made a habit out of completing impossible catches while starring at the University of Puget Sound (UPS).

Phil Carter (#22), captain of the 1979 Wilson High School track team, scores his first touchdown for Notre Dame, where he was the leading ground gainer through his senior year (courtesy Jim Daulley).

The PLU football team thanks its fans for their support during a successful pursuit of the 1999 NCAA Division III National Championship (PLU).

Lawyer Milloy (#9) earned All-America honors at the University of Washington and won a 2002 Super Bowl championship with the New England Patriots (photo by Ethan Jansen, courtesy University of Washington).

Randy Roberts holds the ball for Clint Scott, one of the best place kickers to ever wear a Logger uniform and the 1969 National All-Time career scoring leader in the NCAA (all-levels) for kickers (UPS).

Basketball coach Russ Wilkerson (L.) and football coach John Heinrick try to convince Joe Peyton, a member of the Army Special Forces, to turn out for their respective teams at UPS (SSM, 1910).

An exhuberant Fife High School team celebrates their successful state football championship in 1939: bottom row, L. to R., Howard Bryan, Masaru Tamura, Tom Pruett, Ben Holdener; middle row, L. to R., Kenji Yaguchi, Willie Hamanishi, Yohei Sagami, Frank Dreyer, Joe Trucco; back row, L. to R., Seiichi Yamada, Bob Vinson, Pete Cereghino, Pete Mello, Frank Spear, Frank Evancich, Milt Iida (courtesy Ben Holdener).

Chad Johnson, a 2000 graduate of Pacific Lutheran University, was a three-year starting quarterback for the Lutes and the Gagliardi Award Division III national player of the year (PLU).

Cornerback Marcus Trufant was the 11th pick in the first round of the 2003 NFL draft by the Seattle Seahawks (courtesy the Trufant Family).

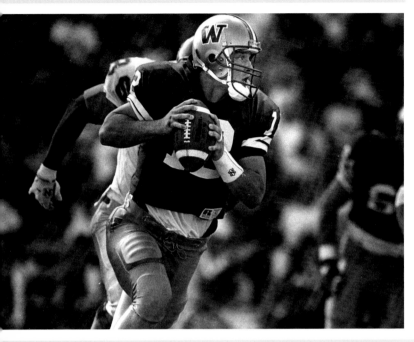

Paul Skansi, a Peninsula High graduate, was a star receiver for the UW Huskies (photo by Betty Kumpf, courtesy University of Washington).

Billy Joe Hobert led the Puyallup Vikings to a 1987 state high school championship and set a championship-game passing record with 374 yards; he went on to a successful career at the UW and in the NFL (photo by Joanie Komura, courtesy University of Washington).

Under the watchful eyes of coach Father Gordon Turner, four members of the 1944 CPS Loggers run through drills: L. to R., Jim O'Brien, Larry Rask, Cliff Schiesz, Al Fairhurst (SSM, 2001.37.2).

the WSU Sports Hall of Fame. In the 1945 season, Hanson set a school scoring record of 592 points, a mark that survived for more than 30 years. At the time, 592 points was a national record and earned Hanson All-America honors.

Stadium High's Clint Names, equally at home on the golf course (see chapter 24, Golf) or the basketball court, may have staged the most spectacular shooting display in state high school tournament history. He scored 39 points against the state's number-one-ranked team, Richland, in a 64–63 Tiger win in 1957. With Stadium leading 7–6, Names made 22 consecutive points for the Tigers on 10 field goals and two free throws. He finished with an 18-for-28 shooting night. He went on to play at UW.

Steve Anstett of Bellarmine Prep was another tall and talented Tacoman. As a senior in 1960, he was second in the City League scoring race by a mere two points to Stadium High star Charlie Williams. Anstett tallied 27 points and 27 rebounds in one game against Lincoln. At the University of Portland, Anstett scored 1,213 points and grabbed 893 rebounds to become the school's career leader in both categories, and he earned team Most Valuable Player honors all three years. Anstett, of course, played during an era in which college athletes could not compete in varsity athletics during their freshmen seasons. Anstett returned to coach his high school alma mater from 1967 to 1995, amassing 326 wins while competing in nine state basketball tournaments.

Tacoma Community College Titans won the 1971 Northwest Athletic Association of Community Colleges basketball crown with a final win over Walla Walla: back row, L. to R., Stanley Edwards, Clyde Strickland, Bruce Larson, Dean Ecklund, coach Don Moseid, Ron Oughton, Jim Carkonen, Mark Belvin, Jim Savitz; front row, L. to R., Mark Seil, Bob Frier, Charles Nicholson, Dennis Bitz, Dave Hunter (courtesy Don Moseid).

Wilson High School produced three outstanding "big men." One of the biggest in Tacoma prep basketball history was 6-foot 9-inch, 245-pound Bob Sprague, who dominated the rebounding department in both high school and college in the early '60s. Jim McKean, another Rams center who earned All-League and All-State honors in high school, enjoyed a fine college career at WSU, where he earned All–Pacific 8 honors as the team's senior scoring leader. He graduated from Wilson in 1964 after three years as a starter, in an era when successive annual starts didn't often happen. Kevin Field, at 6 feet 10 inches, was an All-Leaguer who as a senior at Wilson High School in 2002 averaged 18.3 points and 10.4 rebounds per game, shot 45 percent from three-point range, and went on to play at Oregon State University (OSU). As a four-year letterman at Wilson, he scored more than 1,000 points.

Marty Morin, a Peninsula High School Seahawks scoring star, became one of Tacoma Community College's top players en route to a basketball scholarship to Boise State in the late 1960s. Ev Cunningham of Laughbon was a 1972 All-State selection after scoring 23.8 points per game.

A Bellarmine player who led the city in scoring was Craig Hilden, a two-time All-City choice who averaged 19.5 points per game as a senior in 1967. Bellarmine's Bob Johnson twice earned All-City honors and averaged 16.3 points as a senior in 1971, including 27 against Lincoln's city champs. Bellarmine produced another scoring whiz in 1975 graduate Joel Diggs, a first-team All-City player who averaged 19.7 points per game to lead Tacoma high school players. He went on to play for Central Washington University (CWU).

Lincoln High, a powerhouse in the 1970s, had several standouts, among them Ron Lund and Clarence Ramsey. Lund averaged 24.9 points per game as a junior forward and 17.2 as a senior guard, earning All-City honors both years. He went on to play at UPS. Ramsey, a transfer from Mississippi, averaged 22.1 per game as a junior and 23.2 as a senior and was All-State while leading the Abes to a combined 42–6 record. He also led the 1972 state tournament in rebounding, with 40 in two games. At UW he became one of the Huskies' top 10 all-time scorers.

Bellarmine's Jim McPhee, whose brother Bryce was a standout on the Lions' 1980 state runner-up team, averaged

23.6 points per game as a senior. Like his brother, Jim went on to earn multiple honors for Gonzaga. In fact, Jim still ranks number two on Gonzaga's all-time scoring list, with 2,015 points from 1986 to 1990, trailing only Frank Burgess, another Tacoma resident, who scored 2,196 points from 1959 to '61.

Jake Guadnola, a two-time Narrows League and All-Area selection, led the Bellarmine Lions to two state tournament appearances. A 1994 Bellarmine grad, Guadnola is the school's all-time leading scorer. Casey Calvary is another Bellarmine graduate who starred at Gonzaga. Calvary twice earned All–West Coast first-team selection at Gonzaga and was a second-team All-America and Gonzaga's Male Athlete of the Year in 2001. Brandon Merritt, yet another Bellarmine product, was a member of EWU's 2004 NCAA tournament team after two great seasons at Tacoma Community College (TCC).

Josh Barnard, who graduated from Bethel High School in 1999, scored 22 points for the UW Huskies in a game against the University of California–Los Angeles (UCLA) before he finished his college career as Merritt's teammate at EWU.

Two of Bethel's best players under longtime coach Mike Mullen were Herb Jones and Mike's son, Pat Mullen. The 6-foot 5-inch Jones was an All-League and All-State performer with double-digit scoring and rebounding averages who earned a scholarship to the University of Montana in 1983. He was killed in an auto accident en route to Montana during his sophomore year. Pat Mullen still holds the South Puget Sound League (SPSL) record for assists, averaging 9.4 per contest in 1985. He also ranks near the top in steals with 3.9 per game and a record 78 steals in one season. Now Bethel High's head coach, Pat played at UPS, where he earned National Association of Intercollegiate Athletics (NAIA) All-District recognition.

Don Moseid, a 1954 All-State pick in helping Stadium High place third at the state tournament, was an outstanding scorer at UPS. Bobby Sloan of Stadium High was one of the state's top scorers in 1964, averaging 24.2 points per game. He was followed at Stadium by first-team All-City players Fred Cain and Sam May. Cain led the state in scoring in 1971 with a 29.5 average, getting 49 points against

West Bremerton and 43 versus Mount Tahoma. May averaged 17.9 points per game and earned a scholarship to Duke. He later transferred to UPS, joining Cain in college.

Mount Tahoma High School's first teams featured Ron Cey, who went on to baseball stardom at WSU and then as an All-Star third baseman for the Los Angeles Dodgers. Cey was an All-City high prep basketball standout, averaging 20.2 points and scoring a single-game high of 38 against Wilson in 1966. He played T-Bird basketball with Bobby Moore, who as Ahmad Rashad went on to a brilliant professional football career with the St. Louis Cardinals and Minnesota Vikings. Team captain Bruce Malfait was another T-bird star, with an 18.5-per-game scoring average and All-City honors on the first Tacoma team to finish its regular season unbeaten.

In 1995, a Sumner Spartan became the talk of the state. Josh Steinthal had a record-setting career at Sumner High, the only player in that program's history to have his jersey number retired. He was selected to All-State, All-Area, and All–Pierce County teams and set a SPSL scoring record with 29.5 points per game. He was 3A state scoring champion during the 1995–96 season, averaging 32.1 points per game. His 1,251 career points and 21.2-points-per-game average are still Sumner's best ever. He also established school records for three pointers and career and free throws made in a season. Steinthal graduated fifth in his class with a 3.94 grade point average and he earned the Dean's List recognition at OSU, where he played collegiate basketball. Steinthal ranks third on OSU's single-season and career lists for three-point field goals made. Twice he earned All–Pac 10 academic honors.

The Alt Heidelberg basketball team was the 1937–38 Tacoma City and Pierce County League champions in addition to winning the Pacific Northwest championship: back row, L. to R., Joe Salatino, unknown, Kellstrom, Hal Lee, Gene Gunderson, coach Bill Libke; front row, L. to R., Bill Lemmon, Bill Dahlke, Dutch Holsteine, Bob Huegel (SSM, 2123).

In 1979 Foss provided Tacoma with its first 7-footer, Ron Burns, who eventually played at Whitworth College in Spokane and averaged 24.2 points per game during his three years with the Falcons. In 1984 Brian Wright was another Foss star and top scorer, with a 17.7 points-per-game average, who later played for the WSU Cougars.

Franklin Pierce High School featured Jim Van Beek, who joined Lincoln High's Roger Iverson in forming two-thirds of PLU's "big three" during the 1950s golden years of Lute basketball. Another FPHS product, Rod Tripp, averaged 26.4 points per game as a senior in 1979, a league record that stood for 11 years, and 23.5 points a game as a junior.

Stan Nybo, a first-team All-State player for Rogers High School in 1973, is the second-leading scorer in school history with an average of 16.2 points per game. A 6-foot 4-inch guard, he also ranks as the Rams' best-ever rebounder with 576. The top scorer in Rogers' boys' basketball history is Tyce Nasinec, who then played four years at CWU. He tallied 1,203 points as a Ram in the mid-1990s, averaging 22 points per game. Michael Palm was an outstanding Rogers center in 1998 who went on to become WWU's all-time rebound leader and second-leading scorer.

Puyallup High had its share of top players as well. After averaging 18.5 points as a PHS senior, Ron Crowe played at UW, then transferred to WWU for the 1959–60 season. He was the conference scoring leader with 20.7 points per game, tallying 40 in one game, and led the Vikings to their first-ever NAIA national tournament appearance. Another Puyallup player who starred in college was Doug Spradley. At Gonzaga he finished as the Bulldog's 10th-leading all-time scorer, with 1,427 points; 605 points were during his senior season of 1988–89.

Two of Puyallup High's best football players also deserve recognition for their basketball acumen (see chapter 23, Football: Pro and Semipro). San Francisco 49er Gail Bruce, a dominant football player at UW, was a standout prep football and basketball player at Puyallup High in 1941. National Football League (NFL) quarterback Damon Huard actually led state 3A players in 1990 in scoring as a junior with an average of 24.6 points per game, and as a senior he averaged 25.8 and garnered first-team All-State honors in leading the Vikings to a 21–7 record. Other Vikings to mention include

Brandon Bakke, who went on to play at Fresno State; Dane Looker, now a wide receiver with the NFL's St. Louis Rams; and a foursome of UPS standouts, guards Earl Tallman (1953), Dan Bogrand (1968), and Jerry Williams (1980), and 6-foot 9-inch center Bryan Vukelich (1992).

Rod McDonald, a 1963 graduate, may have been the best player to come out of Clover Park High School. He starred at Whitworth College, along with fellow Warrior Jack Pelander, and then played professionally for the Utah Stars in the ABA. McDonald was an NAIA All-America selection at Whitworth, where for 37 years he held the school scoring record with 1,807 points. He once scored 51 points in a college game against the University of Redlands.

Other Clover Park cagers of note are the 1940s trio of Wes Saxton, Harry McLaughlin, and Willie McLaughlin. They all became standouts on Marv Harshman–coached teams at PLU. Harry McLaughlin, a PLU Hall of Fame member, led all Northwest college players in scoring as a senior, averaging more than 23 points per game. Brian Hagbo, two-time All-League and an All-Stater in 1976, had a 17.5 points-per-game scoring average.

Alphonse Hammond was a standout player for Lakes High School in the 1980s. He became a member of the Centralia College Hall of Fame before transferring to UPS, where he still holds fifth place in the school's all-time free-throw percentage list. The Lancers also had a top rebounder in Scott Johnson. In 1993 and 1994 he averaged more than 14 rebounds per game after averaging 12.6 to lead the league as a sophomore.

Fife High's Vince Strojan, top scorer in the 1964 state A tournament with 114 points, had a great career at St. Martin's College and has been inducted into the SMC Hall of Fame. He scored a school record of 1,736 points as a Saint and was signed by Dallas in the ABA.

Girls' Championship Teams

Puyallup's Jerry DeLaurenti coached Puyallup from 1974 to '94 and won more than 400 games. His teams won six league championships and made 11 state tournament appearances with a best finish of fourth place.

Among DeLaurenti's standout players was Laurie Wetzel, who led the Vikings to three straight SPSL crowns.

Wetzel was the league MVP as a senior in 1985, made All-League first team twice, and later became an All-America performer at UW in volleyball. Kay Koppelman, Tammy Edmiston, Cindy Edmiston, and Kara Jenkins were other top players at Puyallup.

George Quigley coached at Stadium High School from 1974 to 1988 while also coaching varsity baseball during 12 of those years. His 1975–76 girls' basketball team won the City League and finished eighth at the state championships, and his 1979–80 team also won the city title.

Coach Nancy Wells Rothenberg led Clover Park High School's girls basketball team to its first 4A championship, downing Pasco 76–67 in the 1978 title tussle. The Lady Warriors finished the season with a 25–2 record, the first Pierce County team to secure a state girls title. Delores Krumm, the team's leading scorer, starred in the finale against Pasco with 27 points, including 17 of the game's final 30. CPHS led 46–44 with 11 minutes remaining but pulled away in the final quarter.

Krumm's younger sister Kim was a valuable sixth player

The 1948 Tacoma Fuelerettes won the city women's basketball league and finished third in the Northwest Women's tournament: front row, L. to R., Margaret Heinrick, Joyce Jones, Connie Canonica, Delores Sagmiller, Doris Carlson; middle row, L. to R., Donna Brown, Joyce Nelson, Virginia Glassy, Pat Hankinson; back row, L. to R., coach Dick Penhale, Shirley Soggie, Pat Strachan, Pauline Panter, Joan Benton (courtesy Pat Strachan Stavig).

on the '78 team before becoming a starter in 1979. Captain Dana Jones was the point guard in 1978, leading the team in steals; Jan Lyle averaged nine points and nine rebounds per game as forward. The Warriors had two 6-footers in the post position: Robyn Clark, the leading rebounder, was always one of the first players down court; Teresa Hansen averaged three blocked shots per game. Clark went to OSU to play college basketball and later became the women's athletic director at OSU.

The following year the Peninsula Seahawks swept aside all opposition for a 27–0 record and the state 3A championship in 1979. Coach Paul Berg's cagers defeated Hanford High School in the title game, 52–46. The high-flying Seahawks zipped to a 24–12 lead with 18 points from Kim Larson, the regular-season league-leading scorer, and 15 more from Mary Ann Stoican. Hanford rallied for a 34–33 lead late in the third quarter, but Larson hooped a pair of buckets to give Peninsula the permanent lead. Stoican, with 15 rebounds, and sophomore Larson, with 10 caroms, led the backboard assault for the winners. Janelle Rice and Karen Uddenberg provided solid support in Peninsula's quest for the championship. Berg coached five years at Peninsula, then 19 at neighboring Gig Harbor High, and his teams made 10 state tournaments appearances while winning more than 300 games.

The Lincoln Lynx basketball team of 1947 coached by Norm Mayer (MB).

Nobody in the city, however, can top the 22 years that Jim Black invested at Foss High School, from 1978 to 2000. He finished with 323 wins against 168 losses, and the Falcons won nine league championships and advanced to state tournaments on six occasions. The Falcons enjoyed back-to-back 20–0 regular seasons and three straight state tournament trips from 1995 to 1997. Black also had the honor of winning both a Grid-Go-Round football championship and a Hoop-Go-Round basketball championship in 1983.

Among his top players were 6-foot 4-inch center Tatum Brown (who went on to play at the University of Arizona), All-America high school performer Debbie Weston (who also played at SU), forward Onitia Frazier, Collete Stewart (who played at EWU and coached at Puyallup High), and Bianca Ryan from Australia, a pure shooter who twice hit 10 three-pointers in a row.

Myrtle Peterson coached Lincoln High School's quintet for six years and made four state tournament appearances; the Abes were runner-up in 1980, losing to Garfield, 59–58. Her career record of 113 wins and just seven losses, however, bordered on perfection.

Clover Park won the 4A title a second time in '82. Coach Jim Angelel and team topped Auburn, 52–47, for the coveted state crown and finished the year 25–1. That lone loss came at the hands of Bellevue High in the opening game of district play, but Clover Park bounced back to defeat Garfield, Richland, and Blanchet to set the stage for the showdown game with Auburn.

Donya Monroe, Clover Park's top player, was one of the state's best-ever female hoopsters. She was an All-State tournament first-team choice and the tourney's MVP. Monroe averaged 20.2 points per game in high school and 10 rebounds. Selected by *Parade Magazine* as a prep All-America, Monroe was invited to play in the Dial All-American Game in New York City and received a tryout with the 1984 U.S. Olympic team. Other starters for the CPHS champs were Kathy Taylor, Michelle Clark, Netra McGrew, and Allison Lotspeich.

Another successful Tacoma coach was Mike McKay of Wilson. In his six years with the Wilson Rams (1989-94), he won three Narrows League championships and made two state tournament appearances. Top players for McKay

were Debbie Miller, Shannon Parker, and sisters Jennifer Kubista and Christy Kubista. Jennifer now is athletic director for Tacoma Public Schools.

Outstanding Players

Franklin Pierce High boasts Julie Kurrus and Patty Line: Kurrus, voted Most Valuable Player by the Central Division of the Seamount League in 1981, averaged 19.6 points per game. Line averaged 21.1 points as a freshman, a record that stood for 14 years.

Other top performers include Wendi Tibbs of Gig Harbor High from 1979–83 (who went on to play for UPS), Kelly Larson at Rogers High from 1985–89 (PLU), and Kim Larson (WSU) and Kathy Rue (UW) of Mount Tahoma High, from 1985–89 and 1982–85 respectively. Sarah Silvernail of Fife High also was outstanding, leading the Trojans to second in the state tournament in 1983, but her volleyball ability overshadowed her hoops. She was an NCAA All-America in volleyball at WSU.

Bellarmine's Chelle Flamoe averaged 25.9 points per game in 1985, which still stands as a district record. The Lions also produced the Butler sisters, Kim and Julie, who went on to play in college at Santa Clara University.

Lisa Graber graduated from Spanaway Lake High School in 1991. As a senior she led the state in scoring, with a 30.3-points-per-game average, and that same year she set a state record for most free throws made in a season, going 112 for 138. She was a member of the All-State team in 1991 and was an All-SPSL team selection for three years. She attended EWU on a basketball scholarship.

Dawn Lewis of Curtis High also ranks high with 27.1 points per game in 1992 and 19.7 a year earlier. Her rebounding records are even more impressive: 19.3 in '92, 17.3 in '91, and 15.1 in '93.

But it is Kate Starbird of Lakes High School who is considered the best player to come out of the region. Stanford University's all-time scoring star and College Player of the Year in 1997, Starbird is now a veteran of the Women's National Basketball Association (WNBA), having played with Utah, Seattle, Sacramento, and Indiana. She played the 2004 season in Spain, where she averaged 18.7 points per game. Starbird scored 2,553 points in her prep career (the best in state history) and averaged 29.3 points per game as a senior. Her 20.9 average and 2,215 points are all-time marks at Stanford, where she was an All-America performer.

Although Starbird is arguably the most successful female player from Pierce County high schools, many others have competed well and played hard. Ashley Blake graduated from Lakes High School in 2002. As a senior she led the state in scoring, with a 24.5-points-per-game average, and for her career she averaged 20.6 points per game. Her senior year she was 3A Player of the Year, All-Area Player of the Year, Seamount League Player of the Year, the *Tacoma News Tribune* Player of the Year, and a member of the Academic All-State first team. She attends CWU on a basketball scholarship

Following an NBA career with the New York Knicks and Detroit Pistons, Whitworth College grad Phil Jordan played Tacoma semipro basketball (MB).

In 2004 there were some new faces on the scene in girls' basketball. Shaunte Nance of Foss High was the Narrows League MVP and starred in the state tournament with games of 20, 13, and 23 points. Mount Tahoma High freshman Renesha Pate displayed promise for the future, with 29 points against Monroe High in the state tournament, and leading the T-Birds in the other two tourney games with 17 and 16 points, respectively. Two players with aspirations of playing Division I basketball include 6-foot 3-inch Ebonee Coates of Curtis High and Nikki Scott, a 5-foot 7-inch wing player who helped lead Gig Harbor to an eighth-place finish in the 4A state basketball tournament in 2004.

Clearly, high school basketball in Tacoma–Pierce County has its share of big moments and star performers across all levels and classifications of play. These headliners are just the tip of the area's basketball iceberg.

CHAPTER 12

BASKETBALL:
COLLEGE PLAYERS

*Jake Maberry of the UPS
Loggers drives to the hoop
(UPS).*

Community Colleges

Tacoma Community College (TCC) has a rich tradition in Northwest community college basketball circles, with championships in both men's and women's competition. A trio of coaches—Don Moseid, Ron Billings, and Carl Howell—shared in the success of Tacoma's men's program. Each of them has claimed one or more Northwest titles while coaching at TCC.

A college star at Seattle University (SU) and University of Puget Sound (UPS), Moseid was the head coach at Mount Tahoma High School prior to his TCC assignment. He was the first coach to give the TCC Titans credibility, winning 20 games or more in seven of his nine years at the Tacoma campus. In 1971 and 1974, his teams won the Northwest Athletic Association of Community Colleges (NAACC) Championship Tournament.

At TCC Moseid had 188 wins and 71 losses, coaching players such as Tommy Williams, Ron Oughton, and Bruce Larson, all of whom went on to start at UPS. Lincoln High's Tom Patnode and Dean Ecklund were other TCC starters. So was Maynard Brown of Los Angeles, who became one of the top scorers in the Ivy League after moving on to Cornell.

Coach Moseid attracted other quality players from out of state: Gary Juniel from Arizona was MVP of the Northwest community college tournament in 1974. Don Aaron was another Californian who starred at TCC. So did Floyd Haywood, a 6-foot 5-inch transfer from Trinidad and the brother of Seattle SuperSonics star Spencer Haywood. Dave Hunter, out of Jefferson High in Federal Way, was a top scorer in the South Puget Sound League (SPSL), at TCC, and later at Seattle Pacific University (SPU). Dave Oliver of New Orleans advanced to play at Central Washington University (CWU) after playing well for TCC.

Former Lincoln High coach Ron Billings, who with the Abes compiled one of prep basketball's glossiest records, also had quite a coaching career at TCC. Billings won 169 games and three Northwest crowns, and in his first two seasons at TCC he won back-to-back championships. TCC won in the finals in 1982, besting Walla Walla, 66–59, on Walla Walla's home court. Jon Carr, out of Washington High, and point guard Ron Billings Jr. (the coach's son) led the Titans to the upset win. They both were named All-Tournament, and Carr was picked as MVP. The next year, freshman Dave Danforth had 31 points in the 78–66 win over Centralia in the second title contest in 1983, and Sam Tuttle was named tournament MVP with 36 tourney points, 11 assists, and some outstanding defense.

The Titans made it three championships under Billings in 1986. No coach had won three championships previously, but a 74–66 verdict over Clark Community College decided the issue. Cornelius Williams, a 6-foot 2-inch forward from Lincoln High, was named the tourney MVP with 51 points in three games and 16 in the title tilt. Guard Bobby Barnette also was named All-Tournament. He had a game-high 22 in the decider.

With only eight able-bodied players, coach Jerry Shain was apprehensive about Titan women's chances in a three-day, three-game schedule at Yakima in 1986. It was TCC's first-ever appearance in the tournament (women's tournaments began in '79), but the TCC squad won its last 17 games in a row, to finish 23–4, beating Green River and Skagit Valley three times each during that stretch. The Lady Titans dumped Green River, 70–57, in the finale as Holly Hovey, a 5-foot 10-inch sophomore from Puyallup, tallied 17 and was named the tournament's MVP. She had 42 points in the three games. Ruth Ann Rufener, a 6-foot 1-inch sophomore from Clover Park High School, scored 54 points (22 in the championship game) and joined Hovey on the All-Star team.

With Coach Billings's win on the men's side, it was the first time one community college took both men's and women's championships in the same year. For the women, it was quite a season, since they'd started with a 1–3 record.

Carl Howell spent 10 seasons as TCC coach with a record of 236–83, and he developed quite a reputation for sending his players on to four-year programs. Division I NCAA schools alone claimed 25 players from Howell-coached teams. Howell's 2002 Titans won the Northwest Tournament Championship with an amazing 30–3 record. TCC topped Big Bend Community College in the title game, 88–78, for Tacoma's sixth community college championship. Josh Barsh, who later signed to play at Montana State, and Khary Nicholas, an EWU signee, were named to the All-Tournament team along with Fabrizio Mendiola, giving TCC three All-Tourney selections. Barsh was the MVP, while Nicholas led the Titans in the win over Big Bend with 24 points.

No Pierce College team has been able to finish in the top six of postseason play, but one of the Pierce Raiders, Bob Webb, was besieged by offers from major-college programs. Webb played for coach Ray Kinnaman at Fort Steilacoom Community College (as Pierce was formerly known) and performed well enough to earn a scholarship from John Wooden at UCLA. Webb was a member of the national champion Bruins the next year, earning an NCAA championship ring in St. Louis in 1973.

Pacific Lutheran University Men's Teams

Cliff Olson is listed as PLU's very first basketball coach; his record from 1938 to 1941 was 43–16, the best winning percentage in school history at .729. The next two years, however, were easy to forget. The Lutes were 3–16 and 0–17 during that stretch under two different coaches before calling on Hall of Fame coach-to-be Marv Harshman. In the next 13 years, he brought 236 wins to the Parkland campus before assuming the head coaching duties at Washington State University (WSU) and then University of Washington (UW). The Harshman era is remembered as the most exciting ever for Lute basketball.

Marv Harshman seems like a theme in this history of Pierce County sports. He was born in 1917 near Lake Stevens, Washington, attended Lake Stevens High School, and graduated from PLU in 1942, where he played both football and basketball. As a PLU student, Harshman was Little All-America (1941), All-Conference (1938–1941), team Most Valuable Player (1939–1941), the Washington Intercollegiate Conference (WInCo)'s leading touchdown scorer for three straight years as fullback (1939–41), and a two-time basketball All-American. In 1945, when he began coaching basketball at PLU, he also played basketball for the Tacoma Mountaineers.

During the Harshman years, PLU streaked to the front of the class among the Northwest's small-college cagers. A 27-game winning streak, four straight trips to the National Association of Intercollegiate Athletics (NAIA) playoffs, a third-place and second-place national finish, four Evergreen Conference championships, and a 51–3 record from 1956 to 1959 were many of the highlights. Among the recruits "Harsh" brought to PLU was Gene Lundgaard, a shooting star from Anacortes who would become Harshman's successor as coach for 17 years and win more games—280—than any other PLU hoop strategist.

Lundgaard and "High" Harry McLaughlin stole the headlines for the Lutes at this time. McLaughlin was the highest-scoring player in the Northwest, with nearly 24 points per game, in the mid-1940s. His duels with University of Puget Sound's Rod Gibbs were so heralded that neither gym at PLU or UPS could hold the crowds, necessitating a move to the Tacoma Armory. McLaughlin not only could score, but his ball handling rivaled that of a Harlem Globetrotter!

Lundgaard was more steady than spectacular, but his deadly shooting was devastating to Lute opponents; he dominated a strong UPS team in 1951 when the Lutes beat the Loggers five straight, the final by a single point (on a Lundgaard buzzer-beater) for a coveted trip to the NAIA championships. In the process he set a single-game scoring record in the UPS Fieldhouse with 38 points against the Loggers.

By the time Harshman retired in 1985, his coaching career had covered 40 years at PLU (1945–1958), WSU (1958–1971), and UW (1971–1985), where collectively he amassed 642 victories. "Harshman earned the admiration

In the late 1950s the Lutes' basketball team featured the dynamic "Big 3:" Chuck Curtis (#30), Jim Van Beek (#35), and Roger Iverson (#11) (PLU).

CHAPTER SPONSORED BY

COLUMBIA BANK:

Tacoma-based Columbia Bank is committed to serving its customers and the communities around it. With 34 branches in Pierce, King, Kitsap, Thurston, and Cowlitz counties, Columbia and its employees have sponsored Three-on-Three Basketball, the Tacoma Rainiers, and the Mariners, in addition to countless local sports leagues. But the bank's dedication goes beyond sports, reaching into academics, music, the arts, businesses, universities, and youth groups. Corporate offices can be reached at: Columbia Banking System, Inc., 1301 A Street, Suite 800, Tacoma, WA 98402; P.O. Box 2156, Tacoma, WA 98401-2156; (253) 305-1900 or (800) 305-1905; www.columbiabank.com.

and undivided attention of every team he coached," reports his Naismith Memorial Hall of Fame biography compiled in 1985, the year of his induction.

"Beginning at Pacific Lutheran, he coached four NAIA District 1 basketball champions. His 1957 team finished with a 28–1 record, and his 1959 club finished runner-up for the NAIA national title. In 13 years at WSU, Harshman produced three second-place teams in the conference. Harshman concluded his coaching career at UW, where he was selected NCAA Division I Coach of the Year in 1984 and Pac-10 Coach of the Year in 1982 and 1984. Four of his UW teams won 20 or more games, with 11 of 14 squads winning at least 16 games. Harshman, who served as a member of the U.S. Olympic Committee from 1975 to 1981, coached the U.S. [basketball team] to a gold medal in the 1975 Pan American Games."

The years of Evergreen Conference competition were fierce. Not only were PLU and UPS in the upper echelon of league play, so were CWU, Eastern Washington University (EWU), and Western Washington University (WWU). It was almost impossible for one team to break away from the pack, and the excitement reached an all-time high.

But PLU ended all that in 1955 with the enrollment of Chuck Curtis, Roger Iverson, and Jim Van Beek. Former *News Tribune* sportswriter Earl Luebker explained:

Chuck Curtis … Roger Iverson … Jim Van Beek. Three young men in the right place at the right time.

The place? Pacific Lutheran College. It was a college when the Terrific Trio played in Parkland, not a university as it is now.

The time? The basketball seasons of 1955–56, 1956–57, 1957–58, 1958–59. Those were magical, glory years of college basketball in Tacoma as Curtis, Iverson, and Van Beek teamed to form the nucleus of a monopoly in the old Evergreen Conference, the likes of which had never been seen before. They made the PLC Memorial Gymnasium rock on its foundations and made the National Association of Intercollegiate Athletics tournament in Kansas City their home away from home.

Better individual basketball players have and will come along, but it is unlikely that three of their talent, skills, and chemistry will arrive at one small college at the same time. "It was a miracle, really," said Marv Harshman, who coached them through three years. Gene Lundgaard, who coached the Terrific Trio during its senior year at PLC, did not disagree with the miracle assessment. "They were the keys to the best team PLC has ever fielded," Lundgaard said.

The trio under Harshman and Lundgaard led the Lutes to four Evergreen Conference championships, posting a 51–3 record over four years, winning 38 consecutive league games and going unbeaten (36–0) in their last three years. Curtis and Iverson made the All-Conference team all four years they were at PLC. Van Beek was something of a laggard—he made it only during his junior and senior years.

They had four trips to the NAIA tournament in Kansas City, finishing third in 1957 after a one-point (71–70) loss to champion Tennessee State in the semifinals and second in 1959, again losing to Tennessee State (97–87) in the title game. Two of their four losses in Kansas City were to three-time champion Tennessee State. The other two defeats were to top-seeded Western Illinois, 72–67, in 1956 and Georgetown, Kentucky (92–91) in overtime in 1958. Those two losses both came in the second round.

No doubt about it, the Curtis–Iverson–Van Beek era at PLC was a magical time. "Community and fan support were unbelievable," Van Beek said. "Memorial Gym was the place to be. At times, it seemed as if we were the only game in town."

How did the three arrive on the PLC campus at the same time?

Curtis made the relatively long haul from Richland. Iverson and Van Beek didn't have to travel so extensively—Iverson played his high school basketball at Lincoln in Tacoma, and Van Beek was from Franklin Pierce, just a couple of dribbles away from the campus.

Curtis was recruited by UW, and Iverson actually spent a little time with the Huskies. But both ended up in Parkland to the surprise and delight of Harshman.

"We were lucky to get Chuck," Harshman said of the 6-foot 5-inch All-Stater. "We didn't have much to offer back in those days, and I think we were only an afterthought after we managed to come up with some money for room and board for his girlfriend from Richland who wanted to come to PLC. Roger wasn't happy at UW and decided he could be happier at PLC. We were happy that he made that decision. Van Beek wasn't heavily recruited. He was a 6-foot 3-inch center in high school, but we felt that he had some potential."

Curtis and Iverson fit in immediately, starting as freshmen and making the All-Evergreen team as yearlings. Van Beek was a late bloomer. He didn't start until he was a sophomore. "We started using Jim as a forward," Harshman said, "and then we moved him to guard. That turned out to be the place for him." Lundgaard said, "Jim might have been the best of the three, as he matured after college. He might have stood the best chance to make it in the National Basketball Association if he had chosen to go that route."

Curtis played the high post in Harshman's high-low post offense as if the position had been invented for him. He could pass off to the open man and drive or shoot from the key. "He was the quickest big man I'd ever seen," Harshman said. The 5-foot 9-inch Iverson was a master of the fall-away-jumper, a shot that had Harshman often saying, "No, no, no," when Roger launched it and "Yes, yes, yes," after it swished through the net. He might have been the team's leading scorer if they had the three-pointer back then.

The 6-foot 3-inch Van Beek was a competent, efficient player who could shoot from long range, drive, and play tough defense. "He was probably the best defensive player we had," Lundgaard said. "It was always a good defensive team, but that was often overlooked because of the things they could do on offense," Harshman added. "The three provided us with weapons, but we had a good supporting cast over the years. You have to have that to win as many games as we did, but they gave us something to build around. All three had the ability to be innovative and all had an uncanny instinct for the game. They always seemed to make the right choices. I learned a lot about coaching in those three years I was with them."

"It was a bit of luck that the three of us got there at the same time," Van Beek said. "The chemistry was unbelievable. We complemented each other, and we had two great coaches,

Bob Sprague, a 6 feet 9 inches center from Wilson High, played for the Loggers and participated in the 1964 Olympic Trials (UPS).

Harshman and Lundgaard. Harsh was one of the greatest. Rog and Chuck were superconfident. They always thought we'd win. I was the doubting Thomas. I always felt that if we played well and things went right, we stood a chance."

Both Marv Harshman and Gene Lundgaard admit that the Pacific Lutheran magic went beyond the Terrific Trio, to team members such as Bob Roiko, Norm Dahl, Bill Williams, and Rich Hamlin. Phil Nordquist, Jack Sinderson, Jack Hoover, Dennis Ross, Denny Rodin, Mick Kelderman, Al Gubrud, Ardeen Iverson, Bruce Alexander, Chuck Geldaker, and Ralph Carr were others. Even Lute Jerstad—now among the canon of Pierce County folk who have climbed Mount Everest—was a part of the Pacific Lutheran basketball magic.

With the help of their fellow hoopsters and coaches, the Lute trio of Curtis, Iverson, and Van Beek played basketball and won. They collectively wrote some rather exciting chapters of sports history in the process.

Lundgaard followed Harshman with 17 years of solid coaching, although the demise of the Evergreen Conference prompted some changes in opponents and program direction for Lute basketball.

In 1967 the Lutes shared the Northwest Conference championship and they repeated that effort in 1973 and 1978. They also won the league title outright in 1968, 1971, 1974, 1979, and 1980. By 1976 Ed Anderson had taken over as head coach and he won 119 games until 1983. Then Bruce Haroldson became the Lute leader, winning 250 games until 2002.

What goes around sometimes comes around, and in 2003 Marv Harshman's son David was given the assignment to coach future PLU teams. David didn't come without some credentials. He was an assistant to Jud Heathcoate at Michigan State University when the Spartans, led by Magic Johnson, won the NCAA championships, and David also was an assistant with the Seattle Supersonics in the NBA.

The Iverson–Curtis–Van Beek trio did not hog all the hardware at PLU. Over time, six other Lutes have been given NAIA All-America honors, Doug Leeland became an Academic All-American in 1967, 13 Lutes were named to All-District teams, 22 were named to All-Conference teams, and five were named MVPs or Players of the Year.

The All-America choices were Hans Albertson (second team in 1962), Curt Gammel (third team in 1963), Tom Whalen (second team in 1964), Gammel again (first team in 1966), and Don Brown, Geoff Grass, and Seth Albright (all honorable mentions in '91, '93, and '97, respectively). Albright also was named to third team in 1998.

In 1964 and '65, Whalen and Gammell were selected NAIA District 1 Players of the Year. In 1984, '85, and '86, the Northwest Conference named three PLU players as league MVPs: Ed Boyce, Jeff Valentine, and Dan Gibbs. From 1980 to 1991, Dave Lashua, John Greenquist, Dan Allen, Mike Cranston, Paul Boots, and Don Brown joined Boyce, Gibbs, and Valentine as NAIA District 1 All-Stars. Lashua was picked twice.

PLU's "official" games spanned 65 years and produced 941 victories. Attaway, Lutes!

University of Puget Sound Men's Teams

Every decade of UPS basketball seems to have a major moment or a bona fide star player, beginning in the '20s. Harry Enochs was the first. Twice the Logger captain, in 1924 Enochs tallied 131 of the team's 381 points, averaging 10.1 per game on a team that averaged 29. Frank Wilson followed, named to three successive All–Northwest Conference teams before moving on to become an Amateur Athletic Union (AAU) All-America while playing for the great San Francisco Olympic team, coached by Clyde "Cac" Hubbard, former UPS athletic director. (In fact, sensational play in the national AAU tournament in Kansas City won Wilson recognition as the outstanding guard in the United States.) Wilson and the Loggers of 1928 handed UW a 35–21 defeat, one of only six suffered by the Huskies en route to 22 wins and the Pacific Coast Conference Northern Division championship. It was an "iron man" performance by the Loggers, who played the entire game without substitution.

In the '30s, Erling Tollefson had 11 points in UPS's 30–29 victory over UW in 1937, and Tom Cross enrolled at UPS to become a member of the first UPS team to win a Northwest Conference hoop title. He became the team's leading scorer in 1941–42 and then played on Tacoma's only professional basketball team, the Tacoma Mountaineers.

The '40s began with Norm Walker being chosen to the All-Northwest Conference team as a freshman, a feat he repeated as a sophomore while setting a school record with a 15.8-point-per-game scoring average. Tragically, Walker was killed in a traffic accident before the start of his junior year. Teammate Harry Werbisky, also named All-Conference as a frosh, had died a year earlier from a tooth infection, ending one of the most promising athletic careers in college history. He had been a brilliant three-sport star at nearby Stadium High and seemed certain for a similar career at UPS, helping lead the Loggers to their first Northwest Conference title.

In the late '40s, John Heinrick was a high school football coaching legend in Tacoma, one of the finest teachers and motivators in the Northwest. Moving from Stadium High to nearby UPS in 1948, Heinrick quickly won the Northwest Conference basketball title and contended every year for the newly formed Evergreen Conference (EvCo). Many local athletes returned home from the service and utilized their GI bills instead of athletic scholarships to enroll at UPS. The Loggers joined PLU and Whitworth to challenge CWU, EWU, and WWU in the EvCo ranks.

Heinrick's 1948 arrival on campus to coach the hoopsters resulted in yearly runs at conference crowns and district NAIA playoffs. It also triggered the enrollment of a host of talented basketball players who became outstanding high school coaches in the state of Washington. Jake Maberry of Lynden was first to arrive, transferring from WSU. A free-

The St. Joseph's A. C. team was the 1934 champions of the Church–Commercial Basketball League: standing, L. to R., manager George Karpach, Joe Kocha, N. Mladinich, F. Sakalik, Bert Kocha, A. Ribar, coach A. Berilla; sitting, L. to R., F. Svoboda, captain C. Paulik, John Paulik (courtesy Barbara Kocha Harrison).

throw shooting wizard (82 percent in his career), he also ranked as one of the smoothest ball handlers in Logger history. Given the name of "Automatic" Jake, Maberry set school records for most free throws in a game (16), season (192), and career (450).

In the 1948–49 season, the state basketball spotlight shifted to the Tacoma Armory. There UW, fresh from twin wins at the University of Illinois and one of the favorites to win the Pacific Coast Conference, visited "tiny" UPS.

Except the Loggers weren't tiny. With the transfer of rangy Rod Gibbs (a 6-foot 7-inch center from UW) and backups such as 6-foot 6-inch Bob Rinker and 6-foot 6-inch Bill Richey, UPS was not short on height. Dick Brown, a strong 6-foot 4-inch forward who also excelled in football, and sharpshooting Bobby Fincham, the team's leading scorer, led an upset. Gibbs controlled the boards with 11 rebounds,

Tim Evans played forward for University of Puget Sound's 1976 national basketball championship team (UPS).

Fincham had 15 points, and Brown held UW star Sammy White (later a Boston Red Sox catcher) to seven. The Loggers downed the Huskies, 48–41. Brown, a former star at Stadium, was a major factor in leading the Loggers to their first NAIA national tournament in Kansas City.

Fincham's ability to score should have been no surprise. The former Stadium High star had been the Northwest Conference scoring leader as a freshman, became team captain, and was a four-year starter and All-Conference selection. In 1946 he had back-to-back outbursts against the College of Idaho in the old campus gym, hitting 41 and 33 points in successive starts. Considering the usually lower team scores of that era (College of Idaho totalled 73 points in the two games, to Fincham's 74), those individual achievements were major.

Gibbs also starred in the next two years, leading the Loggers to the NAIA tournament in 1949 and '50. His duels with PLU's Harry McLaughlin were the talk of the town. McLaughlin led all Northwest collegians in scoring, with Gibbs in hot pursuit, but it was defense and rebounds that paid off for the Logger big man. In their senior season, Gibbs accepted the challenge and held McLaughlin to nine points in all three meetings. "Hot" Rod had 23, 17, and 19 points in those matchups and added a handful of fouls to his all-time UPS record for most personal fouls.

Russ Wilkerson, Warren Moyles, Dan Inveen, Don Moseid, Ron Brown, and Bob Bafus all followed, and Heinrick taught them well. Not only did they star on the court, but they took his coaching lessons with them to highly successful high school and college coaching assignments. Maberry became a legend in his hometown of Lynden, winning 531 games and four state titles with a 40–15 state tourney record. At Goldendale High, Wilkerson's teams dominated the Yakima Valley annually for six years (winning 19 of 20 in the 1961 regular season) and placed high in every state tourney he qualified for prior to his advancement to UPS coach in 1962. Moyles brought North Kitsap teams to place high in state tournaments before coaching a Northwest AAU championship team in Tacoma in the '60s. Inveen battled Tacoma's powerful Lincoln High teams for city titles regularly while coaching Wilson High and then became Tacoma Public Schools athletic director. Moseid had an unbeaten regular season (20–0) at "new" Mount Tahoma High and later coached TCC to seven 20-win seasons, five league titles, and two NAACC championships. Bafus returned home and had a Hall of Fame career at Colfax, where he won 604 games and back-to-back state titles. Brown was still coaching (42 years) at Centralia in 2003 with 568 victories, the second-best mark in the state among active coaches. Clearly, Coach Heinrick had an impact on these players' lives and the coaching philosophy they espoused.

In the early '60s, Wally Erwin returned to campus after a three-sport career at UPS to coach basketball. One of his early recruits was the biggest man ever to play at UPS to date: Bob Sprague, a graduate of neighboring Wilson High. He was 6 feet 9 inches and 245 pounds. Sprague set six school records in three seasons (a bout of mononucleosis took away his senior year) and was chosen to be a candidate for the national team in the Olympic trials of 1964. He averaged 21.8 points per game and grabbed 758 rebounds, scoring 35 points against Whitworth and 32 against Division I SU, and retrieving 32 rebounds against SPU (nine more than the entire Falcon team), still a UPS single-game record.

By 1968 Wilkerson replaced Erwin at the helm of the Loggers and recruited a trio of run-and-shoot Arizona cagers who had played at Phoenix College. Their impact was immediate: Dave Lindstrom, Argie Rhymes, and John Smith joined Logger superfrosh Charles Lowry, and UPS won its first 13 games. Lindstrom's 47-point effort against St. Martin's College that season still stands as a school record for most points scored in a single game. Smith led all UPS scorers for the season (1,002) and later became a Harlem Globetrotter. Rhymes, destined to be one of most successful high school coaches in Phoenix history, with more than 500 wins, still holds two school records for free-throw attempts, and he was a relentless rebounder.

A year later, Wilkerson decided to give up coaching and in 1969 the Don Zech era began. Junior-college transfers Ed Huston and Howard Clark and major-college transfers Chet Hovde and Mike Jordan joined the Phoenix trio and Charles Lowry to establish UPS as near-unbeatable. Only three last-minute losses (one by a single point, another in overtime) kept UPS from an unbeaten record.

The "Ed and Charles Show" dominated Northwest college basketball headlines for three years as UPS hammered small-college teams and took on every Division I foe willing to play. When the Loggers smacked the University of Montana by 25 points in Missoula, the Grizzlies proclaimed them the "best team" they had played all year (Montana had just beaten UW the week before).

Following these consecutive 24-win seasons that started his UPS coaching career, Zech had his first national title opportunity in 1971. The Loggers were primed, with 23 wins and a regular season–ending rout of Division I SU. In that home finale, Charles Lowry climaxed a great four-year career with a 36-point performance. He graduated to the NBA and the world-champion Milwaukee Bucks but not before the effort of his life in the Division II semifinals.

Unfortunately for the Loggers, a spill by scoring leader Ed Huston (26-point-per-game average) in the next-to-last game of the regular season resulted in a broken arm and his loss for the nationals. Lowry gamely tried to fill the void and outscored Old Dominion All-America Dave Twardzik (later a star guard with Portland in the NBA) 36–9 in a one-point loss to the Monarchs at Evansville, Indiana. UPS had its winning-shot attempt swirl out at the buzzer in the single-elimination final-four round.

In 1976 Zech's UPS men's program scaled the heights to become the first Northwest team ever to win the NCAA Division II Championship. Zech's championship team topped North Dakota (80–77), Old Dominion (83–78), and Tennessee Chattanooga (83–74) to claim the crown, winning the final 13 games of the season for an overall record of 27–7. In those 34 games, the sweet-shooting Loggers connected on 50.8 percent of their shots, the best in school history.

Curt Peterson, a 7-foot center from Seattle, led the Loggers with a 20.9-points-per-game average on 57.1 percent shooting and a free-throw shooting mark of 84.2 percent. Bremerton's Rick Walker and Tim Evans of Blaine, both All-State prep stars, averaged more than 15 points a game for the tall and talented Tacomans, who had a starting lineup averaging 6 feet 7 inches.

The other usual starters on that 1976 team were 6-foot 8-inch forward Brant Gibler of Bremerton and 6-foot 5-inch guard Rocky Botts of Tacoma's Wilson High. All five starters played their high school basketball in Washington state. Among the reserves who played most often were sixth-man guard Mark Wells of Curtis High, freshman center Phil Hiam of White River, 6-foot 6-inch forward A. T. Brown of Compton, California, and speedster guard Jimmy Stewart of Las Vegas, Nevada. Completing the squad were guards Matt McCully of Federal Way (Jefferson High), Mike Strand of Seattle, Mike Kuntz of Wenatchee, Bill Greenheck of Kirkland, and 6-foot 6-inch forwards Mike Hanson of Wilson High and Steve Freimuth of Omak.

Peterson was named the NCAA Tournament MVP, while the unheralded Gibler, with 22 points in the title

Charles Lowery had a stellar career at University of Puget Sound before enjoying a brief stint in the NBA (UPS).

game, also was named to the All-Tournament team. Walker, Gibler, and Peterson received All–Western Region honors a week earlier, while Evans and Peterson were selected on the All-Northwest team.

How dominant was the UPS program? The Loggers were 23–1 against college division foes (splitting games with NAIA powerhouse CWU) and 4–6 in 10 games versus Division I (major-college) teams.

The national championship was particularly enjoyable for Zech since he had predicted early in the season that his '76 team would "win it all." No stranger to success, Zech took 11 UPS teams to postseason tournaments.

Following Zech's championship years from 1970 through 1976, the Loggers won a Western Region championship in 1979 behind 6-foot 8-inch All-America center Joe Leonard and smooth-shooting 6-foot 6-inch southpaw forward Eric Brewe; that team was ranked number one nationally in the NCAA's Division II final poll of the year.

As the '80s dawned, UPS teams had three straight 20-plus-win seasons and another 100 wins. Maurice Selvin arrived via McChord Air Force Base as Zech's final long-range bomber, benefitting from the three-point shot rule that hadn't existed for the likes of Lowery, Huston, and Lindstrom before him. Selvin averaged 21.9 points per game.

By '89, Zech decided that 21 years of college coaching was enough. The Loggers were well prepared for the future, however, and so he retired to spend more time with his family and 15 grandchildren.

Team success didn't result in any 20-win seasons in the '90s although the Loggers managed some solid individual marks. Under coach Bob Niehl, Puyallup High's Brian Vukelich was the Loggers' big threat at 6 feet 9 inches. He had 1,270 points and 779 rebounds in his career, in the top five among school record setters.

Other Loggers who starred under Niehl were Matt Droege, Jon Mitchell, Mark Schultz, Mike Miller, and Pat Mullen. Droege, from Cottage Grove, Oregon, is third all-time in rebounding at UPS with 793 and third in most field goals with 753 (in 1,350 attempts). He scored 41 points in one game against Lewis and Clark State College and twice was an All-League choice. He also was a first-team All-Region selection.

Mitchell holds the third-highest field goal percentage mark in Logger history: 56.3 percent. He and Schultz both earned All-District NAIA honors along with playmaker Mullen. Miller made more three-point field goals than any other Logger—154—and attempted the most three-pointers: 420.

By the year 2003, in 80 seasons, UPS cagers had won 1,146 games under 15 different coaches while losing only 889. Don Zech coached 21 of those years, enjoying 11 seasons with more than 20 wins and compiling a career record of 405 wins and 196 losses.

Coach Eric Bridgeland now guides UPS basketball fortunes in NCAA Division III ranks. His sights are set on creating a new dynasty, and his opening shots in 2003–04 resulted in a 24–3 regular-season mark and a berth in the NCAA postseason tournament. A loss in the quarterfinals at home came when the eventual national champion, Wisconsin Stevens Point, claimed a 100–85 win.

But the Loggers discovered that they were competitive on a national level in Division III, and most of Bridgeland's team returns for another try (only one starter, All-Star guard Matt Glynn, graduated in 2004). The Loggers look loaded for another crack at nationals.

Pacific Lutheran University Women's Teams

Back in 1926, Polly Langlow of PLU scored 270 points in 13 games, setting what was most likely a national women's scoring record, according to research conducted by former PLU sports information director Nick Dawson. "The advent of the College Female Athletic Association, which believed that women would be damaged by too much exercise, put intercollegiate athletics for women pretty much on hold until the 1960s," reported Dawson. Despite the lack of national score-keeping, Langlow's feat is impressive even by today's standards, as is that of her team, the 1926 PLU Dianas, as they were known, which scored 431 points in a 13-game season. Historical records suggest that there was a mix of college, amateur, and high school competition that made up the schedule. It wasn't until 1972 that the Lady Lutes took the floor in their first intercollegiate competition, finishing with a rather modest 9–10 record and continuing with only seven winning seasons in their first 25 years.

Corky Deetz coached the first PLU women's team and had a three-year record of 33–21 before Kathy Hemion took over in 1975. Although the Lady Lutes competed in the Association of Intercollegiate Athletics for Women (AIAW) national tournament in 1980, Hemion's best season was 1982 when the Lutes won 18 games. Mary Ann Kluge then coached PLU for 12 years with solid seasons in '89 (18–9 record) and '97 (17–9). She was named Northwest Conference Coach of the Year at the end of the 1988–89 campaign.

After coaching both boys and girls basketball teams and tennis for seven years at nearby Lakes High School, Gil Rigell began coaching the Lutherans in 1997, and they have won 77.1 percent of their games since he arrived. A PLU alum, Rigell played varsity tennis in college. Rigell's basketball teams posted 20 wins or more in his first six seasons before an 18–6 record in 2003–04. With a career record of 145–43 at PLU, Rigell has taken the Lute women cagers to NCAA national tournaments in 1999, 2000, 2002, and 2003. A 7–4 record in NCAA national play has included at least one victory in every tourney appearance. In 1998 they competed in NAIA Division II nationals but they lost in the first round.

Rigell's teams have won or shared four conference championships, and he was selected as Northwest Conference Coach of the Year in 1999. In 2002 they reached the quarterfinals of the Division III championships before losing to Wisconsin–Stevens Point. That Lute team compiled 23 wins, the most in a single season in PLU history.

The most decorated players in PLU history are Kim Cobray, Kelly Larson, Tara Millet, and Becky Franza. Cobray accounted for five of the top-10 scoring performances in a single game while wearing the black and gold. In 1998 she hit for 34 and 33 points in two games, 31 and 29 in 1996, and 29 in 1997. She was a four-time selection to the All–Northwest Conference first team and the only PLU player ever to be named Most Valuable Player in the league (1997). Cobray also was a second-team NAIA All-America in 1998 and PLU's all-time leading scorer, with 1,730 points. She also holds the record for single-season scoring mark of 492 points and the most steals in career (289) and season (102).

Larson twice was named first-team All-Conference and twice second-team. She was PLU's career record-holder in assists, with 440, and second in career scoring, with 1,545 points. Three times she set a single-game record for steals, with 11, all during the '87 season, and she ranks fourth in career steals, with 190. She also ranks as the school leader in free-throw percentage, with 84.5 percent for a season and 79.1 percent for a career. Currently she is the only women's basketball player in PLU's Sports Hall of Fame. She was inducted in 2002.

Millet was a three-time All-Conference first-team pick and was named Conference Player of the Year in 1999. She also earned honorable mention All-America honors in 1998.

Becky Franza was another three-time All-Conference first-team choice. She ranks second in the PLU record book for career assists (423), three-point field goal percentage (34.7 percent), and free-throw percentage (75.5 percent) and third in career steals (193).

Tanya Wilson holds the single-game scoring record at PLU, with 36 points on January 28, 1995. Others with 29 or

Stadium High and University of Puget Sound grads Tom Names (L.) and Don Moseid take it to the hoop (UPS).

more points include Tasie Hampton (33), Melanie Bakala (30), Gail Ingram (29), and Tara Millet (29).

Jessica Iserman holds the single-game PLU rebound record with 23, versus Western Baptist in 2001. She also had 19 earlier against Whitworth. Millet had a 21-rebound effort against SU in 1998.

Significant PLU team records incude 95 points scored in one game against Lewis and Clark College, 69 rebounds grabbed in a single game against Lewis and Clark, a .654 shooting game against CWU, and a perfect 12-for-12 free-throw shooting performance against UPS.

With Rigell returning for the 2004–05 season, look for the Lady Lutes to continue their winning ways. The records say there's a 77.1 percent possibility.

University of Puget Sound Women's Teams

Women's basketball at UPS celebrated its 30th anniversary as an intercollegiate sport in 2002. Evalyn Goldberg would be proud. Goldberg was captain and MVP of the first Lady Logger basketball team and of the varsity volleyball and softball teams as well. She may have been the best all-around female athlete in school history and is the only woman to win the Ben Cheney Award as outstanding UPS athlete of the year. Upon her graduation, she also became the first woman basketball coach at UPS.

Prior to Goldberg's ascent to coaching, three men led the Lady Logger program. Chuck Bingham was the first varsity women's coach in 1973, and after two seasons, Brian Steberl and Tom Knutson were co-coaches. After Goldberg coached for two years, Sally Leyse coached for nine years, with back-to-back season records in 1986 (20–8) and 1987 (23–8). Dr. Beth Bricker then coached for eight years; her 1997 team went 22–5 with a 15–1 league record. Both Bricker and Leyse were honored by their peers with Coach of the Year designations during their UPS seasons.

Coach Suzy Barcomb became the third women's basketball coach at UPS to win Coach of the Year recognition and the first female coach in Northwest Conference history to win a game in the NCAA tournament. Her record after six years with the Loggers is 107–48, and she has recorded three seasons with 20 wins or more, two with 19.

The 2003–04 UPS cagers had the best season in school history, with a record of 23–5, and advanced to the "Elite Eight" in the NCAA Division III Tournament. A come-from-behind 51–46 win over PLU in Parkland triggered the Loggers' trip to the Northwest Conference championship and on to nationals. Junior forward Lindsay May of Richland took charge of the comeback at PLU and led UPS scorers for the year while earning All-Conference honors. (May has tallied 1,187 points at UPS and ranks fifth among all-time Logger scorers, with a season left to go.)

A victory over Linfield College on the road, 68–55, actually clinched the title when PLU lost its final game of the year, and that sent the Loggers traveling. A first-round win in the NCAA tournament, 61–53, at Chapman College in California, and a sensational 70–66 decision over Buena Vista, Iowa, in Crestview Hills, Kentucky, placed the Loggers among the top eight in the entire country. A disputed call as time ran out in their game against eventual national champions from Wilmington, Ohio, however, left the Lady Loggers thinking "wait till next year." The 63–60 loss ended the best season ever for UPS women.

The most prolific scoring team at the school was actually the 1986–87 squad. In a game with Sheldon Jackson State, the Lady Loggers launched 107 field goal attempts and tallied 113 points, 47 field goals, and 77 rebounds. The Loggers claimed a 113–67 victory, with Keely Running scoring 36 points.

The best individual scoring effort in school history, however, came from Kristina Goos, who scored 41 points against CWU in 1995–96. Goos also had 35 against Lewis and Clark State that season. Both Goos and Running appear throughout the record books at UPS. They are one-two in scoring average, with Running at 18.3 per game and Goos at 15.9. Annie Pettigrew (15.8), Lindsay May (15.0), and Julie Vanni (14.1) complete the top five. Vanni and Goos were NAIA All-America selections: Vanni was named to the third team in 1998–99 and Goos to the third team in 1996–97. Wendi Tibbs and Trish Armstrong have been honorable mentions.

Since the start of conference play, Goos has been named to three All-Conference first teams and one second team. Vanni was a first-team choice twice and a second-teamer. May looks ahead to her final season after being named to

first team twice. Other first-team picks have been Lucy Wilson, Tina Garrett, Kasa Tupua, and Wendy Davis.

Also spotted among Logger leaders statistically are Caron Zech and Linda (Zech) deVries, daughters of UPS men's coaching legend Don Zech. Linda was a first-team All–NAIA District performer in 1988–89.

Another prominent name among the women of UPS was Kelly Brewe. Husband Eric was a scoring star of the UPS men's team, and Kelly did her share with the women's five (once tallying 33 against Northwest Nazarene). They earned a mention in *Sports Illustrated* in 1981 for being a unique husband-and-wife hoop duo at UPS!

Lakes High School graduate Kate Starbird played at Stanford before joining the professional ranks as a member of the Seattle Reign, seen here in 1997 playing against the San Jose Lasers (SSM, 1991.1.5).

CHAPTER 13.

BASKETBALL:
AMATEUR AND PRO

Chuck Gilmur played in the NBA from 1946-51 and locally for the Cheney Studs (SSM, 2000.4.44).

In the years before the National Basketball Association (NBA) was formed, regional professional and amateur leagues existed throughout the country. Young men from Tacoma and Pierce County were playing basketball by the early 1920s. "No one could have had more fun," player Fred Osmers said. "The whole town, lumber camp, or village had a town team or company team. … We often found small-town teams who had played together all the way through the lower grades, high school, and beyond. Eatonville, for instance, had a town team made up of former members of the Eatonville High School team that went to Chicago for the National Interscholastic tournament." With nothing for the teams to do all winter but practice, the local competitions were keen and well followed by the public.

Osmers played amateur basketball in both Tacoma and Seattle from 1920 to 1934, and his life as a hoopster illustrated what the sport must have been like for many players during this era. While in Tacoma, Osmers first played for the McCormick Brothers team and then for the Y Outing

Club sponsored by the YMCA. He also was part of the John Dower Lumber Company, Lacey Farm Dairy, and Wheeler-Osgood teams during the course of his 14 years of playing basketball.

In his autobiography, Osmers included newspaper reports of the many City League basketball teams, players, and episodes of tournament play, providing a portrait of a lively spectator sport loved by many Tacomans. He also introduced the world of exhibition games. These competitions combined the best local basketball talent against traveling teams formed on the basis of race or ethnicity. In the 1930s in Tacoma, spectators were shown the basketball wizardry of Olson's Terrible Swedes, the House of David, the Los Angeles Hotentots, and the Harlem Globetrotters.

The Lincoln High School gymnasium was the venue for one such game in the mid-1930s, when Osmers and Hal "Stork" McClary's team lost to the famed House of David club. "After their displaying a fine passing game and a near-perfect game, together with a brand of comedy that kept the crowd in an uproar," reported one newspaper at the time, "the traveling House of David basketball team lived up to its reputation." Trick passing amazed the spectators, while the Tacoma players had a difficult time following the ball in this 38-to-33 mishap.

Various league championships also were a feature in Pierce County's steady amateur schedule year after year. George Karpach was one of the more successful coaches. His St. Joseph's Athletic Club team ruled the Commercial, Church, and Crusade Leagues for a decade in the late '20s and early '30s. But in the city championships, several different teams prevailed, many with players who stayed together as a team but switched sponsors. Some favorites included the Cammarano Bottlers (with Twang Root Beer across their jerseys), Pacific Mutual Fuel, and the Tacoma Shipyard Sheetmetal five. Lorne Merkle, Bill Lemmon, and Bob Heugel were the mainstays of those teams, which also featured former prep stars Carl Herness, Al Libke Jr., Howard Willis, Wally Brebner, Bob Pullar, and Erling Tollefson.

In the 1936 Berlin Olympics, the United States basketball team beat Canada, 19–8, to win the gold medal in a game played outdoors, in the pouring rain. The American coach was James Needles of Tacoma, Washington. But it was not until 1946 that the Basketball Association of America was organized, and three more years passed before it merged with the National Basketball League to form today's NBA.

When the Northwest tournament was first sponsored in 1930, basketball play in the region was linked to the Amateur Athletic Union (AAU). Winning teams from throughout the state would gather at the University of Washington (UW) Athletic Pavilion for the playoffs. In 1938 the Tacoma team to beat was the Alt Heidelbergs with players Hal Lee, Hal McClary, Bill Dahlke, Jack Holstine, Lyle Kellstrom, Joe "Salty" Salatino, Bob Huegel, and Gene Gunderson.

"The Tacoma Heidelbergs gave a sample of their power in the last period of their game with Mount Vernon," reported the *Seattle Daily Times.* Holstine and Dahlke were top scorers for a game that gave Tacoma 60 points against the 28 made by the Mount Vernon Parkers. Top scorer for the Skagit County team was guard Marv Harshman at 11 points, who by the end of the year would make his way toward Pacific Lutheran College (now PLU). After next

beating the Victoria Dominos, the Heidelbergs faced the Seattle Cammaranos for the Northwest finals.

"Tacoma, after long years of trying, has finally hit the jackpot," reported the *Seattle Sunday Times,* and the team was on its way to Denver for the AUU championship games. "Bill ("Hands") Dahlke and Jack ("Dutch") Holstine, former stars of Washington State College [now WSU], were the siege guns," the newspaper continued. Holstine was selected as a first-team All-Star; Dahlke, along with Lyle Kellstrom, to the second team. Hal Lee was voted an honorable mention slot, as was Mount Vernon's Marv Harshman. Within a decade, Hal Lee was a referee for the Pacific Coast Professional Basketball League.

Although at the time Tacomans weren't drawn to basketball as they had been a decade before, amateur basketball competition remained popular in the postwar years. Families and individual players continued to pursue recreational basketball for years to come.

Scott Names, a classic example, began playing basketball in 1926 on Tacoma's YMCA team. "When he was just 13," a newspaper reported later on, "he poured 40 points through the hoop as Tacoma defeated Seattle for the Northwest championship." Even while attending Stadium High School, Scott Names continued to play amateur basketball outside the school setting. In 1932 he was part of the Washington Hardware team that won the city championship that year. By 1958 Scott had "played with some 50-odd Pierce County quintets," according to one source. That year he also played for Foshaug's Puyallup City League champions, a team that also included his two brothers, Paul and Sid.

While Scott Names played for the Tacoma Municipal League team Generals in 1953, runner-up in the Pierce County AAU tournament, his son Tom had just graduated from Stadium High. Tom Names became a high-scoring basketball forward in high school, and then attended the University of Puget Sound (UPS), where he was a starter for three seasons. He continued as an amateur hoopster, playing for the Harmon Company and Plywood Tacoma teams.

Younger brother Clint followed Tom to Stadium. In 1957 he became a member of the All-State team, setting a scoring record of 39 points against Richland in the class 2A state tournament. At UW he maintained an 11-point scor-

Harry McLaughlin was not only a star on the basketball court for the PLU Lutes, but he also played for the famed House of David team (MB).

ing average while graduating with a degree in engineering. When his work took him to California, he played with the San Francisco Olympic Club. Lured back to the Pacific Northwest, he joined the Tacoma Cheney Studs team for the 1964–65 season. Team members also included Don Moseid, Bruce Alexander, George Grant, Gus Kravas, Jim Van Beek, and Larry Poulson. Coach George Grant was responsible for adding Clint Names to the roster of what newspapers called a "crack AAU team." And that they were. By March 1965, the Studs were on their way to Denver and the national AAU tournament.

By the end of 1968, Clint Names was the coach, general manager, and player for the newly formed Plywood Tacoma team composed of many of those who had played for the Cheney Studs the year before. New additions included Curt Gammell, Mark Anderson, Steve Anstett, Gary Wortman, Ted Werner, Vince Strojan, Lynn Nance, and Jim Harney (who also coached). Dick Burrows of Tacoma Plywood agreed to sponsor the team so that former collegiate players, and current high school and college coaches, could keep abreast of the game.

Their start was not overwhelmingly promising. They lacked a home court, for instance, and found themselves practicing in the Western State Hospital gymnasium. Even so, Plywood Tacoma ended the 1968–69 season with a 22–1 record and a trip to Springfield, Massachusetts, for the National Amateur Basketball Association (NABA) games, a tournament linked to the National Collegiate Athletic Association (NCAA). The Plywood hoopsters went all the way to the final game but lost to the Brittany Zips of Milwaukee by a score of 74–73.

The team continued to make its way to NABA championship games. In 1970 they made it to the semifinals. The following year they won the championship, beating the White Gloves Maintenance team from Houston by a score of 94–86, and they won again in 1973. "The Tacomans are back home after winning the national title," reported *News Tribune* sports editor Earl Luebker, "proving that old basketball players never die, they just dribble away."

By this time it was clear that the Plywood Tacoma team was unique. "That Tacoma recreation team is one of about 25 statewide," *News Tribune* reporter Mike Jordan explained in 1974. "The teams are composed mostly of former college stars, some of whom might have had a shot at the money game but because of circumstances—or choice—play recreational basketball instead." More than one newspaper reporter emphasized how much fun the Plywood team had playing the game and the importance of player camaraderie.

In 1974 Tacoma hosted the NABA national tournament, held at PLU. And though the Plywood team made it to the finals once again, they lost to the Minneapolis Kings by a score of 94–88. Other participating teams included FBI, featuring former UW Husky Lynn Nance, and a Houston entry with Ken DeSpain, a former teammate of NBA great Elvin Hayes. The 6-foot-and-under division had a more local flavor to it: Tacomans Dave Harshman and Tom Tommervik, sons of the two "Marvelous Marvs" of PLU fame, played in the championship game.

The Plywood Tacoma hoopsters were not the only recreational team to achieve success on the court. The 38th Street Club won the AAU Tacoma title in 1948. Rod Gibbs, a 6-foot 7-inch center who later played at UPS, was the cornerstone for the team, which also included Buster Brouillet, Dex Hutton, Wally Brebner, Harry Lang, Marty North, Dip Loveland, and Rod Belcher. In 1959 Jim Harney, who had captained Seattle University's NCAA runner-up team in a championship battle with Kentucky, joined Tacoma's Alt Heidelberg AAU squad. Harney had 32 and 26 points in successive games to decide the Northwest championship.

The seasons that followed were the most spirited in AAU history. The existence of the Northwest AAU league attracted big crowds to games at Seattle Pacific University (SPU), UPS, and PLU.

Tacoma's Pederson Fryers unsuccessfully battled Seattle's Kirk's Pharmacy and Federal Old Line (FOL) for top honors in both 1960 and '61 finales. Coach Warren Moyles, an eight-year scoring star in the league, watched in disbelief when his team lost a 15-point lead and a loose ball rolled away from five Fryers as the gun sounded to signal a 62–61 Kirk's win in 1961. Doyle Perkins had hit a

jump shot with 25 seconds remaining the year before as FOL took a 70–68 verdict.

That was the start of the fierce Seattle-Tacoma rivalry that dominated AAU basketball for several years, and fans turned out in unprecedented numbers to watch regular league games and tournament action. Coach Ron Billings, a three-sport star at PLU, took over as Pederson Fryer coach for Moyles, who remained as a player.

Billings combined ex-PLU stars Roger Iverson and Jim Van Beek, UPS grad Don Moseid, Gary Goble (a 6-foot 10-inch center from Oregon State University), and University of Oregon's Denny Strickland and Glenn Moore into a solid contender for national consideration. Moseid, Iverson, and Van Beek placed among the top 10 scorers in the league for six straight years.

Tacoma lumberman Ben Cheney sponsored the team and the Cheney Studs battled Kirk's, Federal Old Line, and a powerful new Fort Lewis team for AAU honors. The Studs never finished less than second in league play, twice

The 1936 Cammarano Brothers basketball team competed in the Tacoma City League: L. to R., Pete Davis, Joe Salatino, Les Colbo, Bob Houston, Forrest Weingard, Hugh Kraft, Frank Ruffo (SSM, 137).

THE MOUNTAINEERS AND STUDS

The Tacoma Mountaineers, owned by Ed Mays and Milton Bay, was the City of Destiny's new franchise. Tom Cross, Marv Harshman, Irv Leifer, John Katica, Bob Graff, Bob Voelker, J. Voelker, Ernie Endress, and Earl Platt were the initial team members. Tom Werner was coach.

The Mountaineers barely lasted the 1947–48 season. Indeed, by February 1948, the team was in financial trouble. Apparently Ed Mays was ill and his associates were unable to continue the management of the franchise; Milton Bay told the league board that he wanted to sell the Tacoma team. The board decided that if Tacoma did "not accept our reasonable offer to buy their team that we concede and then we will cancel their franchise on the grounds of mismanagement and unpaid bills due." Minutes of board meetings are rarely a clear indication of what really transpired at the time, but it appears that the Tacoma franchise owners were writing bad checks and failing to pay the players.

Shortly before he died, Tom Cross recollected what happened next:

At the end of the season, they took this group, with Tom Werner still coaching, and made arrangements with Major Hal Wright, Special Services officer at Madigan Army Hospital, to play under the auspices of the Madigan Mountaineers. In addition to the old Tacoma roster, they added Al Brightman, voted Rookie of the Year for the Boston Celtics, and Chuck Gilmur, who had become coach of the Lincoln High School basketball team and was an All–Pacific Coast Conference center at UW in 1943. Gilmur had played for Red Auerbach with the Washington Capitols and finished his professional career with the Chicago Stags.

Another player who joined the club was Sammy White, an outstanding UW basketball athlete who was also a top-rated catcher for the Boston Rex Sox for many years. Dean Nicholson, who had taken the position as coach of the Puyallup High School team, also came on board, and Dean later coached the team when they left Madigan to become the Cheney Studs. While playing for Madigan in the early 1950s during the Korean War years, there were many patients—wounded servicemen—who enjoyed the successes of this great team.

One of the great Cheney Studs basketball team members was Bob Houbregs, All-American at UW known for his famous hook shots, and the O'Brien twins. Johnny was an All-American while at SU and Eddie was a great point guard. Another UW great, Joe Cipriano, joined the team as well. He later went on to coach at the University of Idaho and the University of Nebraska. Other team members included Jack Johnson, Dan Inveen, and Gene Lundgaard. For a number of years, the Cheney Studs traveled with the "Harlem Clowns," playing all over the Northwest, Alaska, and California and entertaining fans near and far.

The Mountaineers play an exhibition game against the Harlem Globetrotters (SSM,1998.6.5).

winning the Northwest league championship and twice taking first in the Northwest AAU tournament.

When the Studs belted Fort Lewis 97–74 in 1962 behind Iverson's 29 points plus 17 by Moseid and 16 by Van Beek to win the AAU tournament, Kirk's created a controversy that began the downfall of AAU competition locally.

Kirk's had added Husky star Bill Hansen to its roster and played him in a tourney game against Renton despite a rule against using college players. The rule had been in effect in the Northwest for 15 years, but the national AAU committee upheld Kirk's right to its actions and invited Kirk's as an at-large tournament entrant.

When the Studs objected and announced they would not trek to Denver for the finals under such conditions, two prominent Northwest AAU officials resigned in support. The national AAU committee then rescinded its invitation to Kirk's but did not reinvite the Studs.

The Cheney cagers remained together for one more season and won the 1963 Washington State Amateur Tournament, which had affiliated nationally with the new Basketball Federation of the United States. In an all-Tacoma championship game, the Studs topped Rucker's Florists, 61–50. Van Beek had 28 points and was named All-Tournament along with Rucker's Tom Names. An ankle injury sidelined Names in the early stages of the title tilt, hurting Rucker's upset bid.

Women's Amateur Teams

Amateur basketball for women was popular in Tacoma in the early 1930s, with the Carstens Packing Company team from 1932–33 being one of the contenders for the City Girl's Basketball League championship. Coached by Paul Benton, the Carstens Vagabonds, as they were known, were one of six teams in the league. It wasn't until the early 1950s, however, that the sport really blossomed in Pierce County, and in 1951 the Tacoma Fuelerettes competed in the inaugural Washington State Women's Invitational Tournament hosted by the Richland Women's Basketball Association. Whitworth College won the first state invitational, with the Fuelerettes being awarded the Sportsmanship Trophy.

The team had traveled over to Richland with just seven players available; with only five players left in one of their games, the players were warned to avoid fouling out at all costs. It wasn't too long before Joyce Jones forgot to heed those words as she drew her fifth foul. With only four players remaining, the club had to forfeit the game, but their good sportsmanship and attitude were duly rewarded.

It wasn't until the 1955 tournament in Seattle that a Pierce County team finished in the top three as the Women's Air Force (WAF) of McChord claimed second place with a 5–2 record, losing to the Little Biddy Buddies of Seattle in the 12-team affair. The McChord entry was coached by Mary Edge and was led by Lois Jensen.

Other Pierce County area teams included Kena's Kids, coached by Margaret Zepeda, and Puyallup's River Road Merchants, coached by Marion Ingram. Kena's Kids included such players as Delores Sagmiller, Joyce Jones, Betty Rowan, Carol Kalapus, Margaret Heinrick, and Pat Stavig. Puyallup team members included Pat Fullerton, Marjorie Johnson, Eileen Anderson, Dorothy Miskar, and the Falaschi sisters—Loretta, Noreita, Christine, and Margaret. The only local official involved was Delores Sutherland, who worked at Eatonville High School at the time. Later on, Suzanne Koenig and Alma Stewart donned the pinstripes to referee games.

A formal, organized women's basketball program was established in 1956 with the creation of the Tacoma–Pierce County Women's Athletic Association. Aligned closely with the Metropolitan Park District and supported by Pierce County Parks and Recreation Department director Tom Cross, the association hosted the first-ever Washington State Basketball Tournament, at Baker Junior High and PLU. Key members of the association included Marion Ingram, Pat Stavig, Delores Sagmiller, Louise Mazzuca, Margaret Zepeda, Dot Miskar, Mary Edge, Shirley Johnson, and Eileen Anderson.

The first state tournament involved eight teams, including the McChord Jets and the River Road Merchants from Pierce County. The Freems team of Seattle won the tournament, while the Merchants finished third and won the Sportsmanship Award. First-team All-Stars included forwards Lois Jensen and Pat Fullerton of the Merchants, and second-team All-Stars included guard Loretta Falaschi of Puyallup.

NATIVE AMERICAN SPORTSMEN

Lewis Francis Sockalexis, grandson of a Penobscot chief, is considered by many historians to have been the first Native American in major league sports. In the late 1890s he stepped up to the plate for a team known today as the Cleveland Indians. On Tacoma's fields and courts, many Native American athletes have followed in his inspiring footsteps.

One of the earliest local Native American sports teams was formed at the Cushman Indian Industrial School, which started in 1860 as a one-room day school for Puyallup Indian youth. As it grew into a boarding school, drawing Indian students from the Northwest and Alaska, it inevitably sprouted athletic clubs as well. According to various *Tacoma Daily Ledger* articles, in 1913 the boys had football, basketball, and wrestling teams while the girls excelled at basketball.

Many Native individuals have made their mark on our history as well. Roslyn's Jimmy Claxton dreamt of playing professional baseball since age 13, when he began as a left-handed catcher in the "coal miner's league," competing in the small Cascades communities of Roslyn, Black Diamond, Buckley, Carbonado, Ravensdale, and Wilkeson. He was the only Native American recruited to the Oakland Giants. According to Keith Olbermann of *Sports Illustrated*, a fan who was part Native American helped get Claxton signed with the Oaks, Oakland's Pacific Coast League team. It didn't last long, however. Sports historian Mark Macrae says, "He would only see action in two games, both on Sunday of Memorial Day weekend in 1916. He would pitch a total of two and one-third innings as a professional in the Pacific Coast League."

Claxton was dismissed when Oakland manager Harold Elliot learned that he was also part African American, a bias that had not yet been overcome. However, says Macrae, Claxton's semi-pro baseball days continued for years to come: "According to his family, at age 61 he pitched and won a two-hitter." He retired as a Tacoma longshoreman in 1958. He was the first Native American (and African American) player to appear on a baseball trading card and, just months before his death in 1970,

he was inducted into the Tacoma–Pierce County Sports Hall of Fame.

Outfielders "Indian Bob" Johnson and his older brother Roy were born on the Cherokee Nation Reservation in the Oklahoma Territory and moved to Tacoma at an early age. Both men had long and varied pro baseball careers: Roy played for 10 years from 1929 to 1938, splitting most of his time between the Detroit Tigers and the Boston Red Sox, and Bob played in the major leagues for 13 years, from 1933 to 1945 mainly with the Philadelphia A's. Interestingly enough, each brother ended his career with a .296 batting average. They both then played with the Seattle Rainiers of the Pacific Coast League; Roy in 1944 and 1945, and Bob in 1947 and 1948. Later, Bob managed the Tacoma Tigers of the Western International League during the 1949 season.

Puyallup tribal leader Bob Satiacum was better known in the 1960s and '70s for his activism, staging "fish-ins" for treaty fishing rights (and even enlisting Marlon Brando's support at the time). He was an athlete as well, however, playing basketball at Lincoln High School in 1947. Doug McArthur, who went to Lincoln during Satiacum's time, says, "He was a star basketball player. We called him 'chief' but didn't know he really was one." In 1947, his senior year, he became a starting forward after having been on the reserves. "He was a great passer," says McArthur. That same year Lincoln won the Tacoma city championships and qualified for the state tournament.

Born on the Colville Reservation in eastern Washington and members of the Nez Perce Tribe, Hank and Mel Piatote made their mark in Puyallup playing both basketball and baseball. Hank lettered two years in both sports, under basketball coach Carl Sparks and baseball coach Carl Wasmund, and rubbed elbows with such stars as Tom Absher, Tony Banaszak, Sid Names, Jim Ball, and Dave Dailey, before graduating in 1949. Mel lettered for three years in each, graduating in 1951, and continued playing basketball at Central Washington College under Leo Nicholson.

Another pair of brothers Harry and Willie McLaughlin, who were members of the Sioux tribe, played basketball at Clover Park High School and started their college careers at Washington State College. In 1946 they both transferred to Pacific Lutheran. Harry was known as "the court magician" in the media because of his excellence and showmanship on the court. Marv Harshman, who was the PLU coach at the time, said he was the "most colorful player I ever saw at Pacific Lutheran." Harry's collegiate basketball career lasted from 1946 to 1950, and he was inducted into the PLU Athletic Hall of Fame in 1994. According to Dave Girrard, PLU's current sports information director, he was PLU's third leading scorer of all time. His first two years, he was the Washington Intercollegiate Conference (WInCo) all-league selection; his junior and senior years he earned Evergreen Conference All-Star honors when the school switched conferences. He never averaged less than 12.9 points per game.

Older brother Willie was a three-sport athlete at Clover Park High. In addition to basketball, he was halfback on the football team and competed in track and field, where his best 110-yard high hurdle time was 16.6 seconds. He also cleared 5 feet 10 1/4 inches in the high jump and 11 feet 5 inches in the pole vault. In 1943 he was selected by the coaches association to be on the Pierce County League's all-star team. He continued participating in basketball and track at PLU but quit after his sophomore year. Post-college, he eased into bowling and golf and in 1951 he was crowned club champion at Meadow Park Golf Course.

Pitcher Chico Thayer fell in love with baseball in 1948 at the age of 15. "I was so fascinated watching the pitchers I had to give it a try. I got a couple of gloves and a ball and my cousin and I started pitching." His friends cobbled together a team and he joined: "When I walked to the mound the first time, I was so nervous, my knees were shaking."

Thayer, who was born into the Cowlitz tribe, came to Tacoma from Anacortes in 1951. He pitched in the Major Fastpitch League and participated in 29 regional tournaments during his career, winning nine Most Valuable Player trophies. During his most successful season, he pitched 46 winning games out of 60 and on one particularly long day in the 1950s, he pitched and won five consecutive games with a total of 54 strikeouts.

A member of the Nomalaki Wailiki Tribe, California native Phil Jordan had a long and fruitful basketball career and made Tacoma his home after marrying his college sweetheart. In 1954, he led Whitworth College to a 21–4 record and earned NAIA Third-team All-American honors for himself. By his junior year of 1955, he was averaging 28.8 points when the six-foot-ten athlete chose to leave Whitworth midseason, taking his talents to the professional level, most notably as center for the New York Knicks. He was there (though sidelined with the flu) on March 2, 1962, when Wilt Chamberlain scored his record-setting 100-points in a single game. Jordan later was a top play for Seattle's AAU Buchanan Bakery team and also played for Rucker's Flowers of Tacoma.

Mike Jordan (no relation to Phil) "was a man among boys," says Doug McArthur, the University of Puget Sound's athletic director from 1969–78. An "outstanding" player, Jordan averaged 20 points a game at Seattle University before transferring to UPS, where he "scored in double figures and was a good rebounder." McArthur recalls a UPS game at PLU when Jordan arrived late because he had encountered bad weather driving home across the state after visiting friends on the Colville Reservation. "He just barely got there before game time—he [scored] 36 points in the game, it made all the difference."

Chief Leschi High School won the Boys Class B high school state basketball championship in 1998, finishing with a 25–3 record, in their first-ever appearance at the state tournament. They also participated at the state tournament in 1999 and 2004 but did not place. In 2004 they were led by brothers Sean and Marty Wallace, with sophomore brother Curtis waiting in the wings to assume the leadership role. At season's end, Sean, a four-year starter, ranked as the school's all-time leading scorer and Marty was No. 2 on the list.

Native American athletes continue to participate in sports due to increasing opportunities at Chief Leschi High School, as well as at local parks and recreation programs, and it is only a matter of time before more outstanding accomplishments are seen on the fields and courts of play.

—The Puyallup Tribe of Indians generously sponsors this history.

The Tacoma Mountaineers: L. to R., Tom Cross, Marv Harshman, John Katica, Bob Graf, coach Tom Werner, Ernie Endress, Bob Volker, Jack Volker, Irv Leifer; ballboys Dennis Heinrick (L.) and Dick Wells (SSM, 134).

Tacoma's Cheney Studs claimed back-to-back top honors at the Washington State Women's Basketball Tournament in 1965 and 1966. Coached by Sandy Molzan, the Studs included Virginia Gilson, Pat Karman, Carol Van Brunt, Jan Chase, Barbara Blatter, Pat Lacey, Kay Bentley, and Judy Chindgren. Karman, a physical education teacher at Lakes High, scored 21 points, and Lacey added 18 as the Studs beat the Jolly Green Giants of Spokane, 75–54, to win the state crown in 1966.

A turning point for women's sports occurred in 1969 when Tom Cross asked Molzan to accept a permanent position on the staff of the Pierce County Parks and Recreation Department as women's recreation supervisor. When she turned him down, he asked her to accept the job part-time to supervise women's and girl's league play in basketball, softball, slow pitch, and volleyball.

In the 1970s some of the more competitive teams participated in the Evergreen Traveling League with Olympia, Bremerton, and Seattle, but Pierce County continued to offer an independent recreation league that included top area teams such as Buttons Veterinary Clinic and Pozzi Brothers.

By 1973 the county program had grown so fast that both the Pierce County and Metropolitan parks departments were running separate programs. It also had reached a point that a part-time employee could no longer handle the load, so Karen Moorhead took over fulltime in 1972; Molzan continued to assist while working for the Cheney Lumber Company as a sales coordinator. Women in Pierce County at last had gained equal opportunity to play organized amateur basketball and share the courts with the men.

Exhibition Teams

Another basketball entity that generated interest and enthusiasm in that era was the Cheney Studs Courteers. Organized by Gene Anderson of the Cheney Lumber Company, their emphasis was on entertainment rather than competition. The youthful Courteers learned the ball-handling skills and trick shots made so famous by the Harlem Globetrotters and became extremely professional in their abilities. Soon they were popular halftime entertainment at major college and NBA basketball games throughout the West. Denny Brand, Rob Norwood, Tom Mack, Wayne Hoff, Don Wonders, Pete Wonders, Tom Rogers, George Brown, Jeff Smith, and John Salatino were some of the members of the Courteers.

Pro Players

Although Tacoma's lone pro basketball venture, the Mountaineers, failed at the gate, some professional players with a Tacoma connection made the grade. Frank Burgess, a Gonzaga University All-American who settled in Tacoma as a federal judge, played for the Hawaii Chiefs of the ABA in 1961; Phil Jordan, a great star at Whitworth College in 1954, played in the NBA for the New York Knickerbockers, the Cincinnati Royals, and the Detroit Pistons. (As a sophomore at Whitworth, Jordan led his 1954 team to a 21–4 record and an NAIA National Tournament appearance where he garnered third-team NAIA All-America honors. He was averaging 28.8 points per game his junior season when he was expelled after 10 games for throwing a brick through a window of the college president's house!) Chuck Gilmur, who coached Lincoln High in the 1950s, played for the Chicago Stags and Washington Capitals for six years. Those three closed out their basketball careers in Tacoma, playing on various recreational league teams.

Charlie Williams, who starred at Stadium High and Seattle University (SU), also starred professionally in the ABA. He averaged 20.8 points per game with the Pittsburgh Pipers and led them, along with Connie Hawkins, to the championship. In his six-year career in the ABA, he averaged 16.2 points per game, also playing with Minnesota, Memphis, and the Utah Stars. Rod McDonald, a Clover Park High and Whitworth College star, enjoyed three seasons in the ABA, also with the Utah Stars.

UPS great Charles Lowery enjoyed pro success in the NBA, although a broken leg shortened his career after a couple of seasons. He was sixth man on the Milwaukee Bucks' NBA champion team in 1972–73 and a teammate of Kareem Abdul-Jabbar. Hiram Fuller, who prepped at Stadium High in the late '90s, made his pro debut in 2004 with the Atlanta Hawks.

But in the last 30 years, organized amateur basketball in the region has lost its spectator appeal. "Mike Dahl took an elbow in the tummy, but dove for the basketball anyway. He made a super play, saving it from going out of bounds," reported Mike Jordan in 1974. "But not a fan cheered his effort. In fact, the gym was empty except for the players. Only a few people cared about the game, and even fewer knew that it was going to be played. Dahl and his Plywood Tacoma teammates play their hearts out several times a week. … And for what?

"Love of the game!"

CHAPTER 14

BICYCLING

A. D. Browning, owner of Browning Bicycles near 52nd Street and South Tacoma Way, photographed this group of local enthusiasts (Browning Collection, TPL, Image 147).

Bicycling in Tacoma began in 1888 with the formation of the Wheelman's Club. Competitive racing was not on the minds of the 35 charter members, although they did race their high-wheeled bicycles on the wooden sidewalks of downtown Tacoma, much to the chagrin of local pedestrians. Urban hill climbing was more fun. In 1889 the Tacoma Wheelmen sponsored a hill climb that began on Pacific Avenue and headed up unpaved 11th Street, with the winner determined by how far he got up the hill. Prince Wells, owner of a local bicycle shop, won the contest by making it the three blocks to Market Street.

By the 1890s, the new safety bicycle replaced the high-wheel model. Now women and youngsters joined the men in wheeling around the city. And as the sport grew in popularity, so too did the businesses catering to the local Wheelmen membership, which had expanded to 2,750 by 1897. Tacoma Avenue from South Ninth Street to South 17th became a "bicycle way," where cycling businesses predominated. There was Frank Fentress, a Sterling bicycle dealer; Jack Mullholand sold the Tribune cycle; and W. A. McNeeley peddled the Cleveland. The Horst Brothers sold the Eagle bicycle, while the Wheeler Novelty store had White bicycles as well as Newton- and Libby-built wheels. In all these shops, bicy-

cle talk reigned and the finer points of the different machines were discussed. On summer evenings, "bicycle way" became a racing course as representatives from the various companies sought to sell their product by demonstrating its speed.

One of those who frequented "bicycle way" in the 1890s was Cleveland Bicycle repairman and Tacoman George Sharick, who became one of the nation's best racers. At his first event, at Ocasta, California, Sharick cleaned up the prizes, claiming all the day's trophies from cameras to badges. His brother John, who was also racing, convinced Sharick to enter the money race in which the prize was $150. In the third race, Sharick broke through the rope barrier while riding at top speed, flew into the crowd, broke his bike, and was himself scratched up. But he still managed to win the money prize and move into the professional class of bike racing. For the next six years, the Tacoma native rode for several different manufacturers, with the circuit taking him from Winnipeg to Baltimore.

In the British Columbia coast circuit, Sharick was far in front of his nearest competitors in terms of the percentage points earned. The national races were much harder, however. In 1898 at Woodland Park in New Hampshire, for instance, he came out first in the opening race but finished second in the third. His biggest win was for an $800 purse at the Pacific Coast championship, held in Sacramento, California.

Tacoma bicyclers were especially fond of road racing during the early years of the 20th century. Their favorite route went the 15-mile round trip from "bicycle way" to Rigney Hill in South Tacoma. Store owners also sponsored shorter races for young boys, held on a citywide network of bicycle paths, funded by members of the Wheelmen's Club.

Times were changing, however. As early as 1899 newspapers were correctly predicting that the automobile would soon make the bicycle obsolete. Paved roads replaced the riding paths, and automobile racing replaced the bicycle. The Wheelmen survived as an organization throughout the

decades of the 20th century, but it was not until the 1970s and 1980s that bicycle racing again emerged as a serious sport.

The gasoline shortage of the mid-1970s provided the impetus by pointing to the bicycle as an alternative mode of transportation. By 1975 Clover Park High student Tim Carlson and Tacoman Steve Curry, who worked in a local bicycle shop, were competing in local races sponsored by the U.S. Cycling Federation. Carlson qualified for national competition in 1981, but injuries kept him from attending. Curry was in the state's top 10 in track racing that same year and won the Longacres-sponsored Doo-Dah Criterium in 1982.

By the end of the 1980s, the Steilacoom Racing Club joined the Tacoma Wheelmen in sponsoring local cyclists, with Peninsula High School student Mike Porter its most

Bicycling in Stadium Bowl, ca. 1938 (Richard Studio Collection, TPL, Image D-7388-15).

successful member. In 1989 he won the Washington Trust Classic held in Spokane. The following year Porter, along with teammates Mike Kloeppel and Dan Reinkensmeyer, competed in the nationals held in San Diego. Then in 1991, Porter was one of 10 Americans selected to be a member of the U.S. National Junior Road Racing Team that competed in France.

The 1980s also introduced bicycle motocross (BMX) to the youngsters of Pierce County. Here the venue was the River Valley BMX dirt track constructed within Sumner's Riverside Park. It has hosted both national and state championship events, including the first American Bicycle Association Washington state competitions in 1986. One of the first to use the track was Puyallup High School student Gary Ellis, who in 1983 led the nation in amateur point standings. Tacoman Clarence Perry was the national leader as a professional cruiser.

Other racing and endurance events have crossed the path of local bicyclists. The Tacoma Wheelmen's Club, continuing a tradition that began in the 1890s, sponsors the "century ride," a 100-mile test of pedaling endurance. Pierce County Parks and Recreation has sponsored the Tour de Pierce. In 2002 Tacoma's Wright Park was the competitive venue for the Redline Cup, a cyclocross event sanctioned by the Union Cycliste Internationale. All these events, along with competitive road racing and the BMX, are a part of the county's sports history that will be around for years to come.

The Tacoma Times and Metropolitan Park District sponsored the first annual bicycle meet in 1938; every child who participated got a Double Cola and Hambone candy bar (Richards Studio Collection, TPL, Image D-7387-8).

CHAPTER 15

BOWLING AND LAWN BOWLING

Ted Tadich bowled the first sanctioned 300 game in city history in 1938 (SSM).

Many in the Tacoma area think that bowling evolved with the emergence of Earl Anthony in the early 1960s, though others are cognizant of the legendary Ted Tadich, who began a storied career in the late 1920s. However, the first mention of the sport actually dates to the 1870s in the Steilacoom area, and by the turn of the 20th century the A Street Alleys, Pacific Alleys, and Prince's Alleys were in operation in Tacoma. In fact, Prince's Alley had a six-team league (each team comprised of five men) in 1910, including the Scandinavian Americans, Fidelity Trust Company, the National Bank of Commerce, the Bank of California, the Pacific National Bank, and the Post Office. Among the early individual standouts was C. C. Collins, who bowled the first recorded 700 series in 1916 and carried a 190 average during 48 years of league play.

Over the next 10 years, bowling continued to grow with the addition of the YMCA Alleys, the Corby-Hayes Alleys, the Elks Lanes, the Tacoma Bowling Alleys (consisting of five lanes in the Tacoma Building), and the Dupont Club. The Commercial, Church, and City Leagues were formed during this time. In 1921 the Imperial Alleys were built at Ninth and Commerce Streets, and a year later two six-team leagues, the City and the Commercial, were competing in the center.

Mike Berry, Bill Herdman, Bill Leftwich, and Bertha McCormick were active in the sport at that time. Herdman was elected the first president of the Greater Tacoma Bowling Association (GTBA) when it was formed in 1935 and served four years in that capacity. He was a member of its first Hall of Fame.

Bertha McCormick was a pioneer in Tacoma bowling not only as a longtime competitor but also serving for many years in an official capacity with several leagues as well as in an administrative position with the local association. In a 1971 interview, she recalled that she first started bowling in 1921 when there were no women's leagues.

"We started with eight sets of doubles, and we made up teams for matches against other cities and towns in 1924. There was no one else to bowl against in those days. We were fortunate to get into the Commercial League with the men in 1929, and the first ladies league was organized in 1932. We had 12 girls . . . four teams with three members each. The next year we had six four-girl teams and it kind of progressed from there. We built up the A and B Leagues next, and look what we have now." She also recalled when the foul-line man sat on a platform up on the wall, bowling was 10 cents a line, and the pin-setters were paid 2 cents.

During that time, bowling balls had only two holes rather than the conventional three holes found today.

McCormick, the first women to bowl in the men's City League, was honored in 1966 as the first inductee into the Tacoma Women's Bowling Association (TWBA) Hall of Fame and was given the organization's first life membership. She founded the Northwest Women's Bowling Association and was the group's secretary on three occasions, the TWBA's secretary for three years, secretary of the Commercial League for 16 years, and the men's City B League secretary for nine seasons.

Another pioneer in women's bowling was Bessie Trowbridge, who bowled for 45 years, starting in 1928 at the Cooper Lanes in South Tacoma, and didn't miss a City League tournament until 1974, the year she was inducted into the TWBA Hall of Fame.

The 1930s

In 1928 Ted Tadich, one of the biggest names in Tacoma bowling history, started what became an illustrious 60-plus-year career. Tadich (who stood just under 6 feet 2 inches and weighed 200 pounds) was a standout area baseball player

Jordan's Bread–Commercial League team, 1940–41: L. to R., Mary Kancianich, Dennie Radonich, Isabelle McCormick, Bertha McCormick, Fannie Gambo (photo by Richard R. Moyer & Co., courtesy Tacoma Women's Bowling Association).

From L. to R., Coley Anderson, George Boscovich, Frank LaFleur, Charlie Mettler, Woody Harter, Ernie Stowe (courtesy Greater Tacoma Bowlers Association).

(see chapter 8, Baseball: The Early Years and Amateurs) before he became the dominate force in bowling.

A testimony of his athleticism, Tadich shot a 634-plus three-game series the first time he bowled, and in his first tournament he rolled 695 series in the doubles competition with Lou Vitalich. He carried a composite 198 average in his first year of league play in the City and Commercial Leagues, and nine years later he recorded his highest average, a 219 mark, in Seattle's Major League.

Tadich went on to establish many firsts in regional bowling, including the first American Bowling Congress–sanctioned 300 game in Tacoma on December 21, 1938, at the Broadway Lanes. He also had the city's first 800 series—an 808 effort—which stood for 34 years. He was the only man to sweep all of the events in the Northwest International Bowling Congress tournament. He won the NIBC all-events with a 1,919 total in 1937 and in 1946 with a 1,851; teamed with Vitalich to win the 1934 doubles with a 1,294; took the singles competition with a 717 in 1938; and was a member of the 1955 title-winning Heidelberg Beer team from Tacoma, which piled up a 2,882 pinfall.

"There have been some real tough shooters in the NIBC over the years," Tadich recalled in an interview years later. "When I won those titles, the tournament was scratch. And I shot more than 2,000 scratch all-events three different years and didn't win the title."

Tadich remained active until just a year before his death in 1994 and during his career recorded 13 perfect games, five of which were sanctioned; he had seven 299s and rolled 700-plus series a whopping 129 times. These accomplishments were achieved during a time when high bowling scores were relatively rare compared to the megascores of later years. In fact, after Tadich's 300 game in 1938, it was a dozen years before the next sanctioned 300 was bowled in Tacoma, by Bill Eggleston.

Tadich bowled with some of Tacoma's great teams, including the Heidelbergs, Pacific Match, Hub Clothiers, Columbia Beer, and Jensen Fuel. His teammates and opponents during the 1930s and 1940s included other Tacoma bowling greats such as Jimmy Radonich, Vitalich, John Artoe, Primo Artoe, Bill Herdman, Len Leftwich, Mike Berry, Vic Johnson, and Frisco Burnett.

The TWBA was formed in 1933 with one four-team league consisting of three ladies each, and the GTBA had 16 members when it was formed in 1935. In addition to Bill Herdman (president), Vance McClure was the secretary, a post he held for 12 years. In 1937 a Tacoma women's team comprised of Mildred Fleming, Dani Radonich, Fannie Gamble, Bertha McCormick, and Isabel McCormick set a Northwest tournament record with an 854 team average.

During the 1937–38 season, the third annual men's City Tournament drew 46 teams and 130 bowlers in the doubles and singles. The third-annual Ladies City Tourney in April 1938 had 15 teams. "Practically every woman league bowler in Tacoma is entered in the tourney," reported one newspaper article. During the 1938–39 season, there were 684 league bowlers, including about 100 women.

A number of girls from Aquinas Academy started bowling at the Broadway Alleys under the instruction of Fern Coles in the fall of 1938. The first Tacoma high school league was established at Stadium sometime after that, with four teams competing over a 15-week schedule at the Broadway Alleys. Stanton Stowe was the club president, Ted Wakefield was the vice president, Harry Hescox served as secretary, and Max Dubois (later a Stadium High basketball coach) was the treasurer.

The 1940s

In 1940 the Coliseum Lanes opened, with "no posts" in its advertisement (i.e., no spectator obstructions), at 13th and Market Streets; the 10-lane South Tacoma Bowl opened at 52nd and South Tacoma Way; and Sixth Avenue Lanes opened with six lanes. A year later the Cross-town Bowling League was formed, with one team from each of eight centers—Broadway, Play-Mor, Sixth Avenue, HiWay, Coliseum, K Street Recreation, Puyallup, and Ruston. It was a scratch league, with an 875 limit on teams, that ran through the summer into mid-September. The eight lanes at the North End Alleys at 26th and Proctor (which remains in business today as Chalet Bowl) were added during the 1941–42 season.

In 1943 the first Tacoma versus Seattle All-Star match was bowled, and two years later the ladies' All-Star teams from the two cities joined in the competition; these rivalry matches continue today, enhanced by junior and senior All-Star teams in the 1980s. In 1945 the *Tacoma Times* sponsored the first Tacoma Match Play Tournament, the forerunner of the present-day Tacoma Masters Tournament, the showcase event for Tacoma's high-average bowlers.

Joe Wilman, one of the country's greatest bowlers, was stationed at Fort Lewis at this time and was named chairman for the Match Play event. He was joined on the committee by James Murdock, Bill Eggleston, and Jerry Warden, who came up with the tourney idea.

The original tourney consisted of 12 head-to-head matches and was scored under the Petersen Points system, in which one point is awarded for each victory and one point is given for every 50 pins knocked down during each game. Tadich was the first champion, defeating Frank Barker by a 57.17–57.13 Petersen Points margin. The following year, Frisco Burnett beat Tadich for the title, plus a trip to and entry in the Bowling Proprietors Association of America World Championship tournament; the doubles teams of Ann Lucchesi and Babe Penowich bowled a 1,238 series, one of the highest sets in the nation in 1946.

On January 17, 1948, the Midway Bowl opened with 12 lanes at 38th Street and South Tacoma Way. Tadich and Bob Varner were the co-managers and owners, along with Arnold Miller and R. L. "Sandy" Sanderson. Two years later, Frank Magrini bought out all of the owners except Tadich, and the two operated Midway until 1961, when they opened New Frontier Lanes.

Immediately following World War II, the emergence of the so-called Lincoln High "Whiz Kids" began: Earl Johnson, Jim Stevenson, Frank Dal Santo, Gary Walton, Urban Schmidt, and Howie Pagel were high school students talented enough to defeat most of the adult teams in Tacoma and the Northwest.

Earl Johnson went on to national acclaim during the 1950s, '60s, and '70s and was elected to the American Bowling Congress (ABC) Hall of Fame in 1987. Known as "Twirly" because of his delivery, he won three City Match Game championships and was a member of the Tacoma All-Star team on two occasions in the late 1940s and early '50s following a stint in the Army during the Korean conflict. Johnson was tabbed for a spot on the famed Falstaff's Beer team, headquartered in Chicago and captained by fellow ABC Hall of Famer Buddy Bomar. Johnson helped the Falstaff's team to the ABC tournament team title in 1956, and five years later he won the singles crown with a 733 pinfall when the Classic Division for professional bowlers was inaugurated in the ABC tourney. He bowled for Minneapolis in the one-year (1961–62) existence of the National Bowling League and went on to win five Professional Bowlers Association (PBA) tour championships in a six-year span. During a 13-year PBA career, Johnson earned more than $103,000. Johnson remained in the Minneapolis

Peggy Moran Ruehle lets it fly (SSM, 2002.19.8).

area following his retirement from the tour, working as a bowling center manager.

Fellow "Whiz Kid" Jim Stevenson also became a star in Tacoma and the Northwest, bowling on the PBA national tour for a number of years. He later owned and operated Lincoln Lanes.

On October 9, 1948, the Jensen Fuel team shot a 3,217 scratch total, believed to be the highest ever (at that time), with John Artoe rolling a 661, Primo Artoe a 619, Bill McClelland a 551, Johnson a 682, and Tadich a 704. Later in the season, the Jensen team added a 3,137 total to its record. That same year, Tadich was named to the All–West Coast bowling team, and the men drew a record 180 teams for its City League tourney. Mrs. Charlotte Murphy, the owner of North End Lanes, started the state junior bowling tournament this same year, and "Whiz Kids" Jim Stevenson and Frank Dal Santo teamed to win the doubles title.

Dot Pollen, who went on to become a member of the TWBA Hall of Fame, bowled an all-time ladies' record 663 series in 1949, which included a 262 game at Lincoln Lanes. Later that year, Earl Johnson again grabbed the bowling spotlight when he won the City Match Game title by the largest margin in the history of the event, defeating Lefty Hansen, 162.41–143.44 Petersen Points. Just over a week later, Tadich had the fifth 300 game of his career and his second of the year at Midway.

The 1950s: The Advent of Television Coverage

Chuck Riley shot what is believed to be the first 300 game by a left-hander, at the Narrows Bowl (located at Sixth Avenue and Stevens Street) in 1951, but it was Frisco Burnett who won the year's City Match Play title, with a record 32-game total of 159.02 Petersen Points, a 6,852 pinfall, and a record 214 average. He went on to become the first Northwest bowler to reach the finals of the National Match Game Championship in Chicago; he climbed as high as second heading into the final day of competition before falling back to finish 10th in the 14-man qualifying finals.

Tadich won the 1952 Match Game title while Burnett was automatically seeded into the nationals because of his 10th-place finish the year before. The two squared off in a 42-game match held at seven Tacoma bowling centers.

LAWN BOWLING

Lawn bowling practically died out following the American Revolution because of its negative associations with the English. Scottish immigrants renewed an interest in the game, however, following the Civil War, and by 1899 it reached the Pacific Northwest. In fact, Croatians in Old Tacoma created a bocce bowling green near the present-day Spar Tavern. This is where Ted Tadich, one of the city's outstanding 10-pin bowlers, got his start.

The Tacoma Lawn Bowling Club is today's local manifestation of what one reporter called a sport with "an image problem. The English sport, with its eccentric balls, manicured grass greens, and white jackets, is seen by most of the rest of the world as an activity for the geriatric set." While that might be true, lawn bowling has its corps of regional, national, and international competitions, in which Tacoma lawn bowlers have played a significant role. The club's green in Wright Park has produced two championship women bowlers, Pat Boehm and Margaret Feldsher. The organization also hosted the World Championship Lawn Bowling tournament in 1982.

Lawn bowlers compete in a Northwest tournament at Wright Park in 1938 (Richards Studio Collection, TPL, D7285-2).

Tadich won easily with a 193.34–182.08 Peterson Points margin and a 8,409–8,283 pinfall advantage and went on to finish 10th in the nationals, matching Burnett's finish of the previous year. Tadich was voted into the Pierce County Sports Hall of Fame in 1962.

On January 15, 1953, Dave Tuell Jr. became the youngest bowler at age 16 in the nation to bowl a 300 game.

A member of the Jensen Fuelers team in the adult class B Major League at North End Alleys, Tuell had been playing basketball and missed the first game of the evening. After arriving two frames into the second game, he shot a 172 and then bowled his 300 game.

Tuell enjoyed a long and prestigious career on and off the lanes in Tacoma. He was one of the originators of the

All-Star Travel League, which started in the early 1960s and remains a premier league 40 years later. He also served as the first co-chairman (along with Bob Herron) of the GTBA Masters tournament and won the event in 1974. Tuell began competing on the PBA Senior Tour in the early 1990s and cashed in a number of national tourneys. Tuell was Earl Anthony's first sponsor on the PBA tour and also sponsored other big-name pros, including Tacoma native Gary Mage and Brian Voss. Off the lanes, Tuell had a successful law practice for many years and was a Tacoma School Board member for 18 years.

After the Premier League, which limited membership to those with a 180 average or higher, was started at South Tacoma Bowl during the 1953–54 season, locals enjoyed competing with Dick Hoover, one of the greatest names in bowling history, while he served at Fort Lewis. Thus began a new era in Tacoma bowling.

In February 1955, the brother-sister team of Larry Pentecost and Della Pentecost rolled a 1,215 scratch total, the highest scratch score in the country, in the Mixed Doubles Division of a Christmas tournament, which drew 1,421 entrants nationwide. The Pentecosts' score with handicap was 1,218, good for second place in the event. Larry, who went on to enjoy a long and successful career as one of Tacoma's top bowlers, won the second GTBA Masters tournament. That same month, Ted Tadich bowled the 45th 700-plus series of his career, and the following month Hoover won the All-Army bowling title.

In November 1955, Frisco Burnett returned from Chicago, where he and Johnson had competed in the high-powered Classic League, and later won the first Western Washington Match Game Championship. Around the same time, the first live bowling show was televised on Channel 13, featuring Tacoma Match champ Ocky Sciacqua, competing against Seattle Match Game champ Pete Trynasty, and Jacki Pagni, the high-average lady in Tacoma, facing Seattle's Alma Denini.

Automatic pinspotters were installed at the Midway Bowl in 1955, the first in Tacoma. In September 1956, an additional 48 lane beds were installed with the opening of the Lakewood Bowl, Paradise, and Bowl-Mor, and a number of other centers announced that they were installing auto-matic pinsetters. A year later, Villa Bowl opened in Lakewood and Tower Lanes opened on Sixth Avenue, bringing the total number of centers in the area to 14. By 1960 the number of bowling centers in the county had grown to 17, including Pacific Lanes and Bowlero. The others included Fort Lewis, Sixth Avenue, Lincoln, Midway, Paradise, Villa, Puyallup, the Elks, Downtown, North End, Daffodil, Gig Harbor Secoma (in Federal Way), and Narrows.

Babe Penowich continued to be a dominate force among the women bowlers, selected Washington State Women Bowler of the Year in 1953, 1956, and 1957. She had the highest average in the state on three occasions during that time and was inducted into the TWBA Hall of Fame in 1967. The Babe Penowich Memorial Award is now given annually to the woman who wins the association's City Tournament all-events title each year.

The 1960s

Many bowling stars emerged during the next 40 years, but none shone brighter than the legendary Earl Anthony, considered by most to be the greatest bowler in the history of the sport. Anthony, a Tacoma native, was an outstanding baseball pitcher as a teenager and didn't start bowling until he was 21 years old while working in the warehouse of West Coast Grocery.

He adapted quickly to the lanes, and after two years in Tacoma-area leagues and honing his game in pot matches, he ventured out on the national PBA tour in 1963. However, after three tournaments in Seattle, Portland, and Spokane, he returned to Tacoma, realizing that he was not yet ready for national competition. Anthony continued to work on his game for the next seven years before returning to the tour, where he was an instant national star.

During the 1960s, he was a member of the Carling All-Stars team, along with other Tacoma bowling standouts such as Denny Krick, Paul Garrison, Gary Curry, Larry Fulton, and Rod Pardey. Anthony also competed in the All-Star Travel League and in area and state tournaments. In 1967 he won the GTBA Masters tournament at Pacific Lanes and was a Masters finalist on a number of other occasions. Anthony returned to the PBA tour in the summer of 1970, winning the first of his record 41 national tour events—fittingly, at the Seattle Open at Ballinger Bowl.

Other career highlights include a PBA record of 45 titles, 41 on the national tour; four seniors and two ABC Masters titles (1977 and 1984); five PBA National Championship titles (1973, 1974, 1981, 1982, and 1983); two PBA (Firestone) Tournament of Championships titles (1974 and 1978); 141 top-five finishes on the PBA national tour; a PBA record of 14 consecutive years with at least one title; the PBA Player of the Year a record six times; a six-time Bowling Writers Association of America Bowler of the Year; and *Bowling Magazine*'s first-team All-American a record 12 consecutive years.

Anthony was the first bowler in history to reach $1 million in career earnings and retired with $1,261,931. He was inducted into the PBA Hall of Fame in 1981 and inducted into the ABC Hall of Fame in 1986. He also is a member of the GTBA, the Washington State Bowling Association (WSBA), and Northwest Bowlers Association Halls of Fame. And in 1974, he was named Washington State Athlete of the Year by the Tacoma Athletic Commission.

During his heyday on the tour, Anthony drew praise from many of his contemporaries as well as from past legends. In a 1975 interview with Mike Ingraham, himself a member of the GTBA and Northwest Bowlers Association Halls of Fame in recognition of his 21-year career as the sports writer for bowling with the *Tacoma News Tribune,* the great Don Carter, whom Anthony surpassed as the greatest bowler in history in many people's eyes, had only praise for the Tacoman: "Earl is just fantastic. I didn't think anyone could dominate the tour like he has the last two years with all the talent there is in the PBA. Someone can always get hot for a few weeks, but no one can compare with what he has done.

"He does the same thing every time. He is slow to the line and his speed control is so good... the ball reacts the same way on every shot," Carter said of Anthony's game. "Earl has the best on-the-lane speed control of anyone I've ever seen. He is able to adjust to lane conditions quickly and can throw the ball at any angle."

Although Anthony was a star on the national tour, he maintained his Tacoma residence through 1978 and continued to bowl in the local Travel League when time permitted.

In a 1972 Travel League playoff at New Frontier Lanes, Anthony rolled his first 800-plus series, an 838, based on games of 279–279 and 280.

Anthony was treated with near-hero status by his hometown fans, and on September 24, 1977, the city celebrated him at the Tacoma Bicentennial Pavilion. Tacoma Mayor Gordon N. Johnston declared that Saturday to be Earl Anthony Day and the festivities, co-sponsored by the GTBA and Greater Tacoma bowling proprietors, drew a good-sized crowd, including fans, friends, bowling competitors, and bowling dignitaries from throughout the Northwest.

In 1978 Anthony moved to the Dublin, California, area, where he purchased two bowling centers, and later settled in Cornelius, Oregon, west of Portland. After his retirement from the national tour in 1983, he taught and acted as a spokesman for bowling. He later became one of the nation's top television bowling commentators and a highly sought-after banquet speaker. Anthony's sudden death in 2001 at the age of 63 shocked and saddened the worldwide bowling community.

In 1961 Billie Sulkowsky became the first women to bowl a 300 game in Tacoma, achieving the feat at Tower Lanes. Women's leagues became more popular, junior leagues were in place at all of the centers by the end of the decade, and senior citizen leagues began forming. With the addition of the 32-lane New Frontier Lanes in 1961, Tacoma bowlers had a large variety of centers in which to compete, and the sport continued its unprecedented growth for the next 20 years. For instance, Ozetta Allen bowled the first women's 700-plus series, a 703 effort, based on games of 234, 225, and 244 at the Lakewood Lanes during the 1962–63 season. Ted Pullis bowled only the second 800-plus series in Tacoma bowling history. In addition, the Tacoma All-Star League was formed in 1961 and has been the proving ground for Tacoma bowling stars ever since.

The Match Game tournament was dropped in the early 1960s, and after a two-year void, the area's top bowlers were given another scratch event when Jim Stevenson suggested at a GTBA meeting that Tacoma develop some kind of match play championship with the winner representing the city at the ABC Masters. The first GTBA Masters tournament was held in 1964 at Sixth Avenue Lanes, and Jim

Melin bested a starting field of 55 to win the championship.

The following year Art Childers took over as the Masters committee chairman a week before the event and although it drew only 37 participants, the seed was planted. Under Childers' guidance, the event grew to become the city's premier yearly tournament. It was held in a different center each year, on a rotating basis, a system that remained in place into the mid-1990s. In 1966 the Carling Brewing Company joined the GTBA as a co-sponsor and the five-man finals were televised for the first time.

Television remained part of the Masters for the next six years, with a PBA tour star brought in as the guest commentator each year. Seattle star Johnny Guenther, a future PBA and ABC hall of famer, was the guest commentator for the first few years, and other notable stars including Dick Ritger and Dave Soutar also appeared. Eventually Carling dropped its sponsorship and the television portion of the event was eliminated for nine years before being aired again on cable TV.

The 1970s

Despite the loss of television coverage, the Masters continued to thrive during the 1970s, setting records for numbers of entries, capping out with an all-time marks of 189 in 1979 and 1980. With a downturn in the economy and an overall decline in bowling, entries leveled off to an average of about 130 during the 1980s and 1990s.

A number of Tacoma's biggest bowling stars were crowned Masters champions from the mid-1960s through the mid-'90s. Earl Anthony won his first televised bowling tourney when he captured the 1967 title at Pacific Lanes, while Denny Krick and Jim Melin, intense Anthony rivals during the '60s and early 1970s, have been the only three-time Masters champions. Jeff Mattingly, a PBA national tour standout during the late 1970s and 1980s, won the 1984 Masters. To stay in tune with the changes in bowling, the Masters added a Senior Division in 1985 for bowlers over the age of 55, which remains a popular segment of the tournament.

THE FOLLOWING DEDICATED BOWLERS ARE PLEASED TO SPONSOR THE HISTORY OF BOWLING:

Jim and Margie Oleole

Bunny Tuell

Dr. Lance Lorfeld, Lakewood Chiropractic Center

Bob Hansen Jr.

Jerry and Vicki Williams

Sallie LeMarr, in memory of her husband Jene "Spinner" LeMarr

and son Jene "Tony" LeMarr

The Tacoma 600 Club bowling of 1950: L. to R., Babe Penowich, Dot Pollen, Peggy Ruehle, Carmen Mitchell, Pat Georgetti, Evelyn Stein (courtesy Tacoma Women's Bowling Association).

While Anthony was the dominate star during the 1960s and 1970s, a number of others were in the Tacoma bowling galaxy. Krick, a three-time Masters winner, joined Anthony on the national tour in 1970 and was named PBA Rookie of the Year. The talented right-hander remained on the tour for only for a short time before family obligations took over and he returned to Tacoma. Other Tacoma standouts who tried their luck on the tour, with varying success, during the 1970s included Rod Pardey, Brian Jennings, Bob Gunstrom, and Jerry Williams.

Although a number of bowlers ventured out on tour, Larry Fulton elected a different path. He remained in Tacoma, kept his amateur status, and was one of the city's standout bowlers into the 21st century. Fulton won two regular Masters tournament and one Senior Masters and was named to the Tacoma All-Star team a record 22 times, through 1996.

Bowling was a family thing for the Fultons. Larry's wife, Nadine, began bowling in 1965 and won the City Tournament singles competition twice and was on the TWBA All-Star team 13 times. Her highest game was a 298 and her highest series through 2004 was a 792. When she was inducted into the TWBA Hall of Fame in 1994, she and husband Larry (inducted in 1984) became the second husband-and-wife team honored. The first were Telli (1976) and Jacki Pagni (1969).

Margie Junge Oleole, one of the area's all-time women's standouts, started bowling in 1958, made the All-Star team for the first time in 1962, and continued to be on the team during the next four decades. In 1966 she led the TWBA with a 182 average and has had the city's top average for women three additional times, the latest in 1997 with a 208. In 1984 she rolled a 744 series at Lincoln Lanes; she is believed to be the only woman in Tacoma sports history to both bowl a 300 game (in 2002 at Tower Lanes) and record a hole-in-one in golf (in 1988 at Fort Lewis). Fulton and Oleole are the only Tacoma women to be inducted into the Washington Women's Bowling Association Hall of Fame.

On the junior scene, 17-year-old Joe Gorski grabbed the national spotlight in 1968 when he bowled a 300 game and a 785 three-game series. The 300 was the first ever recorded in junior competition in Tacoma, and the series was the top effort ever, in any competition, by an area youngster. Gorski's 785 stood up for the remainder of the 1967–68 season as the top series mark among all Greater Tacoma bowlers, including adults.

As in all sports, there were many behind-the-scenes movers and shakers who were rarely in the spotlight. In 1970 Cleve Redig, owner of Bowlero Lanes, was elected president of the Bowling Proprietors Association of America (BPAA). Dez Issacson, a longtime Tacoma proprietor (at Lakewood Lanes and Tower Lanes), was given the Vic Lerner Award by the BPAA, for service beyond the call of duty in the national trade organization.

In 1971 one of Tacoma's longtime bowling leaders, Ernie Stowe, resigned after a 24-year stint as the GTBA secretary. Stowe, only the second GTBA secretary, had published a bowling newspaper during the 1940s and 1950s and was secretary of WSBA. He also was the secretary for seven bowling leagues in Tacoma at the time of his resignation from the GTBA post. He is a member of the GTBA Hall of Fame and was a charter member of the WSBA Hall of Fame, along with Tadich and longtime Tacoma bowling official Joe Stemp.

Art Childers was elected by GTBA board of directors to succeed Stowe. A GTBA vice president at the time of the appointment, he had been the chairman of the Masters Committee for the past six years, during a time when it was setting records for number of entries each year. In 1971 he was the chairman of the state bowling tournament and helped attract an all-time record of more than 1,200 teams

to the event in Tacoma. Childers resigned as the GTBA secretary in 1984 and was succeeded by Don Norrell.

Five GTBA presidents and directors have gone on to become presidents of the state association: Red Wakefield, 1955; Ocky Sciacqua, 1960; Art Childers, 1971; Joe Nole, 1978; Don Smith, 1983; and Dick Orr, 1989. Former GTBA presidents John Bulger and Dave Tuell Jr. both were ABC directors. Tacoma also had more than its share of women leaders, including longtime TWBA secretary Jacki Pagni, Peggy Race, Fran Seiler, and current secretary Billie Norrell. Jan Chase, an outstanding athlete who excelled on the bowling lanes, served as TWBA president and then became an official with the Woman's International Bowling Congress (WIBC), based in Greendale, Wisconsin.

On the lanes, Jack Veckman, a 29-year-old right-hander, wrote his name into Tacoma bowling lore when he shattered Tadich's 34-year-old three-game series record, with an 815 set at Puyallup's Daffodil Bowl in 1972. Veckman, an elementary school teacher, started his series with a 257 game, rolled a 300, and closed with a 258 to establish the new record.

During the early 1970s, bowling became prominent in the area schools. Through the efforts of Lou Dales, then manager of Bowlero Lanes, and several other proprietors/managers, 17 Tacoma and Pierce County high school boys' and/or girls' teams competed in the City and County varsity bowling program in 1972. Eight Tacoma-area bowling centers—Bowlero, Tower, Secoma, Daffodil, Lincoln, Paradise, New Frontier, and Villa—joined with the schools to sponsor the program. The school leagues continued to be popular, and state tournaments were later added.

Tacoma was finally rewarded for its position as the hotbed of bowling in the Northwest when it was announced in August 1974 that the PBA would hold its Resident Pro National Championship event at New Frontier Lanes in December. Tacoma responded to the opportunity to host a professional tournament with 256 amateurs participating in the pro-am, a figure that amazed PBA as well as Tacoma bowling officials. Ray Orf of St. Louis won the event.

In 1976 Tacoma sent another of its young lions, Jeff Mattingly, out on the tour. The right-hander enjoyed a 10-year pro career that included a national tour championship in 1978 and earnings of more than $172,000 (during a time when first place in PBA tournaments averaged from $10,000 up to $25,000 for "major events"). Mattingly's career was cut short when he was killed in an auto accident in the winter of 1986–87.

Bowling was at its peak during the 1970s, with approximately 25,000 men, women, and youngsters competing in local leagues. Mixed leagues became popular; the sixth annual 1976–77 City Mixed Tournament drew a record 350 teams, snapping the mark of 216 set the previous year. The new 36-lane Paradise Village opened in 1976 with automatic scoring machines. The machines were first introduced on the commercial market in the late 1960s, and after they were installed at Paradise, other Tacoma centers were quick to follow suit.

The 1980s

Brian Voss, who was stationed at Fort Lewis, earned a number of area and regional honors before venturing onto the national tour scene. He won his first PBA title in 1983 before leaving the area and going on to win 22 titles through early 2004, with career earnings of $2,085,688, fifth on the all-time PBA list. Voss was the PBA Player of the Year in 1988, winning two titles and leading all money earners with $225,485. Voss was inducted into the PBA Hall of Fame in 1994.

Tacoma again burst onto the national bowling scene in 1984 when the first of three Ladies Professional Bowlers Tour (LPBT) national events was held at the newly built, 40-lane Narrows Plaza Bowl and Entertainment center. Jeanne Maiden, at the time an Ohio resident who later married Tacoma sports figure Stan Naccarato and moved to Tacoma, won the first tourney; Aleta Sill won in 1985; and Leila Wagner, a former Seattle resident, claimed the 1986 crown. All three tournaments drew large crowds as the city's fever for bowling continued to amaze national bowling officials.

Maiden has bowled at least 25 perfect games, including a record 23 by a right-handed woman and consecutive strikes of 40. She won nine national and five regional LPBT titles and holds the WIBC records for a six-game total (1,693 pins), nine-game total (2,353), and 18-game total (4,452). She was Tacoma's first woman to bowl an 800 series, a feat she accomplished in 2002 with an 820 three-game set at Tower Lanes.

Tacoma reached its bowling zenith in January 1987 when the BPAA's $500,000 Seagram's Cooler U.S. Open tournament was held at Narrows Plaza Bowl. The tournament, which was the richest in bowling history (a $500,000 prize fund, with $100,000 going to eventual winner Del Ballard Jr. of Richardson, Texas), was the first on the PBA's winter tour that year; it was televised nationally. The tournament was especially significant for Tacoma bowling fans because Anthony ended a 3-1/2-year retirement to compete in the event.

Tacomans packed Narrows Plaza Bowl throughout the week, and on the morning of the five-man finals, a line of people snaked outside the bowling center waiting to purchase tickets.

The 1990s and Beyond

Although bowling remained its main focus, Tacoma lanes, like bowling alleys across the nation, were becoming a family entertainment centers. Bowlero opened the first full-service restaurant, cocktail lounge, and child-care center; New Frontier introduced pull tabs; and Pacific Lanes opened the first public card room. By the mid-1990s, nearly every bowling center had most, if not all, these amenities. In December 1995, Tower Lanes, under the co-ownership of Lou Dales and Vern Issacson, removed eight lanes and installed an indoor 18-hole miniature-golf course.

Bowling continued at a high standard in the late 1980s and into the mid-1990s. Jerry Ledbetter, a former Masters champ and area standout, earned a berth on the Team USA, which represented the United States when bowling was introduced to the Winter Olympic Games for the first time in Helsinki, Finland, in 1987. That same year Joan O'Rourke, a 1972 graduate of Mount Tahoma High School, bowled the second 300 game in Tacoma women's history, on December 9 at Narrows Plaza Bowl.

On December 23, 1991, Dave Hanson stunned the area and set a new all-time record series of 878 at New Frontier Lanes with games of 278, 300, and 300. The effort was even more remarkable since Hanson was on duty as a desk man at the center at the time and was running back and forth from the control desk and the lanes between frames. Other notable high series were a pair of 886s by Simon Little in 1990 and Adam Prichard in 1995.

A number of area bowlers ventured out on the national tour during the late 1980s and early 1990s, including Scott Alexander, who won a PBA title in 1995. In addition to Dave Tuell, Darrel Curtis of Kent, a regular bowler in Tacoma leagues, joined the PBA Senior Tour and won two championships, in 1991 and 1993.

Besides Nadine Fulton, among the area's top women bowlers during the 1970s, 1980s, and 1990s were Margie Oleole, Gerry Garrett, Luann Moore, and Rhonda Hanson. Moore was named to several junior All-Star teams before joining the adult leagues at age 17, and she was named to her first of 10 TWBA All-Star teams at the age of 21 (in 1977). She won the Babe Penowich Award on four occasions and won two Triple Crowns in the Classic League at Lincoln Lanes. At the state level, she was on the winning teams of 1982, 1984, and 1986, and she won the singles title as well as the doubles (with Nadine Fulton) while setting a state record with a 1,361 pinfall. She and Fulton also won the doubles in 1998, and in 1996 Moore won the all-events, setting a record with a 2,007 pinfall. Moore's high game was a 299 and her top series was a 779.

Today bowling continues to be a vibrant part of the community, an activity shared by high-average bowlers as well as once-a-week players, youngsters, and senior citizens, who enjoy the companionship, competition, and camaraderie of bowling.

From L. to R., Dave Tuell Jr., Carl Johnson, unknown, Wally Jenks, Ken Hand (courtesy Greater Tacoma Bowlers Association).

CHAPTER 16

BOXING

Frankie Williams as a young boxer, ca. 1920 (SSM, 1997.20.2).

Many young boxers in the country got their start participating in the amateur Golden Gloves bouts designed to encourage a positive lifestyle for young people. The program was initiated under the sponsorship of the Chicago Tribune in 1923. The Tacoma Athletic Commission (TAC) began sponsoring the local event in 1949. A variety of venues were used for the boxing tournament, including the Tacoma National Guard Armory, the University of Puget Sound (UPS) Fieldhouse, and the Tacoma Dome Convention Center. Stan Naccarato was a key promoter of the tournaments and the ring announcer for the events for more than 40 years.

Some of Tacoma's boxing greats began their amateur and professional careers as Golden Gloves champions. Others got their start earlier in the century. Some of the best known include Freddie Steele, Pat McMurtry, Sugar Ray Seales, Leo Randolph, and Davey Armstrong, along with Mike McMurtry, Chalky Wright, Dave Davey, Bob McKinney, George Wright, Oscar Moore, Bobby Pasquale, Myron Watkins, Robert Linton, Vincent Jones, Frankie Armstrong, Al Armstrong, Dennis Armstrong, Rocky Lockridge, Dewayne Jamison, Johnny "Bump City" Bumphus, and Emmit Linton Jr.

One of the most famous heavyweights in Tacoma boxing history was Frank Farmer, who was born on December 2, 1889, in Sumner but resided in Kapowsin. Known in his early years as the "Kapowsin Logger" and later as the "Old Bald Eagle," Farmer's ring career spanned 23 years. He reportedly won his first fight by knockout in 1907, although his first documented bout was on July 4, 1911, against Eddie White.

Farmer was known as a smart fighter who brought experience and ring smarts to his craft as well as physical strength. According to sportswriter Elliott Metcalf, Farmer could master all but a small group of fighters in the country. His known record reads like a who's who of famous boxers, from the Welterweight (147 pounds) through the Heavyweight Divisions. They included Fred Fulton, the Minnesota Plasterer; Jimmy Clabby, the Indiana Wasp; Jack Dillon, the Hoosier Bearcat; Tommy Gibbons; Fat Willie Meehan; Gunboat Smith; Kid Norfolk; and Bill Tate.

Farmer was undoubtedly Tacoma's longest-running main-event attraction. After professional boxing was shut down by most local authorities on the West Coast throughout 1912, Tacoma Eagles' promoter George Shanklin called on Frank Farmer to headline the first experimental four-round bootleg card when boxing returned in early 1913. Farmer came through with a winning decision over Billy Ross. When the authorities agreed to allow six-round bouts later that year, Shanklin chose Farmer for top billing in the main event, which again he won. Over the years, Farmer also boxed at many other Tacoma venues, such as the Moose Hall, Glide Rink, Tahoma Hall, the Auditorium, Greenwich Coliseum, and the Garden Athletic Club.

During one season, Farmer fought as the main attraction on nine straight Eagles' boxing cards without losing a bout. The most notable of these was his battle with future Boxing Hall of Famer Jack Dillon, the former world light heavyweight champion. Known as the "Giant Killer," Dillon had planned to use the Tacoma match to launch a lucrative West Coast tour, but these plans were derailed by Farmer's quick fists.

Nationally known fighters who were used to fighting 10-, 15-, and 20-round battles were reluctant to bring their hard-won reputations to the shorter bouts allowed in the West Coast states. Often a local fighter who was used to the shorter distance could "steal" a win in a shorter bout before his more-famous Eastern opponent could get warmed up. Sometimes special "arrangements" were made between managers to protect their fighters from such an outcome.

Inigo Luchessi (L.) promoted professional boxing in Tacoma in the 1950s–80s; Tommy Egan (R.) was the California welterweight champion and won a 10-round decision over Tommy James at the Tacoma Ice Palace in 1947; and Virgil Larson fought as an amateur at the Starlight AC during his years at Lincoln High, Gonzaga, and College of Puget Sound (courtesy Ruggles Larson).

After Farmer's draw with top middleweight contender Al Sommers at the Rose City Athletic Club in 1916, it was discovered that their managers had previously agreed that the fighters should box to a draw. As a result, the manager of the club barred the participants from the facility forever.

Farmer was set to fight Sgt. Al Ross in 1917 at the Eagles Lodge. As a special promotion, Charlie Lewis of the local Burnside hat store offered a new cap to each winner. Not to be outdone, his competitor, Art McGinley, offered a new one to each loser. All 14 boxers on the card received new hats—as well as their purses!

A year later, Farmer won a six-round decision over Mick King, the former Australian claimant for the world middleweight title, to annex the Pacific Coast Heavyweight Championship. According to a *News Tribune* account, "When the decision was given to Farmer, the crowd acted as no other ever did at a Tacoma fight. Bankers, loggers, fishermen, and men from every walk of life leaped into the ring."

Pat McMurtry stayed in shape with a strict regimen that included jumping rope (courtesy Pat McMurtry).

On October 20, 1920, Farmer was matched at Civic Arena in Seattle with legendary African-American fighter Sam Langford. The match was looked upon with special interest because Langford, though past his prime, was recognized as one of the greatest fighters who had ever laced on a glove. Former heavyweight champ Jack Johnson had refused to defend his championship against Langford because Sam had given him his hardest fight in 1905, just two years before Johnson had won the title. Jack Dempsey admitted that as a young fighter coming up, he was afraid of Langford and refused several opportunities to fight him. Intimidated for the only time in his career, Farmer made his poorest showing ever in the Northwest, losing a four-round decision. As a result, he was not asked to fight again in Seattle for almost three years.

Farmer, however, remained Tacoma's top heavyweight drawing card. On January 12, 1922, Eagles' promoter Shanklin again called on Farmer, this time to headline the inaugural boxing card at a newly built Eagles Lodge against nationally ranked heavyweight contender Jack McAuliffe from Detroit. For the first time, Farmer failed to post a win at the Eagles as McAuliffe recorded his 11th KO in 11 straight bouts. According to Elliott Metcalf, the fight with McAuliffe ended Farmer's career as a national top headliner.

Farmer earned more than $100,000 in the ring, a goodly sum for that era. He married, bought a farm, and was raising a family but by 1930 he confided to Metcalf that he had lost his home and family and was broke. On March 3, 1930, at more than 40 years old, he was matched to fight Sparkplug Boyd in a small-time show in Tacoma for a purse of probably no more than $25. He pleaded with his sportswriter friends not "to queer this one. Don't rap it. Give me a break. … I'm broke … flat broke. I need the money," then he went into the ring against their advice to fight his younger opponent. Ahead on points halfway through his next-to-last round, he came out of a clinch with his arms hanging loose at his sides, collapsed in the ring, and died. A coroner's inquest found that his death was caused by heart failure rather than by his opponent's blows.

The day after the fight, Metcalf wrote that "Frank wasn't hit by a blow hard enough to cause fatality." He "carried a brooding, bleeding, tired heart that was torn to shreds through grief that extended over long months."

Frank Farmer held at various times the Light Heavyweight Championship of Canada, the Pacific Northwest Heavyweight Championship, the Pacific Coast Light Heavyweight crown, and the Pacific Coast Heavyweight title. Though the research organization BoxRec credits him with 118 professional fights, Elliott Metcalf estimated the number at closer to 400. Although the total number of battles may be uncertain, there is no uncertainty that Frank Farmer was one of the most colorful and popular fighters in Tacoma sports history.

Promoter George Shanklin

Technically speaking, professional boxing between 1910 and 1933 was illegal—during Farmer's career—but the actual enforcement of the state law forbidding prizefighting was left to local authorities. Tacoma, like a lot of other communities around the country, allowed four- or sometimes six-round boxing "exhibitions" at private clubs on a "members only" basis. To become a club member, one had only to purchase a ticket at the door.

In October 1910, the Tacoma Eagles Lodge leased the old Germania Hall at Ninth and Pacific Avenue to stage a boxing exhibition between heavyweights Lee Croft and Jack Lester. The man in charge of the promotion for the Eagles was George Shanklin. It was the first boxing show in Tacoma with a definite scheduled starting time, a printed program, no delays between bouts, and seat ushers. The Eagles continued to promote shows under the direction of Shanklin for the next 25 years or more. During that period, no fighters were ever unpaid for their services and no boxing fans ever received less than full value for their money.

Shanklin's sponsorship allowed Tacoma boxing fans to witness top-notch battlers from Tacoma and nearby: heavyweights Joe Bonds, Young Hector, and Frank Farmer; light heavyweights Fred Lenhart, Leo Lomski, and Joe ("Sparkplug") Boyd; welterweights Billy Wright, Ted Krache, Johnny Jordan, Dode Bercot, and Bobby Harper; and lightweights Bud Anderson, Frenchy Vaise, Johnny O'Leary, Doc Snell, and Wildcat Carter. World middleweight champions Freddie Steele and Al Hostak both were introduced to Northwest fans in Shanklin shows. Future world champion junior lightweights Mike Ballerino and Tod Morgan both

made Tacoma a base of operations for ring activity in the early 1920s. Shanklin also was a mentor for Eddie Marino, Jack Connor, and Dave Miller.

Near the end of his career as a promoter, Shanklin was honored for his 25 years in boxing. Those in attendance at the Winthrop Hotel banquet in 1935 included members of Tacoma's business community as well as Freddie Steele, Seattle boxing promoter Nate Druxman, Bobby Harper, and the legendary Mike Gibbons from St. Paul, Minnesota. A year later, on August 20, 1936, in his first fight after taking the middleweight championship from Babe Risko, Steele fought Jackie Aldare on a Shanklin card at the standard rate for a main-event fighter. It was Steele's way of paying back Shanklin for his efforts in launching Steele's career earlier.

Trainer Eddie Marino

Eddie Marino, originally from Seattle's Georgetown, completed a career of 168 professional bouts. Marino was the lightweight champion of Canada and had fought the great featherweight champion Abe Attell for the world's featherweight championship. The prominent featherweight fighter returned to the Pacific Northwest shortly before World War I to train and manage fighters. During World War I he was a boxing instructor for the Marines, and after the war he opened up his own gymnasium at 719-1/2 Commerce Street in Tacoma. Although Marino was already an astute trainer, Shanklin helped to establish him as a boxing manager and gym owner.

During his 10-year Tacoma tenure, Marino handled Tex Vernon, Heinie Schumann, Frank Farmer, Mike O'Leary, Harry Braner, Irving Seldon, and Frankie Murphy, all capable men but none of championship caliber. Discouraged by financial adversity and his inability to develop a future champion, he decided to give up boxing. In 1930 he returned to Seattle, opened a cigar store, and created a makeshift gym behind the shop. At this time, after he had given up his dream, he discovered Al Hostak and trained him to become a world middleweight champion.

Eddie Marino's boxing legacy did not end with his departure from Tacoma. Both Dave Miller, Freddie Steele's manager, and Jack Connor, manager as well as Steele's first and only trainer, cut their boxing teeth as Marino's assistants at the Commerce Street gym. Homer Amundsen, who became the foremost boxing teacher in the Northwest during the 1940s and 1950s, learned to box from Marino and fought on the amateur boxing shows staged by Marino at his gym.

Marino is still revered today as an outstanding boxing trainer and teacher. His prime pupil, former middleweight champion Al Hostak, called him "a professor of boxing." Pat McMurtry's trainer, Bob Jackson, termed him "the master of them all." His influence can be traced all to way to Auburn's Greg Haugen, whose first boxing teacher was a student of Homer Amundsen.

Dave Miller and Freddie Steele

Born in Boston, Dave Miller moved to Seattle at an early age, ran away from home at age 13, and crossed the border to Vancouver, British Columbia, where he sold peanuts at a racetrack. While there, he crashed the gate to see future world lightweight champ Freddie Welsh fight and became hooked on the sporting life. He tried a little boxing and fought enough amateur bouts to convince himself that he was not a coming champion. During World War I, he worked in the Tacoma shipyards and began hanging around Eddie Marino's gym.

By the late 1920s and early 1930s, Miller was part owner of a boxing gym and managing a stable of professional boxers that included Don Fraser, Jimmy Britt, Frankie Britt, Neil Kilbane, Harry Ketchel, Fred Lenhart, and Jimmy McLeod. But his best fighter was the future middleweight champion, Freddie Steele.

Steele, born December 18, 1912, in Tacoma, began hanging around Miller's gym sometime in 1927, running errands, carrying water bottles, and packing fighters' grips. At first Miller paid no attention to the scrawny, weak-looking 106-pound youngster until Steele prevailed upon his uncle, Emmett Angle, a close friend of Miller's, to take him to the gym's office for a proper introduction. Angle told Miller how badly Steele wanted to learn how to box and asked him to look after Steele so that he didn't get hurt or into any trouble.

At first Miller refused to take Steele's pugilistic aspirations seriously. Steele was put to work after school as an office boy, errand runner, and golf caddy. All the while, Steele worked out every day in the gym, absorbing tricks from the other fighters and begging Miller to use him in a curtain raiser. Miller finally relented but told him he would have to wait until after his 15th birthday. At 115 pounds, Freddie Steele fought his first Tacoma bout in January 1928, and by the end of the year he was undefeated in 12 fights. Dave Miller finally took notice, outlined a training routine, and saw to it that Steele was properly handled and fit to fight.

Steele, who wasn't to meet his birth father until many years later, described Miller as "everything to me, my manager, my dad, my adviser." Throughout much of his boxing career, he lived in a room at Miller's Lincolnshire Hotel in Tacoma, where the desk clerks were instructed to make sure Steele was home before curfew. Steele later explained that after every fight, Miller would lay out the purse money on a table and deal out each share. Then he would give Steele $10 for spending money and make him deposit the rest of his share in the bank. Steele would them have to return the passbook to Miller.

At the age of 17, in his first professional bout as a middleweight, Steele knocked out Jimmy Farrar in three rounds. Steele continued unbeaten in his first 30 fights, winning 26 and drawing four. His first loss came in 1931, when Tony Portillo beat him. He lost again in 1932 to Tommy Herman in a four-round bout held in Los Angeles. After the loss to Herman, he was undefeated for 46 bouts. On July 30, 1936, Steele challenged Syracuse, New York's Babe Risko for the World's Middleweight Championship, fought at Seattle's Civic Stadium. Promoted by Nate Druxman, Steele won the event and went on to take the NBA crown in a 10-round decision over a boxer named Gorilla Jones. Steele defended his championship four times after that. After Steele became champion, he and Miller traveled all around the country, with Steele winning all his fights, including three title defenses.

At the time of Miller's death on August 25, 1937, Steele was training for a title defense against top contender Ken Overlin, scheduled for one week later. Steele dedicated his effort to Miller's memory and knocked out Overlin in four rounds, the only time when future middleweight champ Overlin was ever counted out. After the fight, Steele was

CHAPTER SPONSORED BY:

272-1208
OFFICE (24 HRS)

564-6966
HOME

"C.J." Johnson
BAIL BONDS
"SINCE 1951"

620 SO. 11TH STREET • TACOMA, WA 98405

For Clarence "C.J" Johnson, *endorsing* athletics is the best form of participation. Though he played high school football in 1941, he has mostly been a supporter of the Tacoma Athletic Commission (TAC): "I like what they do for sports scholarships; no one else seems to award them," he says. This year will be the 57th year for the Golden Gloves, a statewide amateur boxing championship—and a huge source of scholarship funds for the TAC. The event is the second longest-running Golden Gloves competition in the country and sponsored by the TAC, USA Boxing, the Boys and Girls Clubs of Pierce County, and the Tacoma Boxing Club. Johnson, father of three girls and grandfather of one, has been posting bonds since 1951 and still operates C.J. Johnson Bail Bonds. "Anything you bump up against outside of the ring, give us a call," he laughs. He recently celebrated his 80th birthday on a trip to Alaska with all of his family.

C.J. and Jimmie Johnson, married for 55 years.

still so distraught about Miller's death that he broke down and wept openly in the ring.

Following Miller's death, Steele lost the edge that had made him such a great champion. Not only did he lose his manager and trainer, he lost a mentor, a financial advisor, and his best friend.

In 1938 he also lost his NBA title to Seattle's Al Hostak by a knockout in the first round. Hostak told Seattle boxing manager and promoter George Chemeres that he hadn't fought the real Freddie Steele that day in Seattle. "What happened is that Steele's manager, Dave Miller, had died and that broke Steele's heart," Chemeres explained. "He lost his desire to fight." The record speaks for itself. Steele lost only two fights in the 139 he had prior to Miller's death. He lost three out of six afterward.

After the Hostak bout, Steele retired at the age of 28, but he did come out of retirement one more time. On May 23, 1941, he was knocked out in the fifth round by Jimmy Casino in a fight held in Hollywood.

Both Stan Naccarato and George Chemeres remember Freddie Steele's finesse as a boxer. "I sat on my dad's lap and watched Freddie Steele fight Babe Risko," said Naccarato. "Steele's loss to Hostak was tragic. That's when he wasn't training anymore. But he was one helluva fighter." For Chemeres, "[Sugar] Ray Robinson was the best fighter, pound for pound, ever. I would have liked [to see] Freddie Steele in his prime fighting Ray Robinson. I would have paid to see that one."

Freddie Steele began a second career in the movies (video catalogs list his acting credit as Fred Steele). According to his daughter, he made 15 films in eight years. For some, he provided the footwork for boxing movies or had a nonspeaking role. His most famous appearance was in the *Story of G.I. Joe*, a movie based on war correspondent Ernie Pyle's stories, starring Robert Mitchum and Burgess Meredith.

Freddie Steele's trainer in the 1930s was Jack Connor, who was also a boxing and wrestling matchmaker. But Connor first became known in the 1920s as the manager and trainer of Johnny Jordan, a prominent light/welterweight, and Eddie "Kayo" Roberts, a world-rated welterweight. Roberts parlayed a one-round knockout (in an overweight match) of then world champ Joe Dundee into a coast-to-

coast campaign that made him one of the most financially successful local fighters of the era. Connor, who was active as a boxing trainer well into the 1950s, was coined "Tacoma's Mr. Boxing" by the *Tacoma News Tribune*'s sports editor Dan Walton.

Trainer Homer Amundsen

Homer Amundsen became interested in boxing in 1919 while eavesdropping on postfight discussions between hotel patrons where he was a bellhop. Curious, the 16-year-old bought a ticket to one of George Shanklin's fight cards and became hooked. He enrolled in boxing classes at the Tacoma YMCA and then became a student of Eddie Marino's. He fought some amateur bouts on a few of Marino's weekly

Jack Dempsey (L.) visited the Pacific Northwest in 1921 and on other occasions to referee bouts and help sell U.S. War Bonds (SSM, 1816).

amateur boxing shows, but his slight frame convinced him that his future lay in the business end of the game.

Amundsen's first gym was a makeshift ring constructed in a shed in his backyard. When success followed, he moved to the Starlight Athletic Club. He trained hundreds of amateur boxers during his 30 years as a teacher.

Amundsen was a firm believer that a young fighter should be trained thoroughly in the fundamentals of footwork, balance, and leverage. He told Charles Leseman in a 1954 interview that "it is wrong to change a fighter's natural style. The art of training is not to alter his style but to encourage and improve it. An apprenticeship in boxing must be served the same as in any trade, usually three to four years. Boxers today are rushed along too fast."

Amundsen's first notable student to graduate to the professional ranks was young George Dixon, who fought up and down the Pacific Coast. In the late 1940s, Amundsen developed heavyweight Dave Davey, who left Tacoma to campaign in the East. Davey fought two memorable battles with Dan Bucceroni, a leading contender for Rocky Marciano's heavyweight title. Amundsen's two most famous students were Tacoma boxing legends Pat McMurtry and Mike McMurtry, title contenders in the 1950s.

Tacoma's Boxing Luminaries

Rocco Marchegiano, a 1947 Fort Lewis private at the end of World War II, responded to a notice posted at the base by a Tacoma gym looking for sparring partners. Harold Bird, his manager at the time, brought Rocco to the gym to spar against "Big Bill" Little. When Rocco saw Big Bill, he was amazed at his height. Rocco couldn't hit him—he just kept swinging and hitting nothing but air. Bird told him that was enough, gave him his $8 for the effort, and sent him back to the base, where a year later he won the Fort Lewis heavyweight title. "I nearly stayed in the Army," Rocco later explained, "but decided to get out and have a try at baseball." Instead, he entered Golden Gloves competition as Rocky Marciano—and retired in 1956 as the undefeated heavyweight champion of the world.

Although the early years of Tacoma boxing included visits from many noteworthies, such as Tommy Burns, Joey Maxim, and Jack Dempsey, the story of Marciano's young

history here underscores the vibrancy and strength of the local boxing scene, even without such luminaries.

Longtime Tacoma Athletic Commission (TAC) director Frank Pignatario was involved with the local boxing scene ever since he witnessed the first Golden Gloves event in 1949. "I remember that local trainer Jack Connor had a fighter by the name of Eddie 'Kayo' Roberts who was a helluva puncher, thus the nickname 'Kayo.' Jack got him a match with Joe Dundee, who was a top contender at the time. Roberts stopped Dundee with a first-round knockout on December 4, 1926, in San Francisco, which was a big upset. The rematch was in New York's Madison Square Garden a month later. Eddie was a tough guy to handle. Jack had to lock him in his room in Manhattan, but somehow he got loose. Jack couldn't find him, but Eddie did show up on the day of the fight. Well, he was way out of it and lost a 10-round decision despite having Dundee down early in the fight."

Pignatario also recalled Jimmy Fitzpatrick, "a nice middleweight fighter. He fought four-rounders. He later joined the Tacoma police department. And Harry Weinstone was a devoted TAC member who loved to work with the Golden Gloves. He usually was the observer at the weigh-ins and also did some amateur boxing in his youth. Chi Chi Britt and Wild Cat Carter were two old-time fighters in the '20s and '30s. They were considered good, hard club fighters."

Ruggles Larson began boxing at Stewart Junior High School in 1946, continuing while attending Lincoln High School and during his time with the U.S. Marines. He first started training at Homer Amundsen's Starlight Athletic Club, located above a meat market at 1114-1/2 Market Street between 1948 and 1950. The facility then moved to an upstairs area of the Memorial Gym on the College of Puget Sound (now UPS) campus. There was just enough room for a ring, a couple of sparring bags, and space to skip rope and shadow-box. In 1951 the pugilists moved from the North End to 917-1/2 Commerce Street and formed the Central Boxing Club.

In 1967 Ruggles decided to create the Monteczuma Boxing Club to promote fighting with local boxers in the region from Vancouver, British Columbia, to Eugene, Oregon. At the time he was covering the Pacific Northwest as a writer for *Ring* magazine and thought he would be able to take advantage of his connections to resurrect boxing. But pro sports were taking a foothold on spectator participation and fans' discretionary income; unfortunately, people were not willing to come out to watch boxing as they had in the past, and thus ended Ruggles' promoting career.

The Tacoma boxing community opened its arms to Muhammad Ali, even after he was stripped of his heavyweight boxing title and licenses following his refusal to join the U.S. Army. Tacoma businessman Morley Brotman, along with Dick Francisco, tried to get the Washington State Athletic Commission (WSAC) to reinstate Ali's professional license. When the attempt failed, the two, according to sports writer Stan Farber, "researched the possibility of putting together an Ali–Joe Frazier heavyweight title fight aboard a Boeing jumbo jet" because "no state then would have control of a license." Even though the aerial bout never materialized, Ali was in Tacoma during the state hearings on his license, visited the Tacoma Boy's Club, and

wowed spectators by hitting the punching bag so hard it was knocked off its ceiling supports.

Actual fighters were not the only ones to grace the local boxing scene. Inigo Lucchesi ranks as one of the top old-time promoters, along with Jack Connor and Paavo Ketonen. Lucchesi organized two sold-out matches between Pat McMurtry and, first, Ezzard Charles and then Willie Pastrano, held in Tacoma's Lincoln Bowl in 1956. He did the same a decade later for George Wright, who fought Randy Sandy and Phil Moyer in sellouts at the Tacoma Armory.

The TAC trio of John McCallum, Dr. Charles P. Larson, and Jimmy Rondeau was also influential in the sport, locally and nationally. McCallum, a sports writer whose entries can be found today in the *Encyclopaedia Britannica*, is best known for his history of the world heavyweight championship. Dr. Larson was a Tacoma pathologist with a national reputation as a crime expert. In 1957 he was appointed by Governor Albert Rosellini as chairman of WSAC. He was also a boxing enthusiast who in 1960

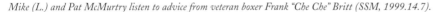

Mike (L.) and Pat McMurtry listen to advice from veteran boxer Frank "Che Che" Britt (SSM, 1999.14.7).

became president of the National Boxing Association (NBA) and was the World Boxing Association (WBA)'s first president the next year.

Larson was president when Emile Griffith KO'd Benny Paret in 1962 in the 12th round of their welterweight title fight in Madison Square Garden. Paret was so badly hurt that brain surgery was required. Larson said it appeared that Paret's head was impaled in the ropes or against the turnbuckle, and his head being in a fixed position when he was knocked out may have been the real reason for the injury. He said, "A study of the pictures of the Paret-Griffith bout may indicate that some redesign of the turnbuckle or change in the ropes will help. We want to do everything possible to prevent such injuries," Larson added. Larson then proposed a number of changes to the safety code designed to reduce the likelihood of future tragedies.

Jimmy Rondeau was regularly in the ring as referee in Tacoma after he moved his family from Bremerton in 1942. From 1946 to 1968, he refereed for Golden Gloves bouts in Tacoma, Seattle, and Portland. When Governor Dan Evans appointed Rondeau to the Washington Boxing Commission in 1970, he could no longer referee Washington bouts, but he could still be found in the rings of foreign countries. The most famous fight he refereed was when George Foreman defeated Ken Norton in Caracas, Venezuela, thus giving Foreman the right to fight—and lose to—Muhammad Ali for the heavyweight title in 1974.

"Looking back on my years in the ring and on the sidelines," remembered Rondeau, "the most interesting contests were held at McNeil Island federal prison. Cy Rubado was the prison's boxing coach. He occasionally matched inmates who were constantly fighting each other in the prison yard. His instructions [to me as referee] would sometimes be, 'Let this go until someone doesn't want to get up.' Sometimes it was a heavyweight up against a lightweight, but [it was] always interesting."

The McMurtry Brothers

Pat McMurtry had a wonderful career in the ring. As a boxer, he climbed as high as fifth in the world heavyweight ranks. He is remembered particularly as a participant in the two fights that drew the largest boxing crowds in Tacoma history.

On July 13, 1956, Pat McMurtry battled and won a 10-round decision over former champion Ezzard Charles at the Lincoln Bowl. Charles was in the twilight of his career. Indeed, he fought just two more times and lost them both. Nevertheless, this was a big win for McMurtry.

Two months later, Pat was at it again. This time he took on Willie Pastrano at the Lincoln Bowl while 11,000 people watched. Pastrano was seven years away from winning the light heavyweight title against Harold Johnson. Pastrano won the 10-round bout, but that fight, along with the Ezzard Charles bout, established McMurtry's reputation as one tough guy, pushing him up in the rankings.

Pat McMurtry and his younger brother Mike got their boxing start at the Starlight Athletic Club on Market Street in Tacoma. The gym was on the top floor of the building, situated over a butcher shop, a grocery store, and a bakery. Homer Amundsen, McMurtry's manager, owned the building along with Kelley's Gym at Ninth and Commerce. "Kelley's was dingy, lighting was poor, the wood was rotten, and there was always the smell of wintergreen from the rubdowns the guys got," Mike McMurtry remembered.

"That was when boxing was boxing, not like the carnival it is today," Pat McMurtry said. "I started when I was six years old. Dad put gloves on us. Every Christmas we got a pair of boxing gloves. That was the known package under the tree. When my parents were first married, my dad told my mother that they were going to have two sons and they both were going to fight. That is what he got. Mike had 214 amateur fights and lost seven, and I had 105 and lost two."

Mike McMurtry got hurt in his first professional bout, against Ken Kass, and never boxed again. Prior to that, the younger McMurtry boxed for Gonzaga and Idaho State. He won the 1954 National Collegiate Athletics Association (NCAA) heavyweight boxing title, went into the Marines after college, and in 1959 had the fight against Kass at Seattle's Sick's Stadium as a preliminary to his brother's main event. Three day's later, the doctors found a blood clot in Mike's brain and operated.

"I am paying for it, no question about it," Mike admitted later on. "If you get hit around the head—I don't care what anybody says—it will take its toll." But in the next breath, Mike McMurtry also acknowledged that "if I had to do it all over, I would do the same damn thing. I enjoyed what I did. I had a lot of fun, especially in college. I traveled 20,000 miles just fighting. I was real good with the capitals of the states."

One of Pat McMurtry's big highlights came when in 1958 he fought and beat George Chuvalo at Madison Square Garden in New York City. Chuvalo, who was the Canadian heavyweight champion at the time, rarely hit the canvas, but he did that night. "I was the first to put him down," Pat McMurtry admits proudly. "Referee Rudy Goldstein started the count, but George jumped right up. Chuvalo was very tough but a nice guy."

"The win over Chuvalo should have been a stepping stone to a showdown with heavyweight champion Floyd Patterson," maintained Peter Bacho, author of *Boxing in Black and White*. "After the Chuvalo fight, sports writer Harry Grayson approached McMurtry and his father, Clarence, about a deal he had in mind. McMurtry would have to move to Boston and have Sam Silverman promote him." Clarence rejected the deal and Pat agreed to a decision that eliminated his chances of becoming a heavyweight champion.

Instead, he fought Nino Valdes in 1958 and Eddie Machen in 1959. Pat McMurtry lost both bouts and his career ended. For him "the losses were unexpected," continued Bacho. "It galls McMurtry to believe he could have beaten Patterson. … He has memories of ring victories and dramatic knockout punches against quality opponents and the glowing accounts of old-time fight fans who saw him box in person or on television.

"Tacomans could boast of Pat McMurtry, a legitimate title contender and potential heavyweight champion. He was homegrown—one of Tacoma's own—starting with his hard-nosed, blue-collar roots on Tacoma's South Side. His fans had known him since his early amateur days in the 1940s, often watching his bouts in person or following his career through the sports pages of the *Tacoma News Tribune* and the region's other dailies. In an era before major-league sports arrived in the Pacific Northwest, McMurtry was arguably the region's biggest sports star."

Sugar Ray Seales won an Olympic gold medal in 1972 (courtesy Tacoma News Tribune).

Sugar Ray Seales

The Seales family came from the Virgin Islands, landing in Tacoma by happenstance. In a game of war among a group of friends, Ray Seale's brother Wilbur had gotten hit in the eye. When the condition worsened, an uncle stationed at Fort Lewis encouraged the family to move to Tacoma, where there were better medical facilities. The family settled in 1963 one block from the downtown Tacoma Boys Club located at South 25th and Yakima. The three Seales brothers—Charles, Wilbur, and Ray—soon found their way to the club and into the ring.

Their introduction to the sport had begun in the Virgin Islands. "We were already into boxing," Ray Seales explained. "Our dad had boxed three years in the U.S. Army and taught us." The three brothers arrived at the Tacoma Boys Club at a momentous time. They joined the four Armstrong brothers—Davey, Dennis, Al, and Frankie—along with Leo Randolph, Dale Grant, and Mitchell Mayes. With so much talent, the club was soon recognized as one of the best boxing clubs in the country. The team ultimately stayed together until after the 1976 Montreal Olympics.

Seales obtained the "Sugar Ray" moniker early in his career. He reminded people of a young Sugar Ray Robinson, who, like Seales, was left-handed. Although Robinson eventually converted to a right-handed boxer, Seales never did. Using his speed and power, Ray Seales moved to the top. He won just about every amateur title there was. In 1972 he qualified for the U.S. Olympic team and won the gold medal in the 139-pound class at the Munich games.

Seales turned professional in January 1973 and compiled a record of 70 wins, six losses, and four draws. Along the

Dave "Davey" Strandley was a heavyweight contender in the 1950s—and a marbles champion in grade school (courtesy Leonard Strandley).

way, he won the North American Boxing Federation (NABF) middleweight crown. But the game extracted a serious cost when Sugar Ray suffered repeated detached retinas in both eyes, making him now legally blind.

Ray Seales will always be remembered, and not just because there was a Ray Seales Day in Tacoma after he won the Olympic gold. There is also an annual Sugar Ray Seales Day in the Virgin Islands: Every April 14, the government shuts down for the holiday.

Leo Randolph

Leo Randolph was another boxing graduate of the Tacoma Boys Club. He began boxing when he was nine years old, and by the end of his amateur career 11 years later, he acquired a record of 160 wins and seven losses. In 1976, at the age of 18, he became the youngest American to have ever won a boxing gold medal, winning in the Featherweight Division at the Montreal Olympics.

After that victory, Randolph returned to Tacoma, graduated from Wilson High School, and in 1978 turned to professional boxing. Two years later, he became "the first Tacoman since Freddie Steele to get a shot at a world boxing championship, in the first world title bout in Washington since the Floyd Patterson–Pete Rademacher match," according to the *Tacoma News Tribune* in 1980. On May 4 of that year, in the Seattle Center Arena (now Key Arena), Randolph won the WBA featherweight crown with a 15-round knockout of champion Ricardo Cardona.

Before the end of the year, however, Randolph retired from professional boxing at the age of 22 with a 17–2 record. A knockout handed to him by Argentina's Sergio Palma was the crowning blow, although his coach, Joe Clough, doubted that Randolph's announced retirement was for real. "He retired a couple of times when he was a young kid," Clough explained to a newspaper reporter at the time. "The first time was when Rocky Lockridge beat him at the Tacoma Boys Club. He was then 10 or 11 years old. A loss gets to him mentally, although he's never been hit as hard and as often as Palma hit him."

Randolph explained matters differently. For the young boxer, his Christian background was a factor in his retirement. "People used to ask me how I could be a Christian and go in the ring and beat up people. My defense was that I was doing it as a sport. I didn't have evil intent. I never had the intention of hurting people. I didn't have a killer instinct. Boxing took me all the way to the top. But some decisions I made, in hindsight, I might do different. If I had to do it all over, I definitely would study the books. I would use schooling as my number-one priority."

He is now one of Pierce Transit's most famous bus drivers. "Most people are kind of amazed that I'm driving a bus," Randolph told a reporter when he was 31. "Right now, I'm just as content as I could be."

Coach Joe Clough and Davey Armstrong

Randolph's coach, Joe Clough, kept amateur boxing alive at the Tacoma Boys Club in the 1960s. "They had the Tacoma Golden Gloves there already," explained Jack Dean, a former Kitsap County detective who assisted Clough at that

time. "But Joe put Tacoma on the map as far as amateur boxing goes. I remember the first time I saw Joe. He had two little kids matched at a show I was putting on at South Kitsap High School [in Port Orchard], but by the time he got to the show he had only one kid. I had promised to feed his kids, and after the show he showed up at the Beachcomber Restaurant with 17 kids. I looked at him and said, 'I thought you had only one kid.' He looked at me and said, 'You promised to feed my kids'."

Dean continued: "I had to scramble with the restaurant to feed them. The owner didn't want to at first and I thought I would have to pay the bill out of my own pocket. The owner was mad, but he finally agreed to feed the kids. So they all ate. But I thought to myself, 'This is the last time I'll invite this guy over to a show'."

As it turned out, Dean and Clough became good friends and coaching colleagues. Nobody, it seemed, could

A powerful right jab sends an opponent to the ropes (courtesy Ruggles Larson).

resist Clough. In 1976 he hitchhiked with Dean back to Montreal for the Olympics. Because Clough was not an official coach with the U.S. team, he was not allowed in the housing area where the boxers stayed. But Leo Randolph snuck food out to Clough and Dean every night during their stay at the Olympics.

Davey Armstrong remembered Clough with fond memories: "If it were not for Clough, a lot of kids, especially in the Tacoma Hilltop area, would not have had the chance at the success they did get. Joe was a good man, a very good man. Yes, he was: a very good man. Joe taught us a lot. You have to remember that in the late 1960s and early 1970s, there was discrimination, and maybe there still is. Our boxing team was predominately black. Not too many whites would stick up for us. Joe was one of them. Here he was, a white guy, saying to people, 'If my fighters can't stay in this hotel, I can't stay in this hotel.' There were times when we didn't have food or money to go on trips, and Joe would lend us the money to get food or go on the trips. If our mom or dad didn't have money, he would provide for us. Every holiday he would invite all his fighters over to his place and feed us turkey. All of us kids would have a nice holiday."

Davey Armstrong is perhaps the most accomplished amateur to come out of Tacoma; he went on to achieve a 24–3 record as a professional. "I guess I was blessed—actually I was blessed," he admits. "I made two Olympics, the 1972 Munich and the 1976 Montreal games."

Most people mistakenly believe that Armstrong won bronze medals in both Olympics. In fact, he did not medal at all. He lost in the quarterfinals both years, losing in 1976 in a controversial decision to Angel Herrera of Cuba, who went on to win the gold. Armstrong is repeatedly told by people who claim they saw the fight on television that he won the bout with Herrera. But Armstrong has never seen a replay. He called ABC to get a copy of the fight and the network told him that they did not have it in their archives.

Armstrong was headed toward a professional title match when he decided to retire from boxing. In what was the last of his 27 professional fights, he was beaten by Stevie Ramirez of San Jose, California. "He was winning the fight and in the fifth and sixth rounds I had him out," Armstrong remembered. "According to a story that appeared in the *Sacramento*

Bee, this guy was on PCP. His corner slipped him some PCP at the end of the sixth round." According to the account, Ramirez, revived due to the drug, slaughtered Armstrong.

Looking back, Armstrong said that he does not regret the boxing experience, except perhaps turning professional. "Turning pro was my last resort. I didn't really want to do it. I didn't have any interest in boxing by then, but I needed money. I would have liked to have gotten a boxing scholarship because education was more important to me than boxing."

Coach Tom Mustin

For 37 years, Tom Mustin has volunteered his considerable skills, time, and knowledge to the youth of Tacoma, primarily at the Al Davies Boys and Girls Club, where he has supervised the Tacoma Boxing Club for more than a quarter century. Almost single-handedly, he recruited and trained hundreds of volunteer coaches and, with them, trained and developed thousands of youngsters.

A 1964 graduate of Stadium High School, Mustin's hobby was boxing. In 1983 he coached at the Junior World Championships and in 1990 he coached at the Goodwill Games in Tacoma. He was an alternate coach for the U.S. Olympic team in 1992 and 1996.

He was rewarded for his accomplishments as one of America's finest boxing coaches when he was selected as head coach for the U.S. team that participated in the 1995 Pan-American Games in Argentina, the 1998 Goodwill Games in New York, and the 1999 World Championships in Texas, where his team won four gold medals and finished as the number-one team in the world. In 2000 Mustin was named head coach for the U.S. Olympic team that participated in the summer games in Sydney, Australia, where they finished with two silver medals and a bronze.

Over the years, boxing in Tacoma has provided youngsters with the opportunity to channel aggressive impulses into constructive behavior. It has enabled participants to become more self-confident, better disciplined, and more productive. It has allowed them to learn valuable lessons about growing up and taking responsibility for their actions. In the process, many have become ambassadors for the communities where they live and examples for others to follow.

CHAPTER 17

CREW

Jim Fifer (L.) and Duvall Hecht (SSM, 1949).

Before collegiate rowing was introduced to Pierce County, George Hunt from Puyallup and Robert D. Martin and James Fifer, both from Stadium High School, all made their mark as successful rowers. Hunt graduated from Puyallup High School in 1933 and then attended the University of Washington (UW). In 1936 he was a member of the UW crew team that represented the United States in the Berlin Summer Olympics, where they won the gold medal.

Martin graduated from Stadium in 1942 and attended UW, where he joined the crew team. In 1947, following service in the Navy during World War II and his return to UW, he finished third in the collegiate nationals in the eight-man races.

The Huskies then won the national title in 1948, but for Martin that was just the beginning; he raced in 15 events and didn't lose a single one. He won the national championship in the four-oared with coxswain event and then topped the year off in London with an Olympic gold medal in the same event. "It is a real sense of satisfaction when you accomplish something like that," remembered Martin. "It takes a while to sink in that you are the best in the world." In the semifinal race of the Olympic trials, the team set the

world record for the event, which remained on the books until 1961. In 1981 Martin was inducted into the UW Sports Hall of Fame as a member of the 1948 men's four-oared crew.

James Fifer graduated from Stadium High School after Martin. "He grew up watching the UW row," explained his wife, Mary Ellen Fifer. "He always wanted to row." Like Martin, he was called into service during World War II as a pilot. He managed to keep his flight hours and still train for rowing. After the war, Fifer rowed for Stanford University, where he served as crew captain and later as a graduate coach. Fifer's initial Olympic experience came in 1952 when he and partner Duvall Hecht competed in the pairs with coxswain event with Jim Biggs at Helsinki in 1952 and lost in the semifinals.

While at Stanford, Fifer befriended another crew enthusiast, Dan Ayrault, who had attended Tacoma's Lowell Elementary and Jason Lee Junior High Schools between 1944 and 1948. At Stanford Ayrault, elected captain of the crew team his junior year, was instrumental in the construction of a crew house on campus. By this time too, Ayrault's father—a retired rear admiral in the U.S. Navy—had settled on American Lake in Pierce County. Dan and teammate

Conn Findlay, along with Fifer and partner Duvall Hecht, found practicing on the lake far more congenial than on Seattle's Lake Washington. And the food on the training table prepared by Ayrault's mother was equally attractive.

In July 1956 the foursome traveled to participate in the Olympic trials held at Lake Onondaga, near Syracuse, New York. In the pairs without coxswain event, Fifer and Hecht upset the 1952 Olympic champions to earn a spot on the Olympic team. Likewise, Ayrault and Findlay won the pairs with coxswain event, with Kurt Seiffert, to qualify by defeating the Detroit Boat Club entry.

Fifer and Hecht claimed their first Olympic win two months later in Melbourne, Australia, in the pairs without coxswain race, and Ayrault partnered with Findlay and Seiffert to win a gold medal in the pairs with coxswain event.

In 1960 Ayrault found himself once again part of the U.S. rowing team, competing in the Rome Olympics. Joining him was an elite group of rowers from throughout the United States who had trained at UW prior to the Olympic trials. Among them was Clover Park High School and Husky graduate John Sayre, who in 1958—his senior year at UW—was part of the men's eight-oared crew competing at Henley-on-Thames, England. The crew lost to the Soviet Union at the games in England but won the Moscow Cup later that year, defeating the Leningrad Truds by 1-3/4 lengths on the Khimkinskoe Reservoir. The win led to an induction for the entire crew into the Husky Hall of Fame in 1984.

The 1960 Olympics were good for Ayrault and Sayre, who joined with Rusty Wailes and Ted Nash to win a gold

George "Shorty" Hunt, a Puyallup High grad, was a member of the University of Washington crew team that won a gold medal at the 1936 summer Olympic Games in Berlin: L. to R., Don Hume, Joe Rantz, Hunt, Jim McMillin, Bob Moch (kneeling), John White, Gordy Adam, George Day, Roger Morris (courtesy the George Hunt Family).

medal in the four oars without coxswain event. Coming from last place 500 meters into the final, this Lake Washington (Seattle) Rowing Club crew representing the United States rowed through the field, catching the leaders from the Soviet Union in the last 300 meters. Then stroke Sayre lifted the beat to 39 per minute, then 40, and finally 41 as the Americans opened up daylight on the Russians. Italy came on fast to take second, with the U.S. four winning by about a half length in a time of 6 minutes, 26.26 seconds to claim the championship. It was Ayrault's second gold medal in rowing.

Collegiate Rowing Comes to Tacoma

Fourteen young Pacific Lutheran University (PLU) students arrived in Seattle one morning in 1967: Their gift from UW, an eight-person rowing shell christened the *Loyal Shoudy* was waiting for them. Just one problem. How could the fledgling PLU crew program, with barely any funds, afford to transport the 60-foot vessel back to their boat house on American Lake? The answer at first seemed like a joke, but the brisk wind nipping at the young men's bare faces assured them that there was nothing to laugh about on this day until their voyage was complete.

On that day, December 18, 1967, PLU's crew grabbed the attention of the nation's rowing community as it rowed the 55 miles from Lake Washington, through the Ballard Locks, and across Puget Sound to Steilacoom. "So many people said we were crazy," said Jim Ojala, one of the 14 oarsmen. "They told us we couldn't do it, that we were nuts to even try. Then we *had* to do it."

Not only did the young men try, they completed their trip in nine hours. Like all great adventures, it was neither easy nor without incident. "At one point we had four men rowing and four bailing, and the water was still rising in the bottom of the boat," explained oarsman Rich Holmes. "Any more and we just couldn't have made it. I've never been so cold in my life."

The water continued to splash into the boat, and the crew members continued to rotate from the frigid conditions of the *Loyal Shoudy* to the warmth of the two escort boats. Finally, after hours of rowing and bailing, the oarsmen arrived in Tacoma. "Everybody felt a sense of personal

accomplishment," said Ojala. "We had proved something to ourselves."

Although the trials of the Sound had made the boat impossible to use for racing, the *Loyal Shoudy* made a great practice boat and, more important, remained an example of what it takes to be a great oarsman. On that day, the crew demonstrated that their hearts and desire were greater than any PLU budget. On that day, the fledgling Lutes crew program proved it was maturing as it set out on the waters to row home. Indeed, on that day the dedication and eagerness to succeed shown by the PLU crew exemplified exactly what it took to bring this sport to Pierce County.

Every sport has its founding father, and although Paul E. Meyer did not invent rowing, he is the pioneer most responsible for bringing the sport to the Tacoma area. In 1963 he brought his rowing expertise, which included several national titles at UW in the early 1920s, to the University of Puget Sound (UPS) as a volunteer coach. In that year, he organized the first-ever Pierce County collegiate crew.

To get started, Meyer tapped his alma mater for equipment. UW graciously responded, loaning the UPS Loggers a shell. Meyer and his crew went about finding themselves a building and dock to house their new boat. They found the perfect place in a National Guard armory at Camp Murray on American Lake. The guard also made a dock available. Although the archaic building was not the greatest place to house a crew, it served the purpose. "It wasn't the best place," said Al Lawrence, an early UPS oarsman and coach. "But it did have showers, lockers, and heat from several old coal stoves. It also gave us a place to work on the boats."

Six months after Meyer formed the crew at UPS, he helped PLU start its program. Much as at UPS, at PLU rowing was not supported by the school because of the expense. But just as with the Loggers, the determination of the Lutes and Meyer prevailed. The young men repaired an old shell given to them from UW and moved in with their crosstown rivals at the National Guard complex. Not only did the two schools share facilities, they also shared Meyer as their head coach.

In March 1964, PLU was ready to join the Loggers on the water for a series of practice races that also included another opponent, Charles Wright Academy. Charles Wright had acquired an eight-person boat, but having no other high schools with which to compete, the academy had to practice with the local colleges. In that first year of rowing, none of the schools competed in an official regatta. However, in a preview of what would become the Meyer Cup in 1965, UPS was pitted against PLU in a practice race on American Lake. And though the Loggers had six months' more experience than PLU, the Lutes won the race.

Before the start of the first competitive season, a group of Tacoma and Seattle enthusiasts formed the Tacoma Rowing Association (later renamed the Tacoma Amateur Rowing Association, TARA). The organization was formed as a parent body to Pierce County collegiate and high school rowing. The group, headed by R. W. May, Corydon Wagner, Paul Meyer, Robert Smith, and Connie Engvall, helped to equip the various crews.

UPS and PLU clearly had a symbiotic relationship. When one crew did well, it drove the other team to compete even harder. Meyer's intent was to use the competitive nature of the two crosstown schools to raise the level of the sport within the region. Meyer's legacy continued under future UPS coaches such as Al Lawrence, Dan Lamberth, Mike Willy, and Sam Taylor.

As the 1960s came to an end, PLU and UPS finally had their chance at an official regatta, the Western Sprints. This competition placed the two clubs in heats against experienced teams with plenty of financial backing, such as UW and Oregon State University (OSU). Although the two Tacoma teams did not fair too well in the sprints, the two schools returned home for the first running of the Meyer Cup. The race is now considered the oldest dual-school trophy race on the West Coast. PLU won the first race and has

Tacoma's first intercollegiate crew race was held on American Lake in 1964 (PLU).

dominated the competition ever since, although UPS has won it as many as three years in a row. The UPS crew attended the national rowing competitions for the first time in 1969. Charles Austin, Jerry Wilson, Al Lawrence, Bruce May, Dave Wilson, Larry Lopez, Ned Rawn, and Rick Peterson composed the Men's Eight team.

Because PLU and UPS had to compete against the big National Collegiate Athletics Association (NCAA) Division I schools, most thought that the Meyer Cup would be the biggest race of the year for these two small schools. However, in 1970 the Lutes almost pulled off the unimaginable. Malcolm Klug, Conrad Hunzinker, Jim Puttler, Bruce Dahl, and Ralph Niels took their four-person shell with coxswain to the International Intercollegiate Rowing Cham-

pionships and almost won the whole thing. After upset victories over East Coast powerhouses University of Pennsylvania and Harvard, PLU was lent the Quakers' boat and some coaching for the finals. "Ted Nash [Penn's head coach] took us out for a workout the morning before the race," said Niels. "He taught us an awful lot in that half hour." Fledgling PLU finished third behind only Rutgers and Massachussetts Institute of Technology.

The cheers of 1970 turned to tears a year later when the Camp Murray boathouse burned to the ground, destroying everything. While UPS and PLU began to rebuild, they moved to new temporary locations. The Loggers moved to Tacoma's Blair Waterway and worked out of a meat-packing plant; the Lutes used the officer's beach at Fort Lewis. The

This University of Washington crew team, which included Tacoman Bob Martin, won a gold medal in the 1948 summer Olympics in London (SSM, 1948).

two schools hopped around from warehouse to warehouse until 1980, when contractor George Jewith, brother-in-law of a Logger oarsman, helped the crews construct a new boathouse at the east end of American Lake. TARA continued to help with the funds and took care of the lease until the organization dissolved in 1990.

In 1972 women's crew made its debut at UPS; PLU followed three years later. In 1976 the women began their first competitive season. Then in 1978, the women's crew teams from PLU and UPS started their own version of the Meyer Cup, the Lamberth Cup, named for UPS coach Dan Lamberth.

In 1983, 13 years after PLU stole the show at the national championships, the men Loggers set out to do them one better. UPS won the Meyer Cup and then won the Hart Trophy—a competition for small independent schools—along with the Cascade Cup. However, at the Northwest championships they finished second to OSU.

Paul Andrews, John Bronson, Erik Glatte, and Peter Jackson, along with coxswain Randy Dolan, went to the nationals that year. They finished ninth in a field of 18, with Glatte named to the National Lightweight Team after the race. And as the Loggers made their mark on Onondaga Lake in Syracuse, New York, the Lutes lightweight women's four made a strong showing at the Women's Collegiate Nationals on Lake Wingra in Madison, Wisconsin.

Even though both schools have a minimum of funds and no scholarships to use for recruiting, they have enjoyed considerable success during their short crewing histories. Both schools have won the Laffromboise Cup—a race for small-school varsity eights—at the Northwest championships. Besides the success of the school teams, several individuals have gone on to make a name for themselves in rowing.

Olympic Contenders

The Lutes sent coach Doug Herland to the Los Angeles Olympics in 1984 as coxswain for a two-man crew; however, Herland, who suffered from brittle bone disease, did not meet the minimum weight requirement for a coxswain. Therefore, said his Web-site biographer, Trudy Williams, "He carried with him a four-pound bag of birdshot," now displayed at PLU. In a 1985 interview, Williams continued,

Herland said that "there is not a better fitness activity [than rowing] for anybody. Anybody, if they have bad knees or bad legs or bad ankles, can have problems running. But they can row. I have my problems, but I can row 10 miles a lot better than I can run a half mile." Herland's boat won a bronze medal in the event.

In 1991, following Herland's death, PLU posthumously awarded him the Distinguished Alumnus in Sports award for all he had done to promote rowing, especially for the disabled. Having just acquired a new crew shell, PLU named it *Herland's Legacy* in his honor. A second one was named *Doug "Herley" Herland*. "He could have never tried, but he just kept plugging away," remembered colleague Doug Nelson, PLU coach and rower. "He made a tremendous impact on rowing."

Another PLU Athletic Hall of Fame inductee is Dave Peterson, who ended his four years of crew as commodore (captain) of the team. He went on to coach the sport at PLU from 1975 to 1985. "Dave taught that there is something very magical about rowing," one of his students remembered, "and those who learned about rowing from Dave—as distinguished from learning how to row—share that magic to this day."

Pam Knapp Black, a 1984 graduate of PLU, was team commodore in her junior and senior year and went on to compete nationally. She was the first rower in PLU history to win a gold medal at nationals and won numerous races during her collegiate career. In 1986 Black joined the U.S. National Rowing Team, which placed second in women's pairs at the Goodwill Games in Moscow and took ninth place at the Rowing World Championships in Nottingham, England. Competition in the U.S. Sports Festival women's four in 1987 and in the U.S. Olympic team trials in 1988—where her team took second place in women's pairs—are additional achievements.

Tacoma's Rowing Clubs

Rowing clubs in Pierce County have never flourished, but in the recent past four clubs discovered what they hope is the secret to keeping afloat. The Riptide rowers formed in 1993, making their home at Woodworth and Company on the Thea Foss Waterway. Ted Atkinson, a Woodworth employee, had always liked to take his shell out on the Thea Foss Waterway. "It is fun to get out there and row," said

Atkinson. "Other people saw me out there in my boat and eventually they tracked me down. They told me that they had a shell in their garage or something and asked if there was a place down on the water where they could put it. Eventually we built a boathouse and formed a rowing club. I guess you could call me the commodore." When Atkinson moved to Montana in 2001, the group disbanded, but the Commencement Bay Rowing Regatta they founded is still held annually.

Bill's Boat House on American Lake is a small facility that rents boats out to anglers. It is also home to the other three rowing clubs in Pierce County. The American Lake Rowing Club first opened in 1988 to anyone interested in rowing. The club's coaches teach novice rowers, and the boathouse includes a weight room and a storage area for the shells. "This facility is great for rowers," said PLU coach Doug Nelson. "It gives serious rowers and young rowers the chance to get away from the grind of life and be at peace." The Rainier Rowing Club was founded in 1994 at the Pocock Center in Seattle and moved to American Lake in 2002.

The Commencement Bay Rowing Club that shares Bill's Boat House consists of local high school students. Young women from Charles Wright Academy formed the club in 1991. When students from other area schools expressed interest in joining, the club's coach, David Robertson, created an interscholastic coeducational program.

"The club is an umbrella of Pierce County schools," explained Robertson. "Any student from any Pierce County school can join. If they have enough people from that school to fill a boat, they can compete under that school's name. Otherwise, we can fill a boat with a group of kids and they can compete as the Commencement Bay Rowing Club. It is great way for everyone to have a chance to compete."

Despite suffering from brittle bone disease, Doug Herland became a coxswain and later coach of Pacific Lutheran University's crew program (PLU).

CHAPTER 18

CURLING

Curling was first introduced at the Lakewood Ice Arena in 1949 (TPL).

Curling, like golf, is a Scottish import, a sport that originated there in the 16th century. It took some time, however, for the game to capture the imagination of Americans and become a competitive sport. Interestingly, women curlers were ahead of the men in creating a national organization, founding the U.S. Women's Curling Association in 1947. Chicago hosted the first national men's championship in 1957, and one year later the U.S. Curling Association formed.

John Johnsen, a Lakewood Ice Arena manager and skating coach, introduced the game to Tacomans in 1949, when the Lakewood Curling Club began playing at the arena when the rink was not used for ice skating. Walt Swanson, John Blair, Marv Tommervik (one of Pacific Lutheran University's greatest football players; see chapter 21, Football: High School and Rugby), Bill Ristine, Ed Stevens, and Gil Richards were some of the members of that first curling club.

With the exception of Johnsen, these men were not professional athletes. Swanson worked at Foss Tug. Stevens managed the Lakewood Country Store. Eugene Riggs, Woody Wilson, R. D. MacRae, and James Shanklin, other early members, were doctors. Chauncy

Spike Griggs, another early member, was a lumber baron. Curling was a sport in which players from all walks of life could enjoy its unique and intriguing aspects. For instance, the Lakewood Curling Club also included real estate developer William Riley, Keith Pederson, Lloyd Clements, mortgage banker George Hamill, psychologist David Jenkinson, brothers Charles and Ray Howard Wright, Jim Stevens, Gene Grant, Walt Hutchinson, and restaurant owner Anton Barcott.

Steve Brightman, a Metro Park employee at Wright Park's conservatory, was one of the club's more active members. He began curling in 1952 and continued for 30 years; as president of the Lakewood organization, he was dedicated to helping promote and foster the growth of the sport locally. Brightman traveled extensively to curl, and for nine straight years he attended an international meet in the Central Highlands of Scotland, where 12 nations were represented. He was also a member of the Granite Curling Club based in Seattle, regarded as one of the top clubs in the country because it represented the United States in several international competitions.

The Lakewood players went to bonspiels, as curling tournaments are called, in nearby Seattle, Bellevue, and Everett. They also competed in Portland, Oregon; Vancouver, British Columbia; Chicago; Toronto; Quebec City; and Scotland.

Time has not been kind to the sport of curling in Pierce County. When the Lakewood Curling Club formed, Johnsen was credited with establishing the sport's first competitive venture on the whole West Coast. By the 1970s, however, the curlers were having a hard time finding a place to play. They moved to the Sprinker Recreation Center following its 1976 opening, in hopes of attracting new curlers. Unfortunately, the plan proved unsuccessful, because the small membership could not afford the cost of ice time. The group then leased a building at South 24th Street and Pacific Avenue in Tacoma and constructed their own rink. By the early 1990s, however, the rising costs of maintaining the facility, plus a declining membership, meant the end of the Lakewood Curling Club.

At the first team curling competition in 1949 at the Lakewood Ice Arena, three curlers sweep the ice to help control the stone as it slides toward the target behind them: L. to R., Anton Barcott, later the owner of Harbor Lights; Al St. Pierre, a Boeing firefighter; Don Gilbertson, a high school junior who ran the arena snack bar (Richards Studio Collection, TPL, Image D37937-1).

CHAPTER SPONSORED BY:

Curlers William and Ann Riley, George and Geneva Hamill, and Dave Jenkinson—in memory of his late wife Jean—along with supporter Zenta Jones, are pleased to sponsor the history of curling. As members of the Lakewood Curling Club, the three couples competed for 20 years in bonspiels in Washington, Oregon, and Canada. Together they won the Johnny Walker Tournament's Consolation Championship Trophy in Scotland in 1975. The club, which at its peak had about 80 athletes, ended its run in 1990, though Dave Jenkinson is still active in the sport.

CHAPTER 19

EQUESTRIAN SPORTS

Chuck Richards participated in the 1971 Pentathlon World Championships in San Antonio, Texas (courtesy Chuck L. Richards).

Foxhunting conjures images of red-coated lords and ladies mounted on fine steeds, following hounds as they chase a critter around the English country-side. There was a reason for the hunt historically: Sheep farmers in Great Britain wanted the fox population controlled. In the American West, the coyote was hunted for the same reason. Although many farmers simply went out and shot coyotes to protect their livestock, the more well-to-do made a sport of it. And thus, so-called foxhunting made its way to the Pacific Northwest.

By the turn of the 20th century, however, there was no apparent need for organized hunts to separate "vermin" from livestock in Pierce County. Instead, according to one reporter at the time, the advent of golf was inspiring hunters. When the Tacoma Country and Golf Club established its roots in Lakewood, "Golf was the sport of the lumber barons, and their homes soon sprang up around both American Lake and nearby Gravelly Lake." Chester Thorne was one such entrepreneur who built an estate on American Lake north of present-day Tillicum. He then hired Tom Bryan to head his gardening staff, little knowing that this Irishman would introduce foxhunting to Tacoma's elite.

Bryan soon met Major James E. Mathews, a Canadian who had established a riding stable near 80th Street and South Tacoma Way, and gave him some hound dogs to start a foxhunting club. When the new endeavor was organized in 1926, Major Mathews called it the Woodbrook Hunt Club. In 1929 the group moved its headquarters to land presently on the edge of McChord Air Force Base just north of the Tacoma Gun Club range. Members viewed "riding to hounds" as an exciting tradition, though it was not a competitive sport per se. "The idea is to enjoy riding your horse out in the wild while appreciating the work of the hounds seeking and chasing the scent of the game." Over the years, their venue remained the prairie lands of the Fort Lewis military reservation, but the hounds did not go after any real game. Instead, they followed animal scents created artificially around the given course.

Although the Woodbrook Hunt Club did not consider foxhunting a competitive sport, it did sponsor other equestrian competitions ranging from "the finest and smoothest gymkanas" to harness racing. By 1950 the Woodbrook stables were home to the Tacoma Union of Washington Horsemen, the Lariettes (a state champion women's drill team), the Pierce County Sheriff's Mounted Posse (state champions in the 1950s), and the Washington State Governor's Guards.

Harness racing was also a part of the Pierce County equestrian-sports landscape in its formative years. There is evidence, for example, that in 1899 the sport was part of the racing venue at Harry Morgan's track, located in the present-day Proctor District of Tacoma. More official records begin in 1948, when the Edward B. Rhodes post of the American Legion sponsored a four-day July event at the Washington Harness Horse Association (WHHA)'s half-mile track, located in South Tacoma near McChord AFB. The race lured competitors ranging from 83-year-old John Richmond, Tacoma's Mrs. Cy Duryea, and 15-year-old Jerry Buck driving "Maxie Hal."

Racing lasted for only five years at WHHA's South Tacoma track. Although the local organization was licensed by the U.S. Trotting Association, the sport was not popular with state officials who, in 1953, denied a state license for the track. State Senator Gerald G. Dixon and WHHA president A. Burwood Kennedy, along with Tacoma sports enthusiasts,

This is one of the first races of 1948 held on the 1/2-mile Washington Harness Track in South Tacoma; note the simple chalk board where race results were posted and the open platform where the announcer calls the race over a P.A. system suspended from a utility pole (Richards Studio Collection, TPL, Image D34299-18).

tried to reinstate the sport, to no avail. From then on, King County's Longacres was the venue for horse racing.

In the 1960s the Valley Riding Club, Meridian Riding Club, Parkland Riding Club, Peninsula Pleasure Riders, and Gig Harbor Horsemen—among others—were all organized under the umbrella of the Washington State Horsemen. In addition, up-and-coming show jumpers competed internationally through the American Continental Young Riders.

The promotion of unique breeds of horses is also a part of the county's equestrian history. In the 1940s, owners of Tennessee walking horses were introducing a new phase of riding to horse fanciers through exhibitions at Woodbrook Hunt Club. By the end of the 20th century, Arnold's Walking Horses in Gig Harbor was breeding and showing championship Tennessee walkers. Arabian horses had been introduced to Pierce County by the end of the 1950s, and in 1978 Glenn Ash, W. Glenn Johnson, and William G. Viert—of Spanaway, Roy, and Tacoma, respectively—incorporated Region V of the International Arabian Horse Association.

Over the years, equestrian competition has not received much press. Publicity usually arose under unique and therefore newsworthy circumstances: a fire at Woodbrook in 1950; the potential loss of riding grounds if a cross-base freeway were constructed along the boundary between McChord AFB and Fort Lewis. Public perception has also played a role in the lack of interest in the sport, one in which horse racing is considered a venue for gamblers and fox-hunting is a preserve of the elite.

The evolution of the sport of polo in Pierce County, however, shows that minds can change. Initially, like fox-hunting, polo was associated with the upper classes. But by the end of the 20th century, when the Tacoma Polo Club began to play on grounds located southeast of Roy, the sport had become a family affair and a competitive venue for players throughout Washington and Oregon. Polo has proven available for anyone to enjoy, whether riders or spectators.

CHAPTER 20

FENCING

Maxine Mitchell competed in four Olympics and was a four-time winner of the U.S. national championship in women's foil (courtesy Marty Tetloff).

Fencing as a recreational sport dates back to the earliest Egyptians; like many forms of modern-day play, it evolved from military traditions and battle. During Roman times, fencing was a part of the life-or-death gladiatorial games. Spain, Italy, and France pioneered fencing as play during the early years of the modern era, when refined gentlemen viewed competition with swords as part of an education that also included dance, literature, and the arts.

Organized recreational fencing was present in the United States by 1891, the year the Amateur Fencing League of America (AFLA) formed. And though it became part of the Olympics in 1896, fencing has never become a popular spectator sport for the majority of Americans. Often termed physical chess, fencing involves a set of moves that can apply to different strategies. The time between fencing moves or turns, however, is measured in milliseconds. Although a great amount of lively action is associated with fencing, a competitor can succeed only through the harmonious combination of mind, body, and weapon.

Fencing was never just a sport for men, and it is interesting to note that one of the first media references to the sport

in Tacoma related to the Annie Wright Seminary. School administrators at this private academy viewed fencing as a proper sport for young women in the 1920s. Two left-handers, Margarita Irle and Elizabeth Bona, stood out in a sport reserved for only majors in physical education, as seen in the 1941 College of Puget Sound (now UPS) Yearbook. Fencing for men at UPS was also in place by this time, and Pierre Carroll instructed the fencing program.

The sport did not take hold in Tacoma, though, until the late 1940s, when Jack Nottingham started a fencing program. Born in the city, he began fencing at an early age; however, it was not until after the Second World War that he seriously pursued the sport. Following training under the legendary Aldo Nadi, Nottingham returned to the Puget Sound region. He had dreams of teaching world-class fencing at a time when the sport was centered in art schools and private athletic clubs. He subsequently moved on to Portland, Oregon's Reed College—where he coached an impressive collegiate win record—and then to San Francisco, where he ran a private club called Foil Circus in his home until his death in the early 1990s. He was considered the "best fencing teacher this country has ever produced" by fencing master

Charles Selberg, a fencing Olympian, former University of Santa Cruz professor, and one of Nottingham's pupils.

Fencing competitors, coaches, and teachers tend to have superior mobility and fluidity. Leon Auriol, who emigrated from France to Seattle in the early 1960s, was no exception. According to his Web-site biography, Auriol aimed to "jump-start Seattle fencing" following Nottingham's failed attempt. Word soon got around that a fencing master was in the region, and Auriol found himself commuting between Vancouver, British Columbia, and Portland, Oregon, giving

Lt. Chuck Richards (L.) fences with a member of the Brazilian team during the Modern Pentathlon at Fort Sam Houston, Texas, in 1969; he was the Modern Pentathlon National Champion in 1970, 1971, and 1972, placed 4th in the team competition and 9th individually in the '72 Olympics, and was a three-time military Pentathlon champion (courtesy Chuck L. Richards).

lessons. Tacoma became a regular stop on his itinerary, and into the 1970s Auriol taught fencing at the YMCA, Charles Wright Academy, Clover Park High School, and UPS.

One of Auriol's Tacoma students was Harald Hillemann, a Polish-born émigré who began fencing at age 13 as part of his military training while still in Europe. At age 36, Hillemann started fencing again at a program at Hudloff Junior High School in Lakewood. Later he began teaching the sport at the YMCA and YWCA, Wilson High School, and Mason Junior High School in Tacoma. Today, at age 83, Hillemann is still coaching the sport of fencing locally.

Maxine Mitchell was one of the best women fencers representing the United States in Olympic tournaments. Mitchell was born in Leroy, Washington—now one of the state's many ghost towns—but the family moved to Los Angeles, where she received her training as a fencer. Later in life, she and her husband, Dorcie, a fencing coach, moved to Tacoma. In between these stays, Maxine Mitchell became an Olympian in 1952 (Individual Foil, Helsinki), 1956 (Individual Foil, Melbourne), 1960 (Team Foil, Rome), and 1968 (Team Foil, Mexico City). She also won the U.S. national championships in women's foil in 1952, 1954, 1955, and 1958 and was one of the oldest Olympic competitors in the games' history when she competed in 1968.

Much of Tacoma–Pierce County's fencing activity centered in the local schools, with Charles Wright Academy a major focus. In April 1963, the school hosted the Northwest International Fencing competitions. Mindy Slikas, a fencing instructor at Charles Wright, was instrumental in luring the games to the school. The Tacoma Fencing Society sponsored classes taught by Leon Auroil. This organization's president, Dr. Hugo Van Dooren, was also vice president of the Western Washington Division of AFLA. Tacoma Community College (TCC) had a fencing program coached by Phyllis Templin, one of Harald Hillemann's former students. "Swashbuckler's Deadly Art Now Tame Sport" headlined a *Tacoma News Tribune* article in 1977 that featured Lisa Krueger Clark and Theresa Turpin, two of Templin's students.

Fencing Clubs

Pierce County fencers organized the Blue Steel Fencing Club at Fort Lewis in 1977. Sgt. Robert Riddle coined the

"blue steel" moniker, basing it on a quote from fencing great Aldo Nadi: "The shining blue reflections of the blade impress you still more ominously than its point. Suddenly you look up and see a pair of eyes glaring at you with defiance. They shine even more than the blade. They are bluer than the blue steel. The effective stare of the veteran."

Bruce Burch, whose fencing career started in high school in 1950 under master Irving Kipnis, was a Blue Steel coach who began teaching locally in the late 1970s. Before joining the club, he was an Olympic contender in the late '50s and an All-American fencer and Western Region champion in all three weapons: foil, épée, and saber. While at the University of Arizona, Burch was one protégé of Maestro Anthony Greco, a fifth-generation fencing master.

Under the Blue Steel club auspices, men as well as women competed against local civilian fencers, hosted demonstrations, and continued to build the legacy of the sport locally. In 1986, for example, Veronica A. Carter and Juan A. Lopez, both in the U.S. Army, fenced with Babette Beckham, Srey Hakry, and Chris Hedegaard at Wilson

High School. Rex Schwartz and Kent Powell, two longtime active club members, also began fencing during this time, while former Korean national champion and Army Specialist Mun Kim was assistant instructor in 1978 during his Army service at Fort Lewis.

More recently, Marty Tetloff formed the new Metro Tacoma Fencing Club in 1998. Tetloff began fencing in 1976 at California State University–Sacramento, studying under Judy Agid. He was a National Collegiate Athletics Association (NCAA) fencer for two years and in 1989 attended the U.S. Fencing Association (USFA)'s Coaches College for Foil at the Olympic Training Center in Colorado Springs. (Harald Hillemann attended the same school for saber in 1994, and Bruce Burch completed courses there in saber and epee in the early 1990s). Tetloff began his fencing program with the support of the Boys and Girls Clubs of South Puget Sound at around the same time when the Blue Steel organization shifted its venue from Fort Lewis to Charles Wright Academy. In 1999 the Metro Tacoma and Blue Steel clubs merged to become the Metro Tacoma Fencing Club, Blue Steel, with Bruce Burch as head coach and Harald Hillemann and Marty Tetloff as assistant coaches.

Within three years of the merger, numerous fencers were competing regularly in USFA-sanctioned tournaments. Kyle Nix qualified for the 2002–03 Junior Olympics in foil. Brennan Johnson qualified in foil for the Junior Olympics in 2004. Other active club junior fencers included Thomas "Max" Jasper, Abigail Jasper, and Colin Moyer (Charles Wright Academy), Phillip "Alex" Corley and Nick Manley (Tacoma School of the Arts), Mike Ede (Covenant High School), Carolyn Hill (Curtis High School), Schyler Lujan (St. Patricks School), Cody Havrilak (North Beach High School), and Geoff Oberhofer (Foss High School). All these students competed successfully in local and regional tournaments and qualified as a team for the nationals in 2003. The Metro Tacoma Fencing Club, Blue Steel, also has a strong veteran fencing contingent; Don Penner, Marty Tetloff, and George "Murph" McCall qualified for the summer nationals individually and as a team in 2003.

Fencing is not one of Pierce County's best-known sports, even though it has been a part of Western culture for centuries. It is an endeavor, however, in which the competitor learns agility and cunning, while mentally working through strategic intricacies. You rarely see the results of local or international competitions in the newspaper sports pages. But those who are learning and competing in Tacoma hope that someday their names will be among the champions in the sport.

Kent Powell's lunge is foiled by Philip "Alex" Corley (R.), a member of the Metro Tacoma Fencing Club's 2004 Junior Men's National Team and a competitor at the U.S. Fencing Association's Division III National Championships (courtesy Metro Tacoma Fencing Club).

CHAPTER 21

FOOTBALL:
HIGH SCHOOL AND RUGBY

Dick Zatkovich, Wilson High and UW grad, coached the Lakes Lancers to a 1997 state title (photo by John Moore, courtesy University of Washington).

Exactly when football was first introduced to high schools in Tacoma and Pierce County is anybody's guess, but the somewhat fuzzy reports that exist in old newspapers indicate that it occurred prior to the turn of the 20th century. In fact, a Tacoma high school yearbook of 1898 mentions a game played between Tacoma and Seattle and refers to an ongoing competition: a five-game series in which the winner gets to keep a $50 silver cup trophy. It's safe to say that high school football now spans 100 years in Tacoma.

In 1904 the *Tacoma Ledger* reported that a Tacoma team downed Olympia 6–0 behind the play of captain Ralph Boggs and fleet Ernie Tanner. In 1905 the Tacomans beat Olympia again 28–0 but lost to Seattle 16–9. That set the stage for a Thanksgiving Day Seattle–Tacoma matchup at the YMCA grounds in Tacoma. Tanner kicked a field goal and fullback Henry Jacobus plunged across from 1 yard out on fourth down to give Tacoma a 10–6 win, their first win over Seattle in four years. Captain Ben Nutley's key block resulted in Seattle yielding its first touchdown of the season.

With only one local high school in the city, the Tacoma school board decided to allow games with high schools in Aberdeen, Hoquiam, Olympia, Everett, Bellingham, and Seattle. Thanksgiving Day was set aside for special competitions. Tacoma played Seattle High School at Athletic Park in Tacoma in the first Turkey Day contest, in 1909. The final score showed 0–0, but the Tacomans were credited with victory because visiting teams in those days had to win "or they lost."

In 1914 the school boards in both Seattle and Tacoma agreed to no more intercity play because of "rudeness." That prompted some kind of player strike in Tacoma, probably because the only games scheduled were between the different classes at Tacoma High School, newly renamed Stadium High School. It wasn't until October that the new Lincoln Park High School was duly recognized by athletic planners, and the first Lincoln-Stadium clash was scheduled for November 7 "to determine the city championship." Stadium tromped Lincoln Park, 28–0, igniting an intense crosstown rivalry that existed for nearly 50 years.

The Lincoln-Stadium Rivalry

When the 1920s arrived, Cliff Marker and Herman Brix were Stadium's headliners. Brix played football at Stadium and the University of Washington (UW) and won a silver medal in the shot put at the Amsterdam Olympics of 1928 (see chapter 44, Track and Field). Then he became a movie star in Hollywood as one of the early Tarzans. Marker was a four-year letterman in football and basketball at Stadium who also competed in discus and shot put. He not only played football at Washington State University (WSU), but also joined the Canton (Ohio) Bulldogs in the national professional ranks, where he played alongside the legendary Jim Thorpe.

The first annual Thanksgiving Day game between Lincoln and Stadium was played in 1922. The Abes were known then as the Railhewers and the Stadium Tigers at that time were called the Toreadors. Lincoln won that game, 28–7. Stadium turned the tables in 1923 with a 6–0 decision, but in '24 a 40-yard field goal by Lincoln's Rick Johnson made the difference, with the Abes winning, 3–0. In fog so thick you barely could see the field, Stadium trimmed

Ends Earl Platt (L.) and Sig Sigurdson (R.) form a goalpost to give Marv Tommervik kicking practice in 1940 while coach Cliff Olson looks on (SSM, 2002.4.1).

Lincoln, 13–3, in 1925, and the Tigers repeated in '26 with a 20–0 whitewash. From 1921–27 Myron "Chief" Carr coached Stadium's football and track teams, after graduating from Montana State University. Two of his top athletes were Herman Brix and Jimmy Dupree, one of the first great African American football players in Tacoma. He then taught for five years at Gault Jr. High School where he coached Hal Berndt, who became a top track sprinter. Carr moved over to Lincoln to serve as head football coach for two seasons before spending 1950–57 back at Stadium as the school's athletic director.

Lincoln's Carl "Kak" Wasmund ran the length of the field in the closing seconds of play in 1927 for a 14–7 victory, but Stadium retaliated in '28 with a 13–0 comeback. The largest crowd in the young rivalry watched the '29 affair, with Lincoln claiming a 13–7 win at Stadium Bowl before 10,000 excited fans. When Stadium missed an extra point in 1930, Lincoln took it again with a 7–6 victory. The '31 Lincoln team, already crowned state champions, routed the Tigers, 32–6. Their season featured two big wins, a 20–0 drubbing of Centralia, with Tommy Mazza, Ole Brunstad, and Jess Brooks scoring touchdowns, and a lopsided Turkey Day game. Stadium threw 44 passes, an incredible number in that era, but completed only 15. A long pass in the final minutes of the '32 game ended in another Lincoln win, this one 12–6; the 1933 game was a scoreless tie.

With the 1934 season, Stadium began a long victory streak. Under coach and Stadium alum John Heinrick, the Tigers won seven in a row. A 0–0 tie in 1941 stopped the winning streak, and coach Eddie Schwarz produced a 13–0 Lincoln win in 1942. With the element of a contest restored, 12,000 fans turned out in the Stadium Bowl in 1943, but there were no cries of victory because neither team scored. Stadium's Bob Nelson caught Lincoln's fleet Bobby McGuire after a long run deep in Tiger territory in the final stages of the game to preserve the deadlock.

That set the stage for one of the greatest Turkey tilts of all, in 1944. In spite of a pouring rain that lasted all day, Lincoln mustered a second-quarter touchdown on a pass from Dean Mellor to Len Kalapus to give the Abes the "mythical" state championship (the official version wasn't established until 1973). Both teams had been unbeaten dur-

ing the season and Stadium hadn't been scored on. Lincoln scored 242 points in nine games under first-year coach Phil Sorboe, a Lincoln alum, yielding just 13 points. Installing the T formation, Sorboe rated his backfield the best he'd ever coached. The "Three Ms and a K" were Mellor, Al Malanca, Bobby McGuire, and Kalapus. McGuire, dubbed "Twinkletoes" by sportswriter Ed Honeywell of the *Tribune*, tallied 18 touchdowns during the season, nine on plays of 30 yards or more, while Kalapus hammered across for 10 touchdowns and kicked 17 extra points.

Tacoma fans saw a future National Football League (NFL) Hall of Fame kicker win the 1945 game when Sam Baker's extra point gave Stadium a 7–6 win. Teammate Walt Espeland's long pass to Paul Johnson tied the game prior to Baker's boot.

This early Thanksgiving Day rivalry wasn't the only football played, of course. In Tacoma several coaches enjoyed gridiron success in that same era. Al Hopkins became an assistant coach at Lincoln in 1927 and was promoted to head coach within two years. By 1930 the Abes won the city championship, followed by city and state titles in 1931. Lincoln's "Big Three" players in 1930 were Frank Stojack, Gene Reardon, and Beverly Schuster. Jess Brooks led the Abes to their state championship, along with Leonard Atkins, Kenny Johnston, and Emanuel Srsen.

John Heinrick began his career at Bellarmine Prep in 1927 but switched to Stadium High in 1934, and the Tigers began to roar. They won seven straight Thanksgiving games (outscoring the Lincoln Abes 111–14 in that stretch) and seven city titles. The Stadium Tigers claimed the state title in 1946 with a 21–6 Turkey Day win, and Heinrick left to coach football at UPS. Fullback Sam Baker, a future running great at Oregon State University (OSU) and a record-setting NFL kicker, provided the inside punch, and the Tigers were loaded with speedy backs to the outside. Quarterback and team captain Garry Hersey called on Ray Spalding, Walt Espeland, and Milt Gust for long gainers. The line was anchored by center Ed Notley, and the tackles were two of Stadium's finest, Bill Kowalski and Bill Greco. The 1947 Bellarmine Lions, under coach Andy Slatt, featured a stable of speedsters in Denny Vye, Otto Fink, and Bob Fink, behind heady quarterback Paul George. The

Lions lost their first game of the season, 13–7, to Longview but stayed unbeaten the rest of the year.

There was a different twist to the prep scene in 1948 when Mooseheart, Illinois, journeyed west to tackle the Stadium Tigers in Stadium Bowl in what was billed as the "first East-West intersectional high school game." The Moose Lodge suggested the game, which needed approval from both the Washington and Illinois Athletic Commissions. Washington Governor Mon C. Wallgren even got in the act, along with Congressman Thor Tollefson and Tacoma Mayor Val Fawcett. The Ramblers, who arrived via train, went on to railroad Stadium, 14–6. Mooseheart enjoyed an undefeated season that year.

Bob Levinson, an assistant to Heinrick since '45, took over the Tigers in 1947, and that was Bellarmine's cue to win its first-ever city football championship. Lincoln also gave Levinson's team a rude awakening, with five wins and two ties in seven Thanksgiving games, until the Tigers finally rocked the state in '54 with a 13–7 upset over the unbeaten Abes in the season finale. In '56 Levinson staggered Lincoln again with a 6–0 win featuring Dave Kerrone's 55-yard scoring jaunt in the fourth quarter. When Levinson was inducted with the first class into the Washington Interscholastic Activities Association (WIAA) Hall of Fame, his football and track coaching successes were rewarded: He won two state championships in track and field and eight league championships in football. His 1965 Stadium High football team was unbeaten, with a 9–0 record, and his '67 victory over Mount Tahoma was regarded as one of the greatest high school upsets in Tacoma history.

Norm Mayer took over at Lincoln in '45, winning more games than any coach in Lincoln history. Two unofficial state championships and a state title in 1948 were credited to Mayer in his first 12 years at the helm. He finished his 23 years at Lincoln with 140 wins and became Tacoma's district athletic director in 1970. When his unbeaten '48 team captured the Thanksgiving Day game from Stadium, 13–7, it earned the state's number-one ranking by Associated Press (AP). Art "The Arm" Viafore quarterbacked that big victory in front of 14,000 fans. The Abes' continued popularity with fans and media throughout the state in 1952–54 was thanks in part to many spectacular runs by Luther "Hit and Run"

Carr. In setting three school records, he scored more touchdowns than any Lincoln player ever, set a new school mark for pass interceptions with a 100-yard return versus Yakima, and tied a school standard for longest punt return with an 80-yard touchdown trip against Stadium in 1954. Phil Sorboe (1929) and Earl Hyder (1952) also had 80-yard returns. The Abes sent five players from this era to the UW, where they all emerged as starters: Carr, Jim Jones, Duane Lowell, Jack Walters, and Jim Heck.

Pierce County Schools

Neighboring Pierce County high schools had their share of early success as well. Coach Carl Sparks built a dynasty at Puyallup High (one that lasted more than 50 years), while Ed McCoy battled him at every turn with the Sumner Spartans. McCoy's coaching skills and successes were apparent when, in three successive seasons, Sumner played for the league title—unfortunately, the Spartans lost each time in the final game to Puyallup, Renton, and Buckley. After teaching and coaching for 13 years, McCoy served as Sumner's principal for another 18 years before becoming President of the WIAA. Bill Vinson took Fife High to the head of its class with year after year of solid coaching, Ed Niehl developed a winning program at Bethel High, as did Eldon Kyllo at Franklin Pierce. Gerry Austin took both Clover Park and Lakes High Schools to a new level of achievement. Doug Funk coached at White River High School for 27 years.

Vinson coached first at Eatonville, but Fife is where he made his mark. In 1939 he led the Trojans to an unbeaten season and the state B football championship. Fife edged Poulsbo, 7–0, in the final game of the year at Bremerton, with Masaru Tamura scoring on a 1-yard plunge after left tackle Joe Trucco blocked a punt on the Poulsbo 10-yard line. Pete Mello converted the extra point. Fife enjoyed huge success that year with a 46–0 win over Tenino, a 19–0 verdict over defending league champion Onalaska, a 19–7 decision over Kapowsin, a 24–6 win over Montesano, a 32–0 blanking of Yelm, a 46–6 rout of Orting, a 36–0 whitewash of Roy, a 58–0 thrashing of Federal Way, and a 40–0 victory over Clover Park. Halfback Frank Spear was the team's top scorer, with 180 of the team's 327 total points. None of the

1940 Stadium High School football team: back row, L. to R., Jack Wilson, Wes Hudson, Marion Klarich, Roy Murphy; front row, L. to R., Fred Angus, Austin Fengler, Rod Giske, Chuck Horjes, LaVern Miller, Bill Gustafson, Dick Beckman (courtesy Cindy Lumsden).

19 points allowed came as a result of a scrimmage play. That year Vinson coached not only football, but also basketball, baseball, and track, all to league titles.

In the early '40s, Vinson coached one of Pierce County's best all-around athletes ever: Don Paul. Paul starred in football, basketball, and baseball and won a state track championship in the broad jump, too. The 1942 Trojans, led by Paul's triple-threat performances, were unbeaten in seven games: His running, passing, and kicking led the way for a Pierce County League championship. Two other big plays also figured in Fife's success, namely Jack Schlumpf's 98-yard pass-interception runback against Federal Way and Roy Herting's leaping pass reception that gave Fife a 15–12 win over Clover Park, cinching the title.

The Trojans repeated their title in '43 but finished with a 6-1-1 record, losing only to Bellarmine of Tacoma.

Against Clover Park, Paul scampered 139 yards in 23 carries, and against Shelton he ran for 25 yards on the opening play, threw a touchdown pass for 30 yards, and ran a pass interception back for a 30-yard touchdown. In the NFL he became a four-time Pro Bowl selection.

When Bill Vinson retired in 1953 after 32 years of coaching, he was asked about the greatest players he ever coached. Obviously Don Paul's name was mentioned first, but Frank Spear was acknowledged in almost the same breath. "Let's just say that they were both great running backs, but World War II interrupted Frank's career." Vinson also was quick to pick his best team, the 1939 state champions, and he singled out the two guards on that team—Ben Holdener and Frank Evancich—as the best linemen he'd ever had, while center Frank Dreyer and halfback Pete Mello also drew raves.

One other Fife football story from the Vinson era is worth noting: The Fife quarterback on the 1941 team was Kenji Yaguchi, who was also the class valedictorian and a champion wrestler. Instead of graduating with his '42 class, however, he was sent to Camp Harmony, an internment camp at the Puyallup Fairgrounds. Like thousands of other Japanese Americans, he had to start life all over again following World War II. But at Fife High School, Yaguchi joined the class of 2002 on graduation day, receiving his diploma some 60 years late, but accompanied by a standing ovation.

Carl Sparks' legacy at Puyallup included 95 wins, 31 losses, and 12 ties—and that's just in football. He also coached basketball from 1941 to 1950 and continued in football until '57. He was Puyallup's first athletic director from 1957 until his death in 1969; the stadium in Puyallup was dedicated in his memory on September 11, 1987.

THE TACOMA CHALK STORY

A former Lincoln High School Abe under coach Norm Mayer in the 1950s, Bill Ochs remembered, "Any ballplayer that played for our coach knew that he gave a 'chalk talk' before each game, furiously diagramming plays on his chalkboard. The manager's job was to make sure he had plenty of chalk, because coach would also use it during halftime when we went into the old block house down in Lincoln Bowl. During the game, however, Coach Mayer would actually pull chalk out of his pocket and literally eat it which would make his lips all white. Coach could often be heard yelling at the manager that he needed more chalk and the manager would say, 'I gave you some, coach!' But Coach would just reply, 'I ate all that, give me more.'"

"If you were a manager, the last thing you wanted to do was run out of chalk," agreed teammate Joe Williams.

The 1945 Puyallup team could lay claim to an unofficial state championship because the Vikings were undefeated in one of the state's toughest leagues. With Buster Brouillet scoring 81 points (he scored 96 the season before), Puyallup edged Renton, 9–0; dumped Buckley, 19–6; throttled Enumclaw, 38–0; bested Kent, 12–0; waxed Auburn, 51–0; blanked Sumner, 20–0; topped Clover Park, 22–13; and dropped Highline, 27–6, on Thanksgiving Day for the Puget Sound League (PSL) crown. Brouillet became the first Viking runner to gain more than 1,000 yards and was a unanimous choice for the All-League team. He also was first-team All-State in basketball that season (see chapter 11, Basketball: High School Players). Center Glenn Rickert, tackle Darrel DeTray, end Roy Burke, and guard Jack Barker were other first-team football choices. The next year Jack McStott led Puyallup with a scoring total of 151 points, tops in the PSL.

Bob Ryan was another successful Puyallup coach; he had a 43–27–5 record with the Vikings, but was 24–3–1 in his final three seasons, winning three straight PSL championships before taking his first college job at his alma mater, University of Puget Sound (UPS), in 1965. Ryan's successor, Jerry Redmond, had a record of 85–59–4 at Puyallup, two league championships, and six league runner-up finishes before he retired in 1980.

Ed Niehl started the Bethel Braves on their way to gridiron success with a 15-year coaching stint of 66 wins and 38 losses, winning 16 in a row over two seasons in 1957–58. The Braves were crowned "mythical" state A champs in '58 after winning two straight Pierce County League (PCL) titles, following a 1955 season during which they were unscored upon. Gary Gregg led the offense, with 845 yards in 115 carries, and Tom Jones added 403 yards in 88 rushing attempts. The Bethel attack, mixing in some single wing, was sparked by guard Carl Schriver. Niehl became the athletic director in '56 and retired in 1981.

Ed Tingstad followed Niehl as Bethel football coach and later as district athletic director. The Tingstad name was prominent, however, because all three of his sons were three-sport athletes and earned scholarships via the Pierce County Scholar–Athletes of the National Football Foundation. Ed Jr. quarterbacked the Braves to state playoffs in

1983 with brother Mark as a tight end and linebacker; Ed became a WSU running back, and Mark was the second leading tackler in the Pac-10 for Arizona State's 1987 Rose Bowl champions. Youngest Tingstad David quarterbacked the Braves three years after his brother then went on to Boise State as fullback in the NCAA Division IAA playoffs of 1990.

A decade later it was Coach Eric Kurle, however, who brought Bethel to the brink of a state championship. His 2000 Braves finished 11–3 behind quarterback John Durocher with a 20–3 loss to Pasco in the 4A title tilt. In 2003 the team once again won the South Puget Sound League crown but bowed to unbeaten Bothell in the state playoffs. Zach Fletcher was the running star in the league decider with 207 yards and two touchdowns against unbeaten Puyallup.

The 1960s and '70s

Although the '50s gave Lincoln teams the edge more than half the time, 1958 marked a new era for Tacoma high school football. Wilson High opened its doors in the west end, and under the auspices of coach Harry Bird the Rams claimed some of Stadium's stars in that first class and won the City League title. In '61 they did it again, and also took the Capital League. But they lost to Lincoln, 14–0, on Thanksgiving Day, spoiling an unbeaten season. The two rivals had tied 7–7 two weeks earlier, earning Wilson the City and Capital titles. Lincoln's Abes, however, had some of their greatest teams during the ensuing decade, providing Tacoma fans with ongoing fierce competition.

Led by the phenomenal Donnie Moore, the 1962 Abe team was called "the best in 17 years" by coach Norm Mayer. They were voted number one in the state AP poll

The 1946 Stadium Tigers were undefeated, lead by co-captains Wells Anderson and Bruce Andreasen (Richards Studio Collection, TPL, Image A25364-7).

after beating Wilson, 14–7, in the annual Turkey Day contest; Moore rammed across for both touchdowns (from the 22- and 1-yard lines), and Dave Williams booted the extra points. "If we were best, Wilson was second in the state," Mayer stated. Moore continued to run wild in '63, scoring 122 points with 19 touchdowns and gaining 1,082 yards. (The 19 touchdowns eclipsed the 18 set by Bobby McGuire as a school record in 1944.) On Thanksgiving Day, Moore ran for 143 yards in 17 carries, including a 48-touchdown gallop, as the Abes dumped Stadium, 21–7. Moore finished his Lincoln career with 2,353 yards gained and 32 touchdowns.

Gerry Austin coached football for 23 years at Lakes High School, then Clover Park, before becoming the district athletic director. He compiled an overall record at both schools of 118–53–8, winning four PSL championships. At Clover Park he twice took the Warriors to Thanksgiving Day games in Seattle for those mythical state title games against Ballard and Garfield, only to lose hard-fought decisions in both cases. In 1964, with Austin's son Rick as quarterback, Lakes had one of its best seasons, finishing 9–0–1, the tie coming at Puyallup in the mud at season's end. On a yardage tie-breaker, Puyallup was awarded the right to play for the All-League title by a margin of 11 yards. Jim Vest lead the Viks to three consecutive Puget Sound League titles and went on to play linebacker at WSU. A three-sport letterman in track and field, football, and basketball, he was the first-ever athlete to be chosen as a national All-American in football.

Mount Tahoma High followed right behind Wilson High School, opening in 1960, but as a new school it took

THE TACOMA NOMAD RUGBY CLUB

Relatively new in the City of Destiny, rugby has yet to capture the imagination of locals except for a few enthusiastic spectators and players. An offshoot of traditional European soccer, the game was first officially played in Tacoma following the foundation of the Tacoma Rugby Club—the Nomads—in 1974. Ed Winskill and Jeff Carlson spearheaded the organization, now a member of the Pacific Coast and Pacific Northwest Rugby Unions.

The Nomads were named after the Glouchestershire, England, team, the Stroud Nomads. The club's goal is to foster national and international competition, including the development of youth rugby. To this end, the Nomads created the Tsunami high school–age team in 1987, and they can point to Dan Kemp as proof of the program's success. In 1995 this Wilson High School senior was selected to be part of the U.S. Junior Team scheduled to play in Australia. Three years later, guided by coach Chad Nestor, the Tsunamis became the Pacific Northwest High School Champions and went on to the nationals in Indianapolis, where they placed 11th in the country.

Throughout their existence, the Nomads have won or placed in various championships carrying such exotic names as the Armadillo Classic, the Bald Eagle Day Cup, Yakima's Tourney of the Gods, and the Skagit Valley Ruggerfest. Along the way, the team won the Tulip Fest Tournament and went to the National Sevens in Connecticut— where they finished seventh. At the National Sevens again in 2000, the Nomads finished fourth in the country.

In keeping with its goal of fostering the sport both locally and nationally, the club plays exhibition games whenever it has a chance, during halftime at UPS football games or in the Tacoma Dome. In 1986 the Nomads hosted the Japanese national rugby team. They've also established a strong rapport with both Fort Lewis and McChord enlisted personnel.

the Thunderbirds a few seasons to catch up. By 1966 this South Tacoma team took the first of back-to-back championships. They whacked Lincoln, 33–12, on Thanksgiving Day behind the touchdown antics of Mike Gomsrud, Donnie Falk, and Bobby Moore. The latter, who later changed his name to Ahmad Rashad and had a great NFL career, led the way during the City League campaign by scoring 76 points and catching 21 passes for 355 yards.

Mount Tahoma's success continued in '67, running its winning streak to 14 straight games under coach Joe Stortini. Moore had another terrific season with nine touchdowns, 11 extra points, and 65 total. He rushed for 560 yards, caught 15 passes for 203 yards, and finished his Thunderbirds career with 202 points (just 10 shy of Lincoln High's Dave Williams, also a future NFL star). Unfortunately, he and his teammates experienced what many have called "the biggest upset in Tacoma history," when Stadium intercepted six passes in the Thanksgiving Day finale, shut down Moore, and won 7–0 in the rain and mud. Rob

Myron "Chief" Carr, football coach at Stadium and Lincoln High Schools, in 1925 at Stadium Bowl (courtesy the Myron Carr Sr., Family).

Benedetti was the scoring hero, intercepting a Rod Bolek pass and racing to the end zone from the 6-yard line, then kicking the extra point. Stadium coach Bob Levinson credited Ralph and Rich Pettus, along with middle guard Joe Newman and linebacker Larry Henley, for their stellar efforts on defense.

During this same period, Fife High experienced another shot at the state championship in its division. The Trojans won two Seamount League titles and 15 straight games under coach Rick Daniels, and in 1967 they topped the AP poll with a 10–0 record following a huge 21–6 victory over Peninsula High. Fullback Tom Merritt gained 240 yards in 25 carries against the Seahawks, but Fife only led 7–6 at the half. Then Bob Lightfoot intercepted a pass to trigger a 77-yard drive, Merritt scored again in the third quarter, and Fife's defense took over the game. Daniels praised those front five: 235-pound ends Mick Spane and Fred Swendsen, plus Al Zampardo, Steve Berg, and Louie Ulrich.

Eldon Kyllo was the first football coach at Franklin Pierce High School, where he served 15 years with a 56–32–4 record and two league titles. In one of the tightest races in history, his Cardinals won the PSL crown in '61 with a 14–13 edging of Renton. Four teams finished with 8–1 records, but the lads from Franklin Pierce earned the nod. The Cards also won the South Puget Sound League (SPSL) in '67 with a 21–0 win over Federal Way. (It was 1982 before Franklin Pierce claimed another undisputed league championship. Coach Mike Roberts got his team through the regular season unbeaten, a first for the Cards, and finished 12–1, losing only in the state title game to Arlington by a 16–3 margin.)

Wilson High figured in the next three state championships, and in 1970 the Rams gave longtime coach Bird a Thanksgiving Day treat in Hawaii with a 38–6 win over Punahoe before 10,361 fans. Wilson had passed on Tacoma's traditional Turkey Day tilt and instead played the best Hawaii had to offer. It was their ninth straight win without a loss, and it gave the Rams a chance to claim state titles in both Hawaii and Washington. Bird called it "my best team, and my greatest win."

Quarterback Doug Gall led the Rams machine, with speedy Wilson Morris and rugged running back Don Dowl-

1930s football action in Stadium Bowl (SSM).

ing operating an option style offense. Punahoe hadn't seen such play during the season, and a film exchange may have duped the Hawaiians a bit. Bird sent them Wilson's win over Clover Park, featuring four touchdown runs by Morris, who scampered for 196 yards in six carries. With Punahoe keying on Morris, Gall passed for two touchdowns and ran the option for another, while Dowling hammered across from 17 yards and one down to trigger the win. Gall, Morris, Dowling, tackle John Whitacre, end Marc Clinton, and center Tom Bucsko were all named to the All-City team that year, with Dowling and Whitacre selected on both offense and defense. Coach Bird died during his 16th season as head of Wilson High's football program, with a record of 82 wins, 40 losses, and nine ties. He was one of the state's most respected football and wrestling coaches.

It was Bellarmine Prep's turn to shine in 1971 and '72. Coach Ed Fallon's Lions had two fine seasons in a row, losing only once each year. Bellarmine's title in '72 was the result of a 7–1 season and an offense that averaged 267.9 yards per game. Mitch Mullans scored seven touchdowns for the Lions, Larry Smith had five touchdowns and two extra points, and Pat Medved tallied four touchdowns. The Wilson Rams were second in the standings, but the Bells beat them, 15–6, and topped Stadium, 28–8, for two of their biggest wins of the season. Fallon was a highly successful coach, both at Bellarmine and earlier at Orting. He had a 42–21–4 record at Bellarmine and an overall mark of 104–36–6. Two of his Orting teams were unbeaten and state poll champs—both AP and United Press International (UPI)—with 9–0 records in 1964 and '65. Quarterback Mike Carrigan, 6 feet-4 inch-end Terry Rudnick, and Dick Dryer starred on those Orting teams. Brothers Casey and Andy Carrigan and Dan and Bill Hobert were other standout players.

Mount Tahoma returned to the forefront after the Wilson Rams' golden run and Bellarmine's successes. The Thunderbirds, however, had their perfect season ruined in the '74 state title tilt, losing to unbeaten Blanchet (Seattle) and UW-bound Joe Steele, 14–6.

Coach Doug Funk had well over 100 wins at White River High—and that as a 1A school playing in a 2A league. All-time stars Greg Baker and Mark Ross lead the ground game. Funk's 1976 Seamount League champions were considered his best-ever team, quarterbacked by Randy Johnson and led by Greg Kaelin's superb running ability and the all-around play of All-State center and defensive end Bruce Kirk.

The WIAA Kingbowl

In 1973 the WIAA introduced its playoff system by classification, which began the official state championships, and the Kingdome served as the initial home of the title games. The event was eventually called Kingbowl.

A Tacoma team didn't win the contest until the third year, when a three-year-old 4A school did it. The Foss Falcons, coached by Jack Sonntag, went undefeated in 12 games for top honors, besting Richland, 17–7, in the title tussle. Sonntag remembered the three years it took to create a program and win a championship. In '73 he had 17 sophomores starting in the program, and by the time they were seniors, they were experienced and very good.

Halfback Wyatt Baker, injured two weeks before the game, scored the first touchdown against Richland on a 3-yard first-quarter plunge to climax a drive of 80 yards. He gained 41 yards en route, then stepped out for the rest of the game. A 35-yard field goal by Dean Bentley made it 10–0 at halftime, and quarterback Reggie Grant connected on a 40-yard pass to Les McCully for the final Foss tally.

Baker and running mate Dewey Brawley were both named to the All-State team, along with wide receiver Keith Brown. Other top performers for Foss were defensive end Zach Hill, guards Mike Durrett and Brian Stowe (a sophomore), and centers Scott Davis and Todd Davis. The two brothers filled that position for Foss teams for six straight years.

That same year, the Sumner Spartans won the 3A state championship (then 2A) behind a rugged defense. Coached by John Anderson, Sumner blanked West Valley of Spokane at Highline Stadium in the rain, 11–0. The Sparts had dropped a 14–3 decision to Shelton the year before. The win over West Valley, which ran Sumner's unbeaten record to 12–0, was played before nearly 6,000 fans. On the game's third play, Daryl Crook intercepted a pass for Sumner and returned it 38 yards to the West Valley eight. Three plays later, fullback Pat Spooner crashed across with a second effort from the 1-yard line, and quarterback Carl Boush swept in for a two-point conversion and the only touchdown the Spartans needed.

Sumner advanced to the 4A ranks in 1977, but Anderson's team was not the least bit intimidated. This time, in the Kingdome, another Spokane school, Gonzaga Prep, fell to the Spartans, 12–7, who finished their season 12–2. They had to advance to the playoffs the hard way after finishing second in their league. With an 8–7 playoff win over Central Kitsap behind them, the Sparts then blanked Bellarmine, 15–0; downed Columbia River, 22–14; and thumped Garfield of Seattle, 34–14. Getting to the title game was mostly a Ron Arca show. The 185-pound junior fullback gained 492 yards in 90 carries in four playoff contests. In the quarterfinals at Vancouver, he carried 29 times for 173 yards and two touchdowns, and in the semifinals against Garfield he lugged the leather 151 yards in 22 carries, including a 72-yard touchdown run to break the game open. Arca also scored the two touchdowns in the championship game.

Anderson coached football at Sumner 23 years, 16 as head coach, and his teams won 114 games, lost 49, and tied six. They won five league championships and made four state playoff appearances. In '77 he was named State Coach of the Year and in '88 he was the state's Athletic Director of the Year.

Peninsula High took its turn in the spotlight in 1978, with Larry Lunke coaching the Seahawks in a pass-happy offensive scheme called "run and shoot." The Gig Harbor–based 'Hawks completed a perfect 13–0 season in 3A football with a thrilling 35–34 championship win over Pullman High.

With 20,000 fans looking on, Peninsula twice erased 13-point Pullman leads. The team motto was "bring home the fish," a reference to the fishing heritage of the harbor, and the Seahawks did exactly that. Quarterback Steve Hunt was the engineer, and fullback Mike Hull scored three times, one on a 53-yard run. Trailing 27–14 in the third quarter, Hunt passed to Paul Skansi for gains of 12, 22, and 25 yards on successive drives, and Hull banged across from short yardage twice for a 28–27 advantage. Pullman took a 34–28 lead after a disputed pass interception by the 'Hawks' Rob Carlson was disallowed.

Skansi, who later became a top pass receiver for UW and the Seattle Seahawks, had never returned a kickoff for a score before, but he found a way. With 7 minutes, 11 seconds left in the game, he gathered the kick at his own 12-

yard line and set sail to the left. Then he cut back to the middle of the field, where Hull and Tony Williams provided a block that sprung him free. He raced down the right side-line, staying inbounds by no more than 6 inches, and sprinted untouched for the score.

When Hunt then kicked the winning point after touch-down (PAT), the 35–34 victory was preserved. Skansi fin-ished the season with 85 pass receptions for 1,506 yards and 14 touchdowns. Not bad for a guy who was playing his first year as a wide receiver in only his second year of football.

In 1979 it was time for another Tacoma team to take home the 4A trophy. Coach George Nordi's Mount Tahoma Thunderbirds were top-ranked in the state by AP, and their Pierce County neighbor, Rogers High of Puyallup, was sec-ond, both with undefeated marks. The UPI poll reversed that, listing Rogers at the top. Pat Hoonan guided the Rogers Rams through 12 straight games and beat Wenatchee in the semifinal game in falling snow at Wenatchee, 27–20, while Mount Tahoma topped Evergreen, 21–7.

The championship game turned out to be the Mike Vin-divich show. The speedy Mount Tahoma halfback rushed for one touchdown, caught a 4-yard pass for another, tossed a 33-yard pass for a third, and returned the second-half kickoff 92 yards for a fourth. He carried the ball 20 times for 126 yards as Mount Tahoma demolished Rogers, 37–3. Quarter-back Brad Gobel completed seven of 11 passes for 61 yards and two touchdowns and ran 10 yards for another.

In Hoonan's 18 years at Rogers, his teams won or shared five league championships and qualified for the playoffs in seven of the last nine years he coached. His overall record with the Rams was 88–72–3.

The 1980s and '90s

What could Mount Tahoma do for an encore? Win back-to-back to back, of course, which they did, downing Issaquah, 21–3, in 1980. It was the first repeat state championship in Kingbowl history, and Vindivich was involved again.

Teaming with option quarterback Fred Baxter, Vindivich and the team's quickness proved to be the difference in the game. It was the 23rd consecutive victory over a two-year period for coach Nordi's group. Baxter set the tone early with a 56-yard keeper to the Issaquah 10 on the second play of the

game. Over the course of the evening, Baxter carried 16 times and gained 126 yards. A 9-yard touchdown keeper in the fourth quarter iced the game as Mount Tahoma's defense refused to yield a touchdown for the second straight win. Vindivich, named All-State for a second time, threw for one touchdown and ran 17 yards for another. He gained 94 yards in 17 carries, with Issaquah keying on his every move.

A 14–0 championship victory over Cashmere gave Eatonville the 1985 1A title in Kingbowl IX. Eatonville fullback Brandon Jumper scored all 14 Cruiser points in the first half on two touchdowns and a two-point conversion. In the game, he rushed for 165 yards. Mark Simons completed five passes for 135 yards for the champs, and Mike Vanning intercepted two passes on defense. Jumper's prep career pro-duced an all-time state rushing record of 5,910 yards and 76 touchdowns.

Puyallup claimed the 1987 4A crown by upending the defending state champion, the Gonzaga Bulldogs of Spokane, 27–21. Billy Joe Hobert set a championship-game passing record with 374 yards, hitting 18 of 32. Hobert hit Aaron Savage with a 53-yard scoring pass in the third quar-ter to give the Vikings the lead, but a 78-yard Gonzaga drive put the Bulldogs back in front; then Hobert went to work again. He fired a bullet to Danny Thurston for 84 yards and the go-ahead tally. Thurston, son of former Puyallup receiver and UPS record-setter Dan Thurston, set a Kingbowl record with nine catches for 200 yards. The win was the eighth in a row for the (11–2) Vikings. Hobert became a star UW quarterback and played in the NFL.

The Vikings were coached by Mike Huard, the father of three outstanding Puyallup quarterbacks (Damon, Brock, and Luke) who reached the finals in both '91 and '92 but couldn't repeat as champs. However, all three Huard sons played National Collegiate Athletic Association (NCAA) Division I football, and as head coach, Mike's record at Puyallup was 143–38 in 17 seasons. He won nine SPSL titles, had four undefeated regular seasons, was SPSL Coach of the Year nine times, and was inducted into the state's Football Coaches Hall of Fame in 1997.

The Huard family dominated football for several years as Damon, Brock, and Luke each played quarterback for Viking teams. Damon was a high school All-American and the Vikings were 14–4 with him at the helm. (He also led the state in scoring in basketball as a senior; see chapter 11, Basketball: High School Players.) Brock also was a prep All-American, and his teams were 16–3. Luke became Puyallup's all-time passing leader, throwing for more than 60 touchdowns while leading his team to a three-year record of 29–5. Unfortunately, none of those terrific Viking teams could duplicate the '87 effort.

There *was* an SPSL team of Vikings that did repeat, however: the Curtis High School Vikings took back-to-back state championships in 1989 and '90 under coach Bob Lucey, a Bellarmine Prep and UPS football star.

The 1989 honor came in Kingbowl XIII, with Deron Pointer in a starring role as the Curtis Vikings downed Kentwood, 25–0, in the 4A finale. Pointer was the son of former Tacoma Cubs outfielder Aaron Pointer, who later became a highly respected NFL official. Deron had two pass interceptions in the game, returning one for a touchdown, and he caught five passes for 37 yards and rushed three times for 38. He later played collegiately at WSU and professionally in the Canadian Football League. The Curtis defense as a whole held Kentwood to a mere 129 yards of total offense.

Lucey's Vikings were on top of the state again in 1990 with a 30–14 thumping of Newport. Brian Jensen was the passing star of the game, connecting on nine of 11 passes for three touchdowns. Two of those tosses went to Justin Sundquist and the other to Jay Dumas. Singor Mobley was

The 1964 Stadium Tigers won the City League title and tied Bremerton for the Cross-State Championship: back row, L. to R., coach Bob Levinson, Jim Booth, Bob Botley, Eddy Smith, Eddie Morris, Charles White, Rich Smith, Aubrey Reed, Phelon Cole, Herb Godfrey, Ted Kintz; front row, L. to R., Ellis Caine, Andy Levesque, Bill Hays, Bob Hunt, Bill Paton, Steve Mikkelson, Tom Greenwood, Rick Keely, Tom Benedetti, Gil Johnson, Mike Irwin, Nick Pergvich (courtesy the Bob Levinson Family).

a two-way standout, with 10 tackles on defense and 54 yards rushing in the first half. Brian Smith also had 10 tackles for Curtis. Mobley followed Pointer to WSU, where he starred before playing in the NFL.

Eatonville also jumped back into 1A championship contention in 1990, sinking Ephrata, 10–6, in Kingbowl XIV. The gritty Cruisers had to hang on to win, handing Ephrata its first loss of the season in 13 games. Quarterback Eric Snyder tallied the lone Eatonville touchdown on a keeper, and kicker Tom Zurfluh had a field goal and the PAT. Tracy Davis rushed for 61 yards in the defensive duel, in which Eatonville concluded the season undefeated (13–0). Snyder kept the ball out of Ephrata's hands in the late stages of the game, drawing three straight offside penalties that erased a third down and 21 yards and got the all-important first down, a critical turning point of the game.

Two years later, coach Steve Gervais brought Eatonville back for a third title try. A come-from-behind 26–23 victory over Zillah was the result. Trailing 23–0 with 8 minutes, 45 seconds left in the third quarter, the Cruisers worked some magic and tallied the last 26 points without a Zillah answer. Another 13–0 season belonged to the champs. Quarterback Bobby Lucht, an All-State performer, handled the Cruiser passing attack, completing 16 of 26 for 162 yards. Eatonville had three fourth-quarter touchdowns, with Joe Dorn, Ben Zurlo, and Tom Zurfluh in starring roles. Dorn scored the winning touchdown with 26 seconds left in the game, while Zurlo rushed for 140 yards, 102 in the second half, and Zurfluh had 98 receiving yards. At 8,938 yards, Lucht's career passing yardage was fourth best in state history.

Tacoma Baptist had two back-to-back seasons that landed them in the class A championship games of 2000 and 2001. The Baptists were 22–4 during that time but lost the title games to unbeaten Colfax and unbeaten Royal. Running back Josh Bousman (6 feet 3 inches and 210 pounds) was the big gun for coach Mark Smith. The state 100-meter champ in his division, Bousman scored 64 touchdowns in his final two seasons at Tacoma, gaining 2,217 yards as a junior and 2,075 yards as a senior (he missed one game). The Steilacoom Sentinels also had two of its best seasons then, winning league titles in both 2001 and 2002.

The Gridiron Classic in the Tacoma Dome

The Curtis Vikings established a new standard for 4A schools when the state championship playoffs became known as the Gridiron Classic and moved to the Tacoma Dome. Bob Lucey's classy 11 looked totally at home crushing Kamiakin, 49–7, for all the marbles. The Vikings thus became the first of the 4As to win three state titles.

The elusive Elijah Baker carried only six times but gained 153 yards and scored a touchdown for the winners. Sam Gage ran for 63 yards. The Vikings averaged 10 yards per play. Quarterback Matt Salzman threw only 11 times but completed five for three touchdowns. Jake Sampson caught a 60-yard touchdown pass, and tight end Jeff Cowart gathered in a 20-yard scoring toss.

Richland tried to stop Curtis in the 1996 contest, but the Bombers did not have enough firepower and Curtis won its fourth 4A championship by a 34–15 margin. Lucey thus became the only coach to win the coveted crown four times. Elijah Baker found the Tacoma Dome turf to his liking, with touchdown dashes of 67 and 50 yards plus a 2-yard scoring plunge. Matt Salzman threw only six passes this time around, but five of them were caught, one by Terry Tharps for a touchdown. David Baker and Jake Sampson also stood out offensively. On defense, the Curtis quickness was evident. Ronnie Griffin intercepted two passes and Charlie Englemann picked one and returned it for a touchdown. Richland could muster only 38 yards in 25 carries on offense.

Lakes High School stole the spotlight in 1997 under coach Dick Zatkovich. The Lancers completed an unbeaten 13–0 season with a 21–17 defeat of Ferndale to become the only team in the state, in any of the classifications, to enjoy a perfect year. The champs trailed Ferndale, 17–0, at halftime when a field goal was good on the last play of the half, touching off a field celebration that triggered Lakes' determination to come back after intermission.

And come back they did, with touchdowns by Brandon DeLeon on a pass from Tracy Kirby, a 1-yard plunge by Brian Bennett, and two extra points by Jacob Estrada. Still down, at 17–14, Lakes turned to its bag of tricks with 1 minute, 32 seconds remaining. A 43-yard double pass from Kirby to Derrick Williams (older brother of Lakes future receiving star Reggie Williams) to Michael Westbrook produced the winning touchdown.

Zatkovich left Lakes after 16 seasons as head coach, with a record of 123 wins and just 39 losses, intending to retire. The lure of coaching proved too much, however, and he decided to take the same position at Lincoln in 2000. The Abes program needed a boost at the time, and Zatkovich provided it. His first team was 4–5, his second 5–4, his third 7–2, and his fourth 9–3. That one earned him a playoff spot and a near-win over Ballard's finalists despite the loss of two star performers just before the game. Coach Zatkovich earned a great deal of respect statewide for his decision to suspend the pair prior to such an important game because of a team rule infraction.

The Lakes program was inherited by Dave Miller, who was an assistant coach there for 14 years. He promptly won four straight league titles with a regular record of 37–1 and an overall mark of 43–5. Three times his teams had unbeaten regular seasons; the Lancers went to the state playoffs in all of Miller's four years, seven straight times overall.

During that stretch, two Lakes players set state championship records: Matt Griffith passed for 325 yards against Skyline in 2000 (setting total offense and passing yardage records), and Reggie Williams caught eight passes in the title tussle for 151 yards (both catching and yardage records). Williams took his skills to UW and became the top draft choice of Jacksonville in the NFL in 2003.

Many outstanding students of Tacoma and Pierce County high schools excelled in football while comparable numbers went on to play in college and the professional ranks. The high school gridiron represents the true spirit of competition and sportsmanship, and the region's game continues to inspire and excite both the players and the fans.

CHAPTER 22

FOOTBALL:
COLLEGE

Ron Medved, Bellarmine Prep and University of Washington graduate, played defensive back for the Philadelphia Eagles from 1966–70 (SSM, 330.02).

The history of Pacific Lutheran University (PLU) and University of Puget Sound (UPS) football is centered around great coaches, from Roy Sandberg to Frosty Westering. Sandberg's stay at UPS was brief, but his teams dominated small-college play in the Northwest in the early '30s. Westering is truly a legend, after 32 years (1972–2003) winning four national championships at PLU. His 305 wins rank in the top 10 among the nation's winningest college coaches.

Other coaches include the Loggers' John Heinrick (1948–1964), who was recognized nationally by the Helms Foundation as a charter member of its Hall of Fame. Cliff Olson, Marv Harshman, and Marv Tommervik's collective successes brought PLU nationwide publicity in the '40s. Bob Ryan took the Loggers to a new level when they stepped up to National Collegiate Athletic Association (NCAA) Division II competition in the '70s. Paul Wallrof (1973–77) and Ron Simonson (1978–84) followed suit.

The Early Years

The UPS Loggers got a 25-year head start on the PLU Lutes in bringing football to campus, playing their first game in 1901 and going 2–2 in their first season of play. The maroon and white beat Tacoma High School, 10–0; walloped Centralia High, 61–0; lost to Port Townsend High, 31–6; and fell to the University of Washington (UW), 16–6.

By 1903 the Loggers improved, completing their first unbeaten season unscored upon. The 6–0–1 record included a 0–0 tie with the Washington State University (WSU) Cougars and a win over Idaho, 11–0. The Loggers also whacked Whitworth College, 35–0, in what was then a crosstown battle since Whitworth also was located in Tacoma, and trimmed Nevada, 10–0, in the season finale.

It took a PLU chemistry professor, Anders W. Ramstad, to round up enough Lutherans to form two 11s, and most had never tossed a pigskin before. As such, PLU started slowly too, losing to Lincoln High, 42–0 one year and 18–0 the next. In the '20s the Loggers played and competed well in the Northwest Conference with teams like Linfield, Whitman, Willamette, and Pacific. In 1929, with All-Conference players John Garnero (1st team tackle), Frank Gillihan (2nd team quarterback), and Don Shotwell (honorable mention end), they stepped up to tackle UW in the first night game ever held in the Northwest, a November meeting in Stadium Bowl. A 73–0 shellacking followed, one of the most significant setbacks in school history. The Loggers never did beat the UW but did come within a touchdown in 1933. By 1931 the black and gold was ready to challenge UPS, however, and a new crosstown rivalry was born. The Loggers won the inaugural meeting, 20–0. PLU had trained for two weeks, the Loggers only four days, but fullback Chet Baker's kicking (punts of nearly 60 yards on several occasions) proved to be the difference in the game played under the lights at Stadium Bowl. The victory settled a duel between Baker and PLU's Red Carlson.

UPS dominated the series throughout the '30s. Coach Sandberg brought Tacoma its first Northwest Conference championship in 1932, with a record of 7–1–1. A 25–0 win over the Lutes opened the season, but Willamette tied the Loggers, 0–0, midway and Columbia University of Portland marred a perfect season in the finale, 6–0. In '33 the Loggers were undefeated in league play and yielded just 12 points, but the Lutes and Loggers didn't play. The highlight of the season was a hard-fought 14–6 loss to the UW Huskies.

After a lapse of six years, the UPS-PLU rivalry was renewed and the Lutes were much improved. The Loggers still prevailed, but it took a long pass from Bill Madden to Richie Rowe and a 1-yard touchdown plunge by Warren Gay to culminate a 55-yard winning march. The night contest drew 7,000 excited fans to Stadium Bowl.

Two more years went by before the two met again, but this time PLU was ready, with the "Marvelous Marvs": Harshman and Tommervik. It was coach Cliff Olson's first

The CPS football team of 1946 included two pairs of brothers: L. to R., Dick Hermsen, Vic Martineau, LaVerne Martineau, Jack Hermsen (SSM, 2001.2.1).

win over the Loggers but not his last. Harshman scored twice, and PLU used three teams during the game, claiming a 47–0 victory. Steve Daley of UPS led the ground gainers with 95 yards, but Tommervik had 93 for PLU in two fewer carries. The rivalry was one-sided no more.

PLU in the 1930s and '40s

Olson earned the moniker "Father of PLU Sports." From 1929 to 1948 he was Lute athletic director; he also coached football, basketball, baseball, golf, tennis, and track. His football squads practiced behind Harstad Hall on a rocky dirt field that became known as the "Parkland Pebbles." At first the team passed the hat at games played in old Lincoln Bowl to finance the athletic program Olson dared to build.

But build it he did. The Lutes had an eight-game winning streak starting in 1939 and twice defeated national power Gonzaga. The Lutes' 16–13 thriller over the Bulldogs in 1940 gained national recognition for the program, with Harshman booting a field goal from the 29-yard line with 16 seconds remaining. The victory came before 15,000 in Stadium Bowl. It was Harshman's first-ever try at a field goal, and it took 11 consecutive pass completions by Tommervik and company to reach the 29. PLU had trailed 13–0 at halftime, but a series of forward passes and laterals, mostly by Tommervik, enabled the Lutes to tie their heavily favored opponent, 13–13, then win the contest on a kick by Harshman in what remains one of the most legendary games in the history of Tacoma football. Tommervik was an outstanding halfback and passer, twice being named to Associated Press (AP) Little All-America teams. Harshman was selected to the All-America team at fullback by the *New York Times*.

In 1947, PLU's 11 shared the Evergreen Conference (EvCo) title, finished the season unbeaten, and won the Pear Bowl in Medford, Oregon, beating favored Southern Oregon College, 27–21. The SOC Red Raiders had won 15 straight games coming into the bowl, but two fourth-quarter touchdowns by PLU provided victory. The Lutes finished 7–0–2, with the ties going to Eastern Washington University (EWU) and Lewis and Clark College. Playing before some big crowds during that regular season, PLU opened at home against St. Olaf's College of Minnesota,

and 8,000 fans, mostly Lutherans, turned out. Another 13,000 watched PLU trounce UPS, 19–0.

Don D'Andrea, a 280-pound All-America center, anchored a PLU line that had "Pete" Peterson and Eldon Kyllo at guard and tackle beside him. The Washington Intercollegiate Conference (WInCo) League champs featured the running of fullback Jack Guyot and halfback Frank Spear, a genuine one-two punch.

Olson's football record at PLU was 64–33–6, including the school's first undefeated season, 8–0, in 1940. In three years as basketball coach, he was 43–16. When he retired in '48, guess who the Lutherans called upon to replace him? The "Marvelous Marvs"!

PLU Coaches

Marv Tommervik and Marv Harshman took control of both the football and basketball fortunes and pitched in to coach some baseball as well. Tommervik was head football coach for four years and had a 19–10–6 record before leaving education to become a business leader in the Parkland community. After taking over for Tommervik, Harshman was 27–28–2; he coached PLU basketball to national small-college prominence at the same time.

Jim Gabrielson and Roy Carlson followed "Harsh" at the football helm, but the two combined for just 44 wins (Carlson won 37) against 73 defeats, and in 1972 Frosty Westering was hired.

Two of Westering's favorite sayings were "Attaway!" and "The big time is where you are!" Westering made his players feel that they were indeed in the big time. He rarely referred to the word *winning* and maintained that "the game is not against the other team, the game is us against our best self, and we don't know how good that is." He kept his program simple. Practice at PLU started when Westering got there, whether it was 3:15, 3:30, or 3:45. He often stopped halfway through practice for a snack break. He told stories and talked Scriptures—but make no mistake: his teams were always ready to play.

Under his mom-and-pop approach, PLU appeared in 15 National Association of Intercollegiate Athletics (NAIA) Division II playoffs and four NCAA Division III playoffs. They won the 1999 NCAA Division III title by winning five straight road games during the playoffs. They won NAIA championships in 1980, 1987, and 1993 and were national runners-up in 1983, 1985, 1991, and 1994. None of Westering's teams ever had a losing season.

He coached 25 NAIA and NCAA All-America first-team players, was NCAA Division III Coach of the Year in 1999, NAIA Division II Coach of the Year in '83 and '93, and a seven-time Northwest College Division Coach of the Year. His is one of the all-time top 10 coaching records in the country.

When Westering retired in 2004, his son Scott was elected to replace him, keeping it all in the family. Scott was an All-American performer at PLU, playing for his dad in the '70s, and served as PLU's offensive coordinator since 1983. A PLU assistant coach for 23 years, he was a star on the first PLU national championship team and is a member of the PLU Hall of Fame.

The "Marvelous Marvs," Harshman (L.) and Tommervik, teamed up to coach PLC in 1948 (courtesy Tacoma News Tribune).

Frosty Westering never coached against John Heinrick of UPS. Heinrick retired eight years before Frosty arrived from the Midwest. But longtime sports fans in Tacoma believe that the ultimate matchup would have been Heinrick versus Westering.

UPS in the 1950s–'70s

Heinrick was a coaching legend in the City of Destiny at both Bellarmine Prep and Stadium High School before taking the helm at UPS. From 1948 to 1964, he won 89 games and tied 12 while losing 46. In 38 years on the local scene, he won 217 games and tied 27 against 101 losses. During many of those seasons, he was athletic director, Fieldhouse manager, and basketball coach at UPS in addition to his football duties. His record against PLU was 29 wins or ties against just five losses (24–5–5), and he won or shared five EvCo titles, beating teams such as Western Washington University, Central Washington University (CWU), and EWU in the process.

A charter member of the National NAIA Football Coaches Hall of Fame in 1957, Heinrick also was selected as the first honorary coach of the Methodist University college All-America team in 1962. He was inducted into the Tacoma–Pierce County Hall of Fame and the Washington State Sports Hall of Fame.

Heinrick was the consummate teacher, leaving a lasting impression on Tacoma's youth. He taught history and coached more than 400 players who themselves decided to become teachers and coaches. Garry Hersey, who played for him at both Stadium High and UPS, was quick to talk about the respect Heinrick's players had for him. "At Stadium our big game of the year was a Turkey Day game with Lincoln, and coach told us he didn't want to see us talking with any girls the week ahead of that game. I didn't talk to my girlfriend [later his wife] for a whole week. You wouldn't see that happening today."

Joe Stortini, who later coached at Wilson and Mount Tahoma High Schools, played at Lincoln but quarterbacked for Heinrick at UPS. He remembered his coach as "expecting the best from you on the field or in the classroom. He taught us to play to win, to do our best, but never to get hung up when we lost."

"Respect" was the one word most of Heinrick's players used when they were asked to remember him. There have been many coaches in Tacoma over the years, but players for Heinrick said "there was only one coach."

Appropriately, when Heinrick retired in '64, one of his former players became the top Logger. Bob Ryan left his glossy record at Puyallup High School to restore some of the glory to a UPS program that had just experienced a one-win season. The Loggers were competing in the EvCo at the time, and the gap between the league's state schools and private schools was beginning to widen. PLU left the EvCo for the Northwest Conference in '65, giving the Loggers a new direction as well.

UPS decided on a bold new athletic step: to become NCAA Division II independents and to travel more for games to areas and states where the student body could relate to the opposition. No longer a commuter college, now a good share of UPS's students hailed from California, Oregon, Hawaii, and Colorado.

It took time for the Ryan "Express" to get underway. The schedule, the level of competition, the recruiting, even the school colors were about to change. At no time in the school's history was there more modification to the football program than in the decade-plus from 1967 to 1978.

Crosstown Rivals: 1960s–'70s

During these early adjustments, PLU easily topped the Loggers twice in 1965, 23–7 and 14–0. Quarterback Tony Lister did much of the damage, scoring in the first game and handling the ball 43 times (a PLU record) in the second. He

Members of the 1940–41 Pacific Lutheran College football team included three sets of brothers: L. to R., Sterling and Marv Harshman, Murray and Blair Taylor, Marv and Bob Tommervik (courtesy Howard Clifford).

was 11 for 23 passing in that one, for 139 yards, with a touchdown toss to Mike McKay.

But Ryan's first collegiate win came in the season opener of 1966, and there was no slowing the Loggers after that. Lister scored the game's first touchdown for PLU, but the Loggers answered with 17 points on a pass from Randy Roberts to Pat Larkin, a 37-yard field goal by Clint Scott, and a touchdown run by Jerome Crawford.

Ryan-coached teams won the next year, 37–0, with Mike Price intercepting a PLU pass on the game's first play, Bob Botley tossing a 41-yard touchdown pass to Dan Thurston, Jerome Crawford returning a pass 22 yards for a score, and Al Roberts tallying twice. Price, a UPS team captain, became an assistant coach at UPS upon graduation and later head coach at Weber State and WSU. Roberts became head coach at Garfield High in Seattle and an assistant coach at UW and spent years coaching in the NFL.

The Loggers took six decisions in a row against the Lutes until the Frosty Westering–led team of 1974 netted PLU a 38–27 win at Franklin Pierce Stadium in Parkland. Rick Finseth threw three touchdown passes for the winners—two to Mark Clinton, who caught a total of seven for 145 yards. Doug Gall was UPS's big gainer, with 168 yards rushing. Then four more Logger victories, two of them in the Kingdome in Seattle, followed.

The rivals' indoor battles in Seattle were classic. With 13,167 fans looking on in 1977, PLU declined a successful field goal and took over on the UPS 5-yard line due to a Logger penalty, only to be held on the next four plays without scoring, and the Loggers won, 23–21. The next year, with PLU leading, 7–6, at halftime, Steve Levenseller returned the second-half kickoff 98 yards to score, and UPS never looked back, winning 27–14. Pat O'Loughlin had 97 yards rushing for the Loggers; Scott Westering caught six passes for 85 yards from brother Brad for the Lutes.

UPS in the 1970s–Present

The UPS domination of small-college football in the Northwest was firmly established by that time. Ryan left UPS following the 1972 season to coach at the University of Hawaii (UH), and his assistant, Paul Wallrof, replaced him for the '73 campaign. Ryan had won 43 games against 27

losses and five ties during his tenure, but the statistics were misleading because most of the losses came at the hands of out-of-state foes such as UH, Santa Clara University (SCU), Sacramento State University (SSU), Simon Fraser University (SFU), Portland State University (PSU), Cal Western, and Humboldt State University (HSU). Against Northwest foes, his teams rarely lost, and they won the Northwest small-college poll four times in his last five years.

Twice the Loggers were the third team out for a berth in the Camellia Bowl in Sacramento. In 1968 the NCAA picked HSU (8–1) and Fresno State (6–3), leaving the 8–2 UPS record on the outside despite both losses (one to UH) being in the last 90 seconds. In '69 the UPS 11 were 7–2, with losses to UH and SSU in the final game of the year. The latter came on the heels of the announcement that Montana and North Dakota, both unbeaten, had been selected for Camellia Bowl play.

Wallrof was one of the most popular UPS coaches ever, with both his players and the fans. Dubbed "Big Wally" by his admirers, he played the part: 6 feet 4 inches and 255 pounds, give or take a few. Wallrof had been a UW tackle under three coaches—John Cherberg, Darrell Royal, and Jim Owens—and was an ex-Marine. The Goofy Goose Drive-in, a restaurant near Baker Stadium where the Loggers played their home games, even named a hamburger after him: the Big Wally Burger!

Fabled Slippery Rock State College of Pennsylvania provided Wallrof with his first college challenge. On a rainy Northwest Saturday afternoon, with extra bleachers ringing the field, the Loggers took a 13–7 decision over the "Rock" and gave Big Wally his first win as head coach. A 16-yard touchdown pass from Mike Mickas to Robin Hill and two field goals by Mark Conrad, one a 48-yarder late in the third quarter, proved the difference. Conrad's booming punts kept the Pennsylvanians at bay much of the game before a crowd of 6,000 appreciative fans.

Wallrof had a record of 31 wins and 18 losses with one tie in five seasons, continuing to campaign as an NCAA independent. The Loggers finished 6–3 in 1973, one of the losses to UH. The 1974 season wasn't typical for the Loggers, however, and the UPS gridders finished at 4–5, including that loss to PLU.

Wallrof decided to bag his wishbone offense in '75 and hired two of the best prep coaches in the Tacoma area to install a new one. Joe Stortini, who had led Mount Tahoma High to the state championship game a year earlier, and Ed Fallon, with a 42–21–4 record in eight years at Bellarmine Prep, were ready to combine their talents and put some go in the Loggers. A big 34–20 win over SCU and a 7–3–1 record in 1975 brought the Loggers back to postseason consideration.

The Loggers won five straight out of the gate in 1976, including a 37–7 pasting of Willamette and a 34–14 triumph over SSU in Sacramento. Chico State then took a 16–15 verdict at Chico to derail the UPS 11, but Brent Wagner's extra point with 11 seconds remaining gave UPS a 28–27 edge over SFU. (Noted actor James Garner watched Wagner's winning boot from a box seat at Baker Stadium on the campus where his daughter was going to school and dating Wagner.)

The Loggers then faced PSU—and the nation's leading passer and total offense leader, June Jones. PSU topped UPS, 29–25, but not before the Loggers tied the score at 22–22 and marched 53 yards to a fourth-down-and-1-yard play at the PSU 4-yard line. A 14–13 loss to SCU the following week left Wallrof's crew only six points away from an unbeaten season.

The Loggers finished 6–4 in '77, Wallrof's final season. He stepped aside as head coach but remained on the staff when good friend and fellow coach Ron Simonson was named to the position. A season-ending loss to Montana, 18–17, was a tough one since UPS was within easy field-goal reach in the final minutes, only to lose a fumble and the game. The highlight of the year was that 23–21 win over PLU in the Kingdome.

About that time, a new administration at UPS began to discuss changes in the athletic program, making football a target for less support. Simonson, ever the competitor, took charge, winning 50 games from 1978 to 1984, a percentage of 71.5 percent, despite the shadow of doubt that surrounded the program. In 1978 he was 9–1 and in 1981 he was 10–2, one of the best-ever marks by a UPS team.

Simonson's debut was in Missoula, where the University of Montana seldom loses. The Loggers won 23–12 as nose guard Mark Scott and linebacker Mark Madland led a stout UPS defense. The Loggers had 11 quarterback sacks (four

by Scott), and Madland had 12 tackles. Ivy Iverson tossed two touchdown passes, a 17-yarder to Bill Hines and a 16-yarder to Keith Brown, in the Logger win.

UPS finished its season with a 56–7 thrashing of CWU to once again be considered for playoffs, but a 28–13 loss to University of California–Davis (UCD) proved to be the difference: two California teams were among the eight picked for the national title chase. (Cal Poly San Luis Obispo was the other.) Among the Loggers' big wins were a 7–0 win over SCU and a 34–21 spanking of PSU.

In 1979 UPS finished 7–4, winning all its home games, losing four on the road, then dumping SFU in Vancouver, British Columbia, 21–9, to end another good season. Ivy Iverson set quarterback records with his season of 2,016 passing yards and 17 touchdown passes.

After a 6–3 season in 1980, the Loggers came away with the first 10-win season in school history in 1981 and, finally, got the nod from the NCAA for postseason play. The Loggers' only loss during the regular season was to Big Sky Conference foe Weber State, 31–10, at Weber State in Utah. In reaching the magic number of 10, UPS downed seven California schools, all with strong Division II programs, including SCU and UCD, en route to their playoff opportunity. Only EWU played UPS among the Washington state teams, and EWU ended number three in the national NCAA poll.

Without question, it was one of the finest records in UPS history, particularly since the opposition was so strong. It was a shame to end it with a loss, but the Loggers did, hosting North Dakota State at Highline Stadium in a Division II NCAA playoff game by a 24–10 count. UPS was one of eight teams in the country to be selected, and the Loggers did themselves proud. It was 10–10 with 5 minutes, 5 seconds left in the game.

Simonson called it quits at UPS in 1984. He finished 7–3, 6–5, and 5–4 as players began to leave the school and new recruits were wary to join because of a growing perception that the program had little support from the school administration. Losing football games became commonplace, and eventually UPS returned to the Northwest Conference, where the Loggers went 0–15 in the 2001, 2002, and 2003 seasons.

PACIFIC LUTHERAN COLLEGE FOOTBALL, 1939—41

(Editor's note: Pacific Lutheran College began its football program in 1926, with A. W. Ramstad its first coach. In 1929 Cliff Olson became both athletic director and football coach for teams called the Gladiators before the school adopted the Lutes moniker. Olson lifted his players to championships for three years running, starting in 1939 and ending two days before the United States entered World War II. David James, a Tacoma News Tribune *reporter at the time, was responsible for publicizing the Lutes' exploits nationwide. He wrote this memoir in 1993 at the age of 83.)*

Every so often some small, unknown school pops up, grows like Jack's beanstalk, and becomes the talk of the nation. So it was with Jim Thorpe's Carlisle Indians before WWI. They cooled off mighty teams of that period. Then we have Slippery Rock, not so much for victories as for a unique name that intrigued sports writers for years. Then along came Pacific Lutheran College (PLC), literally unknown outside Pierce County, until it got just the right breaks in 1939 to gain a national reputation as the Cinderella of college football.

PLC became news because it had so little. It had no football field. It had no goal posts. It had few jerseys that matched. It was the Little School that Had Nothing. All it could do was win football games: 23 out of 25 over its three-year span as Washington Intercollegiate Conference (WInCo) champions. It conquered Gonzaga's powerful independent teams twice and closed out its remarkable three seasons with a win over College of Pacific, coached by the famous Amos Alonzo Stagg, known then as the grand old man of football.

I was doing general-assignment reporting, along with a column on southwestern Washington high school sports called "Southwest Breezes," for the *Tacoma News Tribune* when athletic directors at Bellingham, Ellensburg, Cheney, PLC, and St. Martin's formed WInCo in 1939.

My introduction to Clifford O. Olson, coach and athletic director at PLC, came that summer when he invited me to become secretary of the "Winko" League, as it was called. As I recall, I was to be paid $25 monthly to keep the standings and statistics and do weekly publicity. No writers at either the *News Tribune* or the *Tacoma Times* covered PLC sports at that time. So I asked sports editor Dan Walton (a grand fellow) if I might cover what were then called the Gladiators during the 1939 season. Dan said I was the first reporter ever to ask for that assignment, and if I could enjoy it he was willing to send me out.

I soon learned why sports writers spurned driving out to PLC in Parkland. Coach Olson had come to PLC as athletic director, coach, and fundraiser in 1929 after his graduation from Luther College, where he had played fullback at 160 pounds. Since PLC's founding in 1895, the small Lutheran college had lived year to year. Some years the faculty received only part of their salaries. It was a case of faith and sacrifice. It is important to recall this decade, 1929–38, during which Olson scrimped and saved and did everything from sell tickets to stripe the field, wash the towels, and coach. He scheduled anyone who would play his team, be it high schools, junior colleges, or other small colleges as little known, sportswise, as PLC. Olson's school had about as much glamour as a three-wheeled buggy. ⟶

I found the 1939 squad working out on a playground behind Old Main....Olson's players dressed in whatever jerseys, sweatshirts, pants, or jeans they could scrounge. They practiced goal kicking over a fir bough projecting at about regulation height. The playground was too rough and gravel strewn for injury-free scrimmage, so Olson had his boys throw the ball. They ran lateral plays, short and long, passed, and short-kicked until they became skilled at "keep-away." Their home games were played in the dirt in the old Lincoln High School Bowl, where the board bleachers were so full of stickers and slivers that most fans—of whom there weren't many—stood all during a game.

How Olson managed to recruit players when he had no scholarships to offer puzzled other coaches. It was mainly through his convincing personality that he encouraged players overlooked at area high schools to come to PLC and get an education. He got small-paying after-school jobs wherever he could find them. He arranged board and room or batching quarters. Luck played a part, too. Among what were to become big names in Northwest football were Marv Harshman, "Big" George Anderson, George Broz, Gordon Huseby, and others who tried a year at the University of Washington and withdrew for various reasons. Olson persuaded them to continue their education at PLC. Arlington High School had produced the Tommervik brothers—Tim, Bob, and Marvin—all from a Lutheran family with faith in PLC.

Little did Cliff Olson know in 1938 that he had acquired a player who would become rated along with Sammy Baugh of Texas as the best passer in college football during the next three seasons. Marv Tommervik became famous as "Tommy-gun," a halfback so evasive he rarely ever was sacked. He might run backward 20 yards to complete a 40-yard gainer to his superlative ends, Earl

Platt and blond Icelander Sig Sigurdson. He could run, kick, and pass with such ability he was named on the Little All-America first teams of 1940 and 1941. In combination with Marv Harshman, the signal-calling fullback who likewise gained Little All-America honors, Tommervik and his fellow Lutes made delicious copy for sports writers.

After winning seven out of eight games in 1939, losing only to Central Washington College on a windy day in Ellensburg, the "little school with nothing" was evidently more than a figment of imagination. It had quality and ability. Crowds began flocking to PLC games. Lincoln Bowl couldn't hold them all, and PLC switched the games to the Tacoma Stadium [Stadium Bowl] in 1940.

Promotion of the Lutes became systematized. Sports editors George M. Varnell of the *Seattle Times* and Royal Brougham of the *Seattle Post-Intelligencer*; Dan Walton of the Tacoma News Tribune and Elliott Metcalf of the *Tacoma Times*; Gail Fowler of the Associated Press, Seattle; Russ Newland of the Associated Press, San Francisco; L. H. Gregory of the *Oregonian* in Portland; Paul Zimmerman of the *Los Angeles Times*; and sports writers of *The New York Times* and *New York Sun* all kept the Lutes in the public eye. Spaulding's Record Book asked for weekly reports. In addition to doing coverage for the *News Tribune,* I sent regular reports to the above sources.

The seven games PLC won in 1940, giving it a record of 14 wins and one loss in two years, had the Northwest wondering just how good the Lutes really were. The test came when the Tacoma Hot Stove League proposed the Lutes play Gonzaga University, then a power in West Coast football with an All-America quarterback named Tony Canadeo. The game was scheduled for November 29, 1940, in Stadium Bowl. Gonzaga, coached by Puggy Hunton, came to town licking its chops over making an easy meal of a bunch of Norwegian hicks. Played before one of the largest crowds ever to see a game in Tacoma, it was a contest that etched its way into history. Gonzaga eased through a 13–0 lead in the first half. Everyone except Cliff Olson and his squad expected the slaughter to continue.

No way. The Lutes responded with a spectacular display of laterals and Tommervik passes to gain a 13–13 tie. With 16 seconds left in the game and the Lutes on Gonzaga's 29-yard line after completing 11 successive passes, Marv Harshman attempted the first field goal of his career. He made it, and the Lutes scored an unforgettable 16–13 win.

That sensational victory over Gonzaga did more than underscore PLC's national reputation. It brought Tacoma out of the doldrums it was feeling over the collapse of the Tacoma Narrows bridge. To this day, the victories are credited with creating the spirit and drive that built Pacific Lutheran University

into the reputable institution it is today. Incidentally, two weeks after defeating Gonzaga, the Lutes turned to basketball, at which they were equally adept, and stunned Hec Edmundson's University of Washington Huskies, 40–30, in a preseason game that brought the small Parkland school another slathering of national publicity.

Gonzaga was so miffed about its loss, it asked for a rematch, which it got at the opening of the 1941 season. This time, with 22,000 watching in the Stadium Bowl, the Lutes collared the Bulldogs, 26–13. With Tommervik throwing and Marv Harshman commanding both the attack and defense, the Lutes marched into their third "Winko" League championship. Then two more games were scheduled to test their ability. Coach Matty Matthews brought his Portland University team to Tacoma on November 21, 1941. The Lutes lost for the first time in 19 games, 20–6. Cliff Olson was not one to alibi, but it was a weakened team that night. Marv Harshman was out with the flu and three other regulars were out with injuries. ⟶

College action in Stadium Bowl (SSM).

The Lutes had one more game, and it was a big one: against College of Pacific, coached by Amos Alonzo Stagg. Olson considered this opportunity to meet America's best-known coach a highlight of his career. Again playing before a filled Stadium Bowl, the Lutes defeated College of Pacific, 13–6, on December 5, 1941, two days prior to the Japanese attack on Pearl Harbor.

Most of the Lutes entered military service for the duration of World War II. At one point, Marv Tommervik and Marv Harshman were stationed at San Diego and played with a Navy team that trounced the University of Southern California. Sports writers quickly recognized Tommervik as the passer who had led PLU to so many wins.

In three seasons, the Lutes had grown from nobodies to the country's best-known small-college team. Tommervik was named to the Associated Press Little All-America team in 1940. Harshman and Earl Platt received honorable mention. The following year, the *New York Sun* placed Harshman on its All-America first team, and Tommervik again was named to the Associated Press Little All-America team.

Comparisons between football teams of yesterday and today are difficult because so many things have changed. Today's game is played with platoons and specialists who are on the field in only offense or defense. Uniforms are well padded and helmets have face masks. The Lutes played all of their games on dirt fields, sometimes at night under weak lighting. More than half their games over the three-year span were played in muddy conditions. Tommervik's passing becomes all the more remarkable when it is remembered that he threw a soggy ball inflated with a rubber bladder. All players stayed in the game, whether on offense or defense. They had no face protection, and padding was far thinner than in today's uniforms.

As I read about modern football and the few players who seem to get a full education and graduate, I recall how Cliff Olson stressed education among his players. Most, if not all, of the players in 1939–41 earned their diplomas and went into teaching and coaching. Shortly before his death in 1989, coach Olson told me he was proud of the athletic records "his boys" had accomplished. But he also said he was even more proud of how they became good citizens and educators. PLU honored Olson by naming its modern sports field house for him.

Two men who gave Cliff Olson strong support during these years were Charles "Baron" Barofsky, assistant coach, and Dr. Jesse Pflueger, team physician and trainer. Olson was a serious, determined man who had just the right counterpart in the merry-minded "Baron" and the morale-building Dr. Pflueger. Barofsky had been known as the "Marinette Barrel" when he played football at Marinette High School in Wisconsin. Short and pudgy, he ran like a barrel so effectively that he was compared with the great Red Grange. Dr. Pflueger was a father figure beloved by the players, always with a word of praise for their efforts.

If any one trait featured the Lutes, it was their ability to laugh at themselves and accept the publicity about their "poverty," which endeared them to nationally known sports writers. They were content to be called "the nimble Norwegians" even though some weren't Nordics. They kept stiff lips when asked if it was true that they gained strength by rubbing themselves with "lutefisk oil" before each game. Barofsky loved to claim this made his linemen so strong, opponents could hardly stand to be near them. In three seasons, the Lutes built a reputation that has never faded. To this day, football fans speak with admiration of the years when the "Flying Circus" at Parkland was the talk of the land.

But there are signs of hope: A 33–27 double overtime loss to PLU in 2004 was the closest the Loggers have come to the Lutes in 16 years. And, after two challenging years as head coach, Phil Willenbrock appears to have the Loggers headed in the right direction, completing the season with an overall record of 5–4.

Crosstown Rivalry in the 1980s

PLU, meantime, was a program on the move. The Lutes were dominant in the Northwest Conference and met success, first in NAIA national competition and then NCAA Division III playoffs.

The Lute-Logger series was halted for three years, however, after the 1979 game in which UPS won a 29–14 verdict at Baker Stadium. Quarterback Ivy Iverson passed for 212 yards as the Loggers erased an early PLU lead of 8–7. Programs going in "different directions" was cited as the reason for the split. But once the Logger program was settled in the NAIA, PLU agreed to resume the rivalry in 1983. A record crowd of 14,830 in the Tacoma Dome watched PLU win, 13–10, as Jeff Rohr rushed for 177 yards and kicked two field goals.

UPS turned the tables in '84 as Mike Oliphant had 129 yards in 17 Logger carries and the Loggers prevailed, 32–22. PLU then ambushed the Loggers, 54–13, in '85 and shaded the Loggers, 22–18, in '86 when Jeff Yarnell threw a trio of touchdown passes for the Lutes.

The 1987 game was the last hurrah for the struggling UPS program. The Loggers claimed a 24–7 victory, with Mike Oliphant rushing for 171 yards and three touchdowns. But Frosty Westering's team was on the rise and destined never to lose another game to the crosstown foe. Westering lost seven of eight initially, won three of five when the rivalry resumed, then took 17 in a row before retiring. In his coaching finale, he toppled the Loggers, 40–14, after trailing 14–6 at the half.

PLU in the 1980s–'90s

The Lutes' memorable national-champion seasons with Westerling occurred during this time. The 1980 march to the championship was a first for PLU, and the Lutes dumped Wilmington, Ohio, 38–10, with Chris Utt earning the Offen-

sive Player of the Game award and Scott Kessler realizing the defensive player award. In the 1987 drive, PLU tied Wisconsin–Stevens Point, 16–16, in the Tacoma Dome, but it was later learned that WSP had to forfeit all of its games for use of an ineligible player. PLU's Pat Dorsey was named Offensive Player of the Game, but NAIA records showed "vacant" for defensive player (a WSP player) and maintained the tie result.

The 1993 title was decided in Portland, Oregon, and the Lutes busted Westminster of Pennsylvania, 50–20. Quarterback Mark Weekly was the Offensive Player of the Game and Jason Thiel was the defensive star. Weekly set a national record with six touchdown passes against Cumberland, Tennessee, and earlier in the playoffs he was named All-American by the NAIA, along with linebacker Ted Riddall.

Weekly still holds 15 PLU records, including 4,065 yards of offense in a single season, 10,977 in his career, the most pass completions by a quarterback (33 game, 226 season, 644 career), and passing yards of 3,722 for a single season and 9,737 for his career. Twice he had six touchdown tosses in a game, and he threw 46 touchdown passes in 1993, 115 in his career.

A Lincoln Abe with 32 touchdowns in 1962, Don Moore enjoyed further success as a running back at UW (photo by James O. Sneddon, courtesy University of Washington).

PLU's road show in 1999 was the most amazing championship tale of all. The Lutes logged more than 16,000 miles to down five playoff opponents and finish with the greatest number of wins in school history, 13–1. Clearly, the NCAA Division III title didn't come easy.

The journey started in Salem, Oregon, where PLU turned the tables on Willamette, the only team to beat PLU, 29–20, during the regular season. With Chad Johnson (Westering's grandson) throwing for three touchdowns in a 16–32 performance for 232 yards, the Lutes scored 21 unanswered points in the second half to win a 28–24 decision.

The second round took PLU to Waverly, Iowa, where Wartburg waited, but a 49–14 Lute pasting took care of that. Anthony Hicks, a UW transfer, scored four touchdowns, gained 125 yards on 21 carries, and caught five passes for 50 yards; Johnson completed 14 of 18 passes for 175 yards.

It was on to Collegeville, Minnesota, for the quarterfinals and a crack at touted St. John's. Trailing 9–0 near the end of the first half, Lute Jacob Croft went 4 yards and the Lutes were down, 9–6, at halftime. Two fourth-quarter touchdowns upset the Johnnies' hopes as Kyle Brown caught a pass from Johnson for 18 yards and Hicks ran across from 3 yards out to seal the deal. Hicks gained 141 yards in 17 carries for the game, and Johnson was nine-for-18 and 72 yards.

The semifinals and San Antonio, Texas, were the next stop for Frosty Westering's high-flying gridders, and the Lutes further elevated their game. A 49–28 verdict over Trinity sent them into the Amos Alonzo Stagg Bowl to play for the national championship. Johnson was 16-for-22 passing and 235 yards and Hicks scored four touchdowns, gained 92 yards in 18 carries, and caught five passes for another 83 yards.

From its start in Salem, Oregon, PLU finally realized its goal in Salem, Virginia. A huge Rowan team from New Jersey awaited the frequent-flyer Lutes, considered the underdogs by most. But a 42–13 PLU win settled the nation's number-one Division III argument. All-American Johnson passed for 276 yards with 18 completions in 28 tries. Two of his completions to Todd McDevit went for touchdowns. The ever-present Hicks carried 22 times for 73 yards and caught five of Johnson's spirals for 78 more. The 13 Lutheran wins were the most ever by a PLU team.

Notable Players

At UPS, 25 football players are in the Athletic Hall of Fame: Ralph Bauman, Bruce Blevins, Jess Brooks, Dick Brown, Roy Carlson, Mark Conrad, Jimmy Ennis, Dave Ferguson, John Garnero, Frank Gillihan, Bob Hunt, Bob Jackson, Dan Keuhl, Bill Linnenkohl, Bill Madden, Bob Mitchell, Mike Oliphant, Joe Peyton, Clint Scott, Jack Sprenger, Burdette Sterling, Joe Stortini, Dan Thurston, Frank Wilson, and Warren Wood.

All of them were either All-Conference, All-Northwest, or All-America. In fact, eight were first-team All-America choices. Warren Wood, a fullback who gave up his position to become a guard as a senior, was the only Logger in history to play in the East-West Shrine Game. He was the blocking star of the game, enabling Eddie LeBaron to run wild in a West victory. Wood and Southern Methodist University fullback Dick McKissack were singled out for their stellar offensive performances. Mike Oliphant bypassed football in high school to play soccer, but he set several UPS rushing records and was drafted in the third round, playing for the Washington Redskins and Cleveland Browns.

At PLU, the Lute Hall of Fame includes: George Anderson, Ron Billings, Ross Boice, Evans "Red" Carlson, Mark Clinton, Don D'Andrea, Tom Gilmer, Larry Green, Marv Harshman, Glenn Huffman, Steve Irion, Rick Johnson, Erling Jurgensen, Scotty Kessler, Craig Kupp, Eldon Kyllo, Elmer Peterson, Earl Platt, Steve Ridgeway, Greg Rohr, Sig Sigurdson, Blair Taylor, Marv Tommervik, Scott Westering, John Zamberlin, and the 1947 Pear Bowl football championship team. Again, most of these Lutes were either All-American, All-Northwest, or All-Conference. John Zamberlin, now the head coach at CWU, played seven seasons in the NFL with the New England Patriots and the Kansas City Chiefs. He was All-American at PLU as linebacker.

Obviously, many outstanding individual players contributed to the colleges' winning seasons. The stream of talented coaches at PLU and UPS also paid off: PLU had four "best" teams, all winning national titles, and UPS probably would rank Simonson's 1981 squad at the top, the only Logger team to win 10 games and one of the eight finalists for the NCAA Division II championship.

CHAPTER 23

FOOTBALL:
PRO AND SEMIPRO

Harry Lee Vawter played left tackle for the South Tacoma Athletic & Commercial Club (courtesy Nick Nickolas).

Professional and semiprofessional football has been a part of the Pierce County sports landscape since 1935, the year future wrestling champion Frank Stojack joined the old Brooklyn Dodgers of the National Football League (NFL). When he returned home two years later, he played tackle for the semipro Tacoma Beer Barons (later called the Alt Heidelberg team), sponsored by the Columbia Breweries. Club officials for the team included J. F. Lanser, president; Bill Libke, business manager; R. Parkhurst, secretary-treasurer; Mike Tucci, coach; and Howard Clifford, publicist. Tucci was founder of the construction company still bearing his name, and Clifford achieved notoriety when, as a *News Tribune* photographer, he was one of the last people on the old Narrows Bridge prior to its collapse in 1940.

The Barons played home games in Lincoln Bowl against such teams as the West Seattle Yellow Jackets and the Enumclaw Silver Barons. Notable players for Tacoma besides Stojack included Norm Iverson, Jess Brooks, and Joe Salatino. Iverson was a former All-American from Idaho. Brooks emerged from the College of Puget Sound (now UPS) and is considered one of the greatest athletes to come from that school. Joe Salatino, another great athlete, was an All-Coast

quarterback at Santa Clara University at a time when the quarterback was also the blocking back on offense. After Mike Tucci, Eddie Schwartz coached the team and later became coach and athletic director at Lincoln High School.

Tacoma Indians

Today's professional football developed during the post–World War II era. While the NFL teams concentrated primarily in Eastern and Midwestern cities, the Pacific Coast Professional Football League had its own regional teams and fans. There were three teams in Los Angeles and one each in San Francisco, San Diego, Salt Lake City, and Tacoma—the Tacoma Indians.

"They won seven games, lost four, averaged about 13,000 fans for five Sunday games at Stadium Bowl, managed to get a spot in the championship game due to a quirky forfeit by the rival San Francisco Clippers, quickly gathered to travel to Los Angeles for the title game, were trounced 38–7, and never played again," reported Bart Ripp in the *News Tribune*. The year was 1946.

Al Davies owned the Tacoma Indians. His Birchfield Boiler company, located on the Tacoma tide flats, was the

Indians' headquarters. Steve Slivinski was the coach. He was a University of Washington (UW) guard and linebacker, and the Washington Redskins selected him in the 11th round of the 1939 draft. One year later, he was part of the Redskins team that defeated the Chicago Bears, 73–0, for the NFL championship. One of his Bears opponents was Lincoln High School's Leo Artoe.

The Indians roster included Gene Walters, Chuck Newton, Joe Rettinger, Jack Norton, Bob Erickson, Byng Nixon, Dick Greenwood, Bill Mayther, Harry Cusworth, John Tsoutsouvas, Sig Sigurdson, Earl Platt, and Earl Younglove.

But the two most famous players were Pacific Lutheran College (now PLU)'s "Marvelous Marvs"—Tommervik and Harshman. Owner Davies paid both of them a bonus to play for the Indians rather than an East Coast team. "Davies gave us the extra money because he thought that we would draw fans," remembered Harshman. The "Marvs" had an outstanding season.

"We rarely practiced," Harshman recalled. "Slivinski occasionally called a practice at Renton High School, since many of us worked in Seattle or attended graduate school at UW. [Harry] Cusworth drove to Sunday games from Cle

After careers at Peninsula and the UW, Seattle Seahawks wide receiver Paul Skansi scrambles with a reception from quarterback Dave Krieg (SSM, 1891).

Elum, where he worked in a coal mine." The team took the train south for games in Salt Lake City, Sacramento, Oakland, Los Angeles, and San Diego. They flew to Hawaii to play the Warriors.

It's not clear why the Tacoma Indians lasted only one season. Former coach Steve Slivinski concluded that owner Al Davies lost interest. Additionally, the NFL expanded the team rosters to include Los Angeles, and by 1950 the San Francisco 49ers had joined the nationwide professional football network.

Tacoma Tyees

Semiprofessional football returned to Tacoma in 1962. Ben Hammond was the founder, general manager, and coach behind the endeavor. Hammond was a UW gridiron alumnus who played under coaches John Cherberg and Darrell Royal. While there, he earned All–Pacific Coast Conference honorable mention as a linebacker his senior year. His induction into the U.S. Army, however, ended his potential career as a newly drafted San Francisco 49er. Hammond then joined the semipro Seattle Ramblers team and played two seasons with them before moving to Tacoma in 1962.

Working locally for West Coast Grocery Company made playing in Seattle unrealistic, so Hammond decided to start a team in Tacoma. He was able to attract players while he served as line coach for John Heinrick at UPS and by playing slow-pitch softball at Peck Field. Through his efforts and a few well-known athletes in the area such as Jerry Thacker, Herm Magnuson, Ed Lund, and Mel Mathews, the Tacoma Tyees were born, attracting players from local high schools. The group joined the Northwest Semipro League (NSL), locally playing Seattle, Portland, Eugene, Spokane, and Bellingham on Sundays at Bellarmine's field or Lincoln Bowl. During the team's four years of existence, other top players included quarterback Doug McClary, halfbacks Raoul Ancira and Mike McKay, and fullbacks Jim McCuen and Curt Bagby, as well as Len Manke, Mike Roberts, George Jasmer, Skip Davies, and Jim Walton.

The Tyees finished their first season in 1962 with a 5–5 record and followed that with an 8–2 second-place fininsh

the next season. On November 22, 1963, the team bused to California to play the Eureka Forresters. Even though President John F. Kennedy was assassinated on their way down, everything was all set up for the game, so they went ahead and played it the following day. On November 23, 1963, the Tyees played in the only football game on the West Coast, losing 6–0.

They put it all together and won the league championship in 1964; however, the team folded after the 1965 season. Unfortunately, that year the NSL joined the newly formed Continental Football League, which expanded the number of teams in the organization. Even though the City of Tacoma, the Chamber of Commerce, and local businesspeople were providing financial assistance to the Tyees by this time, traveling to places such as San Jose, Sacramento, and Las Vegas was beyond the resources of the team. Sadly, the Tacoma Tyees went the way of the Beer Barons.

Pierce County Bengals

Another semipro football team emerged, however, when Ed Bemis founded the Pierce County Bengals. Bemis grew up in Tacoma, graduated from Lincoln High School in 1943, and went on to play baseball and football at UPS. Football was always his favorite sport, and when the two-year-old Northwest International Football League (NIFL) decided to expand in 1973, Bemis was on the office doorstep with a $50 check in hand to apply for a franchise.

As founder and general manager, Bemis arranged for the team to play its home games at Spartan Stadium in Sumner. The club took the league by storm in their first year of existence, winning the NIFL title with a perfect record, although they did lose to the NIFL All-Star team, 14–7, before a crowd of 3,000 to end the season.

The Bengals had plenty to growl about, showing their tenacity on the field as they compiled an impressive 88–8–1 record in the first nine years of competition. In fact, all of their losses were either pre- or postseason games. In 1977 the Bengals won the West Coast championships by defeating the San Jose Tigers, 28–27, and in 1979 the Pierce County squad again knocked off San Jose to earn the national championship as crowned by *Pro Football Weekly*.

The Bengals disbanded in 1982, only to reorganize as the Auburn Panthers. Bemis reacquired the team again in 1987, kept them in Auburn for two more years, and then moved them to Sparks Stadium in Puyallup in 1989. One year later, he turned over the reins of the ball club to Ron Baines.

The Pierce County Bengals provided great satisfaction for Bemis, giving many players a chance to further their football-playing days and possibly earn a football scholarship to college. Players held out the hope that a pro football scout might find them as the perfect diamond in the rough. Some were successful in the endeavor. Mike Oliphant was playing in the league for the Auburn Panthers, was scouted by UPS, and ultimately became one of the Loggers' all-time top running backs and went on to a pro career. He still holds several UPS records for touchdowns, with 16 in the 1986 season and five in one game versus Whitworth, and for points scored (96 season).

Bob Ferguson was the most famous of the former Pierce County Bengal players. Prior to graduating from UW in 1973, he was a second-team All–Pacific 8 Conference linebacker his junior and senior years. His ultimate expertise, though, was his ability to spot talent in other players. He was the perfect scout for Dallas, Buffalo, Denver, and Arizona football teams during his career, which ensured Super Bowl appearances for the Buffalo Bills between 1990 and 1993, along with Denver Bronco wins in 1997 and 1998. In 2003 Bob Ferguson became the general manager of the Seattle Seahawks, where he oversees the Seahawks' college and professional scouting departments. He played high school football at Federal Way but has Tacoma roots since his parents are alums of Lincoln and Stadium Highs. His father Dave Ferguson, in fact, was a Stadium yell king in the '30s. Another Bengal was Tony Apostle, a star running back at Wilson High and UW, now the superintendent of schools in Puyallup.

Ron Baines, a former Lincoln High athlete, carried on the Bemis tradition of doing everything possible to keep the team playing, in the roles of owner, equipment manager, and head uniform washer. He actually played on the team until he was 47 years old and still coaches today. His record as a player-coach in 28 seasons with the Bengals was 201 wins, 62 losses. At one time, the team won 107 straight games.

At the age of 53, Baines looked back on his possibilities as a player and reflected that he made some wrong decisions. "I'm just trying to make sure the guys who play for me don't make those same mistakes." After playing wide receiver at the University of Montana and being drafted by the Buffalo Bills, he left the professional camp before the season because he was homesick. Since he could run the 100-yard dash in 9.4 seconds and high-jump 6 feet 10 inches at the time, he probably would have succeeded in the pros.

Tacoma Express

There was one other Tacoma team—sort of. When the Minor League Football System began its first year of play in 1989, one of its charter members was the Eastside Express, originally participants in a local semipro league. In order to identify with the metropolitan Seattle area, they changed their name to the Seattle Express and played games in Snohomish, Washington.

In 1990 the team moved its operation to Tacoma in an attempt to take advantage of what the staff referred to as the "intensely sports-minded nature of the South Puget Sound region." Under the colors of the black and gold, the team's intent was to be part of a developmental system for the NFL and the Canadian Football League (CFL).

Due to the Goodwill Games being held in the Pacific Northwest, the Tacoma Express played an exhibition game in the Tacoma Dome against the Moscow Bears on July 2, 1990, the first-ever football game between a team from the United States and a team from the Soviet Union. The Bears, largely a group of former Olympians from the Soviet Union trying to learn a new game, lost 61–0 to the Tacoma club before a sparse crowd.

The Express then hit the road for their first four games of the season in Oklahoma City, Fresno, and twice in Colorado Springs before returning to Tacoma for their home opener on August 11 playing before 200–300 fans at Stadium Bowl. Not counting the exhibition victory against the Bears, the Express had a 1–6 record before running into problems. The league withdrew support of the club on September 7 because the team was a financial drain on the league's coffers; the operation was shut down for good.

Notable Players

Of course, young football players in Tacoma–Pierce County are like many others around the country. If they play in high school, they aspire to play in college and in the professional ranks. Approximately 52 players, primarily in the NFL and CFL, have performed at the highest level of the game.

The first was Cliff Marker, a captain of the Stadium High football team and a member of the Washington State University (WSU) Hall of Fame. In 1926 he reportedly played for the Canton (Ohio) Bulldogs alongside the legendary Jim Thorpe, and in 1927 he was a member of the NFL champion New York Giants.

Phil Sorboe had been a star athlete at Lincoln High and WSU. He played for the Boston Redskins in 1934; the Chicago Cardinals in '34, '35, and '36; and Brooklyn in '36. Sarboe passed for 1,133 yards and rushed for 243 yards in

his brief pro career before deciding on a coaching career at Central Washington University (CWU), WSU, and Humboldt State. He also coached one year at Lincoln High, where his 1944 team was undefeated and won the "mythical" state title.

Leo "Jelly" Artoe, who went to Santa Clara University out of Lincoln High, became an All-NFL tackle with the Chicago Bears in 1942. He was also the first NFL star to flee the league for the new rival All-American Football Conference (AAFC), signing for $15,000 with the Los Angeles Dons. His signing, along with nearly 100 others who switched, eventually cost both leagues more than $5 million.

Don Paul, the pride of Fife High and the Palouse (at WSU), was drafted by the Chicago Cardinals in 1950, playing there as a running back for three seasons before he joined the Cleveland Browns and became an All-League

This Tacoma Indians backfield looked ready to face the Oakland Giants in a 1946 Pacific Coast Professional Football League game at Tacoma Stadium: quarterback Marv Harshman (in front) lead Northern Division scorers with 38 points; behind him, from L. to R., are halfback Tip Lockard, fullback Bob Barrett, and famed "Tommygunner" of PLU halfback Marv Tommervik (courtesy David Eskenazi).

defensive back. He carried the ball 73 times for the Cards, gaining 469 yards, for a 6.4-yard average. He also caught 48 passes for 690 yards, 14.4 yards per catch, for seven touchdowns. On defense for the Browns, he had 34 pass interceptions for 593 yards and a touchdown. He also had 113 punt returns for 902 yards and two touchdowns and 57 kickoff returns for 1,417 yards (24.9 per return).

Sam Baker, who prepped at Stadium High and starred at Oregon State University (OSU), was drafted by the Los Angeles Rams in 1952. He had been OSU's all-time rusher at fullback with 2,043 yards in his Beaver career. Traded to the Washington Redskins, Baker saw limited action (17 carries and 17 punts) before military obligations took him away from the game. Upon returning in '56, Baker took up placekicking, and that brought him NFL fame. He led the NFL with 17 field goals in 25 attempts (68 percent, which was good at that time) and punted 59 times for a 42.5-yard average.

By 1957 Baker led the league in scoring, with 77 points on 14 field goals, 29 extra points, and a rushing touchdown from a fake field goal. In '58 he led the league in punting,

with a 45.4-yard average on 48 punts, a long of 64 yards, and no blocks.

Baker moved to Cleveland in 1960 to replace Lou Groza, in brief retirement, and led the league with 44 points after touchdown (PATs) in 46 tries, but he only punted in '61 when Groza returned to the Browns. Dispatched to Dallas in '62, Baker again led the league in extra points (50 of 51) and scored a career-high 92 points before being traded by coach Tom Landry to the Philadelphia Eagles, along with two others, for standout receiver Tommy McDonald.

Baker flourished as an Eagle. He set a record with 16 field goals in his first season, had a back injury that took its toll in '65, but came back with a new record of 18 field goals in '66 with a 72 percent success rate, including 14-for-14 inside of 40 yards. He also booted a 51-yarder at Pittsburgh, a team record at the time. A blocked extra point in the season finale was his only PAT miss of the year.

Overall, Baker kicked 90 field goals for the Eagles in 153 attempts, had 475 points, and had 205 PATs in six seasons in Philadelphia, where he was an All-League punter

The Tacoma Tyees semipro football team: back row, L. to R., founder and coach Ben Hammond, unknown, Vic Miller, Mel Mathews, Sonny Louckes, Dave Larson, Len Manke, Joey Jasmer, Skip Davies, unknown, unknown, Ed Lund; middle row, L. to R., Jim Walton, unknown, Harold Burg, unknown, unknown, Dave Bishop, unknown, unknown, unknown, Thurston, Jim McCuen , unknown; front row, L. to R., unknown, Herm Magnuson, Dick Fournier, unknown, Buck Buchanan, Raoul Ancira, Swede Wilson, Jim Trinchinni, Bill Thompson, Jerry Thacker, Hanson (courtesy Chris and Bill Thompson).

and twice a Pro Bowl choice. On three occasions, he kicked four field goals in a game; his 12 consecutive successful field goals remains a team record.

At his retirement in 1969, Baker's "book" showed 179 field goals in 315 tries (third all-time in the NFL), 977 total points (fourth all-time), 703 punts for 29,938 yards (42.6-yard average), and 110 straight games in which he scored—a league record.

Dave Williams, a three-sport Lincoln High star and UW receiver, was a first-round draft pick by the St. Louis Cardinals (second receiver taken behind Gene Washington of Michigan State) and played seven years in the NFL with the Cardinals, San Diego Chargers, and Pittsburgh Steelers. After two seasons in the World Football League (WFL) with Southern California, he became the first Seahawks player signed in the expansion draft of 1975. Unfortunately, he suffered a leg injury during an off-field Seahawks promotion and was forced to retire by 1976. During his NFL career, Williams caught 183 passes for 2,768 yards and 25 touchdowns, averaging 15.1 yards per catch. He was fifth in the league in catches in 1969. He also rushed occasionally, with six carries for 69 yards, averaging 11.5 yards per carry.

Before he retired, Williams was assigned No. 80 by the Seahawks, just prior to Steve Largent joining the team. "As I was leaving the locker room," Williams remembered, "I met Steve and told him he could have my jersey, my shoes, pads, anything he found of use, because my career was finished. Damned if he didn't do pretty well! I tell my grandkids that my jersey is in the NFL Hall of Fame, but it just has a different name on it."

Ahmad Rashad was an all-around athlete at Mount Tahoma High School, where he was known as Bobby Moore; he was a phenom in football and track and started on a basketball team that had an unbeaten regular season. He starred at the University of Oregon (UO), where he was a record-setting running back. In the 1971 season, he carried 249 times for 1,211 yards and seven touchdowns, and he became the first player in UO history to rush for more than 100 yards in five straight games. He also set a school record that stood for 30 years, with 285 yards rushing in a single game.

In 1972 Rashad was drafted by the St. Louis Cardinals, in 1974 he went to the Buffalo Bills, and then he achieved NFL stardom in seven seasons with the Minnesota Vikings. Rashad earned Pro Bowl recognition four straight years from 1978 to 1981 and ranked among the top 10 in the NFL for receptions five times, including 80 in the 1979 season, second best in the league. He was third in the league in receiving yardage that year, with 1,156 yards, and fifth in touchdown pass receptions, with nine. Currently he is an NBC sports commentator.

Ron Medved prepped at Bellarmine and had a stellar career at UW, where he was team captain. At UW he played offense, was a Hula Bowl selection, and had a series-record touchdown run against Stanford of 88 yards. He also gained 97 yards and scored a touchdown against Ohio State in 1965. Medved was a defensive back for the Philadelphia Eagles from 1966 to 1970.

Another Mount Tahoma/UO graduate starred professionally, in the CFL: Vince Goldsmith was All-City, All-State, and All-American in football at Mount Tahoma; he was a two-time state champion in the shot put and still holds the state record in that event at 69 feet 11.5 inches. In 2000 he was chosen to the Washington state All-Century team. At UO Goldsmith was Athlete of the Year in 1977, started on the defensive line for four straight years, and was named to the Oregon Hall of Fame in 2002. He was team Rookie of the Year in '77, team MVP in '79 and '80, All–Pacific 10 Conference and All-Coast in both years, and second-team All-America. He played in both the Hula Bowl and Japan Bowl and won the Morris Award as the Pac 10's outstanding defensive lineman.

In Canada he was CFL Rookie of the Year in '81 and was named to the All-CFL team in 1981, '83, '86, and '88. He was Saskatchewan MVP and Outstanding Defensive Player in 1983 and set a team sack record of 21. His 130 total sacks is third all-time in the CFL, and he is a member of the Saskatchewan Hall of Fame. In 1989 his team won the Grey Cup Championship.

CFL also was kind to Washington State University (WSU) Cougar Mike Levenseller, a Curtis High graduate. At Curtis he had 116 receptions in a season, a league record. In the Palouse (WSU) he had 121 receptions (third on the Cougar list) for 2,061 yards (second all-time). In 1976 he caught 67 passes for 1,124 yards, still season records at WSU.

Puyallup High and UW grad Damon Huard played for the NFL's Miami Dolphins from 1998–2000 (SSM, 1999.9.1).

Levenseller was drafted by the Oakland Raiders and played for Tampa Bay and Buffalo for a year, then for two at Cincinnati, before heading north of the border. He played four seasons in Canada, highlighted by a 19-catch game for 138 yards in 1984 at Saskatchewan. He also coached in the CFL, from 1986 to '91, when his Toronto team won the Grey Cup. That success was a sendoff to WSU, where he returned the following year and has been an assistant coach ever since. He now is the Cougar offensive coordinator.

Ray Horton joined the UW football program after a fine prep career at Mount Tahoma High and became one of the best defensive backs and punt return men in Husky history. In 1980 he averaged more than 13 yards per return and brought one back 73 yards for a touchdown against University of Southern California. He was an All-America pick in '81 and played in both the East-West Game and the Hula Bowl.

Horton played as a corner and a safety in the pro ranks for 10 years with both Cincinnati and the Dallas Cowboys and in the 1989 Super Bowl against San Francisco. He also coached the secondary team at Cincinnati, Detroit, and Pittsburgh. Horton credited high school coach George Nordi as his most positive influence. In his sophomore year in college, he tired of football and was set to quit school to become a firefighter. Nordi told him to "forget about four-alarm fires and capitalize on the opportunity at the UW." Horton listened to his coach.

Paul Skansi never even gave a thought to pro football in high school. He hardly thought about college football. Coming from Gig Harbor, he planned to become a fisherman. In his only season as a high school receiver, however, Skansi teamed with quarterback Steve Hunt for 1,506 receiving yards, still the fifth-best mark in state history. His Peninsula High team went 13–0 and won the state 2A (now 3A) championship.

Skansi's 89-yard touchdown gallop sealed the deal as his Peninsula High team nipped Pullman, 35–34, and UW came calling with a "late" scholarship offer. He became a Husky and caught 138 passes at UW, a record he held for many years. Drafted by Pittsburgh, he ended up a free agent and was signed by the Seattle Seahawks in 1984. He played for the 'Hawks for eight seasons and caught 166 passes for 1,950 yards. After a year with Ottawa in the CFL, Skansi became a regional scout for the San Diego Chargers in 2000.

Lawyer Milloy, from Lincoln High and UW, joined the New England Patriots in 1996 before Buffalo plucked him away in 2003. As a prepster, he was one of the nation's top recruits after rushing for 1,056 yards as a senior, scoring 15 touchdowns, and intercepting seven passes at safety. A top baseball prospect as well, Cleveland drafted him out of high school as a pitcher, but he elected to attend UW. He played three years of baseball as a Husky and excelled on the football field. He was picked on six All-America first teams and was the first defensive back in Husky history to have more than 100 tackles in two straight years (106 in 1994 and 115 in '95). Milloy forfeited his senior season to become eligible for the NFL draft.

He was a four time Pro-Bowl choice with the New England Patriots, starting 106 straight games, longest on the

CHAPTER SPONSORED BY

THE TACOMA–PIERCE COUNTY SPORTS COMMISSION:

In 1989 a group of local business leaders banded together to raise money to attract the NCAA Women's Final Four basketball tourney to Tacoma. The event was held for two years in the Tacoma Dome and was a huge success. As such, those same leaders decided that there needed to be an organization in Tacoma that worked to bring more sporting events to the region. Fred Shanaman recalls that, "Seattle and other cities already had such organizations in place, so we needed to keep up." After reaching an agreement with city officials, the Tacoma–Pierce County Sports Commission (TPCSC) was born in 1992. Thirteen years later, the TPCSC remains the sole organization in the area designed to create and support amateur athletic events in our region.

The TPCSC has a rich history of economic impact through encouraging sports tourism and local sports organizations and was proud to lead the drive in the mid-90s to keep football's Gridiron Classic in Tacoma. That drive continues to this day, as it is part of the "Inside Backers," a group formed to raise money to replace the playing surface for state football championships at the Tacoma Dome. Additionally, through the "Amateur Athletic Fund," it has contributed over $100,000 to local sports organizations helping them create or host various sports championships and events. Over the years such events have resulted in more than one million hotel-room nights and an estimated influx of $165,000,000 to the city.

The TPCSC remains committed to the local sports scene by supporting the organizations that are already strong in our region but at the same time looking for new groups that need our assistance.

The Tacoma–Pierce County Sports Commission is a proud sponsor of this history and will continue to fulfill its mission of "economic development through amateur sports." For questions about TPCSC or for information about the Amateur Athletic Fund grants, go to www.tacomasports.com or contact Tim Waer, Executive Director, (253) 284-3260.

team. He was defensive captain for the Patriots and led the team in tackles four straight seasons, with marks of 151, 173, 121, and 113. He had 16 tackles in a '98 game against San Francisco and 755 in his six Patriot seasons, which included the Super Bowl championship of 2002. In 2003 the salary cap sent him off to Buffalo.

Chad Eaton, a standout at Rogers High in Puyallup and at WSU, was a 306-pound defensive lineman who played five years with New England and two with Seattle before an injury left his NFL future in doubt. Many consider him the best lineman ever produced by Pierce County. In 1995 he had 77 tackles and 2-$\frac{1}{2}$ sacks as a Patriot.

Puyallup High School developed three quarterbacks, Billy Joe Hobert and brothers Damon and Brock Huard, for UW and the NFL. A third Huard brother, Luke, played college football at North Carolina; completing the football family, father Mike was one of the most successful coaches in Washington prep history, at Puyallup High.

Damon Huard, the oldest of the three brothers, was an All-America high school football player who led the state in basketball scoring as a junior as well. At UW he became a passing leader in several school categories. He played mostly as a backup quarterback for Miami (six years) and New England. He was a Super Bowl champion with the Patriots in '02. His record as a starter is a glossy 5–1 and he earned NFL Player of the Week honors in his first start at Miami.

Brock Huard was the Gatorade Player of the Year nationally in high school at Puyallup, where he led the Vikings to a 16–3 record in two seasons. At UW he south-pawed his way to several school passing records, too. In 2000 he and Damon became the only two brothers ever to start at quarterback on the same day for two different NFL teams. Brock was a Seattle backup, for the most part, for four years before assuming that role in Indianapolis behind Peyton Manning. Then he returned home to play again in Seattle.

Being a backup is not strange to Jon Kitna, a product of Lincoln High and CWU, who developed into a Seattle Sea-hawks starter, then moved to Cincinnati, where the Bengals watched him become a bona fide star, and was asked to back up Carson Palmer, the Bengals' "future franchise." Kitna had a great 2003 season and was named Comeback Player of the Year, even though he had a solid 2002. His '03 stats showed 324 pass completions, 3,591 yards passing, 26 touchdowns, and a 62.3 percent completion percentage. He was the only NFL quarterback to take every single snap during the sea-son—1,078—and also was the only Bengals player to play on every offensive snap.

Marcus Trufant hasn't had enough time in the NFL to demonstrate how bright his star will shine, but the former Wilson High and WSU speedster appears to have a brilliant future. He started every game as a rookie cornerback and led the team in pass breakups as the Seattle Seahawks' number-one draft choice. Trufant was an ESPN All-America selec-tion at WSU and an All–Pac 10 Conference defensive back. He had 11 pass interceptions and more than 400 yards in returning punts, a school record. At Wilson he was captain of football, basketball, and track teams; was All-State; and gained 1,967 yards while scoring 30 touchdowns. He also had 48 tackles and eight interceptions in the Rams second-ary, leading his team to the runner-up position in the state 4A championship.

Other Contributors

Players aren't Pierce County's only contribution to pro foot-ball. Milt Woodward, a baseball player at UPS and a sports writer for the *News Tribune,* was a Stadium High graduate who became founder, president, and commissioner of the American Football League (AFL). In that role, he helped the NFL's Pete Rozelle merge the two leagues and create the first Super Bowl.

Al Ruffo went from Tacoma to Santa Clara University, where he was inducted into the Bronco Sports Hall of Fame. He was the owner and first coach of the San Fran-cisco 49ers. Later he became mayor of San Jose.

Dana LeDuc was a track and football star at Washing-ton High in Parkland, but his claim to fame on the profes-sional football front came as a strength and conditioning coach. He is considered one of the best in the business for the NFL teams of Miami, Seattle, and St. Louis.

Look for more of the region's players in the years ahead. Future stars are on the rise, such as Reggie Williams of Lakes High School, the UW's all-time best pass receiver and a top draft pick by Jacksonville in 2004.

CHAPTER 24

GOLF

Ken Still gets fired up after another successful putt (SSM, 2014).

Golf, like many other sports, has unclear origins. The Chinese played a form of the game as early as 300 BC; the Romans under Caesar used club-shaped branches to hit feather-stuffed balls. By the Middle Ages, both the Dutch and the Scots were playing a game similar to the modern form. Indeed, in 1457 King James II of Scotland banned golf, as bowling previously had been banned, because it interfered with military training. The ban did not last long, however, and when Mary, Queen of Scots, played the game in 1567, she was considered the first known woman golfer. By 1754 Scotland's Royal and Ancient Golf Club at St. Andrews became the world's first formal golf course.

The first golf club established outside Great Britain was in 1786 in Charleston, South Carolina. A century passed, however, before the game really captured the imagination of American sports enthusiasts. In 1894 the U.S. Golf Association, later renamed the Amateur Golf Association of the United States, was founded, with the first U.S. Open played the following year. The U.S. Women's Amateur tournament was instituted in 1895, but women's golf underwent several organizational changes prior to the formation of the Ladies Professional Golf Association (LPGA) in 1950.

In the Northwest, a ship's manifest for a Hudson's Bay Company employee arriving at Fort Nisqually in 1846 listed golf clubs among the man's belongings. Although there is no record of where Pierce County's first golf game was played, perhaps this unnamed Scot practiced his swing on the prairie grasses near where the Tacoma Golf Club located its first course several decades later.

Golf was formally introduced to Tacoma with the arrival from Scotland of Alexander Baillie in 1892. He came as the representative of the trading firm Balfour, Guthrie, and Company. On his entry into the country, he encountered customs officials who had not heard of the game of golf. After Baillie described the game, the customs agent entered the clubs as garden tools!

Baillie joined other avid Tacoma golfers who had arrived before him and established the Tacoma Golf Club in 1894, the first organization of its type in the West. These men and women were aware of the limitless prairie land south of the city close to where the Northern Pacific Railroad had constructed its repair shops. The links were located south of the shops, between what is now South 62nd and 76th Streets and South Tacoma Way, and they constructed a clubhouse at South 62nd Street and Junett.

The Tacoma golf season then was a little different than today's. "The golfer cannot enjoy the sun," reported the *Tacoma Sunday Ledger* in 1898. "It makes the grass on the South Tacoma links grow too long and interferes with the play. The course becomes soft with dust and it is practically impossible to play during the summer season. The light snow of January or the fine rain of the winter is better suited to golf." Tournament play therefore took place between October and June.

On Thanksgiving Day, men and women played for silver and gold cups. In 1898 the men's champion was Chester Thorne, who, the newspaper explained, was "holder of the Thorne cup, offered by himself." Mrs. Stuart Rice was the women's champion. New Year's Day awarded the Balfour medal, offered by Balfour, Guthrie, and Company to Charles Mallott, who was the first and only holder of this medal and a former caddie at the South Tacoma links in 1898. Another man, W. A. Eberly, held the course record at this time, shooting an 87 for 18 holes on December 27, 1897. Within a year of the *Ledger* account, Tacoma golfers formed the Pacific Northwest Golf Association (PNGA), on February 4, 1899, making it the second oldest golfing organization in the nation. Founding members included the Victoria and Waverley golf clubs in British Columbia and Oregon, respectively, along with those from Vancouver, British Columbia, Seattle, and Spokane, in addition to Tacoma. The first PNGA championship tournament was held in April 1899 at the Tacoma Golf Club links, with

This Summit View team participated in the Tacoma Golf League in 1931 (SSM, 1089).

Tacoma residents Charles Mallott and Mrs. Melbourne (Amelia) Bailey the first winners. Since that year, the Tacoma club has hosted PNGA tournament play 21 times.

The prairie land used by the golfers was owned by the Northern Pacific Railroad, and as industrial development progressed along the rails, it became coveted real estate. By 1904 the golfers had to move. The R. B. Lehman farm, located on the eastern shore of American Lake, proved the ideal location, so in 1905 the club merged with the local country club and was renamed the Tacoma Country and Golf Club (TCGC).

By the 1920s, champion golfers were playing throughout the Pacific Northwest, but they were unknown outside the region. Therefore, local enthusiasts challenged the Western Golf Association, headquartered in Chicago, to a match. The best Northwest golfers were to play the best from Chicago and the Mississippi Valley in St. Paul, Minnesota. The Pacific Northwest team, which included Chuck Hunter Jr., an 18-year-old from Tacoma, won the challenge 9–7. The victory prompted one newspaper reporter to ask, "How come they have eight players away out there on the other side of the Rockies who are good enough to come here and give the best in the Middle West a trouncing?"

The South Tacoma neighborhoods near the original club produced some of the Northwest's best professional golfers and instructors. Al Feldman and Neil Christian both grew up in the Manitou area. Feldman, who was a professional for 57 years prior to his death in 1990, was also a golfing instructor throughout his career. He started playing golf competitively in 1954 and won the Northwest Open in 1957. His greatest claim to fame was holding four tournament titles at the same time—the British Columbia, Montana, Oregon, and Washington Open championships—all of which he gained during the 1966–67 season. Between 1924 and 1939, Neil Christian won the Northwest Open three times but twice lost the title in a playoff. He also won the Washington Open three times. Brothers Gene and Gordy Richards, who lived in South Tacoma just east of the original links, were two former TCGC caddies to become professionals. In fact, more than 50 other caddies followed the same path.

New Courses

In 1915 W. F. Jowders and W. B. Beal announced the construction of a new 18-hole golf course west of Manitou in southwest Tacoma. The course was designed by John Ball, a noted golf architect of the time, and was to be privately owned but open to the general public. The name of this new facility was Meadow Park.

"There is a demand for such a course," explained Jowders. "The growth of the game in Tacoma has been nothing less than marvelous. Most of the courses in Tacoma … do not enjoy the use of grass putting greens, and this should prove an attractive feature. The fact that we are within the city limits is another thing that should find favor in the eyes of golfers who have not the time to make longer trips." The course was built adjacent to the streetcar line, and promoters hoped that the train company would create a station stop at the clubhouse door.

The public nature of Jowder's private enterprise, though new to the Pacific Northwest, was common elsewhere. "It has been done for years in England, and some of the cities in the east have courses of this character. A public course is much cheaper than a regularly organized club for the players, and for this reason I believe that a properly equipped golf course, although privately owned, will prove a success in Tacoma." The course opened to the public in November 1917 and is the second-oldest course in Pierce County still in use.

In 1919 a short nine-hole course was added to Meadow Park, but it was subsequently renamed the Williams Nine, after J. Ralph Williams. Williams, a Park Board commissioner for 28 years with the Metropolitan Park District, had saved Meadow Park from becoming a housing development. Naming the short course for him was an appropriate recognition of his years of service.

The next course of note was developed in Fircrest. Like Meadow Park, its members pointed to its proximity to Tacoma and its location along the streetcar line as selling points to potential members. Fircrest also advertised the quality of its links design as a major amenity. The golf club itself was organized in 1922. J. W. Anderson, manager of the Tacoma Land and Improvement Company, was credited at the time with locating the golf course just west of Regents

CHAPTER SPONSORED BY
BILL GAZECKI:

Bill Gazecki, a former president of the Tacoma Athletic Commission and a contributor to the sports museum, dedicates the history of golf to his friend Ken Still. Still's extensive golfing career included 26 years on the Professional Golfers Association (PGA) Tour, with him competing in six Masters, 13 U.S. Opens, and seven PGA championships. He also teamed up with Jack Nicklaus, Raymond Floyd, Dave Hill, Lee Trevino, Miller Barber, Dan Sikes, Gene Littler, Tommy Aaron, Billy Casper, and Dale Douglas to compete against Great Britain and Ireland for the 1969 Ryder Cup, which ended in a first-ever tie. Stills won the 1969 Citrus and Milwaukee Opens, the Kaiser Open, and the CBS Golf Classic in 1970 (partnered with Gene Littler), and played on the PGA Senior Tour at age 50. His best major finishes included fifth place in the 1970 U.S. Open and a sixth-place tie in 1971 in the Masters. Locally, Still conquered nearly every local; some of his top scores include: Allenmore, 62; Brookdale, 65; Fircrest Golf Club, 62; Meadow Park, 62; and Tacoma Country Club, 63.

Park. Residents in this developing suburb soon changed its name to Fircrest and incorporated as a municipality.

The golf club hired links architect A. Vernon Macan to design the course. "I believe Fircrest will provide not only an excellent test of the game, but a maximum amount of fun and amusement," Macan wrote in 1923 while the course was under construction. "Laying out a golf course is something in the nature of a Chinese puzzle, the main difference being that when the solution or design is finally settled on there is no definite proof that it is right."

The same newspaper article reprinted a letter sent to a Fircrest board member from William Tucker, a nationally known golf course and turf expert. After praising the quality of Macan's design, Tucker pointed out that Tacoma's golf courses were not simply for the amusement of local enthusiasts. "There is no doubt in my mind," Tucker said, "that a real high-class course will add interest and promote greater publicity to your town, and I believe such a course will induce golfing tourists to dwell a few days at Tacoma to have a round of golf. This any golfer will do if a course warrants it and is perfectly willing to pay $2 to $3 to have the

privilege." Since its opening in 1923, the Fircrest course has attracted such golfing celebrities as Bing Crosby, Babe Ruth, Sandy Koufax, Ben Hogan, Arnold Palmer, Billy Martin, Lee Trevino, and Nancy Lopez.

John Ball, designer of the Meadow Park and Allenmore golf courses, as well as many others in the United States, had a son, Ray W., who was the builder for his father's courses but also designed courses on his own. And, in an unusual twist, Ray Ball also became a golf pro (see Golf Pros later in this chapter). While still at Fircrest, Ray designed a new course on the shores of Lake Steilacoom and was present at the dedication in 1929 when Bill Yost, city amateur champion and another student of Ball's, teamed with Roger Peck, also a former city title holder, to beat Tacomans Walt Delin and Bill Noonan. A year later, Ray built the Allenmore course for his father and in 1931 opened Parkland's Brookdale facility, with a record-breaking 68 strokes.

The development of golf courses continued, including the Linden Golf Course (1926), Lake Steilacoom (1928), Parkland (1929, renamed College in 1937 and University in 1971), Highlands (1930), and Fort Lewis (1936). Two other courses in play during the 1930s that did not survive the decade were the Green Fairway on the Tacoma-Seattle Highway near the Puyallup River Bridge and nine holes at Paradise Valley on Mount Rainier.

Two of the earliest driving ranges in Pierce County included the Lakewood Range and the 38th Street Range. Originally a pre–World War II partnership between John Rudy and Chuck Congdon, the Lakewood Range was established in the late 1930s and operated up until 1979. Bart Hogeberg ran the 38th Street Range from 1950 to 1967, but he is most noted for his patents on three automatic tee systems. The first two, established in 1942 and 1943, involved photoelectric cells; he received a third patent in 1957 for a new system involving air-solenoid technology.

The Brookdale course was the vision of a Pierce County pioneer. In 1931 Frank Mahon formed the Roselawn Recreation Company and carved new links out of the family's donated land claim situated east of Spanaway. He called the course Brookdale after the nearby community of that name.

Allenmore opened near the corner of South 19th and Cedar Streets the same year. Owners Sam Allen and W. J.

Dinsmore hosted a large delegation of the local golfing fraternity at the grand opening in August. Included among the dignitaries was Mayor M. G. Tennent, who led the procession "by sending the first ball, a gold-hued pellet, off a silver tee."

Links mushroomed during the latter half of the 20th century to include such courses as Fort Steilacoom (1951), American Lake Veterans Hospital (1956), Artondale (1960), North Shore (1961), McChord's Whispering Firs (1962), Lake Spanaway (1967), Oakbrook (1967), High Cedars (1971), Madrona Links (1978), Canterwood (1988), Lipoma Firs (1989), the Classic (1991), and Sumner Meadows (1995). Over the years, both the Metropolitan Park District of Tacoma and Pierce County Parks assumed a greater role in managing what W. F. Jowders considered "pay-as-you-play" golf. Between membership-based clubs, private operations, and publicly run facilities, golf is now one of the county's main participant sports.

Women's Golf

Jane Bradley is generally credited with generating interest and involvement in women's golf in the Tacoma area, from

On its opening day in 1931, Allenmore Golf Course featured an exhibition match with several of the top female golfers in Pierce County, including: L. to R., Mrs. E. E. Perkins of Fircrest, Mrs. Dean of Fircrest, Mrs. John (Jane) Bradley of Tacoma Country and Golf Club, Mrs. L.T. (Helen) Murray also of TCGC (courtesy Lowell Butson).

the 1930s. She encouraged girls to become involved in junior golf, including Joan Mahon, Ruth Canale, Mary Carter, Ruth Busch, Amy Lou Murray, Helen O'Brien, and Jeanne Walters.

Marjorie Jeffries Shanaman played to a 2-handicap by the time she was 18 in 1925 and was a medalist in the qualifying round of the first Tacoma City Women's Amateur. She defeated Mrs. Guy Riegel, the 1926 PNGA champ, 1 up in the quarterfinals and Elizabeth Curran, the 1919 PNGA champ, 8 and 7 in the 36-hole finals. She beat Riegel again, 1 up, to win the State Women's Championships in 1928.

Joan Mahon Allard developed her golfing skills as a teenager at Brookdale, her father's course, and went on to win the State Women's Public Links Championship three times and Tacoma Women's City title five times. Ruth Canale Ward got her start at the Lake Steilacoom Golf Course under the watchful eye of pro Ray Ball. Thanks to his efforts, she won the Washington State Junior Girls title in 1933 at age 13. Ruth and Joan soon became known as the "Brookdale golfing twins," trading off tournament wins, playing in exhibitions—and beating male golfers on a regular basis. Ruth's winning ways culminated with the Tacoma City Championships two straight years in 1940 and 1941, though she continued regularly to add club championships to her record before retiring in 1980.

Amy Lou Murray Young, granddaughter of the first PNGA women's champion, Amelia Bailey, was runner-up in the 1957 PNGA tournament, defeating defending champ JoAnne Gunderson, 1 up. She was also TCGC women's champion 14 times and runner-up 16 times. She was a U.S. Golf Association Women's Committee member from 1955 to 1970.

For Amy Lou Murray Young, golf was steeped with family tradition. Besides her grandmother's success in 1899, Amy Lou's mother, Mrs. L. T. Murray, was a runner-up in 1938 for the TCGC title, and Amy's sister Anne won the tournament in 1941 and 1944. Amy's daughter, Lowell Young, won the tournament in 1972 and 1978 and was runner-up three times. And, finally, Amy's daughter-in-law, Barbara Young, was runner-up in 2002 and champion in 2003.

Other top women's golfers included Wylma Blackadder Hodgins, a 17-time club champion at Linden; Shirley Baty;

Barbara Hulscher; Mardee Smith; and Shirley McDonald Fopp, a multiple State Public Links champion.

Golf Pros

One of the earliest golf pros in the area was Jim Barnes, who came from Cornwall, England, and served as pro at TCGC from 1910 until 1913. He then went on to win the Northwest Open four times in five years, the first Professional Golf Association (PGA) championship in 1916, the U.S. Open in 1921, and the British Columbia Open in 1925.

In 1916, at the age of 25, Ray Ball worked at Tacoma's Meadow Park, where Neil Christian was one of his students. Ten years later, Ray became a golf professional at Fircrest, where he gained a reputation "as a home professional as distinguished as the golfing nomads who travel around the country devoting the larger part of their time to tournament play." Ray Ball's professional golf career followed the courses he helped to design and build. After leaving Fircrest in 1931, he became pro at Lake Steilacoom and remained there until 1935, the year the golf club disbanded. He then moved on to Allenmore. By the outbreak of World War II, he had taught thousands of golfers throughout his professional career but counted Bill Yost (state and city champion), Virgil Cliff (city champion), and Mrs. Dewey Busch (city women's champion) as three of his most memorable pupils.

It was Chuck Congdon, however, whom players remember as one of the finest club professionals in the country. Congdon was 55 and in his 30th year as a golf pro at TCGC when he died in 1965. "He was an acknowledged master at the craft of teaching," noted former *Tacoma News Tribune* golf writer Jack Sareault, "one of the finest in the land. His students included more than a dozen national champions and a variety of touring pros, men and women."

He was also a contender in any tournament that he entered. Congdon won the Canadian Open in 1948, the U.S. Senior Championship in 1960, the British Columbia Open seven times, and the Washington Open four times. He rated one of his best competitive rounds of golf an 8-under-par 62 in the third round of the 1964 Seattle Open, a PGA tour stop held at Broadmoor Golf Club in Seattle. (In the same tournament, Tacoma professional Ockie Eliason shot a hole-in-one worth $10,000 but missed the cut. Ironically, Billy Casper, who won the tournament, received only $5,800 for his victory.)

Patricia Lesser Harbottle, who first met Congdon when she was a 15-year-old golfer, remembered his teaching style. "He would analyze my swing for 15 minutes before making a correction. He'd stand there and look, and I'd be waiting and waiting for him to say something, hoping he would say the right thing. He could see what I was doing wrong, but wouldn't actually tell me. Instead he would suggest what I should do." During one lesson, Congdon suggested that they play a round of golf instead. He gave Pat two strokes for the nine holes, at five cents a hole. Shooting from the men's tees, Pat won the match 32 to Chuck's 35—and won a quarter for her effort.

Many golfers who started out during the golf pro days of Ball and Congdon made their mark later on. Jack Walters was 16 in 1929 when he won the first of his 17 Northwest Lefthanders Championships. He was a student at Stadium High School at the time. Walters became the glue that bound together the left-handed golfing fraternity in the Pacific Northwest, one of the few concentrations of lefties in the country. He twice won the National Association of Left-Handed Golfers Championship, first in 1953 at French Lick, Indiana, and then in 1960 on the Fircrest Golf Club course. He went on to become a member of the board of governors for both the national and international left-handed associations and was instrumental in bringing the tournament back to Fircrest in 1973.

Tacoma professional Ockie Eliason, who made the hole-in-one at Broadmoor in 1964, enjoyed more success at the Northwest Open than any golfer around. In 1955 and 1956 Ockie became the last golfer to win back-to-back titles at the event. He was low professional, tying for second place overall in 1954, tying with Ken Still for second place in 1957, and tying for second again in 1958. He retired in 1986 after 20 years as golf pro at Allenmore.

Other golf pros of the era included John Rudy, who spent 30 years as head pro at the Fircrest Golf Club until retirement in 1983, and Al Mengert, Congdon's replacement at TCGC. Mengert was the U.S. Amateur runner-up in 1952 and won the Washington Open three straight years

before moving from Spokane to Tacoma. He went on to win the 1966 Northwest Open while golf pro at TCGC. Dave Leon, who was runner-up in the U.S. Junior Amateur in 1957 as a Tucson, Arizona, teenager, has been the head pro at Linden since May 1972.

Junior Golfers

The PNGA, involving Washington, Oregon, Idaho, Montana, and British Columbia, added junior boys in 1955 and girls in 1956 to its tournament program. Boys' champions included Storm Gleim (Puyallup High) in 1977; John Bodenhamer (Lakes High), 1978; Todd Erwin (Bellarmine Prep), 1979; Patrick Brownfield (Bellarmine), 1987; and Peter Wooding (Bellarmine), 1989. Erwin became a teaching professional and won the Washington State Open four

Pat Lesser Harbottle takes a swing, ca. 1950s (courtesy John and Pat Harbottle).

times. One of Wooding's sisters, Audrey, won the 1985 Junior Girls' Tournament. Then his other sister, Michelle, won back-to-back women's titles in 1986 and '87.

The Tacoma Golf Association (TGA), spearheaded by Frank Dempski in 1958, inaugurated an annual match-play tournament for juniors. Bea Williams began doing the same for Tacoma-area girls almost simultaneously, promoting junior golf programs regularly at Meadow Park Golf Course.

Joan Teats of Tacoma was another person instrumental in giving junior golfers more tournament opportunities. She

George Wise was a top golfer in the area and won the 1930 Steilacoom Lake Club Championships (MB).

was the driving force behind the formation of the Washington Junior Golf Association (WJGA) in 1977, with competition offered in eight and under, 12–14, and 15–17 age groups for both boys and girls. The juniors advanced to the state tournament through qualifying rounds. The Girls Junior Americas Cup followed a year later, pitting 18 teams from 11 Western states, two Canadian provinces, and Mexico.

High school golf was invitational on a statewide basis until the Washington Interscholastic Activities Association (WIAA) recognized a state tournament in 1970. Wilson High School, led by individual champion Russ Bloom, wasted no time claiming the first-ever state title, with members Ron Stenger, John Thielade, Scott Shelton, and Phil Carmichael teaming up for the crown. Bloom and Thielade then teamed up with John Gazecki and Harold Bonnell to win the Northwest community college title for Tacoma Community College (TCC) in 1971. In fact, TCC enjoyed success on the links with Northwest Athletic Association of Community Colleges (NAACC) team titles in 1971, 1990, and 1991; tournament medalists included Russ Bloom (1972), Tim Mark (1975), and Seig Boettcher (1979).

Along with the Rams, Lakes, Curtis, Clover Park, Bellarmine, Washington, Gig Harbor, Lakes, and Life Christian High Schools have accounted for 14 boys state titles in various enrollment classifications; Bellarmine High School has won five of those championships, with Pat Brownfield and Dusty Brett each winning an individual title as well. Brett also won the Washington Junior title before moving on to a fine collegiate career at Stanford University.

Steilacoom in 2002 (2A) and Bellarmine in 2003 (4A) are the only local high schools to win the state girls' championships. Mark Bender, who coached the Lions to the title, handed over the reins to his daughter Hailey, a four-year varsity golfer for Bellarmine, who continued her golfing career at the University of Washington (UW) and earned club champion honors at Fircrest in 2002.

Life Christian Academy has experienced considerable success on the links, winning the 2003 boys state A title lead by seniors Brandon Hjelseth and Taylor Ferris. The Eagles then duplicated the feat in 2004 behind freshmen Chris Teeny and Andrew Putnam, who won medalist honors with a final round score of 68 including a hole in one.

Top Amateur Golfers

John Harbottle met Patricia Lesser while attending Seattle University (SU) in the 1950s. "She was the first woman to play for a men's college team," Harbottle said of his wife in 1986. "In fact, she was such a good player, that first year she was the number-one player in five of our 13 matches—played from men's tees and got along well with everybody." By 1955 Lesser won the U.S. Women's Amateur Championship in addition to the U.S. Junior Girls Championships. In 1954 and 1956 Lesser played on the U.S. Curtis Cup against Great Britain and Ireland, and numerous other tournaments victories placed her in the PNGA Hall of Fame in 1985.

Tacoma dentist John Harbottle was not too far behind his wife as an amateur winner, becoming one of the city's top players. He was low amateur in the 1982 U.S. Senior Open and runner-up in 1986, then co-medalist in 1988 and medalist in 1993 in the U.S. Senior Amateur Championships. Harbottle also won the PNGA Senior Amateur tournaments in 1988, 1990, 1992, and 1993.

In the 1960s and 1970s, Bob Johnson, George Lanning, Ed Eisenhower, John Bodenhamer, and Clint Names were golfers of note. Johnson, a 1958 graduate of Stadium High School, was on the PGA Tour from 1964 to 1967, earning a second-place finish in the 1966 Azalea Open. Lanning retired from the Air Force at McChord in 1968 and became head golf pro at Oakbrook in the early 1970s. He carded a 60 in the pro-amateur Washington Open in 1977 and 1979 and qualified for the PGA Senior Tour, playing for nine years until his untimely death at the age of 58. According to Jack Sareault, Lanning was one of the best left-handed golfers in the nation.

Lakes High School graduate John Bodenhamer was 16 years old when he shot a 13-under-par 55 on May 10, 1978, on the Fort Steilacoom course—the only golfer from Pierce County to break 60. A former state amateur champion (1981) who played golf at Brigham Young University, Bodenhamer has served as executive director of PNGA since 1990.

Ed Eisenhower was the older brother of President Dwight David Eisenhower, who may have introduced Ed to golf when he became commander at Fort Lewis in the 1930s. Ed was a Tacoma attorney for 47 years until his death

in 1971. He took up golf at the age of 35 and became the TGCG champion at the age of 66. By 1969 he began shooting his age or under and was an age-shooter for 12 years in a row, missing only one year in 14, and that was by a stroke—the day before his birthday.

Clint Names is representative of many of the outstanding amateur Pierce County golfers. He started playing the game at 11 years old, graduated from Stadium High School, and went on to UW, lettering in both basketball and golf. In 1961, while still a Husky, he won the Big Five Conference in golf. By the end of the 1970s, he won the Tacoma City Amateur Championship and successfully competed in the Northwest Open, the U.S. Amateur tournament (as Tacoma's only representative), and the Fircrest Amateur several times.

Names also won the Pat Boone Celebrity Golf Classic at Ocean Shores in 1969, won the TGA Champion of Champions meet in 1971, and was the Fircrest Golf Club champion at least five times. Among the Names family papers is a scorecard for the 1971 Fircrest Championship in which Clint toured the course in 65 strokes, the first time the score had been achieved since the 1950s when Frank Marolich also shot a 65. In 1971 Clint was named Tacoma area Golfer of the Year.

Another golfer of note was Brian Haugen, a Puyallup High School graduate who won the Pacific Coast Amateur in 1980. Since this event was inaugurated in 1967, only eight Washington golfers have ever won this, Haugen being the first one from Pierce County. And, 24 years later, Michael Putnam, a student at Pepperdine University and graduate of Life Christian High School, became the second, with his victory in August 2004.

Doug Doxsie played twice for the University of Puget Sound (UPS) in the National Collegiate Athletics Association (NCAA) Division II tourney. He also became a club professional. He not only holds the head pro position at the Seattle Golf Club, but he also is in his second two-year term as president of the PGA's Pacific Northwest Section, an area embracing Washington, Oregon, Montana, and northern Idaho.

Pacific Lutheran University (PLU) qualified four teams (1974–76 and 1984) for the National Association of Intercollegiate Athletics (NAIA) national tournament and, in 2001, for the NCAA Division III nationals. The Lutes also had individual national qualifiers in Jay Robinson, Mark Clinton, Greg Peck, Scott Mattson, and Todd Gifford. Since it began golf competition in the Northwest Conference in 1966, PLU won 21 team crowns, shared another, and accounted for 17 individual titles, two each by Clinton, Jeff Clare, and Tyler Kalberg.

The history of golf in Tacoma and Pierce County is not complete without a word about Tom Tuell. In 1982 Tom took the sport into a new dimension by becoming the Golfing Gorilla, wearing a gorilla suit whenever he participated. He was 31 years at the time, played to a plus-3 handicap, and was an extremely long striker of the ball. The Golfing Gorilla idea was his way of promoting golf and providing the game with a character celebrity. He knew he had a marketable idea when he was accepted at all stops on the PGA tour. Tuell played exhibitions with such golf greats as Jack Nicklaus, Arnold Palmer, and Byron Nelson, and in 1984 he became the 12th member of the 350 Club, a select worldwide group of golfers who can hit a ball at least 350 yards.

From Amateur to Pro

Precious few from Pierce County have tested the demands of the pro golf tour. Jim Bourne, the North Shore course's co-owner, played in the late 1950s, and Bob Kelly was an Oakbrook assistant when he played in 1977. Doug Campbell played in 1979 and 1980, lost his card, and played again in 1982.

Brian Mogg went from Lakes High School to four years on the Ohio State University team, then also into professional golf. Mogg played in 1986 and 1988 and on the inaugural Ben Hogan Tour in 1990. He won both the Northwest Open and Washington State Open in 1989 and has been operating the Brian Mogg Performance Center since 2002 in Orlando, Florida. Recently he was named one of the top 100 teaching pros in the U.S. by *Golf Magazine*.

Patty Curtiss of Fircrest, the 1975 PNGA Girls' runner-up and 1979 PNGA Women's runner-up, went into parallel careers, with dual credentials as an LPGA teaching professional and athletic trainer in the Spokane area and Southern California.

The first from Pierce County on the LPGA tour was Audrey Wooding, a Bellarmine and Stanford graduate from Tacoma who played during the 1994 season. Her sister Michelle qualified and played on the LPGA for two years (1998 and 2001) and played on the women's Futures tour for eight years.

Of all of Pierce County's professional and amateur golfers, Ken Still was the most successful. He played the PGA tour for 23 years, having turned pro in 1953. He played on the pro tour full-time starting in 1960 and then joined the Senior Tour when he was 50. Still competed in six Masters, 13 U.S. Opens, and seven PGA championships during his outstanding career. He captured tour victories in the 1969 Florida Citrus (winning $23,000 for his first victory) and Milwaukee Opens, won the Kaiser Open in 1970 in a playoff with Lee Trevino and Bert Yancey, and then partnered with Gene Littler in 1970 to win the CBS Golf Classic in a playoff with Orville Moody and Miller Barber. And he played against and with some of the most notable golfers in the world, including Ben Hogan, Sam Snead, Jack Nicklaus, Arnold Palmer, Gary Player, and Chi Chi Rodriguez.

Still described his most memorable moment as the time when he played the Houston Invitational in 1967. In the opening round, he ended with a 7-over-par 78 for the course at the Houston Champions Golf Club. "I made [airplane] reservations on Friday afternoon from Houston to Seattle-Tacoma," he recalled, "thinking I would probably miss the cut. Friday I shot a 2-under-par 69, making the cut by two strokes. The plane I was to take from Houston was hit by lightning and all 87 aboard were killed. I've always been a believer in never quitting, and it really came true in this instance."

Still's greatest achievement, however, happened two years later, when in 1969 he joined Nicklaus, Raymond Floyd, Dave Hill, Trevino, Barber, Dan Sikes, Littler, Tommy Aaron, Billy Casper, and Dale Douglass to compete against Great Britain and Ireland for the Ryder Cup. In 1927 Samuel Ryder, a British seed merchant, had first conceived of a tournament between the best American and British players, with the professional golf associations from both nations selecting the players to compete.

"While American dominance rendered the previous

tournament meaningless as a competitive event," reported the British Broadcasting Corp. (BBC) Web site, "it's hard to think of a better example of Ryder Cup golf than Royal Birkdale [England] in 1969." Eric Brown, British captain, "had earlier instructed his players not to look for American balls if they landed in the rough, and during one of the four balls on the second day the captains had to come out and calm the warring players." The competition ended in a tie, 16–16, the first tie ever in the Ryder Cup. Ken Still and Dave Hill beat the British competitors in four balls, 2 and 1. Still lost by one hole in the singles.

The most recent golfing champion from the area is Puyallup's Ryan Moore. His victories started in 2000 with the American Junior Golfers Association Thunderbird Junior, the Trophy Lake Junior, the WJGA Championship, and the Washington State High School Championship. Moore was also the Pacific Northwest Junior Boy's Amateur Player of the Year in 2002, along with being the three-time South Puget Sound League (SPSL) Player of the Year.

After high school, Moore went to the University of Nevada at Las Vegas (UNLV), where his status as a champi-

onship golfer continued. Following the 2001–02 season, he received an All-America honorable mention, as well as being named the Mountain West Conference freshman of the year. In 2002 he won the U.S. Amateur Public Links Championship with a 10-and-9 victory over Lee Williamson at The Orchards Golf Course in Michigan. His margin of victory was the second highest in APL finals history.

By the time Moore was a junior, he had become a member of the U.S. 2003 Walker Cup squad, in addition to representing the NCAA and the USGA at the 2003 Palmer Cup. Not only was he one of two male amateur golfers to represent the United States in the 2003 Tournament of the Americas, but he also made the cut at the 2003 Masters Championships. He won the 2003 Toyota Men's Collegiate Championship, was runner-up at the Western Refinery All-American Classic, earned second-team All-America and first-team Mountain West Conference honors, and was named UNLV's Olympic Sportsman of the Year for two straight years.

In 2004 his success continued: He won the NCAA Championships, followed by victories in the U.S. Amateur

Jack Walters (far R.) won the National Left-handers Championships in 1953 and 1960, the latter on his home course at Fircrest (courtesy Fircrest Golf Club).

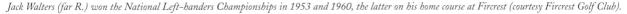

Local dentist Dr. William Burns poses with Babe Ruth at Fircrest in December 1926, when Ruth was in town to star in a vaudeville show at the Pantages Theatre (MB).

Public Links, the Western Amateur Championships, and the Sahalee Players Championships, all in a span of 10 weeks. Moore capped a sensational year by adding medalist and team honors at the World Amateur Team Championships in Puerto Rico.

Many Tacoma and Pierce County golfers have been inducted into the Halls of Fame for the sport. The PNGA Hall of Fame honored Patricia Lesser Harbottle, along with her husband, Dr. John Harbottle; Chuck Hunter Jr.; and Jack Walters, the noted lefty. The Pacific Northwest Golfers Hall of Fame includes Jim Barnes, Neil Christian, Charles Congdon, Gordon Richards, Jim Bourne, Al Feldman, George Lanning, Ken Still, and Ockie Eliason.

A September 1898 *Tacoma Sunday Ledger* article announcing the opening of the new golf season provided a revealing headline: "Great Fun, But It Costs Lots of Money: This Month Opens the Pacific Northwest Season of Golf, the Game on Which, Since It Entered Our List of Out-Of-Door Sports, Americans Have Spent Fifteen Million Dollars Yearly." Where all the money went was a mystery to the reporter, but he assured his readers that the large expense ($125 per golfer per year) "need not deter anyone from learning the game. It may be played economically if the player will take care to suppress the natural inclinations." Many readers must have heeded the reporter's advice, for by the end of the 20th century golf was competing with softball and baseball as the country's number-one participant and spectator sport.

CHAPTER 25

GYMNASTICS

Yumi Mordre of Franklin Pierce High School competed for the University of Washington where she became the first Husky gymnast to earn an NCAA title, winning the vault and balance beam events (photo by Bruce Terami, courtesy University of Washington).

Gymnastics as we know it today was introduced to the United States by German and Czech emigrants early in the 19th century. The sport was also a part of the original Olympic Games; in ancient Greece, the term gymnastics applied to all exercises practiced in the gymnasium—or school—hence, the sport's name. When the Olympics were revived in 1896, men's gymnastics were included as a scheduled event; women's competition was added in 1936. It was the riveting performances of Russia's Olga Korbut and Romania's Nadia Comaneci in the 1970s that made gymnastics so popular in the United States.

In Pierce County, gymnastics was a part of the public schools' physical fitness curriculum by the 1930s, but there is no clear indication that schools took it as seriously as other sports until the 1970s. Those who wanted training at an earlier age went to private clubs or local dance schools. The latter often included simple gymnastics as a part of a student's training regimen, and since dance was needed in gymnastics competition, studio instruction proved invaluable. Lew Ballatore's School of Dance was one such studio in Tacoma, where Ballatore taught from 1955 to 1979.

Joe Rooney founded the Puget Sound School of Gymnastics (PSSG) in 1972. Two years later he sold the facility to its director and coach, Brad Loan. Through the efforts of the club, Tacoma was the venue for the Pacific Northwest Open Invitational Women's Gymnastic Meet for 15 years. Loan told the *Tacoma Review* in 1979 that "girls like gymnastics because it is a difficult sport which they can excel in without having to be compared with boys."

Loan's star gymnast at this time was Lochburn Junior High School ninth grader Roni Barrios. By 1979 she was a five-time national balance beam champion and a two-time parallel bar champion, and she had won the state championship five years in a row. The year before, she won three medals at the National Sports Festival in Colorado Springs and went on to place in the top 10 in the Senior Elite Division in 1980 and 1982. After graduating from Clover Park High School, Barrios went to California State University–Fullerton and was named to the World University Games team in 1983.

In that same year, Franklin Pierce High School's Yumi Mordre became the top gymnast in the area. Mordre made the U.S. Senior Elite Team and went to the Pan American

Games, where she won gold medals in the floor and team competitions and won a silver medal in the all-around event. Mordre went on to become the United States' fourth best gymnast at the world trials and competed for the United States in the 1983 Budapest World Championships. Mordre was the alternate for the 1984 U.S. Olympic team featuring Mary Lou Retton.

Mordre later attended the University of Washington (UW), where she became the first female gymnast to earn All-America first-team honors, something she achieved seven times. In 1987 she became the first Husky gymnast to win National Collegiate Athletic Association (NCAA) titles, one for the vault and one on the balance beam. She was inducted into the UW Athletic Hall of Fame in 1995.

In 1967 Wilson High School's Carrie Eggimann was the City League's top all-around performer. The following year she won subregional titles in four individual events as well as the all-round title. Initially, practicing proved to be a challenge. "In the 10th grade," Eggimann said in 1977, "we had trouble getting the gym for practice. We turned out from about 6:45 a.m. to 8:00 a.m. each morning." Challenges such as this, and the growing popularity of the sport among young women, might explain why in 1981 John Smith formed a second training facility: the North American Sports Academy Gymnastics (NASA Gymnastics) in Gig Harbor.

In 1982 PSSG's Kelly Baker was named to the Junior National Elite Team after placing fifth at the U.S. National Championships. She also placed fifth in Japan and was selected to compete for the U.S. team in the United States versus China competition of 1982.

Michelene Meyers of Rogers High School in Puyallup was ranked 11th and was named to the U.S. Junior Team in 1987. She won a silver medal in the team competition at the Argentina International Gymnastics Invitational in the same year and was on the gold medal–winning team at the Japan Junior International Invite in Tokyo in 1986 and 1987. The PSSG also had two Elite National all-around champions, Puyallup High's Elli Maulding and Catherine Williams; Williams became a three-time state all-around champion and set three school records at the UW. Foss High School's Marilyn Anderson, also with PSSG, was

named to the Elite National training squad in 1988 and went on to star at Oregon State University.

Young girls of middle school age excelled in gymnastics during the 1990s, especially those living in the peninsula area of Pierce County. The Tacoma YMCA gymnastics program produced one winner in 1990, when 12-year-old Kim Dougherty placed first in the floor exercises at the Washington State 8-Open Competition and moved on to Tampa Bay, Florida, for the YMCA National Gymnastic Meet. Kelsi Kemper, from Goodman Middle School, was the only known rhythmic gymnast in Pierce County. Even though she lived in Gig Harbor, she trained in Russia and Lithuania and had a Bulgarian coach. At the U.S. Olympic Festival in 1994, she returned home with a team gold medal.

In the 1990s, John and Linda Smith used architectural plans, taken from what was then the Soviet National Training Center in Moscow, to construct a new state-of-the-art facility they owned in Gig Harbor. Mt. Tahoma's Lindsey Lauderdale trained there and won the 1992 National All-Around and Floor Championship titles in the USA Independent Gymnastics Club National Championships. It was Tiffani White, however, who brought real prominence to the Smith's program. A Puyallup High School student, White earned five national titles between 1994 and 1997 at the Elite National level and led the Pacific Northwest All-Stars to a team gold-medal victory over Mexico. Team members Hali Saucier of Peninsula High and Gig Harbor High's Danielle Crowley each won International All-Around titles and also competed at the Elite Level. White went on to compete for OSU while Saucier shifted to spring board diving at Louisiana State University.

The PSSG remained powerful as well during this time, led by Junior Elite National All-Around Champion Heidi Prosser of Curtis High. In 1993 Prosser won a bronze medal against the best in the world at the Japan Junior International Invitational in Osaka. More recently the club trained Wilson High School's Onnie Willis, who was named to the Junior Elite National Team in 1996 and then won the Junior Olympic National All-Around title in 1998. Willis considered her team's win at the 1998 Junior Olympic Nationals her greatest athletic thrill. In 1999 the Tacoma Athletic Commission named her Athlete of the Year, just before she became a

University of California–Los Angeles (UCLA) Bruin. While there, she won the NCAA all-around event in 2000.

Men's gymnastics existed in the '60s and early '70s in Pierce County, but Title IX legislation caused its demise at the high school and college level, and by the '80s men's programs existed only at the club level. From 1984 to 1992, PSSG and NASA Gymnastics offered men's gymnastics and Taft Dorman, Andrew Davis, and Matt Childers all began their training at NASA. All three were instrumental in Michigan State qualifying for the NCAA National Championships for the first time in 40 years, with Dorman, a 2000 Curtis High graduate, receiving a full gymnastics scholarship after his medalist performance on the still rings

at the Junior Olympic nationals. Due to financial losses, however, competitive men's gymnastics gave way to an emphasis on more recreational programs.

Today gymnastics is flourishing in the region with numerous clubs, YMCA programs, and junior high and high school programs. There are more than 75 programs in the state of Washington, compared to 15 in the early 1970s. Gymnastics training is often considered the best form of physical education, which could explain the sport's continued growth in popularity. But more likely, as long as the Olympic Games inspire dreams of athletic success, there will be girls and boys learning gymnastics.

Brad Loan, coach at Puget Sound Gymnastics and a longtime developer of elite national-caliber gymnasts (courtesy Puget Sound Gymnastics).

CHAPTER 26

HANDBALL

A U.S. Open National Invitational Singles Champion in 1971 and 1972, Gordy Pfeifer turned pro in 1973 and attained a top ranking of third before retiring in 1983 (courtesy Gordy Pfeifer).

According to the U.S. Handball Association, handball is defined as "a game where two adults lock themselves in a room and bash a small ball against the walls with their hands." Four walls plus a ceiling comprise the most popular arena for the game, although handball is also played outdoors on three-wall and one-wall courts.

Hitting a ball with the hand for sport was known to the Egyptians and pre-Columbian Americans thousands of years ago. Alexander the Great introduced the sport to Italy, and by the time the Roman Empire collapsed, handball was played throughout Europe.

Historians of the game debate when and where handball was first introduced in the United States. The first courts may have been built in Brooklyn in the 1880s; or the game may have been first played in San Francisco in 1873. There seems to be agreement, however, that the sport came to America with Irish immigrants, suggesting that handball could have been played here as early as the 1840s, when famine brought many Irish to these shores.

By the 1920s, Tacoma was producing championship handball players, a trend that continues to this day. The city has had many champion players; an approximate count of

championships includes at least 15 state opens, 14 state masters, eight Northwest regional opens, two Northwest regional youth championships, six nationals, and one professional win.

In the 1920s, 1930s, and 1940s, most of the play was at the old YMCA at Seventh and Market Streets. In the basement was a 2-foot by 40-foot court that had a low 18-foot ceiling (regulation height is now 20 feet). There also were two courts at the original Elks Club building located at 565 Broadway. Allan Browne, Pete Sabutis, Fred Osmers, Charles "Rip" Revelle, Bob Holder, and Harry Westbrook were some of the standout players from that era. Westbrook, in fact, was the Tacoma City Champion in singles from 1923 to 1935, won the Northwest YMCA singles title in 1926 and 1928, and teamed up with Rip Revelle to win back-to-back Tacoma City doubles championships in 1939 and 1940.

In the late 1940s, the YMCA decided to build two new handball courts that were 23 feet by 46 feet—larger than the U.S. Handball Association (USHA) specifications of 20 feet by 40 feet. The players asked the YMCA to conform to the fledgling USHA court guidelines, but the organization chose to conform to the dimensions set by the older Amateur Athletic Union (AAU). As a result, most of the players left the YMCA and began playing at the Tacoma Elks. These two courts were also oversize, at 21 feet by 42 feet, but they were at least closer to regulation size. With this exodus to the Elks, the fraternal organization became the hub of handball for players in Tacoma. From the 1950s on, every Tacoma City Champion who went on to win state or regional championships were members of the Tacoma Elks.

In 1965 the Elks Club moved to its current location on South Union Street. Two regulation-size courts were built, with more than 200 players vying for playing time. In the 1950s and 1960s, outstanding local players winning state or regional titles included Bill Faraone, George Baydo, Bill Reed, Archie McClean, Lea McMillian, and Ernie Johnson.

In 1965 Gordy Pfeifer was introduced to the sport of handball. He soon entered, and won, a novice tournament at the Elks, and an amazing handball career was launched. In 1969 he won the national YMCA singles crown. This was the first of his 16 national, world, and professional titles. Beginning in 1973, he toured professionally and ranked consistently in the top four players in the country. Pfeifer, the dominant player in the Pacific Northwest, remained a top national player well past his retirement. He was a man who hated to lose, even when playing for fun.

In six months, Pfeifer went from novice to being one of the best players in Tacoma. "Then I ended up teaming with

The 1942 Tacoma Elks Club handball team has been considered the strongest in Tacoma history: back row, L. to R., Harry Westbrook, Al Howe, Bob Holder, Fred Osmers; front row, L. to R., manager Bill Boudwin, Orville Stewart, Al Ziegler (SSM, 359).

THE HISTORY OF HANDBALL IS DEDICATED TO AND SPONSORED BY THE FOLLOWING PLAYERS AND CONTRIBUTORS:

Raoul Ancira	Gil Mendoza
Al Cail	Dr. Anthony J. Milan
Doug Cail	Mike Morehart
Dennis Cruchon	Kent Morrell
Jim Driscoll	Dick Pfeiffer
Ron Ewing	Randi Platt
Jim Kraft	Steve Sand
Lea McMillan	Martinson, Cobean & Assoc., P.S.

Lea McMillian, one of the better players around the area at that time, and we went to the nationals," remembered Pfeifer. "We won our first match and then met up with the top two players in the country and lost. That was my first exposure to competitive, top-notch handball. I got to see what real handball was like."

In 1968 Pfeifer teamed with Bob Schonig and made it to the national semifinals. The duo lost to Jimmy Jacobs and Marty Decatur, two of the nation's top singles players. The next year, Pfeifer won the first of 17 major titles when he, back with Lea McMillian as partner, won the national YMCA doubles title. Pfeifer's second major championship came in 1970, when he won the Canadian national handball championship by defeating former child movie star Stuffy Singer, another champion player in the United States.

Pfeifer turned professional after winning back-to-back U.S. Open National Invitational singles titles in 1971 and 1972. For the next 10 years, he competed on the USHA circuit and reached a third-place ranking by the time he retired in 1983. "I was in my late 20s before I ever started the game," Pfeifer explained after his retirement. "Matter of fact, I played my best between the ages of 40 and 43. Most of the players are done in their mid-30s, so I was a late bloomer. I still could have played. I was in good enough condition and was improving, but I had just won the World Invitational singles and doubles at age 43, beating the top three players in the world. I felt I couldn't do better than that at my age."

Firefighters Play

Tacoma, like many major cities in America, has a rich tradition of firefighters who play handball. Throughout America, many fire stations have handball courts. The first station to have a court in Tacoma was No. 6. Built in 1895 at Ninth and A Streets, it later became the fire department's headquarters and was renamed Station No. 1. Prior to World War I, when the fire department stopped using horses to pull the water tanks and switched to engines, a hay loft was converted into a handball court. From these humble beginnings came such players as Bob Nice, Roger Pennington, Walt Savisky, Tom Haneline, and Myron Schmidt.

FRED OSMERS REMEMBERS

The old YMCA in Tacoma had a handball court, in addition to their basketball gymnasium. I slipped into the Y for a steam shower almost every day while healing from a basketball injury. Lyle Johnson, a top handball player at the time, was alone on the court. I stood on the balcony watching him for about 10 minutes. He called to me to come on down and hit a few. I replied that I had never played handball in my life, to which he answered, "Well, it's about time you started! You should know that anyone who can play tennis should be able to play handball. Tennis originated from this sport."

I took him up on his offer and began a 20-year career playing the game. And it was a great game, the best half-hour to two-hour workout of any sport I ever watched or indulged in. You can play it just as hard as your constitution and desire dictate. You contact a ball about the size of a golf ball, wearing a heavy leather glove because the ball is heavy and hard. The game is usually played by hitting the ball with an open hand. I, however, hit the ball with a closed fist.

In those days, Tacoma had but two handball courts, one at the YMCA downtown and one at the old Elks Club just a block from city hall. The courts were in use around the clock for six days each week. In 1931 the Washington Athletic Club (WAC) in Seattle completed its new facilities, which included two of the finest handball courts in the country. Television, of course, was unknown, so there was lots of available time in which to indulge ourselves in this indoor game.

Competition was keen in the Puget Sound area, and Tacoma developed some of the top players in the country. Between 1925 and 1950, Harry Westbrook won the Tacoma City title at least

eight years running and the Northwest title several times. He and his partner, Rick Revelle, won the doubles Northwest title over a several-year stretch. Following Westbrook by at least 10 or 12 years was Ernie Johnson. Ernie won both City and Northwest titles before moving to Portland, Oregon, where he represented the Multnomah Athletic Club as their number-one player. Those two, in my opinion, were the best. Robert Holder would be my choice for third all-time player.

My career as a competitive handball player ended on a Saturday night, the night before Pearl Harbor, when the Elks team, of which I was a part, was defeated by the WAC team. During that game, I injured my left leg. It took 13 months to really recover. But my handball days were over, along with my hope and plans for winning the Northwest doubles title.

My partner would have been Chuck Carroll, who in 1928 had been an All-America football fullback. He was a major in the Judge Advocate General's Office at Fort Lewis and played handball in Tacoma during his assignment at the base. We teamed up in doubles, and I was convinced we would take the Northwest title. He put more power into his shots than anyone I had ever seen. We won every match we played together. The Army, however, assigned Carroll to another post, and that bubble burst. But with my injury not long after, I would have been out anyway. I guess that's the luck of the draw. It just wasn't meant to be.

—FredOsmers, from an undated autobiography

Schmidt was introduced to handball in 1954, one day after he reported to Harold Fisk as a rookie firefighter. And during the course of more than 40 years of playing, he proved a prolific winner. Schmidt, a fist-hitter like Fred Osmers, got his training from Doug Fournier, a bus driver for the city. "Doug belonged to the Elks in downtown Tacoma and drove a bus," remembered Schmidt. "I lived down at the end of the transit line and often took the bus because with my fireman's badge I rode free. Quite often the driver was Doug. I started talking handball with him. It went from there and he invited me over to the Elks to watch him play." Fournier schooled Schmidt on the fire station's court, teaching him the intricacies of fist-hitting.

Schmidt once estimated that he had won at least 50 tournaments. These included city and firefighters' championships, along with Washington and Northwest regional titles. One of his most memorable wins came during the U.S. National Championships in 1980, when Schmidt was playing in the semifinals. He was down 10–1 in the tie-breaking game and was on the verge of losing the match if his opponent scored just one more point. Instead of giving up, he told himself to stay in the game and give it his all. The results were dramatic: he came back to win the match by scoring 11 straight points.

Bob Holder (second from L.) congratulates Al Ziegler for winning the YMCA championship, as Harry Westbrook (R.) looks on (MB).

From that moment on, he knew he could play with the best and made it a personal goal to become a national champion. In 1988 he achieved that goal by winning the Super Singles Division. In 1993 he won the U.S. National Singles Championship, Super Veterans' Division, in Baltimore, Maryland. Even though he's now retired from the Tacoma Fire Department, Schmidt continues to play handball. He also continues to win.

Notable Players

The military was also a source for many great handball players in Tacoma, and even though there were courts at McChord Air Force Base and at Fort Lewis, many players decided to join the Elks. Some of the Army's most successful players included Army Col. Dick Pfeiffer and Lt. Gil Mendoza; the Air Force had Sgt. John Mooney and Lt. Kris Schaumann.

For the past 25 years, players such as Ron Ewing, Steve Sand, Al Cail, Doug Cail, and George Cobean have risen to the forefront at the state and regional level, honing their game at the Tacoma Elks and then traveling to compete throughout the Pacific Northwest.

When the Elks opened its membership to women in 1995, Randi Platt became the first female player to join in 1996. And for the sake of competition, Randi has always chosen to play against men, to improve her strength and her game. Today about 100 active players continue to represent Tacoma and the Elks.

Unlike other professional sports, handball has not captured the public's imagination. "Handball, being played on a four-walled court, in a very small enclosure, could never be a spectator sport," explained Fred Osmers in his memoirs. "There is no way a sizable audience could view a match." This circumstance in turn means that corporate sponsors are hard to come by. Most of the professional players fund their own competitions, clearly making the sport a labor of love rather than a profession.

CHAPTER 27

HORSESHOES

Floyd Sayre was the state horseshoe champion in 1925 and president of the Tacoma Horseshoe Pitchers Association (courtesy Vennard and Jan Lahti).

The sport of pitching horseshoes evolved from the ancient game of quoits, one of the five games in the ancient Greek pentathlon. Originally, iron or rubber rings called quoits were thrown at a target, but by the Middle Ages peasants had replaced the quoits with horseshoes. In the United States during the Civil War, the sport became popular in the Union military camps. Following the end of hostilities, soldiers took the game home with them, where they created pitching courts throughout the nation.

There is no record of a horseshoe tournament in this country until 1910, when a competition was held in Bronson, Kansas. Four years later, the same state witnessed the formation of the Grand League of the American Horseshoe Pitchers Association, followed by the National League of Horseshoe and Quoit Pitchers in 1919. The two organizations consolidated in 1921, and four years later members changed the name to the National Horseshoe Pitchers Association (NHPA). Tacoma players were a part of this organization.

The sport, long a favorite in rural communities, also became widely popular in the nation's cities during the 1920s and 1930s. A likely reason is the mass movement of farmers and other outlying residents into the cities following

World War I. Horseshoe pitching was also easily adaptable to city life, and in Tacoma as elsewhere, courts sprang up all over the urban landscape. The game was obviously affordable for poorer folk; because of this, a social stigma often was attached to horseshoes, and some referred to it as "barnyard golf."

Although Leroy Hopkins of Hopkins Pharmacy is considered the father of horseshoe pitching in Tacoma, it's not clear when local horseshoe enthusiasts moved beyond sandlot pitching to serious competition. By 1923, however, Floyd Sayre was recognized as a potential champion. That year he received a letter from C. O. Gregory of the Puyallup State Bank congratulating him for his record established at the first annual picnic of the Pierce County Horseshoe pitchers. "You are making a splendid showing," Gregory wrote, "and I urge you to develop into an all-class, that you may be eligible for the National Tournament to be held next year. It would be a pleasure for me to hear of the Northwest sending a contestant to such a tournament."

Sayre went on to become state champion in 1925 and was president of the Tacoma Horseshoe Pitchers Association (THPA). That year, the organization completed its official courts on the former Central school grounds located at South Fourth and St. Helens Streets, a project undertaken with the assistance of the Tacoma School Board. The new facility was enclosed and lighted, allowing year-round play. At the dedication, Sayre competed against Clarence Swan, who became state champion in 1928.

Also in 1925, THPA sponsored and dedicated a second court, at Point Defiance, with the help of the Metropolitan Park Board. "The court shows the true American spirit of cooperation between public officials and private energy, and this energy is fittingly represented in the game which combines the good luck of the horseshoe with the skills of the participant," H. E. Veness told a newspaper reporter. Veness was a horseshoe pitcher for the Four L Band, a group of men who competed in addition to providing music for the dedication. THPA obtained official sanction to hold Washington State Championship tournaments at the Point Defiance courts.

Local competitive events pitted both individuals and commercial teams against each other. Newspapers regularly provided detailed reports of the games and winners of league play. Competitions were also a time for socializing. One Christmas, for example, the games—involving 36 horseshoe pitchers—were wrapped around a party of food, exhibition pitching, music, and acrobatic stunts.

By 1929 THPA embarked on a campaign to interest more people in the sport. Physical education instructors from the Tacoma schools were the first to hold what were called "special horseshoe pitching contests." There were also

Horseshoes was a popular pastime in the 1930s and '40s (TPL).

games for Tacoma realtors, carpenters, lawyers, physicians, school principals, and city officials. All of this was part of a program entitled Play Horseshoes for Health, one that even got local druggists to embark on their own league play.

This period also saw the introduction of a Commercial Horseshoe League by the Metropolitan Park District's playground and recreation department. Sponsors for the various teams included the St. Paul and Tacoma Lumber Company, Wheeler-Osgood, the Northern Pacific Railroad shops, Hunt Mottet, and Standard Oil. During the 1920s and 1930s, Tacoma horseshoe players enjoyed their greatest years.

On the eve of the Depression, horseshoe competition was tightly woven into the park district's playground program. Local boys and girls were pitching shoes on more than 15 courts located in playgrounds scattered throughout the city's neighborhoods. To generate further interest in the sport, the park district held a citywide tournament at Wright Park in 1929. The *Tacoma News Tribune* provided prizes for the winner of the Men's Division and for all the boys and girls entered in the playground tournament. (It's not clear why there was no competition for adult women.) The results proved that Floyd Sayre had not lost his touch. He beat Edward Lindbeck for the City Championship, winning six straight games.

Robert Hager is credited with organizing the citywide tournament. He was president of THPA at the time, and he also worked as supervisor of physical education for the school district. Hager, along with Walter F. Hansen, superintendent of recreation, came up with the idea of a game *really* called "barnyard golf." It was horseshoes played like a game of golf with "18 separate pegs in box contraptions to be shot from raised platforms—the tees." The pegs were 40 feet apart and the course was laid out in Franklin Park, a stone's throw from Hoodlum Lake. Once again, Floyd Sayre and Clarence Swan played at the dedication of this uniquely Tacoma game.

In 1938, on the eve of World War II, the THPA club installed eight new courts at Wright Park at a cost of $200. By that time, tossing the "equines' hoofpads," as one reporter put it, was an entertaining spectator sport. "There are a lot of angles to this shoe-pitching game," a writer noted. "A player must be careful of his stance, know how to judge the distance and know how to turn the shoe in mid-air to make it light by the pins. And to be able to do that, one has to study the game."

However, the sport was never the same after World War II. People still played but not in the numbers seen before the war began in 1941. But THPA has persevered and is still linked to the Washington State Horseshoe Pitchers Association. It hosts a series of state-sponsored tournaments each year, including the Gilbo Open, the Tacoma Memorial, and the Tacoma Turkey Shoot. Bob Hoerner, current president of the organization, even created a traveling horseshoe pitching museum to promote the sport locally.

Although the City of Destiny has not been blessed with championship players in recent history, the game is still a joy for those who toss the shoes. It's "not that much fun to watch," local player Cyril Kitchen said recently, "but it is certainly fun for those who gather at Wright Park." There is plenty of competition when people from all over the state come to play what Kitchen affectionately called "farmyard horseshoe pitching."

DON'T CALL IT "BARNYARD GOLF"!

The game of horseshoes is a true American game. It was at one time a game played by people of all classes in this country, and yet real careful study has not been given to the game and, naturally, very few horseshoe pitchers have learned the game from a scientific standpoint.

When the name of "barnyard golf" is mentioned, the average individual gets the impression that it is more or less a joke, but I will assure you that if you try to learn the game from a scientific standpoint, it is no joke. The game of golf is without question a perfectly high-class sport. But, all in all, the game of horseshoes is altogether too good a game to be cheapened with the above-mentioned familiar name.

The sport readers perhaps do not realize that the game is taking as prominent a place as it has all over the country. We have two national magazines which devote every inch of space to the game of horseshoes. There are several factories over the country which are kept busy and are usually well behind with their orders in making a standard shoe which is used in all regulation games.

During the last two or three years the game has come to the front to a greater extent than ever in its history. Followers of the sport have found that it is entertaining and one of the most scientific of all sports. We have in the city of Tacoma somewhere about 20 men, with whom I am personally acquainted, who are learning the game from a scientific standpoint—in other words, pitch what is known as an open shoe—that is, a shoe pitched so that it comes open at the peg consistently.

There are a number of private horseshoe courts in the city, the largest one being located at Hillsdale, at the end of the McKinley Park carline, where the Tacoma City Horseshoe League will open its schedule Tuesday night.

People of all classes, rich and poor, participate in the game. They can spend as much or as little money as they like. Our worst difficulty at present is the fact that there are no downtown, centrally located, public courts for participants or spectators. However, the Kiwanis Club, in conjunction with the school board, is planning at the present time to construct courts, close in, downtown, which will be open to the general public and can be used 12 months in the year. All spectators will be privileged to attend any of the league games.

—A. S. Walferton of Tacoma Horseshoe Leagues, *Tacoma News Tribune*, ca. 1925

CHAPTER 28

HYDROPLANE RACING

Harry Reeves gets ready to test the U-19 Coral Reef in 1960, an unlimited hydroplane owned by Austin Snell (SSM, 1997.6.9).

Boat racing in and around Tacoma has always been popular. Competition of inboards, or limited hydroplanes, is an institution at Lake Spanaway and Lake Tapps; the outboards, or unlimited hydroplanes, have a long tradition at Silver Lake near Eatonville. Drivers of many unlimited hydros, or thunder boats (as they are often called), have plied their trade on these waters in boats longer and more powerful than the limited hydros.

In 1956 the *Miss B&I* became the first unlimited hydroplane to represent Pierce County. Owned and driven by Bob Gilliam, a private in the U.S. Army at the time, the *Miss B&I* was built in the Fort Lewis hobby shop. As the story goes, Gilliam even had full colonels at work sanding down the decks. Powered by an Allison engine, *Miss B&I* attended the 1956 Seattle Seafair Regatta but did not qualify for the race. Apparently Bob took her out for an after-hours test run on Lake Washington in almost total darkness and ran over the racecourse log boom, where she suffered hull damage. A few weeks later, on Flathead Lake at Polson, Montana, Gilliam vindicated himself by beating Norm Evans in the *Miss Seattle* and winning the Copper Cup.

In 1962 B&I Stores of Tacoma sponsored a second thunder boat. The "new" *Miss B&I* was the old *Gale IV*, built in 1954, which had also raced as *Wildroot Charlie, Miss Everett,* and *Cutie Radio.* She was owned and driven by Bob Miller, who had been a crew member on the original *Miss B&I.* Using stock equipment and an Allison engine, the Miller team participated at five of the six races on the 1962 Unlimited Hydro tour. The boat's highest finish was fifth place in the Governor's Cup on the Ohio River at Madison, Indiana.

One of the most popular race boats of all time was Austin Snell's *Coral Reef.* With Harry Reeves driving, she was the pride of Pierce County at the 1958 Gold Cup in Seattle, where she finished a surprise second. Designed and built by Lea Staudacher in 1957, the *U-19* craft originally campaigned as *Miss Rocket,* named after Snell's Rocket U-Save service stations. During its first year and a half of operation, the *U-19* was the epitome of mediocrity, lacking both speed and reliability.

On the eave of the 1958 Gold Cup, *Coral Reef* was lightly regarded, having never before qualified for a final heat. But pilot Reeves was fresh from a victory the previous

Bob Gilliam sits in the Miss B & I of Tacoma preparing for a test run (SSM, 1997.8.1).

weekend in the 136-cubic-inch Class national championship race on Seattle's Green Lake. After qualifying 10th in a 17-boat field, the *Coral Reef* came alive on race day with heat finishes of second and first in the preliminary action.

In the final heat of 30 miles, Reeves went all out after Jack Regas and the Rolls-Royce Merlin-powered *Hawaii Kai III*, leaving the rest of the field far behind. At the finish line, it was Regas taking the checkered flag five seconds ahead of Reeves. But to hear the *Coral Reef* crew cheer their driver when he returned to the dock, you would have thought they were the victors.

In the years that followed, the *U-19* remained a familiar and popular craft even when it became the property of Bob Fendler from Phoenix, Arizona, and no longer represented Pierce County. Regardless of what name was painted on the boat at any given race, *Coral Reef* would always be just that to her countless local fans.

Of all the individuals who have represented Pierce County in the Water Sport of Kings, none stands taller than George Henley. Although short and stocky in build, "Smiling George" was a giant of a man behind the wheel of an unlimited hydroplane. During a career that lasted from 1970 to 1975, Henley won 12 out of 34 races entered, for a winning percentage of 0.353.

A veteran limited hydro pilot, Henley started his thunder boat career as a crew member on the likes of the *Miss B&I* and *Coral Reef*. His first unlimited ride as driver was in the *Burien Lady*, owned by Bob Murphy. The team's modest budget notwithstanding, Henley raised many eyebrows when he finished a strong second in the 1970 Seattle Seafair Regatta, winning the final heat and defeating the overall winner, *Miss Budweiser*, in the process. Later Henley saw action with Bob Fendler and Lincoln Thrift's *7 1/4% Special* and Jim McCormick's *Red Man II*. Henley's best finish was

George Henley of Eatonville piloted the Miss Pay 'n Pak to two straight national unlimited championships, 1973–74 (SSM, 1970).

second place in the 1973 Champion Spark Plug Regatta at Miami, Florida, with Lincoln Thrift.

Then came the historic 1974 racing season, when Henley joined forces with owner Dave Heerensperger and crew chief Jim Lucero on the "winged wonder," *Pay 'n Pak.* After having paid his dues with the low-budget teams, Henley had a ride that was truly commensurate with his ability. The *Pay 'n Pak* already had won four races and the National High Point Championship in 1973 with Mickey Remund as driver. It was up to Henley to do it all over again.

In his first appearance with *Pay 'n Pak,* in Miami, Henley experienced mechanical difficulty after winning both of his preliminary heats. But a week later in Washington, D.C., Henley won the President's Cup on the Potomac River, beating the likes of Bill Muncey in *Atlas Van Lines,* Leif Borgersen in *U-95,* and Howie Benns in *Miss Budweiser.* There could be no doubt about it. Henley had achieved the big time.

He followed that win with victories at Owensboro, Kentucky; Tri-Cities and Seattle; Dayton, Ohio; San Diego; and Madison, Wisconsin, becoming the first driver to win seven High Point races in a single season. One particularly memorable contest was the American Power Boat Association (APBA) Gold Cup on Lake Washington at Sand Point. All day long, Henley battled side by side with *Miss Budweiser,* driven by Howie Benns, sharing the same roostertail on extremely rough water in perhaps the greatest performance of his career.

After that stellar 1974 campaign, Henley decided to retire from unlimited hydro racing and to concentrate on his Eatonville-based marina business. Heerensperger soon discovered that it was easier to find someone to help run Henley's business than it was to find someone to replace Henley in the cockpit of the *Pay 'n Pak.* Like very few drivers before or since, Henley could guarantee results. But his price was high, as *Pay 'n Pak* boat owner Heerensperger readily attested. So Heerensperger became Henley's partner, and the rest is history.

Following his brief retirement from the sport, Henley rejoined the *Pay 'n Pak* team at the third race of the 1975 season in Owensboro. In the short time that Henley had been away, *Weisfield's,* chauffeured by Bill Schumacher, had

garnered most of the glory and appeared likely to unseat *Pay 'n Pak* from its national championship throne. On the first lap in the first heat at Owensboro, Henley's boat spun out and then went on to blow an engine. *Pay 'n Pak* was forced to withdraw, and the race went to *Weisfield's.* All hope of retaining the High Point crown appeared lost.

Despite a formidable deficit in points, however, George sparked *Pay 'n Pak* to one of the great comebacks in hydroplane history. The *Pak* took third at the next race, in Detroit, and then found the winning combination a week later in Madison, where Henley retained his title in the Indiana Governor's Cup, decisively beating *Weisfield's.* This was followed with victories in Dayton, Tri-Cities, Seattle, and San Diego. The end result was a third-straight season title for *Pay 'n Pak,* which scored 8,864 points to 8,213 for *Weisfield's.* Never before or since has one boat's momentum been so effectively halted by the performance of another boat.

In his last season of Unlimited Class participation, "Smiling George" won more races than any other driver and averaged more points per race than anyone else. The pride of Eatonville and Pierce County had no worlds left to conquer. His legacy to the sport is a standard of competitive excellence that few drivers in any racing category have ever achieved.

More recently, Gig Harbor's Terry Troxell has emerged as the latest local unlimited hydro driver to enjoy success. "I got my start in the '50s when I was five years old. My grandfather, a crewman on the *Slo-Mo IV,* took me down to the shop and put me in the boat. I sat there for one and a half hours while he worked on the boat, and I just decided I was going to race hydros. I started racing when I was 20 and have been doing it for more than 35 years." Driving the *Znetix II* in 2001, Troxell captured the first unlimited race of his career at the Columbia Cup in Kennewick, Washington, with an average speed of 144.849 miles per hour. With 30 years of experience racing limiteds in Pierce County, Troxel has changed his focus to the Unlimited Division with the *U-16 E-lam.*

In the early 1960s, sports fans in the Seattle-Tacoma area, thanks to station KTNT in Tacoma, were treated to live weekly television broadcasts of outboard racing on summer evenings. These were APBA-sanctioned events for hydroplane and runabout classes held on the Port of Tacoma Industrial Waterway.

THIS HISTORY OF HYDROPLANE RACING IS SPONSORED BY:

Armand Yapachino

and the

Tacoma Inboard Racing Association

The Tacoma Inboard Racing Association (TIRA) has, for many years, been a driving force in Pierce County's long-standing love affair with boat racing. One of TIRA's most eloquent representatives, both on and off the racecourse, was the nationally ranked 280-cubic-inch Class team of Armand Yapachino and his son Neal. Year after year, their Ed Karelsen–crafted *Joya Mia* was one of the best and fastest 280s in the country. It won a houseful of trophies for the father-and-son team.

Armand Yapachino started racing in the '50s after watching the unlimiteds on Lake Washington. His first boat was a vintage 280 craft called *One Meatball*. Neal followed in his father's footsteps and qualified as a driver at Lake Spanaway in 1970. In addition to driving, Neal served as commodore of TIRA and as a member of the APBA Inboard Racing Commission. He stepped up to the big time as pilot of the *Miss Tri-Cities/Mark & Pak* unlimited hydroplane in 1978. Neal had a second thunder boat ride lined up in 1980 when he suffered fatal injuries driving a 225-cubic-inch Class hydroplane at Sweet Home, Oregon. Tragically, he never realized his Unlimited Class ambition.

Hydroplane racing enthusiasts more recently have discovered an increasing interest in Limited Class boats. Spanaway Lake, featuring 8- to 22-foot boats with modified to stock engines, is the venue of choice for APBA's Region 10, the largest region in the country, covering Washington, Oregon, Idaho, and Montana; yearly competitions are held on the lake in May.

Even old-timer Armand Yapachino continues to find joy in his *Joya Mia*, placing first locally, second in the Pacific Northwest, and third nationally in 2003. "Racing is a challenge," Yapachino said. "To be number one, a driver must establish balance upon the water, be ever conscious of time, be aware of the other drivers around you, and hope that there are no mechanical failures." Drivers are "competing with the fastest boats in the country right here on Spanaway Lake," he concluded. "The experience is beyond belief."

Frank Woods (L.) and Ed Longozo hang on as the Coral Reef is lowered into the water (SSM, 1997.6.15).

CHAPTER 29

ICE HOCKEY

George "Wingy" Johnston (SSM).

The Pacific Coast Hockey Association (PCHA) was formed in 1910 at Nelson, British Columbia, when Lester Patrick and Frank Patrick received permission from their father to go ahead with plans to build ice arenas in Vancouver and Victoria. These two cities, along with New Westminster, banded together to form PCHA. Thus was ice hockey born in the Pacific Northwest.

In 1938, the Tacoma Hockey and Skating Club formed, with about 40 members who enjoyed either ice hockey or social ice skating. The Cammarano Brothers Pioneers were the first real hockey team from Tacoma, though they initially had to play in an independent league in Seattle. Team members included Norman Bain, Carlysle Melquist, Marvin Steinback, Don Fraser, Ed Weir, Louis Weir, George Arcand, Russ Heglund, and Lon Bishop. One of the team's members, Louie Weir, set out to establish a local league, the Tacoma Ice Hockey League (TIHL), with himself as president.

The league made its debut on December 28, 1938, at the Lakewood Ice Arena. Because of the "less than regulation ice surface," reported *Tacoma Times* sports editor Elliott Metcalf, "the clubs will play five-man hockey instead of the customary six-man game." This picked up the pace and intensity of the game and proved to be very popular with the fans.

"An overflow crowd turned out," *Tacoma News Tribune*'s Howie Clifford also reported, "and was treated to thrills, spills, fights and considerable first class hockey as the Alt Heidelbergs upset Cammarano Brothers, 8 to 3, in the opener, and the Medosweet Dairies came from behind to down Griffin Fuel, 7 to 4, in the nightcap." The season ended on April 18, 1939, when Griffin Fuel defeated the Alt Heidelberg squad to claim the first-ever TIHL Championship. For the next several years, the Tacoma City League program flourished and the popularity of the game expanded to the surrounding communities.

In 1944–45, the Pacific Coast Hockey League (PCHL) formed as an amateur league because the National Hockey League (NHL) had claimed territorial rights to Seattle, Vancouver, and Portland and demanded a large fee for the territory, which the PCHL objected to paying. Tacoma joined the PCHL in 1946 following the opening of the Tacoma Ice Palace, located at South 38th and Union Streets. Hubert Hahn built the structure as the newest addition to the Tacoma sports scene. The Tacoma Rockets, under the ownership of Ron Moffat and David Downie, who also doubled as the team's coach, took local hockey to a higher level of amateur play.

Later on in the 1940s, the name of the ice palace was changed to the Tacoma Ice Arena. At the same time, arena owners Fred Urban and Sam Bergerson bought the ice hockey team from Downie, Moffat, and Gordon Teel and raised the team into the professional ranks. The new owners hired Muzz Patrick, a standout with the NHL's New York Rangers, to coach the team. Patrick was the son of the legendary Lester Patrick, after whom the NHL's Patrick Division is named. (His nephew, Craig Patrick, served as general manager for the 1991 defending Stanley Cup champion Pittsburgh Penguins.)

Earl Luebker, longtime sports editor for the *Tacoma News Tribune,* covered the Rockets and also served as their official scorer. In 1983 he reminisced about the teams' heyday:

> A mutual love affair developed between the fans and the Rockets. The line of Pee Wee Read, Ronnie Rowe, and Wingy Johnston had a certain magic about it. Doug Adam had an uncanny knack of getting the puck into the net.
>
> Then there was defenseman Joey Johns, the man the opposing fans loved to hate. Buck Jones, another defenseman, also made his mark on the opposition. Buck didn't smoke or drink and his most violent expletive was a loud "Golly, gee whiz"—but he managed to lead the league in penalties.
>
> Goalie Doug Stevenson was another crowd favorite. There was the night when he stopped a puck with his forehead midway in the first period. The game had to be stopped while he was taken to the dressing room for a quick repair job. After 10 or 12 stitches, he returned to the ice and finished a shutout.

Other popular players included Dick Milford, Neil Andrews, Bill Giokas, Norn Gustavsen, Alex McKay, Harry Bell, Charlie Macdonald, Wayne Brown, Hub Anslow, Ted O'Connor, Bart Bradley, Mark Marquess, Babe Pratt, Doug Toole, Andy Lambrecht, and Warren Godfrey. Godfrey went on to have a distinguished career with the Boston Bruins and Detroit Red Wings.

The Rockets' first season resulted in only 16 wins out of 60 games and a lock on last place in the league. Tacoma's fans, however, were treated to a game between the Montreal Canadiens and the National League All-Stars. Tacoma was the only American city in which the two clubs would play, and top performers included Maurice "The Rocket" Richard and Toe Blake for the Canadiens and Sid Abel and Ted Lindsay for the All-Stars.

Despite an influx of talent, thanks to the resourcefulness of Muzz Patrick, the Rockets never won a league championship although they did record three straight second-place finishes for the 1947–49 seasons. During the 1949–50 season, the top three scorers in the PCHL were all members of

TACOMA'S FIRST FAN CLUB

Local fan clubs date from the post–World War II era, when Jim Boland and Evelyn Brellenthin organized a bus trip for ice hockey fans to go to an away game for the Tacoma Rockets. And in 1949 the Tacoma Rockets Fan Club held its first official meeting at the Tacoma Ice Arena, under the direction of officers Boland and Eddie Asp, with a mission to "help underprivileged children in the community, plan for the betterment of home games, organize bus trips for out-of-town games, and plan dances and picnics."

One early fund-raiser was the sale of hockey buttons. When selling the item was prohibited during games, the organization developed a new sales technique: club member George Mills walked the ice arena wearing the buttons on his coat. "I didn't have to ask people to buy them," Mills explained, "but when they came up and asked where they could get one, I was only too happy to oblige."

The first organized hockey league was formed in 1938 by Louie Weir of Griffin Fuel; representing the original four teams were, L. to R., Lon Bishop of Cammarano Bros. Pioneer Beer, Norm Bain of Medosweet Dairies, Weir, George Goldsberry of Alt Heidelberg, and Ed Weir also of Griffin Fuel (courtesy Lonnie Weir).

the Rockets: Ronnie Rowe (91 points), George "Wingy" Johnston (90 points), and Mel Read (87 points).

Patrick coached the Rockets through the 1952–53 season, the club's last years of play. The team by then was a losing proposition. Travel costs were becoming excessive as expansion took the Tacoma team to the Canadian prairie cities of Edmonton, Calgary, and Saskatoon for games. According to Lynn Faulk, team treasurer and business manager, problems with updating the local arena's deteriorating ice-forming pipes was the final economic blow.

Amateur Hockey

There was more to ice hockey in Tacoma than the professional team, however. Through the organizational abilities of Tom Cross and the enthusiasm of Joey Johns, along with the entire Rockets team, a new high school league was initiated in 1948. The program was a natural extension of the local youth recreational hockey games already offered. And at the time of its formation, the Tacoma High School Hockey League was the first of its kind in Washington State.

Practice sessions were held at the Tacoma Ice Arena on Saturdays, with four schools—Lincoln, Stadium, Bellarmine, and Clover Park—participating the first year. In the first-ever high school league game, Clover Park defeated Stadium, 6–4, with Jim Mulvey scoring three goals for the victorious Warriors. Lincoln followed up with a 9–1 victory over Bellarmine when Jack Folsom tallied a goal and three assists and Ernie Posick added a goal and two assists for the Abes. The contest was played before 2,500 fans at the Ice Palace. Clover Park went on to win the league title, however, with a 5–0–1 record. Although this program lasted only through the 1950 season, young hockey players still used the Lakewood Ice Arena.

Danny Stewart, who worked weekends at the Lakewood Ice Arena as floor manager, approached Johnny Johnsen, the rink manager, about forming a youth hockey program. With Johnsen's blessing, Stewart started calling some of the former high school players to come out and help coach teams. It was hard for old players such as Jim Beaty, Len Webster, and

CHAPTER SPONSORED BY

THE PNAHA AND THE TAHA:

The history of ice hockey is dedicated to Youth Hockey and the people who made it happen in Tacoma and Pierce County: Donna Kaufman, president of the Pacific Northwest Amateur Hockey Association (PNAHA) for the past eight years, founding administrator of the Southwest League, and the Tacoma Amateur Hockey Association (TAHA) President, Secretary, and Scheduler; Rob Kaufman, PNAHA Coaching Director and Director of Player Development & Evaluators; John Cope, Pat Williams, Tom Spina, and Jim Keller, all past TAHA Presidents.

TAHA accomplishments include:

- Creating and hosting the annual Daffodil Tournaments
- Bantams 1993-1994 State Champs
- Bantam Tier II Team 1996 State Champs
- Squirt Tier II Team 1996 State Champs
- Hosted 1997 State of Washington Tier II Championship
- Hosted 1998 Regional Tier II Championship, where the local Bantam team lost by only one point in the final game to a Los Angeles team that went on to take the National Championship
- Midgets 2000-01 Southwest League Champs

Ernie Posick to turn Stewart down because he was always there helping them out if they wanted to skate, work as rink rats, or get their skates sharpened. This effort was the impetus for what eventually became the Tacoma Amateur Hockey Association (TAHA).

TAHA moved its program to Sprinker Recreation Center when it opened in 1976. The lure of a full-size sheet of high-quality, maintained ice to practice on and a new environment were attractive to the group, and the growth of youth hockey increased significantly. Yet another new venue, the Puget Sound Hockey Center, subsequently opened in the 1990s enhancing the growth of youth and adult hockey even more.

Pro Hockey Returns

On September 27, 1983, the Los Angeles Kings played an exhibition game against the Calgary Flames—the first professional hockey game in Tacoma since the Rockets' 1952–53 season. But it was not until 1991 that the "new" revitalized Tacoma Rockets took to the ice at the Tacoma Dome as a part of the Western Hockey League (WHL).

"The first two seasons of operation by the fledgling Rockets were filled with record-breaking excitement," reported Tacoma Rockets Hockey Club director of media relations Ron McGrath. "In their 1991–92 inaugural campaign, they proved they were worthy inhabitants of the huge Tacoma Dome, one of the largest hockey arenas in North America." The Rockets smashed one attendance record after another during their first year of play. "On the ice," McGrath continued, "Tacoma also etched two playing records: the most points (53) and the most wins (24)." At the time, the Rockets' achievements were the all-time WHL marks for the first year of operation by an expansion club. Following the 1992–93 season, three Rockets won player awards as the best in the WHL: goalie Jeff Calvert was named the Most Valuable Player; Michal Sykora was honored as the best defenseman; and playmaking center Jamie Black was selected as the most sportsmanlike player.

Bruce Hamilton, president and general manager of the Rockets, credited the entire organization for the initial successes on the ice. Coach Marcel Comeau, who was named Coach of the Year following the 1992 season, was especially important to the team. So too, in Hamilton's eyes, was the scouting staff led by Lorne Frey.

But a franchise team with successful players can have losses. By the end of the 1992 season, many of the players who had led the Rockets to record-breaking play had been drafted into the NHL. Among those who left were defenseman Thomas Gronman, winger John Varga, and blueliner Michal Sykora. Others who joined the exodus were high-scoring winger Allan Egeland and goalie Todd MacDonald.

The Tacoma Rockets did not survive too many more seasons, and loyal fans were outraged, although few were certain who to blame for the city's second loss of its ice hockey team in a half century. The anger did not last long, however. On January 23, 1997, the West Coast League (WCL) awarded another expansion franchise to Tacoma under the ownership of Bruce Taylor.

The Tacoma Sabercats hit the ice scoring. They won the Northern Division title with a 42–19–3 record but lost to San Diego in the league finals. During the 1998–99 season, the Sabercats were Northern Division champions once again. This time, however, in a game played in the Tacoma Dome they beat San Diego 6–4 to win the league championship, 4 games to 2.

In those first three seasons, Dan Shermerhorn was WCHL MVP and Rookie of the Year for the 1997–98 season; Scott Drevitch and John Olver won back-to-back honors as defenseman and coach of the year, respectively, for the 1997–98 and 1998–99 seasons; and Alex Alexeev won Defenseman of the Year while Blair Allison was crowned top goaltender during the championship season.

The Sabercats won their third consecutive Northern Division title in 2000, but it proved to be the team's last hurrah after they lost the championship to Phoenix. By the time the season ended, coach and general manager John Olver resigned and owner Bruce Taylor sold the team to California writer and producer Barry Kemp. The following year, the Sabercats suffered their first losing season. Losses of this kind meant a dwindling audience, and by 2002 the Sabercats were no more.

When *Tacoma News Tribune* columnist Dave Boling wrote about the opening Sabercats game in November 1997, he said that "this was a fine game. But will this thing survive or will we all have to go through the collapse or the defection of another team just when we grow attached to it?" Ice hockey has always been able to attract those passionate about their hockey and happy to have a team again. Unfortunately, as for both the old and new Rockets before them, there were not enough of those passionate fans to keep professional hockey in Tacoma.

Goalie Doug Stevenson (L.) and teammate Andy Lambrecht squeeze Cal Stearns to push him to the outside, ca. 1949 (SSM, 1999.16.80).

CHAPTER 30

MARBLES

In May 1943, Joe Holmquist of Edison Elementary out shot a field of eight district winners to become the Tacoma grade-school marble champion, winning a $25 war bond (Richards Studio Collection, TPL, Image D14517-3).

The origins of the game of marbles date from antiquity: Augustus Caesar played with nut marbles as a child. Archaeologists found engraved stone marbles in North American Indian mounds. Jewish children used filberts in a similar game during Passover. Presidents Washington, Jefferson, and Lincoln all played the game. Warren G. Harding in 1922 gave his presidential approval to what newspapers called the "first marble championship of the world," played between Jersey City and Washington, D.C., boys. It was a sport for children, and in the United States competitions were open to both boys and girls of all races and ethnicities.

Tacoma entered the National Marbles Tournament its founding year. Editors of the Scripps-Howard newspaper chain were the organizing force behind the event. In 1923 the company "decided to sponsor a truly national tournament, inviting winners from contests all over the United States to participate." Newspapers or city parks departments sponsored the local competitions.

Tacoma's Lloyd Williamson played in the National Marbles Tournament after beating Erling Bergerson for the city championship and Portland's Creed Lall for the Pacific Coast crown. "Lloyd plays a smiling, calm yet rapid game,"

the *Tacoma Times* reported during the regional tournament. "Just tell them back in the Pacific Northwest that I'll do my best tomorrow" was his comment to the reporter. "I feel pretty good, gee."

The Atlantic City Chamber of Commerce paid Williamson's expenses to compete in the nationals, and he was still in the running after two days of play against challengers from Pennsylvania, Ohio, Missouri, and Texas. The Columbus, Ohio, lad won, but during the championship games contestants were treated royally in Atlantic City's finest hotels. Some 5,000 fans watched tournament play.

Before the computer industry revolutionized play, marbles was a major playground sport. Boys and girls congregated during recess to play this game in which the object was to hit the opponent's "pip" out of a circle; if you did, it was yours to keep. Everyone had their sure-shooter sphere, and games were played until you or someone else had all the marbles. Reformers called it a game of chance. For them, this childhood game played at recess was really underage gambling.

Marbles championship play continued throughout the 1930s and 1940s. Paul Lucien won the local honors in 1931 (he later became the 1940 city table-tennis champion; see sidebar in chapter 43, Tennis). Sacred Heart's Jimmy Collins won the Berry Pink trophy and gold medal in 1940. District champions that year were Vernon Keister, Dale Henderson, and Dave Strandley, who became an outstanding heavyweight boxer under the name of Dave Davey (see chapter 16, Boxing). Collins, when interviewed in 2004, remembered that he was always playing marbles with Dean Pitsch and Virginia Glassy.

Glassy also remembered her days playing the game. "We played marbles during recess at Sacred Heart School. When the bell rang, the nuns would remind us to wash our hands before we went to the classroom. It seems like they were always outside watching us play." Glassy was better than her brothers at the sport. When they played, they lost their mar-

bles. She, in turn, would challenge the winners and, on behalf of her siblings, retrieve the marbles from the neighborhood boys.

Vern Keister, a 1940 runner-up and 1941 city champion, was a master at knocking the marbles out of the ring. "I could take my shooter and stick it right in the middle of the ring," he remembered. Once it was there, the opponents' marbles were sitting ducks. Vern acquired the name of "rubber-knuckle Keister." And in a gesture popular with his classmates, he "willed" his marbles to one of his teachers, because, he said, the teacher had lost his own!

In 1943 Spike Thorpe, Mike Dillon, Richard Brammer, Ed Thygesen, Jerry Harding, Bob Schlichte, Billy Pitt, and Joe Holmquist competed for the city grade-school marbles

The four boys who were crowned district marbles champions for the 1940 citywide competition: L. to R., Vernon Keister of Gault, junior high champion; Dale Henderson of Sherman, North End champion; sharp-shooter Jimmy Collins, a 12 year old at Sacred Heart, city champ; Dave Strandley, South End champion. (Richards Studio Collection, TPL, Image D9813-3).

Wearing "Marble King Tournament Champion" badges, boys kneel to shoot in the 1943 grade school championships at Lincoln Bowl (Richards Studio Collection, TPL, Image D14517-4).

championship. Lincoln Bowl was the venue for games sponsored by the *Tacoma Times* and the Tacoma School Board (Robert Hager was supervisor of health and physical education at the time). Holmquist won the competition and a $25 savings bond and was featured in the newspaper.

Serious marbles play rarely survived childhood. By the time a youngster was in high school, other sports attracted the shooters' attention. Girls, too, were less welcomed as time went by. "While the boys played marbles, girls played jacks" was the way that Bill Pitt's wife, Jeanne, explained the change. But even in old age, the former marbles whizzes remembered their past glory. Holmquist remembered winning the Pacific Northwest championship in 1945; Bill Pitt recalled that marbles was, indeed, like gambling. Whoever won the most marbles was champion for the day. Your goal was to win them back the next. It was, for Pitt, like a poker game.

Mike Dillon won third place in the 1943 championship games. "I asked my dad to buy me a bag of marbles," he said some 60 years later. He then lost them in play, along with the marbles from the family's Chinese checkers set. Then Dillon's fortunes changed. He started winning. "I kept winning and winning and stored the marbles in quart jars. It didn't take me too long before I had about nine quart jars filled with marbles." But Dillon retired from marbles championship play in the seventh grade and started playing baseball. (He became one of the finest amateur and professional pitchers from Tacoma, playing for the 1956 Stanley Shoemen team that won the national baseball championships; see chapter 8, Baseball: The Early Years and Amateurs.)

By the end of the 20th century, marbles disappeared from the playgrounds of America. There is no clear explanation why a game that had captured the imagination of children for so many years ceased to entertain. The story of the playground game's end is ironic. You can hear young people today say that a person has "lost his marbles," referring to someone not thinking too clearly, without any idea of the origin of the phrase.

CHAPTER 31

MOTORCYCLE RACING

Don McLeod races at the Graham Speedway in 1971 (courtesy Don McLeod).

Motorcyclists began to organize themselves nationally with the creation of the Federation of American Motorcyclists, headquartered in Brooklyn, New York. The group did not survive World War I, but its existence symbolized the emergent popularity of the motorized cycle during the early years of the 20th century. By 1924 the American Motorcycle Association (AMA) formed. "An organized minority can always defeat an unorganized majority" was the group's motto, pointing to its efforts to challenge early local restrictive ordinances designed to keep motorcycles off city streets.

Tacomans were introduced to the sport in 1912, when W. P. Glasgow's motorcycle shop at 10th and A Streets was one stop on a Seattle-to-Portland (and return) road race sponsored by the Seattle Motorcycle Club. Tacoma's two entries were Ray Day riding a Flying Merkel and Arthur Wisner on a Harley-Davidson; both tied for first place with perfect scores after racing on a rough Pacific Highway still not ready for mechanized transportation.

By the following year, motorcycle racing was a part of the Fourth of July Montamara Festo in Tacoma (see chapter 6, Automobile Racing). The Advertising Club sponsored the event, and businesspeople competed to have the race run on their particular downtown street by bidding on the prize money awarded the winners. Tacoma Avenue merchants won the bidding war by offering a $30 prize to the first-place winner. Unfortunately, it's not recorded who won the city's first race that sped from South Seventh to South 23rd on Tacoma's only asphalt-paved downtown street.

During the decades to come, motorcycle racing blossomed in Pierce County. On May 31, 1922, Wells Bennett—speed king of the motorbike world—shattered the 24-hour world endurance record when he circled the Tacoma Speedway track at an average of 73 miles per hour. Over that 24 hours he logged 1,562.2 miles.

In 1928 the American Legion sponsored a Fourth of July celebration in Stadium Bowl that featured fireworks, a military spectacle, Gyro clowns, Japanese wrestlers and fencers, model airplane flights, a wall-scaling contest, the Portland Turnverein gymnasts—and a new event called "motorcycle polo." Eatonville's Dan Ceccarini, also known as "Tacoma Dan," was one of the polo team competitors.

The Tacoma Motorcycle Club (TMC), which formed in

In 1928 the Indian Cycle Company, located at 450 St. Helens Street, was owned by Max H. Steinhart (courtesy Dr. Wayne D. Herstad).

1926 amid all this activity, established racing facilities near South 11th Street and Marine View Drive by the 1930s. Some of the earliest winning racers were Larry Strong, Curtis Day, Roy Rogers, and crowd favorite Cliff A. "Red" Farwell.

Red Farwell began racing in 1933 and by 1947 he had held the title of Pacific Northwest Champion for seven years. He also won the Bob Knox Memorial Trophy in both 1938 and 1941 (a race sponsored by TMC to honor member Bob Knox, who died tragically in a traffic accident in 1938). Until 1946, Farwell had never raced outside the Pacific Northwest. That year, however, he entered the Daytona and finished seventh among the nation's most competitive racers.

Both men and women were a part of the Tacoma organization. Dorcas Sizer, a member then and club historian years later, once wrote of an impromptu race through the wilds of southern Pierce County. "Every Sunday, at some time or another, the whole gang is out at the course, spading, raking, blowing stumps, or collecting garbage," Dorcas wrote in 1941. "Last Sunday, however, the girls got tired of this Sunday work and suggested a run. Flora Whitney, Vera McElroy, and Juanita Marquez ... made out a secret destination run ... over very dusty roads around Fort Lewis, Camp Murray, and some of our smaller lakes."

In 1947 TMC bought property south of Puyallup, constructed a track, and continued hosting the annual Bob Knox Memorial Day race, among others. But then urban sprawl caught up to the Puyallup Raceway, and members moved the facility farther south, where they constructed the Graham Speedway on 80 acres of farmland. Tacoma's Emil Ahola was one champion who utilized the Graham track during these early years of racing. In 1965, competing in his second year of the Expert Class, Ahola won the national point championship for the motorcycle time trials and road racing under the AMA's jurisdiction. Earlier in the season, he won the Washington State Championship and the Northwest regional title as well.

Again, suburbanization encroached on the motorcyclists. Neighbors began to complain about the noise, and soaring property values forced the club to sell. The club remains active, however, through membership ranging from teenagers anxious to test their skills to older riders whose former racing days have been replaced with rides on the back roads of the Pacific Northwest.

In addition to the Graham Speedway, racers also used what they called Blue Baron Hill. It was not much to look at: a gravel scar carved out of salal and ferns above a nondescript cinder-block building that was the headquarters for the Blue

Baron Motorcycle Club. From the clubhouse, however, it appeared almost vertical and must have been a challenge just to get to the top, let alone beat the clock. The hill sits on the edge of the South Tacoma peat bogs near where the end of South 56th meets Tyler Street.

Lincoln High School's 1958 graduate Don McLeod is one Blue Baron alumnus. He began his sports career as a roller-skating speedster (see chapter 36, Skating: Roller) and moved on to stock car (see chapter 6, Automobile Racing) and motorcycle racing, where he participated in hill climbs, scrambles, poker runs, and other competitions at the Graham Speedway and on Blue Baron Hill. McLeod held the Blue Baron Hill Climb record for five years.

In 1965 McLeod won the overall national point standings in the AMA's Novice Division; the following year, he then won the overall in the Amateur Division. In 1967 he placed 15th in the Expert Division and earned a national

Don McLeod (#112) surges to the lead on his Harley Davidson in a 1965 novice race at the Graham Speedway (courtesy Don McLeod).

ranking of 83 in 1968. Only 100 such awards are given out in the United States. Emil Ahola was the first Tacoman to earn his national AMA number; McLeod was the second. In fact, Tacoma gained national prominence in 1965 when three riders from the same city were named national champions—the first time one city had done so all in the same year—Ahola (Expert Class), McLeod (Novice Class), and Bob Smith (Amateur Class).

Bob Malley was another Blue Baron racer. He began in 1960 and by 1962 was the leading scrambles rider in the Northwest. He went into professional racing the following year and at the end of the season ranked fifth in the novice standings. By the mid-1960s, Malley had achieved Expert status in the AMA and was a leading competitor on the Western Region racing circuit.

Most motorcyclists, however, remember Malley better as "Bouncing Bob," who in 1970 became the Western Region starter for nationally sanctioned competitions. Malley credits Dave Welsh for launching his career as a starter, one that began in 1968 at the Graham Speedway, where he was the man with the flag who made sure that no racer jumped the line. Malley decided to add some flair to the task, to do something different and interesting for the fans. He initially got his "Bouncing Bob" moniker because his starting antics included a challenge to see how high he could jump above the motorcycles when beginning a race. After a chat with motorcycle daredevil Evel Knieval, who reminded him that as a starter "you are always a performer," Malley took tumbling lessons and added cartwheels to his starting repertoire. The result was electric. Racing fans anticipated and loved the gymnastics performance as a prelude to the waving of the green flag. By 1982, however, electric lights had replaced Malley's cartwheels and a motorcycle era came to an end.

Malley did more than race and start motorcycle competitions. By the 1970s, he also sponsored two local clubs. One, Young Hotshots, was for youngsters ages six to 16, organized to teach young riders the art of motorcycling and safe riding techniques. The second club was formed in 1969 in conjunction with McNeil Island prison inmates, some of who had achieved Expert Class racing status before their incarceration. The inmates conceived the program themselves as a way to combine their love of motorcycles with developing skills as mechanics. The program was the first of its kind in the federal penal system.

Pierce County continues to harbor new racing careers. In 1989 Gig Harbor High School student Jay Whipple competed in the National Motocross Association National Championship races held that year in Ponca City, Oklahoma. Meanwhile, Tacomans Dale Zlock and Dan Zlock of Zlock Racing became known for their superior bike construction. In 1989 two of their creations placed seventh and ninth in the prestigious Daytona 200 motorcycle race, a showing considered the best finish for Pacific Northwesterners at that time. From 1995 to 2001, they raced in the Formula USA series, an unlimited engine and chassis class, and won three national championships.

Blue Baron Hill, where the motorcycle club once hosted climbs up the gravel scar, is no more. Puyallup Raceway Park and the Graham Speedway are also remote memories for Pierce County motorcycle racers. Miles of logging roads, pastures, and forgotten gravel pits are now the imaginary racing venues and training grounds for those with motorcycle racing on their mind.

Blue Baron Motorcycle Hill Climb, August 1948 (courtesy Dave Allen).

CHAPTER 32

MOUNTAINEERING

Alma Wagen taught math at Stadium High, but her passion was mountaineering and, in 1915, she hiked completely around Mount Rainier (Mountaineers Photographs Scrapbook 2, TPL).

Pierce County's landmark Mount Rainier has intrigued and challenged climbers for generations. Even from the days of early exploration and first ascents, county residents have impacted the mountain and the sport of climbing and, to this day, remain active in mountaineering.

The first recorded expedition to the mountain was in 1833 when Dr. William F. Tolmie, an employee of the Hudson's Bay Company, entered the western side of what is now Mount Rainier National Park, using the Puyallup Valley as his approach route. His principal mission was to collect botanicals for medicine.

The first recorded attempt of the summit was in 1857 by a group led by Lt. August Kautz. They used a southwestern approach, climbing a glacier route to the west of the Nisqually Glacier. Kautz was able to climb to the 14,000-foot summit saddle, but he did not reach the exact summit point before turning back because of darkness. The glacier route he used now bears his name. Kautz did make mountaineering history, though: his climbing party was the first in North America to use alpenstocks fitted with metal spikes and boots fitted with metal cleats, which he designed and made at Fort Steilacoom.

Philemon Van Trump and Hazard Stevens are credited as the first to reach the summit, a feat accomplished on August 17, 1870. They employed the pack and lowland guide services of James Longmire and an Indian guide named Sluiskin who led them to the Mazama Ridge area just below the glacier line. After they attained the summit, it was too late in the day to safely descend, so they spent the night there, finding shelter in ice caves formed by hot volcanic steam vents.

Noted naturalist John Muir climbed Mount Rainier in 1888, staying a night at what is now called Camp Muir, located above Paradise, on the mountain's most popular climbing route. The first woman to climb the mountain was Fay Fuller, who lived in the Tacoma area; she achieved the summit on August 10, 1890, wearing, it should be noted, a thick flannel dress! The alpenstock she used on that historic climb is on display at the Shanaman Sports Museum of Tacoma–Pierce County.

After Fuller's expedition, the business of mountaineering instruction and guiding became a career for a number of Pierce County climbers. Many clubs, guiding companies, educational programs, and retail stores participated throughout the area's history in assisting local residents to explore and enjoy the mountain environment. Local climbers, and many from all over the world, have used Mount Rainer as training grounds. The famous 1963 American Everest Expedition attempted Rainier during September 1962 as part of their preparation, but they were unable to reach the top due to bad weather.

Luther "Lute" Jerstad, born in Minnesota, moved to Gig Harbor with his family in 1949, where high school friends introduced him to mountaineering. A basketball star and graduate of Pacific Lutheran University (PLU), Jerstad began climbing in the 1950s and worked as a guide on Rainier from 1960 to 1962, reaching the summit more than 40 times. On the basis of this experience, he was invited to join the 1963 American Everest Expedition and became the second American to stand on the top of the world, reaching Everest's 29,028-foot summit three weeks after Seattle's Jim Whittaker. Jerstad also carried a movie camera to the top and recorded the first footage from there. He died of a heart attack in 1998 just 500 feet short of the 18,192-foot summit

At age 77, Bronka Sundstrom became the oldest woman to summit Mount Rainier when she reached the peak led by guide Jason Edwards in 2002 (courtesy Jason Edwards).

of Mount Kala Patar in Nepal, and two years later, at the request of his family, Jerstad's ashes were carried to the summit of Mount Everest.

Seattle-born Lou Whittaker has lived in Ashford for many years, becoming a fixture at Mount Rainier as co-owner and chief guide of Rainier Mountaineering, Inc. (RMI). Since 1968, RMI (co-owned until 2001 by Tacoma attorney Gerry Lynch) has employed many local climbers as guides and led thousands of customers to the top of Rainier via the Camp Muir Route from Paradise.

Other well-known Pierce County climbers include Jason Edwards, from University Place. A local teacher, Edwards successfully completed climbs of the "Seven Summits," the highest point on each continent, and worked as a guide for many years at Mount Rainier, where he accomplished nearly 300 climbs. Edwards summited Everest in 2001 after four previous attempts. In 2002 Edwards climbed

PIERCE COUNTY CLIMBERS WHO CONQUERED MOUNT EVEREST

Luther Jerstad	May 22, 1963
Chris Chandler	October 6, 1976
Phil Ershler	October 20, 1984
Robert Link	May 7, 1990
Ed Viesturs	May 8, 1990
Mark Tucker	May 10, 1990
Eric Simonson	May 15, 1991
George Dunn	May 15, 1991
Brent Okita	May 21, 1991
Dr. Mark Rabold	May 16, 1993
Dave Hahn	May 19, 1994
Jason Edwards	May 24, 2001
Jason Tanguay	May 15, 2004

Mount Rainier with 77-year-old Bronka Sundstrom, from Ashford, the oldest woman to reach the mountain's summit. Tacoma native Craig Van Hoy is another mountaineer who recently completed his quest to climb the highest peak on each of the seven continents; he's only the eighth person from Washington to accomplish this feat.

Joe Horiskey, from Eatonville, has guided at Mount Rainier since 1968 and is perhaps the guide with the longest career of continuous guiding on the mountain. In 1975 Horiskey led the first RMI commercially guided expedition up 20,320-foot Mount McKinley in Alaska. Denali, as it's known, is the highest summit in North America, and Horiskey currently has 24 expeditions there to his credit. He was also a climber on the Lou Whittaker–led 1982 expedition to the north face of Mount Everest.

On this expedition, Pierce County's most prolific female climber, Marty Hoey, fell to her death at the 26,000-foot level. Hoey, who lived in Wauna, had attended Annie Wright School in Tacoma. At the time of her death, many considered her the top female climber in America, with numerous ascents of Rainier, McKinley, and Aconcagua to her credit, as well as expeditions to the Pamir range and the Himalayas.

Dee Molenaar was a mountain guide on Mount Rainier from 1940 to 1941, was a Mount Rainier National Park ranger from 1948 to 1952, and was also involved on some of the earliest of the American-led Himalayan expeditions. The author of several books, including the popular *Challenge of Rainier,* Molenaar has also drawn and published numerous landform style maps of Mount Rainier and other mountainous regions.

Bill Lokey conducted research, sponsored by the Foundation for Glacier and Environmental Research, on the summit of Mount Rainier in 1971 and 1972. This included mapping steam caves and discovering a small lake about 150 feet below the surface, in the Western Crater, during an extended stay of 49 nights and days on the mountain's top. As director of emergency management for Pierce County from 1986 to 1997, he led the county's volcanic hazards management efforts, which the U.S. Geological Survey recognized as a national model during his tenure.

Like Lute Jerstad, Tacoma's Eric Simonson began mountain climbing while a teenager and member of the Tacoma Mountaineers, a local outdoor organization formed in 1912. Simonson first climbed Mount Rainier in 1970 and now has summited Rainier nearly 300 times. He started guiding in 1973 for RMI and since 1997 has run his own guide service, Mount Rainier Alpine Guides, leading climbs via the Camp Schurman route and the Emmons Glacier. Simonson summited Everest in 1991 and is also a "Seven Summiter." His other company, International Mountain Guides, conducts climbs worldwide. "I am a mountain guide," he told a *Tacoma News Tribune* reporter just before his successful assent of Mount Everest in 1991. "My job is to bring my clients home alive. In my book, safety is the first priority. Making the summit is the second priority and having fun is the third. I like to describe myself as a professional worrier. I always have to be thinking."

Simonson led the Mallory and Irvine Research Expeditions to Mount Everest in 1999 and 2001, searching for clues to the fate of George Mallory and Andrew Irvine, who disappeared at 28,000 feet on Mount Everest in 1924. His team's discovery of Mallory's remains in 1999 was an international event, and the artifacts from Simonson's 1999 and 2001 expeditions were displayed at the Washington State History Museum in Tacoma. The exhibitions, both very popular and well attended, made it clear that mountaineering history continues to be of interest even to nonclimbers. The story of these expeditions is told in *Ghosts of Everest* and *Detectives on Everest*, which Simonson co-authored.

Other key figures in modern mountaineering hail from the Pierce County area. One of America's best-known high-altitude mountaineers is Ed Viesturs, who started his climbing career at Mount Rainer, where he worked as a guide throughout the 1980s and early 1990s, living in Ashford during the summer. Viesturs has made more than 100 successful climbs of Rainier and participated in several expeditions to McKinley, in addition to his well-known quest to become the first American to ascend the 14 highest 8,000-meter peaks of the world. He has climbed 12 to date. In the process, Viesturs has achieved six ascents of Mount Everest and distinguished himself on dozens of expeditions. In his most recent ascent of Mount Everest, he became one of only two non-Sherpas to reach the summit for the sixth time. He is also the only American and one of only five people to climb the six highest peaks in the world without supplemental oxygen.

Dave Hahn has lived in Ashford and spent his summers guiding on Mount Rainier since the early 1980s, with well over 150 successful ascents of the mountain. Additionally, Hahn has made dozens of expeditions to McKinley, Mount Vinson, Cho Oyu, and Everest, where he has had five successful ascents. A member of both the 1999 and 2001 Mallory and Irvine Research Expeditions, Hahn was one of the climbers who found the remains of George Mallory. Along with his 2001 teammates—Jason Tanguay, Tap Richards, Andy Politz, Loppasang Temba Sherpa, and Phurba Tashi Sherpa—Hahn was awarded the David A Sowles Memorial Award by the American Alpine Club for distinguishing himself, with unselfish devotion at personal risk or sacrifice of a major objective, in assisting fellow climbers imperiled in the mountains. During the off-season, Hahn has lived and worked for many years at Taos Ski Valley in New Mexico and also in Antarctica.

The Tacoma area's latest big-league climber is Jason Tanguay, who started working as a guide at Mount Rainier during the summer while attending Whitman College. After graduating with a degree in biology, he settled in Tacoma and attended the University of Puget Sound to obtain his teaching credentials. In addition to his more than 75 ascents of Rainier, Tanguay has accomplished expeditions to McKinley and Cho Oyu and was also a member of the 2001 Mallory and Irvine Research Expedition. On that trip, he participated in the highest mountaineering rescue in history and helped to save the lives of several climbers trapped at 28,750 feet, though it cost him his own personal shot at the summit. In 2004 Tanguay returned to Everest and reached the summit via the South Col Route with a team from International Mountain Guides, of Ashford. Tanguay currently lives in Tacoma with his wife, Karina, and teaches at Vashon Island High School.

Besides the slopes of Mount Rainier, the region is also the home of an important man-made climbing and training rock: Spire Rock, in Spanaway at Sprinker Recreation Center. Developed in the early 1970s, it is still a focal point for beginning climbers as well as those looking to improve their skills. Spearheaded by Wayne Cooke and a host of volunteers, with support from Washington National Guard units and the Pierce County Parks and Recreation Department, Spire Rock has been used by numerous mountaineering groups as well as Edwards, Horiskey, and Simonson and other local guides as an entrée to major climbs throughout the world.

Climbers from all over the world continue to use Mount Rainier as a training ground for the Seven Summits. Likewise, local mountaineering, both as a sport and a business, continues to evolve and grow; it is a centerpiece of American climbing.

CHAPTER 33

RACQUETBALL AND SQUASH

Vicki Panzeri was ranked #1 in the world in racquet-ball in 1989 (courtesy Vicki Panzeri).

In 1950 in Greenwich, Connecticut, a former tennis pro named Joe Sobek developed a game he called "paddlerackets." It was played on a handball court and designed to keep his tennis players in shape during the long winter months. Sobek was later recognized as the undisputed originator of the sport we now call racquetball. Little did he know at the time that the game would become not only an Olympic sport but also a multimillion-dollar industry.

Racquetball evolved in 1969, followed by the formation of the International Racquetball Association. This organization, in turn, became the American Amateur Racquetball Association, and its international competition was held in St. Louis, Missouri, with Dr. Bud Muehlteisen, a dentist from San Diego, the first champion.

The Tacoma Racquetball Club was formed at McChord Air Force Base in 1969. Its founding members were M. Sgt. Dick Hassan, who worked in the base's legal office; Lt. Eli Lee, a C-141B aircraft pilot; M. Sgt. Alvin C. Metz, a C-141B crew chief; and Sid Williams, a civilian employee in the 62nd Supply Squadron's Base Service Store. Within a year, the club's membership had grown to 46 players.

Canada had an excellent team of racquetball players, and early in 1971 they invited McChord to play. The resulting games became the first of many such invitationals that are still going on today.

Art Redford, Park Weaver, Dan Bueler, and Sid Williams later formed the Washington Racquetball Association in 1972. This organization published a monthly newsletter and held the first major racquetball tournament, the "Daffy Open," at Pacific Lutheran University that same year. The first open drew the cream of racquetball's crop at the time from the hotbed of the sport: California.

In 1972 the sport turned professional, and at Fort Lewis a young woman named Vicki Panzeri stepped onto a racquetball court for the first time. In 1979 Panzeri joined the pro tour, where she was known for her aggressive game style and nonconformist attitude. She had the best season of any player on the circuit in 1982–83 and as a result was voted the Most Improved Player by the World Professional Racquetball Association; her ranking jumped from 14 to 4 in one year. By the 1984–85 season she had claimed the number-two spot among women professionals, a position she

SQUASH:
A DIFFERENT RACQUET GAME

Although squash courts are not in abundance in Pierce County, with perhaps no more than three accessible to the public, one local athlete took advantage of the courts to make it to the top. Former Tacoman and Charles Wright graduate Mark Alger started playing squash at the Tacoma Lawn Tennis Club in 1972 at the age of 12. He became the tennis club's champion two years later, in addition to being the semifinalist at the Canadian Junior Squash Nationals. By 1979, Alger was a member of the Australia-bound U.S. National Squash Team, the first time a West Coast player was so honored.

The next year Alger turned pro and won both the Pacific Coast Men's Championship and the U.S. National Men's Championships. After several years on the World Professional Squash circuit, Alger went on to win the Men's 30+ U.S. National Championship in 1991 and 1992. A decade later, he was still competing, becoming the quarterfinalist at the 2001 Australian World Masters Squash Championship games held in Melbourne. His enthusiasm for the game propelled Alger to construct a regulation squash court in his home in Palmer, Alaska, and he devotes his spare time to introducing his adopted community to the game.

ers could be found at the 565 Club on Broadway, the original YMCA facility on Market Street, and the present-day Elks Club on Union Avenue. Those playing racquetball in Gig Harbor went to the Town and Country Club.

Racquetball facilities have grown along with interest in the sport. Today there are more than 100 racquetball courts in the county. They can be found at Fort Lewis, McChord Air Force Base, Madigan Hospital, the YMCA, health clubs throughout the region, the University of Puget Sound, the Lakewood Racquet Club, and Sprinker Recreation Center, along with numerous courts at apartment houses and condominiums.

Some of the more active players in the early years from Pierce County besides Williams and Redford included Rhett Kirk, Jerry Henderson, Mike Call, Eli Lee, Gene Elias, Larry Roehr, Javier Figueroa, Jim Julich, Al Metz, and Dick and Donna Reinhardt. Over the years, however,

Sid Williams was largely responsible for the growth of racquetball throughout Pierce County in the 1970s–80s (SSM, 1876).

hung onto for 12 years before retiring to Bellevue, Washington. After a lengthy time away from the game, Panzeri returned in October 2003 with partner Beth Neff of Puyallup to place second in the women's Elite Division at the U.S. Racquetball Association's National Doubles Championships in Minneapolis, Minnesota.

The military and college courts are not the only places where racquetball is played in Pierce County. By the 1970s and 1980s, there were established handball courts in the Tacoma area, where racquetballers also found a home. Play-

Williams did more to promote racquetball statewide than perhaps any other person. His tournaments were legendary and it was not uncommon to find him providing instruction for everyone, from beginners to advanced players, at three or four different facilities each week. He continued to play in tournaments almost every weekend, adding title after title to his resume. A testimony to his longevity in the sport, he teamed up with fellow Tacoman Ace Untalan in 1989 to win the Men's National Masters Championship in the 55+ Division in Multnomah, Oregon.

Tacoma's Mark Alger (R.) runs around Jay Gillespie's forehand drive on his way to victory in the 1981 U.S. National Squash Championships (courtesy Ham Biggar and Mark Alger).

CHAPTER 34

RIFLERY AND SMALL ARMS COMPETITIONS

Lt. Chuck Richards takes aim in the shooting event during the 1970 Modern Pentathlon Trials in Fort Sam Houston, Texas. (courtesy Chuck L. Richards).

Tacoma, like most communities at the end of the 19th century, formed its own National Guard units that served during the Spanish-American War, the Mexican border campaigns, and World War I. But it was most likely in 1894, when Washington held its first trap-shooting tournament and local marksmen first gathered. Five years later, the city hosted the competitions on the tide flats near the head of Commencement Bay.

Frank L. Baker, then president of the Tacoma Gun Club, suggested the grounds of the Camp Lewis Military Reservation, as Fort Lewis was known then, in 1919 as a site for the club. And since the U.S. government was encouraging shooting sports as an adjunct to military preparedness, the new army reservation seemed a logical place. By 1920 the gun club was allowed to use land that is now a boundary between Fort Lewis and McChord Air Force Base north of the Mount Rainier ordnance depot. The club was still there in 1951, when member Arnold Riegger won the overall event's highest average at the American Target Shooting championship held that year in Illinois.

The Tacoma Rifle and Revolver Club, located on Chambers Road near Charles Wright Academy, however,

claims to be Washington's oldest facility, in operation prior to 1889. There were also college Reserve Officers Training Corps (ROTC) programs for young riflemen and -women, and in 1937 Tacoma's Stadium High graduate Sigred Bergerson won the ROTC rifle championship at the University of Washington (UW). Three years before, she had won the women's state championship and the national women's "Dewar" rifle title.

The Tacoma Sportsmen Club was organized in 1933, pointing to a change in focus for local sharpshooters, one that continues into the present. Rifle and small arms competitions became more linked to hunting and to recreational target shooting. In addition, lovers of the sport began to look back in time and introduced new competitions using antique weaponry. The club created rifle, pistol, skeet, trap shooting, and archery ranges in 1946 that were used in competitive sports. The facility, located south of Puyallup off Canyon Road, still exists today.

Over time, existing organizations and new facilities emerged for the benefit of arms competitors, including the Gig Harbor Sportsmen, the Paul Bunyan Rifle and Sportsman Club, and Tacoma Rifle and Pistol. The Sumner

Sportsmen Association concentrates on skeet-shooting; Eatonville's Upper Nisqually Gun Club caters to riflemen and -women living in eastern Pierce County.

One appeal of target shooting is that everyone—young, old, men, and women—can compete. Earl Colson Jr., a 19-year-old Tacoma scattergun expert, won his second all-around championship at the Washington State Trapshooting Association tournament held in Port Angeles in 1941. His main competitor was Buckley's George Young, making the competition an exciting Pierce County affair. At the end of the regular round, both men were tied with a score of 317 out of a possible 350. Colson shattered 186 out of 200 in the 16-yard event, 89 out of 100 in the handicap, and 42 out of 50 in the doubles. He then defeated Young in the final shoot-out.

Colson's winning streak continued into 1941. In June that year, he swept three out of four events at the state championship tournament held in Spokane. He blasted 198 birds to win the singles, scored 338 for all-around honors, and broke 49 out of 50 clay pigeons to win the doubles award. The following month at the Pacific International Trapshooting Championships in Portland, Colson won the high all-target trophy, with 729 out of 770 birds brought down. He tied for second in the 16-yard target shooting event.

In 1942 Tacoma's Irene Paulson achieved the National Rifle Association (NRA) championship for the 50-foot rifle course. Franklin Pierce High School teenager Pamela Mary Gress was awarded the Distinguished Rifleman Medal in 1955. "Tacoma's Annie Oakley," 13-year-old

The Annie Oakleys of the Mount Rainier Rifle League in 1949: back row, L. to R., Mrs. Larry (Ida) Walsh, Mrs. Harold (Violet) Perrin, Irene Paulson, Janice Muzzy, M. Thornberry; front row, L. to R., Mrs. Leonard Price, Mrs. Bart (Augusta) Rummel, Mrs. Grant Ackerland (Richards Studio Collection, TPL, Image D38323-1).

Dorothy Kippie became the first girl ever to win the state junior rifle championship in 1963.

Kippie went on to become one of the area's accomplished shooters. In 1967 she was recipient of the Alice D. Molt trophy, an NRA award presented to the high-scoring girl in the NRA Sectional–National Indoor Championships: Kippie scored 391 out of a total of 500 points and was challenged to hit an aggregate of 10 shots in the prone, standing, sitting, and kneeling positions, in addition to hitting at 50 feet with metallic sights on an A-17 target. She also won a bronze medal in riflery at the Munich Olympics six years later.

Stadium High School's Jack Rummel achieved a new national shooting record for juniors and second place in the Overall Sharpshooter Class, which included adults, in the NRA matches held in Ohio in 1956. That same year, University of Puget Sound (UPS) band director R. L. Wheeler was high aggregate scorer in the Washington State Small Bore Rifle Championship held at Mount Vernon, Washington. Roy dairy farmer Richard Amundsen defeated Hoquiam housewife Gertrude Backstrom in a pressure shooting competition in 1956, winning the North Pacific States Regional Pistol Championships held at the Tacoma Police Range.

In the 1980s Claude Kinard, Jay Waldron, Robert V. Coghe, Jim Jensen, and Scott Jones were the county's award-winning sharpshooters. Tacoma Rifle and Revolver Club members Coghe and Jensen competed in the NRA's Midwinter Pistol Championships at Camp Perry, Ohio, in 1984 and both won. Coghe, a 62-year-old retired Air Force master sergeant and shooting instructor, walked away with the Senior Master Championship; Tacoma police detective Jensen won the Sharpshooters Class. Curtis High School's "Hot Shot" Scott Jones, also a member of the McChord Sportsman Club, was named to the All-American Skeet Team in 1988.

Claude Kinard competed for the Paul Bunyan Rifle and Sportsman Club and was sponsored by the Puyallup Shooters Shop, a business he partially owned. His specialty was metallic silhouettes, handgun targets shaped as different-sized animals placed at varying distances. In 1981 Kinard set a record by knocking over 69 of the 80 targets at the International Handgun Metallic Silhouette Association Championships held in Farragut, Idaho. The achievement made him an All-American in his specialty.

Just prior to receiving the award, Kinard lost his legs in a fiery automobile accident. However, the tragedy did not stop him from bringing home two world handgun titles from his next competition, held in Indianapolis in July 1982. In the first event, he shot a perfect 80 out of 80 in the revolver category and then, using his new artificial legs, broke another world title in the standing position by hitting 67 out of 80 targets.

In 1983, the year before Jay Waldron graduated from Puyallup High School, he attended the U.S. Olympic Training Center in Colorado Springs as a trap shooting

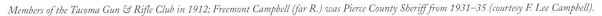

Members of the Tacoma Gun & Rifle Club in 1912; Freemont Campbell (far R.) was Pierce County Sheriff from 1931–35 (courtesy F. Lee Campbell).

Practice shooting at the Gun Club in 1912 (courtesy F. Lee Campbell).

trainee. Following his graduation, he joined the U.S. Army and captured a gold medal at the 1991 Pan American Games in Cuba, breaking 212 out of 225 targets launched from a bunker at speeds of up to 11 miles per hour. By 1992, as a member of the U.S. Shooting Team, he broke 198 out of 200 clay targets, guaranteeing him a place on the Olympic team competing in Barcelona that year. He received no medals for marksmanship at the games but did win a gold at the World Cup competitions held in Mexico City and a silver medal at the Suhl World Cup in Germany, both held the same year.

Matt Dryke began skeet shooting in Sequim but ultimately found his way to the Tacoma Sportsmen Club. He was 16 when he first tried out for the Olympic shooting team and competed in the U.S. championships. He won the Olympic gold at Los Angeles in 1984 and to date is the only American to do so. He "never considered the possibility that one day he'd be an Olympic skeet shooting champion," reported the *Pierce County Herald* in 1992. At least not when he was a junior at Sequim High School. "It wasn't in the back of my mind as a kid," he said then. "But it became a dream when I was introduced to it when I was 16." Following more than a decade of successful competition, Matt Dryke is now a member of the USA Shooting Hall of Fame.

New challenges were added to the common fare of rifles and pistols when the Tacoma Rifle and Revolver Club began to host black-powder meets and Schuetzenfests in 1977. The latter "shooting festival" originated among German-Americans in the 1870s but had died out as a result of World War I. Shooters now use a single-shot Schuetzen rifle in the competitions, many of which were "liberated" during World War II. By the time Tacoma's Chuck Bordman competed in 1984, participants were casting their own bullets and sometimes used replicas of the original. Even so, the purpose is the same: modern-day marksmanship using historical weaponry.

Representing Pierce County at the 2004 summer Olympic Games in Athens, Greece, was 22-year-old Morgan Hicks, a Bethel High School graduate. She participated in the women's 50-meter, three-position event, placing 12th overall. When she picked up her father's rifle at age 13, little did anyone know an international shooting star would emerge. Coach Doug Shellenberger was always impressed with her discipline when she competed at the Paul Bunyan Rifle and Sportsman Club in Puyallup. He was not surprised when she broke three state records and tied national records at the gun club during her senior year at Bethel. She won the coed 2004 National Collegiate Athletics Association (NCAA) Division I Rifle Championship in air rifle prior to qualifying for the Olympics.

CHAPTER 35

SKATING: ICE

Jack Boyle and Patsy Hamm, ca. 1949 (SSM, 2002.35.3).

The Lakewood Figure Skating Club, reported the *Tacoma News Tribune* in 1949, not only was one of the community's most active organizations, it also had attained a broader reputation because of the number of its young ice skaters who participated in national championships. In addition, Tacoma had more skaters participating in professional ice shows than any other city in the country. Many ice skaters were born here. Others came because of the quality of professional coaches. And though not all the champion ice skaters stayed to call Pierce County their home, they all remembered with fondness the Lakewood Ice Arena, whose public life began on the eve of World War II.

When Tacoma industrialist Norton Clapp purchased the former Oakes ballroom on the shores of Steilacoom Lake in 1936, he did it to satisfy his wife's strong interest in ice skating. The future Weyerhaeuser Corporation chairman couldn't have known what converting the quaint old dance hall into the Lakewood Ice Arena would produce in the coming decades.

The ballroom was part of an old bathing and swimming resort originally owned by the Oakes family. During the

Depression, it underwent several changes in ownership; in 1934 it was known as the Towers, a dance hall where Howie White's 10-piece orchestra regularly played. After Clapp purchased it and converted it to ice, the well-known landmark hosted many private parties. Then, in September 1938, the *Tacoma News Tribune* announced the construction of a "modern ice rink and hockey arena" within the facility. "Since it was rumored the arena was contemplated," the newspaper reported, "the management has been besieged by inquiries from hundreds of skating and hockey enthusiasts, showing the tremendous interest in the sports." By December, the Lakewood Ice Arena was opened to the public. The facility immediately became the home of the Lakewood Figure Skating Club (the name was changed to the Lakewood Winter Club in 1948) and remained so until 1982, when part of the building collapsed and it was subsequently demolished.

Even in its heyday it was hardly perfect. It was not full-sized and it often dripped condensation from the ceiling, marking up the ice and sometimes making skating hazardous. But it was Tacoma's own arena, and local skaters held fond memories of the time when the ice was resurfaced by hand and live organists provided the music. Fred Holt was the first Lakewood organist. He had quit dental school in Iowa to come West, where he worked in the shipyards during the day and played the rink's Hammond B3 at night. Holt also wrote music for the Lakewood Winter Club's "Ice Capers," productions held in the arena following World War II. The arena was not just for figure skating, however. In 1949 John Johnsen, then manager, introduced curling to the Pacific Northwest and formed the Lakewood Curling Club (see chapter 18, Curling).

Meanwhile, the City of Tacoma got its own arena, the Tacoma Ice Palace, located at South 38th Street and Union. Hubert Hahn built the structure in 1946 as the newest addition to the Tacoma sports scene. "Despite numerous material delays and skyrocketing production costs," the *Tacoma*

News Tribune reported, "initial use of the rink will come [in October] when turnouts begin for the Tacoma Ice Hockey club." Hahn also planned to have the rink opened to the public for ice skating.

Marlene Jackson Thurston devoted most of her life to skating, and in her mind Tacoma figure-skating nostalgia includes taking her 78 rpm records to the public sessions at the ice palace in the late 1940s. "I used to bring my old 78s so they could play music for the public sessions," Jackson Thurston recalled. "They had a large pipe organ that was also used to play music. There were two ice arenas in town … and no Zambonis [ice resurfacing machines]. In those days, they scraped the ice with a tractor pulling a blade, then hosed the ice and squeegied off the extra water for a fast resurface effort."

A popular Ice Follies number in 1951 was called "The Roaring Twenties" and featured the comedy team of Tacoman Dick Rasmussen and Bill Cameron: in front, L. to R., John Mulvey, Cameron, Rasmussen; in back in white hat is Tacoman Wayne Earley; in back with face obscured is Tacoman Bill Boyle (SSM, 2002.44.3).

Jack Boyle grew up in one of Tacoma's best-known skating families, graduated from Stadium High School in 1949, and teamed with Patsy Hamm to place fourth in the senior pairs event at the U.S. championships. He toured with the Ice Follies, Holiday on Ice, and other shows, but he still had fond memories of his years in Tacoma. "I loved to skate, and the Lakewood Ice Arena and the Tacoma Ice Palace were my favorite places to go," he said. The Lakewood arena in particular brought back special memories. "I remember Fred Holt at the organ, Bert Flake on his tractor preparing the ice, Mrs. Beeler and Alice Flake working in the box office, and the good hamburgers and hot fudge sundaes in the snack bar."

Dora May Coy, who made a name for herself as an international and Olympic judge of figure skating, served on the executive committee of the U.S. Figure Skating Association. But she was most active in the Lakewood Winter Club and proud of the skaters it produced. "Many famous names have come from our skating 'factory': Jimmy Grogan, Lois Secreto, Marlene Jackson, Pat Firth, the [Larry] Hamm and [David] Riggs duo, Patsy Hamm, and Jack Boyle, just to name a few," Coy wrote during the 1960s in documenting the club's history. "We have contributed more skaters to the professional shows than most any other club in the nation."

Dora May Coy was there for the first public performance at the Lakewood Ice Arena, on December 17, 1938. Female skaters wore street-length skirts. Some male skaters wore black tights. "The rink was brand-spanking-new, decorated elaborately in Swiss chalet fashion, with murals painted on the walls … and authentic German beer steins on the shelves," she wrote. "The opening number of the first show was an introduction to school figures, and the participants were Joe Jenae, Britta Lunquist, Myrtle Girten, George Monnier, and Sparky Bourque. There was also a waltz, a 10-step, and a pairs number by National Junior Pairs Champions Betty Lee Bennett and John Kinney, pupils of John Johnsen." Johnsen, who became coach at the Lakewood arena at this time, executed a solo number called the "Sailor's Hornpipe."

CHAPTER SPONSORED BY
THE LWC AND THE LSF:

The Lakewood Winter Club (LWC) and the Lakewood Skating Foundation (LSF) are proud sponsors of this history. The LWC has been a member of the United States Figure Skating Association since the 1930's, supporting ice skating in Pierce County where it has produced world and Olympic team members, national skating champions, and top competitive figure skaters. Due to the costliness of supporting a competitive figure skater and operating an Olympic-sized skating rink, contributions to the non-profit LSF are greatly needed. (The LSF is a 503c organization and contributions are tax free.) You can contact an officer of the LSF Board of Directors by calling the Sprinker Recreation Center at (253) 798-4000.

The original Lakewood Winter Club (SSM).

Diane Jacobsen (L.) and Patsy Hamm (R.) were partners in the ladies pairs competition (SSM, 2002.27.9).

The Early Years

Many people believe that Lois Secreto epitomizes early ice skating in Pierce County. Secreto began skating at the age of eight. "At the time, I was very involved with tap dancing," she remembered, "as I think all little girls were trying to be the next Shirley Temple. After that first time on ice, however, I couldn't think of anything else. Little by little, the tap dancing faded out and skating was in." Soon she was one of Johnny Johnsen's students and, in 1942, won the Northwest Juvenile Girls title.

When barely a teenager, Lois Secreto teamed with Jimmy Grogan and, in 1945, they won the Pacific Coast Junior Pairs competition. She also placed second in the Junior Girls event. One year later, Secreto won the Northwest Novice Ladies title, followed by the Northwest Senior

title in 1947 and a second in the Pacific Coast Senior Ladies event in 1950. The latter win qualified her for the national championships, where she tied for first place with Tenley Albright in the freestyle skating event.

Following her amateur competitions and graduation from Stadium High School, Secreto joined the Shipstads and Johnson Ice Follies but returned to Pierce County two years later to marry and to teach ice skating at both the Tacoma Ice Palace and the Lakewood Ice Arena. "I absolutely loved teaching. To be able to take a complete beginner and watch them progress was so exciting."

During these formative years, no one achieved more as a competitive skater than the colorful Jimmy Grogan. "He started skating as a rink rat at the Lakewood Ice Arena," said Secreto, his first partner. Left motherless at 12 in 1944, Grogan made his home with U.S. Army Major Floyd Moore and his wife, Emily, who was active in the Lakewood Figure Skating Club. When the Moores were transferred to California, Grogan went with them.

At 16, he earned a spot on the 1948 U.S. Olympic team at St. Moritz, Switzerland, and took sixth. Four years later, in 1952, he skated to an Olympic bronze medal at Oslo, Norway. But he had the misfortune of peaking at the same time as the incomparable Dick Button. Grogan finished second four times at the world championships, twice behind Button (1951 and 1952) and twice behind Hayes Alan Jenkins (1953 and 1954), and was second behind Button four times (1948–1952) at the U.S. championships.

After leaving competition, Grogan was a spectacular show skater with Arthur Wirtz's Hollywood Ice Revue and Ice Capades. He was also instrumental in developing the Ice Castle Training Center at Lake Arrowhead, California, and coached there from 1985 until his death. In 1991 Grogan was inducted into the U.S. Figure Skating Hall of Fame.

One of the main reasons Tacoma turned out so many figure skaters was the cozy atmosphere of the Lakewood Ice Arena. In addition, the club shows often attracted talent seekers for touring shows. Dick Rasmussen became the first Lakewood skater to venture out on tour in 1943. He tried out for the Ice Follies during its spring run in Seattle and was accepted. Two years later, the show dipped into the Lakewood "farm club" and enlisted the talent of Margaret Clark.

John Mulvey and Patricia Hoyt began touring in 1947.

Soon there was a string of Tacoma skaters touring with the Ice Follies, including Wayne Earley, Diane Jacobson, Marlene Jackson, Jodi McDaniels, Sally Price, Lois Secreto, Larry Hamm, Patsy Hamm, Billie Baker, Dave Riggs, and Jean Jensen. At one point, three members of the same Tacoma family—Bill, Jack, and Eleanor Boyle—were touring with the Ice Follies.

Jim Stephens, owner of the Highland Ice Arena in Seattle, recalled the summer ice shows in Tacoma in 1947 and 1948. "We put on an ice show in the summer called Gay Blades," Stephens said. "We had great dance sessions in the

summers, with Lakewood and Seattle members joining with four professional couples. We had dance cards where you signed up your partners in advance, and there were so many that some dances were run in two or three flights to allow plenty of room and all an opportunity to skate."

When ice skaters recounted their fondest memories, music and the snack bar always seemed to come to mind. Organ music was the essence of skating, and Fred Holt at Lakewood, along with Esther Vanderflute at the Tacoma Ice Palace, provided the tunes. The snack bar was a place for "skating mothers," remembered Lois Secreto. They "would sit on the big sofas behind the glass window in the snack bar

Jimmy Grogan, ca. 1952 (courtesy Pat Firth Hansen).

where it was warm and watch their kids skate." According to Don Gilbertson, who was a rink rat at the time, the arena snack bar was a place where both World War II– and Korean War–era soldiers congregated. "My mother and I found that on Sundays between afternoon and evening [skating] sessions, these G.I.s had nothing to do. We set out checkerboards, Chinese checkers, and cards and always made some kind of homemade meal for those men."

Coaches

Two of Tacoma's great figure-skating coaches were John Johnsen and Kathy Casey. Johnsen came first, in 1939 through 1941 and again in 1948 through 1968. Casey began teaching in 1962 and continued until 1990. Together, they may have taught more skaters in the area, and produced more champions, than all other coaches combined.

Born and raised in Denmark, John Johnsen started skating at the age of six. At age 16 he moved to Calgary, Canada, where he joined the Glencoe Skating Club. After teaching in Seattle, he was hired as the teaching pro when the Lakewood Ice Arena first opened to the public. Pat Hoyt, Dick Rasmussen, Patty Greenup, and John Kinney were some of his successful young skaters at the time. He stayed at Lakewood until 1942, when he became a counter-intelligence agent for the United States in Denmark and other northern European countries. Following the war, he taught in San Francisco but returned to Lakewood in November 1948 as head pro and manager.

Johnsen took over as the pro for skaters Patsy Hamm, Jack Boyle, Sally Price, Diane Jacobsen, Nancy Roberts, and Joan Winters. He stayed for 20 years, although hepatitis and failing health slowed his contributions significantly for the last 10 years of his time in Pierce County. He also laid the groundwork for a large number of Lakewood skaters to join the Ice Follies and other touring shows.

With Johnsen's health failing, Kathy Casey, a former skater from Great Falls, Montana, was hired to teach at the Lakewood Ice Arena. For the next 28 years, she taught scores of skaters until leaving in 1990 to replace Carlo Fassi as skating director at the Broadmoor World Arena in Colorado Springs, Colorado. During her later years in Tacoma, Casey served as president of the Professional Skaters Asso-

ciation for six years and also served on the Olympic Coaches Committee.

Like Johnsen, Casey turned out a string of strong show skaters. Later, she produced a woman's junior world champion in Jill Sawyer (1978) and taught school figures to Rosalynn Sumners, the women's world champion in 1983 and Olympic silver medalist behind Katarina Witt at Sarajevo in 1984. She also led skaters such as Jim White, Scott Kurtilla, Scott Williams, and Scott Davis to national achievements. Davis, who graduated from Curtis High School, followed Casey to Colorado Springs and won the U.S. Senior Men's Championships in 1993 and 1994.

The husband-and-wife coaching team of George and Leah Mueller came to Lakewood in 1942, to replace Johnsen when he left for war service. Prior to their arrival, they had taught in Boston, Toronto, St. Louis, Philadelphia, and Long Beach, California. They remained for six years and were particularly fond of the area—especially the small "patch" of ice downstairs at the Lakewood arena that was used for school figures. "We intend to develop the younger skaters of Tacoma and use this fine championship material you have here," Leah Mueller said at the time. "We like the Northwest and your beautiful Lakewood arena. That patch downstairs—we shall train all our stars there in complete privacy until they want to show off upstairs."

In 1946 Jim and Dorothy Stephens became the first pros at the Tacoma Ice Palace. They were teaching outdoors on natural ice in Edmonton, Alberta, at the time Hubert Hahn hired them to run the skating program for the new facility. Among their top performers were Marlene Jackson, who graduated from Stadium High School in 1952 and skated professionally for the Ice Follies; Lois Secreto; and Joan Schenke. The Stephens also ran a successful summer program in 1947 and 1948, from which one skater—Erica Batchelor—went on to win a woman's world championship for Great Britain. Even though the Stephens moved on to the Portland Ice Arena in 1948 and then to Seattle in 1951, they remained a part of the regional skating scene through their ownership of the Highland Ice Arena.

Patsy Hamm left her mark on Tacoma skating both as a competitor and as a coach. She partnered with Stadium High School's Jack Boyle to finish as high as fourth in national pairs competitions in the 1940s. As a coach, she helped develop the Lakewood brother-and-sister team of Judi and Jerry Fotheringill into two-time U.S. pairs champions. Hamm, who grew up in Eatonville before moving to Lakewood at the age of nine, did most of her skating and teaching at the Lakewood Ice Arena. "I know that once skating gets in your blood," Hamm once said, "it stays there. Skating, both on my own and while teaching, has always been a major highlight of my life. And one never knows when one makes a difference. In fact, the last time I skated was just last year when I was teaching my first granddaughter to skate."

Competitive Skaters

Between 1953 and 1994, the ice arenas' coaches led seven Pierce County skaters to national championships: Patricia Firth (1953), Joan Schenke (1956), Judi Fotheringill and Jerry Fotheringill (1959, 1963, and 1964), Robert Madden (1960), Jill Sawyer (1977 and 1978), and Scott Davis (1993 and 1994). Some of these performers provided reminiscences of their experiences for a 2002 reunion that celebrated the history of figure skating in Pierce County.

Patricia Firth was U.S. Junior Ladies National Champion in 1953. She and her sister Mary "first discovered Lakewood sometime in the late 1940s. At first sight, we loved the picturesque Swiss chalet–style ice arena on the lake with the cozy snack bar. It just felt good skating there. We remember taking lessons from the Muellers on the small patch of ice in the basement. It was great for working on figures and spins during the busy public sessions upstairs.

"Though I was the little 'sis' who tagged along after Mary, I became serious about 'my' skating at age 10, in summer school, skating with Dick Button and a treasure trove of other top skating stars of the time. During the 1948–49 season, we discovered John Johnsen. Under Johnny, I came to love figures (my forte) and I knew that someday I had to teach. Johnny, who based his teaching on the principles of physics, never failed to answer my plethora of questions. In the summer of 1950, we achieved the gold test at Lakewood, and what a wonderful feeling it was. That was followed in 1951 with my first-ever title—Northwest Senior Ladies—and a third-place Junior Ladies at my first nationals. In 1952

I placed first in the Pacific Coast Senior Ladies Division and second at nationals in Junior Ladies; and in 1953 I successfully defended my title at the Pacific Coast championships and then won the Junior Ladies National Championships. The national title put me on the road to world [competition]s and a seventh-place world standing. Being on the 1955 World Team was the experience of my life.

"I signed to skate professionally at the Empress Hall Theatre Production in London, and while they were trying to get me a work permit, I taught dance in the summer of 1955 at Lakewood. When they were unable to get me a work permit in London, I started teaching full-time in Great Falls, Montana, where one of my first star pupils was Kathy Casey. She was only 14 years old at the time but she did pass her fifth, sixth, and seventh tests that year—a real testament to her ability to pick up and execute figures. I went on to teach in Butte and Missoula, Montana; Omaha, Nebraska; and Bellevue and Lynnwood in Washington state.

"Some of my favorite memories over the years include the spectacular ice shows with the live organ music, the challenge of doing eight shows over two weeks, fabulous costumes, and lots of pretense, glamour, and glitz. I also recall creative choreography so you could squeeze your program into Lakewood but stretch it into a regular-size ice surface for competition, plus skating with speed without hitting the barrier. One time when I was trying not to be late for practice and was running to the rink, I got stung on the ankle by a yellow jacket. The next day was my seventh test and I could barely lace my boot over that swollen ankle.

"Overcoming challenges made us strong, and I still love and religiously follow skating, but as an armchair spectator. It was a wonderful atmosphere to grow up in, as those truly were the 'good old days'."

Joan Schenke repeated Firth's national title three years later. She grew up in the north end and attended Jason Lee Junior High School. Schenke remembered, "My dad loved hockey and so we went to Tacoma Rockets hockey games when the team was formed in 1946. The games were at the newly opened Tacoma Ice Palace, and after meeting the skating pros, Jim and Dorothy Stephens, Dad decided I should take some lessons. I do remember how much I loved taking lessons from the Stephenses and how nice they were to me. I

SHORT-TRACK SPEED SKATING

The surge of in-line skaters in the 1990s needed a venue for training during the winter, and crossing over to ice was a natural. Short-track ice speed skating was an exhibition sport at the 1992 Winter Olympics but became a full medal sport in 1994. The first athlete in the area to successfully accomplish this was Tacoman K. C. Boutiette, who was named to the U.S. team.

In 1993, through the efforts of Jerry Suhrstedt, a member of the Northwest Speed Skating Association, the Tacoma Speed Skating Club (TSSC) was formed to further the growth of short-track ice speed skating in the area. The TSSC's home base was at Sprinker Recreation Center in Parkland, and Suhrstedt was the head coach, with Gary Gandee and Roger Mosiman serving as assistant coaches. The club participated in several competitions in Eugene, Oregon, at the Lane County Speed Skating Club as well as at rinks in British Columbia.

Mosiman, a longtime resident of Gig Harbor, was the perfect complement to the efforts of Suhrstedt. A native of Minnesota, Mosiman started ice skating at age four and lived across the street from a winter sports park where skating was commonplace. The park hosted the annual U.S. Outdoor Speed Skating Championships, and Mosiman competed in it for six years. He won a North American title in a U.S.–Canadian competition and set two world speed-skating records in the 13- and 15-year-old age groups.

In addition to Boutiette's involvement in the club, another bright star on the horizon was a very young Apolo Anton Ohno. Both Ohno and Boutiette started on quad roller skates, converted to in-line skates, and then, ultimately, converted to ice skates. A natural on ice after having skated for only a couple of months, Ohno competed in the B.C. provincial championships and took first place. He then skated in the U.S. national championships and took first in one race and fourth overall.

TSSC eventually relocated to another facility and ultimately disbanded due to a lack of available ice time, but the careers of Boutiette and Ohno continued to blossom, leading to outstanding performances.

In the 1998 Winter Olympics held in Nagano, Japan, Boutiette placed eighth in the 10,000-meter race with a time of 13 minutes, 44.03 seconds; finished 14th in the 5,000-meter race in a time of 6 minutes, 39.7 seconds; and claimed fifth in the 1,500-meter race in a time of 1 minute, 50.04 seconds. Competing in the 2002 Olympic Games in Salt Lake City, he took fifth in the 5,000-meter, the race of his life, in which he held the Olympic-record pace for several minutes. His time was 6 minutes, 22.97 seconds, which shaved almost nine seconds off his personal best in spite of not qualifying for a medal. The charismatic Ohno, now a Seattle resident, won a gold medal in the 1,500-meter and a silver medal in the 1,000-meter at the Winter Olympics held in Salt Lake City in 2002.

Although there are no short-track speed skating venues or clubs in Pierce County at present, when these two competitors take to the ice every four years, it creates excitement and hope that future champions will have an opportunity to achieve their dreams as Boutiette and Ohno have done—and as Mosiman did more than 60 years ago.

feel strongly that Jim and Dorothy provided the foundation for my skating and the motivation that went with it.

"When the Stephens moved from Tacoma, I also made a move and started taking lessons from John Johnsen at the

Patty Gilroy and Robert Madden, silver dance champions in 1958 (SSM, 2002.47.2).

Lakewood Ice Arena. To this day, I still consider John Johnsen a very gifted teacher. He had many national and international skaters over the years, and he did it teaching on an undersized rink that was a real disadvantage, in my mind. My career flourished under his guidance, and in 1956 I won the US. Junior Ladies Championship. That was followed up next year with a runner-up finish to Carol Heiss in the Senior Ladies Division at the 1957 U.S. National Championships, a third-place finish in the North American Championships, and a seventh-place finish in the World Championships.

"Of all the awards and medals I have won, including the national title, the Lois Secreto Award I won in 1956 meant the most to me because of the type of person Lois was. She was a most gracious person and she has always remained in my mind over the years. Throughout life we come in contact

with people who are very special. She is one of those people who encouraged you to be the best you could be through example."

The brother-and-sister team of Judi and Jerry Fotheringhill won the U.S. Pairs National Championship in 1959, 1963, and 1964. Like many kids, they started skating during the Saturday-afternoon public sessions at Lakewood. "We were being looked after by our two teenage aunts, who thought it would be fun to take us skating for an afternoon," explained Judi. "This led to a series of group lessons taught by a young, energetic professional, Patsy Hamm. During the course of the public lessons, she recognized that Jerry and I were brother and sister and took a particular interest in us because she had been a pair skater and thought we fit the ideal for a young pair team.

"In the years to come, Jerry has been quoted as saying, 'Well, our parents wanted us to do something together, and I refused to put on a ballet outfit, and Little League wouldn't let Judi play, so this seemed to be a good compromise.' By 1959 we had won the U.S. Junior Pairs title and now this was getting serious. There was always a problem coming from Tacoma, in that the rink was not regulation size and we had never skated our entire program through—we had to constantly do the program in sections because we couldn't fit it all in our little rink. We had to make early-morning trips to Seattle to practice the program on a full-sized rink.

"By 1961 we were really on the verge of breaking into the top three at the national Senior Pairs level, but due to a very poor performance in Colorado Springs we placed fourth and were not selected for the international team. Disheartened, we returned to Tacoma and came to grips with the idea of early retirement. All this changed when that year the Boeing 707 carrying the U.S. team to the World Championships went down in Brussels, Belgium, killing all aboard. We were now the top remaining pair in the country and felt some sense of opportunity, if not responsibility, to revive our career.

"Off we went to Sun Valley to spend the summer training and working in the resort. A reporter from the *Denver Post* saw us perform and reported back to the powers that be at the Broadmoor in Colorado Springs that they should have us skate for them. Within a year of that move, and under the tutelage of Carlo Fassi, Jerry and I were on our first World Team, succeeded by our first National Senior Pairs title, and, finally, our being named to the 1964 Olympic team.

"Patsy Hamm was our first pro, and emotionally she remained with us through all the years. After just the first few years and as our career improved, we were passed on to Johnny Johnsen, the head pro. His brother, Hans, was the pro at Sun Valley; he was a great help in arranging our summer there. We were very lucky with all of our coaches. Patsy, to our young eyes, was filled with enthusiasm and made the whole thing seem like an adventure. After we had moved on with Mr. Johnsen, Patsy sent a little leprechaun doll as a good-luck token for us to take to competitions. This, along with her encouraging spirit, went with us every time, and I think it lives in the boxes with all of our skating memorabilia today."

The Skating Scene

Other people whose presence made sure ice skaters had an easy ride included Ray "the Deacon" Shirk, Robert H. Williams, Danny Stewart, and Bert Flake—keepers of the ice, managers of the rink rats, and sharpeners of skates at both skating rinks. But it was Al and Iria Beeler who kept

Socks and skates were among the accessories sold at the Lakewood Ice Arena; Shirley Lander (R.) is the sales clerk (TPL).

the Lakewood Winter Club and the Lakewood Ice Arena together during much of their shared history. Iria started working at the rink as a bookkeeper in 1954 and became the manager in 1968, a job she held until 1982.

"Al became very active in the [Lakewood Winter] club," wrote Kathy Casey in the *History of Figure Skating in Pierce County,* "and was president for eight years. He also held other offices … and served on the board of directors for over 25 years." Al Beeler became a qualified gold judge for figure and freestyle skating and built props for the countless annual ice shows held at the Lakewood Ice Arena.

In the 1970s, Pierce County Parks made plans to expand its Harry Sprinker multipurpose sports facility to include a recreation center. Since the Lakewood rink was too small to accommodate competitive skaters, the Lakewood Winter Club "expressed a keen interest in renting ice time for club programs, occasional competitions, and their competitive skaters to have a chance to practice freestyle programs on a regulation-size sheet of ice."

When the Lakewood Ice Arena's roof collapsed and the arena closed for good in 1982, the Beelers lost their second home. The club, and the Beelers with it, moved full-time to the Sprinker Recreation Center. The Tacoma Ice Palace's fate was similar to that of the Lakewood facility. After the Tacoma Rockets' demise in 1953, the Ice Palace was renamed Tacoma Sports Arena and became a venue for boxing. The building, abandoned for a period, became more diversified, with an amusement center filling the original ice rink and a printing shop encompassing a basement. In March 1986, the roof collapsed, thus ending the life of another ice rink in Pierce County.

However, in 1987 the Lakewood Winter Club hosted the U.S. National Figure Skating Championships, with the Sprinker Recreation Center the venue for the Compulsory Figures competition. Since then, the center has been home to the club for more than 25 years, remaining the only full-service ice rink in Pierce County, with hockey, broom ball, public sessions, and both competitive and recreational programs for all ages. The Lakewood Winter Club, with its national reputation for excellence, along with Sprinker Recreation Center, keeps ice skating at the forefront of Pierce County sporting activity.

CHAPTER 36

SKATING: ROLLER

Walt Clifton competed at the King's Roller Palace in downtown Tacoma (SSM, 2003.14.2).

Roller-skating has been around for more than 200 years. British inventor John Joseph Merlin introduced the first pair of skates at a masquerade ball in London in 1760. His was not a good beginning for the sport. Although he was a genius as an inventor, he was a lousy skater; at the party he crashed into a wall, doing serious damage to both a mirror and himself.

It was not until 1937, however, that the first official U.S. Amateur Speed Skating Championship races were held. Dance and figure championship competitions followed two years later. By 1979 roller-skating had become a part of the Pan American Games. Most regional competitions were held at either the Oaks Roller Rink in Portland or the Adams Roller Bowl in Tacoma, because of these venues' long-standing reputation for excellence.

Roger and Dolores Adams met in the 1930s, when he was a floor guard at Earle Page's Midway Skating Rink located at 38th and South Tacoma Way, and their engagement followed various sessions of trick skating together at the rink. They created a roller-skating dynasty whose significance still exists today: daughters Rolores (Skip) and Lanette and son Roger. Skip later bore two additional championship skaters: Tom Peterson and Lin Peterson.

Roger and Dolores Adams started married life managing the Roller Bowl, located near the B&I at 8006 South Tacoma Way, living upstairs with their growing family. Skip Adams Peterson remembered the clamp-on skates of the era. "Young skaters could earn tips by hammering the clamp-ons to skaters' shoes. They used a solid spike or iron to push the shoe soles down under the clamp. You then had a leather strap wrapped from the heel over the instep. If the skaters wore clamp-on skates, they also wore a skate key around their neck to tighten up the clamp attached to their shoes." Don Hamblin, who started skating in 1947 and went on to become a national singles and doubles competitor, earned his tips by helping Fort Lewis soldiers strap on their clamp-ons.

Skip also remembered the pipe organ, played by Jess Curtis. "The organ pipes hung in the middle of the skating floor. It was an open ceiling. One night I spent three hours in the loft above the rink with the organ pipes. I couldn't hear for days!" The music was silenced following a fire in 1951, one that destroyed the entire facility. The Adams family then opened the Tacoma Roller Bowl at 7455 South Tacoma Way, the largest in the state at the time. Roger Adams was honored as a Life Member of the Roller Skating

Patty Berg, a top LPGA player, and Fircrest Head Pro John Rudy (courtesy Fircrest Golf Club).

Patty Curtiss hits a shot (courtesy Fircrest Golf Club).

Jack Walters was a two-time National Left-handed Association champion (SSM, 106.1).

Joan Mahon (shown here) and Ruth Canale were known as the "Brookdale Twins" (courtesy Joan Allard).

Dusty Brett won a 1995 state high school 4A title while competing for Bellarmine Prep before moving on to play at Stanford University (courtesy Fircrest Golf Club).

In the space of only 10 weeks, golfer Ryan Moore won the 2004 NCAA Division I title and four more amateur championships (courtesy University of Nevada–Las Vegas Athletic Department).

Ken Still always remained loyal to his home course at the Fircrest Golf Club, where he worked initially as a caddy and later as an assistant pro (courtesy Fircrest Golf Club).

Marjorie Jefferies Shanaman won the state women's championship in 1928 (courtesy Fred Shanaman).

Ted Elvert (R.) gives a young Clint Names some putting pointers (courtesy Fircrest Golf Club).

Pat Harbottle enjoys a ticker tape parade in Seattle, celebrating her 1955 U.S. Amateur Championships victory (courtesy John and Pat Harbottle).

Teeing off on the first hole at Fircrest Golf Club during the 1960 Carling World Open; Ernie Vossler won the event (SSM, 2002.17.1).

Yumi Modre was the Senior International Vault champion in 1992 (courtesy Puget Sound School of Gymnastics).

Tiffani White won the National Elite Championship title on the balance beam in 1996 over a strong field of future NCAA standouts (courtesy John D. Smith, NASA Gymnastics).

A Wilson High grad who went on to UCLA, Onnie Willis won a share of the all-around title at the 2001 NCAA Women's Gymnastics Championships and earned All-American honors on the parallel bars, beam, and floor (courtesy Puget Sound Gymnastics).

The crew of the U–19 Miss Rocket in 1957, owned by Austin Snell (SSM, 1997.16.4).

Armand Yapachino and his limited hydroplane Joya Mia have been one of the mainstays on the local circuit for years (courtesy Armand Yapachino).

George Henley of Eatonville drove the Miss Pay 'n Pak unlimited hydroplane to the national championship in 1974 and 1975 (SSM).

Neil Andrews of the Tacoma Rockets (SSM).

The Rockets' Dick Milford (lower R.) battles to score (SSM, 1999.16.85).

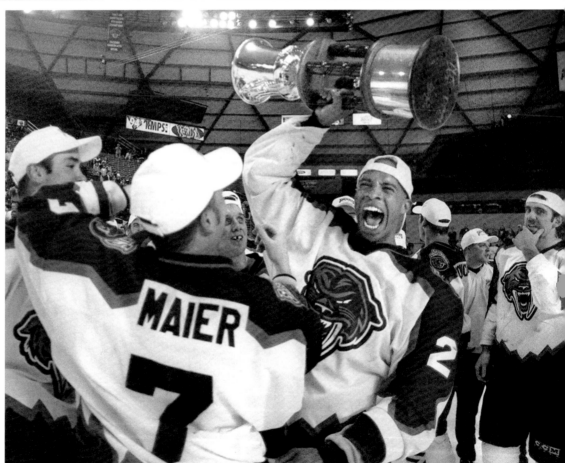

Tacoma Sabercats celebrate winning the West Coast Hockey League championship's Taylor Cup in 1999 (SSM, 2002.10.3).

Joey Johns was a hard-nosed defenseman for the Tacoma Rockets (SSM).

Members of the 1948 Tacoma High School Hockey League All-Star First Team: L. to R., Grant Anderson (Lincoln), Jim Beatty (Lincoln), Russ Fowler (Lincoln), Carl Peterson (Stadium), Gordon Early (Clover Park), Gary Anslow (Bellarmine) (MB).

Cheney Studs' 12-and-under 1953 Pee Wee hockey team in action at the Tacoma Ice Palace (courtesy the Cheney Family).

Official starter Bob "Bouncing Bob" Malley entertains the crowd with his race-start routine—early in his career and, at top of page 345, later on pavement (SSM, 276.2).

Red Ehret competes in the Blue Baron Motorcycle Hill Climb, 1949 (courtesy Dave Allen).

"RED" EHRET

Dan Ceccarini (third from L., in white shirt), also known as "Tacoma Dan," prepares to play motorcycle polo as part of the 1928 Fourth of July festivities at Tacoma Stadium (courtesy Dr. Wayne D. Herstad).

Paul Allen, owner of Allen Motorcycle Sales, spent many hours preparing motorcycles for the Blue Baron Hill Climb (courtesy Dave Allen).

Taking a turn on the dirt tracks was no easy feat (courtesy Dave Allen).

Motorcyclists enjoy a day of riding at Pt. Defiance Park in 1928 (courtesy Dr. Wayne D. Herstad).

Mountain extremes appeal to many Tacoma climbers (courtesy Susan Jerstad).

In 1963 Lute Jerstad became the first person from the state of Washington—and only the second American—to stand on top of Mount Everest's 29,028-foot summit (courtesy Susan Jerstad).

Judy and Jerry Fotheringill were the 1963 U.S. National Pairs Champions (SSM, 2002.43.1).

Patty Hoyt performed for the Ice Follies in 1946 and later married fellow Tacoman figure skater Wayne Earley (TPL).

Scott Davis, 1983 and 1984 U.S. National Champion (SSM, 179).

The comedy team of Larry Hamm (top) and David Riggs (bottom) performed their "In the Park" routine in the 1954 Ice Vogues show produced by Sonja Heinie for Holiday on Ice (SSM, 2002.36.5).

George and Leah Mueller taught at Lakewood Ice Arena, shown here in 1942 (SSM, 2002.30.07).

Lois Secreto and Jimmy Grogan were crowned the 1945 Washington State and Pacific Coast Junior Pairs Champions (SSM, 2002.37.4).

Diane Jacobsen (L.) and Patsy Hamm in 1948 (SSM).

At age 11, Don McLeod won the Juvenile B Speed Skating Division U.S. National Championships; he skated one more season before moving on to yo-yos, motorcycle racing, stock car racing, and sprint car racing (courtesy Don McLeod).

Lin Peterson takes a turn on an outdoor track in Oregon in 1980 (courtesy Rolores "Skip" Peterson).

Northwest Roller Rink operators crowd onto the Steve's Gay 90's Restaurant cable car in 1954, which ran from 54th and South Tacoma Way (courtesy the Adams Family).

Adams Roller Bowl Drill Team, ca. 1960 (courtesy the Adams Family).

Tom Peterson in 1981 (courtesy the Adams Family).

Racing winners in 1964, including Roger Adams (standing, far R..) (courtesy the Adams Family).

1950 College of Puget Sound Ski Team: back row, L. to R., Don Gassaway, Don Gilsdorf, Weldon Howe, Russ Read; front row, L. to R., Don Boesel, Chuck Jorgenson, Chuck Howe, Dr. Bob Springer (courtesy Chuck Howe).

Richie Nelson of Lincoln High School competed in the Tacoma Junior Ski Association's boys' championships at Paradise Valley (courtesy Joe LaPorte).

The Tacoma News Tribune ski school staff readies for a busy day at Crystal Mountain, ca. 1960s (courtesy Joe LaPorte).

David Krussow was a national soap box derby champion in 1966 (SSM, 2029).

The 1946 soap box derby race on what was then a new course, down Sixth Avenue from Jackson Street towards the Narrows Bridge (MB).

Frank Paige (in R. car) at the start of a 1946 soap box derby race (MB).

The FC Royals 77 team won the 1998 U18 National Championship under coach Brian Van Blommestein, displaying the obligatory "We're #1" sign, and 13 of its players from Tacoma–Pierce County went on to play Division I soccer in college (courtesy Brian Van Blommestein).

Tara Bilanski of Puyallup High was a three-time team MVP at the UW and ranked in the top four in virtually every statistical category (courtesy University of Washington).

The Heidelberg Soccer team (courtesy Norm Ruffner).

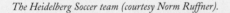

The 1934 Whetstone Soccer club played in a Seattle league: front row, L. to R., Henry Hademan, Jimmy Harrison Sr., Bob Marten, child mascot Ockie Larsen Jr., Oscar Larsen, John Marten; middle row, L. to R., Jimmy Harrison Jr., John Dobbs, John Wilhelm, Sparky Borgen; back row, L. to R., Dr. Whetstone, Eddie Colbo, Sonny Bailey, Carl Wilhelm (courtesy the Bill Bailey Family).

Winston Del Llano of the Tacoma Tides warms up with a few quick drills (SSM , 2002.4.30).

A Tacoma Stars trading card featuring Preki (SSM).

Joey Waters' trading card (SSM).

The 1963–64 Tacoma Soccer Club Juniors, coached by Frank Hall (courtesy Frank Hall).

Pacific Lutheran University's title-winning players in action (PLU).

John Rockway, Tacoma Teamsters pitcher during the 1943 season, warms up prior to game (courtesy Aldyth Rockway).

The 1951 Tacoma Fuelerettes (also known as Pacific Mutual Fuels): front row, L. to R., Donna Brown, Dorothy Anderson, Shirley Soggie, Joyce Jones; middle row, L. to R., Kathryn McHugh, Patsy Strachan, Ellen Schmidt; back row, L. to R., Delores Benjamin, Gloria Malley, Mary Jane Brammann, coach Bill Stavig, Patsy Hankinson, Sue Kauth, Margaret Heinrick (courtesy Pat Strachan Stavig).

The Paramount Electric slowpitch team won the Housewives League in 1965 (SSM, 1747).

This Lincoln Furniture fastpitch team from 1947 included: back row, L. to R., Bob Ryan, Jim Sulenes, owner/sponsor Ralph Johnson, unknown, Rod Giske; front row, L. to R., Howie Martin, Lorne "Shorty" Campbell, Ray Mahnkey, Chuck Horjes, Roy Murphy, Tip Lockard (courtesy the Cindy Lumsden Family).

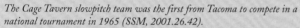

The Cage Tavern slowpitch team was the first from Tacoma to compete in a national tournament in 1965 (SSM, 2001.26.42).

Miriam Smith Greenwood was a member of the 1976 U.S. Olympic swim team (courtesy Dick Hannula Sr.).

Wilson High grad Kaye Hall won a gold medal in the 1968 Olympic Games (SSM, 223).

Chuck Richards at the finish of the pentathlon's swimming event at the 1972 Summer Olympic Games in Munich, where he established new Olympic and world records with a 3 minutes 21.7 seconds for the 300-meter pentathlon freestyle (courtesy Chuck L. Richards).

Megan Quann, double gold medalist at the 2000 Summer Olympic Games in Sydney, Australia (SSM, 2001.4.3).

In 1963 Mike Stauffer (L.) and Chuck Richards became the first Tacoma swimmers to qualify for the U.S. National Senior Championship Meet (courtesy Dick Hannula Sr.).

Janet Buchan Elway represented the U.S. in the World University Games in Mexico City and won the 400-meter individual medley (courtesy Dick Hannula Sr.).

Dick Hannula, coach and founder of the Tacoma Swim Club (courtesy Dick Hannula, Sr.).

Dave Trageser, a Puyallup High graduate, holds the single-season record for most wins at Pacific Lutheran University with a 34–1 record in 1978 (PLU).

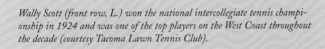

Wally Scott (front row, L.) won the national intercollegiate tennis championship in 1924 and was one of the top players on the West Coast throughout the decade (courtesy Tacoma Lawn Tennis Club).

U.S. Open mixed doubles champion Pat Galbraith played his high school tennis at Bellarmine Prep (SSM, 1269).

Dana LeDuc, a 1971 Washington High grad, took second in the shotput at the NCAA Championships in 1974 (courtesy Dana LeDuc).

Jack Higgins was the best collegiate sprinter in the state in 1962 (UPS).

Coach John Sharp stands with his 1954 Lincoln High 880-meter relay team: L. to R., Vic Eshpeter, Luther Carr, Jim Jones, Dick Hagen (SSM, 263.10).

Pole vaulting brothers Mike (L.) and Casey Carrigan (SSM, 2001.26.33).

Vince Goldsmith of Mt. Tahoma High School set the state shotput record with a toss of 60 feet 11 inches in 1977, a high school record that still stands today (courtesy Vince Goldsmith).

John Fromm won the "Triple Crown" of U.S. javelin throwing—national titles in NAIA, NCAA, and AAU competition—in the late 1950s (PLU).

Jim Daulley lead the Wilson Rams track team to four state titles (1975, 1978, 1980, 1981); two of his top runners were Calvin Kennon (L.) and Darrel Robinson (R.) (courtesy Jim Daulley).

Chuck Richards at the finish of the 1500–meter run while competing in the 1972 Olympic pentathlon event (courtesy Chuck L. Richards).

Herman Brix (R.) with John Kuck (L.) and Emil Hirschfeld at the 1928 Summer Olympic Games in Amsterdam (courtesy Herman Brix).

Gertrude Wilhelmsen (R.) gets ready to mount a training bar on board the S.S. Manhattan, en route to the1936 Olympic Games (courtesy Gertrude Wilhelmsen).

Stewart Junior High School track team with Howard Olson (back row, third from L.) (SSM, 2002.25.20).

Dave Williams earned 12 varsity letters at Lincoln High School in football, basketball, track, and the decathlon and was the 1963 state high hurdles champion (SSM, 2001.33.5).

Fife High School's 1992 volleyball team at state finals: L. to R., Tina Buck (obscured), Kira Grass (#44), Lenny Llanos (standing), Angie Beauchene (#21), coach Jan Kirk, Sarah Copps (#14), Sarah Silvernail, Heidi Pasinetti (#10), Rhonda Austin (obscured), Amber Borgamanerio (obscured), Frankie Fitterer, Shawnna Sessler (courtesy Jan Kirk).

The first local to play volleyball at a Division I school, Julie Kurrus spikes the ball for the University of Washington, where she was a walk-on who then earned a scholarship (courtesy Julie Kurrus).

Puyallup High grad Cristal Morrison was selected the Gatorade Player of the Year in Washington in 2004 (courtesy Mike and Dianne Morrison).

Sarah Silvernail was a standout performer at WSU after leading the Fife Strojans to a state championship in 1992 (courtesy Washington State University).

Jeff Gotcher sits firm in 1987 state semi-finals (courtesy Jeff Gotcher).

Sumner's David Olmstead was state champion in the 135-pound division in 1984 (courtesy David Olmstead).

The 120-pound 1953 state champion Vic Eshpeter of Lincoln High School receives the Harry Sorenson Memorial Award as the tournament's outstanding wrestler from Bill Tomaras, Washington State College coach. (courtesy Vic Eshpeter).

Frank Stojack was crowned King of Wrestling in 1953 (SSM).

Larry Gotcher at the 1988 NCAA Division I championship semi-finals (courtesy Larry Gotcher).

The annual Mat Classic, the high school wrestling state championships, at the Tacoma Dome (courtesy Washington Interscholastic Activities Association).

Moonglow III, owned by Dave Nielsen (courtesy Ken Ollar and Guy Hoppen).

Rink Operators of America because of his local and national contribution to the sport. The Roller Bowl remained in operation until 1984, when high rents led to the sale of the property, which was converted to a used-car lot.

Of Dolores and Roger's two daughters, Lanette was the championship skater. At five years old, she won the Primary Girls Freestyle Championships and was the first Northwest roller skater to win the U.S. National Roller Skating Championships, in 1949 and 1950. "Her skating was highlighted by her fiery red hair and the speed and grace with which she could spin," sister Skip remembered. "Her expression was exciting and you loved to see her perform." Lanette went on to win nationals in Elementary Girls Artistic Singles in Cleveland, Ohio, in 1952 and nationals in Juvenile Girls Speed in Washington, D.C., in 1954. With her sister Skip as coach in 1957, Lanette placed second at the national championship in Novice Ladies Artistic Singles in Lincoln, Nebraska. She married Ted Werner, known for his basketball achievements at Washington State University and with the amateur national powerhouse Plywood Tacoma team. Together they owned National Skate Distributors.

Skip Adams Peterson coached for 25 years. Her primary focus at the Tacoma Roller Bowl was coaching speed skaters such as Jim Flaherty, Steve Clemons, Mara Jones, Dana

Lanette Adams, 1949 freestyle national champion (courtesy the Adams Family).

Fred Johnson was the Northwest Speed Skating Champion in 1922 (courtesy Marjorie Johnson).

Jones, Desi Lewis, K. C. Boutiette, and Doug Glass. But her most outstanding skating accomplishments were her two children, Tom and Lin, who skated all the way to the Pan American Games.

Tom Peterson started speed racing at age three and won his first national title two years later. In 1967, only eight, he won the Juvenile D speed competitions at nationals. He continued to compete, winning eight world championships along the way, events that took him to Italy, Argentina, Belgium, Colombia, Brazil, and New Zealand. Sister Lin Peterson was also a speed skater. "She could keep up with and beat most of the boys in her age group," her mother proudly recalled, and her ability led to numerous state, regional, and national championships.

Brother and sister also competed as a team in mixed relay speed skating events and were recognized as the most outstanding duo in the sport worldwide. For them, racing did not necessarily take place on a paved track, as one might imagine. When the two won their first world championship, in Como, Italy, in 1979, the course was on a paved road in a park with numerous winding turns.

Their crowning achievement was the 1979 Pan American Games held in Puerto Rico. To get there, Tom Peterson first won top honors at the 41st annual U.S. Amateur Roller Skating Championships, held in Lincoln, Nebraska. Representing the Tacoma Roller Bowl Speed Club, he won four gold medals and defeated Chris Snyder, then defending champion. Lin won the Junior Ladies Overall Division title by setting three new speed records. Together, Tom and Lin won the Senior Two Mixed 3,000-meter Relay.

Tom and Lin's arrival in Puerto Rico marked the first time roller-skating was an event at the Pan American Games. Tom won four gold medals, two in track competitions, one in cross country, and one—with Chris Snyder—in track relay. Lin received a bronze in track competition and a silver in the track relay. Following these victories, the two continued to compete and as a team won the Senior Two Mixed Relay event at the U.S. Championship five times.

Although the Adams family dominated the sport, Pierce County produced many other national champions, as well as successful coaches such as Chuck Reece, Rich Schuyler, Lanny Werner, Pat Pattison, Helen Lisk, and Tom Torgesen. Don Norlen, who previously trained with Skip Adams Peterson, became an artistic coach and guided Pat Shannon and Jim Collyer to singles championship competition.

Other rinks in Pierce County included Puyallup's Tiffanys, University Place's Skate King, the Summit at Fort Lewis, and Spinning Wheels in Spanaway. King's Roller Rink opened on 27th and Pacific Avenue in 1931, and Walt Clifton, who was a "skate boy" at the time, remembers Japanese sailors holding skating parties at the rink prior to World War II.

Skating rinks formed clubs and also held their own dancing revues. In 1959 Tacoma Dance and Figure Club presented the "Paris in Orbit" show at the Tacoma Roller Bowl as a fund-raiser for skaters wanting to compete nationally. That same year, Rita Gardner, a Clover Park High School senior, became Roller Skating Queen for the state of Washington at the 15th annual Amateur Roller Skating Championships.

Not all championship competitions ended on a happy note. Don McLeod remembered how his championship win was actually lost by a last-minute shift in the finish line during the 1952 national competition in Denver, a move that occurred without telling all of the racers. McLeod crossed the original finish line first, but lost the race because he had not been told of the change. The experience soured him on the sport. A sixth grader at Park Elementary School at the time, Don quit and turned to a different kind of racing—cars and motorcycles—where he enjoyed considerable success (see chapter 6, Automobile Racing, and chapter 32, Motorcycle Racing).

Roller-skating remains a popular amateur sport and form of recreation in Pierce County. Clamp-on skates with keys are no more; carrying their precious keys, skaters now negotiate the pathways of local parks on inline skates. That form of recreational exercise might herald the beginnings of a new championship skater.

Lanette Adams and dance partner Paul Snyder in 1954 (courtesy the Adams Family).

In 1974 the Adam's Tacoma Roller Bowl was located at 7455 South Tacoma Way (courtesy the Adams Family).

CHAPTER 37

SKIING

Gretchen Kunigk-Fraser wearing her team uniform for the 1948 Winter Olympics in St. Moritz, Switzerland (SSM, 1926).

On July 30, 1917, the *Tacoma News Tribune* reported the successful completion of a ski-jumping tournament held on Alta Vista, a knoll located above Paradise Inn on Mount Rainier. This was the first recorded snow sport competition in Pierce County, and it brought ski jumpers from as far away as Norway. Indeed, Tacoma's O. M. Overn, who organized the event, maintained that most of the 50 spectators that year were Norwegians who had relatives or friends competing in the tournament. The winner was Olga Bolstad of Seattle, but Tacoma's O. P. Saether came in third. (Throughout the first years of ski jumping on Mount Rainier, women competed alongside men.)

With the success of this first tournament, local enthusiasts of the sport formed the Northwest Ski Club and sponsored a second competition in 1918, when Tacoman Sigurd Johnson defeated Olga Bolstad. Pierce County's Hilmar Nelsen placed third. "So successful was the meet," reported the *Tacoma News Tribune*, "and so enthusiastic was the crowd that made the long trip into the snow lands that those in charge have determined to make this an annual sport classic."

The Rainier ski-jumping tournament continued to attract competitors and spectators from outside the region, even though conditions were not always ideal. Some years torrential rains made the ski-jumping slope a soggy mess. Other years, unseasonable snows blocked snowplows, forcing participants and observers to hike through the drifts to Paradise. Whatever the weather conditions, Tacomans claimed the distinction of being one of the few cities in the world that successfully staged a ski tournament in midsummer!

Chris Bakken of Roy was a prize winner in 1920, when competitors and spectators were filmed for the first time. In the next decade, the ski-jumping event became an arena reserved for men, with women and girls participating in what the newspapers called "gliding contests," a reference most likely to cross-country skiing. Likewise, a 1922 newspaper report of the ski-jump classic noted there was to be a 5-mile ski race. As with the gliding contests for women, this race was probably a cross-country event, indicating that local skiers were becoming more interested in speed competitions.

The 1930s were the heyday of competitive skiing on Mount Rainier. Clubs flourished: the Pacific Northwest Ski Association (PNSA) organized in 1930, followed by the

Washington Ski Club (WSC) in 1933 and the Tacoma Ski Club in 1934. WSC sponsored the first Silver Skis Race on Mount Rainier, in 1934, along a course from Camp Muir to Paradise Valley. The competitors left Paradise shortly after daylight for the almost three-hour trek to Camp Muir.

"It was a ski racing spectacle never seen before or since," reported *Seattle Post-Intelligencer* sports editor Royal Brougham. "Sixty contestants starting together at the sound of a shotgun, plunging, poling, falling and flying from Camp Muir at Rainier's 10,000-foot level to Paradise Lodge, more than 4,500 feet and four miles below." The winner was Don Fraser, in a time of just under 10 minutes. In the ensuing years, the Silver Skis Race was considered one of the major races in the country, drawing champions from all over the skiing world. It ran until 1942, when it ceased operations during World War II, and then continued again from 1946 to 1949.

In 1935 the National Ski Championships and the Olympic tryouts both were held on Mount Rainier. But skiers demanded a lift; so, following approval from the Department of the Interior, Chauncey Griggs and David Hellyer, who represented a private corporation managing tourist facilities in the national park, funded its installation. The rope tow, fueled by Ford V-eight engines and wheels, made ski competition on the mountain a whole lot easier.

Stadium High School and College of Puget Sound (now UPS) graduate Shirley McDonald learned to ski on Mount Rainier, winning the women's national downhill champi-

Male skier airborne on the slopes of Mount Rainier (SSM).

MOUNT RAINIER SKIERS IN THE MOVIES

The slopes of Mount Rainier were the setting for several motion pictures during the early years of the film industry, providing local skiers an opportunity to have small roles or act as stand-ins for the stars. The first chance came in 1937, when director Sidney Lanfield chose the back side of Alta Vista as the setting for the Sonja Heinie—Tyrone Power film "Thin Ice." The movie featured Heinie as an ice-skating instructor who falls in love with Power, playing an incognito prince, and proved to be one of the former Olympic gold medalist's most successful films.

There are scenes in the movie that portray both Sonja Heinie and Tyrone Power skiing, something that neither was able to do. So local skier Otto Lang, who started the Rainier National Park Ski School in 1937 at Paradise, came to the rescue and doubled for Power. Wade Perrow stood in for Heinie on the slopes, persuaded by his brother Marshall, who had joined Lang in the Rainier ski school endeavor.

Twentieth-Century Fox's production "Ski Slopes" began filming during World War II. Twelve Northwest skiers had parts in the movie including Joe LaPorte—a member of the 1941 Bellarmine Prep ski team—Dottie Warter, Elaine Solum, and Tacoma News Tribune reporter Howard Clifford, who played the character of Oscar in the film.

Clifford's reminiscences regarding the production might indicate one reason why the movie cannot be found in video catalogs today: "I remember that the cameraman was called away to military service before they got too far into the project, leaving Jack Kuhne, the producer, to do both jobs. Well, Jack loved his Scotch and needed it to get through the ordeal. The only problem was that it was during prohibition and ration cards were required to purchase liquor. So, Jack sent Joe LaPorte and myself to Tacoma to round up some scotch. We were ingenious! We went to the Police Department and came away with 12 cards that had been confiscated from individuals currently residing in jail. Filming happily continued…"

---

onship as well as the downhill, slalom, and combined in the Far West Kandahar event. The only female to win the Women's Silver Skis Championships twice, McDonald was a member of the 1940 U.S. Olympic team, but competitions were cancelled because of the onset of World War II.

The war years also introduced a new type of skier to the slopes of Mount Rainier. The National Ski Patrol had been formed in 1938 to rescue stranded snow enthusiasts. Within two years, the patrol was given a military function, with special units incorporated into the Army at Fort Lewis. The 87th Regiment of skiers camped at Longmire and were trained in winter combat on Mount Rainier before becoming one of three regiments to form the 10th Mountain Division in Europe.

When Shirley McDonald trained on Mount Rainier before the war, her coach was Merritt Cookingham, a graduate of Stadium High School. He began teaching the sport at Paradise in the mid-1930s under Jim Gillespie. Following the war, he continued under Marshall Perrow. Merritt's most famous student was Gretchen Kunigk Fraser.

Gretchen Kunigk was born in Tacoma on February 11, 1919, and at the time of her death in 1994 was still known as America's Lady of Skiing. Her interest in the sport undoubtedly came from her Norwegian mother, who campaigned for the development of public skiing on Mount Rainier. Prior to Gretchen's marriage in 1939 to Donald Fraser, a member of the 1936 Olympic ski team, she attended UPS and became a member of the school's team.

In 1940 Gretchen Fraser was named to the Olympic ski team, along with McDonald. Even though the games were not held that year, Fraser competed nationally during this time, winning the downhill and alpine combined championships in 1941 and the national slaloms in 1942. Other victories included the Silver Belt in Sugar Bowl, California, and the Snow Cup at Alta, Utah.

Fraser made headlines throughout the world at the 1948 Olympic games in St. Moritz, Switzerland: she became the first American skier ever to win a gold medal. She followed her top honor in the slalom with a silver medal in the alpine combined event. And in 1952 she served as an advisor/manager for the 1952 U.S. Olympic ski team.

Although Fraser retired from the sport following her Olympic victories, skiing always remained a part of her life. Prior to the 1948 games, Fraser taught riding, skiing, and swimming to injured war veterans. Following the war, her interest in using sports as a rehabilitation tool was extended to the Special Olympics. Her lifetime of commitment led to her induction in 1957 into the first class of the Tacoma–Pierce County Sports Hall of Fame, the National Ski Hall of Fame in 1960, and the UPS Sports Hall of Fame in 1989.

While Fraser was winning honors on the slopes in 1948, Chuck Howe, a member of UPS's ski team from 1946 to 1950, was helping the campus ski club acquire the Deep Creek Lodge Recreation Area. In order to have a place to

Hiking the 2-½ mile trek from Narada Falls to Paradise to ski in 1934 was a long and slow endeavor (SSM, Loc. 301.11).

train, the college student body purchased this recreational site on Forest Service property, which consisted of two lodges and seven cabins. Howe spearheaded the acquisition and was appointed student manager to oversee the area, a highly unusual arrangement for a college at the time.

Later, Howe was also instrumental in organizing intercollegiate ski meets that included both UPS and Pacific Lutheran College (now PLU) in the competitions. The UPS Loggers were aided by the appointment of Shirley McDonald and her husband, Martin Fopp, one of the world's top competitive skiers and a former national downhill champion in Switzerland, as instructors. "With the appointment of the Fopps," reported Seattle's Dan Coughlin, "Northwest skiing gets a shot in the arm. If other ski towns get the same idea, maybe Washington will take its rightful place among the leaders of the sport."

Martin and Shirley Fopp (MB).

Chuck Jorgensen, a 1947 Stadium High graduate, was one of UPS's skiers at this time. After college he enlisted in the Army in the Counter Intelligence Corps and was stationed in Japan during the Korean War. Jorgensen and the First Cavalry Division, of which he was a part, hosted the Far East Ski Championships in 1952. Jorgensen had his skis and boots shipped to Japan, practiced constantly, and won both the downhill and slalom events.

Howe and his wife, Jane Creswell Howe, later began teaching at the Tacoma Ski School, which had been rejuvenated following World War II. Joe LaPorte, certified by PNSA as an advanced instructor, served as the chief instructor for the school, which was sponsored by the *Tacoma News Tribune* and the Metropolitan Park District. LaPorte served in this capacity from 1952 to 1965, with Don Gilsdorf as his assistant; Stan Olsen then took over the reins for 10 years.

The ski school was an incredible success. Free lessons were given to more than 100 students per day on the weekends, and participants paid only for their transportation and insurance. Another unique ski program was Sunday high school ski parties sponsored by the local PTAs, Tacoma Police Department, and the Tacoma Athletic Commission (TAC). The program was initially offered only to Tacoma high school and junior high students and later expanded to include others in Pierce County.

The first year, the ski school was held at Paradise Valley, but it later moved to other Washington locations such as Snoqualmie Summit, Ski Acres, and Crystal Mountain. According to LaPorte, "We'd make the kids get their gear on and then sidestep up the hill to pack down the slopes first. Our goal was to introduce youngsters to skiing—not to develop hotshot champions." After leaving the Tacoma Ski School, Joe started up the Cascade Ski School in the late 1960s, which was geared to adults who wanted to ski midweek to avoid the crowds. (He subsequently sold the business to Shirley and Martin Fopp, who ran the very successful school for many years.)

A core of highly qualified and certified instructors taught thousands of youngsters from the 1930s through the 1970s. Some of these instructors included Marshall Perrow, Wade Perrow, Merritt Cookingham, Dave Cookingham, Joe LaPorte, Shirley and Martin Fopp, Les Gilsdorf, Don

haeuser executive Everett Griggs II, and Dave Grossard, then a timber cruiser for the White River Lumber Company. The group's first choice was Corral Pass, a mountainous area used to train soldiers in cross-country skiing during World War II. In the eyes of those planning a new resort, the hills were not challenging enough for sport skiing. They therefore turned their attention to Forest Service land a few miles south of Corral Pass: the land surrounded an old mining claim near the headwaters of Silver Creek.

Even though promoters considered the site ideal, it was not until 1955 that investors from both Seattle and Tacoma formed Crystal Mountain, Inc., and produced the study needed to convince the Forest Service that the location was ideal for a ski resort. Once "persuaded the area could support

Joe LaPorte and another ski school instructor debate conditions on race day (courtesy Joe LaPorte).

Gilsdorf, Stan Olsen, Dennis LaPorte, Larry LaPorte, Dick Vanderflute, Mary and Jim Monroe, Jack and Janine Tangney, Joanne Torgerson, Eddie Aylsworth, Bob Mick, Rick Myers, Benny Robertson, Dinah Effinger, Dick Kilham, LeRoy Ritchie, Mary Ambjor, Don Hermsen, Ron Bloom, Gordon Bostwick, John Ditter, Chuck and Jane Howe, Lindy Aliment, Buster Arenes, Nancy Creswell, and Richie Nelson.

In spite of enthusiasm for and the success of the Tacoma Ski School, the days of Mount Rainier's rope tow were numbered. Throughout the postwar years, a constant campaign urged the Department of the Interior to approve the development of a public ski resort on the mountain. The national parks, however, were not conceived for this kind of use, and Rainier was expected to be preserved as a wilderness. The creation of ski slopes on its hills would damage its pristine nature. Snow sport enthusiasts would have to find another location.

The quest began in 1949, when Seattle's Mel Borgersen began looking for a site in the Cascade Mountains. He was soon joined by Tacomans Mary Lee Griggs, wife of Weyer-

WATER SKIING

Joe LaPorte was an avid snow skier and a member of the Bellarmine ski team, but he thoroughly enjoyed trading in his snow skis for water skis each spring. LaPorte first started up the Totem Ski Club on American Lake in 1950, which served the needs of both water and snow skiers. Arnie Forsberg put the money down, and the club purchased a clubhouse and dock on Silcox Island in American Lake. They then raised funds to pay back Forsberg by sponsoring dances or putting on water carnivals and shows throughout Pierce County, such as at the Browns Point Improvement Club's annual salmon bake or the Tacoma Athletic Commission's water carnival.

LaPorte became very accomplished in performing various water-skiing maneuvers and tricks for the crowds. Other skiers who participated in the water shows included Lloyd Gammersvik, Bob Hentze, Charles Schuler, Harold Seaberg, Dale Andahl, Howard Clifford, and Don Gasaway. All eight men were granted life memberships in the American Water Ski Association, which is also affiliated with the International Water Ski Union of Geneva, Switzerland. Women who took part in the water shows included Norma Holt, Lucille Fleischmann, Karen Peterson, Ethel Compton, and Junise Nelson.

Skiers (L. to R.) Jim Grenier, Ralph Laudin, and Joe LaPorte, members of the Totem Ski Club, practice on American Lake for an upcoming water carnival appearance (courtesy Joe LaPorte).

From Mount Rainier to Crystal Mountain, and from the first ski jump in 1917 to later-day racing, Pierce County's winter slopes have been the training ground for young Olympic hopefuls. But more important, thousands of men, women, and children have learned not only to ski, but to enjoy and appreciate our winter wilderness.

The Flying Kilometer, temporarily grounded, on Mount Rainier in 1936 (SSM, 301.31).

a resort," explained the *News Tribune* reporter Skip Card, "the Forest Service in 1958 sought proposals for what it called the Crystal Mountain Winter Sports Area." Four years later, the facility was ready for snow sports enthusiasts. At the time, when then Governor Albert Rosellini cut the ribbon to open the new resort on November 22, 1962, he announced that "they will soon be calling Sun Valley 'the Crystal Mountain of Idaho.'"

Bill Coghill was another founder of Crystal Mountain. He had moved to Washington from Wisconsin in 1959 to work for Weyerhaeuser. He brought his love of skiing with him and joined the Tacoma Mountaineers. When he learned about the creation of a ski resort in the county, he offered to help by acquiring the topographic maps needed to design the ski courses for the resort and to aid the Mountain and Ski Patrol. He was also a member of the patrol for 23 years. Coghill helped on the first World Cup race held at the resort in 1966, coached Phil Mahre and Steve Mahre of Yakima when they were 13 years old, and even at 75 remains active as a coach and racer.

Skiers take a break to gaze at Rainier, ca. 1940 (SSM).

CHAPTER 38

SOAPBOX DERBY

David West won "best designed car" in 1968 at the Soap Box Derby National event; this racer is on display at the Shanaman Sports Museum (SSM, 1184).

There was a time in Pierce County when the most-anticipated event of the year was not the Daffodil Festival or the Fourth of July air show and fireworks spectacular. From 1936 to 1973, the one event the entire area rallied around was the annual Soapbox Derby. For nearly four decades the race, sponsored primarily by the *Tacoma News Tribune* and local Chevrolet dealers, gave area boys a chance to design and race soapbox cars.

Praise for the event was communitywide. In a 1954 letter to the newspaper, a writer commented that "the Soapbox Derby makes every boy who participates a better citizen for tomorrow. He learns how to plan, how to use tools and to complete a project he has started. We regard every boy a winner, regardless of where his racer finishes." The next year the *News Tribune* called the building and racing of soapbox cars an "example of community teamwork in building better boys. The Soapbox Derby gives boys a chance to join up with a constructive gang. There's no better way to keep boys interested and busy. And busy boys are better boys."

The sport began in 1933 in Dayton, Ohio, during the early years of the Depression. When *Dayton Daily News* photographer Myron E. Scott witnessed three boys racing homemade engineless cars down a hill, he proposed a formal race with a prize for the winner. In time, the sport gathered interest and expanded outside the Dayton area, especially after Scott convinced Chevrolet to sponsor the derby as a national youth promotion. Within a year, and with the *Daily News* encouraging city newspapers to sponsor the local races, winners from 34 cities traveled to Dayton for the first national championship. Sponsorship interest from the United States' four major tire manufacturers, all located in Akron, prompted relocation of the soapbox derby headquarters to that city, where they were staged since 1935.

Tacoma entered the competition in 1936. The city's first champion was Ellsworth Staley, a 14-year-old Gray Junior High School student. Eugene Riggs and Harold Freiter followed as winners in 1937 and 1938. Contestants used the South Yakima Street hill between 25th and 29th Streets as their racing venue. The year Freiter won, the Tacoma Goodrich Silvertown store provided the repair pit near the starting ramp, and National Guards installed a communication system to connect the starting and finishing lines. Jerry Geehan and Mac McAllister broadcast a play-by-play of the race action on radio station KVI.

"Derby Hill" continued as a racecourse until the outbreak of World War II in 1941. The sport was discontinued during the hostilities but was resumed again in 1946 at a new location: the roadway running from Jackson Avenue toward the newly collapsed Narrows Bridge. The hill was a steep one, and "several rows of heavy tarps were hung from cables to slow down the racers," 1946 champion Frank Paige remembered. Some of the "racers went all the way through the first two sets of tarps before coming to a stop."

Paige entered the Soapbox Derby in 1946 because of the urging of his older brother, Dick, who had missed the opportunity because of the war. Noting that the course was rather steep, Earl Paige was determined to help his son overcome any fears and get used to the course ahead of time. He tied a rope around the back of the soapbox car and then attached it to the front of his '38 Chevrolet so it would serve as the brakes for the racer. They did a trial run, and his dad then pulled Frank back to the top for another practice run. They quickly discovered that the brake system was inadequate, and minor adjustments were made. "A few more trips down the course and I got rid of my fear of the hill real quick," recounted Frank. "I honestly believe that those practice runs were a big factor in my victory. Not being afraid of that hill was the best preparation my dad could have given me."

Use of the Narrows Bridge hill for derby racing lasted until 1948, the year former Pierce County Executive Joe Stortini won the event when he was a boy. When plans were completed for constructing the second Narrows Bridge, derby sponsors had to find another place for the race. Their choice was on St. Helens Avenue, with the starting ramp in front of the *Tacoma News Tribune* offices at Seventh and the finish line just down the street at Ninth and St. Helens/Broadway. The next year, they raced on the South 38th Street hill from Lincoln Heights toward Tacoma's baseball stadium, located near South Tacoma Way.

In spite of changing locations, the championship race continued to be a local community event. In 1953, for example—the year Duane Hopper won the trip to the national contest—the phonographic industry's Music Performance Trust funded a concert performed by the Tacoma musicians' union and radio station KTNT broadcast the derby.

Life was also short for the South 38th Street site, but only because the Kiwanis organization had completed a new, permanent home for the annual race in 1957. Kiwanis Derby Hill, located at South 19th Street and Bantz Boule-

Kiwanis Derby Hill, located by Cheney Stadium, was the last site of the local soap box derby races (SSM, 1188).

TACOMA'S SOAPBOX DERBY CHAMPIONS, 1936–1973

1936	Ellsworth Staley	1957	Jimmy Stewart
1937	Dr. F. Eugene Riggs	1958	Dave Marzano
1938	Edwin "Harold" Freiter	1959	Warren Lusier
1939	Dave Gabbert	1960	John West (second place at nationals)
1940	Don Davenport	1961	Stan Gorski
1941	Edward (Ned) Bliss	1962	Gary Marzano
1946	Frank Paige	1963	Joel Gorski (ninth place at nationals)
1947	David Baird	1964	Greg Schumacher (national champion)
1948	Joe Stortini	1965	Don Campbell (fourth place at nationals)
1949	Duane Swanson	1966	David Krussow (national champion)
1950	Harold Jardeen	1967	Rick Petereson
1951	Richard Johnson	1968	David West
1952	*No race due to newspaper strike*	1969	James Maddock
1953	Duane Hopper	1970	Scott Corvin
1954	Harold Harvey	1971	Brent Michaelson
1955	Don Frederickson	1972	Bob Sargent Jr.
1956	Bobby Booth	1973	Gary Mahoney

vard near present-day Cheney Stadium, cost $100,000 to construct. The track was modeled after the one in Akron, allowing racers to reach speeds of 30 miles per hour. With a new track that both boys and girls could practice on, Tacoma racers began to make a name for themselves at the national championships.

The competition in Akron was fierce, and racers had to qualify through five or six heats before reaching the final championship run. John West finished second in 1960 and was awarded the best-constructed racer in the country. In 1964 Greg Schumacher, age 14, won the national title and with it a $7,500 college scholarship and an all-expense-paid trip to the New York World's Fair. When he returned home, Tacoma held a ceremony in his honor. Schumacher credited the intense competition of Tacoma's race in preparing him for the All-American Derby. "Getting through Tacoma gave us confidence for nationals," he told local derby historian Gary Brooks. "To win in Tacoma was a lot tougher than in many other cities."

Two years after Schumacher received his hero's welcome, David Krussow received the same treatment. When he returned to Tacoma as the 1966 national champion, he was given a parade and police escort to the top of Kiwanis Derby Hill, where he greeted his well-wishers.

Soapbox Derby racing was a sport that united fathers and sons and established friendships that could last a lifetime. The Marzanos were one such family. Jim raced in the second annual derby in 1937. Later on he became director of workshops sponsored by the Kiwanis, and from 1950 to 1973 he personally instructed numerous racers throughout the area. "The derby was more than a hobby for me," Marzano remembered. "When I was 12, I was drawn to it. I met probably 80 percent of the friends I have today through the Soapbox Derby." Altogether, he advised 20 boys who won Tacoma titles. John West was the first of his pupils to place at the All-American Derby.

Two of Jim's pupils were his sons, and both became Tacoma champions. David Marzano placed second in the

Tacoma race in 1956 and 1957 and won it all in 1958. At the national in Akron, David placed second in his heat, losing to the eventual national champion from Muncie, Indiana. Four years later, in 1962, brother Gary won the Tacoma title. However, after he won his preliminary heat with the fastest time of the day at the national championships, his racer was sabotaged by another participant's father.

The Campbell family provided another Soapbox Derby legend. Clarence Campbell and his sons were involved with the event for 30 years. Clarence competed from 1936 to 1938. He then advised his sons when they decided to build cars and participate. Jim raced from 1955 to 1957 and Larry competed in 1961. Youngest son Don was the Tacoma champion in 1965 and placed fourth in the finals in Akron, Ohio.

The Gorskis and the West brothers were also family winners. Stan Gorski took top honors in the local race in 1961; his brother Joel won the Tacoma race in 1963 and went on to place ninth at the national championships. John West, the local winner in 1960, made the most of his visit to Akron, placing second overall, winning the Fastest Heat Award, and being recognized with the Best Constructed Racer Award. Then a student at Curtis Junior High, West also received a $4,000 college scholarship. In 1968 not only was his brother David crowned the Tacoma champion, but in Akron he brought home the trophy for the Best Designed Racer as well, which is currently on display at the Shanaman Sports Museum at the Tacoma Dome.

By the 1970s, however, the popularity of the Soapbox Derby was waning. The All-American Derby is still run each summer in Akron, but the attention it now receives is nowhere near what it used to be. The loss of corporate sponsors is the main reason: Locally, the *Tacoma News Tribune* dropped its sponsorship in 1968. Nationally, Chevrolet abandoned the sport four years later. "With today's changing lifestyles," explained Chevrolet general sales manager Robert D. Lund, "young people in America have different needs, attitudes, and interests. To keep pace with the changes, we must develop creative new programs that are responsive to

CHAPTER SPONSORED BY
DR. JOHN WEST:

Dr. John West says he learned a lot from his youth spent racing soap box derby cars. He was introduced to—and got hooked on—the sport after admiring a neighbor's derby car. "I was fascinated by the lines and beauty of it." He later worked on his own cars side-by-side with his father Roy, who, he says, "taught me how to see a vision come true, how to obtain a goal, and how to do intricate things with my hands."

West spent three years building and racing cars with his father and younger brother, David, who later raced in the All-American Soap Box Derby and won the "best designed racer" award.

In 1960, West had the opportunity to work for a year with coach Jim Marzano, "my soap box derby hero." He admired Marzano's passion and knowledge of the sport and says, "Jim was smart and a winner. Our families have become true friends." West himself excelled and that same year won second place in the All-American Soap Box Derby as well as driving the fastest heat of the day. West also had the fastest average time and won the "best constructed racer" award. It was the most hardware ever won in a single world derby championship, and he became the first Pacific Northwesterner ever to place in that annual competition. He won a $4,000 college scholarship and later spent time working with other soap box derby hopefuls through the Tacoma Athletic Commission. Today he still uses some of the skills he acquired building racers: "Those fine motor skills were the foundation for the needed artistry in my endodontics practice today."

modern attitudes." With Chevrolet's announcement, and as local dealerships followed its lead, other newspapers and civic organizations also ceased to sponsor the event.

It was about this time that Akron derby officials discovered that some competitors were cheating in the designs of the soapbox cars. Among the clearly defined rules that each youngster was to follow when building a racer, one was that only $40 could be spent in its construction. Some contestants, however, were spending up to $2,000, using illegal molds and welded parts to make the car sturdier and electromagnetic boosters to provide an extra punch at the start.

There is no evidence that Tacoma's entries in the All-American Derby race used any of these illegal construction techniques to get an edge on their opponents. But the national scandal was another reason why soapbox racing in Tacoma could not find a new local sponsor. The official race ended in 1973. Yet the demise of the Soapbox Derby in Tacoma should not cast a shadow on its importance in the community nor what it meant to those who participated. Countless youngsters gained valuable lessons and skills from this event, and the derby provided a rallying point for throngs of Tacomans each summer.

Greg Schumacher, 1964 national champion (SSM, 2027).

CHAPTER 39

SOCCER

Forward Steve Zungul joined the Tacoma Stars during the 1986–87 season for their playoff run and was considered the greatest indoor soccer player in the world (MB).

"The Tacoma soccer football team will play its first game of the season at Seattle tomorrow," reported the *Tacoma Daily News* on October 30, 1909. The Seattle game, played in Woodland Park against the Thistles, ended in a tie. At the Tacoma opener at Athletic Park the following week, the local soccer club beat the Seattle Rangers, 2–1. By December, Tacoma led the league, followed by the Rangers, Thistles, Renton, and the Celtics. The lead did not last long, however: within a month, the Seattle Rangers were at the top for the rest of the season.

Soccer competition between Tacoma and Seattle reflected the general animosity with which the two cities regarded each other. This was a time when grown men fought (verbally at least) over whether "The Mountain" should be called Rainer or Tacoma. On the soccer field, things sometimes got a little nasty. "Rough Soccer" headlined the *Daily News* on January 17, 1910, after the Seattle Rangers ousted Tacoma from first place in the league. "Frequently in the game yesterday the Rangers and Tacoma players tangled up and mixed it with their hands when the playing became brisk. The Rangers goalkeeper became so irritated when the Tacoma players worked the ball close up

to the goal that he picked up hands of mud and threw it at the players." During one field collision, a Rangers player broke his nose. The Tacoma player's head was cut.

Small crowds of enthusiastic fans regularly attended soccer games at Athletic Park throughout the early years of the 20th century. And the local players of the Northwestern Soccer Football Association (NSFA) took the game seriously enough to recruit players who had migrated from Great Britain. For instance, in 1913, when Tacoma hosted the Mathew Dow Cup, to be awarded to the Northwest champions, the newspaper introduced local fans to goalie G. Stewart, formerly of the South Wales Birkenhead Club, winners of the Nelson Cup in 1912; Donald Harris, a Scottish import; and F. A. Martinetti, from England. Even with all the new talent, however, the Tacoma team recorded loss after loss throughout the season.

At the time, reporters liked to blame the field official. "Unless referees are chosen by the soccer league who can give impartial decisions, the game is not likely to advance," said a *Daily News* report in 1913. "McGafferty [the referee] won the game because he showed real good form in making his decisions to suit Seattle players. This probably occurred because a relation of his was in the Seattle uniform." Complaints aside, soccer did continue and Tacoma won the state championship during the 1924–25 season. Four years later, the Cammarano Brothers soccer team won the Brown Brothers Cup.

Dr. Whetstone's soccer team was popular in Tacoma in the 1930s. In 1937 his team of dentists beat Gilt Top by a score of 2–1, with Aggie Neilson scoring both goals. Also that year, Victoria, British Columbia's Wednesday League All-Star team hosted the Whetstone team in an international competition. Victoria won the contest 3–1, with center forward Jimmy Martin Jr. scoring the only Tacoma goal, with offensive support from fullback Eddie Colbo and goalkeeper Sonny Bailey.

Early accounts of soccer matches played at the old Athletic Field were often a continuous litany of maneuvers through mud. In 1931, however, construction began on a new indoor Northwest soccer and sports center called Exhibition Hall, located off Puyallup Avenue at Bay Street. Dedicated in 1941 by Mayor Harry P. Cain, the building, later called the Soccer Centre and now known as Arena Sports, still exists as an indoor sports facility.

Stadium Bowl was also a venue for soccer games. In the 1930s, for example, players from the British cruiser HMS *Danae* met an All-Star team picked from the Tacoma City League rosters. The Young Men's Business Club sponsored the exhibition game. Prior to the all-star event, the *Danae* crew had slaughtered the Fort Lewis team by a score of 7–0 and the Tacoma team by an 11–2 decision. Prominent baseball players Joe Bowers and Sonny Bailey were added to the Tacoma team in the hopes that his majesty's sailors would not win again.

Junior Soccer

Many urban schools had adopted soccer as a "standard grammar school game," and Tacoma was no exception. Players from the local adult soccer club volunteered to coach such fledgling players as Michael Mozel from the Edison Tigers. "The boys are enthusiastic about the game and are fast learning to keep their places on the field and 'pass' the ball, instead of kicking it over to their opponents," the *Daily News* reported in 1913. Given the known pugilistic tenden-

cies of the big boys when they played the game, one school principal was relieved to witness the sportsmanlike spirit shown by the youngsters as they "played a vigorous and clean style of soccer [and] took a beating without trying to fight the game out orally afterward."

Although junior soccer continued into the 1930s, it was not until after World War II that the sport's popularity exploded. Local schools and private clubs developed programs for both young men and women, and championship competitions became equal in status to those of their American football cousins.

In 1961 the city had its first postwar youth team. John Haas and Walter Greisinger had formed the Tacoma Soccer Club (TSC) for adult play the year before, with the club's two teams participating in the Greater Seattle League. After watching boys playing rather disorganized matches prior to

Stadium High School grad Jeff Durgan was playing for the Seattle Sounders when he faced the legendary Pele of the New York Cosmos, in this North American Soccer League exhibition game (SSM, 1106.371.00).

the games played by the club, the older members decided to sponsor a junior team for the youngsters. Thus the Tacoma–Pierce County Junior Soccer Association (TPCJSA) was born. The TSC juniors, consisting of boys ages nine to 12 coached by Frank Hall, played a five-game season against elementary schools at Jane Clark playfield. Members of that first team included Mike Lay, Terry Lay, Greg Black, Gerald Porsche, Richard Porsche, Dennis Zamberlin, Bill Whitby, Danny Blowers, Dan Whitehurst, Clark Casebolt, Mike Howard, Harold Hayward, and Larry Yarberry. Other teams that participated during the first two seasons included Marymount Academy, University Place Pedersons, and University Place Wilhelms.

The Tacoma Youth Soccer committee, consisting of Bill Aiken, George Black, and Frank Hall, was then formed in 1962 as an adjunct of TSC. The committee met to organize and operate a junior league more formally than it had the previous year. The winner of the first season of league play was the North End Wanderers (later known as the Tacoma Wanderers). The North End Wanderers and North End United took part in the second annual United States–Canadian soccer exchange, in 1963, which was played in a snowstorm in Vancouver, British Columbia.

The first Five-a-Side tournament was held that spring. The play, limited to youngsters, consisted of five players on the field plus one substitute. The game originated in England as something comparable to spring training in baseball and football. Quick play of seven-minute halves with a three-minute break in between was designed to condition the soccer "booter" for championship play. It was around 1974 that the Lakewood Soccer Club initiated this popular tournament, which was played on 17 fields at Fort Steilacoom County Park. Under the guidance of Harvey Tess and Skip Rash, this tournament was at one time considered the largest youth soccer tournament in the United States. Due to competition from indoor soccer arenas, however, and more playing opportunities in the spring, the tournament ended in the early 1980s.

The 1960s were growth years for soccer in Pierce County. The Washington State Youth Soccer Association (WSYSA) formed during this period, and TPCJSA expanded. Under Dr. Kurt Blau's leadership of the Tacoma group, the Metropolitan Park District made more fields available for play. The sport was also publicized widely both during the Daffodil Festival in 1967 and an exhibition played at Cheney Stadium between double-header baseball games.

The Tacoma Wanderers continued to be the team to watch. In July 1967, they became the first American-school team to tour England. The Wanderers presented keys to the City of Tacoma to the Lord Mayors of each English city they visited. Tim Loth of the team also became the first Tacoman to receive a college soccer scholarship, to the University of Denver. That same year, Doug Howard organized the first Pacific Coast International Convention, which took place in Portland. Age brackets, ball size, and rules and regulations were all coordinated at this meeting and carried on to the national organization that was later formed. In addition, the City of Destiny hosted the first state tournament for 12-year-olds, with the Cheney Studs winning the title. Roman Strug and Frank Hall formed a 12-and-under select team to play in Portland and San Francisco; Strug took his Cheney Stud Hustlers to England during the 1970–71 season.

As the popularity of soccer grew, Pierce County became a consistent venue for tournament play. During the 1976–77 season, for example, a boys' under-16 team from Nuneaton, England, as well as an under-19 team from Braunschweig, Germany, visited Tacoma. The following year, 191 teams participated in league play under the direction of Kelly Bendixen. Due to the efforts of soccer referee Gary Lindgren, the ties between TPCJSA and the Pierce County Soccer Referees Association were strengthened considerably. TPCJSA conducted the second annual North American Youth Soccer Championship for boys under 16. The regional winners from the West, Midwest, South, and East, plus four top Canadian regional teams, met to determine the U.S. Youth, Canadian Youth, and North American Youth Soccer Champions. The Western Regional representative for the competition was the Tacoma Kickers, coached by Frank Hall. This same year, three of the association's junior players were drafted into the pros: Danny Vaughn by the Detroit Express, Leif Redal by the Los Angeles Aztecs, and Cliff Brown by the Seattle Sounders. Darrel Oak, who had been drafted earlier, was already playing for the Seattle Sounders.

Girls' Soccer

In the 1972–73 season, the formation of the first girls' leagues occurred, and thanks to the hard work of Bob Matson, 16 girls' teams participated. The following year, eight clubs were formed under the overall leadership of Al Bacon, TPCJSA president.

The Lakewood Soccer Club was home of the successful Sounderettes. This team of local high school girls won three straight state championships and one regional title by 1979. Christy Hansen, Carol Donohoe, Denise David, and Kimm Feir were from Lakes High School. Sandi Gordon, Becky Carle, and Trish Gordon were from Clover Park. Bethel High School was represented by Patty Affriseo, Monica Hudson, and Stacy Howe; Washington High School by Micki Furlong; Charles Wright Academy by Gail Gardner; Bellarmine Prep by Mary Giusti; Stadium High School by Kris Egge; and Lincoln High School by Denise Boyer. In 1980 the team, coached by Larry Feir, competed in the Helsinki International Soccer Cup games and the Sweden-based Gothia International Soccer Cup competition. The Sounderettes were the official U.S. entry for the Gothia Cup games.

The Sounderettes were not the only women's team to move beyond the bounds of a local field. Tacoma's Nortac Sweetfoot-Carrera went to the national junior championship games in 1980. Team members, coached by Dan Swain, were Denise Chalmers, Colleen Clancy, Cindy Emery, Paula French, Laurie Johnson, Tracy Johnson, Dori Kovanen, Tammy McIntosh, Karen Medved, Martha Murray, Kappy Names, Anne Nierbergall, Jeanne Oak, Sue Ray, Dawn Shelstad, Sue Strinsky, and Sandy Wilson. Of these players, Stadium High's Dori Kovanen was a member of the North Carolina Tarheels when they won four National Collegiate Athletic Association (NCAA) Division I National Championships. As a freshman she was named a first-team All-American; after graduation she served as assistant coach at Stanford University and played on the U.S. national team. In 1990 Kopachuck Middle School soccer players Vanessa Sage, Heidi Martin, and Beth Fleming were selected to play on the Washington 15-and-under team competing for the Dana Cup in Denmark and the Gothia Cup in Sweden.

The Tacoma Dome during a Tacoma Stars championship game (SSM).

Although state soccer championships began in 1981, it wasn't until 1987 that Bellarmine became the first Pierce County team to win a girl's state crown. They won additional titles in 1994, 1996, 2000, and 2004 under co-coaches Mary Rink Campbell and Jenny Phillips (for the first two crowns). Under former Tacoma Stars standout Joey Waters, the Lions defeated for the 2004 championship their cross-town league rival Stadium Tigers, who were also coached by a former Stars player John Baretta. Narrows League Bay Division MVP Megan Sweeney tallied the game-winner on a put-back, and forwards Corrine Baldassin and Dolly Enneking added the rest of the goals. The team finished the season 21- –0–2. Waters accomplished a rare feat in 2004 as his boys team at Bellarmine also won the Narrows League and 4A state championships and was voted National Champions by the National Soccer Coaches Association of America.

Then there was the Football Club Royals (FCR). By 1996 this organization, under a coaching staff of Dan Swain, Jim Lane, and Brian Van Blommestein, consisted of 11 teams for young women ranging in age from 11 to 19 years. "This is a program that knows success," reported the *News Tribune*. "On July 25, the club will send its under-17 and under-18 teams to the Youth National Championships in Indianapolis." Prior to that year, the teams had won both state and regional championships, and the under-18 team had twice been the defending champions of the illustrious Washington, D.C.-Area Soccer Tournament.

Collegiate Soccer

The Washington, D.C.-Area Soccer Tournament had actually begun in 1970, at the insistence of the young women themselves, as a way to prepare for collegiate sports at a time

The 1928–29 Cammarano Soccer Team won the Brown Brothers Cup: back row, L. to R., secretary T. Mackie, J. Cook, A. Taylor, L. Colbo, B. Palo, playing manager P. McLeod; front row, L. to R., J. Crawford, A. McLeod, J. McDougal, J. Devaux, A. Dugan (MB).

when women's soccer was not high on the list of sports priorities. As a result of the tournament, and as soccer became more prevalent on college campuses, two-thirds of Royals graduates received college scholarships by the 1980s. Gretchen Gegg (Bellarmine Prep) followed Kovanen to the University of North Carolina a year later, won a national championship, and played on the U.S. national team for four years. Gregg later became the first U.S. woman to play professionally, as well as the first U.S. player to compete in Japan. Celeste Davis (Franklin Pierce High School) won an NCAA Division I national title while competing at Barry University, and Mary Rink played and coached at Pacific Lutheran University (PLU) before returning to coach at her alma mater, Bellarmine Prep. Tara Bilanski (Puyallup High

School) was co-captain and an academic All-American at the University of Washington (UW) before moving on to coach the Portland State University women's soccer team. UW coach Lesle Gallimore credits former FRC players, including Bilanski, for the Huskies' recent strong performances in NCAA soccer tournaments.

Perhaps the most talented girls team were the FCR 77 Club formed in 1988. The team won its first state championship in 1989, won the next seven state titles, added a regional crown in 1998, and capped off the year by winning the under-18 national championship in Indianapolis, Indiana. This team consisted of 12 players from Tacoma–Pierce County who went on to play Division I in college. Coach Brian Van Blommestein's record during his eight seasons with the team was 310–25–10; all his teams combined earned 21 state championships, four regional titles, and two national championships in his 15 years with FCR.

Pierce County women did not have to travel far to play championship university soccer in the 1990s. The coaching achievements of Dr. Colleen M. Hacker at Pacific Lutheran University (PLU) is the reason. By the time Hacker retired in 1995 after 15 years of coaching soccer for the Lutes, the women's team had played for the National Association of Intercollegiate Athletics (NAIA) national championship five consecutive years. The Lutes won the title in 1988, 1989, and 1991 and placed second in 1990 and 1992. During the years Hacker coached, the Lutes women had an enviable 232–59–18 record. She remained on the PLU faculty following her retirement from coaching and was the sports psychologist for the Women's U.S. National Soccer Team when it won a gold medal at the 1996 Olympic Games, the 1998 Goodwill Games, and the 1999 World Cup, along with a silver medal at the 2000 Olympic Games.

Tacoma Community College (TCC)'s women's team burst onto the soccer scene in the mid-1990s with three consecutive Northwest Athletic Association of Community Colleges (NAACC) championships in 1996, 1997, and 1998. Between Jerrod Fleury, coach for the first two years, and Amanda Roberson, who guided the team to their third title, the Titans accumulated a 53–3–4 record in their championship years. The Most Valuable Player of the 1998 title run was Sheryl Williams; her efforts were complemented by Taya Addison, who tied an NAACC single-season scoring mark with 24 goals.

By the 20th century's end, young boys and men were again working their way to playing championship soccer. In 1999 the FC United 80 team, coached by Seth Spidahl, earned its national championship winning the under-18 crown in Orlando, Florida. The team won the Surf Cup in San Diego and the Tampa Bay Sun Bowl in Tampa, Florida, en route to amassing a 40–2 record while allowing only 18 goals the entire season. Six players from Tacoma–Pierce County were key to the team: Scott Burcar (Bethel High School), Matt Pritchard (Bellarmine Prep), Zac Tallman (Gig Harbor High School), Christian VanBlommestein (Washington High School), and Paul Troyer and Chris Raymond (both Curtis High School). The following year, the men's team at TCC joined the championship parade, under coach Shawn Edelman, with a NAACC title.

Pro Soccer

Although women's soccer in the region focused primarily on the amateur and collegiate nature of the sport, Jeff Durgan, Mark Peterson, and Jeff Stock—whose names are often linked because they began playing soccer together at an early age—all went professional the moment they had a chance. The trio originally played together on the Norpoint Royals team in the early 1970s under John Duggan, who founded the team and coached at UPS from 1979 to 1987. The pinnacle of the Royals' success came in 1977, when Norpoint finished second in the national junior soccer tournament and ended the season with a 33–1–2 record. In 1978 Durgan, Peterson, and Stock were selected to attend the Western Region U.S. National Youth Soccer training camp. Later that year, they played in the North and Central American Caribbean under-19 soccer championship games in Honduras. And before the ink was barely dry on their high school graduation diplomas, the three were playing professional soccer.

Durgan was a first-round fourth-draft choice of the New York Cosmos, and in 1980 players elected him the North American Soccer League (NASL) Rookie of the Year. He beat out former teammate Mark Peterson, who as striker for the Seattle Sounders scored 18 goals and broke the league rookie record of 10. Stock signed an Olympic contract with the Seattle Sounders in 1978, although playing professional soccer was not his initial choice. "He had visions of playing professional baseball," *News Tribune* sports editor Ted Pearson said in 1982. "After all, father Wes had carved out a lengthy major league career as a pitcher and coach, so it was almost second nature for Jeff to look to the diamond." Sounders scout Jimmy Johnston changed Stock's mind.

Tacoma and Pierce County schools produced a slew of professional soccer players besides these three, many of whom played for pro teams in their own backyard. From Stadium High came Cliff Brown, Chris Hellenkamp, Darrel Oak, and Leif Redal, who all played for West Coast teams. Tim Barto, Jamie Deming, Mike Farmer, and Wilson High School's Dan Vaughn were others. Soccer started as a varsity sport in 1974 during Vaughn's senior year, when he was co-captain with Mike Graham. Following his graduation from Mount Tahoma High School, Dale Mulholland found himself playing on a Russian professional team. Lincoln High School's Carl Milford played for the American Soccer League's Tacoma Tides. Bellarmine Prep's Mike Enneking, Foss High School graduate Brent Goulet, and Homer Screws of Washington High played for the NASL Tacoma Stars. Goulet was also on the U.S. national team.

In 1970 John Haas, together with his son Henry, Dr. Stanley Mueller, and Morris McCollum, and two others from Seattle, formed the area's first semiprofessional team, called the Sea-Tac Soccer Club. From June through August, they played 18 games against the Vancouver Spartans, the

Vancouver Cougars, and the Victoria Royals in what was called the Western Canadian League. The team's roster included TSC players, and its team played several games at Baker Stadium on the UPS campus, sometimes attracting as many as 750 spectators.

Coached by Frank Fletcher, the Sea-Tac team included Tacoma players Mike Ruffner, Dave Clayton, Bob Lynch, Coke Mead, and Manuel Arenas. Norm Ruffner, a longtime volunteer for the Junior Soccer Association, managed the team, which included trainer Mike Ryan, broadcaster Bob Robertson, and publicist Stan Farber. In addition to their regular league games, they played three exhibition matches at Seattle's Memorial Stadium against Newcastle United of the English first division, as well as against visiting teams from Israel and Vienna.

Unfortunately, the Sea-Tac team was stocked with "weekend warriors" well past their prime, compared to the three Canadian teams, which included well-conditioned professionals, many of whom went on to play in the NASL. As a result, the club finished with an 0–17–1 season record. Nevertheless, this effort was a prelude to the advent of professional soccer in the area.

Another team that was comprised mainly of Tacoma–Pierce County players was the Mueller Barons formed in 1979 by Norm Ruffner. "I started the team by getting Henry Mueller to come and watch a game, and he liked our style and gumption so much that he agreed to sponsor us," Ruffner recalled. The Barons competed in the men's Washington State Premier League for five seasons and won the state championship in 1980. The Mueller Barons played the Seattle Sounders to a 1–1 tie in an exhibition game and served as a farm club for the Sounders, Portland Timbers, and Vancouver Whitecaps of the North American Soccer League. Local players on the team included Dan Strug, Chris Hellemcamp, Mike Enneking, Leif Reidal, Coy Anglin, Mike Hoag, Jim Diedrich, Jamie Deming, Mark Richards, Earl Nausid, Jimmy Vaughn, and Jeff Ruffner.

INDOOR SOCCER'S FANS

Indoor soccer spawned many Tacoma Star boosters; Adam's Thunder, the Bleacher Bums, and the Dancing Stars were just some of the team's fan clubs. But Art Huggins was the team's number-one fan. His contribution to the sport included a billboard located on Canyon Road near his home enlivened with his own poetry, such as this 1986 offering:

The Tacoma Stars are still around,
Striving hard to gain some ground.
Come on down and watch them play
The greatest sport there is today.

Like George Mills of hockey's Tacoma Rockets Fan Club (see chapter 29, Ice Hockey), Huggins's coat was festooned with soccer buttons, but his were not for sale. "It was love at first sight for Art Huggins and indoor soccer," *News Tribune* reporter Earl Luebker told readers in 1986. "Once Higgins saw the Stars he was hooked."

Tacoma Tides

Before the Tacoma Stars, there was the American Soccer League's Tacoma Tides. Governor Booth Gardner was part owner of the team that organized in 1976. (Gardner, in

Tacoma Stars forward "Preki" was named the league's best passer for the 1987–88 season (courtesy Tacoma News Tribune).

fact, has been called Pierce County's number-one soccer dad. He often rearranged his schedule as governor so that he could coach the girls' soccer team, on which his daughter played. His interest in the sport was so strong that he helped to organize a professional woman's soccer league and was the commissioner of the newly organized National Soccer Alliance.)

Gardner joined Stan Naccarato to introduce a new generation of Tacomans to professional outdoor soccer. While Gardner served as president of the Tides, Naccarato was general manager, the same role he held concurrently for the Tacoma Twins baseball club. The pair then hired New Yorker Dan Woods as head coach. At age 29, he was one of the youngest coaches in the United States to obtain his class-A license.

Team players were an international mix. They came from India, Brazil, Great Britain, South Africa, Bolivia, and Jamaica. Stateside players joined from as far away as New England but also included Tacoma's Carl Milford, a Lincoln High graduate whose father, Dick, was a member of the Tacoma Rockets pro hockey team in the 1940s. Top players the inaugural year of the Tides included Dave Chadwick, Roy Sinclair, and Pepe Fernandez. Another local player was backup goalie Bruce Arena, who went on to coach the UPS soccer team and in the late 1990s was chosen as head coach for the U.S. Olympic men's team.

The Tacoma Tides lasted only one season due to insufficient funds and dwindling attendance. Professional soccer hibernated for seven years before a new arena opened its doors to play: this time soccer would be an indoor game.

The first major sports event in the Tacoma Dome, held on August 2, 1983, was a soccer game—part of the EuroPac Cup International Competition—held between the NASL's Seattle Sounders and the Sports Club Internacional of Brazil. Brazil won by a score of 2–1 in a playing environment that was less than amicable. Reporters noted the "untranslatable verbal exchanges" between Brazilian and American players. The Brazilian interpreter threw a water bottle at the Seattle goalie when the latter refused to shake hands with a member of the Brazilian team. "The first major sports game in the Tacoma Dome ended in shame and an international incident of sorts," said sports writer Stan Farber. But the fans still loved the game, and watching indoor soccer in the Dome provided an impetus for the formation of the city's Major Indoor Soccer League (MISL) team.

Tacoma Stars

Talk of such a team began when the owner of the Denver Avalanche MISL team put the franchise up for sale. He offered it to a group of Tacoma investors headed by John Best, former owner of the Seattle Sounders soccer team. The group envisioned professional soccer play in the Tacoma Dome beginning with the 1983–84 season. Seattle Sounders owner Bruce Anderson also wanted the Avalanche, and both interests lobbied Tacoma Dome manager Mike Gebauer for the honor of playing in the Dome. Strong Tacoma names were behind the Best campaign, including four representatives of the Weyerhaeuser family and John Long, former owner of Atlas Foundry, so ultimately the group won the rights.

Best had little time to put a team together. By August the schedule was already in place—the opening game would be against Los Angeles in the Dome on November 5—but the team had no name. Residents were invited to submit their choices, and among such possibilities as the Turtles, Tacos, Flakes, and Whiz, Best settled on the Stars. Kevin Welsh, coach of a 13-and-under league bearing the same name, was the winner. "We liked our name, and we were willing to share it," Welsh told the *News Tribune.* Once designer Chuck Pennington produced the logo and Best selected Bob McNab as coach, Tacoma's first major-league soccer franchise was ready for play.

The first two seasons of Tacoma Stars play was, to say the least, a challenge. Midway through the first season, Best replaced coach Bob McNab with Freddie Goodwin, in hopes of improving the Stars' 1–11 record. The losing record was more likely due to the last-minute effort of creating a new team than to bad coaching. Even so, the beginnings of a competitive team were present during those first two years of play. Tacomans Mark Peterson and Chris Hellencamp were two recruits. Other players were Dale Mitchell, goalie

John Baretta, and Danko "White Shoes" Grgic. Jimmy "The Smurf" Sinclair, Ralph Black, and Charlie Carey were the only players with extensive MISL experience.

But in the third season, everything changed. Best fired Goodwin after the 1984–85 season, rehired McNab, and then replaced him again with former Seattle Sounders coach Alan Hinton. At the same time, the Stars began to acquire new players, including Stadium High School graduate Jeff Stock, who at the time was recovering from injuries sustained while playing for the Sounders. Rookies Preki Radosvljevic and Lu Stojanovic, both players from the Red Stars in Belgrade, Serbia, joined newcomers goalie Mike Dowler, Greg Blasingame, and Fran O'Brien. Tony Chursky,

Pepe Fernandez of the 1976 Tacoma Tides boots it away in an American Soccer League professional match (SSM, 2002.4.27).

Tim Barto, Mike Enneking, Gary Heale, Ray Evans, Bob Lenarduzzi, Jimmy McAllister, Neil Megson, Ralph Black, and Joe Waters were the returnees. Then came Keith Furphy and Steve Zungul, "King of the Major Soccer League," who had been the Most Valuable Player for five of the MISL's seven years of existence.

The introduction of the newcomers was electrifying. Zungul captured the fans with his devotion to the sport. "I love soccer," he told Earl Luebker after arriving in Tacoma in February 1986. "I'm still single, so I can love soccer more than anything. It's ecumenical all over the world, every place but this country. Maybe we can make it here. We'll give it a try in Tacoma." He, along with Radosvljevic, became true sports icons because of their stature among the league's best players.

By April 1986, the Tacoma Stars qualified for the Western Division playoffs and became "a significant sign post in Tacoma sports history," according to reporter Bart Wright, covering "the first playoff series by the first tenant of the Tacoma Dome." The San Diego Sockers were the team to beat, with the winner advancing to the finals against Minnesota. The Stars didn't make it, but close to 20,000 fans packed the Dome for the series end.

Fans, however, can be fickle, and by 1988 attendance was down and the entire MISL realized it was in financial trouble. In order to survive, each franchise was required to post a $400,000 bond or be removed from the roster. Players were told that if they would not accept a payroll cut, the league would go out of business. They agreed to a reduction in salaries, saving the league for another season. Even so, Stars' owners still struggled to find the funds to pay the bond. Newspaper headlines at the time tell part of the story. "Tigers' Naccarato issues S.O.S.: Save Our Stars," read one in June 1988. When the money was still not forthcoming, the Tacoma Stars folded.

A month later *News Tribune* sports editor Pete Wevursky wrote, "Tacoma's bereaved Stars fans are advised against rushing to join Wednesday or Sunday night Parcheesi leagues to fill their cultural void just yet. They still might have indoor soccer games around which to structure their winter lifestyles." Wevursky was referring to an effort by James Manza to resuscitate the team. Former Stars goalie Joe Papaleo introduced Manza to former coach Alan Hinton. Within a month of the Stars' demise, Manza had pulled together a group of 28 local investors and was welcomed into the MISL as a "new" expansion team. Wayne Pieper, president of the Tacoma Stars Satellites booster club, offered the club's help in promoting ticket sales. The new Stars would use the Tacoma Soccer Centre for its headquarters and practice arena.

"Stars to officially twinkle, again, today," headlined the *News Tribune* on August 4, 1988, even though coach Hinton still had the task of recruiting players. Neil Megson was the first to sign, followed by Mike Dowler and the brothers Schmetzer—Walter, Andy, and Brian. By the time play resumed in November, Peter Ward, Peter Hattrup, Dave Hoggan, Ali Kazemaini, Joey Waters, Bill Crook, Bernie James, Homer Screws, P. J. Johns, and Preki Radosvljevic were added to the roster. Although all the players agreed to a pay cut, Preki's sacrifice was the greatest. At the time of the Stars' reorganization, he was playing for the Estrela Amadora in Portugal. If Hinton wanted Preki in Tacoma, a contract buyout fee of $54,000 was necessary. Preki himself paid the fee.

During the new season, Preki had a Most Valuable Player year, and the Stars went again to the playoffs. But the team lost to the Wichita Wings, three games to one, and injuries plagued the Stars players, while the MISL faced continuing financial instability. The history of the Stars over the next three years was more about whether indoor soccer was going to survive as a league rather than about team play.

In the end, indoor professional soccer in Tacoma died for good in 1992, though not for lack of trying. In November 1991, the Stars' owners brought former Tacoma Tigers general manager Stan Naccarato on board as executive vice president. His charge was to sell the team to a public that was not purchasing enough tickets to the soccer games. He tried, but as he told *News Tribune* columnist Bart Wright, "the hole was too deep." Tacoma could not muster the fan base to economically support the team. "Death watch over as Stars die mercifully," wrote Wright. He also provided the epitaph: "Tacoma Stars, 1983–1992; They Had Fun While It Lasted."

CHAPTER 40

SOFTBALL: FASTPITCH

Margaret Zepeda convinced owner Harry Esborg of Hollywood Boat & Motor to sponsor a fastpitch team for which she coached and played third base; she was later inducted into the Texas Softball Hall of Fame (MB).

At Chicago's 1933 World's Fair, 70,000 fans enjoyed a nationally organized softball tournament for the first time. That same year, 13-year-old Tom Cross pitched and played the outfield for the Fisher Drug team in Tacoma.

By 1935 more than 1,000 teams played fastpitch softball in the state, and Leonard Thomas and Trevor McLain were two of the area's best fastpitch pitchers. McLain was the first of the windmill hurlers. Thomas pitched several no-hit, no-run games for teams that won both city and county titles, and he was one of the few ever to outpitch McLain.

In 1938 the Tacoma Elks began nearly 65 years of sponsorship by entering a team in the Pro-Service-Vets League, one of four city leagues at the time, though commercial and church-fraternal teams also had leagues. John Rappin was the first Elks manager, and his batteries were pitchers Ted Goranson and Harry Mounsey and catchers Ed Cartozian and Bill Wieking. Recruiting some of the better players in Tacoma over the next few seasons enabled Rappin and the Elks to become one of the top teams in town by 1940.

Earl Mahnkey, considered a top shortstop, and Ed Sabol were teammates on those early Elks teams, and both were later named to the Tacoma–Pierce County Baseball-Softball Oldtimers Hall of Fame. Karl Miller, an outstanding base stealer who perfected the hook-slide, also starred for years locally.

During the '40s, softball was incorporated into the war effort, with countless businesses and industries sponsoring league competition as a way to enhance home-front morale. The Tacoma Tigerettes became one of the city's first women's fastpitch team, and players such as Betty Keffler, Teddy Davis, Bebe Blake, and Hildegard Sierman were the mainstays. Their star player was Gertrude Wilhelmsen at shortstop and center field: she had competed in track and field at the Berlin Olympics in 1936 before turning to softball. She also was inducted into the Tacoma–Pierce County Baseball-Softball Oldtimers Hall of Fame.

Leonard Thomas, along with John Rockway and McLain, continued the "big three" among the local men's pitchers, and the 1941 season was filled with highlights. The Tacoma Teamsters set an all-time City League record for offense with a 31–7 win over the 239th QMX. All-Rails completed an unbeaten regular season with a 16–0 mark, led by pitchers McLain and Sam Tipton. In the semifinals of the annual Pierce County Inter-League Championship, Tom Cross pitched and batted the Veneermen to a 10–3 win over the Puyallup Druggists. Trailing 3–1 early, Cross hit a two-run homer to tie the score and then doubled with the bases loaded to send three more across and seal the win. The Veneermen edged All-Rails, 1–0, the next night, with neither team getting a base hit through five innings, but lost to the Elks, 3–2, in the final as Len Thomas twirled a three-hitter. Thomas once pitched in three county tournament games and was credited with two shutouts and a no-hitter, but his biggest thrill came when he pitched against the tour-

ing "King Kong Kelly" at Lincoln Bowl. John Rockway tossed a no-hitter in the finals of the Pierce County Metro League. Later he became the first Metro Amateur Softball Association (ASA) commissioner for Tacoma.

A Golden Era

From 1940 to '42, the Pacific Northwest did not participate in the World Tournament, but that all changed in 1943 when the Tacoma Teamsters became the first Northwest entry to participate. It signaled the start of a golden era for the sport in Tacoma and Pierce County. Several servicemen stationed at nearby Fort Lewis and in the Tacoma Coast Guard were instrumental in this shift, as they proved to be among the nation's elite fastpitch hurlers. Woodrow Red,

The 1945 Stores–Machinists fastpitch team won the city, county, state, and regional championships and finished third in the World Softball Championships: back row, L. to R., George Naku, George Robinson, Chuck McMillan, John Carbone, Jim Stores, Vern From; middle row, L. to R., Hal Holcomb, Paul Larson, Clyde Olson, George Roket, John Hudson; front row, L. to R., Kermit Lynch, Bob McCarty, Hal Blumke (courtesy Gay Roket Hartman).

Hal Blumke, Kermit Lynch, and Bob McCarty became the new pitching heroes of the next decade, dominating the local softball scene and giving the area its first taste of regional and national levels of play.

Two Tacoma brothers, Dick Pease and George Pease, made a significant contribution to the sport as well. After playing softball in high school in the '30s, the Pease brothers decided to form a team and name it for a neighborhood friend who was killed in the war, Wes Hudson, one of Stadium High School's all-time great athletes. Their Wes Hudson Athletic Club (HAC) won several league titles in years following. Roger McDonald was a HAC star, hitting four home runs in one game, two in the same inning.

The 1943 Tacoma Teamsters defeated Kauffman Buick of Spokane, 9–3, to win the Washington State Softball Championship behind the four-hit pitching of Woodrow Red. George Roket led the team at the plate with five hits in six tries, scoring three times and driving home two runs. He was named to the All-State team along with Red, catcher Hype Jensen, second baseman Bill Ruehle, and shortstop Bob Huegel. Manager Clyde Olson then took the club to the World Tournament in Detroit, Michigan, but they lost a pair of 2–1 games to Cincinnati, Ohio, and Kodak Park of Rochester, New York.

Red, a Coast Guardsman stationed in Tacoma, had pitched his Arkansas team to state and regional championships in both 1941 and '42 and later returned to his home state to toss many more shutouts. He was still doing it in 1951 when he lost a 1–0 championship game to legendary Herb Dudley of Florida in the national finals. From '46 to 1970, he was named to so many All-Star teams that they quit counting.

In 1945 the Stores-Machinists of Tacoma played in the first game of the 13th annual world softball tournament in Cleveland, Ohio. Hal Blumke tossed a two-hitter to defeat Phoenix, Arizona, 2–1, in the final frame. After eight innings of scoreless play, Phoenix took a 1–0 lead in the ninth, only to yield the winning rally as George Roket stole home on a double steal and Kermit Lynch singled home the deciding run.

Several days of rain followed, but a 1–0 win over Merced, California Army Base was next as Blumke struck out nine and allowed just two hits. A walk to Paul Larson and singles by Roket and Hernandez accounted for the lone run of the game in the third inning.

Another 1–0 victory, this one over Houston, Texas, featured Blumke's one-hit pitching and a towering home run in the eighth inning by right fielder Bob McCarty. Earl Mahnkey starred defensively at shortstop and had one of Tacoma's three hits.

After the Stores-Machinists' three straight wins, all credited to Blumke, the Fort Wayne, Indiana, Zollners were too much for them. Third-baseman Hernandez had Tacoma's only hit, but the defending national runners-up took a 7–3 decision in semifinal action. Lynch was the losing pitcher when in the fifth inning batter Wildness yielded six Fort Wayne runs.

Flint, Michigan, sent Tacoma home with a 1–0 defeat in the third-place game. Portland's Don Skinner, added to the Tacoma roster for the tournament, outpitched his opponent but lost when his mates couldn't muster a run. It didn't help matters when Bob McCarty was robbed of a home run thanks to a leaping catch by a Flint outfielder in the seventh.

Nonetheless, the Stores-Machinists were one of Tacoma's most successful representatives ever at world competition. Vern From and Les "Whitey" Holtmeyer were two stars from the Stores-Machinists who, joined by Art Lewis and Bob Frankowsky, delivered top performances as local softball moved into the '50s. A slugging catcher, From was a team leader for the Tacoma Elks and the Irwin-Jones Dodgers, the dominating team at the time. Third-baseman Lewis was From's teammate on championship teams, along with Frankowsky, an imposing 6-foot 4-inch pitcher who used a windmill approach in addition to a regular underhand delivery. Lewis was regarded as the best "hot corner" player in the state, making just three errors in 50 games.

Holtmeyer was one of the area's best-ever all-around players. He was named to four state All-Star teams and a regional All-Star team in 1945. A speedy outfielder and outstanding hitter, he was a member of the 1945 Fort Lewis team, which won the Pacific Northwest All-Service Softball Championship. In 1946 he played briefly with legendary pitcher Eddie Feigner and his famous "King and His Court" team, and he played in three national championships, in 1946, 1951, and 1952.

Women's Teams

Women's fastpitch also emerged from the Tacoma City League to contend beyond local competition, with Lincoln Electric and the Sumner Athletic Club (SAC) fielding solid teams in 1945. Bob Huegel coached the Lincoln squad, including players Marion Ricono, Peggy Moran Ruehle, and Betty Rowan, to the Washington State Championship that year and then finished the season trying to unseat Lind-Pomeroy of Portland for the right to advance to the national tournament. But Portland's ace pitcher, Betty Evans, was too much for the Tacomans. They got to first base only twice in two games. Lincoln Electric did come back, however, to win a second consecutive state crown in 1946. The Sumner club, organized and coached by Jerry Kreuger, was a force to reckon with for the next four years.

A familiar name on the fast-pitch scene then was Margaret Heinrick, daughter of legendary Stadium High and College of Puget Sound (now UPS) football and basketball coach John Heinrick. As a 14-year-old, she was asked to catch for the Fort Lewis women's team in the 1946 national championships. She also played several exhibition games against the four-time world-champion Phoenix Queens, billed as the "Ziegfield Girls of Softball."

The emergence in 1948 of the Tacoma Fuelerettes (also known as Pacific Mutual Fuels) and SAC put women's fast-pitch in the limelight. Both teams competed in the state tournament in 1948, but a strong SAC contingent won the 1949 crown, with the Fuelerettes placing third. The SAC entry, coached by Oliver Malley and Bob Chaplin, included the All-Star battery of Ann Kauzlarich and Dora LaFaive Dietz, along with Freida Bostwick, Gloria Malley, Betty Hart, Kate McHugh, Doris Wanberg, Shirley Soggie, and Ann Pyfer, among others.

The Tacoma Fuelerettes entry featured Dee Sagmiller, Joyce Jones, Virginia Glassy, Pat Strachan, Patty Parsons, Louise Baskett, Margaret Heinrick, Dorothy Miskar, Peggy Parsons, Marjorie Johnson, and Ruthe Canonica. Players added the following seasons included Mary Ellen Farley, Sue Kauth, and the Thrasher sisters, Barbara and Beryl. They were coached for two years by Frank Cey, father of Los Angeles Dodgers All-Star third baseman Ron Cey, before Dick Penhale and Bill Stavig assumed the coaching duties.

In the '50s, many women's teams came and went as fastpitch grew. The Brotman Clothiers, Woodmen of the World, Darigold Dairymaids, Shamrocks, Rustlers, Washington Hardware, PVT Club, and the Orphans (so noted because they could not find a sponsor) were all regular league teams and tournament participants. But it was the Hollywood Boat and Motor (HB&M) team, coached by Margaret Zepeda and Carl Benson and featuring Zepeda on third base and pitcher Louise Mazzuca, that raised the sport to another level.

An avid softball player, Zepeda came to Tacoma from San Antonio, Texas, met Harry Esborg, owner of HB&M, and sold him on the idea of sponsoring a women's softball team. She put together a competitive group of players from local recreation leagues, featuring Mazzuca, a 14-year-old pitching phenomenon with a big windmill windup. Among the many players to don the HB&M uniform were Joyce Jones Wolf, Sandy Molzan, Esther Deuel, Jan Chase, Carol Schnuriger Boyer, Alayne Butterfield, Gloria Longo, Peggy Parsons, Patty Parsons, Sue Kauth, Margaret Heinrick, and Shirely "Mac" Olsen.

HB&M played in the Evergreen Travel League against teams from throughout Washington, Oregon, Idaho, and

Louise Mazzuca of Stadium High still holds the record for most no-hitters thrown (three) in a national championship tournament in 1961 (SSM).

1953 Wood Realty Fastpitch Team: back row, L. to. R., Bob Wood, Gordy Bendick, Fran Luhtala, Larry Slovek, Butch Corbin; middle row, L. to. R., Frank Davies, George Karpach, Vern Martineau, Vic Martineau, Dick Yohn; front row, L. to. R., Dick Webster, Wally Brebner, Bill Bellamy, Jack Hutchinson, Jack Hermson; batboy unknown (courtesy Bill Bellamy).

Canada and hosted clubs from Utah, California, and Arizona. Big crowds greeted some of the visiting teams, including an exhibition game featuring the great Charlotte Armstrong of the Phoenix Queens, who lived up to her name when she pitched against HB&M. Famous for pitching from the mound, second base, or center field—it didn't matter—she was unhittable from any of those three positions.

Upon returning to Texas, Zepeda went on to earn the distinction of having the most wins as a coach in the history of Texas women's fastpitch and was elected into the Texas Softball Hall of Fame. Mazzuca's career quickly blossomed when she moved to Portland to play for the nationally ranked Erv Lind Florists. A three-time first-team All-

American in 1959, 1960, and 1961 while with the Florists, Mazzuca still holds the record for most no-hitters thrown in a national championship tournament, with three in 1961. She also shared Most Valuable Player honors two straight years at nationals. Possessor of 19 career no-hit games, Mazzuca was also honored to pitch an exhibition game against the Portland Beavers 3A baseball team. She was inducted into the Pacific Northwest and Tacoma–Pierce County Softball Halls of Fame.

The 1950s

Also during the '50s, as many as eight men's teams joined the City of Sumner League, playing games under the lights

at the high school football field. Cot Zehnder was a stand-out third baseman who remembered a Tacoma team asking Sumner to assemble an All-Star team to play it. Guy Hall managed the first team, and soon they were playing teams from Renton, Olympia, and Portland. As the team matured, it traveled extensively for games and played in state tournaments. Although the club never won a state title, it finished as runner-up one year and competed well.

Three star players from the team—Merle "Butch" Corbin, Fran Luhtala, and pitcher Larry Slovek, all outstanding all-around athletes who graduated from Sumner High School—received offers to join the Irwin-Jones Dodgers in Tacoma. The Dodgers and Tacoma softball blossomed in the years that followed.

Just as enlisted personnel added luster to the county softball ranks in the '40s, the Tacoma Rockets hockey team brought a new wave of softball talent as those players looked for something to do in the off-season. Doug Adam and Alex Watt joined Dick Milford and Joey Johns on the Irwin-

Jones team of 1951, and a dynasty appeared in the making. With the addition of a budding superstar, pitcher Lloyd Blanusa, the Dodgers dominated the local scene. Adam, a 1951 state tournament All-Star, was a team leader and fine shortstop. Watt was one of the best "on-base" leadoff hitters in the game, while catcher Milford caught for pitcher Johns, making up one of the better batteries in the area. Johns previously pitched the Teamsters to the 1947 City Championship and starred for the Tacoma Elks in 1948.

The Dodgers won the regional championships in 1951 and in '52, when they went on to the World ASA Tournament in Bridgeport, Connecticut. They beat Sioux City, Iowa, 5–2, in the opener, with Dick Webster's home run the big blow. The Tacomans then lost a 2–0 decision to Memphis, Tennessee, in two extra innings to set the stage for a dramatic meeting for runner-up with the former defending national champions.

Dow Chemical of Midland, Michigan, took a 3–0 lead into the final frame, but the Dodgers came back with a last-

gasp rally. Don Skinner and Lloyd Blanusa singled back to back, and Bob Frankowsky, playing in his final fastpitch game, pinch-hit and singled home a run. Dow Chemical changed pitchers, and Alex Watt greeted the newcomer with a single, to score Blanusa. With runners at first and third, Wally Brebner flew out to end the game and the Dodgers returned home with a second-place trophy.

In the '53 regionals, catcher/manager Blanusa out-pitched the legendary Bob Fesler of the Renton Cowboys in a 1–0 third-game thriller—one of local softball's best-ever pitching duels—and then hurled a no-hitter in the championship game against Boise, Idaho. Ironically, Boise got to go to the nationals when the Tacomans couldn't raise the necessary funds.

Tacoma was host for the 1954 regionals, the final year of the Dodgers dominance. Ben's Truck Parts and the Dodgers were Tacoma's two entries in the tournament at Peck Field, and Ben's Truck Parts captured runner-up honors behind Renton and four straight wins by Fesler. Renton's 2–0 win over Ben's Truck Parts in the title tilt featured 19 strikeouts by Fesler, who allowed the Tacomans four hits, two by Tom Zurfluh.

Zurfluh was Ben's Truck Part's ace hurler, and he fired a no-hitter at the Eugene, Oregon, Rubenstein's in the opening game. Zurfluh joined Fesler as the pitchers on the All-Regional team, along with Ben's Truck Parts catcher, Bud Thomsen; first baseman Don Maitland; and his brother, infielder Bob Zurfluh. Dodgers outfielder Les Holtmeyer also was chosen.

The regionals moved to Caldwell, Idaho, in 1955 and Wood Realty represented Tacoma. The Realtors were comprised of several former Dodgers players, including first baseman George Karpach, who was selected to the regional All-Star team for the first time in a career that spanned 22 years. He missed playing in the regionals only once in that time and was eventually named to four regional All-Star teams and, later, to the Tacoma–Pierce County Baseball-Softball Oldtimers Hall of Fame.

The Realtors also had two young pitchers who starred for years to come: Gene "Chico" Thayer and Dick Yohn, both destined for the Tacoma–Pierce County Baseball-Softball Oldtimers Hall of Fame. Thayer and Yohn had storied careers. Thayer came to Tacoma from Anacortes in 1951 and played for the Tacoma Moose, who qualified for the state tournament in Walla Walla. He pitched in 29 regional tournaments during his career and won nine MVP trophies. One day he pitched five consecutive games—37 innings—and won all five with a total of 54 strikeouts. In another game he pitched 19 innings, and in his most ambitious season, he started 60 games, won 46, and lost only 14.

Yohn began pitching in the Church League while still in high school at Stadium. He quickly advanced to City League competition and played five years at Tacoma's highest level with Spring Air, Wood Realty, and Irwin-Jones. Before graduating from high school, he was named to the Tacoma Invitational All-Star team along with Northwest pitching legends Jack Hutchinson of Portland and Bob Fesler of Seattle. In 1985 he was inducted into the Pacific Northwest and Seattle Metro Halls of Fame after playing another 16 years with the Federal Old Line, Pay 'n Pak, and Peterbilt teams, all of which consistently played in the national and world tourneys. Yohn made too many All-Star teams to count.

Finishing Out the 20th Century

A wave of slowpitch interest prevailed in the '60s, although some men's fastpitch teams continued to play regularly. Jay Beach was one of the faithful fastpitch performers who persevered, although he admitted to some frustration for the Tacoma teams trying to unseat Seattle's powerful Pay 'n Pak team for most of the decade. Manke & Sons especially gave it their all on a yearly basis, but it was 1974 before the tide turned.

Early in that season, the Manke Lumbermen handed Pay 'n Pak a rare double-header loss, 2–1 and 2–0. John Collins hit a two-run homer to beat them, and the seeds were planted for a rematch at the Northwest Regionals in Spokane. There, the two rivals were tied 0–0 going into the 11th inning when Manke pitcher Gene Thayer walked the leadoff hitter. A decision to change pitchers resulted in a five-run uprising by Pay 'n Pak—and a second game, as Pay 'n Pak needed two wins to claim the title.

The Manke men jumped all over starter Gale McGrath, then Dick Yohn, and Dick Christensen, grabbing a 2–0 lead.

One of the greatest fastpitch hurlers in local history, Woodrow Red practices at the Coast Guard base, ca. 1944 (MB).

Thayer relieved starter Tommy Thomas after Pay 'n Pak tied the score at 2–2 and shut out the defending champs the rest of the way. Four runs in the third inning, highlighted by John Collins' two-run single, sent Manke to the nationals in Clearwater, Florida. Thayer was named the tournament's MVP and selected to the All-Star team with Ken Thomas, Hank Jarvits, Keith Bauer, and Ron Vandergrift. Other team standouts were Lloyd Glasoe, Jay Beach, and Darron Nelson. The Tacomans dropped a 1–0 verdict to Detroit but then suffered a 9–0 defeat at the hands of the top-rated Clearwater Bombers in the national championships.

It wasn't a last hurrah for fastpitch in Tacoma because in 1980 Cheney Stadium hosted the World Softball Tournament. Fourteen teams from around the world competed in the nine-day event, and record crowds attended as the United States took a 3–0 win over Canada in a nine-inning title clash. Longtime Tacoma sports figures Doug McArthur and Stan Naccarato were among the tournament directors, along with ASA Commissioner Steve Orfanos.

The '80s produced two dominant men's teams in Tacoma: B&I Sports and the Cloverleaf Tavern. They competed well in regional tournaments, and the two teams actually merged for the 1985–88 seasons before splitting again to become B&I Sports and Unocal. Mike Koppa and Kevin Moon were B&I's pitching stars, and Koppa was named the regional's most valuable pitcher in 1989. Position players who starred were Lloyd Glasoe, Ken Bauer, Keith Bauer, and Darron Nelson. Cleon Tungsvik was Cloverleaf's ace pitcher.

From 1971 to 1984, former University of Colorado baseball player Ken Stancato played fastpitch for Cloverleaf Tavern and Puget Sound Bank. His teams went to the national championships 10 times during that period, and Stancato compiled a 15–4 record in national competition before changing to modified fastpitch for the latter part of his career.

During that same period, Dan Oliver emerged as one of Tacoma's best fastpitch players. With a lifetime batting average of .325 and 125 home runs, he roamed left field for Puget Sound Bank, B&I Sports, Manke & Sons, and Colonial Cedar. He was selected to 45 All-Tournament teams and five Puget Sound Traveling League All-Star teams. Dan went on to coach B&I Sports and the Cheney Studs men's fastpitch teams from 1984 to 1994. During this time, he won nine of 10 Northwest League titles, and his teams finished in the top 10 nationally in class A softball ranks seven out of nine years. His coaching record was a glossy 462–157.

Tacoma's men's teams once again became national contenders during the '90s. B&I Sports players participated throughout the decade under several sponsorships, such as Chalet Tavern, Pegasus Restaurant, and Greco Homes, disbanding after the 1999 season. But before that, they claimed state and regional titles and finished second in the National Softball Association's (NSA) nationals in 1992, followed by a third-place finish in the North American Fastpitch Association (NAFA) Worlds in 1994. Moon and Koppa remained the pitching stars.

Unocal changed to Cleon's Auto and took third place at the ASA nationals in 1995, fourth at NAFA Worlds in 2000, and fifth at NAFA in 1998. Hall of Fame inductee Cleon Tungsvik was joined by Kevin Moon and Jim Edalgo to form a strong pitching staff. Moon became a two-time

NAFA All-Star. Prominent players for Cleon's included Mike Stroh, Shane Cook, Wayne Farr, Cary Elston, and the brothers three, Mike, Tom, and Keith Tungsvik. Cleon's Auto still competes today.

Women's fastpitch took on a new identity in the '80s and '90s as well, with the introduction of strong high school and college programs, particularly at the local universities of PLU and UPS.

High School and College

No Tacoma area prep team has won a fastpitch state title, but Gig Harbor, Puyallup, and Rogers High Schools have fared well in regional competition since the first state high school tournament was formed in 1992. Rogers was runner-up in the 4A state finals in 1995 and 1997 and finished third the next year under coach Mike Wight. That year they also won the West Central District fastpitch title, the only Pierce County team to ever do so.

In 1995, Dan Oliver started the girls' fastpitch program at Gig Harbor High School, and his teams earned state tournament berths on five occasions. They finished seventh in the 1996 3A state championships and third in the 1997 4A state tournament.

Rogers coach Mike Wight and Puyallup's Tony Batinovich were responsible for the solid records at those two neighboring schools. Batinovich's teams appeared in eight district and four state tourneys in his 12 years with the program, and he amassed more than 160 wins. Among the Tacoma schools, Stadium and Wilson have two state tournament appearances at the 4A level.

Four-time first-team All–South Puget Sound League outfielder Kirstin Wicklander of Puyallup was considered one of the top players to appear at the high school level locally, along with Puyallup infielder Katie Absher, who played collegiately at Purdue, and Rogers' pitching ace Jenny Lybrand.

In the college ranks, coach Ralph Weekly took his first job at PLU in 1986 and won National Association of Intercollegiate Athletics (NAIA) championships in both 1998 and 1992. He was named National Coach of the Year in eight out of nine years at PLU, where his record was 313–94. He was head coach at the University of Tennessee–Chattanooga and coached the U.S. women's team to the gold medal with a 15–0 record at the 1995 Pan American Games Qualifier in Guatemala. He was assistant coach when the U.S. team won its third straight gold medal at the Pan Am Games that same year.

Current PLU coach Rick Noren, who has been at the helm for 10 seasons, recently surpassed Weekly's record, finishing the 2004 season with 320 victories and 79 defeats. His Lady Lutes have advanced to the National Collegiate Athletic Association (NCAA) Division III playoffs five of the past six seasons since becoming an NCAA member in 1999, with a fourth-place national finish to their credit in 2002. That same year, Noren was accorded West Regional Coach of the Year honors, along with being named Northwest Conference Coach of the Year four times. The Lutes have had 43 All-American players, including multiple winners Jewel Koury, Shannon Fritzke, Janell Gunter, Melissa Korb, Sheree Deskin, Karen Stout, Andrea Farquhar, Brenda Dobbelaar, Leta Baysinger, and Jeanine Gardner.

Robin Hamilton has been coach at UPS for 19 years and has had 16 winning seasons while posting a 379–230–2 record. She was named Northwest Conference Coach of the Year five times and produced 10 first-team NAIA All-Americans, eight NAIA All-Tournament players at the national championships, and 70 All-Conference performers.

Twice the Loggers have advanced to national championship games. In 1991 the Loggers finished second, losing to Hawaii-Loa, 5–1, in the title tussle. The 10th-seeded Loggers beat Carson-Newman, Sienna Heights, Minnesota-Duluth, and Emporia State before falling twice to the champions. Pitcher Melody Stanley, center fielder Annie Pettigrew, shortstop Pua'ala Soares, and third baseman Tara Brown all were selected on the All-Tournament team. In 1995, seeded last in a 16-team NAIA field, the team spilled sixth-seeded University of West Florida twice and third-seeded Hawaii-Pacific. A 3–1 loss to Oklahoma City in the final game spoiled the bid, but All-America shortstop Heather Paulson, as well as pitcher Dani Besel and first baseman Kirsten Wilson, were selected to the All-Tournament team.

With the tremendous growth and popularity of girl's fastpitch in the school and club programs from ages 10 on up, the outlook is bright for more champions to emerge.

CHAPTER 41

SOFTBALL: SLOWPITCH

Earl Hyder completes a double play, while teammate Ken DeForrest looks on (SSM, 2000.4.56).

Slowpitch began in Pierce County in 1956 when Tom Cross, then assistant superintendent of Tacoma's Metropolitan Park District, introduced the sport after he saw the game played in Chicago with a 16-inch ball. He concluded that the sport would increase the action and participation on the field when compared to fastpitch softball, a game dominated by pitchers and catchers.

Howell's Sporting Goods, Wylie's Café, and the Tacoma Athletic Commission (TAC) were the three sponsors of teams originally involved in the program. Players on the Howell's team read like a who's who in Tacoma sports history, with such stalwarts as pitcher Frank Gillihan, catcher John Heinrick, Marv Harshman, Marv Tommervik, George Wise, Sonny Bailey, Cross, Chuck Gilmur, Lornie Merkle, Steve Orfanos, and Al Maul. A housewive's league was also formed around this same time, with Carolyn Howard pitching and Sylvia Hannula playing shortstop.

Contributing to the growth of the sport in the 1960s was the appearance of Denny MacGougan's column entitled "Rec Hilites" in the Sunday edition of the *Tacoma News Tribune.* MacGougan helped to promote the formation of not just the slowpitch program, but other recreational activities as well. By the end of the decade, slowpitch leagues included

such divisions as housewives, men 35 and over, and senior boys and girls, as well as teams for various industrial, commercial, government, and church organizations.

The first slowpitch games in Tacoma were played in the highly competitive Metro League at Peck Field using a 14-inch softball, even though a 12-inch ball was used at the national level. However, due to Peck Field's short fences, the 14-inch ball was necessary to reduce the number of home runs in a game. With the opening of the Harry Sprinker Recreation Center in 1969, the Western Washington League was created, and with its much bigger fields, teams could choose between leagues using either size ball. For years, this new league was known as one of the premier leagues in the state.

The number of teams mushroomed with the opening of the South End Recreation Area complex in 1980. At the same time, the Pierce County Parks and Recreation Department hosted the first-ever U.S. Slo-pitch Softball Association (USSSA) tournament. The introduction of the USSSA program greatly enhanced the competition opportunities for teams and players, and in 1993 a new organization called the National Softball Association (NSA) introduced another new program into the area.

Many great slowpitch teams, players, coaches, and umpires have been involved over the years. Among the more noteworthy teams were Alfred's Café, B&I Sports, BJ's All Stars, The Cage Tavern, Champions's Athletic Supply, Cloverleaf Tavern, Coach House, Creekwater Dispensary, Dean's Tavern, Emery Motors, 48th Street Tavern, Heidelberg, Hi Hat, Home Plate Tavern, Little Jim's Pub, Lucky Lager, McKnight's Food, People's Church, Players Tavern, Poodle Dog, Schooner Tavern, Sons of Italy, the Spar Tavern, Spud's Pizza Pete, Tony's Wahzoos, Tucci and Sons, Wested Tires, and Whylie's Café.

The first Tacoma team to compete nationally in slowpitch was Tucci and Sons, in 1964. Players from successful Tacoma-area baseball and fastpitch teams, many of which had finished as national amateur champions or runners-up, formed the nucleus of both the Sports Supply team and the Tucci and Sons team. From 1961 to 1964, the latter team won the Northwest Regional Slowpitch Championships each year, beginning a Pierce County dominance in the sport that lasted for many years.

Marty Erdahl coached the Tucci squad, which competed all season using the 14-inch ball (with a record of 36–2) but had to change its style of play to a 12-inch ball for the national tournament in Springfield, Ohio. An 11th-inning home run by Gordy Pfeifer (see also chapter 26, Handball) against Pine Tavern won the regional crown and qualified

Umpire Bob Maguinez observes the action as two local teams slug it out in a recreational slowpitch game (SSM, 2003.16.8).

the team for its title trip. The Tacomans won their Ohio opener 10–0, against Rhode Island, behind Doug McArthur's rare-for-slowpitch three-hit shutout, but the Kentucky and Wisconsin regional champs followed with 4–3 and 8–5 wins to eliminate the Tucci team. The nucleus of that squad was comprised of players from the former Stanley's Shoemen team, which won Tacoma's first-ever national baseball championship in 1956. They were Dale Bloom, Jack Johnson, Jim Gallwas, Ron Storaasli, and McArthur. Ex-professional players Bill Funk and Al Maul also were on the team, along with slowpitch legend-to-be Pfeifer.

Over the years, the accolades were numerous for many teams, but the first team to dominate the sport in Pierce County was the Heidelberg Beer men's slowpitch team. Between 1965 and 1975, this team won more than 800 games and 60 tournaments in the Open Division, including five consecutive regional championships and seven consecutive appearances at national tournaments. In 1968 Heidelberg finished fifth place in the men's open Amateur Softball Association (ASA) National Championship in Long Island, New York.

Formed in 1968, the People's Church Softball Club was the most prominent local team on the national scene, winning the USSSA Church World 1A championships in 1991 and 1993. Between 1968 and 1997, the club compiled an incredible 1,368–411 win-loss record, played in 21 consecutive Church World 1A Tournaments, won 17 Washington regional and state titles, and went 11 years without losing a Washington State Church 1A Tournament. Manager Steve Shackett was selected to three All-World teams as manager and was inducted into the USSSA Hall of Fame in 1993. Other team members included Shackett's brother Owen, Dan Valentine, Jerry Henderson, Darrell Shively, Ivy Iverson, Curtis Wells, Bob Spellmeyer, and brothers Ralph and Rich Van Dyk, the latter a USSSA Hall of Fame inductee in 1995.

In August 1984, Gordy Pfeifer became the first slowpitch player ever to be inducted into the ASA Northwest Region Hall of Fame. Between 1963 and 1971, he was the dominant player in the Northwest. In 1968, as both player and coach, he led his powerful Heidelberg team to the Northwest regional championships, where he was selected Most Valuable Player, hitting .852. At the world tourna-ment in Long Island, New York, he led the team to a fifth-place finish while hitting .833. He became the only player from the West Coast selected to the All-World team.

During the 1970 Northwest regional games, Pfeifer again led Heidelberg to the title, was again selected Most Valuable Player, and during one stretch had 22 hits in 23 at-bats, with seven home runs. Over the course of his playing career, he was selected to 18 All-Star teams and was tournament Most Valuable Player 10 times. His career batting average was .603, and as a player/coach between 1965 and 1971, his teams compiled a record of 927 wins and 79 losses.

Other noteworthy players in the men's program included Joe Kreger, Dan Lowry, Ken Jones, Dick Zierman, Ed McGrath, Mel Burrell, Ken Schulz, Bob Young, Jim Lane, Marco Malich, Dave Wilsie, Ken DeForrest, Butch Pasquale, Dean Eklund, Dave Benedict, Cal Goings, and USSSA Hall of Famer Dan Luthala.

Officials

The list of slowpitch umpires is as extensive as the lists of teams and players. Those to remember are Bob Maguinez, Earl Hyder, Dave Kerrone, Joey Johns, Joe Bailey, John "Doc" Holliday, Lornie Merkle, Paul Gustafson, Jim Oleole, and Ken Laase, who was inducted into the USSSA State of Washington Hall of Fame in 1995.

Pierce County Parks and Recreation Department and Metropolitan Park District administrators associated with slowpitch softball over the years, besides Tom Cross, include Doug McArthur, Jim Webster, Steve Orfanos, Jan Wolcott, Gary Lindgren, Marc Blau, Aaron Pointer, Sandy Molzan, Karen Moorhead, Debbi Hanson, Toni Turnbull, and Cliff Owens. There has also been Sara Harris of Puyallup Parks and Recreation, Rebecca Giles of Sumner, Traci Williams in Buckley, and Eric Guenther in Gig Harbor.

Women's Teams

Women's slowpitch softball proved as popular a sport as men's play. Beginning with The Cage Tavern team in 1965, women's teams have achieved national recognition through tournament competitions sponsored by a wide array of Tacoma and Pierce County businesses, as well as by local schools, universities, churches, and recreation centers.

The Cage Tavern team formed when the owners of the tavern, Spud Hansen and Harley Otis, posted a turnout schedule in the tavern. The first practice was held at Franklin High School's field, where coaches Bill Herbert and Parry McCrae met more than 30 potential players, many coming from a recently disbanded women's fastpitch team. Hansen and Otis vowed that if the team went undefeated and qualified for the nationals, the tavern owners would finance the trip even if it meant selling the business. The team finished the regular season with a perfect 22–0 record, and Hansen and Otis, true to their word, sold the tavern to help pay expenses for the trip, along with proceeds from cake sales and car washes and a donation from the Carling Brewing Company.

Seventeen players, two former tavern owners, two coaches, and five rabid fans (each of whom paid $50 for the trip) set out for Omaha, Nebraska. Hansen, who went on to sponsor teams in almost every sport in Tacoma and Pierce County, remembered the event. "My partner, Harley Otis, and I were the sponsors [owners] of The Cage—not coaches. All we did was sell the tavern to the highest bidder, jumped on the leased bus, and accompanied the team to the nationals. We did not coach or play—we just paid bills and played around."

In their first game, The Cage were defeated by Cleveland Music with a score of 5–2. The Cage played their second game against the host team from Omaha and lost it 14–12. Even so, the team was honored at the awards ceremony for being the first West Coast team to play in a women's national tournament and for traveling the farthest: 1,700 miles.

Spud Hansen's Pizza Pete became the new sponsor in 1966, a team also comprised of many former talented fastpitch players, as well as housewives, teachers, and businesswomen. Between 1965 and 1971, the team compiled an unbelievable record of 381 wins and 20 losses. In the process, they won seven consecutive state championships. Bill Herbert continued to coach the Spuds throughout its short history. A 1958 graduate of Lincoln High School, he was also a slowpitch player on various men's teams. Laura Herbert, Sandy "Sam" Turnley, Joyce Wolf, Charlene Miller, Jeanine Eshpeter, and Nancy Craig led the roster of players.

Many of these women went on to play on or coach other softball teams.

In 1972 the Pizza Pete club split into two teams, with Jan Chase taking part of the team and Joyce Wolf taking over the balance of the club. Many top players participated in the program, including Pat Kearney, Tammy Skubini, Judy Gray, Nancy Jerkovich, Peg Loverin, Kay Bentley, Mary Haavisto, Linda Rudolph, and Margaret Steeves.

Wolf had, perhaps, the most exciting softball career. A 1950 graduate of Stadium High School, she started playing fastpitch in 1946 under coach Telli Pagni and later played for the well-known Hollywood Boat & Motor fastpitch team. After playing with The Cage and Pizza Pete, Wolf coached the B&E Tavern, her half of the former Pizza Pete, which later became the Creekwater Dispensary and, finally, BJ's All Stars.

In 1972 B&E hosted the Northwest Region 31 Slowpitch Tournament at Peck Field. That first season, they lost to Hamilton's Towing of Bellingham in the finals, but the following year they won seven tournaments, finished third at regionals, and ended the season with a 66–5 record. Playing under the name Creekwater Dispensary in 1974, Wolf's team ended the year with a three-year record of 151–19, with wins in 19 out of 22 tournaments, and finally won the regional championships that were held on their home field at Sprinker Recreation Center. Earning a trip to the national tournament in Elk Grove, California, they became only the second team in Tacoma women's slowpitch history to qualify for the national championships.

In Elk Grove, Creekwater won their first game against a team from Virginia but proceeded to lose their next contest to the powerhouse Miami Dots, eventual champions, and were then eliminated by a Kansas team to finish 17th. Top players that season included the Textor sisters, Alice and Phyllis, Sue Vincent, Ardi Schrag, Darleen Peterson, Vicki Panzeri, Louise Rota, Trena Page, Pat Kearney, Sue Carter, Sandy Molzan, Terri Riffe, Sue Ray, Melodie Fox, and Bev Risner.

Even though its name changed over the years, Metro Tacoma's B&I sports team lasted the longest when it comes to women's slowpitch softball. B&I Sports, along with Ron Erwin, first provided the financial backing. In later years, Whit and Shirley Hemion sponsored the team. The

Hemions enjoyed a long relationship with slowpitch, watching their sons Whit Jr., Jack, and David all play on top local teams, along with daughter Kathy. (A tragic airplane crash en route to the 1978 regional championships in Montana took the life of Whit Jr., one of the most-feared long-ball hitters in Tacoma.) And though Jack and David retired from the sport, Kathy, a 1970 Lakes High School graduate, continued with her winning ways on the field, culminating with a USSSA State of Washington Hall of Fame induction in 1994. Whit Sr. and Shirley were much more than just sponsors of the team; they were great friends with all and helped players time and again with low-interest loans to finance cars and homes.

Throughout the years of play, Jack Thompson, Carl Lopez, Kathy Hemion, Toni Turnbull, Chris Phillips, and Trena Page all coached the championship team. Although it won numerous tournament championships, B&I Sport's best year ever was 1991. The team placed third in the ASA national tournament held in Salem, Oregon, followed by a USSSA regional title. After competing in these two tournaments, several of the team members were named to the All-American and All-Regional teams, including Hemion, Lisa Barron, Carol Auping, and Vicki Miller.

Although winning championships was important to the team, developing friendships and having fun was always the

The first organized girl's softball team, ca. 1950s (SSM, 2122).

first priority for the B&I players. The women continued to play throughout the 1990s, changing the name of the team to OMT (One More Time) and then TOP (Too Old to Play). Along with the name changes came new players, including Rhondi Adair, who was also an All-American. Although the team no longer competes in league play, they still reunite for an occasional tournament where the only rule in force is, according to Adair, "No practicing. Just show up and play the game."

In 1990 the Sting, a slowpitch team of teenage girls from eastern Pierce County and Tacoma, were invited to play in the ASA Hall of Fame Classic in Oklahoma City. The team was one of only a dozen teams nationwide to play in six consecutive world tournaments. Coached by Chris Gibson, it placed as high as fifth in the USSSA World Tournament in 1986 and seventh at the ASA tournament in 1988.

Other Contributions

The first co-ed slowpitch programs were introduced by the Pierce County Parks and Recreation Department in the summer of 1973, and today more than 500 teams throughout Pierce County alone compete at various levels.

In 1991 Pierce County Parks offered the first Half Century Plus slowpitch league for men and women ages 55 and over, and today the program has more than 200 players representing 12 different teams. The masters slowpitch program has blossomed considerably since 1997; Tacomans who have participated on Senior Softball National Championship teams include Joe Stortini, Bill Winter, Chip Cipriano, Lynn Larson, Jim Peterson, Bill Fleener, Bill Wheeler, Earl Birnel, Jack Scott, Jerry Thacker, Bob Young, Mike Vitovich, Dick O'Brien, Ron Mattila, Bill Meyer, Bob Congdon, Bob Fontaine, Fred Barker, and Peo DeCano.

Another significant contribution to slowpitch came from the venerable John Rockway, who was responsible for Pierce County gaining its own ASA Metro status and who served as the first Metro Tacoma–Pierce County ASA commissioner, from 1953 to 1974. He was then succeeded by Steve Orfanos and subsequently by Debbi Hanson, the first woman to hold such a position in the community.

The Metropolitan Park District hosted the first Northwest Region Slowpitch Tournament at Peck Field in the late

CHAPTER SPONSORED IN HONOR OF

THE 1968 HEIDELBERG SLOWPITCH TEAM:

Bob Young, pitcher, infield, Nationals All-American selection in Long Island, New York (1968, Heidelberg), Senior Softball Las Vegas (1999, SeaTac) and Canton, Michigan (2001, Emerald City); Ken Schulz, outfield, pitcher, two-time regional all-star, baseball pitcher at Lincoln High all-state, Western Washington College all-conference; Jerry Thacker, shortstop, Regional MVP, football at University of Puget Sound All-American Quarterback (1969); Butch Pasquale, outfield, regional MVP (1971), power hitter, 40–50 homeruns a year; Marco Malich, outfield, catcher, high batting average, 18 all-star awards; Jim Lane, second base, Nationals All-American selection in Long Island, New York (1968, Heidelberg), high batting average, seven national tournaments; Terry Trowbridge, third base, shortstop, seven national tournaments, numerous all-star awards; Jerry Foss, outfield, pitcher, six all-star awards, three national tournaments; Ken Laase, outfield, leadoff hitter, RBI over 600 for seven consecutive years, 22 consecutive hits; Dick Sam-

laska, third base, three MVPs in Great Falls, Montana, MVP for highest batting average at 700, MVP for defense; Dick Zierman, outfield, pitcher, catcher, five MVP's, power hitter, numerous all-star awards; Al Reil, five years with Heidelberg, second and third bases and shortstop, utility player; Ted Whitney, catcher, 1968 all-star.

1950s. Since then, both Metro Parks and the Pierce County Parks and Recreation Department have been active in hosting numerous state, regional, and world ASA, USSSA, and NSA tournaments each summer in a continuous effort to promote and highlight the game.

"I'll bet you heaven doesn't have enough softball fields," Tacoma Metropolitan Park District's Margaret McCormick said in 1987, explaining the popularity of slowpitch softball throughout the nation. For both men and women amateur softball was, and is, a way for friends and families to stay in touch over the years. "Everybody's friends," another softball player said. "It's a family-type thing. After the game's over, it's still social and everybody enjoys it."

CHAPTER 42

SWIMMING AND WATER POLO

Dick Hannula Jr., won a World University Games Championship in the 400-meter freestyle and the 800-meter freestyle relay in Sophia, Bulgaria, in 1977 (courtesy Dick Hannula Sr.).

Swimming had an accidental beginning in Tacoma and Pierce County. Stadium High School was initially designed as a hotel with an indoor swimming pool as an amenity for tourists. The hotel was never completed, thanks to the Panic of 1893, but architect Frederick Heath convinced the Tacoma School Board that the burned-out shell of the hotel would make an ideal high school. When the doors opened to students of Tacoma High School in 1906, it became the first school in the state to have a swimming pool. Frederick Health next designed Lincoln High School, this time with two swimming pools, one for boys and one for girls starting the school term in the fall of 1914.

From the beginnings of the 20th century, in other words, swimming pools were a given component of high school design throughout the county. In addition, community indoor pools became a part of the swimming landscape. Tacoma's Metropolitan Park District constructed two outdoor Olympic-size pools at Titlow Beach and in the South End. Local swimmers viewed the Titlow pool as a crucial training venue when preparing for national and international competitions.

The successes of swimmers in the national and international arena brought world recognition to Tacoma and Pierce County. The county is home to two Olympic swimming champions, six U.S. swimming Olympians, five U.S. national champions, one individual-event world record holder, several American record holders, and a number of U.S. major international meet champions.

High Schools

High schools provided a major local competitive venue. Lincoln and Stadium dominated swimming prior to World War II. Wally Streeter coached Stadium 17 years and won seven boys' state championships. He later coached at Mount Tahoma High School. Following the end of the war, beginning in the 1950s, the growth of Washington State high school swimming was phenomenal. High school girls' swimming started in the 1970s, and there are now two state championship meets for 4A and 3A schools, with more than 100 teams vying in both the boys' and girls' competitions.

Of the many swimming coaches during the latter years of the 20th century, Dick Hannula stands out as one of the best in the nation. He began his coaching career at Lincoln

High School in 1951 and coached teams to two boys' state titles (one shared with Stadium) in his seven years there. After transferring to the new Wilson High School, he established the longest high school undefeated record in the country achieved by one coach and one high school. From 1959 to 1983, Hannula coached 323 meets without a loss, including 24 consecutive boys' state championship meets. His one tie during this winning streak was with Lakes High School, coached by Mike Stauffer. Hannula's achievements moved beyond the local scene after he published books on coaching swimmers, works that have been translated into several foreign languages. He was inducted into the International Swimming Hall of Fame as an honor coach in 1987.

Tacoma high school swimmers have finished first in the United States on several occasions: Wilson's Dave Hannula (1972) in the 200-yard individual medley; Rod Stewart (1973) in the 100-yard butterfly for two consecutive years, Dick Hannula Jr. (1975) in the 200- and 500-yard freestyle; Mark Smith (1975) in the 100-yard freestyle; Sean Victor (Foss, 1988) in the 100-yard butterfly; Missy Frost (Foss, 1986) in the 100-yard backstroke, and Kathy Garrison (Peninsula High School, 1976) in the 100-yard freestyle. Dick Hannula Jr. broke the existing national interscholastic records in his winning events.

Wilson High School also won boys' state championships under coach Chris Myhre in 1989 and 1990, and coach Dee Loose added another in 1998. Coach Mike Stauffer and Lakes High School won in 1984 and 1985. Curtis High School, with coach Jim Baurichter, won in 1992. Coach Dan Wolfrom of Foss High School was the

In 1970 four Tacoma Swim Club members scored the first points ever for the club at a national championship meet by winning the 800-meter freestyle relay: L. to R., Jack Horsley, Dennis Larsen, Kurt Knipher, Dan Hannula (courtesy Dick Hannula Sr.).

first Washington high school coach to win both the boys' and girls' state championship titles in one year, a distinction accomplished in 1986. Wolfrom also won the most girls' state championship meets of any Pierce County coach: 1983, 1984, 1985, 1986, and 1991. Dave Emery of Clover Park and Rogers High Schools, Craig Brown of Peninsula High School, and Kimo Streeter at Mount Tahoma and Peninsula High Schools also had long and distinguished coaching careers that contributed greatly to the swimming successes of Pierce County. Streeter coached a number-one national high school swimmer, Kathy Garrison, at Peninsula. Streeter was also one of the first two swimmers, along with Earl Ellis, to ever represent the University of Puget Sound (UPS) at the National Association for Intercollegiate Athletics (NAIA) National Championship Meet, back in 1958 for coach Don Duncan. Earl Ellis went on to a distinguished career as head coach of the University of Washington Swim Teams.

Coach Peggy Johnson added a girls' state championship in 1997 at Gig Harbor High School. Rogers High School and coach Heather Hoskins won the girls' state championship in 2002 and 2003. Jerry Hartley coached both Puyallup and Rogers High School swim teams with distinction, but his greatest achievements came in the sport of water polo (see sidebar). During his coaching tenure, he won 11 Washington High School State Water Polo Championships. Ten were consecutive at Puyallup and he added another one as coach of Rogers.

Swim Clubs

The formation of local private swim clubs provided an important training ground for these young swimmers. Dick Hannula, then Lincoln High School swimming coach, founded Tacoma Swim Club (TSC) in 1955 and served as its head coach until 1998. When Hannula retired, Jay Benner replaced him. The Puyallup Swim Club and especially South Sound Swim Club (SSSC) have also provided championship swimmers, under the coaching skills of first Rick Benner (no relation to Jay) and then Dave Kienlen. Collectively, these swim clubs provided the nucleus of swimmers that made high school swimming so successful in the county.

Elite Competitors

Stadium's "hotel–high school" pool was the ripple that started Tacoma–Pierce County swimming on the road to success. This ripple became giant waves from the 1960s to the present. Pierce County swimmers continued to develop national and international elite swimmers, even to the highest Olympic level.

The story begins in 1963 when the TSC qualified the first two Tacoma swimmers for the U.S. National Long Course Championship Meet: Chuck Richards and Mike Stauffer. In 1972 Richards, a Stadium High grad and All-American at Indiana University, was on the U.S. team at the Munich Olympics, where he broke the world record for the 300-meter pentathlon event. Stauffer became an All-American at the University of Minnesota. He then returned to Pierce County to coach the Lakes High School and Lakewood Swim Club (LSC) teams.

Kaye Hall was without a doubt Tacoma's first famous swimming champion. She began her winning career in 1967, when she set a new American record in the 100-yard backstroke and won the U.S. Short Course Championship in that event. Hall then took the silver medal at the Pan American Games. The following year, she set a world record in the 100-meter backstroke at the Mexico City Olympics while winning a gold in the event. She also established another world record while winning the 400-meter medley relay and won the bronze medal in the 200-meter backstroke. At the World University Games in Turin, Italy, in 1970, Hall won gold medals in both the 100-meter backstroke and the 400-meter medley relay. By the time she was inducted into the International Swimming Hall of Fame in 1979, she held the American record in six backstroke events in long course and in short course in both yards and meters.

The 1970s was the swimming decade for the Hannula brothers: Dan, Dave, and Dick Jr. In 1974 the three boys, along with Wilson High School teammate Mark Smith, set a new American Club record for the 800-meter free relay at the U.S. National Championship meet held in Concord, California. The record was short lived. It was broken 20 minutes later by a team from the Long Beach Swim Club; even so, TSC still considered the achievement quite extraordinary.

THE FOLLOWING LONG-TIME COACHES AND SWIMMERS
FROM THE TACOMA AND PIERCE COUNTY COMMUNITY ARE PLEASED TO SPONSOR
THE HISTORY OF SWIMMING:

Jack and Angela Connelly

Don Duncan

Janet Buchan Elway

Kaye Hall-Greff

Dick and Sylvia Hannula

Dan and Margaret Hannula

Bruce Richards, Chuck Richards, Shirley Richards Slade—in memory of our parents Len and Betty Richards

Mike and Sharon Stauffer

Kimo and Ann Streeter

In 1972 Dave set a new American record in the short-course 200-meter individual medley in the Canadian Open Championship meet. He won U.S. National Championship honors in the 400-meter individual medley in 1975 and competed in the World Championship games in Cali, Colombia. Also that year, Dick qualified and swam for the U.S. National Team in the Hapoel Games in Israel. Two years later, he won two gold medals in the 400-meter free event and the 800-meter free relay at the World University Games in Sophia, Bulgaria.

The 1970s also saw a number of young women competing on the national and international level. In 1972 TSC's Barbara Mitchell qualified for the U.S. Olympic swim team and competed in the 200-meter breaststroke in Munich, Germany. Miriam Smith qualified and swam in the 200-meter backstroke at the Montreal Olympic Games. In 1979 TSC's Janet Buchan won the gold medal in the 400-meter individual medley at the World University Games in Mexico City. She also broke the short-course American record for the 400-meter individual medley at an international meet in Paris as a member of the U.S. national team.

Megan Quann is Pierce County's second famous swimming competitor. She was not the only local champion, however. In 1993 Katy Dobner, a student at Puyallup High School, won 10 medals, including two gold relay medals at the World Games for the Deaf in Sophia, Bulgaria. Even so, Quann, a member of SSSC, dominated women's swimming as the 20th century came to an end and a new one began.

Her national and international competitions began in 1998, when she won the 100-meter breaststroke at the U.S. National Championship games and the bronze medal in the 100-meter breaststroke in the Goodwill Games at Long Island, New York. The following year, Quann took second in the 100-meter breaststroke and first in the 400-meter medley relay in the Pan Pacific Championship meet in Sydney, Australia.

The swimming successes continued into the 2000 Sydney Olympic Games, where Quann won gold medals in the 100-meter breaststroke and 400-meter medley and set a new American record in the 100-meter breaststroke. Following the Olympic games, she won the 100-meter breaststroke at the U.S. National Championship meet and swam to a second place in the 400-meter medley relay at the World Championship in Fukuoka, Japan (2001); competed in the Pan Pacific Championship in Yokohama, Japan (2002); and won the 100-meter breaststroke at the U.S. National Championship meet (2003). Quann missed qualifying for the 2004 Athens Olympic games by just a few seconds.

Quann was not alone as a successful competitive swimmer as the 21st century began. SSSC's Jamie Reid was also at the 1998 U.S. National Championship meet and won the 200-meter backstroke event. Two years later, she won the

200-meter backstroke event at Spring Nationals, followed by a gold medal in the 200-meter backstroke at the Santo Domingo Pan American Games in the Dominican Republic in 2003. Sara Platzer, from LSC, competed in the World University Games in Beijing in 2001 and in Seoul in 2003.

TSC's Dana Kirk won the 100-meter butterfly event at the U.S. National meet and competed in the Goodwill Games in Brisbane, Australia, in 2001. She won the 200-meter butterfly at the Olympic trials in 2004, assuring her a place on the U.S. team heading to Athens. Although Dana

LONG DISTANCE SWIMMING

On May 14, 1956, Bert Thomas became the first man in history to swim from Seattle to Tacoma, crossing the frigid 18.5 miles in 15 hours, 20 minutes. The 275-pound ex-logger entered choppy Puget Sound at 11:35 a.m. at Fauntleroy, battled the 46-degree water, and arrived at 3:05 a.m. just east of the Old Tacoma Dock.

Born in Durango, Colorado, Thomas spent his boyhood years in Pe Ell but moved to Tacoma and attended Lincoln High School where he played football before entering the Marine Corps. He was a marine drill instructor in San Diego and later instructed Navy frogmen at Pearl Harbor. Previously, Thomas had swum successfully from Port Angeles to Victoria in July, 1955, negotiating that 18.3 miles in 11 hours, 17 minutes.

In Puget Sound, Thomas swam in what he called his "automatic stroke"—a powerful, distance-eating, overhand sidestroke with which he averaged 24 strokes per minute. He stopped every hour for food, gulping dextrose, hot coffee, and orange juice from a plastic tube. An estimated 5,000 people jammed the dock area to catch a of glimpse of Thomas as he emerged from the murky waters. He was accompanied on the swim by George Peterson, skipper of the boat Memo-

ries, as well as Erling Bergerson, wife Mary, and 12-year-old daughter Sharon.

Two years later, Thomas succeeded in swimming the English Channel from Cape Griz Nez, France, to Dover and then half-way back before being pulled from the water due to exhaustion. When he died in 1972 at the age of 46, Thomas was co-manager of Bill's Boathouse on American Lake.

More than 40 years later, another Tacoma swimmer made waves in long-distance, open water swimming. Jay Benner was on the USA National Team for Open Water Swimming from 1994 through 1996 and won the national championship for 10,000 meters during that period. He swam all over the world on the professional marathon circuit from 1994–2000 and currently holds the record for a double crossing of the Aegean Sea in Greece, a distance of 37.2 miles. Benner attempted a four-way crossing—a feat never before accomplished—of the Aegean in 2002, but completed only 58 miles before being pulled from the water. Benner also has swam races in the Nile River and completed a 55-mile river race in Argentina. He started coaching Tacoma Swim Club in 1997.

A DIFFERENT POOL SPORT: WATER POLO

In the early 1960s, swim coaches discovered the valuable role that water polo could play for their swim teams: it served as an effective but fun way to condition athletes for the competitive swimming season. Anytime teams are picked and goal posts are set up, however, the competitive nature quickly emerges, and since then, Tacoma area high schools have been at the forefront of the sport in Washington since the 1970s.

According to Dick Hannula, "When I was on the swim team at Aberdeen High School from 1944 to '46, we played a version of water polo. But, as I recall, it was right around 1969 when the first 'unofficial' state championship was held in Washington. We started playing water polo at Wilson [High] around 1964, and I coached the team through the 1970s."

Chuck Richards, a '64 Stadium High graduate, recalled playing water polo every year in the fall. "We went to Victoria on one trip to play some teams. It was not a varsity sport and it seemed a bit random as to who had teams and who you played from year to year," said Richards, who went on to set an Olympic swim record in the 1972 pentathlon event in Munich.

In 1970 Wilson High put together one of the strongest teams in the area and proceeded to defeat every club they competed against, including Washington State University, UPS, PLU, and various high school teams. It was common even through the '80s for high schools to schedule games against colleges so team members could play at a higher level of competition. As a club sport, there were no sanctioned leagues or state tournaments, so the students competed in an informal league that over the years included Clover Park, Curtis, Foss, Lakes, Lincoln, Mount Tahoma, Peninsula, Puyallup, Rogers, Stadium, and Wilson High Schools.

Jerry Hartley, former swim coach at Puyallup and Rogers High Schools, is universally credited with developing the sport in the state. "He promoted water polo and was a good coach, competitive, and the 'man' in the state when it came to the growth of water polo," according to Hannula. Hartley fostered the notion that water polo could stand on its own merits and didn't need to be considered a "stepchild" to swimming. Eventually, nonswimmers started to play and soon water polo was attracting individuals besides champion swimmers who wanted to actually learn the game.

According to unofficial records, Wilson won the first "state" championship in 1969 under Hannula, while Hartley's Puyallup club finished runner-up. After another three titles won by Wilson, the Hartley-led Puyallup Vikings then ran off with 10 straight championships, until Jack Connelly's Lakes Lancers team defeated the Vikings in 1983 to end their winning streak. The Lancers dominated the double-elimination event, beating the Vikings 13–1 in a winner's bracket semifinal game and again, 12–6, in the title contest.

But Puyallup came back to win the next three titles, from 1984 to 1986. With the exception of 1988, which was won by Rogers, Curtis High School was the next water polo power to emerge, winning seven titles from 1987 to 1994 under coach Tim Vesey. Since 1995, however, the sport has been dominated by Mercer Island, Bainbridge Island, and Sammamish high schools.

With water polo being a relatively inexpensive sport compared to most and with participation in high-school girl's water polo on the rise, the future of the sport appears bright.

won no Olympic medals, her sister Tara did. Tara placed second at trials in the 100-meter breaststroke and finished sixth in that event at the Olympics. She received a silver medal in the 4 X 100-meter medley relay for her participation in the preliminaries that were required to qualify the U.S. team for the finals. This was the first time two sisters, both from Bremerton, qualified for the same Olympic team, at least in the United States.

The world rankings are the highest achievement awards in world long-course swimming. Only the top 25 in the world achieve this certificate. This achievement level was attained by the following TSC swimmers: Kaye Hall, Barbara Mitchell, Debe Gratias, Miriam Smith, Dan Hannula, Dave Hannula, Dick Hannula Jr., Dennis Larsen, Jack Horsley, Chuck Richards, Janet Buchan, Bob Jackson, Yolande VanderStraten, and Dana Kirk. Megan Quann and Jamie Reid of the SSSC also reached this level.

Colleges

Tacoma and Pierce County have produced hundreds of scholarship swimmers at the college level. The National Collegiate Athletic Assocation (NCAA) Division I All-Americans list is the most prestigious; it includes the following from Wilson High: Mike Stauffer (1961), University of Minnesota; Bruce Richards (1966), Michigan State University; Dan Hannula, Kurt Knipher, Bob Music, and Dennis Larsen (1970), University of Washington; Dave Hannula (1972), Rod Stewart (1973), and Dick Hannula Jr. (1975), University of Southern California; Dave Swenson (1973) and Steve Jack (1974), Southern Illinois University; Saadi Ghatan (1983), Princeton University; and Evan Martinec (2000), Louisiana State University. Other Pierce County high school swimmers completing the men's Division I All-American list include Chuck Richards (1963), Stadium High and University of Indiana; Jack Connelly (1974), Lakes High and Stanford University; Paton McClung (1987), Curtis High and University of California-Berkeley; and Todd Edison (1988), Curtis High and Southern Illinois University.

Wilson High also produced female swimmers who attained All-American status in NCAA Division I: Miriam Smith (1976), University of Southern California; Janet

Buchan (1979), Stanford University; Roxanne Carlton (1982), Southern Illinois University, Dana Powers (1982), University of Nebraska; and K. C. Cline (1988), Brigham Young University. The Foss High swim team and Bellarmine High contributed Susan Lenth (1983), Stanford University. Foss also had Paige Wright (1986), Northwestern University. Gig Harbor High School contributed Jackie Lobdell (2000), University of California–Los Angeles (UCLA). All of these swimmers, boys and girls, also competed for TSC. LSC swimmer Sara Platzer, Lakes High School (2000), also achieved this distinction at UCLA, as did Jamie Reid (2001), Puyallup High School and SSSC, at the University of Florida.

Both UPS and Pacific Lutheran University (PLU) have established successful swimming programs. Gary Chase, coach at PLU, integrated his physiology background into the endeavor and, along with his successor, Jim Johnson, led their teams to top 10 finishes in NAIA collegiate competitions.

Don Duncan started at UPS in 1956, and by the time of his retirement 37 years later, he coached 10 individual national champions in the NAIA and 10 individual champions in the NCAA Division II. In addition, he coached 76 collegiate All-Americans in these two divisions. His greatest swimmer, Bob Jackson, established a NCAA Division II record in the 100-yard breaststroke that still remains on the books at the time of this writing. For 14 years, Wilson High School graduate Dan Seelye held the national record in NCAA Division II in the 100-yard backstroke. When Duncan retired, his successor, Chris Myhre, won three men's and four women's NAIA championships. Sarah Rudolph was the most successful woman swimmer when, under the guidance of coach Rick Unrue, she won five Division II titles while establishing three national Division II records.

The future continues to look bright, with many talented young swimmers and coaches coming of age. The greatest contribution of the Pierce County swimming alums was and will continue to be the successful citizens that have come out of the swimming program. Physicians, lawyers, dentists, teachers, coaches, engineers, and businesspeople attest to the self-discipline, time management, and industriousness that are at the heart of the best swimming programs.

CHAPTER 43

TENNIS AND TABLE TENNIS

John DuPriest competes in the Pacific Northwest Open in 1947 (courtesy Don DuPriest).

Tennis, like so many sports enjoyed today, has a long history stretching back to medieval times. In Tacoma, however, the origins of the game are a bit more recent, beginning when a group of local women met to form a tennis organization in 1886. The Alpha, formed two years later, became Tacoma's first lawn tennis club, featuring four grass tennis courts.

In 1890 the official Ladies Tennis Club was born, and the women shared four grass courts with a men's organization, known as the Tacoma Lawn Tennis Club. The grounds they shared are now the site of the Woodstock Apartments at First and Yakima. The men's clubhouse, an old barnlike structure, was on Division Avenue where a car dealership now stands. By 1904 the two groups combined under the Tacoma Lawn Tennis Club (TLTC) banner. One of a handful of tennis clubs west of the Mississippi more than 100 years old, TLTC was one of the founding members of the Pacific Northwest Tennis Association in 1904.

Courts and a clubhouse were constructed across from Wright Park and the original Annie Wright Seminary on North First Street. Within a year of its founding, TLTC was hosting the Pacific Northwest Open Tennis Championships, an event that has been played in Tacoma every year except for 1945. The Thorne Cup, awarded to the men's singles champion at the Northwest Open in 1895, was named for Chester Thorne, a prominent Tacoma banker and one of the first commissioners of the Port of Tacoma. The Thorne Cup is older than the notable Davis Cup, whose origins date to 1900 in Boston.

In 1903, when the courts had to be moved to make way for the Woodstock Apartments, the Tacoma Land Company offered TLTC land along Tacoma Avenue North adjacent to the present-day Annie Wright School. A new clubhouse was completed in 1905 at 502 Borough Road, the present site of TLTC. According to club historian Suzanne Jordan, the early clay courts "required watering and rolling prior to use, and they became a sea of mud during rainy conditions. However, in freezing weather the courts were covered with water and transformed into a skating rink." Members could also lawn bowl or play croquet on nicer days.

The Pacific Northwest Open Tennis Championships, still held annually at TLTC, is Tacoma's premier tennis competition, consistently one of the top prize money events in the region. The summer competition takes place on the club's six outdoor and two indoor courts, with the Peggy Haley Trophy now awarded to the best woman player, along with the Thorne Cup for men. Initially the Pacific Northwest Tennis Open also included junior and senior matches, but by the '70s these events—while still a part of the Tennis Open—required the use of some 22 courts located throughout Tacoma and Pierce County.

Many national and international tennis greats have found their way to TLTC and had their names engraved as winners of the Pacific Northwest Open, such as Jack Kramer, Bill Tilden, Pancho Gonzales, Maureen Connolly, Rosie Casals, and Don Budge. While in summer Reserve Officer Training Corps (ROTC) at Fort Lewis in 1966, Arthur Ashe played exhibition games and umpired during

the Pacific Northwest Open; even Dean Martin Jr. played in the Pacific Northwest Open once in the 1970s.

TLTC also had its share of local winners and outstanding teachers. Among the latter were Lyle Morton, Gary Linden, Doyle Perkins, Wallace Scott, Jim Verdieck, Dave Rasmussen, Steve Kubota, and Paul Koessler, formerly an All-American at Pacific Lutheran University (PLU). One of the early Pacific Northwest Open winners from Tacoma was May Sutton Bundy, who won the women's singles title in 1911 and 1912. In 1905 she had become the first American to win at Wimbledon.

Wallace Scott, before becoming a tennis pro, and Patty Greenup were also early local tennis winners. Scott, a lefty with a well-documented powerful serve, at one time coached at Stadium and Lincoln High Schools. He won the national collegiate championship in 1924 in Philadelphia

Jay Abbott (L.) and Eddie Schultz won the National Association of Intercollegiate Athletics District I doubles title and finished second in doubles at the Northwest Conference tournament in 1983; Schultz was inducted into the PLU Athletic Hall of Fame in 2004 (PLU).

TABLE TENNIS, OR PING-PONG

The British invented table tennis during the early years of the 20th century and coined the name Ping-Pong for the new sport. It gradually encircled the globe, finding a competitive home from China to Romania. In fact, many Americans know table tennis as the sport that helped the United States reopen diplomatic doors to China during the Nixon administration. Cold war tensions eased a bit when China invited members of the U.S. Table Tennis Association to play in Peking in April 1971. For a short spell, this little-known sport received international attention.

On March 19, 1933, the Point Defiance pavilion was the venue for the first annual Pierce County Ping-Pong tournament. Ping-Pong was popular because it was affordable at a time when the Great Depression left most people with little money but still a desire to play some kind of game. With just a paddle and a ball, a player was set for table tennis. For many tournaments, no entry fee was charged, but players had to furnish their own balls and paddles. A 10-cent donation each night helped cover the costs of trophies. For Depression-era youth, the sport became a lifetime endeavor, and it is not unusual to find some of those people still playing today.

Paul Lucien, a 1937 graduate of Lincoln High School, recalled that table tennis players at that time were part of a league whose home was on the upper floors of the Medical Arts Building. The group later moved across Market Street to the YMCA building, then located at Seventh. Lucien became one of the top local players. In 1940 the Park City Ping-Pong Club held a county singles elimination tournament on five consecutive Wednesday evenings at Jefferson field house. Following Lucien's three straight weeks of victories, the *Tacoma News Tribune* informed readers that "Paul Lucien is the No.1 man in Tacoma competitive ping pong. With two titles already under his belt, Lucien won another Wednesday night, by flashing his shots past Grant Putman in the second open county singles tournament."

Lucien, a left-hander, became known for employing a defensive "chop" game counter to the powerful offensive fireworks of others. His play imparted a reverse spin that his opponents were not used to. Potential competitors against Lucien's wild spin were likely members of the Tacoma YMCA Table Tennis Club, including Karl Kloepper, Phil Garland, Charles Stewart, and Merle Smith.

Tore Frederickson, another Ping-Pong veteran, migrated to the United States from Sweden and started playing the sport at the age of 24, continuing to do so at the age of 81. He, along with many other players, was a part of the Tacoma Table Tennis Club, organized in the 1960s. Their first venue was in a University Place fire station, then the Fircrest Community Center, and now the South Park Community Center. Frederickson remembered the Daffodil Festival Table Tennis Tournament as one of his favorites.

Table tennis, apart from the momentary attention it received in the 1970s, is not a sport that regularly grasps the attention of sports writers. But local enthusiasts love this particular kind of competitive play. Presently the First Congregational Church is a weekly home for table tennis play. The four tables are busy all night long.

and was one of the outstanding players on the West Coast throughout the 1920s. Greenup figure skated in the wintertime and played tennis in the spring and summer. Upon graduation from Stadium High School in 1942, she joined the Ice Follies and skated professionally before returning to Tacoma. She was hired by Jack Heinrick to teach both skating and tennis at Tacoma Community College (TCC). She was a longtime participant in local Pacific Northwest tennis tournaments in addition to teaching at the Tacoma Elks Club and the Oakbrook Country Club.

Schools

While TLTC was home to many local tennis players, schools were developing their own youth programs. Future attorney Wally Cavanagh began playing in the mid-1930s, and by 1939 he was part of a Mason Junior High School team that also included brothers Dick and Ken Burrows, along with brothers Harvey and Harold Mosich. Lyle Morton, whom Cavanagh called his mentor, organized the Proctor Street Tennis Tournament for players under the age of 18. In Proctor tournaments that year, Cavanagh was the singles winner at 15 years old. TLTC sponsored the Center Tournament for young men, where Cavanagh won the title in 1940. The media accolades continued that year, when Cavanagh competed in the City Tournament sponsored by the Metropolitan Park District and played on the courts at Point Defiance Park.

At that time, the Mason Junior High School tennis team was the only one in the city. Cavanagh and his pals were so good that they played against the Stadium High School team before all becoming Stadium Tigers themselves. By the time of his graduation from Stadium in 1944, Cavanagh had been part of a tennis team that took both state tournament and Cross-State League titles. He continued competitive tennis at the University of Washington (UW) until the rigors of law school intervened.

Stadium, Bellarmine, and Lincoln High Schools also had excellent programs during that time. Don Flye, a Lincoln High graduate, was nationally ranked in the Boys 14 Division in 1947 and went on to UW, where he teamed up with Bill Quillian to win the National Juniors Doubles Championship in 1951. Before Flye left college, he was named to the top position on the team his junior year, won three doubles and one singles conference title for the Northern Division of the Pacific Coast Conference, and was a member of the 1953 U.S. Junior Davis Cup team. Thirty years prior, his father, Guy, a Stadium graduate, was also a prominent player in the area.

New youth tennis programs and facilities located throughout Pierce County led to what former Clover Park High School coach Gary Thomas called "the great growth of tennis in Tacoma." Using concrete courts constructed at Clover Park High during the Great Depression, Ed Stevens, owner of the Country Store at Lakewood Center, introduced tennis to locals in the early 1950s. Palmer Koon and Larry Larson, both students of Jim Verdieck, started the Clover Park District Program in the early 1960s. Thomas, coach from 1966 to 1992, also ran the Clover Park summer tennis program from 1973 to 1978, when more than 1,100 young people enrolled. In addition, a Junior Davis Cup League formed for those between the ages of 10 and 16. Competition venues ranged from Vancouver, British Columbia to Oregon. "There was good sportsmanship, and many participants later played interscholastic and collegiate tennis," remembered Thomas. Participating organizations included TLTC, Lakewood Racquet Club (LRC), Clover Park Tennis Club, Oakbrook, the Tacoma Country Club, and Fox Island, where Susan Spencer was the force behind the junior tennis program through the 1990s.

Although Stadium High School is credited as being the first Tacoma high school to win a boy's state high school championship, the school actually tied with Yakima's Eisenhower High School in 1965. Bellarmine won outright honors with back-to-back titles in 1968 and 1969 with a team that included Jim Healy, John Galbraith, and Rod Koon. The Gig Harbor High School boys' tennis team, under coach Lyle McIntosh, posted a glossy 58–0 record in dual matches from 1981 to 1984. This successful run included four consecutive top-four finishes in the 2A state tournament, including third place in 1981 and 1984, second in 1982, and state champions in 1983. Steve Holmes was the state singles champion for the Tides in both 1983 and 1984.

On the girls' side, Charles Wright Academy had four state crowns to their credit. Taryn Anderson of Annie Wright

School won three A/B high school crowns, the last in 2003. Sonja Olejar, another Bellarmine student, won an unprecedented four straight high school singles championships in 4A competition, losing only one set and no matches in her 1989–92 high school career. She went on to star at Pepperdine University. Winning back-to-back 4A state titles in 2003 and 2004, the Lions were lead by doubles champions Alita Fisher and Katie Kennel and singles player Suzie Matzenauer.

Colleges

At the collegiate level, Mike Benson coached the PLU men's team from 1970 to 1999, a total of 30 years. During that time, he amassed an overall won-lost record of 400–196 and 167–18 in conference play. The Lutes won 24 Northwest Conference championships and competed in the National Association of Intercollegiate Athletics (NAIA) Nationals 19 times, finishing eighth twice. Playing for the Lutes from 1976 to 1979, Dave Trageser of Puyallup High School holds the single-season record for most wins, with a 34–1 record in 1978 and 34–2 in 1979. His career record was 125–12, and in addition to four singles championships at the conference and district levels, Trageser reached the singles and double finals at nationals and was named the Outstanding Performer at the nationals in 1978. Other top performers over the years included Eddie Schultz, Doug Gardner, Craig Hamilton, Paul Koessler, Gary Wusterbarth, and Jonathan Schultz. Gardner and Hamilton were both recipients of the NAIA's prestigious Arthur Ashe Award, given for athletic and academic achievements, community involvement, and sportsmanship.

Longtime PLU physical education instructor Sara Officer started the first women's team, in the 1960s, though later on Benson took over and coached six years to finish with a 90–35 record. Carolyn Carlson, under coach Rusty Carlson (no relation), reached the quarterfinals in the national tournament during her 1984–87 career to become one of PLU's top female players.

At the University of Puget Sound (UPS), top players under the direction of longtime coach Steve Bowen included 1998 singles champion and Conference Player of the Year Mari Hrebenar and district singles and doubles champion Lisa Wong in 1993.

At the community college level, Jack Scott's Fort Steilacoom Raiders' team won the men's community college state championship in 1975. Tacoma Community College (TCC), led by player Brian Berg, took second at state under Harland Malyon in 1967, TCC's first year at state, and then went on to make 12 more appearances. Dan Beyette was TCC's top player over the years, and the establishment of the TCC Tennis Club helped to encourage the community to get involved in the sport. Jerry Ogden and Al Epstein then started the Greater Tacoma Tennis Association and ran organized leagues and tournaments on the TCC courts, which helped the growth of the sport for many years.

Prominent Players

Tennis grew tremendously in popularity, both locally and nationally, in the '60s and '70s. Part of the new interest was sparked because tennis got more attention in the national media, including coverage of many charismatic international tennis stars such as Ilie Nastase and Jimmie Connors, and a World Team Tennis league was created, with players ranging from Tom Gorman (Seattle Cascades) to Billie Jean King (Philadelphia Freedom). And who can forget the 1973 "Battle of the Sexes" challenge held between Billy Jean King and Bobby Riggs, played before a televised audience of 37 million?

Increased popularity of tennis in Tacoma led to the start of numerous instructional programs at both private clubs and public facilities. In the late 1970s, tennis enthusiasts rallied to build indoor courts that transformed tennis into a year-round sport and created an environment where the city could provide training grounds for present and future tennis players. LRC was the first private club to invest in indoor courts, opening two in 1968; TLTC soon followed suit in 1975. The Lakewood Summer Festival, an event that in the 1970s drew more than 100 participants for the men's singles, was inspired by George Linthicum. In addition, newer athletic clubs, such as the Town and Country Tennis Club in Gig Harbor (six indoor courts) and the Fircrest Tennis Club (three indoor courts), saw their tennis memberships increase. In July 1976, the first public facility opened when the Pierce County Parks and Recreation Department constructed four indoor tennis courts at Sprinker Recreation Center. Many of these clubs set up interclub team competitions for adults and youth. With the U.S. Tennis Association (USTA) taking a proactive approach in promoting tennis at the grassroots level, the town of Fircrest added six public courts and classes immediately filled up, as did the mixed doubles leagues that were then gaining in popularity.

Other Pierce County residents have also made significant contributions to local tennis history. Garold Gray and John DuPriest were both top players at Stadium High School, with DuPriest attaining a national top 10 ranking in the Boys 15-and-Under Division in the late 1940s. He then played at UPS and won the Evergreen Conference championship while in college. Later on Mike Pazourek achieved a number-one ranking in the country in the Boys 14-and-Under Division. Scott Shogreen, a Curtis High graduate and a rival of Pat Galbraith, went on to play at Pepperdine University before returning to the Pacific Northwest, where at one time he was ranked number one in singles, doubles, and mixed doubles. He was one of the top 35-and-over players in the country, having represented the United States in international senior competitions on several occasions. Jody Rush, a longtime teaching pro in

the community, was ranked number one in various age group divisions in his career. So was Steve Kubota, currently the head pro at Sprinker Recreation Center. Rush also has several national titles to his credit, and beginning at age 40, he represented the United States in international senior competitions. Leona Matzenauer was an active participant in the Masters programs, attaining a number-one ranking in the nation in the Women's 35-and-Over Division in 2000.

Fortunately for the community, a number of individuals volunteered to serve with the USTA's Pacific Northwest Section. For several years, Max Thomas was an area vice president who helped organize the Pacific Northwest Senior Championships. A founder of LRC, Thomas finished runner-up at the USTA Nationals in 1990 in the 75-and-Over Division and, after playing for 78 years, finally retired from the game at the age of 85. Don Ervin played at Stadium

Practicing overhead serves was the order of the day at a local summer instructional camp, ca. 1950s (SSM).

High and then coached the UPS men's team for seven years before serving as vice president for the USTA's Southwest Washington Section for six years. He was also a longtime umpire for Team Tennis and the Virginia Slims and World Championship Tennis Tours. Ervin devoted 42 years on various Pacific Northwest Tennis Association (PNTA) committees, continuing to play at LRC at the age of 81.

Doris Claypool served on the board of LRC and as vice president of the USTA's Southwest Washington Section. She also played in the senior women's events throughout the Northwest and for years helped run the Pacific Northwest Senior Championship games. Peter Kram's involvement included being two-time president of the Southwest Section of the PNTA, serving on numerous USTA national committees, and being a linesman and umpire for both the Virginia Slims Tour and the World Championship Tennis Tour. In 1977 Doctors Eugenia Colen and John Colen were the first Washingtonians to umpire at Wimbledon.

The tennis contributions of Harold and Suzanne Koenig took them from the local courts of Fircrest to elementary schools throughout the county. From the late 1970s through the 1990s, they started mixed league competitions, a program that became so popular the match play crossed county lines to include players from Kitsap and Thurston Counties.

During this time, the Koenigs also taught program staff how to teach tennis because there were not enough pros to meet instruction needs. Local park departments, boys and girls clubs, and the YMCA asked the couple to develop an instructional program so that even those who did not play tennis themselves could teach the sport to beginners. Teaching tennis also took the Koenigs on the road as a part of the Play Tennis America Program (PTAP). Initially sponsored by tennis champion Arthur Ashe through the USTA, PTAP teaches tennis to disadvantaged students in public schools and advocates for neighborhood courts, making the game available to all children regardless of their family's income.

Doyle Perkins created a strong juniors program as tennis pro at the Tacoma Lawn Tennis Club in the early 1960s (photo by J. Mack Koon).

Local pediatrician Dr. George Tanbara's goal is to create tennis opportunities for children so that the sport becomes a lifelong health and recreational activity. Tanbara ranked fourth in 2002 in the Pacific Northwest 80-and-over singles standings and has played against high school state champions for decades. He believes that the tennis experience should be less about competition and monetary rewards and more about playing with family and friends.

J. Mack Koon, a president of TLTC and PNTA, arranged a local exhibit of the Davis Cup. He inspired the organization of local and regional tennis programs. His wife, Dode, was instrumental in developing the tennis program at Bellarmine Prep in the late 1950s. Sons Jamie, Rod, and Palmer were all active players and instructors; Rod won two state high school doubles championships with John Galbraith, Pat Galbraith's older brother. In 1966 the family was presented with the Tennis Family of the Year Award by the PNTA, and in the mid-'70s, they ran the Fircrest Tennis Club.

A Pro

Despite all these important contributions, it's still player Patrick Galbraith who is Tacoma's most successful and best-known tennis champion. He began playing at the age of six and honed his skills as a left-handed tennis machine at Bellarmine Prep, where he won three straight high school state singles titles, 1983–85. Following his graduation from high school, he was recruited by the University of California–Los Angeles (UCLA). Along the way, he won singles titles at the Pacific Northwest Tennis Championships in 1985, 1986, and 1990, becoming only the second three-time men's open singles winner in the tournament's history when he defeated fellow Tacoman and longtime rival Scott Shogreen, 6–4, 6–4. By the time he left UCLA, Galbraith was a three-time All-America doubles player and had won the Pacific-10 Conference singles championship, along with a National Collegiate Athletics Association (NCAA) Division I doubles title in 1989.

By 1990 Galbraith reached the semifinals at the U.S. Open and in 1993 and 1994 he was a Wimbledon doubles finalist with partner Grant Connell, finishing runner-up both times. Together they were the world's number-one-ranked doubles team in 1993, and two years later they won the World Doubles Championships, as well as placing sec-

Jack Kramer played in the Pacific Northwest Open Tennis Championships at the Tacoma Lawn Tennis Club in 1937 (courtesy Tacoma Lawn Tennis Club).

ond at Wimbledon. Galbraith also won the U.S. Open in mixed doubles with Elna Reinach in 1994 and Lisa Raymond in 1996, followed finally by his dream: an invitation to play in the Davis Cup competition. Teamed with Patrick McEnroe, the twosome successfully defeated their Mexican competitors but lost to their Czech Republic rivals. During Galbraith's career, he won at least one Association of Tennis Professionals doubles title for 11 consecutive years and totaled 36 doubles titles with 16 different partners before retiring in 2000 with $2.6 million in winnings.

For more than 100 years, tennis has been played on the clay and concrete courts of Pierce County. The sport formally began as a game for the elite members of TLTC but quickly achieved a broader popularity, thanks to school programs and facilities available at parks and community centers. From May Sutton Bundy to Pat Galbraith, Tacoma's instructors and tennis enthusiasts have produced many champions; then will surely produce many more.

CHAPTER 44

TRACK AND FIELD

R.A.B. Young was a world heel-and-toe champion in the late 1890s (courtesy Helen Young).

The state high school track meet, in its nearly 60 years of official existence, never had been held in Tacoma. But in 1982, when the idea of Star Track was brought forth at Lincoln Bowl, it was as if the meet had come home.

Tacoma and Pierce County have had a long and rich tradition in track and field, one stretching back to the early years of the 20th century and including one of the state's first Olympic medalists, as well as its first woman track Olympian—and this almost 40 years before the advent of girls' high school track. More to the point, however, Tacoma and suburban Pierce County high schools had won 12 of the previous 14 state boys 3A team championships and a half dozen titles in the still-young 2A classification.

But in 1982, the state meet itself was on a losing streak. In the early 1970s, the big-school meet (now 4A) had been wrenched from its historic home at Washington State University (WSU) in Pullman and taken to Seattle, only to be abandoned on the doorstep of the University of Washington (UW). Starting with a desultory final running at the UW in 1976, the meet was bounced around to four different sites in six years, its crowds, coverage, and stature

diminishing. And the fledgling 2A meet (now 3A) was doing no better.

So when Dan Inveen of the Tacoma School District and Dick Kunkle of the *Tacoma News Tribune*, two longtime leaders and innovators in local track, set their sights on bringing the meet to Lincoln Bowl, they knew it was something of a rescue mission—except that they had a lot more than that in mind. Indeed, what they mapped out was a three-day, four-session extravaganza for the 3A and 2A meets combined, complete with opening ceremonies and closing fireworks and a blaze of media coverage.

Their big idea needed a big name, which came from another local sports leader, Doug McArthur: Star Track. After all, they were proposing "to boldly go where no [state meet] had gone before."

And so they did, spectacularly, with large and enthusiastic crowds filling both sides of the bowl and recapturing much of the glory the meet once enjoyed in Pullman. It was just as Inveen and Kunkle had envisioned—and it locked in Tacoma as the center of the Washington track universe.

The timing was perfect too. In 1982 two local athletes, Darrell Robinson of Wilson High School and Ericka Harris of Gig Harbor High School, were far and away the fastest 400-meter runners in the nation and coming to the end of stellar high school careers. Unfortunately, Harris's final meet ended in a muscle pull. But Robinson took the state 400-meter record into uncharted territory—less than 46 seconds—as he led Wilson High to another team title and launched himself on a summer that would end with him the fastest world Junior 400-meter runner of all time.

Soon Star Track had a reputation as one of the best high school meets in the nation, although as far as the Tacoma schools were concerned, it might have become too much of a good thing. Coaches statewide credited the meet with spurring a resurgence in the sport, which ironically helped end Tacoma schools' domination, although Pierce County suburban schools continued to ring up titles. And the meet that went begging in the late 1970s now was coveted across the state.

Of course, the prominence of Pierce County in track and field wasn't confined to the conventional school and open competitions on 400-meter ovals nor the old, cockeyed five-laps-to-a-mile track around Stadium Bowl. Fort Lewis's Cowan Stadium long was the site of the state Special Olympics. The Sound-to-Narrows run, modeled by Dick Kunkle on San Francisco's Bay-to-Breakers and launched

Members of the 1948 College of Puget Sound undefeated track team included: back row, L. to R., Don Danielson, Al Danielson, Nelson, unknown, Chuck Gusto; middle row, L. to R., John Rafto, unknown, unknown, Ron Tuttle, Dick Lewis, Paul Kelly, coach Mitch Angelel; front row, L. to R., Duval Wiseman, Max Walden, Dale Larson, John McCorry, Jack Fabulich (SSM, 1552).

under *News Tribune* sponsorship in 1973, was the oldest of the Northwest's mass-participation road races and is still one of the largest. Puyallup's Sparks Stadium and Lakewood's Harry Lang Stadium were regular venues for district and other competitions. And the University of Puget Sound (UPS)'s Baker Stadium even stood in for the University of Oregon (UO)'s Hayward Field in the filming of the 1997 movie *Prefontaine*.

Not all of the athletes were kids, either; some of them were seniors, including the hundreds who annually ran Sound-to-Narrows, plus Masters track competitors who proved that the sport isn't for only the young. Indeed, some of those folks were among the sport's foremost contributors, such as Tacoma's Fred Shanaman and Puyallup's Ron Mattila. Shanaman, a onetime Dartmouth shot-putter whose donation capped the drive to build the sports museum that bears his family name, returned to his athletic roots at age 57 and established himself as one of the top Masters weight men in the country, placing third nationally in the 60–65 weight pentathlon in 1996. Mattila launched Federal Way's elementary track program in 1972, about the same time he embarked on his Masters career, which continued into the 21st century with bronze medals in the 50- and 100-meter dashes at the Masters World Games in Utah in 2003.

The Early Years

The stories and records of Pierce County track are seemingly endless, the personalities as diverse as the county's population. In the 1890s and early 20th century, for instance, the most famous Tacoma track athletes actually walked into the record books.

Racewalking—heel-to-toe racing—was the rage, and athletes who engaged in the sport were called pedestrians. "It was not so long ago," a Tacoma newspaper writer noted in 1916, "that walking was a sport, avocation and constitutional exercise in Tacoma. Walking clubs were quite the thing, and long-distance walking races were much indulged in by those who were able to swing their pedal extremities with rapidity and continuity. As a recognized sport, champion pedestrians were under the care of trainers, and big prizes were offered to the winners."

Foremost among those champions were the Young brothers. Robert Allen Brown Young was credited in 1896 with breaking five world records in an afternoon's walk. He taught his brother Isaac the sport, and the two of them brought along their youngest brother, William, who in 1905 won the Northwest amateur championship for the mile walk at the Lewis and Clark Exposition in Portland. Of William, a reporter noted, "His friends at the city hall point to his feet, for Bill wears a No. 14 shoe, as evidence that he should be a natural-born walker."

Interest in track and field "athletics" revived worldwide with establishment of the modern Olympic Games in Athens in 1896. The City of Destiny was right in step, with the Tacoma Athletic Club (TAC)'s annual fall meeting that year at Athletic Park including the 100-yard dash, 440-yard run, 1-mile run, pole vaulting, and broad jumping. James Barrager was the Pacific Northwest champion in the broad jump and 100-yard dash, and other local favorites included Eddie Dickson and A. Gallatin Brown, 100-yard dash runners; John Schlarb, George Gregg, and Lewis Parsons, 1-mile runners; and Hilland Kennedy, pole vaulter.

Buckley High's John Ganero hurled the discus 119 feet 6 inches at the annual Pierce County Track and Field Meet in 1924, beating the previous record by exactly 7 feet (courtesy David Eskenazi collection).

The first recognized state high school meets came in 1905 in Seattle and Pullman, where Tacoma was well represented: it was recorded that a Boggs of Tacoma swept the 50- and 100-yard dashes in 5.8 and 10.6 seconds, respectively; a Lawrence won the discus at 111–3; and Harry Watson won the mile in 4 minutes, 54.8 seconds.

One of the early Pullman meet's most impressive champions was Puyallup quarter-miler Talbot Hartley, who in 1927 became the first state runner to break 50 seconds in the 440-yard dash; his 49.6 seconds lasted 14 years as the meet record. Tacoma's 1929 official debut at the state meet was ominous: the city's first two state titles came in the 440-yard dash, with Stadium High School's Orm Pound, and the 880-yard relay, with the Lincoln High team of Michel, Fawcett, Berry, and Johnson in a meet record of 1 minute, 31.5 seconds.

Tacoma's "recorded" history as a producer of young track champions began in 1929, the year the city schools first competed in the state meet in Pullman. Although Tacoma had four champions in the first state meet in Seattle in 1905 and actually played host to the last of a short-lived event called the East versus West meet in 1911, the city and almost everyone else in Western Washington stayed home from the Pullman Interscholastic, which got going in 1915. But when the Pullman meet gained official status in 1924, schools from across the state—although not Tacoma and Seattle—signed up.

Tacoma's success in the state meets of the 1930s was a precursor of things to come. Bert Meier, in 1931 and '32, brought Stadium High's string of state 440-yard dash titles to four, and he also won the 200-yard dash in '32. Stadium, led by Chuck Soper and coached by Ralph Christie, won the team title in '34. Soper, who won his second straight state discus title in 1934 with a national interscholastic record of 190 feet, 6 1/2 inches, went on to collegiate stardom at the University of Southern California (USC). Placing second in the National Collegiate Athletics Association (NCAA) and first in the Amateur Athletic Union (AAU) meet in 1938, he was selected to an All-American team that competed in Europe in that last pre–World War II summer. Starting in 1935, Lincoln High School ran three titles in a row, two under coach Vincent Keyes and one under William Hardie. The Abes' superstar was sprinter Hal Berndt, out of Mitch

Herman Brix was a silver medalist in Amsterdam's 1928 Olympic Games (SSM, 2000.6.3).

Angelel's Mason Junior High program, who swept the state 100-yard and 220-yard dashes in 1936–37 and whose 9.8 seconds in the 100-yard dash in 1937 stood as the City League record for more than 20 years. Three years after Berndt, another Abe, Dick Kenniston, also swept the state 100-yard and 220-yard dashes in 1940–41.

Angelel's coaching began at Mason Junior High in 1929 and he started turning out champions almost immediately in a career that included Stadium High School and UPS. His contributions included his son Jim, longtime coach at Clover Park, as well as a protégé, Bob Ehrenheim, who made Mount Tahoma High School a state contender in the 1960s.

Through the rest of the 1940s, Tacoma's state success was limited. Fife, however, had three state champs, including the multisport star Don Paul, for whom track was no better than a third sport but who beat 'em all with a 21-foot 4 3/4-inch long jump in 1944. Paul went on to star in football and baseball at WSU and spent a long career as a defensive back in the National Football League (NFL; see chapter 10, Baseball: High School and College Players, and chapter 23, Football: Pro and Semipro).

The 1950s brought team championships to Clover Park, under young coach Art Hutton in 1952, and to Stadium in 1954, highlighted by coach Bob Levinson's long career. The Stadium Tigers won it without a single individual champion, but the next year, Stadium's Steve Anderson was the meet's star, sweeping the hurdles even as Yakima won the team title. Anderson went on to excel at UO, just missing the 1960 Olympic team in the decathlon.

Lincoln High also was prominent in the 1950s, breaking the 880-yard relay record two years in a row, led by future UW running backs: 440-yard dash winner Jim Jones in 1954 and long-jump record-breaker Luther Carr in 1955. Carr's 1955 meet record, 23 feet 7 inches, stood for almost 10 years. Lincoln also had a two-time mile champion in Neil Rader, 1950–51, later a two-time Northern Division champion at WSU.

Olympic Contenders

The first and arguably most colorful of Tacoma and Pierce County's track and field Olympians and U.S. national team stars were Herman Brix, Stadium class of 1924, in 1928 at Amsterdam, and Gertrude Wilhelmsen, Puyallup class of 1931, in 1936 at Berlin. Brix came home with a silver medal, and then went on to a career in Hollywood using the stage name Bruce Bennett, most famously as one of the late 1930s Tarzans. Wilhelmsen came home to work the family farm, raise her own family, and continue competing in a variety of sports—including Masters track—into her later years, living to see girls attain equal status with boys in state high school track.

For both, the road to the Olympics started inauspiciously. Amazingly, Brix started small. Literally. "In high school I played in the midget program—I started out at 125 pounds," he said in a 2004 interview. But by the end of his Stadium High career, under the coaching of Myron "Chief" Carr, he was a 180-pounder and still growing ("as big as they make them," said the 1924 yearbook), on his way to UW to compete in football and track.

"Sports were natural for me. I was always interested in glee club and I got to play the lead in *The Pirates of Penzance* … so I really got my start in performing in high school." The acting bug would have to wait, though. In college it was just sports.

"What motivated me at the UW was the fact I had an older brother, Egbert, who was also on the football and track teams, and I was darned if he was going to be better than I was." They overlapped one season on the varsity, and that season—Herman's sophomore year—provided what Herman, a tackle, called "my first big highlight in sports," the Rose Bowl game. By a missed extra point, the Huskies lost to Alabama, 20–19, but the trip wasn't a total loss. "The next day we went over to the studios of Douglas Fairbanks and got a tour as well as having our picture taken with him." That visit was a fortuitous moment in Herman Brix's life.

In Brix's junior and senior years at UW, track took increasing prominence. He won the NCAA shot-put title as a junior, throwing 46 feet 7 3/8 inches, and as a senior he won the national AAU title and then the Olympic Trials, earning his ticket on the boat to Amsterdam.

"John Kuck, two Stanford boys, and I were the weight men for the U.S. team," said Brix. "Eleanor Holm was a 14-year-old diver on the team, and she was so small she could curl up into a ball and the four of us would get our exercise [on the boat] by throwing her from one to the other."

Brix opened his Olympic competition with a throw of 51 feet 8 1/4 inches, shattering the Olympic record by more than a foot and also surpassing the world record of Emil Hirschfield of Germany, who was second. Kuck, "who always threw well in practice but not always in competition," Herman said, was far back in the finals. "I told him to lie down, relax, close his eyes, and imagine he was at home throwing in front of his parents." And on his next throw, Kuck unloaded a put of 52 feet 3/4 inches, breaking Brix's freshly set world record. "I had only one throw left," Brix said, "and couldn't beat him and settled for the silver."

Brix returned to a hero's welcome, complete with parades and banquets, in Tacoma—but that wasn't the same as gainful employment. So, at the invitation of Douglas Fairbanks, he was off to Southern California to compete for the Los Angeles Athletic Club and train at United Artists Studios while starting his acting career. He continued to compete, pointing for the 1932 Olympics in Los Angeles, and extended his personal competitive best to 52 feet 10 inches. But he also soured somewhat on amateur sports when he was left stranded after winning a big meet in Vancouver, British Columbia, because the AAU cancelled a promised European tour. And although he continued to train for the 1932 Olympics in Los Angeles, his movie career interfered in a decisive way when he broke his shoulder while working on the film *Touchdown*. He tried but was unable to get back to full shot-put strength for the Olympic Trials (and the winning put in the Los Angeles games was "only" 52 feet 6 inches). That effectively ended his career, although he was later to throw an unofficial 54 feet 4 inches in an indoor exhibition at UW. It was a different era, one of true amateurism. "I never got one penny for competing," Brix said, and after college he usually had to pay for his own travel.

As Bruce Bennett, Brix took his place among Hollywood's Tarzans—check out the 1938 *Tarzan and the Green Goddess*—but the highlight of his film career probably was a role in the 1948 film *Treasure of the Sierra Madre*, an Academy Award–winner starring Humphrey Bogart and Walter Huston.

Gertrude Wilhelmsen's road to the Olympics pretty much started in her backyard. "Sports was my passion, and I liked to be outside and doing all sorts of sports," she said in 2003. "I was just a natural athlete and I could do all of those things. My father [a German immigrant] brought me up because my mother died in 1920 in the flu epidemic."

Girls' sports in the late 1920s and 1930s were popular in many schools, but it could vary wildly from school to school or town to town, and in many places actual competition was frowned upon. It was not until 1928 that women's track, and just a handful of events, was added to the Olympics.

So in one sense, Wilhelmsen came along at just the right time. Puyallup High, under coach Pop Logan, had girls' track, and Wilhelmsen took part in all the throwing events. Just one year after graduation, she got her first shot at the Olympics, only to finish fourth, one place from the team, in the javelin at the '32 Trials in Chicago. "But I just decided I had to move on and had to keep working to make the Olympics the next time around."

By then, she was married with a child, but said "I found time to train because my daughter would just come with me while I trained or my husband would watch her while working in the pasture."

Her sister Hildegard, a sprinter and hurdler, was in training too—Gertrude would throw the javelin and Hildegard would run to retrieve it. And then her old high school coach came back into her life.

"Pop Logan was working out at Viking Field and saw me training and invited me to come over and train with the boys on the track team, who were doing field events," she said. "I don't mean to brag, but I was pretty good. I was naturally strong, and working on the farm helped make me a little stronger."

By 1936 Gertrude was ready. She and Hildegard traveled to Providence, Rhode Island, for the Olympic Trials, and Gertrude qualified for Berlin in both the discus, second at 116 feet 9 inches, and javelin, third at 119 feet 3 inches. (The shot put was not yet an Olympic women's event.) Hildegard, in the 100-meter dash and 80-meter hurdles, didn't make it.

"Even with the political climate of the 1936 Berlin Olympics, there was no fear—just happiness at qualifying," Gertrude said. "That Hitler was there was of no real concern to me. But an advantage I had over my teammates was the fact that I spoke fluent German, so I could talk real easily with everyone over there. In fact, one day Hitler's men called me over because they wanted to talk to an American athlete, and we had a real nice conversation in German."

She turned down a chance to meet Hitler "because I wanted to watch Jesse Owens run—and I have a picture that I took of him in the race."

Wilhelmsen didn't win a medal in Berlin, but she eagerly pointed out that Puyallup didn't come up empty. "George Hunt graduated from Puyallup High in 1933 and he was on the gold medal–winning [UW] crew team," she said. "Two Puyallup grads on the same Olympic team," she marveled, noting that "the community was very supportive of us and raised money for us to attend the Olympic Trials."

Pierce County claimed only three more track Olympians, but one was a two-time medalist and another was a two-time qualifier. Gig Harbor's Doris Severtsen competed in both the 1968 Olympic Games in Mexico City, placing fifth in the 800-meter run, and the 1972 Olympic Games in Munich. Orting schoolboy Casey Carrigan, in one of the most amazing Olympic Trials upsets ever, pole vaulted his way onto the 1968 team for Mexico City.

And Mac Wilkins, whose discus career blossomed at Clover Park High School before he moved away in his senior year, won the 1976 Olympic discus in Montreal in a career that also included a world record, a berth on the boycotting 1980 team, and a silver medal in 1984 at Los Angeles.

Women's and Girls' Sports

When young Doris Severtsen, growing up at Horsehead Bay on the Gig Harbor Peninsula, discovered she liked running, she probably had no idea that she was on her way to becoming a trailblazer—not to mention a world champion—in a sport that barely even existed in this country at the time.

"When other kids were riding horses and bikes, I was running," said Severtsen, now Doris Heritage. "Most mornings and weekends, I'd go down to the water and walk along the beach or do some running. I'd do it just for the fun of it."

That fun led to her first competitive running, at Artondale Elementary School, and then Junior Olympics with the Mic Mac team in Tacoma, all of which led in turn to her

Doris Severtsen Heritage in mid-stride (SSM, 167).

first barrier: "In high school," in the late 1950s, "girls weren't even allowed to set foot on the track."

Women's and girls' sports often were afterthoughts in America. Interestingly, in the years before World War II there probably was wider acceptance of high school and college girls' sports—although some of it was in a "play day" rather than a competitive context—than there was after the war, when women were expected to leave the workforce and get back to the kitchen. Most high schools had tennis and swimming teams for girls in the 1950s, and in some parts of the country, girls' basketball was huge. Track and field, though, was almost completely the province of dedicated AAU-backed club teams found in most cities, such as the Mic Macs organized and coached in Tacoma by Robert McQuarrie.

Still, Severtsen was lucky. The Mic Macs, where she and sprinter-jumper Cecilia Ley Hankinson were achieving notice up and down the West Coast, were well coached and well traveled, and when Severtsen graduated from Peninsula High School and headed for Seattle Pacific University (SPU), she owned a national record in the 880-yard run and soon linked up with the man who became one of the foremost women's coaches in the country: Ken Foreman.

Under Foreman's coaching and with standouts such as Severtsen and Virginia Husted, SPU became one of the nation's foremost women's track powers, first as the Falcon Track Club and then as an official college team. Severtsen, who along the way had married another runner, Don Brown, won the first of her five straight world cross-country titles in 1967, and in that same year, she won the silver medal in the 800-meter run at the Pan-American Games in Winnipeg. In 1968 she qualified for her first Olympic team and placed fifth in the 800-meter run at Mexico City, in 2 minutes, 3.9 seconds, behind the gold medal of another American, Madeline Manning. The cross-country titles kept coming; she won a silver medal in the Pan-Am 800-meter run in Cali, Colombia, in 1971, and in 1972 she was back on the Olympic team in the 800-meter run—and in the first-ever Olympic women's 1,500-meter race.

At last count, Severtsen was a member of eight halls of fame and only the second woman inducted into the U.S. Track Coaches Hall of Fame. She won 14 national titles and five world titles as a runner; was a member of nine U.S.

national teams; set U.S. records in the 440-yard dash and 880-yard run; and was world record holder in the mile and the 800-, 1500-, 3000-, 5000- and 10,000-meter races. She was head coach of the U.S. national cross-country team and four times an assistant coach on U.S. Olympic and World Championship teams. And she's still coaching at her alma mater, where 10 of her cross-country teams have placed in the top 10 nationally and 36 of her distance runners have placed nationally. The kid who used to run for the fun of it grew up to become synonymous with women's track and distance running—as an athlete, a contributor, and a coach.

Among Pierce County athletes of Severtsen's era, only one other woman, Wilson High School's Judy Durham, reached the national-team level. Durham, who was the first Washington high school girl (and still one of the few ever) to long-jump 20 feet, qualified for the 1971 Pan-Am Games in Cali, Colombia, in the pentathlon. But an injury in the long jump knocked her out of the competition, and she missed out on the '72 Olympic team.

Colleges

For Tacoma and Pierce County track athletes, achieving fame beyond high school usually meant leaving home, even if going only as far as Seattle. And, of course, hundreds of local stars did that, the majority to UW, WSU, or other state schools, in addition to other major track programs across the country. But the recruiting street ran both ways, and PLU and UPS, both with proud athletic traditions, also made some notable contributions to the area's track history.

One of them, indeed, bears a name synonymous with PLU sports: Harshman. But this Harshman, Sterling, older brother of Lute athlete and PLU, WSU, and UW coaching immortal Marv, got into track almost by accident.

The Harshmans were multisport stars at Lake Stevens High School, but most of their track competition was just against each other. Sterling was known for his speed in football, his first love, and in 1935 teammates encouraged him to try sprinting. So he did, only to lose to a Monroe runner named Lee Orr. But Sterling was unaware that both had beaten the Snohomish County record for the 100-yard dash. (Orr went on to place fifth for his native Canada, behind Jesse Owens, in the Berlin Olympics 220-yard dash and later ran on a world-record mile relay team and won an NCAA 440-yard dash championship at WSU.)

While Orr was making a track name for himself and Marv was starting college, Sterling was in the Marines. But when he got out in 1939, Sterling, at Marv's urging, also enrolled at PLU and in 1942 ran 100 yards in 9.6 seconds, a record that stayed on the PLU books until 1989 and still ranks (as does his 220-yard-dash mark) as third best in school history. From there, he went on to a 28-year career as track coach at Puyallup High.

PLU's greatest track hero, however, was a strong-armed lad from Seattle, John Fromm, who in the 1950s dominated small-college javelin throwing nationally, and then stepped up. He won a virtual Triple Crown of national titles—the National Association of Intercollegiate Athletics (NAIA), the NCAA (twice), and the AAU—topping out at 257 feet 1 inch. High jumper Hans Albertson, javelin thrower Verner Lagesson, discus thrower Mark Smith (from Curtis High, now one of the area's coaching mainstays), and decathlete Phil Schot were other Lute national champions setting the stage for a spectacularly successful modern era.

Under Coach Brad Moore, who arrived in 1980, PLU continued as a small-college power. The Lute women won 15 conference titles in a 20-year run and took the NAIA cross-country title in 1988, behind national champ Val Hilden. When the school moved to NCAA Division III in 1998, PLU's teams were second and third in their first Division III national meet.

UPS's greatest sprinter, and possibly greatest track athlete, also came to the sport through the backdoor. Jack Higgins of Anacortes was a basketball player when he got to UPS. But when he left, he was the best collegiate sprinter in the state, running the 100-yard dash in 9.4 seconds, just one-tenth of a second off the world record at the time. His times of 10.3 seconds for 100 meters and 20.6 seconds for 200 meters in 1962 remain far and away UPS's all-time best.

Another UPS multisport star of the '60s who's still on the record books was Joe Peyton, who long-jumped 24 feet 1/2 inch in 1964. He also high jumped 6 feet 8 inches and won a West Coast title, was an All-America football player, and in all earned 11 letters as a Logger. But that hardly covers his contributions to UPS, for Peyton served 29 years as

UPS track coach, retiring in 1997. He is in the NAIA Coaching Hall of Fame and is the only person in the UPS Hall of Fame as both an athlete and a coach.

Among Peyton's standout students were Ken Johnson, NAIA javelin champion in 1975, and Jim Bob Cairns, a two-time NAIA marathon champion. And Dana Boyle was a national champion in both track and cross-country, spearheading the Loggers' run of four NAIA national titles in women's cross-country, 1992–95.

Star Track

When Darrell Robinson ignited Star Track I with his breakthrough 400 meters, setting the stage for a world junior record, there was a certain sense of inevitability about it. The event had become the domain of Tacoma schools, with the nation-leading three-year state-title strings of Keith Tinner of Lincoln High, 1972–74, and Robinson's former Wilson High teammate, Calvin Kennon, 1979–81. So Robinson had to wait his turn; although he won the national Junior Olympics title in 1980 and the state 200-meter title in 1981, he never had beaten Kennon in the state 400-meter!

The 47.3-second time Tinner ran in the 1974 state meet 440-yard dash, then his 46.7-second time in the summer, seemed like marks for the ages. But just seven years later, Kennon ran 47.33 seconds for 400 meters at state and 46.3 seconds in the summer, en route to Louisiana State. Whereas Tinner and Kennon's marks had given them national junior team status, however, Robinson was headed for the U.S. "varsity." His 45.74-second time at Star Track and then world junior record of 44.69 seconds put him on the national team, and soon he was beating the Russians in the U.S.-Soviet dual meet.

Robinson recalled it mainly in terms of wanting to make a big impression at the first Star Track. "We were going to win it, and we were going to win it in style," he said in a 1996 interview. "We were on the fastest track in the state, and we were in very good shape."

For Robinson, the heady success of that summer of '82 was impossible to top. But despite his well-publicized difficulties with college choices—he arrived at the University of Houston in the fall of 1982, only to find its sprint program falling apart—and then his failure in the 1984 Olympic Trials, he remained among the world's 400-meter elite for a half dozen years, winning a national title and competing for the United States in Europe, Asia, and Australia.

Outstanding Coaches and Intense Rivalries

Tinner, Kennon, and Robinson were products of a Tacoma and Pierce County track development system that was particularly robust in the 1960s and '70s, with the Park Olympics and other summer programs at Sprinker Recreation Center augmenting a revived scholastic program notable for outstanding coaches and intense rivalries.

The programs were given impetus by Washington's emergence in the 1960s as one of the nation's foremost high-school track states, and Casey Carrigan became a benchmark of that status through pole vaulting. All the Carrigan boys—Andy, Mike, and Casey—were all-around small-school athletes, and all wound up at Stanford University. But when their father, Paul, built a pole-vault runway and pit on their Orting farm, it was clear which sport was number one. Mike won the vault in the second-ever state class A meet in 1964 in Ellensburg. And then it was Casey's turn.

Casey won the state A title as a freshman in 1966, a sophomore in 1967, and a junior in 1968, when he became the state's first 16-foot vaulter. Then, astoundingly, he was off to join the big boys, vaulting 16 feet 8 ¼ inches at the AAU meet in Sacramento, good enough to be invited to the Olympic high-altitude training camp at South Lake Tahoe, where in September he went 17 feet and made the U.S. team. Carrigan did not place at Mexico City, but his presence there as a not-quite-senior in high school in that most technical of events was remarkable.

Aaron Williams was 1978 state champion in the long jump with a leap of 24 feet 4 inches (courtesy Jim Daulley).

Back home, Carrigan finished his Orting career with another state A title in 1969 and eventually raised the state's all-time best to 17 feet 4 3/4 inches. His Stanford career had disappointments, but he stayed competitive through the mid-'70s, topping out at 17 feet 10 1/2 inches in 1975.

Among other school stars from the 1960s were three guys who, like Don Paul 20 years before, were just passing through on their way to the NFL: Lincoln High School's Dave Williams, state high hurdles winner in 1963; Mount Tahoma High School's Bobby Moore, who upset the high-jump champion in 1966; and Wilson High School's Clyde Werner, shot-put champ in 1966. Williams and Werner played at UW and Moore, who later changed his name to Ahmad Rashad, attended UO; only Williams, an NCAA placer, seriously pursued track in college.

Marv Harshman holds up the starting gun for brother Sterling (far R.) and his teammate on a practice run (courtesy the Sterling Harshman Family).

The Tacoma–Pierce County dominance of the state 3A meet started with Clover Park High School's 1968 team title, then was locked in by Lincoln High's rise to the top in 1969. The Abes won successive titles in 1969–70, shared the title in '71, then won two more in '73 and '74. Wilson High School took over, briefly, in '75. The City League's run was interrupted by Lakes High School in '76, but Lincoln High was back in '77—and then Wilson High won four of the next five, culminating with the Darrell Robinson–led '82 team. Finally, Rogers High School won the wildly competitive '83 meet, meaning that over 16 years, county teams had won or shared 14 titles in the 3A boys state meet—and Clover Park won the girls 3A in 1980.

A state 2A meet also was launched, for boys in 1973 and girls in 1975, and Pierce County started on top when Washington High School became the inaugural champion in both meets. The Washington boys, however, quickly gave way to district rival Franklin Pierce, which won four in a row, 1974–77. Soon thereafter, the new Gig Harbor High School rose to the top of the 2A ranks.

The Lincoln–Wilson state-meet rivalry was relatively short-lived, flaming out in the 1980s, but it dominated the sport as nothing else has before or since. And possibly because of that brilliant intensity, its two coaches, Lincoln's Dan Watson and Wilson's Jim Daulley, both "retired" young.

Watson's teams were built on the dashes, the relays, and the jumps. Tinner, of course was the peerless star of that run, winning five dash titles. He also helped in a couple of the eight relay championships the Abes won under Watson's guidance. It was just part of a remarkable history for the school beginning in 1929: 24 state relays titles, 16 by the boys and eight by the girls. Under Watson, the jumpers were just as impressive as the sprinters: in 15 years, Lincoln won 10 state titles in the jumps as 15 different jumpers scored, accumulating 30 places.

Daulley was coach of four of Wilson's five title teams, turning the reins over to Sam Ring in '82, Robinson's senior year. The Rams were remarkable for their across-the-board excellence. From the late '60s to the early '80s, Wilson had state champions in the 100-meter, 200-meter, 400-meter, mile, high hurdles, shot put, long jump, triple jump, and both relays.

The 1970s were an era of breakthrough individual performances. Lincoln's Joel Braggs became the state's first 7-foot high jumper in 1971, but within years Curtis's Al Darneille and Franklin Pierce's Lu Moore had improved on him. Lincoln's Lloyd Brown was the first to triple jump 49 feet, also in 1971, launching a long run of success by the Abes in the horizontal jumps, but before the decade was out, Wilson's Aaron Williams, another future Husky footballer, had reached 50 feet 3/4 inches in the triple jump as well as 24 feet 4 inches in the long jump. Washington's Dana LeDuc, who reached 63 feet 11 1/4 inches in 1971, was one of five local shot-putters to break the 60-foot barrier before Mount Tahoma's Vince Goldsmith trumped them all, passing 65 feet in 1976 and reaching an amazing 69 feet 11 inches in 1977. LeDuc became one of the nation's top collegiate throwers at University of Texas, then became an NFL strength coach. Goldsmith, who went to the UO, eventually cast his lot with football and had a long career in the Canadian Football League. Lincoln's Tinner dropped his 440/400 best to 46.7 seconds on his way to UW, where he ran on the 1975 NCAA champion mile relay team. Wilson High first showed its speed with Dave Rorem in '69 and Wilson Morris in '71, both sweeping the sprints, en route to collegiate careers at WSU and Oregon State University (OSU), respectively. Rogers High had a hero in Jim Brewster, who shared an 880-yard title as a sophomore, then won both the 880 and the mile in 1973; he later was an NCAA 800-meter finalist at WSU. Larry Ladowski of Bethel High swept the state hurdles and won the national junior champs title. Foss High crowned its first state champ, Jeff Bruce, who won the hurdles in 1976 and went on to WSU and the 1980 Olympic Trials finals in the high hurdles. And Peninsula High's Tom Sinclair extended the state's javelin all-time best to 239 feet 1 inch—and later won the 1979 NCAA title for UW.

Among high school girls, whose state meet became official in 1974, Lakes High School had two '70s superstars in Linda Jones, who swept the 100-yard and 220-yard in both of the first two years, and Sheila Kaskie, who won two state cross-country titles and one track 3,200-meter race. Bellarmine Prep ended the decade with successive girls' state cross-country titles.

Lincoln-Wilson wasn't the only rivalry that defined and propelled the sport in the 1970s and beyond. Indeed, Clover Park High, which actually started the Pierce County domination in 1968, and its younger district rival Lakes High have kept it up into the present day.

Clover Park won state boys titles in what amounted to three eras, under three coaches: Art Hutton in '52, Darold Talley in '68, and Marty Walsh in '92–93—plus the girls' title for Jim Angelel and Jan Erickson in 1980. And those earliest Clover Park title teams were big in the distances, with miler Wes Smylie starring in '68 after he and teammate Bob Brandon had finished 1 and 2 in cross-country the previous fall. At Lakes, the architect of the program, with state titles in '76 and '88, was Warren Logan, who sent a high percentage of his stars on to college programs, several prominent on WSU's dominant early-'80s teams. The Lancers' 1999–01 title run was under former Foss High hurdler Willie Stewart Jr., whose father was the principal at Lincoln High for most of the Watson era.

At the 2A level, it was district rivals Franklin Pierce and Washington High Schools, with the Washington Patriots, under Jon Herrington, winning the inaugural state title in 1973. But then Franklin Pierce took over under coach Tom Buckner, who turned out future college stars as handily as titles in a four-year run, 1974–77, before heading to Mead High School in Spokane. Washington High has been a power ever since, winning back-to-back boys titles in 1989–90 with Mark Smith, the former discus champion for Curtis High and PLU, at the helm and acquiring a new Pierce County League rival in Joel Wingard, whose Gig Harbor athletes won state girls titles in '81 and '83 and the boys title in '96.

The 1980s and '90s

With the introduction of the Star Track era, a greater concentration on speed began to develop. Indeed, the records of not only Darrell Robinson but also Ericka Harris and Donna Dennis were still standing at the millenium. Clover Park's Dennis won the state 3A 100-meter three times and the 200-meter twice between 1980 and 1982, with her 200-meter best of 23.39 seconds still on the books. Two years after Star Track I, she was an Olympic Trials finalist in the 200-meter as a UW sophomore.

Harris won the state 2A 200-meter and 400-meter as a Peninsula High freshman in 1979, then in successive years swept the 100-meter, 200-meter, and 400-meter for the new Gig Harbor High. But it was in the summer after her junior year that she rocketed to national prominence, winning the National Junior Olympics 400-meter in a stunning 51.45 seconds—which for more than 20 years remained three seconds faster than any other Washington schoolgirl has run and among the top 10 all-time best nationally. Sadly, in her senior year her high school career—and, in effect, her entire career—ended in injury at Star Track I, and her brief collegiate career at the University of California never got going.

Among the other fast women runners of the '80s were prospective UW roommates Joyce Schweim of Puyallup High and Angie Tasker of Washington High. Schweim capped her prep career by running the nation's fastest 300-meter hurdles, one of her three victories (100-meter, both hurdles) in the 1986 3A meet. Tasker was the high scorer in two straight state 2A meets, placing in four events in both 1985 and '86 and winning the 200-meter, 400-meter, and long jump (19-plus feet) in '86.

Team champions in that decade included Wingard's Gig Harbor girls in class 2A in 1981—when Harris and middle-distance star Patty Ley won every event from the 100-meter to the 1,600-meter and then were part of a relay victory—and in '83. The Rogers High boys' 1983 victory, under coach Dave Weir, was the last of the 16-year Pierce County run and was led by Kris Durr, who won the 200-meter and 400-meter; his 47.1 seconds for 400 meters ranked fourth in state history, behind Robinson, Kennon, and Tinner. In class 1A, Steilacoom High won three state titles, 1984 and '86–'87, under coach Mike Hanby. Among 2A boys, there were Washington High's successive titles in 1989–90 and Fife's share of the '85 title; former Franklin Pierce High and Central Washington University (CWU) sprinter Steve Slavens coached the Trojans. And Lakes' boys rode sprint strength, amid William Knight's run of three straight 400-meter titles, to their share of the '88 3A crown.

Lakes High School's most memorable '80s hero, though, might have been Curt Corvin, who won two state cross-country titles and then in his senior year the 3,200-meter, one night after running third in what remained the fastest

high school four-man 1,600-meter/mile race—four runners under 4 minutes, 10 seconds—in U.S. history. Indeed, Star Track's initial emphasis on speed gave way to sensational distance running for much of the decade. Ley finished with five state titles, two in cross-country, and Wilson's Michelle Finnvik won three straight 3A 800-meters, 1982–84. The decade ended with a familiar name out in front of 2A distancemen: Andy Maris of White River, winning the 3,200-meter in '89 and 1,600-meter and 3,200-meter in '90, following the tradition of his brother Jerry, the 1978 state cross-country champ.

Bellarmine's Jolene Staeheli was an impressive double winner of the 3A 1,600-meter and 3,200-meter in 1991, on her way to Georgetown University. But over the next three years, another Lion, Sarna Renfro, rewrote the books as the most prolific girl distance champion the state had seen: eight state titles, two in cross-country and three straight 1,600-meter–3,200-meter sweeps. She capped her career in 1994 with 4 minutes, 46.85 seconds in the 1,600-meter, not only erasing the meet record from the memorable Star Track II but claiming the national lead. She went on to compete at Stanford University.

Almost 10 years later, another Bellarmine star was rattling the national lists. Brianna Felnagle, a convert from soccer, came from seemingly nowhere to win the state 4A 800-meter as a freshman in 2001. Then a year later she won the state 1,600-meter and topped a national field in the 800-meter at the Golden West meet in Sacramento. Only 90 minutes after that state 1600-meter run, she lost to Amanda Miller in the 800-meter by a time of 2 minutes, 14.10 seconds to 2 minutes, 14.11 seconds—Felnagle's only loss to date in state track and cross-country events. Her junior year was her first full season of cross-country, and she won the state 4A championship in 18 minutes, 14 seconds, the fastest 4A time since the meet went to a 5-kilometer distance. Later that spring, after recovering from mononucleosis, she became the fastest 4A girls runner, a 1600-meter and 800-meter double winner with times of 4 minutes, 47.71 seconds and 2 minutes, 10.44 seconds, respectively, eclipsing her competitor Sarah Schwald (4 minutes, 52.06 seconds and 2 minutes, 11.04 seconds, respectively). Felnagle also completed a rare triple crown of being the 4A cross-country, 1600-meter, and 800-meter champ. In her senior year, she was undefeated for the 2004 cross-country season, beating Zoe Nelson at SunFair in a time of 17 minutes, 11 seconds, breaking the previous course record of Sarah Schwald and successfully defending her 4A state cross-country title with a new 5-kilometer record of 17 minutes, 53 seconds—the only girl to ever break the 18-minute barrier. With top finishes by Felnagle's teammates, the Lions—under coach Matt Ellis—managed to eke out a team victory over the Gig Harbor Tides, who were led by standout Stephanie Sipes.

The boys' middle distances recently enjoyed a revival in the Puget Sound area in the 21st century, with yet another national champion leader: Courtney Jaworski of Curtis High, who won two straight state 4A and one national junior 800-meter titles, finishing his career with a nation-leading 1 minute, 50.5 seconds at Star Track.

Speed continued to prevail in the old Clover Park–Lakes district rivalry, and it took on a special dimension in the early 2000s with Lakes led by Reggie Williams and Clover Park by Shelton Sampson—both on their way to UW football careers. Williams finished as 2001 sprint champ for the Lancers; Sampson, a year younger, was a six-event winner, three times in the high hurdles, for the Warriors. Williams departed UW early, hoping to follow the long-ago successes of Dave Williams and Ahmad Rashad as an NFL wide receiver.

Speed also was the word at Steilacoom High, which moved up from class 1A to the new 2A classification during the '90s. Darrin Harris, with 21.75 seconds in the 200-meter in 1996, remained on the 1A books as state record-holder, and Alexis Yeater, with 11.95 seconds in the 100-meter dash and 24.52 seconds in the 200-meter event, set lofty standards in the girls' sprints when the 2A started in 1998, while Sentinels teams held relay meet records in both classifications.

Coaches and Officials

None of these extraordinary track and field achievements could have been accomplished without the efforts and contributions of coaches down through the years, nor the work of those officials and athletic directors who run the pro-

grams and run the meets. Certainly, in Pierce County the people behind the Park Olympics, Star Track, and Sound-to-Narrows left lasting impressions. Dan Inveen, a onetime track star himself, was track and field supervisor for the Pierce County Parks Department during the heyday of the Park Olympics and later, after a basketball coaching career at Wilson, became athletic director for Tacoma schools. Dick Kunkle was a *News Tribune* sports writer who dreamed up the Sound-to-Narrows run and then set his mind to bring a state high school meet to Tacoma. He and Inveen coaxed Star Track into being.

They were not alone as supporters of local track and field competitions. Over the years, officials included Inveen's successor district athletic directors, Karst Brandsma and Joe Bullock, and co-directors such as Angie Eichholtz, Ed Tingstad, and Bud Hatley. Longtime officials included Judy Erwin,

Competing for the Pacific Coast Club of Long Beach, Mac Wilkins shows his discus form (courtesy Mac Wilkins).

Jerry Ley, Gordon Jones, Dick Unrue, Jack O'Loughlin, and Esther Wilfong. Important figures from the early Park Olympics days included Chuck Gilmur, Tom Cross, Bill Madden, and Mitch Angelel, along with club coaches such as Rudy Jones, Lloyd Morgan, and Paul Llewellyn.

Star Track also had a spiritual leader in Art Hutton, who formed a founding triumvirate with Inveen and Kunkle until he decided to return to the coaching ranks at Clover Park High School. Hutton coached the school's first state title team in 1952, then went on to a long and productive career at CWU before returning to Tacoma. One of Hutton's most enduring contributions to Tacoma track was his protégé, Sam Ring.

Ring, a Mount Tahoma graduate who ran distances for Hutton at CWU, was a major contributor in his own right, but he also had championship teams throughout his coaching career. In the late 1970s and the start of the 1980s, Ring spent the fall coaching Bellarmine cross-country (girls' state titles, 1977–79) and the spring as an assistant to Jim Daulley amid

Wilson's run of boys' track titles. He then took over at Wilson, for one more state title, after Daulley's retirement in 1982. Ring then spent 15 years as men's and women's cross-country coach at UPS, where the Lady Loggers won four consecutive NAIA national championships from 1992 to 1995.

Another 1960s City League distance star and coaching protégé, a longtime friend and sometime rival of Ring, made a different kind of contribution to the city's track history. Pat Tyson, who ran for Dan Watson at Lincoln High, then at UO, was one of the nation's foremost high school distance coaches, at Mead High School in Spokane, with a run of 10 straight state cross-country titles at one point. But Tyson always loved Star Track and was the most vocal of the Spokane coaches who lobbied to keep the meet in Tacoma. After all, it was, for him, coming home. One of the cherished traditions of his Mead program was to bring as many team members as possible to Tacoma every year and, on the Saturday morning of Star Track, lead them on a run through Point Defiance Park, his old training route and the place where it all started.

Stadium High School track team, ca. 1960s (SSM).

CHAPTER 45

VOLLEYBALL

Lisa Beauchene was a member of two state championship teams while competing for Fife (courtesy Jan Kirk).

In 1895 William G. Morgan, a Young Men's Christian Association (YMCA) instructor in Holyoke, Massachusetts, introduced the game of mintonette to his classes. In developing the sport, Morgan tried to combine the elements of basketball, baseball, tennis, and handball, which he thought would be more in keeping with the young men's wishes for exercise. During a demonstration game, according to one history, "someone remarked to Morgan that the players seemed to be volleying the ball back and forth over the net, and perhaps 'volleyball' would be a more descriptive name for the sport." One year later, Springfield College hosted the first official game of volleyball.

During the early years of the sport, the YMCA remained the focus of competitions. In 1922, for example, the organization held the first national championships in Brooklyn, New York. Some 27 teams from 11 states were represented. Within six years, however, it became clear that the sport attracted a broader base of players, a realization that led to the formation of the U.S.A. Volleyball (USAV). From these small beginnings, volleyball has grown to become an Olympic sport (first introduced in Tokyo in 1964) as well as a venture for professional athletes, scholastic players, and beach recreators.

The 1917 Tahoma yearbook for Stadium and Lincoln High Schools gave "special commendation" to the Lincoln Park 10A girls for being volleyball champions, the first historic record of the game in the area. In the 1929 yearbook, the seniors at Stadium High defeated the juniors 15–9, 15–3, and 15–11 to win the interschool championships, and by 1931 volleyball was "rapidly becoming one of the favorite sports for girls at Lincoln" as well. The young women were not allowed to play other schools but kept their competitions in-house among the various grades. And if the region followed the national norm, throughout the following decades volleyball was played by local church groups, in assorted community centers, and in the schools, where it became a standard component of the physical education curriculum.

During the '50s and '60s, the popularity of volleyball progressed mainly on military bases and in the YMCAs. In 1959 Judge Waldo Stone, a regular paddleball player at the Y on Seventh and Market Streets in downtown Tacoma, found no players available so he stuck his head in the door of the gym and noticed a group of guys playing volleyball. He joined in and for the next 15 years was a regular part of the Noon Crew. By the late '60s, more than 100 men's, women's, and coed volleyball teams were in action through the local parks and recreation programs, so the opportunities were plentiful for people of all ages and abilities. Other regulars over the years included George Weyerhaeuser, Valen Honeywell, Ron Robbins, Orv Harrelson, Harry Slifer, and Glenn Neumann.

By the early '70s, the YMCA group formed a club that practiced in the afternoon and traveled to tournaments on the weekends, playing college club teams at Washington State University (WSU), Oregon State University (OSU), and even the Canadian national women's team in Coquitlam, British Columbia. By this time, others had joined in, one of the most enthusiastic being Russell Perkins, a local dentist. A track and football player at Stadium High School and the University of Puget Sound (UPS), Perkins acquired his interest in volleyball through college intramurals. Perkins, along with his sons Rick and Jeff, formed the nucleus of the YMCA team, which included six other teammates all more than 50 years old.

Women's Volleyball

It was women's volleyball, however, that captured media attention during the latter half of the 20th century. The spark was lit in 1974, when the U.S. Congress mandated (with Title IX) that women's sports were to be funded equally to men's. As a result, female athletes began to be recognized, both in terms of their performance and through the awarding of athletic scholarships. Volleyball quickly became one sport in which women excelled.

The sport was first offered competitively at the high school level in the state in 1973, but the number of teams was so few that only four officials refereed all of the interscholastic and recreational matches in Tacoma. In 1975 White River High School, coached by Trena Page, finished runner-up to Ridgefield for the class 1A state championship, and in 1977 the Washington Patriots, under the tutelage of Pam Spitzer, became the first school from Pierce County to win a state title, defeating Bellingham for the 2A crown.

Tacoma, and especially Pierce County, schools saw their fair share of outstanding players, and a recent poll of local coaches agreed that Sarah Silvernail (Fife, 1993), Laurie Wetzel (Puyallup, 1985), and Lisa Beauchene (Fife, 2000)

were in the top five of the all-time best area players. One of the first players from Pierce County to earn a scholarship at a Pacific-10 Conference school was 1981 Franklin Pierce graduate Julie Kurrus. She led the Cardinals to a 14–1 Seamount League title and a fifth-place finish at the 2A state championships before playing four seasons at the University of Washington (UW).

Cindy Pitzinger, a 1984 Rogers High graduate, moved on to a stellar career at the University of Montana, where she was selected to the All-Mountain Conference team her junior year and also trained with the U.S. Olympic team prior to the Barcelona, Spain, Olympic Games. Laurie Wetzel put the 1985 Puyallup High School Vikings on the map with three South Puget Sound League (SPSL) championships during her career, and she garnered first-team league honors twice, along with a league MVP selection. Wetzel played four years at UW, was a two-time member of

By the end of her Rogers High and college careers, Cindy Pitzinger possessed a 35-inch vertical jump (courtesy Cindy Pitzinger Willey).

the All-Pac-10 first team and a National Collegiate Athletics Association (NCAA) first-team All-American in 1988, and played professionally for the New York Liberties and in Bellinzona, Switzerland, before spending nine years as an assistant coach at the Division I college level.

Coach Jan Kirk firmly established one of the top programs in the state at Fife High School, as her 10 league and district titles attest, along with four 3A state crowns earned in 1992, '95, '96, and '99. Fife High's individual player contributions included four Beauchene family members who helped keep the Trojans at the forefront of success: Angie (1994), Suzanne (1995), Rene (1997), and Lisa (2000). Angie, Suzanne, and Rene each finished their careers with one state title to their credit, and Lisa enjoyed two state championships during her high school career. Lisa then moved on to play at Sacramento State, where she helped the Division I Hornets to four 20-victory seasons as well as three NCAA tournament berths; she culminated her career as the Big Sky MVP. It was Sarah Silvernail, however, a transfer from Yakima, who probably left the biggest impression on the court with her devastating kills during Fife's 1992 state title run. Silvernail then played four years at WSU, where she was a two-time All-American Pac-10 Player of the Year in 1996 and the Pac-10 record holder for kills per game. Ultimately she received the *Tacoma News Tribune*'s and Inland Empire's Athlete of the Year honors. Silvernail was a member of the U.S. national team for two years and played professionally for five seasons before retiring.

At the 4A level, Wilson High School, under coach Steve Gustafson, won seven straight Narrows League titles between 1981 and 1987, but the first 4A state title belongs to coach John Reopelle, who led the Bethel Braves to top honors in 1996. Since then, Tony Batinovich's Puyallup teams have been a mark of consistency at the 4A level, with a fourth-place finish in 1998, third in 2001, and second in 1999 and 2002. Spanaway Lake has made a significant impact in the 4A ranks over the last three years, placing 9th in 2002, 3rd in 2003, and 5th in 2004. The Sentinels were led by Jalen Pendon, voted SPSL Co-player of the Year (with Cristal Morrison) in 2003 and league MVP in 2004. Pendon, who will play next at WSU, was chosen The News Tribune's Player of the Year in 2003 and 2004 and the Seat-

A 1985 graduate of Puyallup High School, Laurie Wetzel was South Puget Sound League MVP in both volleyball and basketball (courtesy Laurie Wetzel-Hayward).

tle Post-Intelligencer's Player of the Year in 2004. The league rival Jaguars of Emerald Ridge claimed back-to-back fourth-place finishes at state in 2003 and 2004.

In the 3A division the White River Hornets grabbed third place in 2003. The Hornets improved on this finish, taking second in the 3A state volleyball tournament in 2004 with a loss to top-ranked Bishop Blanchet High. White River High now has three consecutive state tournament appearances under coach Lenny Llanos.

Two key members of the Wilson Rams' successful teams in the 1980s were Suzanne Vick and Lorrie Post. Vick played collegiately at Eastern Washington University (EWU), where, as a setter, she led the Eagles to a Big Sky Conference title. Post, a first-team National Association of Intercollegiate Athletics (NAIA) All-American in 1990 while at Western Washington University (WWU), led the Vikings to a third-place finish that year in the NAIA National Championships and was a two-time winner of WWU's Female Athlete of the Year. She also finished as WWU's career leader in kills and digs, the former record just recently broken in 2003 after having stood for more than 10 seasons.

Other top players throughout the community included Breen Eddinger and Mary Finnerty of Bellarmine; Corrin

Chapin, Donja Walker, and Jordan Gienger of Bethel; Jennie Rennie of Curtis; Shawna Sessler of Fife; Becky Jones of Foss; Katrina Carlson of Peninsula; Shelley Borovich, Karen Goff, Kristen Goff, Jenny Medl, Kristy Carstensen, and 2003 Washington State Gatorade Volleyball Player of the Year Stevie Mussie of Puyallup; Adrienne Sloboden, Jana Freeman, Tonya Minion, and Julie Jeffery of Rogers; Natasha Kozen, Julie Nordek, and Lora Spencer of Sumner; Michelle Weydert of Washington High; and Jennifer Kubista and Christy Kubista of Wilson.

Christal Morrison, a 2004 Puyallup High grad, was invited as an eighth grader to attend a High Performance Camp hosted by USAV and was given the award of Most Likely to be on the USA national team one day. The next year, Morrison was selected to the U.S. Junior National team, and in the spring of 2002 she spent another two weeks with the junior team and competed at the North Central American and Caribbean Confederation (NorCeCa) tournament in Puerto Rico, where she had seven kills and two aces in a loss to Puerto Rico in the finals. In her junior year, Morrison and teammate Stevie Mussie led the Puyallup Vikings to a second-place finish in the 4A state championships, where she also was chosen MVP of SPSL. By the summer of 2003, Morrison was named the number-one recruit in the nation for her position by college coaches. And she capped off her outstanding high school career by duplicating teammate Mussie's feat as a recipient of the 2004 Gatorade Volleyball Player of the Year in Washington. As a freshman starter at UW in 2004, Morrison helped her team attain their first-ever number-one ranking in the United States.

The newest rising star in local volleyball circles, Kylie Marshall, was selected as an outside hitter on the U.S. Youth National Team in the summer of 2004 and competed in the NorCeCa championships in Puerto Rico. A junior at Emerald Ridge High in Puyallup, she will compete at the Junior World Championships in 2005.

College

In the local college scene, UPS placed fifth in the Association of Intercollegiate Athletics for Women (AIAW) 1981 national tournament, but the college's banner year was in 1993 when the Loggers became the first team outside of Hawaii or California to win an NAIA national championship, doing so under longtime coach Robert Kim, who was named Coach of the Year. The Loggers defeated Hawaii-Hilo, which was seeking an unprecedented sixth national title, by a score of 15–3, 15–8, and 15–11 at the 14th annual NAIA National Championships played on the Point Loma Nazarene campus in San Diego. UPS finished with a 42–6 record for that season, and sophomore Andrea Egans was named tournament MVP.

With coach Mark Massey taking over the program in 1996, the Loggers became one of the few small-college teams in the nation to run a "swing" style offense, patterned after the U.S. Men's National team, and in doing so powered their way to a fifth-place finish at the NAIA nationals in 1997. Making the transition in 1999–2000 to NCAA Division III play, the Loggers dominated the West, winning the Northwest Conference and West Region titles with an undefeated record and advancing to the NCAA quarterfinals, where they dropped a narrow 13–15 fifth game to the number-one-ranked team in the nation on its home court.

Kevin Aoki, successful longtime coach at Bethel High School, was at the helm of the Pacific Lutheran University (PLU) Knights. His team made their first and only trip to the NCAA Division III national championships in 1999, finishing 1–1 while losing to University of California–San Diego, the number-one West Regional seed.

Regardless, PLU and UPS both have had their share of top players over the years. Cathy Flick was a two-time NAIA first-team All-America selection and a two-time NAIA national tournament Most Valuable Player in 1986, when the Loggers finished third, and in 1987. She was the Reebok and American Volleyball Coaches Association Player of the Year both years as well and was also selected District Player of the Year. A team captain and multiple All-Conference performer, Flick garnered the Puget Sound Female Athlete of the Year award twice and was selected into the NAIA National Hall of Fame in 1996. Other Loggers selected to national tournament first teams included Janice Lwin in 1993, Egans in 1995, and Anna Dudek in 1997. Swing hitter Dudek was a two-time All-American and in 1998 was nationally ranked number one in digs and number two in kills in her senior season. In 1999 junior

Eileen Gamache was ranked number one in the Northwest Conference in kills, aces, and digs, all even though she is a mere 5 feet 3 inches. In 2000 senior setter Lindsi Weber and sophomore setter Karen Elmgren were selected as All-Americans, while Gamache earned All-Region honors and freshman Adrian Ougendal was selected West Region Freshman Player of the Year. In 2001 Elmgren repeated as All-American and Ougendal as All-Region, and both attained All-American status in 2002. At PLU, Rachelle Snowden established school records for kills and digs during her 1992–95 career; those records still stand.

Volleyball Clubs

Fortunately for many, club volleyball programs under the auspices of USAV, such as the Puget Sound and Narrows Volleyball Clubs, are frequently organized, affording youngsters the opportunity to acquire and improve the skills necessary to play in high school and college. And for many others, because volleyball can be a lifetime sport, they are able to play well into their 70s in age-group competition.

Jerry Weydert, for example, who is now 55, has been a volleyball player since 1970 and coached at the high school, college, and club levels; officiated at all levels; worked at the 1990 Goodwill Games and the 1996 Olympic Games in Atlanta; and in August 2003 coached the All-Army men's and women's teams in the Armed Forces Championships. He continues to play in the Masters age-group division and in 1990 received Player of the Year honors in the 40-and-Over Masters Silver Division at the USAV championships in Raleigh, North Carolina.

Dave Dempski, who didn't begin playing volleyball until the age of 45 at the YMCA, quickly became involved with the formation of the Tacoma Volleyball Club, which hosted drop-in gym programs, clinics, and summer outdoor tournaments from 1988 to 1995. An avid supporter of volleyball at the regional level as well as having officiated for more than 10 years, Dempski's on-court successes include three golds, two silvers, and one bronze medal since 2000 at the USAV

Members of the 1975 All-Army team at Fort Lewis included two Tacomans Jerry Weydert (#27) and Leala Jew (#19), the first female to ever play on an Army men's team (courtesy Jerry Weydert).

Nationals and Huntsman World Senior Games in St. George, Utah, in the men's 55 and 60 age groups.

Lynn Larson, also a latecomer to volleyball, started playing in the mid-1970s in the local recreation leagues offered by the Pierce County Parks and Recreation Department. He won his first gold medal in 1998 in Dallas on a 60s team, was a member of the All-Tournament team in Columbus, Ohio, two years later, winning the gold medal again, and in 2003 won another gold medal in Minneapolis, Minnesota, in the 65 age-group competition.

Wayne Gardner, who was both a player and a referee beginning in the 1930s, remains a local legend, having devoted almost 80 years of his life to the sport. As recently as 2002, he was still a part of USAV as a referee for local games—at the age of 92. A tireless advocate for the sport, Gardner served as general manger for the Seattle Smashers pro volleyball team in 1978, part of the ill-fated International Volleyball Association. He was elected to the Washington Officials Association's Hall of Fame in August 2004.

Marc Blau, a referee and assigner for 30 years with the Tacoma–Pierce County Volleyball Officials Board, received the National Federation of Interscholastic Officials Association (NFIOA)'s Washington Volleyball Official of the Year award in 1996. Leala Jew, a local referee for 10 years who also officiated at five state championships, became the only female ever to be named to the All-Army men's volleyball team in 1975, a year before a women's program was established. Tacoma's only two nationally rated officials, Walt Gogan and Teri Wood, and NFIOA Volleyball Official of the Year in 2003 Jerry Aeschlimann, a 28-year veteran referee, remain active at the high school and college levels; Aeschlimann has officiated for more than 15 state tournaments in his career.

Over the years in Pierce County, men, women, boys, and girls have played volleyball in their required physical education classes; for fun as a community, church, or recreation endeavor; or as a serious athlete. As a competitive sport, it has proven to be one in which, at least locally, women dominate the courts. But it's the pure love of the game that inspires today's players and those yet to come.

CHAPTER 46

WRESTLING

Jerry Conine, a Fife High graduate, receives his trophy at the 1964 Olympic Trials where he qualified for the Tokyo Olympic Games (courtesy the Jerry Conine Family).

When wrestling was first introduced to local schools, it was valued as a sport that could appeal to young men of all sizes and motivate them to stay in school. Any boy, from a slim 98 pounds to a sturdy 200 pounds or more, could compete in encounters that replicated, with rules, the hand-to-hand combat once practiced on all the world's battlefields. Wrestling was also a part of the original Olympic games.

Competitions between Tacoma's Stadium and Lincoln High Schools were well established by 1930, and Cammarano Brothers provided the trophy for the crosstown winner. Throughout the early years of the decade, wrestling teams from Aberdeen, Shelton, and Fife were added to the list of competitors. The sport was also one of the few during the 1930s in which races easily mixed during competition. Japanese wrestlers were a part of both Stadium and Lincoln teams in 1930, and Lincoln also had the only African American wrestler.

Armand Yapachino, a wrestler for Stadium and state champion in 1944, was known as "the Arm." Not only was he a winning wrestler for Stadium, according to one reporter, he helped the team by "teaching the sophomores

on the squad many new holds" at a time when high school wrestling was still in its infancy.

These first games, called wrestling "smokers," took place in the Tacoma Armory. They combined high school competitions alongside matches between high schoolers and freshmen from Washington State University (WSU). Boxers and professional wrestlers competed in between the student bouts. In 1953 the venue changed when Dr. Bill Thomas, then wrestling coach at WSU, organized the first official statewide tournament in Pullman.

Tacoma's Lincoln High School wrestlers came in second to powerhouse Sedro-Woolley at the first state tournament. Under the leadership of coach Harry Bird, who later coached at Stadium, the team won the championship in both 1954 and 1955 and had four individual winners each year. Bird went on to coach a total of 16 individual state champions and was inducted into the State of Washington Wrestling Coaches Hall of Fame in 1984.

Lincoln's Vic Eshpeter, who later became a wrestling official, was one of the state's first two-time individual champions winning the 120-pound weight classification in both 1953 and 1954. Other winners during Lincoln's championship years included Les Kleinsasser, Jerry Dorfner, Mike Smith, Fred Crothamel, Jack Harding, Dave Cusata, and Gary Markham. A generation of Pierce County wrestlers came and went, however, before a local wrestling team matched the accomplishments of Lincoln High School in the 1950s.

The Lincoln Abes had a serious Pierce County competitor during this time. The Fife wrestling program also began in the 1930s and it was one of the teams participating in the first state championship at Pullman. That year the school took third, but one of its wrestlers—Elsworth Finlayson—individually won in the 138-pound weight class. He did the same the following year, making him another early two-time

champion in the state tournament. Fife coach Harry Sorenson produced another individual state winner in 1955, Lyle Rader in the 175-pound weight class, the same year the team was runner-up to Lincoln.

Fife was also the wrestling home of Gerald "Jerry" Conine. He grew up on a chicken farm in rural Pierce County and as a lad earned a reputation for catching the critters faster than anyone else. His speed and energy were channeled into organized sports when, as a seventh grader, he wrestled a ninth grader to the ground. By the time he graduated from Fife High School in 1957, Conine was captain of both the wrestling and the football teams and won the state wrestling championship at 177 pounds.

Frank Stojack was famous for his airplane spin (SSM, 1999.15.1).

THE HISTORY OF WRESTLING IS SPONSORED BY
BROTHERS JAY AND CHESTER SESSLER:

Jay was an active wrestler in high school, becoming the league and district champion in 1955 and taking third place in the state wrestling finals. His son Jon continued the wrestling tradition at Fife High School. With Chester, Jay

founded Sessler, Inc., a contracting company and today they wrestle with building materials instead of each other.

Jay Sessler (on top) wrestled at 101 pounds in 1957 and finished third at the high school state championships (courtesy Jan Kirk).

A wrestling scholarship took Conine to WSU, where he placed third on the Pacific Coast at 177 pounds for three years in a row. By 1964 he was on his way to the Tokyo Olympic Games as a part of the U.S. team. He won against the Swedish competitor, drew against the Hungarian entry, had a bye in the third round, and lost to the Swiss in the fourth. He was therefore eliminated from the competition but placed sixth in freestyle at 213 pounds.

Conine retired from the sport in 1966 but not before winning the National Greco-Roman Championship. He then moved on to championship competition in handball and racquetball. (Along the way, he began coaching son Jeff, who won the Junior Nationals in racquetball at 18 years old. Coming from a family that never stuck to one sport, Jeff Conine also played baseball and won his second World Series ring when the Florida Marlins beat the New York Yankees in 2003.)

By the 1970s, 212 high schools in Washington sponsored 8,000 wrestlers. And Pierce County had another championship team, inspired by the coaching skills of Warren Depringer and Dan Hensley: Clover Park placed either

first or second in four state championship matches between 1972 and 1978. George Ratcliff, Andy Kacmarcik, and Bill Stout were some of the school's individual winners.

Warren Depringer, an import from Iowa and another inductee into the state Coaches Hall of Fame, started the wrestling program at Clover Park High School in 1959 and remained there until 1970. Of all of his students, he best remembered Dick Sowell, who in 1962 became Clover Park's first state champion. Dan Hensley replaced Depringer at Clover Park and coached the team to three state championships before being inducted into the Hall of Fame in 2003.

But many schools contributed their fair share of wrestler winners. Bethel came in second at the state championships in 1963 and again in 1987. Lakes placed either first or second between 1973 and 1976, while Franklin Pierce achieved second place from 1981 to 1983. Curtis and Peninsula High Schools were champions in 1977, 1987, and 1995, and White River won a state crown in 1995 and finished as runner-up in 2001, 2002, and 2003.

In fact, since 1953, rarely has a year gone by without a Pierce County contender becoming a state champion in some weight class. Sumner's David Olmstead was one of the most successful, winning the 129-pound weight class in 1982 and 1983 and then again in the 135-pound division in 1984. Spanaway Lake's Jeff Gotcher was the 148-pound state champion in 1985, 1986, and 1987, achieving one of the more remarkable records in high school wrestling with a perfect 101–0 (71 by pins) won-lost record. At the time, Gotcher was the first wrestler to go through high school undefeated, and only one other has done it since. Olmstead and Gotcher were the county's first three-time state champions.

Dr. John Bonica was the Light-Heavyweight Wrestling Champion of the World in 1941 and was known as "the Masked Marvel" to Tacoma fans (courtesy Angela Thomas).

Until the late 1980s, high school championship wrestling competitions were held at various venues, including WSU at Pullman and the University of Washington (UW) sports complex in Seattle. When schools were divided into title classifications based on size, new venues were added to support the increasing number of matches, meaning that the meets were scattered throughout the state. In 1988, however, wrestling coaches Mike Hess, Sam Indorf, Shelly Thiel, Steve Anderson, and Jim Meyerhoff considered the possibility of having all the statewide championship matches held under one roof. The result of their deliberations brought the first Mat Classic to the Tacoma Dome in 1989.

"One must understand that we have come from wrestling 'smokers' among 10 schools and horsehair mats to an extravaganza that draws 896 wrestlers, more than 25,000 fans, and media reporters and photographers from more than 125 newspapers, television stations, and radio stations," claimed Cal Johnson, one historian of state wrestling. By 1998 some 24 mats covered the floor of the Tacoma Dome, while Ed Aliverti, the popular Olympic and National Collegiate Athletics Association (NCAA) commentator, announced the various events. The effort needed to organize the Mat Classic is phenomenal, but in 2001 cofounder Jim Meyerhoff became the Mat Classic tournament director, after years of managing the event on the floor.

Meyerhoff attended University of Puget Sound (UPS) from 1966 to 1970 and was inducted into its Athletic Hall of Fame in 1990. He was a four-year letterman in wrestling and team captain for three years and received the Most Inspirational award twice. In 1968 he was the first UPS wrestler to compete in a national championship tournament. Meyerhoff competed again nationally his senior year and ended his collegiate career with a record of 62–10–1 (his marks for the 1970 season were 18–1–0).

Meyerhoff went on to coach at Franklin Pierce High School in 1973 and stayed there until 1985. While there, he led the wrestling team to three runner-up finishes at the state tournament. From 1985 to 1988, Meyerhoff was head wrestling coach at Pacific Lutheran University (PLU), and in his last season the Lutes hosted the National Association of Intercollegiate Athletics (NAIA) nationals. During 18 years of coaching, he produced a 151–111–2 record, an endeavor that has placed him in the State of Washington Wrestling Coaches Hall of Fame and the National Wrestling Hall of Fame. In 1984 he was selected as Wrestling USA's National Man of the Year.

College Wrestlers

Several local wrestling champions continued the sport while in college and beyond. Brent Barnes, a Rogers High School graduate, won a National Junior College Athletic Association (NJCAA) National Championship in the 158-pound classification in 1982 while attending North Idaho College. Barnes became assistant coach to Paul Greeley at Bethel in 1986, the year the school team placed second in the state wrestling championships. Since 1987, he has been wrestling coach at Lake Stevens High School and named Washington State Coach of the Year and National Federation of High Schools Coach of the Year.

Franklin Pierce's Mark Peterson attended Central Washington University (CWU) and placed sixth in the NAIA national championships in 1985 at 126 pounds. He was team captain for three seasons and co-MVP in 1984–85. One year later, White River's Joe Klein placed third in the NAIA national tournament at 126 pounds while wrestling for PLU. State champion in the 141-pound division at the 1995 Mat Classic was Curtis High School's Kirk White. White moved on to become a three-time All-American at Boise State and a 1999 NCAA champion.

Larry Gotcher was almost equal to his brother Jeff, with a glossy high school record of 92–2–1. Larry placed third as a sophomore, second as a junior, and first in the state championships during his three years of competition. Of his 92 career wins, an astounding 82 were pins. And he completed his high school career with 24 straights pins and then won his semifinal state tournament match 25–2 before wrapping up the title with a 17–1 rout. In 1984 Larry became the only high school wrestler ever to win a regional Olympic tournament when he won the trials at the age of 16. He went on to make the final Olympic qualifying squad in 1984, 1988, 1992, and 1996 but missed out competing in the games. As a member of the Michigan Spartans wrestling team, Larry was a two-time All-American in 1988 and 1989 and won the Big 10 championship during the 1989 season. That

same year, he placed fourth in the NCAA Division I championships in the 142-pound weight classification.

Both PLU and UPS have produced top wrestlers of note over the years. Between 1981 and 1987, first-team NAIA All-Americans from PLU include Paul Giovannini, Mark Agostini, Jeff Lipp, Chris Wolf, Adrian Rodriguez, Bob Freund, John Godinho, Brian Peterson, Quoc Mguyen, Tuan Nguyen, John Aiken, and J. J. Hanson.

Bob Hunt, former Stadium footballer and wrestler, had a career similar to teammate Meyerhoff's, and both attended UPS at the same time. Competing in the heavyweight division, Hunt was a four-year letterman in wrestling and participated in two NCAA Division II national championship tournaments. He then went on to a 15-year career as head wrestling coach at Orting, Stadium, and Wilson High Schools and was inducted into the Loggers' Hall of Fame in 1994. Mike Schmid, a 1969 Puyallup graduate, placed seventh at the NCAA Division II national championships in the heavyweight division in his junior year at UPS.

Coaches

Throughout the years, Pierce County saw its fair share of inductees into the State of Washington Wrestling Coaches Hall of Fame. Besides Bird, Depringer, and Meyerhoff, they included Rick Daniels and Larry Brown at Fife; Jim Richards and Ed Arima at Sumner; and Ray Barnes, Dick Pruett, and George Wilfong at Puyallup. Wilfong spent 25 years at Puyallup High while amassing 11 South Puget Sound League and five regional titles. Combined with his predecessor Ray Barnes, the two coaches collectively span more than 37 years at one school.

Pro Wrestlers

But the appeal of wrestling was not limited to the area's amateurs. During the middle decades of the 20th century, Tacoma was one stop on the Pacific Northwest professional wrestling circuit. Crowds congregated at the Tacoma Armory or the Arena at South 38th Street and South Tacoma Way (the old Tacoma Ice Palace) to cheer their favorite athlete along. Local bouts featured such challengers as Bulldog Clements, Cowboy Ace Abbott, The Ram, the Unmasked Marvel (Buddy Knox), "the body beautiful from Hawaii" (Harold Sakata), the

Great Atlas, and the Mighty Midgets. Fans came out in droves long before television remade the sport into an entertainment extravaganza. Newspaper accounts usually credited Paavo Ketonen as the local promoter organizing the events.

Of all the wrestlers competing here, John "Masked Marvel" Bonica and Frank "King of the Northwest Wrestlers" Stojack were the most famous. The two men shared a common background and decided to enter professional wrestling for similar reasons. Both came from Southern European immigrant families and, though not born in Tacoma, made substantial contributions to the local community beyond their athletic accomplishments on the wrestling mat.

Frank Stojack was born in Canada of immigrant parents who moved the family to a small farm in South Tacoma when Frank was seven years old. While at Lincoln High School, Stojack was a 13-letter man and won the Richard Graff Memorial Award for academic achievements and sportsmanship. Football and wrestling dominated his college career, and when he graduated from WSU in 1935, he turned professional in order to save the family farm from Depression-era creditors.

The future champion wrestler began by playing right guard two seasons for the old Brooklyn Dodgers of the National Football League (NFL). Then in 1938 Stojack decided to leave football to concentrate on professional wrestling. Through the next 30 years, he faced hundreds of opponents in thousands of bouts. And in 1954, when fans were asked to vote by mail for their favorite wrestler, the majority of 100,000 respondents elected him "King of the Northwest Wrestlers." The year before, in Spokane, Stojack became the world light heavyweight wrestling champion, successfully using his famous "airplane spin" toss against Gypsy Joe.

Stojack, however, did not view professional wrestling as a career. It was a hobby. He wrestled for fun, with his winnings going to benefit the Boys Club of Tacoma, an organization he helped to create. He was a contractor by trade, a member of Carpenters' Local 470, and became secretary-manager of the Tacoma Chapter of the Associated General Contractors of America in 1964. He was also a politician: he was a member of the Tacoma City Council the year he won the world championship title and later Pierce County Sheriff for several terms. "Frank Stojack was the most distin-

guished celebrity we had," remembered former Tacoma Mayor Gordon Johnston, who also grew up in South Tacoma. "He was a hero to us."

When running for the Tacoma City Council in 1953, Stojack's qualifications for office were questioned by one of his opponents because Stojack was a wrestler and a laborer. "Yes, I am a successful pro wrestler by avocation," responded Stojack, "and I work with my hands in an honorable trade." Participation in professional sports "does not indicate that a man lacks brains," he continued. "Countless of our most successful business and professional men and governmental leaders started as laborers, many as pro athletes." Among the examples he provided was then Pierce County Sheriff Harold Bird, who was a former professional boxer, and Dr. John Bonica—the Masked Marvel.

John Bonica was 27 years old and had been wrestling professionally for eight years when he arrived at Fort Lewis's Madigan Hospital in 1944 as an army physician. His family had migrated from Italy to New York in 1925 so that young John, who dreamed of becoming a doctor, could get the education he needed. Bonica began wrestling in high school and continued while beginning his premed courses at Long Island University, winning the New York City and regional middleweight intercollegiate championships along the way. He turned professional in 1936 in order to pay for his education. First he wrestled under the name Johnny (Bull) Walker. Then he became the Masked Marvel.

The Masked Marvel attended medical school during the day, wrestled at night during the school year, and traveled with various circuses in the summer. He won the light heavyweight championship of Canada in 1939 and two years later was light heavyweight champion of the world, if only for a period of seven months. By the time he ended his wrestling career in 1950, Bonica had—like Stojack—met hundreds of opponents in thousands of venues, including meets with the Northwest wrestling king himself. Opponents also included Jim Landos and Lou Thesz, two of the greatest wrestlers of the time.

Following the Second World War, Bonica left Madigan to become director of the Tacoma General Hospital Department of Anesthesiology. As Dr. Bonica, he was well on his way to becoming an international authority in his medical field. But the Masked Marvel continued to wrestle, competing in meets that blanketed the Pacific Northwest and British Columbia. In 1950, when Dr. Bonica retired from the sport, he began writing what eventually was considered the international Bible of pain diagnosis and therapy, entitled *The Management of Pain.* He remained in Tacoma for another 10 years, then founded the Department of Anesthesiology at the UW School of Medicine and the world's first Multidisciplinary Pain Clinic.

When Dr. Bonica died in 1994, one memorial referred to him as "the Founding Father of the Pain Field" because of his half-century of work "to define pain as a clinical field and a worthwhile subject for multidisciplinary neuroscience." We have the Masked Marvel to thank for Dr. John Bonica's award-winning medical contributions to the world. "For those of us who knew him well," the memorial continued, the doctor struggled daily with his own chronic pain caused by his years of wrestling.

The wrestling ethic has remained with these competitors over the years. "I don't believe that there is such a thing as an ex-wrestler," Joe Klein wrote in 2004. "Wrestling becomes a part of you and it helps form who you become. For those who pursue it seriously, wrestling teaches impeccable work ethics, self-discipline, and self-control. Many wrestlers will attest that these skills helped them succeed in their chosen careers." For professional wrestlers Frank Stojack and Dr. John Bonica, it was public service and an outstanding medical career.

Former coach Warren DePringer agreed. "I still believe that wrestling is possibly the most outstanding sport for young men. It is not a spectator sport but really a participant's sport. It does not discriminate because of height or weight. It requires great discipline and hard work and is extremely technical. Most people do not realize this. It gives one a great deal of self-confidence that lasts through a lifetime."

Vic Eshpeter tries to wrestle his way out of a predicament (courtesy Vic Eshpeter).

CHAPTER 47

YACHTING

Saga, owned by Kirk Hull (courtesy Ken Ollar and Guy Hoppen).

Given this region's historical seafaring context, it's not surprising that the first Tacoma Yacht Club (TYC) formed as early as 1889 and established its boathouse at Manzanita on the southern end of Maury Island. While the world depression that began in 1893 forced the organization to declare bankruptcy, by 1908 TYC was incorporated again, thanks to the efforts of C. E. Hohberg. The Northern Pacific Railroad agreed to provide space in the heart of Tacoma's harbor. Members constructed a boathouse, and by 1909 some 30 sail- and powerboats were moored at the facility.

During World War I, however, the club's lease was canceled due to the war effort. To accommodate boating enthusiasts, the Metropolitan Park Board of Tacoma agreed to lease property at Point Defiance, where the yacht club still finds it home today. The original clubhouse was barged to the new site and placed at the end of a huge breakwater formed by slag produced at the nearby Tacoma ASARCO smelter. To reach the clubhouse, members scrambled down the Point Defiance bluff from their motorcars parked at the top. Despite such challenges, by 1919 the club membership had increased to more than 100 boaters, reflecting the rapid and steady growth that began after the war.

One of the earliest sailboats to race in Puget Sound's waters was the 41-foot-long *Bonita*, owned by Herman Larsen. Herman's father was I. M. Larsen, a sailmaker from Norway who started the Larsen Sail and Awning Company of Tacoma. The company produced and repaired sails, and Larsen's sons Herman, Alf, and Ingolf joined in the business. Herman had the *Bonita* built in 1909 and began racing under the TYC banner. In February 1911, he won the annual midwinter race to Protection Island and, in April, the Metropolitan Cup (the Seattle-Tacoma race) with a time of 11 hours, 55 minutes.

Through the years, TYC has been home to prestigious yachts with histories of their own. One of the most elegant was the *El Primero*, owned by Sam A. Perkins, a Northwest political power broker who at one time owned both the *Tacoma Ledger* and *Tacoma News Tribune* newspapers. Perkins, who was commodore of TYC from 1912 to 1914, once said that "probably more presidents have been entertained aboard the *El Primero* than any other yacht afloat. They include Taft, Roosevelt, Harding, and Hoover."

The club was also home to the *Argosy*, a vessel built in the Martinac yard in 1925 for Dr. Edward A. Rich, a

Tacoma orthopedic surgeon. It was the first official entry when the Capital to Capital race from Olympia, Washington, to Juneau, Alaska, was devised in 1928. The 1,000-mile race, the longest of its kind at the time, was the first race on the Pacific coast sanctioned by the American Power Boat Association (APBA). It attracted national attention, including that of Charles F. Chapman, the reknowned author of *Piloting, Seamanship and Small Boat Handling,* who came here from the East Coast to serve as a crewman aboard one of the boats. Besides the *Argosy,* two other Tacoma boats entered the race: the *Lota,* owned and skippered by Dr. S. L. Blair, and the *Shoofly,* skippered by 20-year-old Herbert Schuh. The race was so successful that on July 4, 1928, all of

the skippers involved met aboard the *Argosy* and formed the International Power Boat Association (IPBA) to perpetuate the race.

TYC was, of course, not the only organization for boaters in Pierce County. The Day Island Yacht Club, the Corinthian, and a club in Gig Harbor also were part of the Puget Sound waterscape. Whether participants or spectators, members of all of these organizations were very much interested in racing.

Sailboat Racing

Serious sailboat racing in Tacoma, however, began in the '50s and within a generation had grown to a fleet of some 60 boats.

Stormy Weather, owned by Govnor Teats, in May 1955 (courtesy Ken Ollar and Guy Hoppen).

The many racing opportunities on Commencement Bay and South Puget Sound included the New Year's Race, the Rowland Series, the Daffodil Race, the Wednesday Evening Series, the Blake Island Race, the Fourth of July Race, the Vashon Island Race, the Horsehead Bay Race, the Al Anderson Series, and the Larsen Trophy Race. By the 1970s, more than 40 regattas were offered throughout the year. Of these, autumn's Wednesday night races from Manzanita to Dash Point and back to TYC were the most popular.

A significant new venture in the early 1950s created a whole new class of sailboats: the Douglas Fir Plywood Association announced plans to develop and sell a plywood boat. The company turned to Ben Seaborn to design the new boat and then talked to Ed Hoppen about building a prototype. Hoppen, a longtime boat builder in Gig Harbor, "was an innovator who did his own thing and was willing to experiment with just about anything," recalled Jerry Smith, a TYC member and longtime sailboat aficionado.

Hoppen, who had built the *Nautilus* sailboat, set out to create what he called the Thunderbird, a 1 Design Class boat, 26 feet long and made out of plywood with a sharp chine. The Thunderbird became one of the first and only class sailboats to be manufactured in Tacoma–Pierce County, although they later started building them out of fiberglass.

After the prototype was developed and deemed seaworthy, the second Thunderbird, called the *Pirouette*, was built for Hoppen himself, and Smith owned the third Thunderbird, called the *Windsong*. According to Smith, "the Thunderbird class really turned out to be one of the most successful 1 Design Class boats in the world."

In 1958 a new group called the Puget Sound Sailing Association (PSSA) was formed "to help more people, particularly youngsters, engage in the sport of sailing," according to a news release at the time. Headed by Des Sessinghaus, the El Toro Class sailors who started the group requested that the park district add an aquatics director to the park staff, "to obtain the maximum pleasure from the fine bodies of water we have."

Dr. Govnor Teats was one of the most prolific racers representing TYC. His *Stormy Weather*, a 42-foot sloop, captured TYC's Sailboat of the Year honors six times in a 12-year span, from 1955 to 1966. He then won again in 1968 with *White Squall* in the Cruise Division. (Teats was out sailing a flattie the day the Narrows Bridge collapsed. According to his son, Roger Deitz, "If Dad had looked over his shoulder while sailing, he would have seen the bridge fall.")

Teats, who served as commodore of TYC, cruised the Northwest waters extensively, circumnavigating Vancouver Island once. In 1959 he crewed for a friend of his in the Transpacific Yacht Race from Los Angeles to Hawaii, one of the most popular and enduring long-distance ocean races in the world, dating back to 1906. In 1959, the same year Teats participated, the largest boat to ever race the Transpac, the 161-foot *Goodwill*, sailed the best time, covering the 2,225 nautical miles in 10 ½ days.

Teats went on to crew in two other Transpac races during his life and also raced in the Cape to Rio yacht race in 1971 aboard the *Greybeard*, a famous sailboat out of Vancouver, British Columbia. This race takes sailors 3,300 adventurous miles across the Atlantic Ocean, heading northwest from Cape Town to Isla da Trinidade and then southwest to Rio de Janeiro. As the fleet draws closer to the

South American coast, skippers need to decide whether to choose the longer route out to sea with stronger winds or a shorter distance along the coast but with potentially lighter airs. According to Tacoman Dave Nielsen, one of three watch captains with Teats on the *Greybeard*, "we were shooting for first-to-finish honors but had to settle for second boat across the line."

The grandaddy of sailboat races in the Pacific Northwest was the Swiftsure Victoria to Lightship race, a 136-mile course that ended just off Cape Flattery in the Strait of Juan de Fuca. Considered the most prestigious, this race was noted for bringing together the greatest yachts along the West Coast. In 1964 Jerry Smith captured the Swiftsure Trophy as overall winner in his 36-foot sloop *Bandit*, and in 1965 another Tacoman, Bill Brasier, took the *Kialoa* to first place in the Class A Division and third overall out of a total of 72 entries. Govnor Teats also won the Pacific Handicap Racing Fleet overall title in 1973 with *White Squall.*

Dave Nielsen had a banner year in 1968 as he made his maiden Swiftsure voyage aboard his new Cal-40 *Moonglow III* and sailed away from some 90 others to win the City of Victoria Trophy for the first boat home. He was also first in Division II and third overall.

Later that year, Nielsen and his crew, which included his wife, Margaret, Irv Smith, Neil McConaghy, Tom Murphy, and Jim Marta, became the first U.S. boat to finish the popular 19-day Victoria to Maui race. *Moonglow III* captured the City of Victoria Trophy for elapsed time for first place in Division II as well as the Maui Chamber of Commerce Trophy in Division II for corrected time. These accomplishments, along with previous wins with his *Moonglow* and *Moonglow II* sailboats, resulted in Nielsen winning Sailboat of the Year accolades in the TYC's Racing Division.

Another noteworthy achievement was that of the sloop *Saga,* which was built in Norway in 1935 and raced in the San Francisco Bay Area before being brought to Seattle in 1949. Hal Palmer moved the *Saga* to Tacoma early in 1956 when he garnered Sailboat of the Year. *Saga,* with Kirk Hull at the helm, subsequently captured the 1959 and 1961 6-meter Class North America World Championships.

Although the list of sailboat racers is long, those considered the most competitive who raced not only in Tacoma-

area events but throughout the Pacific Northwest included Bill Braiser (*Eclipse, Kiaola*), Al Buchan (*Glenco*), John Gordon (*Comus*), Stan Kieszling (*Windsong II*), Bud Larsen (*Chandra*), Neil McConaghy (*Polly Adler*), Bill Johnson (*Rainbird*), Tom Murphy (*Sundance*), Dave Nielsen (*Moonglow III*), John Pokela (*Risque*), Roger Rue (*Cierco*), Des Sessinghaus (*Sierra*), Irv Smith (*Topic*), Jerry Smith (*Bandit*), and Govnor Teats (*Stormy Weather, White Squall*). Al Buchan and Lynn Summers later purchased the America's Cup winning boat, the *Weatherly*, a 12-meter boat, and raced it out of TYC.

Powerboat Racing

In 1949 TYC expanded its programs to include powerboat predicted-log racing, more commonly referred to as a contest. Each skipper pilots his or her vessel over a prescribed course in a time he or she predicts, without access to any means for determining elapsed time. The only instruments allowable are a magnetic compass, a depth sounder, a local chart of the waters, and a tachometer.

In essence, once the course is laid out and it has been determined in what time the racers must finish, each skipper has to estimate not only what time he or she will start the race but also where he or she will be at certain points along the course. The goal is to arrive as close to the official ending time of the race as possible. The difference between the actual arrival time and the ending time of the race determines the winner. These contests closely proximate the conditions encountered in actual piloting, where safe arrival at a destination may require the navigator to accurately assess and compensate for wind, current, and other elements that might cause errors.

IPBA is the governing body for predicting-log contests in Washington and British Columbia. The South Sound and North Sound regions host six events per year, and to be qualify for Skipper of the Year, competitors must participate in at least 50 percent of the area races. South Sound races include the Olympia Governor's Cup, the Gig Harbor Invite, the Day Island Trophy, the Tacoma-Olympia Challenge, and the Jack Hyde Memorial race.

Judd Day won Skipper of the Year honors during the first two years of the TYC's powerboat racing program. Jim

Hanna won the first of four such awards in 1967. Other top skippers from the area included five-time winner Al Molzan and six-time recipient Ray Pond, who was also the first winner of the Jack Hyde Memorial race.

In 1960 Evert Landon was unable to skipper his boat, so he asked longtime friend and fellow boater Bill Kunigk to take his place at the helm so that his boat could still earn points and have a shot at Boat of the Year honors. Bill, brother of Olympic gold medal skier Gretchen Kunigk-Fraser (see chapter 37, Skiing), won top honors, and when he returned Landon was so excited he said, "Let's do it again next year!" Four years later in his own boat, the *Revel,* Landon participated in 11 races, finishing first six times and runner-up once, and took a third, fourth, fifth, and sixth place to win Power Boat Skipper of the Year honors in a landslide.

In addition to IPBA, which oversees local races, the North American Cruisers Association invites skippers from throughout North America to compete in an invitational predicted-log contest held in different locations each summer. The express purpose is the opportunity to compete for a national title. The first such local winner was David Pease, who skippered the cruiser *Whitecaps,* a boat unfamiliar to him, over 35 miles in Santa Monica Bay in California. His score was the best of the 13 entries representing regional champions from throughout the United States and Canada. Other North American Invitational Championships have been won by TYC members Joe Bocanegra (1988), Ray Pond (1994), and Larry Price (1994).

Noncompetitive Sailing

Despite all these accomplishments, competitive racing has never been the dominant focus of boating and yachting in Pierce County. Sailors did not have to belong to a private yacht club to enjoy the waters of Puget Sound. Boathouses were scattered along the shoreline, from Steilacoom to Old Tacoma. The Foss Boathouse located at Salmon Beach and Stewart's Boathouse near the present Old Town Dock were two of the area's earlier facilities. But the original Metropolitan Park District boathouse at Point Defiance was the best known until it was destroyed by fire in 1984. It was acquired by Tacoma in 1913, and by 1956 it was considered the largest boathouse in the country. From here, sports fishermen ventured out to capture the elusive salmon.

Charles N. Curtis established the local Sea Scout program to introduce the educational value of seamanship in 1929. Even today the Mount Rainier Council of Boy Scouts maintains two vintage yachts that link its programs to the nation's boating past. One, named to honor Curtis, was constructed for the Coast Guard in 1931 to chase rumrunners during the days of Prohibition. The second, the *Odyssey,* constructed in 1938, was used to test electronic gear in the development of radar and sonar during World War II.

The waters of Puget Sound have been a sports venue for Americans from the earliest years of settlement. Until the seas run dry, sailors and boaters will race and cruise upon them and in the process will continue to contribute to Pierce County's sporting legacy.

The backfield for the 1949 University of Puget Sound football team included Warren Wood (second from L.) who was selected to play in the 25th annual East-West All-Star Shrine Game his senior year (UPS).

THE PEOPLE
PART III

The following appendices list all of the professional players, hall-of-famers, award-winners, and many other men and women who have contributed in a variety of ways to sports in Tacoma and Pierce County throughout the years.

(Note that throughout these appendices, the following abbreviations are used: HS indicates "high school;" PLU, "Pacific Lutheran University;" UPS, "University of Puget Sound;"UW, "University of Washington;" and WSU, "Washington State University." Various other abbreviations are used to indicate positions.)

Professional Baseball Players (Major League)

Austin, Rick (P): Cleveland Indians, 1970–1971; Milwaukee Brewers, 1975–76.

Baker, Jesse (P): Chicago White Sox, 1911.

Blowers, Mike (3B): New York Yankees, 1989–91; Seattle Mariners, 1992–95, 1997, 1999; Los Angeles Dodgers, 1996; Oakland Athletics, 1998.

Caskey, Craig (P): Montreal Expos, 1973.

Cey, Ron (3B): Los Angeles Dodgers, 1971–82; Chicago Cubs, 1983–86; Oakland Athletics, 1987.

Edwards, Marshall (OF): Milwaukee Brewers, 1981–83.

Edwards, Mike (2B): Pittsburgh Pirates, 1977; Oakland Athletics, 1978–80.

Fournier, Jack (1B): Chicago White Sox, 1912–17; New York Yankees, 1918; St. Louis Cardinals, 1920–22; Brooklyn Dodgers, 1923–26; Boston Braves, 1927.

Hand, Rich (P): Cleveland Indians, 1970–71; Texas Rangers, 1972–73; California Angels, 1973.

Harstad, Oscar (P): Cleveland Indians, 1915.

Herbel, Ron (P): San Francisco Giants, 1963–69; San Diego Padres, 1970; New York Mets, 1970; Atlanta Braves, 1971.

Johnson, Bob "Indian Bob" (OF): Philadelphia Athletics, 1933–42; Washington Senators, 1943; Boston Red Sox, 1944–45.

Johnson, Roy (OF): Detroit Tigers, 1929–32; Boston Red Sox, 1932–35; New York Yankees, 1936–37; Boston Braves, 1937–38.

Kelleher, Mick (SS, 3B, 2B): St. Louis Cardinals, 1972–73, 1975; Houston Astros, 1974; Chicago Cubs, 1976–80; Detroit Tigers, 1981–82; California Angels, 1982.

Libke, Al (OF): Cincinnati Redlegs, 1945–46.

Loughlin, Larry (P): Philadelphia Phillies, 1967.

Lyons, Steve (OF): Boston Red Sox, 1985–86, 1991–93; Chicago White Sox, 1986–90; Atlanta Braves, 1992; Montreal Expos, 1992.

Mosolf, Jim (OF): Pittsburgh Pirates, 1929–30; Chicago Cubs, 1933.

Murphy, Billy (OF): New York Mets, 1966.

Neighbors, Cy (OF): Pittsburgh Pirates, 1908.

Nettles, Jim (OF): Minnesota Twins, 1970–72; Detroit Tigers, 1974; Kansas City Royals, 1979; Oakland Athletics, 1981.

Peterson, Cap (OF): San Francisco Giants, 1962–66; Washington Senators, 1967–68; Cleveland Indians, 1969.

Pointer, Aaron (OF): Houston Astros, 1963, 1966–67.

Pregenzer, John (P): San Francisco Giants, 1963–64.

Rickert, Marv "Twitch" (OF): Chicago Cubs, 1942, 1946–47; Cincinnati Redlegs, 1948; Boston Braves, 1948–49; Pittsburgh Pirates, 1950; Chicago White Sox, 1950.

Sisk, Doug (P): New York Mets, 1982–87; Baltimore Orioles, 1988; Atlanta Braves, 1990–91.

Stock, Wes (P): Baltimore Orioles, 1959–64; Kansas City Athletics, 1964–67. Coach: Kansas City Athletics, 1967; Milwaukee Brewers, 1970–72; Oakland Athletics, 1972–76, 1984–86; Seattle Mariners, 1977–81.

Strand, Paul (P/OF): Boston Braves, 1913–1915; Philadelphia Athletics, 1924.

Whitaker, Steve (OF): New York Yankees, 1966–68; Seattle Pilots, 1969; San Francisco Giants, 1970.

White, Mike (OF): Houston Astros, 1963–65.

Baseball No-Hitters

November 18, 1905: Bobby Keefe, Tacoma Tigers at Oakland Oaks, Tacoma 3–0 (9 innings)

July 11, 1939: Floyd Isekite, Wenatchee Chiefs at Tacoma Tigers, Tacoma 3–0 (9 innings), Western International League

May 30, 1946: Cy Greenlaw, Yakima Stars at Tacoma Tigers, Tacoma 3–0 (7 innings, GM #2) Western International League

August 26, 1962: Dick LeMay, Vancouver Mounties at Tacoma Giants, Tacoma 4–0 (7 innings, GM #2)

September 1, 1963: Jerry Thomas, Denver Bears at Tacoma Giants, Tacoma 1–0 (7 innings, GM #2)

June 22, 1964: Dick Estelle, Denver Bears at Tacoma Giants, Tacoma 2–0 (9 innings)

May 11, 1965: Dick Estelle, Hawaii Islanders at Tacoma Giants, Tacoma 6–0 (9 innings)

June 21, 1975: Tom Norton, Hawaii Islanders at Tacoma Twins, Tacoma 1–0 (9 innings)

July 9, 1978: Jim Beattie, Tacoma Yankees at Spokane Indians, Tacoma 2–0 (7 innings, GM #1)

August 24, 1980: Larry McCall, Spokane Indians at Tacoma Tigers, Tacoma 1–0 (7 innings, GM #2)

May 14, 1985: Tim Conroy, Tucscon Toros at Tacoma Tigers, Tacoma 1–0 (7 innings, GM #1)

June 10, 1991: Pat Werni, Vancouver Canadians at Tacoma Tigers, Tacoma 1–0 (9 innings)

July 3, 2001: Brett Tomko, Tacoma Rainiers at Oklahoma City Redhawks, Tacoma 7–0 (9 innings)

July 7, 2001: John Halama, Calgary Cannons at Tacoma Rainiers, Tacoma 6–0 (perfect game)

Halama's 2001 no-hitter was the first 9-inning perfect game in the Pacific Coast League's history, which started in 1903 and has included approximately 71,250 games played through 2002.

Hall of Fame: Baseball and Softball

Tacoma–Pierce County Baseball–Softball Oldtimers Association (www.oldtimerbaseball.com) Hall of Famers (through 2004):

Baseball

Morry Abbott, Primo Artoe, Rick Austin, Sonny Bailey, Cy Ball, Lou Balsano, Otto Balmer, Tony Banaszak Jr., Ron Billings, Earl Birnel, Les Bishop, Dale Bloom, Frank Bonaro, Ray Brammer, Jack Bratlie, Jess Brooks, Dick Browse, Frank Brozovich, Gordy Brunswick, Luther Carr, Ron Cey, Vern Champagne, Jim Claxton, Gene Clough, Dick Colombini, Howard Davis, Bob Dawson Sr., Mike Dillon, Fred "Buzz" Doane, Ozzie Edwards, Cliff Ellingson, Jim Ennis, Les Faulk, Bob Fredricks, Bill Funk, Maury Galbraith, Jim Gallwas, Holly Gee, Ron Gee, Bill Geppart, Ron Goerger, George Grant, Dick Greco, Al Greco Sr., Cy Greenlaw, Dave Hall, John P. Heinrick, Andy Helling, Joe Hemel, Ron Herbel, Garry

Hersey, Gordy Hersey, Bob Houston, Glenn Huffman, Earl Hyder, Floyd "Lefty" Isekite, Jack Johnson, Rick Johnson, Bob Johnson, Arly Kangas, Rod Keogh, Andy Ketter, Bob Kohout, Vern Kohout, Vic Krause, Earl Kuper, Ocky Larsen Sr., Harold Larson, Tony Lavorato, Rick Lewis, Al Libke Jr., Bob Lightfoot, Bryce Lilly, Chuck Loete, Larry Loughlin, Bob Maguinez, Mel Manley, Harry Mansfield, Floyd Marcusson, Vic Martineau, David Mathews, Allan Maul, Neil Mazza, Doug McArthur, Frank McCabe, Ed McCoy, Barney McFadden, Bob McGuire, Jack McStott, Pete Mello, Lornie Merkle, John Milroy, Dave Minnitti, Phil Misley, Joe Mlachnik, Bill Moe, Vern Morris, Frank Morrone, Dave Molitor, Jimmy Mosolf, Bill Mullen, Ford Mullen, Bill Murphy, Stan Naccarato, Jim Neeley, Bruce Nichols, Harry Nygard, Clyde Olson, Marion Oppelt, Dick Palamidessi, Don Paul, Jim Pelander, Al Pentecost, Cap Peterson, Aaron Pointer, Gilly Portmann, John Pregenzer, Bill Ralston, Fred Rickert, Marv Rickert, Jim Robinson, Rance Rolfe, Pat Rooney, Ernie Ruffo, Frank Ruffo, Pete Sabutis, Joe Salatino, Cliff Schiesz, Hal Schimling, Dick Schlosstein, Marv Scott, Bill Sewell, Otto Smith, Bob Snodgrass, Joe Spadafore, Ray Spurgeon, Ron Staples, Wes Stock, Ron Storaasli, Jack Tanner, Morry Taylor, Elmer Thiel, Erling Tollefson, Rudy Tollefson, Art Viafore, Chuck Viafore, Heinie Vogel, Stan Wallace, Carl "Kak" Wasmund, Pat Weber, Russ Wilkerson, Ray Wing, George Wise, Steve Whitaker, Mike White, Paul "Doc" Wotten, Ed Yusko.

Softball: Fastpitch

Doug Adam, Don Anderle, Jay Beach, Gordy Bendick, Lloyd Blanusa, Hal Blumke, Wally Brebner, Glen Collins, Merle "Butch" Corbin, Frank Davies, Bill Dunham, Bob Frankowsky, Vern From, Lloyd Glasoe, Jack Hermsen, Les Holtmeyer, Hank Jarvits, George Karpach, Art Lewis, Fran Luhtala, Kermit Lynch, Earl Mahnkey, Don Maitland, LaVerne Martineau, Louise Mazzuca, Roger McDonald, Darron Nelson, Dan Oliver, Dean Pitsch, Woodrow Red, Lou Rickenbacker, John Rockway, Bill Ruehle, Peggy Moran Ruehle, Harry Rush, Ed Sabol, Delores "Dee" Sagmiller, Larry Slovek,

Ken Stancato, Pat Strachan Stavig, Gene Thayer, Leonard Thomas, Bud Thomsen, Alec Watt, Dick Webster, Gertrude Wilhelmsen, Joyce Jones Wolf, Phil Yant, Dick Yohn, Lawrence "Cot" Zehnder, Margaret Zepeda, Bob Zurfluh, Don Zurfluh, Tom Zurfluh.

Softball: Slowpitch
Dave Benedict, Earl Birnel, Dave Bishop, Jan Chase, Ken Deforrest, Dick Halleen, Margaret "Maggie" Heinrick, Kathy Hemion, Ken Jones, Joe Kreger, Gordy Pfeifer, Ken Laase, Jim Lane, Lynn Larson, Marco Malich, Dick O'Brien, Butch Pasquale, Joe Stortini, Jerry Thacker, Ken Schulz, Terry Trowbridge, Bill Wheeler, Dave Wilsie, Bill Winter, Bob Young, Dick Zierman.

Broadcasters and Sportswriters
Rod Belcher, Jerry Geehan, Don Hill, Ed Honeywell, Clay Huntington, Bob Robertson, Art Thiel.

Umpires
Joe Bailey, Hal Berndt, Bob Corbin, John Heinrick, John Holliday, Bob Huegel, Joey Johns, Dave Kerrone, Rick Lewis, Ted Lopat, Lornie Merkle, Dave Minnitti, Frank Morrone, Jim Oleole, Gerald Redburg, Clarence Stave, David Van Hulle.

Sponsors
Darold Billings; Billings Electric; Cammarano Bros. Inc.; Ben B. Cheney; Harry Esborg, Hollywood Boat & Motor; Ples Irwin; Len Manke, Cloverleaf Tavern; Spud Hansen, Spud's Pizza Parlor; Tacoma Elks Club; Washington Hardware; Alden Woodworth.

Professional Basketball Players
Burgess, Frank (ABL): Hawaii Chiefs, 1961.
Curtis, Chuck (ABL): Pittsburg Rens, 1961.
Fuller, Hiram (NBA): Atlanta Hawks, 2004.
Gilmur, Chuck (BAA): Chicago Stags, 1946–49; Washington Capitals, 1949–51.
Jordan, Phil (NBA): New York Knicks, 1956–57, 1961–62; Detroit Pistons, 1957–59; Cincinnati Royals, 1959–61;

St. Lous Hawks, 1962–63.
Lowry, Charles (NBA): Milwaukee Bucks, 1972–73.
McDonald, Rod (ABA): Utah Stars, 1970–73.
Williams, Charles (ABA): Pittsburgh Pipers, 1967–68; Minnesota Pipers, 1968–69; Pittsburgh Condors, 1969–70; Memphis Pros, 1970–1972; Utah Stars, 1972–73.

The Professional Bowler's Tour
Earl Anthony, Kenneth Baker, Russell Baker II, Leonard Blakey, Donald Calhoun, Michael Clark, Garry Curry, Jim Duncan, Brian Edwards, Mark Fennell, Stephen Garland, Leslie Horton Jr., Sam Jennings, Earl Johnson, Michael Karch, Michael Kennedy, Denny Krick, Jeff Mattingly, Brad Mensen, LuAnn Moore, Jeannie Maiden Naccarato, Michael O'Rourke, Rod Parday, Robert Pike, William Reach, Mark Rowley, Jim Stevenson, Dave Tuell Jr., April Lord Wittig.

Hall of Fame: Bowling
Greater Tacoma Bowling Association (GTBA) Hall of Famers
1964: Bill Herdman; Jim Radonich
1965: Ted Tadich; Berle Wakefield
1966: Frisco Burnett; C. C. Collins
1967: Telli Pagni; Ernie Stowe
1968: John Artoe; Bill McClelland
1969: Mike Berry
1970: Joe Stemp
1971: *No inductee*
1972: *No inductee*
1973: Earl Johnson
1974: Bill Leftwich; Ocky Sciaqua
1975: Lou Bacalich; Jim Stevenson
1976: Urban Schmidt
1977: Primo Artoe
1978: Ev Olson; John Pasnick
1979: Earl Anthony; Dez Isaacson
1980: Carl Johnson; Larry Pentecost
1981: Brian Jennings; David R. Tuell Jr.
1982: Denny Krick; Joe Nole
1983: John Bulger; Dick Orr
1984: Larry Fulton; Jack Reese
1985: *No inductee*

1986: Don Smith

1987: Jim Melin; Rocky Rockwell

1988: Art Childers; Jeff Mattingly

1989: Jerry Ledbetter; Buck Scholz

1990: Jene LaMarr; Mac McGreevy

1991: Ron Dittmore; Mike Ingraham

1992: *No inductee*

1993: Lee Losk

1994: Larry Gabrielson

1995: Bob Bjorke

1996: Ray Burke II

1997: *No inductee*

1998: Bill Hurlbut; Putney McCormick; Don Norrell

1999: Julius Walker; Fred Wharton

2000: Bob Gunstrom; Bob Hanson

2001: Layton Shirley; Ted Wakefield

2002: Paul Fish; Jay Turner

2003: Frank Dietz

Tacoma Women's Bowling Association (TWBA)
    Hall of Famers

1966: Bertha McCormick

1967: Stella "Babe" Penowich

1968: Dorothy Pollen

1969: Louise "Jacki" Pagni

1970: Mildred Fleming; Mary "Mae" Knight

1971: Patricia Georgetti

1972: Mae Thomas

1973: Evelyn (Bloom) Brock

1974: Bessie Trowbridge

1975: Barbara Gavin

1976: Al Lind

1977: Mildred Greer; Glad Remer

1978: Eleanor "Kit" Campbell

1979: Elizabeth "Bessie" Scott Peterson

1980: Peggy Race

1981: Frances Sieler

1982: *No inductee*

1983: Aggie Thomas

1984: Margie (Junge) Oleole

1985: Marion Marshall; Billie Sulkosky

1986: Anite Kissick

1987: Mary Sears

1988: Jan Greswell

1989: Billie Norrell

1990: Jerry Garrett; Joyce Harrington

1991: Evelyn Garl

1992: Dennie Russell

1993: Florence Raap

1994: Nadine Fulton

1995: Esther Campbell

1996: Viola Waisath

1997: Janice Chase

1998: Garetta V. Ernest

1999: Gwen Terry

2000: LuAnn Moore

2001: Jytte Klein

2002: Shirley Welch

2003: Jan Jelvik

Professional Boxers

(includes weight class)

Anderson, Ole (heavyweight), 1920s

Armstrong, Davey (126 pounds), 1980s

Bailey, Bill (160 pounds), 1950s

Bennett, Leonard (147 pounds), 1930s

Biegler, Bob (heavyweight), 1960s

Britt, Frank "Che Che" (126 pounds), 1920s

Britt, Jimmy (unknown), 1930s

Bumphus, Johnny (135 pounds), 1980s

Bush, Donny (135 pounds), 1940s

Cook, Paulie (126 pounds), 1940s

Croft, Lee (heavyweight), 1940s

Cuevus, Gus (147 pounds), 1950s

Davey, Dave (heavyweight), 1940s and '50s

Davis, Al (147 pounds), 1940s

Delaney, Paul (153 pounds), 1930s

Evans, Billy (147 pounds), 1940s

Farmer, Frank (heavyweight), 1920s and '30s

Findlay, Mike (147 pounds), 1940s

Fitzpatrick, Jimmy (147 pounds), 1940s

Garcia, Rudy (135 pounds), 1950s and '60s

Grant, Dale (175 pounds), 1970s and '80s

Green, Gene (135 pounds), 1960s

Green, Irvin (160 pounds), 2000s

Hall, Jess (heavyweight), 1940s and '50s

Halloway, Hal (147 pounds), 1940s

Hart, Billy (147 pounds), 1930s

Hawkins, Roy (heavyweight), 1940s

Jamison, DeWayne (160 pounds), 1980s

Jasmer, George (171 pounds), 1960s

Jensen, Ernie (160 pounds), 1940s

Johnson, Parrish (160 pounds), 1990s

Johnston, Charlie (147 pounds), 1940s

Ketchel, Harry (126 pounds), 1930s

Larson, Ruggles (135 pounds), 1950s

Lenhart, Fred (175 pounds), 1930s

Little, Bill "Big" (heavyweight), 1940s

Linton, Emmett, Jr. (160 pounds), 1990s

Linton, Robert (147 pounds), 1990s

Lockridge, Rocky (130 pounds), 1970s and '80s

Mack, Sid (147 pounds), 1950s

Marrow, Lacky (175 pounds), 1930s and '40s

McComber, Jock (heavyweight), 1930s and '40s

McKinney, Bob (heavyweight), 1950s and '60s

McMurtry, Mike (heavyweight), 1950s

McMurtry, Pat (heavyweight), 1950s and '60s

Morris, Oscar (147 pounds), 1960s and '70s

Mott, Cecil (147 pounds), 1960s

Nicholson, Larry (135 pounds), 1950s

O'Mara, Sonny (unknown), 1950s

Pasquale, Bobby (175 pounds), 1960s

Passmore, Tommy (unknown), 1940s

Parker, Wayne (160 pounds), 1940s

Randolph, Leo (118 pounds), 1970s and '80s

Reed, Dick "Ritchie" (147 pounds), 1950s

Roberts, Eddie "KO" (160 pounds), 1930s

Sams, Mike (195 pounds), 2000s

Seales, Sugar Ray (160 pounds), 1970s and '80s

Seales, Wilbur (147 pounds), 1980s

Smith, Larry (160 pounds), 1970s and '80s

Snell, Doc (126 pounds), 1930s

Steele, Freddie (160 pounds), 1920s, '30s, and '40s

Stone, Wally (126 pounds), 1940s

Thompson, Jerry (135 pounds), 1950s

Torres, Angelo (126 pounds), 2000s

Torzewski, Brian (heavyweight), 2000s

Vaden, Paul (154 pounds), 1990s

Ward, Davey (147 pounds), 1940s

Warren, Ronnie (160 pounds), 1990s

Watkins, Myron (160 pounds), 1990s

White, Eugene (160 pounds), 1970s

Wright, Chalky (135 pounds), 1930s

Wright, George (160 pounds), 1960s

Yenter, Denny (175 pounds), 1960s

Professional Figure Skaters

The following skaters achieved the highest levels in the testing structure as set forth by the U. S. Figure Skating Association, or the comparable Canadian standards, and earned gold medals in one or more of the following categories: figures, free style, dance, pairs, or moves in the field.

1950: Marlene Jackson; Lois Secreto

1951: Patricia Firth; William Nick

1952: William Nick; Evelynne Olsen

1953: Joby Moore

1954: Patricia Firth; Carol Irwin

1955: Joan Schenke

1956: Sally Price

1957: Annette Kennedy

1960: Marianne Beeler; Jerry Fotheringill; Judianne Fotheringill

1962: Robert Madden

1963: Linda Galbraith; Patty Gilroy; April White

1965: Roseanne Lee

1966: Richard Paice

1967: Diane Puckett

1968: Paul Spruell

1970: Donna Albert; Babs Vasser

1971: Donna Albert; Kathy Gleason

1972: Jim Parr; William Santee; Dawn Weiburg

1973: Marcy Sulenes

1974: Jean-Rene Basle

1975: Jean-Rene Basle; Heidi Broback

1976: Lisa Church; Natalie Flake; Dana Olson

1977: Danette Williams; Kelly Yoshida

1978: Staci Loop; Beth Names; Sally Odekirk; Jill Sawyer

1979: Cory Mims

1980: Carol Jo McCormick; Sally Odekirk; James White

1981: Arnold Alt; Lani Pim

1982: Jean-Rene Basle; Dawn Bialek; Janice Teodoro

1983: Stephanie Heitz; Sherry Slemko; James White

1984: Karen Nolan

1985: Lori Knoll; Michelle Nolan

1986: Michelle Nolan; Jozelyn Winder

1987: Jozelyn Winder

1988: Dawn Gardunia; Kaia Halvorson; Lynette Lagmay; Kelly Moller

1989: Julie Elledge; Andrea Moss; Stephanie Rose

1990: Scott Davis; Leanne Highsmith; Kimberly Kartic; Stephanie Rose

1991: Sarah Gendreau; Leanne Highsmith

1992: Kelly Clark; Heidi Green; Heidi Pelander; James Peterson; Stacey Zimmerman

1993: Lisa Martin

1994: Leanne Highsmith; Richen Woods

1995: Michelle Taylor

1996: Valerie Larsen; Michelle Taylor

1997: Michael Bauer; Robyn Lane; Jim Peterson; Stephanie Rowland

1998: Elena Anderson; Kristen Bagby; Sue Ellen Harris; Merrie Parr; Stephanie Rowland

1999: Lynn Neil; Merrie Parr

2000: Chris Dougherty; Sue Ellen Harris; Lynn Neil

2001: Chris Dougherty; Aanya Reiten

2002: Glenn Patterson; Lindsey Wilson

2003: Tiffany Chaney; Elise Friedrich; Jessica Leatham; Daniel Nam; Aanya Reiten; Andy Riffle; Lindsey Wilson

2004: Jennifer Bourlet

Professional Football Players

Arnold, John (WR): Detroit Lions, 1979–80 (Washington HS).

Artoe, Leo (T): Chicago Bears, 1940–42, 1945; Los Angeles Dons, 1946–47; Baltimore Colts, 1948 (Lincoln HS).

Baker, Sam (P, FB): Washington Redskins, 1953, 1956–59; Cleveland Browns, 1960–61; Dallas Texans, 1962–63; Philadelphia Eagles, 1964–69 (Stadium HS).

Baldassin, Mike (LB): San Francisco 49ers, 1977–78 (Wilson HS).

Bearden, Jerome (n/a): Oakland Invaders, 1984; Denver Gold, 1985 (Wilson HS).

Boose, Dorian (DE): New York Jets, 1998; Edmonton Eskimos, 2003 (Foss HS).

Bruce, Gail (DE, OE): San Francisco 44ers, 1948–49; San Francisco 49ers, 1950–51 (Puyallup HS).

Bush, Lewis (LB): San Diego Chargers, 1993–98 (Washington HS).

Butler, Hillary (LB): Seattle Seahawks, 1998 (Lakes HS).

Coombs, Tom (TE): New York Jets, 1982–83 (UPS).

Eaton, Chad (defensive T): New England Patriots, 1996–98; Seattle Seahawks, 1999–2003 (Rogers HS).

Forsberg, Fred (LB): Denver Broncos, 1968; Buffalo Bills, 1970–73; San Diego Chargers, 1974 (Wilson HS).

Fuller, James (DB): San Diego Chargers, 1992–93; Philadelphia Eagles, 1996 (Stadium HS).

Godfrey, Herb (OE, DE): Cleveland Browns, 1942 (Lincoln HS).

Goldsmith, Vince (LB): Saskatchewan Rough Riders, 1981–83; Toronto Argonauts, 1984, 1988–90; Calgary Stampeders, 1985–87 (Mount Tahoma HS).

Grandberry, Ken (RB): Chicago Bears, 1974 (Laughbon HS).

Hobert, Billy Joe (QB): Oakland Raiders, 1995–96; Buffalo Bills, 1997; New Orleans Saints, 1998–99 (Puyallup HS).

Horton, Ray (S): Cincinnati Bengals, 1983–88; Dallas Cowboys, 1989–92 (Mount Tahoma HS).

Huard, Brock (QB): Seattle Seahawks, 1999–2001; Indianapolis Colts, 2002–03 (Puyallup HS).

Huard, Damon (QB): Miami Dolphins, 1998–2000; New England Patriots, 2002–03 (Puyallup HS).

Hunter, Torey (DB): Houston Oilers, 1995 (Curtis HS).

Jenkins, Fletcher (DE, NT): Baltimore Colts, 1982; Los Angeles Express, 1984 (Lakes HS).

Jones, Jim (DB): Los Angeles Rams, 1958; Oakland Raiders, 1961 (Lincoln HS).

Juma, Kevin (WR): Seattle Seahawks, 1987 (Fife HS).

Keel, Mark (TE): Seattle Seahawks, 1987; Kansas City Chiefs, 1987 (Clover Park HS).

Kitna, Jon (QB): Seattle Seahawks, 1997–2001; Cincinnati Bengals, 2002–03 (Lincoln HS).

Klumb, John "Sticky Fingers" (OE, DE): Chicago Cardinals, 1939–40; Pittsburgh Steelers, 1940 (Stadium HS).

Kupp, Craig (QB): Phoenix Cardinals, 1991 (PLU).

Levenseller, Mike (WR): Tampa Bay Buccaneers, 1978; Buffalo Bills, 1978; Cincinnati Bengals, 1979–80; Edmonton Eskimos, 1982; Calgary Stampeders, 1983–85; Toronto Argonauts, 1991 (Curtis HS).

Marker, Cliff (OE, BB, FB, TB): Canton Bulldogs, 1926; Frankford Yellow Jackets, 1927; New York Giants, 1927 (Stadium HS).

May, Sherriden (RB): New York Jets, 1995–96 (Spanaway Lakes HS).

Mays, Stafford (DE, NT): St. Louis Cardinals, 1980–86; Minnesota Vikings, 1987–88 (Lincoln HS).

McBride, Charlie (BB, LB): Chicago Cardinals, 1936 (Puyallup HS).

McCurdy, Gary (RB): Sacramento Gold Miners, 1993 (UPS).

McQuary, Jack (HB, DB): Los Angeles Dons, year unknown (born in Tacoma).

Medved, Ron (DB): Philadelphia Eagles, 1966–70 (Bellarmine Prep).

Milloy, Lawyer (DB): New England Patriots, 1996–02; Buffalo Bills, 2003 (Lincoln HS).

Mobley, Signor (DB): Dallas Cowboys, 1997–98; Edmonton Eskimos, 2003 (Curtis HS).

Oliphant, Mike (RB): Washington Redskins, 1988; Cleveland Browns, 1989–91; Sacramento Gold Miners, 1993 (UPS).

Paul, Don (DB, HB): Chicago Cardinals, 1950–53; Cleveland Browns, 1954–58 (Fife HS).

Rashad, Ahmad (WR): St. Louis Cardinals, 1972–73; Buffalo Bills, 1974; Minnesota Vikings, 1976–82 (Mount Tahoma HS).

Ruffo, Al (founder, coach): San Francisco 49ers, 1944, 1946–47 (Bellarmine Prep).

Sarboe, Philip John (RB): Boston Redskins, 1934; Chicago Cardinals, 1934–36; Brooklyn Dodgers, 1936 (Lincoln HS).

Scott, Kevin (RB): San Diego Chargers, 1988; Dallas Cowboys, 1989 (Rogers HS).

Shipley, Randy (C, G): Portland Storm, 1974; Portland Thunder, 1975 (PLU).

Sigurdson, Sig (OE, DE): Baltimore Colts, year unknown (PLC).

Skansi, Paul (WR): Pittsburgh Steelers, 1983; Seattle Seahawks, 1984–91; Ottawa Rough Riders, 1991–92 (Peninsula HS).

Smith, Raonall (LB): Minnesota Vikings 2003–04 (Peninsula HS).

Stojack, Frank "Toughie" (G): Brooklyn Dodgers, 1935–36 (Lincoln HS).

Trufant, Marcus (DB): Seattle Seahawks, 2003–04 (Wilson HS).

Washington, Harry (WR): Minnesota Vikings, 1978; Chicago Bears, 1979 (Stadium HS, Foss HS).

Werner, Clyde (LB): Kansas City Chiefs, 1970, 1972–74, 1976 (Wilson HS).

Williams, Aaron (WR): Oakland Invaders, 1984; Denver Gold, 1985 (Wilson HS).

Williams, Dave (WR): St. Louis Cardinals, 1967–71; San Diego Chargers, 1972–73; Pittsburgh Steelers, 1973; Southern California Sun, 1973–74 (Lincoln HS).

Williams, Vince (RB): San Francisco 49ers, 1982–83 (Mount Tahoma HS).

Woodard, Milt (commissioner): American Football League, 1966–70 (Stadium HS).

Zamberlin, John (LB): New England Patriots, 1979–82; Kansas City Chiefs, 1983–84 (Wilson HS, PLU).

The Professional Golf Tour

Barnes, Jim (PGA)

Bourne, Jim (PGA)

Brett, Dusty (Mini Tour)

Brown, Chuck (PGA)

Campbell, Doug (PGA)

Congdon, Chuck (PGA)

Eliason, Ockie (PGA)

Feldman, Al (PGA)

Johnson, Bob (PCA)

Lanning, George (PGA)

Love, Jim (Mini Tour)

Malm, Glenn (Mini Tour)

Mengert, Al (PGA)

Ming, Chris (Mini Tour)

Mogg, Brian (PGA)

Newell, Frank, Sr. (PGA)

Parkhurst, Tom (PGA)

Rudy, John (PGA)

Towns, Ken (PGA)

Wooding, Audrey (Mini Tour)

Wooding, Michelle (LPGA)

Professional Racquet Sports Players

Alger, Mark (Squash)

Chaffeur, Ken (Tennis)

Galbraith, Pat (Association of Tennis Professionals Tennis Tour)

Pazourek, Mike (Association of Tennis Professionals Satellite Tennis Tour)

Pfeifer, Gordy (Handball)

Shogreen, Scott (Challengers Tennis Tour)

Professional Soccer Players

Brown, Cliff, Stadium HS, Seattle Sounders (NASL)

Durgan, Jeff, Stadium HS, New York Cosmos (NASL)

Enneking, Mike, Bellarmine Prep, Tacoma Stars (MISL)

Goulet, Brent, Foss HS, Tacoma Stars, US National team

Hellenkamp, Chris, Stadium HS, Portland Timbers, Fort Wayne, Indiana, Flames

Mulholland, Dale, Mt. Tahoma HS, Seattle Sounders "A" League, pro Russian team

Oak, Darrel, Stadium HS, Seattle Sounders (NASL)

Peterson, Mark, Wilson HS, Seattle Sounders (NASL), Tacoma Stars (MISL)

Reidal, Leif, Stadium HS, Los Angeles Aztecs (NASL)

Stock, Jeff, Stadium HS, Seattle Sounders (NASL), Tacoma Stars

Vaughn, Dan, Wilson HS, Detroit Express (NASL, ASL), Memphis Rogues, Calgary Boomer, Jacksonville Teamen Screws, Homer, Washington HS, Tacoma Stars (MISL)

Milford, Carl, Lincoln HS, Tacoma Tides (ASL)

Waltman, Danny, Bellarmine Prep, Seattle Sounders, Chicago Storm (MISL)

Tacoma–Pierce County Sports Hall of Fame

The Tacoma–Pierce County Sports Hall of Fame was the brainchild of longtime sportscaster, sportswriter, and radio station owner Clay Huntington, who encouraged the Tacoma Athletic Commission (TAC) to recognize the community's great sports stars for their outstanding athletic achievements over the years.

The first Hall of Fame inductees were recognized in 1957 and additional members were added up until the 1970s when the organization ceased honoring local athletes. The Tacoma–Pierce County Sports Hall of Fame resumes its efforts to recognize deserving individuals with the class of 2005.

These Hall of Fame members are recognized for their outstanding sports accomplishments and contributions that have brought significant local and regional acclaim to themselves and to the Tacoma–Pierce County area. Additional criteria includes:

1. Athletes must be retired from active competition. (*Exception:* Individuals in such categories as coach, administrator, official, broadcaster, or sportswriter still active at the age of 70 may be nominated for the Hall of Fame.)

2. Coaches, administrators, broadcasters, sportswriters, and officials must demonstrate significant accomplishments in their field for an extended length of time.

3. Individuals to be considered must be born and raised in Tacoma–Pierce County or must have maintained a significant long-term residence in the community. Exceptions may be made at the discretion of the Hall of Fame committee.

4. Other categories not listed will be considered on an individual basis by the committee.

A committee of past and present local sportswriters and broadcasters, TAC directors, and Hall of Fame members cast ballots to determine the new inductees who are selected from an impressive list of candidates. For additional information, visit www.tacomasports museum.com.

Nominations for future considerations, which should include a detailed description of the individual's athletic career, may be submitted via email to marc@tacomaathletic.com or in writing to: Tacoma–Pierce County Sports Hall of Fame, c/o Tacoma Athletic Commission, P.O. Box 11304, Tacoma, WA 98411.

The Honorees:

1957
Bob Johnson, Baseball
Gretchen Kunigk-Fraser, Skiing
Freddie Steele, Boxing

1958
Marv Harshman, Basketball, Football
Marv Tommervik, Football
Frank Wilson, Basketball, Football

1959
John Heinrick, Basketball, Football Coach
Cliff Olson, Football
Joe Salatino, Baseball, Football
Wally Scott, Tennis
Frank Stojack, Football, Wrestling

1960
Charles Congdon, Golf
Charles D. Hunter, Golf
Roy Johnson, Baseball

1961
Leo Artoe, Football
Herman Brix, Track
Paul Strand, Baseball

1962
Shirley Fopp, Golf, Skiing
Jack Fournier, Baseball
John Kennedy, Basketball Coach, Referee
Phil Sarboe, Football Coach
Ted Tadich, Bowling

1963
Jack Connor, Boxing

Frank Gillihan, Football, Football Referee
Marcus Nalley, Hunting
Don Paul, Baseball, Basketball, Football
Jack Walters, Golf
George Wise, Baseball, Golf

1964
Cy Neighbors, Baseball
Marv Rickert, Baseball
Al Ruffo, Football
Ernie Tanner, Baseball, Football, Track
Frank Tobin, Baseball

1965
Myron "Chief" Carr, Football, Track Coach
Pat McMurtry, Boxing

1966
Dill Howell, Baseball
Elliott Metcalf, Sportswriter

1967
Harold Bird, Boxing

1968
Ben B. Cheney, Baseball
Dan Walton, Sportswriter

1969
Jesse Baker, Baseball
Lou Balsano, Baseball
Tony Banaszak Sr., Baseball
Jimmy Claxton, Baseball
Harry Deegan, Horse Racing
Dick Greco, Baseball
Walt Hagedorn, Baseball
Bob Hager, Athletic Administrator
Frank Hermsen, Baseball
Joe Hermsen, Baseball
Chuck Horjes, Football
Rick Johnson, Baseball, Basketball
Harold "Wah" Keller, Athletic Administrator

Lee Kierstad, Baseball

Bill Libke, Baseball

Cliff Marker, Baseball

Joey Peterson, Baseball

Frank Ruffo, Baseball

Jack Sonntag, Baseball Coach

Lou Spadafore, Baseball

Carl Sparks, Football Coach

Ole Swinland, Baseball, Basketball

Mike Tucci, Football

Bill Vinson, Basketball, Football Coach

Hal Votaw, Baseball

1970

No Inductees

1971

Jess Brooks, Baseball, Football

Gordon Brunswick, Baseball, Basketball, Football

Eddie Carlson, Baseball

Dug Dyckman, Football

Jimmy Ennis, Baseball, Football

Harold "Ox" Hansen, Football

Vince Hanson, Basketball

Ocky Haugland, Baseball

Al Hopkins, Football Coach

Wes Hudson, Football

Everett Jensen, Football

Neil Mazza, Baseball

John McCallum, Sportswriter

Bobby McGuire, Baseball, Basketball, Football

Max Mika, Basketball, Football

Vern Morris, Baseball, Basketball, Football

Jimmy Mosolf, Baseball

Andy Nelson, Baseball

Harry Parker, Archery, Football

Harry Werbisky, Baseball, Basketball, Football

Gertrude Wilhelmsen, Track

Henry "Fat" Williams, Baseball

1972

Art Berg, Baseball

Frankie "Che Che" Britt, Boxing

Ed Honeywell, Sportswriter

Floyd "Lefty" Isekite, Baseball

Vern Pedersen, Football, Swimming

Roy Sandberg, Football Coach

Frank Spear, Football

2005

Morry Abbott, Baseball

Lanny Adams (Werner), Roller Skating

Bruce Alexander, Basketballl Official

John Anderson, Football Coach

Neil Andrews, Hockey

Earl Anthony, Bowling

Davey Armstrong, Boxing

Gerry Austin, Football Coach

Dan Ayrault, Crew

Sam Baker, Football

Roni Barrios (Mejia), Gymnastics

Shirley Baty, Golf

Ralph Bauman, Football

Rod Belcher, Broadcaster

Mike Benson, Tennis Coach

John Best, Soccer Administrator

Ron Billings, Football, Basketball Coach

Lloyd Blanusa, Fastpitch

Dale Bloom, Baseball

Jack Boyle, Figure Skating

Frank "Buster" Brouillet, Football

Dick Brown, Football, Basketball

Ole Brunstad, Football

Janet Buchan (Elway), Swimming

Ruth Canale (Ward), Golf

Luther Carr, Football

Andy Carrigan, Football

Casey Carrigan, Track

Ron Cey, Baseball

Jerry Conine, Wrestling

Tom Cross, Basketball, Official, Athletic Administrator

Chuck Curtis, Basketball

Don D'Andrea, Football

Jim Daulley, Track Coach

Don Duncan, Swimming Coach

Jeff Durgan, Soccer

Ockie Eliason, Golf

Ed Fallon, Football Coach

Jim Fifer, Crew

Pat Firth (Hansen), Figure Skating

Don Flye, Tennis

Fred Forsberg, Football

Jerry Fotheringill, Figure Skating

Judi Fotheringill (Fuller), Figure Skating

Vern From, Fastpitch

Nadine Fulton, Bowling

Doug Funk, Football Coach

Pat Galbraith, Tennis

John Garnero, Football, Basketball, Track

Jerry Geehan, Broadcaster

Rod Gibbs, Basketball

Tommy Gilmer, Football, Track

Evalyn Goldberg (Schultz), Basketball, Volleyball, Fastpitch

Vince Goldsmith, Football

Jeff Gotcher, Wrestling

Larry Gotcher, Wrestling

Cy Greenlaw, Baseball

Jimmy Grogan, Figure Skating

Kaye Hall-Greff, Swimming

Patsy Hamm (Dillingham), Figure Skating

Dave Hannula, Swimming

Dick Hannula Sr., Swimming Coach

John Harbottle, Golf

Sterling Harshman, Track, Football

George Henley, Hydroplane Racing

Garry Hersey, Baseball

Gordy Hersey, Baseball

Don Hill, Broadcaster

Billy Joe Hobert, Football

Ray Horton, Football

Mike Huard, Football Coach

Glenn Huffman, Football, Basketball, Baseball

Bob Hunt, Football, Wrestling, Track

George Hunt, Crew

Clay Huntington, Broadcaster, Sportswriter

Earl Hyder, Baseball

Dan Inveen, Basketball, Administration

Norm Iverson, Football

Roger Iverson, Basketball

Bob Jackson, Swimming, Football

Marjorie Jefferies (Shanaman), Golf

Lute Jerstad, Mountaineering, Basketball

Joey Johns, Hockey, Fastpitch

Sonny Johns, Archery

John Johnsen, Figure Skating Coach

Earl Johnson, Bowling

Jack Johnson, Baseball, Official

Jim Jones, Football, Track

Margie Junge (Oleole), Bowling

George Karpach, Fastpitch

Dori Kovanen, Soccer

Eldon Kyllo, Football

Dana LeDuc, Track & Field

Pat Lesser-Harbottle, Golf

Bob Levinson, Football, Track Coach

Lincoln High School 1944 backfield, Football (Len Kalapus, Al Malanca, Bob McGuire, and Dean Mellor)

Earl Luebker, Sportswriter

Gene Lundgaard, Basketball

Bob Maguinez, Baseball

Joan Mahon (Allard), Golf

Robert Martin, Crew

Jeff Mattingly, Bowling

Steve Matzen, Basketball

Norm Mayer, Football Coach

Tommy Mazza, Football

Louise Mazzuca, Fastpitch

Doug McArthur, Athletic Administration, Baseball Coach

Bertha McCormick, Bowling

Harry McLaughlin, Basketball

Don McLeod, Motorcycle Racing, Auto Racing, Roller Skating

Ron Medved, Football

Lornie Merkle, Basketball, Baseball, Football Official

Jim Meyerhoff, Wrestling

Dick Milford, Hockey

Bob Mitchell, Football

Don Moore, Football

Yumi Mordre, Gymnastics

Don Moseid, Basketball, Basketball Coach

Amy Lou Murray (Young), Golf

Jeanne Naccarato, Bowling

Stan Naccarato, Baseball, Athletic Administrator

Clint Names, Basketball, Golf

Dean Nicholson, Basketball Coach

George Nordi, Football Coach

David Olmstead, Wrestling

Dr. Dave Olson, Athletic Administrator

Carl Opolsky, Football

Cap Peterson, Baseball

Mark Peterson, Soccer

Joe Peyton Track, Football, Basketball

Gordy Pfeifer, Handball, Slowpitch

Cindy Pitzinger (Willey), Volleyball

Earl Platt, Football, Basketball, Baseball

Leo Randolph, Boxing

Ahmad Rashad, Football

Jerry Redmond, Football Coach

Chuck Richards, Swimming, Pentathlon

Bob Robertson, Broadcaster

Jim Rondeau, Boxing Referee, Administrator

Mark Ross, Football Coach

Bob Ryan, Football Coach

John Sayre, Crew

Marv Scott, Baseball Coach

Sugar Ray Seales, Boxing

Lois Secreto (Schoettler), Figure Skating

Doris Severtsen (Heritage), Track, Cross Country

Sarah Silvernail (Elliot), Volleyball

Mark Smith, Track

Miriam Smith (Greenwood), Swimming

Chuck Soper, Track

Bob Sprague, Basketball

Stanley's Shoemen, 1956 National Championship Baseball Team (Stan Naccarato, sponsor; Morley Brotman, sponsor; Doug McArthur, coach/manager; Tom Montgomery, statistician/scorekeeper; Jack Johnson, C; Dale Bloom, P; Mike Dillon, P; Manly Mitchell, P; Max Braman, P; Dick Montgomery, P/1B; Dick Schlosstein, 1B; Russ Wilkerson, 2B/3B; Gordy Hersey, SS/2B; Jim Gallwas, 3B/SS; Bob Maguinez, LF; Earl Hyder, CF/SS; Ron Storaasli, RF; Gordy Grubert, OF; Pat Dillon, IF/OF; Ray Spalding, OF. Monte Geiger, P; George Grant, SS; Jim Harney, 2B—added from Cheney Studs for regional, national tournaments.)

Ken Still, Golf

Jeff Stock, Soccer

Wes Stock, Baseball

Ron Storaasli, Baseball, Basketball, Football

Joe Stortini, Baseball, Football, Slowpitch

Vince Strojan, Basketball

Fred Swendsen, Football

Dave Trageser, Tennis

Dave Tuell Jr., Bowling

University of Puget Sound Loggers, 1976 National Championship Basketball Team (Don Zech, coach; Mike Acres, assistant coach; Jim Schuldt, trainer; Doug McArthur, athletic director; Brant Gibler, F; Rick Walker, F; Curt Peterson, C; Tim Evans, G; Rocky Botts, G; Mark Wells, G; A.T. Brown, F; Phil Hiam, C; Jimmy Stewart, G; Mike Strand, G; Matt McCully, G; Mike Kuntz, G; Steve Freimuth, F; Bill Greenheck, G.; Mike Hanson, F.)

Jim Van Beek, Basketball

Gene Walters, Football

Dan Watson, Track Coach

Clyde Werner, Football

Frosty Westering, Football Coach

Laurie Wetzel (Hayward), Basketball, Volleyball

Tom Whalen, Basketball

Steve Whitaker, Baseball

Mac Wilkins, Track

Charlie Williams, Basketball

Dave Williams, Football

Onnie Willis (Rogers), Gymnastics

Warren Wood, Football

Milt Woodard, Athletic Administrator

Armand Yapachino, Hydroplane Racing

Robert A. "RAB" Young, Racewalking

John Zamberlin, Football

Don Zech, Basketball Coach

State of Washington Sports Hall of Fame

The Tacoma Athletic Commission established the State of Washington Sports Hall of Fame in 1960. Hall of Fame members are recognized for their outstanding sports accomplishments and contributions that have brought national acclaim to themselves and to the state of Washington. A committee of sportswriters and sports broadcasters from throughout the state cast ballots to determine the new inductees, who are selected from an impressive list of candidates. For additional information, visit www.washington sportshalloffame.com. Nominations for future considerations may be submitted in writing to: State of Washington Sports Hall of Fame, c/o Tacoma Athletic Commission, P.O. Box 11304, Tacoma, WA 98411.

Baseball
1962: Fred Hutchinson
1963: Vean Gregg
1964: Earl Averill; Bob Johnson
1969: Earl Torgeson
1974: George Burns; Jeff Heath
1977: Harlond Clift; Gerry Staley
1978: Roy Johnson; George "Rube" Walberg
1979: Jack Fournier; Ray Washburn
1980: Joyner "JoJo" White; Sammy White
1983: Earl Johnson; Ron Santo
1986: Amos Rusie
1989: Ed Brandt; Woody Jensen; Mel Stottlemyre
1994: Ron Cey; Wes Stock
2003: Ira Flagstead; Hubert "Hub" Kittle; Ryne Sandberg

Basketball
1962: Elgin Baylor
1965: Jack Nichols
1967: Eddie O'Brien; Johnny O'Brien
1968: Gale Bishop
1969: Bob Houbregs
1974: Hal Lee
1979: Gene Conley; Bobby Galer
1983: Bill Morris
1994: Marv Harshman; Paul Lindeman; Doug Smart
1997: Fred Brown

1998: Jack Sikma
2004: Frank Burgess, Steve Hawes

Bowling
1994: Earl Anthony

Boxing
1961: Freddie Steele
1965: Al Hostak

Equestrian Sports: Horse Racing
1967: Basil James

Football
1960: George Wilson
1961: Mel Hein
1963: Ray Flaherty; Hugh McElhenny
1964: Butch Meeker
1965: Chuck Carroll
1967: Morris "Red" Badgro
1968: Turk Edwards
1969: Harland Svare
1970: Arnie Weinmeister
1974: Tony Canadeo; Don Heinrich
1977: Sam Baker; Vic Markov; Ernie Steele
1978: Don Paul
1980: Keith Lincoln
1983: Chuck Allen; Ed Goddard; George Reed
1986: Paul Schwegler
1989: Gail Cogdill
1994: Hugh Campbell*; Ray Frankowski; Rick Redman; LaVern Torgeson*; Jerry Williams*
1996: Ahmad Rashad; Bob Schloredt
1997: Jimmie Cain; Ray Mansfield
1998: Don James
1999: Steve Largent
2004: Terry Metcalf
(Asterisk * denotes recognition for outstanding coaching qualifications as well as play.)

Golf
1963: Marvin "Bud" Ward

1970: Harry Givan
1978: Chuck Congdon
1983: Jack Westland
1994: Joanne Gunderson Carner; Ken Still
1997: Anne Quast Sander
1999: Rod Funseth; Pat Lesser-Harbottle

Handball
1994: Gordy Pfeifer

Hockey
1986: Frank Foyston

Riflery and Small Arms Shooting
1964: Arnold Reigger

Skiing
1960: Gretchen Kunigk-Fraser
1966: Olav Ulland
1996: Phil Mahre; Steve Mahre

Swimming
1960: Helene Madison
1962: Jack Medica
1983: Kaye Hall-Greff
1994: Dick Hannula

Tennis
1997: Tom Gorman
1998: Janet Hopps-Adkisson

Track and Field
1961: Herman Brix
1979: Gerry Lindgren
1980: Brian Sternberg
1999: Mac Wilkins
2005: John Chaplin; Doris Severtsen (Heritage)

Yachting: Boat Racing
1979: Billy Schumacher
1986: Bill Muncey
1996: Stan Sayres

Sportswriters and Broadcasters
1968: Royal Brougham
1974: Leo Lassen
1977: Vince O'Keefe
1989: Milt Woodard
1994: John McCallum
1999: Rod Belcher; Clay Huntington
2001: Bob Blackburn; Les Keiter; Georg Meyers; Harry Missildine
2004: Dave Niehaus

Coaches and Administrators
1960: Vincent "Nig" Borleske (Football, Basketball, and Baseball Coach); Hiram Conibear (Crew Coach)
1961: Gil Dobie (Football Coach)
1962: Babe Hollingbery (Football Coach)
1963: Al Ulbrickson (Crew Coach)
1964: Rusty Callow (Crew Coach)
1966: Buck Bailey (Baseball Coach); Clarence "Hec" Edmundson (Basketball and Track Coach)
1969: John Heinrick (Football, Basketball, and Baseball Coach)
1970: Harry Deegan (Horse Breeding Administrator); Jimmy Phelan (Football Coach)
1977: Joe Gottstein (Horse Racing Administrator)
1978: Jack Friel (Basketball Coach); Bill Nollan (Football, Baseball, Basketball, and Track Coach)
1983: Enoch Bagshaw (Football Coach)
1986: Fred "Doc" Bohler (Athletic Director, Football, and Track Coach)
1989: Jim Owens (Football Coach); Torchy Torrance (Baseball Administrator)
2004: Ben Cheney (Administrator); Stan Naccarato (Baseball, Promoter)

Coaches

While there are and have been many excellent coaches deserving our recognition, the following is just a small representation of the "coaching fraternity" in Tacoma and Pierce County. These are men and women who have shaped the lives of our children and our players—in high schools, colleges, clubs, and pro teams—and devoted their time to the sports that we all love.

Tom Ainslie, Golf, Fircrest HS

Kevin Aoki, Volleyball, Bethel HS, PLU

Homer Amundsen, Boxing, Starlight Athletic Club

John Anderson, Football, Sumner HS

Roy Anderson, Football, Basketball, Peninsula HS

Steve Anderson, Golf, Soccer, Franklin Pierce HS

Lee Andry, Tennis, Curtis HS

Jim Angelel, Track, Basketball, Clover Park HS

Mitch Angelel, Track, Mason Jr. High, Stadium HS, South End Athletic Association Striders

Steve Anstett, Basketball, Bellarmine Prep

Ed Arima, Wrestling, Gymnastics, Sumner HS

Ed Armstrong, Wrestling, Lincoln HS

Rollie Arthur, Figure Skating, Lakewood Winter Club, Soccer, Eatonville HS

Leon Auriol, Fencing, Charles Wright HS, Clover Park HS, UPS

Gerry Austin, Football, Clover Park HS, Lakes HS

Curt Bagby, Football, Curtis HS

Donna Albert Baker, Figure Skating, Lakewood Winter Club

Shirley Baker, Volleyball, Spanaway Lake HS

Jim Ball, Wrestling, Curtis HS

Ray Ball, Golf, Meadow Park, Lake Steilacoom, Fircrest, and Allenmore Golf Courses

Vern Ball, Tennis, Lakewood Racquet Club, Fircrest Racquet Club

Joel Balmer, Soccer, Pierce College, Washington HS

John Baretta, Soccer, Stadium HS

Ray Barnes, Wrestling, Puyallup HS

Tony Batinovich, Volleyball, Fastpitch, Foss HS, Puyallup HS

Jim Barnes, Golf, Tacoma Country & Golf Club

Jim Baurichter, Swimming, Curtis HS

Hugh Becket, Basketball, Eatonville HS

Lindsey Bemis, Basketball, Curtis HS

Mike Benson, Tennis, PLU

Lori Benton, Figure Skating, Lakewood Winter Club

Paul Berg, Basketball, Peninsula HS

Dan Beyette, Tennis, Tacoma Lawn Tennis Club

Ron Billings, Basketball, Lincoln HS, Tacoma Community College

Harry Bird, Wrestling, Football, Lincoln HS, Wilson HS

Jim Black, Basketball, Foss HS

Lloyd Blanusa, Basketball, White River HS

Alice Bond, women's sports, CPS

Steve Bowen, Tennis, UPS, Pacific West Tour

Michael Bradley, Basketball, Chief Leschi HS

Beth Bricker, Basketball, CPS

Craig Brown, Swimming, Peninsula HS

Larry Brown, Wrestling, Fife HS

Jim Brillheart, Baseball, Tacoma Tigers

Dennis Buchholz, Basketball, Stadium HS

Tom Buckner, Track, Franklin Pierce HS

Mike Burton, Baseball, White River HS

Albert "Bo" Campbell, Wrestling, Fife HS

Roy Carlson, Football, PLU

Rusty Carlson, Tennis, PLU

Phil Carmichael, Volleyball, Rogers HS

Myron "Chief" Carr, Football, Track, Basketball, Stadium HS, Lincoln HS

Kathy Casey, Figure Skating, Lakewood Winter Club

Gary Chase, Swimming, PLU

Don Clegg, Football, Wilson HS

Jim Clifton, Basketball, Puyallup HS

Joe Clough, Boxing, Tacoma Boys Club

Jerry Clyde, Basketball, Orting HS

Chuck Congdon, Golf, Tacoma Country & Golf Club

Merritt Cookingham, Skiing, Rainier National Park Ski School

Ernie, Cope, Basketball, Football, Eatonville HS, Kapowsin HS

Doug Cowan, Wrestling, Curtis HS

Rick Daniels, Wrestling, Football, Fife HS

Wayne Dalesky, Basketball, Foss HS

Jim Daulley, Track, Wilson HS

Red Davis, Baseball, Tacoma Giants

Chet Dawson, Tennis, Fort Lewis

Jerry DeLaurenti, Basketball, Baseball, Puyallup HS, Orting HS

Warren Deprenger, Wrestling, Clover Park HS

Bob Dezell, Golf, Wilson HS

Patsy Hamm Dillingham, Figure Skating, Lakewood Winter Club

Bob Dinsmore, Basketball, Fife HS

Robert Dirk, Hockey, Tacoma Sabercats

Mick DuBois, Basketball, Stadium HS

John Duggan, Soccer, UPS, Norpoint Royals

Don Duncan, Swimming, UPS

Bob Ehrenheim, Track, Mount Tahoma HS

Ockie Eliason, Golf, Allenmore Golf Course

Earl Ellis, Swimming, UW

Dave Emery, Swimming, Clover Park HS, Rogers HS

Geroge Engelland, Swimming, Stadium HS

Jimmy Ennis, Baseball, CPS

Harry Enochs, Football, Basketball, Baseball, Fife HS

Don Ervin, Tennis, CPS

Ed Fallon, Football, Orting HS, Bellarmine Prep

Al Feldman, Golf, Meadow Park Golf Course

Jim Fish, Tennis, Bellarmine Prep

Bob Fincham, Basketball, Bethel HS

Mike Fisher, Baseball, Tacoma Tigers

Mike Fitzpatrick, Volleyball, Sumner HS

Martin Fopp, Skiing, UPS, Cascade Ski School

Shirley McDonald Fopp, Skiing, Cascade Ski School

Janice Teodoro Forbes, Figure Skating, Lakewood Winter
    Club, Sprinker Recreation Center

Jill Fox-Mullen, Volleyball, Rogers HS

Greg Friberg, Football, Mount Tahoma HS

Doug Funk, Football, White River HS

Bud Galusha, Baseball, Washington HS

Jeff Gardner, Football, Stadium HS, Puyallup HS

Holly Gee, Baseball, Clover Park HS

Steve George, Golf, Bellarmine Prep

Steve Gervais, Football, Eatonville HS, Gig Harbor HS

Chris Gibson, Basketball, Fastpitch, Franklin Pierce HS,
    White River HS

Freddie Goodwin, Soccer, Tacoma Stars

Lou Grant, Basketball, CPS, Eatonville HS

Paul Greeley, Wrestling, Spanaway Lake HS, Bethel HS

Dave Grisaffi, Wrestling, Bellarmine Prep

Steve Gustafson, Volleyball, Wilson HS

Steve Haase, Wrestling, Bellarmine Prep

Colleen Hacker, Soccer, PLU

Merle Hagbo, Baseball, Football, Clover Park HS

Dave Hall, Basketball, Baseball, Fife HS

Frank Hall, Soccer, Tacoma Wanderers

Dick Halleen, Basketball, Rogers HS

Robin Hamilton, Fastpitch, UPS

Rich Hammermaster, Basketball, Puyallup HS

Mike Hanby, Track, Steilacoom HS

Dick Hannula, Swimming, Lincoln HS, Wilson HS,
    Tacoma Swim Club

Ed Hardenbrook, Baseball, Lakes HS

Bill Hardie, Track, Lincoln HS

Dottie Harris, Volleyball, Bellarmine Prep

Marv Harshman, Basketball, Football, Baseball, PLC

Sterling Harshman, Track, Puyallup HS

Jerry Hartley, Water Polo, Swimming, Puyallup HS, Rogers
    HS

Luther "Red" Harvel, Baseball, Tacoma Tigers

Bob Heskett, Wrestling, Spanaway Lake HS

Jack Heinrick, Basketball, Stadium HS

John Heinrick, Football, Basketball, CPS, Stadium HS, Bel-
    larmine Prep

Andy Helling, Baseball, Puyallup HS

Kathy Hemion, Basketball, Volleyball, PLU

Dan Hensley, Wrestling, Clover Park HS

Doris Brown Heritage, Cross-country, USA team, Seattle
    Pacific University

Jon Herrington, Track, Washington HS

Harper Hill, Wrestling, Lakes HS

Harald Hillerman, Fencing, Wilson HS, Hudtloff HS,
    Mason HS, YMCA, YWCA

Alan Hinton, Soccer, Tacoma Stars

Dan Hoffman, Wrestling, Eatonville HS

Pat Hoonan, Football, Rogers HS

Al Hopkins, Football, Track, Lincoln HS

Heather Hoskins, Swimming, Rogers HS

Carl Howell, Basketball, Tacoma Community College

Mike Huard, Football, Puyallup HS

Bob Hunt, Wrestling, Stadium HS

Don Huston, Basketball, Curtis HS

Art Hutton, Track, Clover Park HS, Bellarmine Prep

Dan Inveen, Basketball, Wilson HS

Rod Iverson, Basketball, Rogers HS

Roger Iverson, Basketball, Peninsula HS

Todd Irwin, Golf, Performance Golf

Pete Jansen, Baseball, Gig Harbor HS

John Johnsen, Figure Skating, Lakewood Winter Club

Bob Johnson, Baseball, Tacoma Tigers

Jim Johnson, Swimming, PLU

Michelle Johnson, Basketball, Softball, Pierce College

Rita Johnston, Volleyball, Franklin Pierce HS

Rudy Jones, Track, Soccer, South End Athletic Association Striders, Lincoln HS

Jerry Joyce, Track, Cross-country, Puyallup HS

Jack Justice, Football, Bethel HS

Tim Kelly, Basketball, Lincoln HS

Ed "Eagle Eye" Kendrick, Football, Basketball, Roy HS

John Kennedy, Basketball, Lincoln HS

Joe Kilby, Slowpitch, Fastpitch, Orting HS

Robert Kim, Volleyball, UPS

Jeff Kindle, Basketball, Rogers HS

Jan Kirk, Volleyball, Fife HS

Harold Koenig, Tennis, Fircrest Recreational Center

Suzanne Koenig, Tennis, Fircrest Recreational Center

Mary Ann Kluge, Basketball, PLU

Horace "Pip" Koehler, Baseball, Tacoma Tigers

Palmer Koon, Tennis, Lakewood Racquet Club

Rod Koon, Tennis, Fircrest Recreation Center

Joel Kortus, Basketball, Franklin Pierce HS

Steve Kubota, Tennis, Town & Country Tennis Center, Fircrest HS, Sprinker Recreation Center

Eric Kurle, Football, Bethel HS

Eldon Kyllo, Football, Franklin Pierce HS

Dan Lamberth, Crew, UPS

George Lanning, Golf, Oakbrook Country Club

Joe LaPorte, Skiing, Tacoma Ski School, Cascade Ski School

Art Larson, Track, Puyallup HS

Al Lawrence, Crew, UPS

Linda Galbraith Leaver, Figure Skating, Olympic and world competitors

Bill Lemmon, Basketball, Stadium HS

Sally Leyse, Basketball, UPS

Bob Levinson, Football, Track, Stadium HS

Bob Lightfoot, Baseball, Wilson HS

Paul Llewellyn, Track, Hudtloff HS

Brad Loan, Gymnastics, Puget Sound School of Gymnastics

Whitey Lockman, Baseball, Tacoma Cubs

Warren Logan, Track, Cross-country, Lakes HS

Pop Logan, Track, Puyallup HS

VG Lowman, Basketball, Track, Mason HS, Stadium HS

Bob Lucey, Football, Curtis HS

Mike Lynch, Baseball, Tacoma Tigers

Gene Lundgaard, Basketball, PLC

Larry Lunke, Football, Peninsula HS

Howard Lutton, Football, Franklin Pierce HS

Sean Madden, Volleyball, Bethel HS

Marco Malich, Baseball, Peninsula HS

Harland Malyon, Tennis, Tacoma Community College

Larry Marshall, Baseball, Charles Wright HS, Spanaway Lake HS, PLU

Stacia Marshall, Tennis, PLU

Paul Martin, Baseball, Stadium HS

Mark Massey, Volleyball, UPS

Norm Mayer, Football, Basketball, CPS, Lincoln HS, Tacoma School District

Jimmy McAlister, Soccer, Tacoma Stars

Doug McArthur, Baseball, Stanley's Shoemen

Ed McCoy, Football, Basketball, Track, Sumner HS

Jim McDonald, Baseball, Mount Tahoma HS

Jack McGee, Baseball, UPS

Joe McGinnity, Baseball, Tacoma Tigers

Lyle McIntosh, Basketball, Gig Harbor HS

Mike McKay, Basketball, Wilson HS

Bob McKean, Cross Country, White River HS

Art McLarney, Basketball, Bellarmine Prep, UW

Bob McNab, Soccer, Tacoma Stars

Bob McQuarrie, Track, Tacoma Track and Field

Larry McWhirter, Volleyball, Curtis HS

John Medak, Basketball, Steilacoom HS

Bill Melton, Baseball, Bethel HS

Al Mengert, Golf, Tacoma County & Golf Club

Jim Meyerhoff, Wrestling, Franklin Pierce HS

Dave Meyers, Baseball, Tacoma Rainiers

Frank Michael, Baseball, Bellarmine Prep

Dave Miller, Boxing (Freddie Steele)

Dave Miller, Football, Lakes HS

Roger Miller, Fastpitch, Fife HS

Brad Moore, Track, PLU

Carl Moore, Track, Wilson HS

Lloyd Morgan, Track, Waller Road Roadrunners

Dave Morris, Basketball, Stadium HS

Lyle Morton, Tennis, Badminton, Tacoma Lawn Tennis Club

Don Moseid, Basketball, Mount Tahoma HS, Tacoma Community College

George Mueller, Figure Skating, Lakewood Figure Skating Club

Leah Mueller, Figure Skating, Lakewood Figure Skating Club

Bill Mullen, Baseball, Lincoln HS

Mike Mullen, Basketball, Bethel HS

Pat Mullen, Basketball, Bethel HS

Tom Mustin, Boxing, Tacoma Boys Club, Olympic team members

Chris Myhre, Swimming, Wilson HS

Dennis Nelson, Basketball, Rogers HS

Frank Newell, Golf, Fircrest HS

Jack Newhart, Football, Lincoln HS

Bruce Nichols, Baseball, Rogers HS

Dean Nicholson, Basketball, Puyallup HS, CWU

Ed Niehl, Basketball, Football, Bethel HS

George Nordi, Football, Mount Tahoma HS

Rick Noren, Fastpitch, PLU

Don Norlen, Rollerskating, Tacoma Roller Bowl

Sara Officer, Field Hockey, PLU

Stan Olsen, Skiing, Tacoma Ski School

Cliff Olson, Football, Basketball, PLC

Mark Olson, Swimming, Curtis HS

Dan Oliver, Fastpitch, Gig Harbor HS

John Olver, Hockey, Tacoma Sabercats

Tom Omli, Wrestling, Rogers HS

Bruce Orness, Basketball, Franklin Pierce HS

Trena Page, Volleyball, White River HS

Dick Palamidessi, Baseball, Wilson HS

Marty Parkhurst, Football, Orting HS

Frank Patrick, Football, CPS

Murray "Muzz" Patrick, Hockey, Tacoma Rockets

Frank Pavia, Wrestling, Bethel HS

Doyle Perkins, Tennis, Tacoma Lawn Tennis Club

Marion Pericin, Basketball, Bellarmine Prep, Portland State University

Marshall Perrow, Skiing, Rainier National Park Ski School

Dave Peterson, Crew, PLU

Myrtle Peterson, Basketball, Lincoln HS

Rolores "Skip" Peterson, Roller Skating, Adams Roller Bowl

Tom Peterson, Tennis, Tacoma Lawn Tennis Club

Joe Peyton, Track, UPS

Jenny Phillips, Soccer, Bellarmine Prep

Earl Platt, Football, Basketball, Kapowsin HS

John Pregenzer, Baseball, Orting HS, Washington HS, Franklin Pierce HS

Dick Pruett, Wrestling, Puyallup HS

George Quigley, Baseball, Basketball, Stadium HS

Dave Rasmussen, Tennis, Town & County Tennis Center

Tealy Raymond, Baseball, Tacoma Tigers

Joe Reasons, Wrestling, Clover Park HS, Curtis HS

Ron Rebish, Wrestling, Washington HS

Gerald Redburg, Basketball, Curtis HS

Jerry Redmond, Football, Puyallup HS

John Reopelle, Volleyball, Bethel HS

Hal Rhyne, Baseball, Tacoma Tigers

Terry Rice, Track, Cross-country, Stadium HS

Jim Richards, Wrestling, Sumner HS

Gil Rigell, Basketball, Lakes HS

Sam Ring, Cross-country, UPS

Mary Rink, Soccer, Bellarmine Prep

Ari Roberts, Football, Fife HS

Mike Roberts, Football, Franklin Pierce HS

Bob Robinson, Football, Basketball, Track, Curtis HS

Dan Rohn, Baseball, Tacoma Rainiers

Bob Ross, Basketball, Washington HS

Mark Ross, Football, Steilacoom HS

Sue Ross, Volleyball, Clover Park HS

John Ruby, Basketball, Foss HS

Russ Rudolph, Basketball, White River HS

Jody Rush, Tennis, Pacific West Tour

Roger Russell, Figure Skating, Lakewood Winter Club

Bob Ryan, Football, Puyallup HS, UPS

Mike Sacido, Wrestling, White River HS

Mark Salzman, Track & Field, PLU

Mark Salzman, Cross Country, Basketball, Track Curtis HS

Gary Sambila, Track, White River HS

Roy Sandberg, Football, CPS

Tom Sawyer, Track & Field, Franklin Pierce HS, Washington HS

Del Schaefer, Basketball, Franklin Pierce HS

Dale Schimke, Tennis, Washington HS, Franklin Pierce HS

Lois Secreto Schoettler, Figure Skating, Lakewood Winter Club

Dave Schultz, Tennis, Fife HS

Eddie Schwarz, Basketball, Football, Lincoln HS

Jack Scott, Tennis, Fort Steilacoom Community College

Marv Scott, Baseball, Basketball, Stadium HS, Wilson HS, Woodworth Contractors

Wally Scott, Tennis, Lincoln HS

Jerry Shain, Basketball, Tacoma Community College

John Sharp, Track, Lincoln HS

Jeff Short, Football, Fife HS

Ron Simonson, Football, UPS

Steve Slavens, Track, Fife HS

Don Smetheram, Tennis, White River HS

Greg Smith, Tennis, Lakewood Racquet Club

John Smith, Gymnastics, NASA Gymnastics

Lee Smith, Volleyball, Peninsula HS

Lori Smith, Volleyball, Peninsula HS

Mark Smith, Football, Track, Tacoma Baptist HS, Washington HS

Andy Slatt, Football, Basketball, Bellarmine Prep

Steve Slavens, Track, Fife HS

Steve Slivinski, Football, Tacoma Indians

Dick Snyder, Tennis, Bellarmine Prep

Jack Sonntag, Football, Foss HS

Phil Sorboe, Football, Lincoln HS, WSU, Humboldt State University

Carl Sparks, Football, Basketball, Puyallup HS

Seth Spidahl, Soccer, Tacoma Community College, FC United

Pam Spitzer, Volleyball, Washington HS

Mike Stauffer, Swimming, Lakes HS

Ken Still, Golf, Fircrest HS

Ron Storaasli, Baseball, Lakes HS

Joe Stortini, Football, Mount Tahoma HS, Wilson HS

Bill Stout, Wrestling, Peninsula HS

Kimo Streeter, Swimming, Peninsula HS

Wally Streeter, Swimming, Stadium HS

Jim Sulenes, Football, Golf, Curtis HS

Dan Swain, Soccer, Nortac Sweetfoots, FC Royals

Darrold Talley, Football, Clover Park HS

Greg Talley, Golf, Fircrest HS

Dave Tate, Baseball, Rogers HS

Jim Tevis, Baseball, Rogers HS

Jerry Thacker, Baseball, Orting HS

Gary Thomas, Tennis, Clover Park HS

Joe Thomas, Golf, Curtis HS

Ed Tingstad, Football, Bethel HS

Rick Todd, Volleyball, Puyallup HS, Curtis HS

Larry Tommervik, Basketball, Wilson HS

Marv Tommervik, Baseball, Football, PLC

Mike Tucci Sr., Football, Columbia Beer Barons

Ken Tyson, Golf, Meadow Park and Lake Spanaway Golf Courses

Brian Van Blommestein, Soccer, FC Royals

Jim Verdieck, Tennis, Tacoma Lawn Tennis Club

Bill "Pop" Vinson, Basketball, Football, Eatonville HS, Fife HS

Kathy Gleason Wainhouse, Figure Skating, Lakewood Winter Club, Sprinker Recreation Center

Paul Wallrof, Football, UPS

Carl "Kak" Wasmund, Baseball, Puyallup HS

Joey Waters, Soccer, Bellarmine Prep

Dan Watson, Track, Lincoln HS

Dave Webb, Tennis, Curtis HS

Norm Webstad, Baseball, Tacoma Community College

Ralph Weekly, Fastpitch, PLU

Keith Weller, Soccer, Tacoma Stars

Bert Wells, Basketball, Track, Cross-country, Curtis HS

Bob Wendt, Gymnastics, Rogers HS

Tom Werner, Basketball, Tacoma Mountaineers

Frosty Westering, Football, PLU

Bill Wheeler, Wrestling, Bethel HS

Jim White, Figure Skating, Lakewood Winter Club

Mike Wight, Fastpitch, Rogers HS

George Wilfong, Wrestling, Puyallup HS

Russ Wilkerson, Basketball, UPS

Nancy Williams, Softball, Volleyball, Puyallup HS

Sid Williams, Racquetball, Pierce County clubs

Joel Wingard, Track, Gig Harbor HS

George Wise, Baseball, Lincoln HS

Doug Wisness, Track, Cross-country, Bethel HS

Dan Wolfrom, Swimming, Foss HS

Dan Wood, Soccer, Tacoma Tides

Steve Wright, Tennis, Pacific West Tour

Tammy Wright, Volleyball, Spanaway Lake HS

Gary Wusterbarth, Basketball, Steilacoom HS

Dave Wytko, Slowpitch, White River HS

Ron Urquhart, Basketball, Bellarmine Prep

Jim Verdieck, Tennis, Tacoma Lawn Tennis Club

Leo Young, Tennis, Pacific West Tour

Roy Young, Baseball, Foss HS

Dick Zatkovich, Football, Lakes HS

Don Zech, Basketball, UPS

Officials

Washington Officials Association–Meritorious Service Award recipients

1966: Frank Gillihan (Football); John Heinrick (Football, Baseball); John Kennedy (Football, Basketball); Bob Pullar (Basketball, Baseball)

1972: John G. Fadness (Football); Harold Lockard (Football); Ed McCoy (Football); Joe Salatino (Basketball); George Wise (Football, Baseball, Basketball)

1973: Stan Anderson (Basketball); Joe Beckman (Football); Ed Bucsko (Football); Joe Hemel (Football); Carl Herness (Football); Gene Jack (Football, Basketball); Rollie Nielsen (Football); Ed Stricherz (Basketball, Football)

1976: Tom Cross (Football, Basketball); Bill Funk (Basketball); Glenn Rickert (Football)

1977: Jack Heinrick (Basketball); Robert Levinson (Basketball); Lawrence Merkle (Football, Basketball, Baseball)

1978: Marv Tommervik (Football)

1979: Marty Erdahl (Basketball, Football); Charles Gilmur (Track, Football)

1981: Dale Bloom (Basketball); John Holliday (Baseball); Jack Johnson (Football)

1982: Ed Hillis (Football); Del Michaelson (Basketball, Football); Jerry Snarski (Basketball); Art Viafore (Football, Baseball)

1985: Don Habel (Basketball); Ray Highsmith (Football); Dan Inveen (Football); Mike McKay (Basketball, Football)

1986: Vic Eshpeter (Wrestling); Gordon Junge (Basketball); Dan Watson (Wrestling)

1988: Dean Haner (Basketball)

1989: Aaron Pointer (Football, Basketball)

1990: Marc Blau (Volleyball); George Karpach (Basketball, Football); Dan Spriesterbach (Football); Stan Standifer (Football, Basketball); Jay Stricherz (Football)

1992: Mike Burton (Football); Kirk Dornan (Football); John Miller (Football)

1995: Jerry Aeschlimann (Volleyball); Sharman Carey (Volleyball); Jim Dungan (Football); Wayne Gardner (Volleyball); Merle Hagbo (Basketball, Football); Gil Lopez (Volleyball); Dave Schmidt (Wrestling); Teri Wood (Volleyball); Jim Meyerhoff (Wrestling)

1997: Cal Goings (Football); Clarence Leingang (Basketball, Football); Jerry Meyerhoff (Football); Jan Wolcott (Football)

1999: Rich Hammermaster (Football); Bob Murff (Football); Darron Nelson (Football); Bob Peterson (Football); Jack Stonestreet (Basketball, Football); Bob Holloway (Football, Basketball)

2000: Terry Keister (Football)

2003: Walt Gogan (Volleyball); Lenny Llanos (Volleyball); Cliff Milanoski (Volleyball); Mike Schmid (Wrestling); Toni Turnbull (Volleyball)

Referees and Umpires

There have been many outstanding officials particpating in sports throughout Tacoma and Pierce County; the following individuals, however, have been the most active at the national, regional, and state levels over the years.

Baseball, Softball Fastpitch, and Softball Slowpitch

Joe Bailey, Sonny Bailey, Hal Berndt, Les Bishop, Lon Bishop, Willard Carpy, Tom Cross, Paul Gustafson, Gene Hansen, Al Hodges, John Holliday, Dill Howell, Earl Hyder, Joey Johns, Dave Kerrone, Rick Lewis, Steve Liptrap, Ted Lopat, Bob Maguinez, Randy Martin, Lornie Merkle, Frank Morrone, Stan Naccarato, Jim Oleole, Steve Orfanos, Dick Pease, John Pregenzer, Bob Pullar, John Pyfer, Joe Racquer, Cecil Randle, Gerald Redburg, Bob Royal, Joe Salatino, Art Spencer, Clarence Stave, Dave Van Hulle, Art Viafore, George Wise, Jerry Woods.

Basketball

Bruce Alexander, Stan Anderson, Will Bachofner, Dale Bloom, Abe Cohen, Tom Cross, Marty Erdahl, John Fadness, Bill Funk, Frank Gillihan, Don Habel, Merle Hagbo, Dean Haner, Jack Heinrick, John Heinrick, Carl Herness, Bob Holloway, Bob Huegel, Gene Jack, Jack Johnson, Ken Jones, John J. Kennedy, Vern Martineau, Vic Martineau, Jim McCuen, Lawrence Merkle, Phil Misley, Darron Nelson, Bob Pullar, Tom Rowland, Jerry Snarski, Jack Spithill, Jack Stonestreet, Ron Storaasli, Ed Stricherz, Mark Stricherz, Darold Talley, George Wise.

Boxing

Bill Goodwin (Judge), Ernie Jensen (Referee), Jeff Macaluso (Referee), Joe Macaluso (Judge), Morris McCollum (Judge), Tom McDonough (Judge), Pat McMurtry (Referee), Foire "Piggy" Pignatore (Judge), Billy Richmond (Judge), Jim Rondeau (Referee), Davey Ward (Referee).

Football

Joe Beckman, Ron Billings, Ed Bucsko, Mike Burton, Bob Carlson, Tom Cross, Kirk Dornan, Bob Ehrenheim, Marty Erdahl, John Fadness, Frank Gillihan, Chuck Gilmur, Don Habel, Merle Hagbo, "Pop" Hagerty, Rich Hammermaster, Carl Herness, John Heinrick, Joe Hemel, Ray Highsmith, Bob Holloway, Buddy Horton, Bernie Hulscher, Dan Inveen, Ellis Johnson, Jack Johnson, George Karpach, John Kennedy, Clarence Leingang, Tip Lockard, Art McLarney, Jr. , Lornie Merkle, Jerry Meyerhoff, Darron Nelson, Gil Nelson, Ed Pedersen, Aaron Pointer, Don Sloan, Jack Spithill, Don Spreisterbach, Stan Standifer, Jack Stonstreet, Ed Stricherz, Jay Stricherz, Blair Taylor, Marv Tommervik, Art Viafore, George Wise, Jan Wolcott, Warren Wood.

Hockey

Joey Johns, Ron Scavatto.

Motorcycle Racing

Bob Malley (National Referee), David Welsh (National Starter).

Riflery and Small Arms

Erling Bergerson (NRA Referee).

Soccer

Jack Butcher, Regi Carpenter, Chris Davis, Frank Hall, Peter Loveland, Jack Montgomery, Tim O'Hara, John O'Keefe, Mohammed Saghakeneh, Mike Schmitt, Dave Simon, Dana Reinhart, Chuck Talbot, Jack Taylor, Karl Van Zeben.

Volleyball

B. J. Aea, Jerry Aeschlimann, Debbie Beckwith, Marc Blau, Teddi Bottiger, Wayne Gardner, Walt Gogan, Steve Gustafson, Larry Guzman, Diane Irish, Paul Jensen, Leala Jew, P. J. Jones, Ray Laguana, Floro Llanos, Lenny Llanos, Gil Lopez, Cliff Milanoski, Jim Oleole, Margie Junge Oleole, Jim Ragasa, Jim Stewart, Toni Turnbull, Teri Wood.

Wrestling

Dan Ackley, Bob Ames, Dick Barclay, Terry Beckstead, Andy Cline, Eric Davis, John DeWeber, Brian Dunbar, Vic Eshpeter, Bill Harr, Bernie Hulscher, Jerry Joyce, Stan Kowamoto, Jim Meyerhoff, Tom Moore, Jim Nelson, Bruce Osborne, Jim Pitingoro, Mike Schmid, Dave Schmidt, Dan Watson, Bill Wheeler, Mike Williams.

Sports Broadcasters

The following are among the most prominent sports broadcasters at the national, regional, and local level, as well as those who announced professional baseball in Tacoma.

Belcher, Rod: Tacoma Tigers
Beuning, Thom: Tacoma Sabercats
Calvert, Dick: Tacoma Stars
Curto, Mike: Tacoma Rainiers
Doane, Bill: Tacoma Twins
Field, Bob: Tacoma Rockets
Geehan, Jerry: Tacoma Tigers
Glasgow, Tom: PLU, high school football, basketball
Gordon, Adam: Tacoma Rockets
Halligan, Mason: wrestling, Midget auto racing
Hill, Don: Tacoma Giants, Tacoma Cubs
Howarth, Jerry: Tacoma Twins, UPS

Huntington, Clay: Tacoma Rockets, Tacoma Tigers, high school, college, PAC-10

Jarstad, John: Seattle Rainiers, high school, college

Jordan, Harry: wrestling, boxing

Lambert, Carl: high school football, basketball

McArthur, Doug: high school, college football, basketball

O'Day, Pat: hydroplane racing

Popham, Art: Tacoma Yankees, Tacoma Tugs, Tacoma Tigers, UPS

Robertson, Bob: Tacoma Giants, Tacoma Tigers, UPS, PLU, WSU

Simons, Rod: general sports anchor

Thomas, Steve: PLU, high school football, basketball

Sports Writers

Among the more well-known sports editors and beat writers for the *Daily Ledger* (DL), *Tacoma Times* (TT), and *Tacoma News Tribune* (TNT) are the following individuals.

Bishop, Biddy, TNT Sports Editor

Clayton, John, TNT

Davison, Don, TNT

Dyer, Braven, Los Angeles Times Sports Editor

Farber, Stan, TNT

Green, Ranny, TNT

Honeywell, Ed, TNT

Hong, Nelson, TNT Sports Editor

Hunt, Marshall, New York Times

Huntington, Clay, TT

Ingraham, Mike, TNT

Irwin, Lee, TNT

James, Dave, TNT

Jordan, Mike, TNT

Kahn, Mike, TNT

Kiehl, Jeff, TNT

Krueger, Jerry, Sumner News Index Sports Editor

Kunkle, Dick, TNT

LaRue, Larry, TNT

Lawrence, John, TNT

Lindgren, Gary, TNT

Luebker, Earl, TNT Sports Editor

McGrath, John, TNT

Metcalf, Elliott, DL, TNT, TT Sports Editor

Miller, Paul, TNT

Mottram, Bob, TNT

Page, Tom, Suburban Times Sports Editor

Payne, Bob, TNT

Pearson, Ted, TNT Sports Editor

Phelps, Dale, TNT Sports Editor

Ripple, Bill, TNT

Ruiz, Don, TNT

Sareault, Jack, TNT

Schey, Bill, TNT

Thiel, Art, TNT, Seattle Post-Intelligencer

Walton, Dan, DL, TNT Sports Editor

Williams, Bea, TNT

Williams, Herb, TNT

Wright, Bart, TNT

Woodard, Milt, TNT

Zehnder, Ernie, Sumner News Index

Sports Photographers

The more notable sports photographers for the area include:

Anderson, Warren

Boland, Marvin

Bowen, Chapin

Buck, Jerry

Carmack, Russ

Clifford, Howard

Kellman, Bruce

Larsen, Bruce

Moyer, Richard

Ollar, Ken

Richards, Ed

Richards, Turner

Rudsit, Bob

Sage, Mike

Seman, Clarence

Studios, Smith

Trueblood, William

Wilhelm, Rhiny

Wong, Lui Kit

Zimmerman, Wayne

Behind the Scenes: Administrators, Management, and More

For every sports team that takes the field and for every athlete who competes, there is a multitude of individuals whose efforts provide the opportunities, gear, and venues: administrators, league coordinators, physicians and trainers, ushers and ticket takers, batboys and girls, ballgirls and boys, clubhouse attendants, groundskeepers, and many others. While not inclusive, the following represents just a small number of the individuals who work behind the scenes so that we can participate in and enjoy our sports in safe and healthy environments.

Administrators: Professional Sports

Robert Abel (President, Western International Baseball League); Bobby Adams (General Manager, Tacoma Cubs); Sam Bergerson (Owner, Tacoma Rockets); John Best (President/General Manager, Tacoma Stars); Claudia Best (Assistant General Manager–Baseball Operations, Tacoma Stars); Frank Colarusso (General Manager, Tacoma Sabercats and Tacoma Tigers); George and Sue Foster (Owners, Tacoma Rainiers); Bruce Hamilton (General Manager, Tacoma Rockets); Gavin Hamilton (Chairman, Tacoma Rockets); Kevin Kalal (Assistant General Manager, Operations, Tacoma Tigers, Rainiers); Barry Kemp (President, Tacoma Sabercats); Dr. Charles Larson (President, National Boxing Association); Dave Lewis (General Manager, Tacoma Rainiers); Joe McGinnity (Owner, Tacoma Tigers); Stan Naccarato (General Manager, Tacoma Twins, Yankees, Tugs, Tigers and Tacoma Tides and Tacoma Stars); John Olver (General Manager, Tacoma Sabercats); Roger Peck (President, Western International Baseball League); Rosy Ryan (General Manager, Tacoma Giants); Bruce Taylor (President, Tacoma Rockets); Fred Urban (Owner, Tacoma Rockets); and Milt Woodard (Commissioner, American Football League); Ron Zollo (Assistant General Manager, Tacoma Twins, Yankees, Tugs, Tigers).

Administrators: Amateur Sports

Roy Archer (President, Tacoma City Baseball League); Karl Benson (Commissioner, Western Athletic Conference); Mike Burton (President, National Federation of Inter-scholastic Officials Association); Lorenzo Dow (President, Tacoma City Baseball League); Debbi Hanson (Commissioner, Amateur Softball Association); Ken Jones (President, Washington Officials Association); Steve Orfanos (President, Amateur Softball Association); John Rockway (Commissioner, Amateur Softball Association); Lou Spry (Official Scorer, NCAA College World Series).

Batboys, Ballboys, Clubhouse Attendants, Equipment Managers, Public Announcers, Scorekeepers, and More!

Paul Adams (Tacoma Cubs); Sam Adams Jr. (Tacoma Cubs); Don Auderle (Stickboy, Tacoma Rockets); Jon Armstrong (Tacoma Rainiers); Phil Baldasare (Tacoma Cubs); Tim Bannon (Tacoma Giants); Bob Bianchi (Tacoma Cubs); DJ Birnie (Tacoma Rainiers); Jeff Bopp (Tacoma Rainiers); Don Brisbois (Tacoma Cubs); Randall Brown (Tacoma Twins); Jeff Buhr (Tacoma Cubs); Bobby Burrows (1947 Tacoma Tigers); Jimmy Burrows (1947 Tacoma Tigers); Doug Cail (Tacoma Giants); Brian Chambers (Tacoma Rainiers); John Cheesman (Tacoma Twins); Mike Cheesman (Tacoma Twins); Justin Corley (Tacoma Rainiers); Frank Cumbo (1938 Tacoma Tigers); Marshall Dale (Tacoma Twins); Bob Dawson Jr. (1949–51 Tacoma Tigers and Tacoma Rockets); Gary Dennis; Mike Edling (Tacoma Giants); Tal Edman (Tacoma Rainiers); Adam Ellis (Tacoma Rainiers); Peter Ellis (Tacoma Rainiers); Charlie Engelman (Tacoma Tigers, Rainiers); Jon English (Tacoma Twins); Maceo Faison (Tacoma Twins); Tom Gallo (Tacoma Twins); Dave Geppert (Tacoma Tugs); Charles Hawkins (Tacoma Cubs); Rich Hawks (Equipment Manager, Tacoma Stars); Dennis Heinrick (Ballboy, Tacoma Mountaineers); Jerry Hicks (Tacoma Giants); Ken Higdon (Batboy, Tacoma Yankees and Clubhouse Manager, California Angels); Shaun Holland (Tacoma Tugs, Tigers); Greg Hume (Tacoma Giants); Brian Jensen (Tacoma Tigers); Kevin Johnson (Tacoma Cubs); Steve Johnson (Tacoma Cubs); Terry Jordan (1947 Tacoma Tigers); Mark Kalal (Scorer, Tacoma Rainiers); Harry Kalapus (Clubhouse Manager, 1946 Tacoma Tigers); Rick Keely (Tacoma Giants); Gene

Kelly (1939–40 Tacoma Tigers); Steve Kneeshaw (Tacoma Giants, Cubs); Tom Kneeshaw (Tacoma Giants, Cubs); Frank Kuzmanich (Tacoma Twins); John Lincoln (Tacoma Twins); Billy Lovelace (Tacoma Rainiers); Maury Maenhout (Tacoma Yankees); Doug McArthur (PA, Tacoma Giants); Tim McDonough; Brian McGrath (Tacoma Yankees); Gary McGuire (Equipment Manager, Tacoma Stars); Terry Meisenberg (Tacoma Giants); Tom Merry (Tacoma Rainiers); Phil Miller (Tacoma Tigers, Rainiers); Ryan Miller (Tacoma Rainiers); Jim Montgomerie (Scoreboard Operator, Cheney Stadium); Alex Muller (Tacoma Rainiers); Steve Naccarato (Tacoma Twins); Cory Oberhansly (Tacoma Giants); Jerry O'Connell; Bill Ogden (PA, Cheney Stadium); Denny Oughton; Darin Padur (Official Scorer, Tacoma Rainiers); Jake Parker (Tacoma Rainiers); Rhett Parker (Tacoma Rainiers); Dick Pease (Scorer, Class A Basketball State Tournaments); Rodger Peterson (Scorer, high school, UPS); Kyle Piazza (Tacoma Rainiers); Dave Porter (Stickboy, 1948 Tacoma Rockets); Ernie Posick (1950 Tacoma Rockets); Greg Prince (Tacoma Giants); Jeff Randall (PA, Cheney Stadium); Rob Reagle (Tacoma Rainiers); Ryan Scheffler (Tacoma Rainiers); Charles Spruck (Tacoma Cubs); Brad Spry (Scorer, Cheney Stadium); Gordon Spry (Scorer, Cheney Stadium); Steve Spry (Scorer, Cheney Stadium); John Theilade (Tacoma Cubs); Aaron Trolia (Tacoma Rainiers); Todd Van Buskirk (Tacoma Yankees); Brian Viafore (Tacoma Rainiers); Leland Waite (1949 Tacoma Tigers); Bruce Wallace (Tacoma Yankees); Dick Webster (PA, UPS, Lincoln Bowl); Dick Wells (Ballboy, Tacoma Mountaineers); Mark Wilkerson (Tacoma Twins, Yankees, Tugs); Gene Wellman (1938 Tacoma Tigers); Allan Winsley (Tacoma Cubs); Mark Wojohn (Tacoma Giants).

Groundskeepers

Milt Anderson (Peck Field, Heidelberg Park, Tiger Park, Cheney Stadium); Bob Christofferson (Cheney Stadium, Safeco Field); Dave Grisaffi (Cheney Staduim); Gene Hansen (Cheney Stadium); Leo Liebert (Cheney Stadium); Scotty Ryan (Cheney Stadium).

Physicians

Dr. Charles Abernathy (Golden Gloves); Dr. Sam Adams (Tacoma Giants, Cubs, Twins, Yankees, Tugs, Tigers); Dr. John Bargren (Tacoma Stars); Dr. Don Cummings (Golden Gloves); Dr. John Hilger (Tacoma Rockets and Tacoma Sabercats); Dr. Bob Johnson (Tacoma Giants, UPS); Dr. George Kunz (Golden Gloves); Dr. Jeff Nacht (Tacoma Rockets, Tacoma Sabercats, and Tacoma Tigers, Rainiers); Dr. Robert O'Connell (Golden Gloves, local high schools); Dr. Howard Pratt (Golden Gloves); Dr. Greg Popich (Tacoma Rainiers); Dr. Richard Waltman (Tacoma Tigers); Dr. Robert Wilson (Tacoma Stars).

Ticket Managers, Takers, and Ushers

John Condon (Tacoma Ice Palace); Betty Howes (Ticket Manager, Tacoma Cubs, Twins, Yankees, Tugs, Tigers); Helmer Larson (Peck and Cheney Fields); Grant King (Cheney Stadium); Horace "Pip" Koehler (Ticket Manager, Cheney Stadium); Jerry Lilly (Cheney Stadium); John Melchiorre (Cheney Stadium); Harry McCarthy (Ticket Manager, Cheney Stadium); Ernie Myers (Ticket Manager, Tacoma Ice Palace); Harold Pratt (UPS); Tony Roberts (Ticket Manager, Tacoma Stars); Bob Strobe (Cheney Stadium); Nick Tucci (Cheney Stadium).

Trainers

Dave Andrews (Tacoma Stars, USA men's soccer team); Tip Berg (Tacoma Rockets and 1947 Tacoma Tigers); Walt Horn (Tacoma Tigers); Leo "Doc" Hughes (Tacoma Giants); Gary Nicholson (Tacoma Cubs, Chicago Cubs, PLU); Rob Nodine (Tacoma Rainiers); Randy Roetter (Tacoma Rainiers); Jim "Zeke" Schuldt (Tacoma Tides, UPS); Bruce Snell (Tacoma Stars, USA men's soccer team); Pat Steele (1946 Tacoma Tigers); Harry Westerby (1950s Tacoma Rockets).

ACKNOWLEDGEMENTS

When the Tacoma Athletic Commission (TAC) pledged its support for the establishment of a local sports museum, it signified a major commitment on its part toward the preservation of our sports history, including the publication of this book. Two key book committee members from the TAC who have been supportive of this effort from its inception are owed a debt of gratitude: President Tony Anderson and past president Greg Plancich. Both played an active role in seeing the book to its fruition.

This sports history became a reality through the efforts of a team of hundreds of men and women. It is only appropriate that we show our appreciation for those who have helped, and the accolades start with Caroline Denyer Gallacci, a local historian who teaches American history courses at our universities and colleges and is author of *The City of Destiny*. Caroline spent considerable time reviewing initial rough chapters and writing large portions of the manuscript. She also interviewed many of our community's sports legends to add introspection and personality to the book.

Likewise, one of our local sports icons, Doug McArthur, brought his understanding of sports history, as well as his tireless energy to this project. As he always does, Doug immersed himself in this book above and beyond the call of duty, writing, reviewing, and perfecting various chapters.

The research staff at the Tacoma Public Library's Northwest Room assisted us throughout the project. Brian Kamens, Jody Gripp, Robert Schuler, Glenn Storbeck, and Julie Ciccarelli provided incredible support over the past several years. Gary Fuller Reese, who created the library's special collections, retired before this book went to press, but his foresight in saving valuable historical materials made our research a lot easier.

Donald Sleep, Joe Ursich, Don Davison, Frank Colarusso, Stan Farber, and Nick Dawson proved to be valuable research assistants, as did Ron Karabaich and Mike Sage whose extensive backgrounds in photography aided our effort. The memories of Clay Huntington, Stan Naccarato, Doug McArthur, and Tom Cross were invaluable in helping identify significant dates, events, and people related to the sports history.

To publish a book of this magnitude required considerable financial support and, without the generosity and support of individuals and businesses within the community, this book could not have been possible. We are grateful for their commitment and extend our deepest appreciation for allowing our dream to turn into reality. Sponsors include

Stan and Jeanne Naccarato (Baseball); William Cammarano (Automobile Racing); Chris Hubbard of One Stop Insurance Center, Water Rights, Inc., Niosi Construction, and the Tacoma Badminton Club (Badminton); Ben B. Cheney Foundation (Baseball); Columbia Bank (Basketball); Mel Miceli and family (Basketball); Bob Hanson Jr., Sallie LeMarr, Dr. Lance W. Lorfeld, Jim and Margie Oleole, Bunny Tuell, and Jerry and Vicki Williams (Bowling); C. J. Johnson (Boxing); Cascade Print Media and Mario Menconi (Football); Geneva and George Hamill, Jean and Dave Jenkinson, Zenta Jones, and William and Ann Riley (Curling); Metro Tacoma Fencing Club, Blue Steel (Fencing); Tacoma–Pierce County Sports Commission (Football); Raoul Ancira, Al Cail, Doug Cail, Dennis Cruchon, Jim Driscoll, Ron Ewing, Jim Kraft, Lea McMillan, Gil Mendoza, Dr. Anthony J. Milan, Mike Morehart, Kent Morrell, Dick Pfeiffer, Randi Platt, Steve Sand, and Martinson, Cobean & Associates P.S. (Handball); William Gazecki (Golf); Jim and Judy Keller (Ice Hockey); Tacoma Inboard Racing Association and Armand Yapachino (Hydroplane Racing); Joel Attaway and Forty Below, Inc., Jason Edwards and Mountain Experience Adventure Travel, The Summit Haus, and Eric Simonson and Mount Rainier Alpine Guides (Mountaineering); Shanaman Sports Museum of Tacoma–Pierce County (Tacoma Athletic Commission); Dr. Marv Tommervik Jr. (Umpires and Referees); Leonard Blau, Art and Dallas Redford, and Sid Williams (Racquetball); Lakewood Winter Club (Skating: Ice); Ed and Teresa Andrews, Karl and Susan Entenmann, Les and Diane Gilsdorf, Weldon Howe, Chuck Jorgenson, Chuck Lowe Jr., Rick and Joan Myers, Rich Nelson, Stan and Phyllis Olsen, and Royce and Elaine Ward (Skiing); Dr. John West (Soapbox Derby); Jeff Stock (Soccer); Vern From (Softball: Fastpitch); Heidelberg Slowpitch team of Jerry Foss, Ken Laase, Jim Lane, Marco Malich, Butch Pasquale, Al Reil, Dick Samlaska, Ken Schulz, Jerry Thacker, Terry Trowbridge, Ted Whitney, Bob Young, and Dick Zierman (Softball: Slowpitch); Clay Huntington (Sportswriters and Broadcasters); Angela and Jack Connelly, Don Duncan, Janet Buchan Elway, Kaye Hall-Greff, Dan and Margaret Hannula, Dick Hannula Sr., Bruce Richards, Chuck Richards, Shirley Richards Slade, Mike and Sharon Stauffer, and Kimo and Ann Streeter (Swimming); J. Mack and Dode Koon and family; Pat and Steve Kubota, Dr. Larry and Mary Larson, Harland Malyon and Lee Whitehall, Dr. John Rowlands, Tacoma Lawn Tennis Club, and Dr. and Mrs. Max S. Thomas (Tennis); Dr. Greg Plancich (Track and Field); Tacoma–Pierce County Volleyball Officials Board (Volleyball); Chester and Jay Sessler of Sessler Inc. (Wrestling); Dave Nielsen (Yachting); the Tacoma Public Library (Public Parks, Playgrounds, and Organized Sports); and the Puyallup Tribe of Indians (Basketball and general support).

Additional thanks to the following individuals and community organizations for their generous support: Tacoma Rainiers Community Fund, Priscilia Bahmiller, Lynette Bartoy, Ray Brammer, Francis Browne, Ed and Lucille Freiter, Jan and Vernard Lahti, Al Malanca, John Messina, Ken Spurgeon, Marv Treadwell, and Gary Tucci.

Like any good creative effort, this book needed passionate individuals willing to research and write. We relied on more than 25 people to help with specific chapters. In some cases, they wrote an entire chapter leaving only editing and proofreading to be done. We were fortunate to have the talents and knowledge of several past and present sports writers from the *Tacoma News Tribune* including: Mike Ingraham, who covered bowling during his entire 21-year career and is a member of two bowling Halls of Fame; Jack Sareault, golf beat writer for 22 years and a *Golf World* correspondent for more than 40 years; Bill Schey, a member of the sports department for 28 years covering figure skating in the Pacific Northwest; Craig Hill, who has covered college football and basketball and other sports for eight years and researched crew for this publication; and Bob Payne, who spent 41 years in the newspaper industry, 22 of which were at the *Tribune* specializing in track and field. He has covered two Olympic Games, 15 NCAA meets, and five Olympic Trials and has served as president of the Track and Field Writers of America.

Other significant chapter contributors for whom we are grateful include: Jim Price, an award-winning member of the Society for American Baseball Research and a former sportswriter for the *Spokesman-Review* in Spokane, who has followed Pacific Northwest minor league baseball for more than 40 years (professional Baseball); Sally Dutton (amateur

Baseball); Joe Moelders (Badminton); Dr. Wayne Herstad, local chiropractor, historian, and the preeminent collector of Tacoma Speedway memorabilia (Tacoma Speedway); Ed Williams (Automobile Racing); John Ochs (Boxing); Marty Tetloff, a member of the United States Fencing Coaches Association and founder of the Metro Tacoma Fencing Club (Fencing); Brad Loan, coach and owner of the Puget Sound School of Gymnastics for more than 30 years (Gymnastics); Doug Cail and Fred Osmers (Handball); Fred Farley (Hydroplane Racing); Tom Cross (Umpires and Referees); Dick Hannula (Swimming); and Rod Koon and Gary Thomas (Tennis).

Others providing valuable insight and material for select chapters include: Ron Suslick (Tacoma Athletic Commission history); Jeannette Sieler (Parks and Recreation information); Clay Huntington and Sally Dutton (Broadcasters and Sports Writers); Terry Mosher and Don Morrison (Archery); Bill Cammarano, Bill Seidelman, Dave Fogg, and Walt Austin (Automobile Racing); Bob Maguinez and Bob Snodgrass (Baseball); Kathy Popham who shared Art Popham's cassette tapes of radio interviews (Baseball and Boxing); Marv Harshman (Basketball and Football); Pat McMurtry, Frank Pignataro, Morris McCollum, and Ruggles Larson (Boxing); Joe Landers (Crew); Randi Platt and Bruce Young (Handball); Armand Yapachino (Hydroplane Racing); Mark Wallace and Bob Malley (Motorcycle Racing); Sid Williams (Racquetball); Rolores "Skip" Peterson (Skating: Roller); Chuck Howe, Howard Clifford, and Joe LaPorte (Skiing); Ben Hammond, Jim McCuen, and Ed Bemis (Football); Ken Still and Pat Harbottle (Golf); Gary Brooks (Soapbox Derby); Frank Hall, Norm Ruffner, and Brian Van Blommestein (Soccer); Tim Connelly (Swimming); Jack Connelly, Marc Brouillet, and Tim Vesey (Water Polo); Mike Benson, Peter Kram, and Suzanne Jordan (Tennis); Debbie Sage (Volleyball); Jim Meyerhoff (Wrestling); William Riley (Curling); Joel Attaway, CEO of Forty Below, LTD, a local manufacturer of high altitude mountaineering equipment and formerly involved with the family business BaseCamp Supply, Eric Simonson, and Jason Edwards (Mountaineering); Dave James (Football); Dr. Steve Kneeshaw (Baseball); Stan Olsen (Badminton and Skiing); Ken Campbell, John Bailey, and Dave Nielsen (Yachting); the Tacoma News Tribune, the Spokesman-Review, Jack Pfeifer, Scott Spruill, Mike Hubbard, Track & Field News/Tafnews Press, Washington State University, Pacific Lutheran University, and University of Puget Sound (Track and Field).

Additional contributors whose support also was appreciated include: Rick Guild and the Boys & Girls Club of Tacoma–Pierce County; Brad Moeller and Tim Waer of the Tacoma–Pierce County Sports Commission; Kirsten Olsen and Paula Johnson, Shanaman Sports Museum curators; baseball historian David Eskenazi; Kevin Kalal, Assistant General Manager of the Tacoma Rainiers; baseball statistician Ray Nemec; Dale Phelps, the Tacoma News Tribune sports editor, columnist John McGrath, and sportswriter Don Ruiz; Cathy Brewis, Director of Marketing for the Tacoma News Tribune; Brian Sponsler and Dave Girrard, Sports Information Directors at University of Puget Sound and Pacific Lutheran University, respectively; former UPS Sports Information Director Robin Hamilton; Kellie Ham of Ham Type & Graphics; Mario Menconi and his staff at Cascade Print Media, including Don Kincl, Bryan Ramsey, and production manager Kevin Young; Evan Brown of KLAY Radio; the United States Golf Association; the American Bowling Congress; Matt Zeysing of the Naismith Memorial Basketball Hall of Fame; Jim Daves and Brian Tom of the University of Washington Athletic Department; and Don and Billie Norell, Brad Cheney, Nick Nickolas, Bob Young, Joyce Wolf, Rhondi Adair, Ken Ollar, Guy Hoppen, Bob Farr, John Wohn, Ed Carr, Margie Oleole, Dave Alskog, Bill Bailey, George Karpach, John D. Smith of NASA Gymnastics, Woodrow Red, Gay Hartman, Lornie Merkle, Vicki Panzeri, Greg Smith, Kathy Wainhouse, Loren Zimmerman, Jan and Vennard Lahti, Mark Alger, the Tacoma–Pierce County Baseball–Softball Oldtimers Association, and the Shanaman Sports Museum of Tacoma–Pierce County.

A profound respect for the publishing profession has blossomed as a result of more than two years of intense research and writing. Kate Rogers, owner of Unleashed Book Development in Seattle and editor of this publication, accepted the challenge of molding the unique writing styles of three authors into a cohesive format. Simply put, without

Kate's patience and nurturing this book would not have become a reality. We are indebted to her professionalism and desire to make this book something we can all look upon with pride. Many thanks, too, to her collaborators: copy editor Kris Fulsaas, designer Karen Schober, print manager Elizabeth Cromwell, proofreader Erin Moore, and indexer Carolyn Acheson. A special thanks to writer Niki Stojnic, who worked with Kate to recognize our many chapter sponsors.

And finally, we are pleased to have the University of Washington Press distribute this history to bookstores and other outlets throughout the region. The press's staff has provided excellent assistance, especially Pat Soden, Michael Duckworth, Mary Anderson, and Denise Clark.

Sources

As every sports enthusiast knows, there are thousands of sources covering all facets of the subject. They range from published books and articles, to media presentations and information on the internet. The available data is overwhelming. It also poses a challenge for the historian wanting to put what took place in Tacoma and Pierce County within the broader framework of 20th century American sports history. There are guides, however. David Halberstam's edited anthology *The Best American Sports Writing of the Century* (Boston: Houghton Mifflin, 1999) is one. Another is James A. Michener's *Sports in America* (New York: Random House, 1976), while the North American Society for Sports History has published the *Journal of Sports History* since 1974.

A considerable amount of recent historical research has centered on the integration of racial, religious, and ethnic minorities into mainstream America sports. The edited work of John Bloom and Michael Nevin Willard, *Sports Matters: Race, Recreation and Culture* (New York: New York University Press, 2002) was helpful in writing this history. So too was Brian McDonald's *Indian Summer* (Emmaus, Pennsylvania: Rodale, 2003) and Jane Leavy's *Sandy Kofax: A Lefty's Legacy* (New York: HarperCollins, 2002), works that discuss the integration of Native Americans and the Jewish athlete into baseball. As this book goes to press, Neil Lanclot's *Negro League Baseball: The Rise and Ruin of a Black*

Institution (Philadelphia: University of Pennsylvania Press, 2004) was released.

For those wanting a general introduction to the history of Tacoma, Murray Morgan's *Puget's Sound: A Narrative of Early Tacoma and the Southern Sound* (Seattle: University of Washington Press, 1979) remains the most popular for the early years. Caroline Denyer Gallacci's *The City of Destiny and the South Sound* (Carlsbad, California: Heritage Media, 2001) carries Morgan's story into the 20th century. *A History of Pierce County, Washington* (Tacoma: Heritage League of Pierce County, 1990) provides histories of Pierce County communities, as well as ones covering some of the county's sports' venues and organizations. "Planning the City of Destiny: A History of Tacoma, Washington to 1930," Gallacci's unpublished doctoral dissertation (Seattle: University of Washington, 1999) includes information on the development of parks and playgrounds in the city.

There are few published sources on the history of sports in Tacoma and Pierce County but those that exist are important: Jacob Jordan's *Six Seasons* (Tacoma: Green Dragon Publishing, 1996) tells the story of the 1960–1965 Tacoma Giants. *Please Don't Call Me Tarzan*, by Mike Chapman (Newton, Iowa: Culture House Books, 2001) is a biography of Olympic medalist Herman Brix. Ronald E. Magden's *Furusato: Tacoma–Pierce County Japanese 1888–1988* (Seattle: University of Washington Press, 1988) discusses the role baseball played in the lives of Asian immigrants. *Sunday Afternoon at Garfield Park: Seattle's Black Baseball Teams, 1911–1951*, by Lyle Kenai Wilson (Everett: The Print Shop at the Bend in the River, 1997) includes a section on Tacoma's African-American baseball players. Philip J. Funigiello's *The Challenge to Urban Liberalism: Federal-City Relations During World War II* (Knoxville: University of Tennessee Press, 1979) helps us understand the creation of the Tacoma Athletic Commission. Med Nicholson's "The Ben Cheney Story," published in the Pacific County Historical Society's *Sou'wester* (Volume XXXV, No. 3, Fall 2000) is an excellent biography of this outstanding man. *It Started in the Mountains,* by Joy Lucas (Spokane: Arthur H. Clark Co., 1996) was a useful resource on skiing.

Both public and private institutional archives proved to be a wealth of information. The Metropolitan Park District of

Tacoma and the Pierce County Parks and Recreation Department, along with other local park jurisdictions, have records that helped us to tell the sports story. The Lakewood Winter Club and Pierce County have produced "A History of Figure Skating in Pierce County" (Tacoma, 2002), one of the most valuable of the county's publications. Equally informative is "Celebrate Tacoma's Ice Hockey History" (Tacoma, 2001) produced by Marc Blau. Besides the minutes of its Board of Commissioners dating from 1907, the Metropolitan district has a priceless list of parklands beginning with the first donation in 1883. The files and scrapbooks of the Tacoma Women's Bowling Association and the Greater Tacoma Bowling Association were most helpful, as was Marc Blau's collection of area sports memorabilia and news clippings and the souvenir programs of the Tacoma–Pierce County Baseball-Softball Oldtimers Association.

There are numerous research files held by the Tacoma Public Library and the Shanaman Sports Museum of Tacoma–Pierce County. The library's collections include both photographs and newspaper clipping files; those by sports columnists and reporters were particularly helpful. Of course, the Shanaman Sports Museum exhibits formed the basis of this history, as did its collection of newspaper articles, photographs, personal reminiscences, and event programs, all

laden with historical data. For the sport of boxing, considerable information was gleaned from several issues of *Ring Magazine* and "BoxRec," an internet boxing records archive.

Another major resource was the many personal scrapbooks, newspaper clippings, and photographs shared by the following athletes and organizations: Lloyd Blanusa, Sonny Johns, Dr. Charles P. Larson, Bob Malley, Lornie Merkle, the Names family (Scott, Tom, and Clint), Marion Oppelt, Dixie Million Wheless, Norm Mayer, Bob Carlson, Dave Alskog, the Tacoma Athletic Commission, and Marty Tetloff.

Fortunately, former and present-day athletes love to talk! Many were interviewed by telephone or e-mail as a part of the research for this history and are quoted directly in the text. Others were recorded and filed in the Shanaman Museum's collection. The list of the taped interviews include the following athletes: Lloyd Blanusa, Luther Carr, Tom Cross, Harold Freiter, Vern From, Wayne Gardner, Chuck Gilmur, Dick Greco, Cy Greenlaw, Dick Hannula, Vince Hansen, Marv Harshman, Doris Heritage, Clay Huntington, Joey Johns, Bob Malley, Doug McArthur, Pat McMurtry, Lornie Merkle, Stan Naccarato, Clint Names, Scott Names, Tom Names, Marion Oppelt, Fred Osmers, Peggy Ruehle, Ken Still, and Jack Tanner.

INDEX

SUBJECT INDEX
*Page numbers in *italics* indicate photo caption.